Special to The Daily

the first
One Hundred Years
of Editorial Freedom
at
The Michigan Daily

**Edited by
Susan Holtzer**

Caddo Gap Press

Special to The Daily:
One Hundred Years of Editorial Freedom at *The Michigan Daily*
Edited by Susan Holtzer

Copyright 1990 by Caddo Gap Press, Inc.
Library of Congress Catalog Card Number 90-082935
ISBN 0-9625945-2-0
$24.95

 Published by **Caddo Gap Press, Inc.**
317 South Division Street, Suite 2
Ann Arbor, Michigan 48104
(313) 662-3604

Materials reproduced from *The Michigan Daily* by permission of the
University of Michigan Board for Student Publications.

This volume has been prepared for the Centennial Celebration of *The
Michigan Daily*, October 19-21, 1990. The editor thanks the members of
the Centennial Celebration Committee and The Michigan Daily Alumni
Club, an affiliate of the Alumni Association of The University of Michigan, for their encouragement, cooperation, and assistance in producing
this anthology. Royalties from sales of the volume will be paid to The
Michigan Daily Alumni Club, to be used in the Club's efforts to sustain
and enhance the quality and independence of *The Michigan Daily* during
its second one hundred years of publication.

Special
to
The Daily

table
of
contents

Nearly five thousand people have been part of *The Michigan Daily* in the past one hundred years, fighting like hell to maintain the quality, independence, integrity and courage of what we have always believed to be the finest college newspaper in the world.

This book is dedicated to all of them, and to their successors. And to the next hundred years.

--S.H.

the beginning

Prior to the fall of 1890 the news of the university appeared in two weekly journals, the Chronicle *and the* Argonaut, *respectively by two sets of competing fraternities. Each carried a number of independents on its staff. I was a de jure independent editor of the* Argonaut. *What I was de facto I never found out for I had no duties to perform. Each journal was largely devoted to the group of fraternities which it represented. Neither was representative of the entire University. Both were losing ground.*

In the spring of 1890 a number of us decided that the University needed a real journal. The University had an enrollment of 2153 students. Ann Arbor was a small town of less than 10,000 inhabitants. We naturally could not secure the support of those sponsoring the journals we were attempting to displace. The University of Michigan Independent Association was therefore organized. It was not opposed to any society or group. Its sole purpose was to publish a journal representative in every way of the entire university life and all its activities.

We first planned a weekly to be known as the University of Michigan Independent. *Then after considering a semi-weekly we finally concluded to publish a daily to be known as the* U. of M. Daily. *The summer of 1890 was largely occupied in making preparations. We solicited advertising from Detroit and Ann Arbor merchants and with difficulty succeeded in selling them some space in what still was a non-existent paper. We had to find a publisher. We had no capital whatsoever. We had only an idea backed by a few enthusiasts who were willing to give their time and energy to a worthy cause. Samuel W. Beakes was publishing the* Ann Arbor Argus. *He had faith in our plan and agreed to be the publisher.*

With some hesitation but with confidence in the success of the enterprise, we went ahead. The first Daily *appeared on Monday, September 29, 1890.*

Paying advertisements were not easy to secure. These were the days before automobiles, radios, refrigeration, modern razors, foods with one of the vitamin alphabet, shaving and dental creams, etc. Advertisers of jewelry, clothing, students' books and supplies, musical instruments, took space. Two of the railroads advertised their time tables. The Opera House advertised its current performance.

The Daily *succeeded far better than we had ever anticipated. We built better than we knew.*

—Justice Henry M, Butzel, '92L, and Harry D. Jewell, '91
(from The Michigan Daily 50th Anniversary
Edition, Nov. 16, 1940)

The subscribers were the members of the 'U of M Independent Association' and chose the editors upon the basis of work done in competition. The bylaws provided that 'all moneys which may be left at the end of the college year beyond what is sufficient to pay the expenses of the publication' shall be divided one-fourth to the business managers, one-half to the managing editors, and the rest among the other editors, all on the basis of time spent. I do not recall receiving anything but hard knocks, headaches, and penalties for class cuts during my three semesters' service.

—Ralph Stone, '92L
(from The Michigan Daily 50th Anniversary
Edition, Nov. 16, 1940)

U. of M. DAILY.

VOLUME I.   MONDAY, SEPTEMBER 29, 1890.   NUMBER 1.

FACULTY ANNOUNCEMENTS.

GENERAL BIOLOGY.—The undersigned will be in the Botanical Laboratory on Wednesday between 10:30 and 12:30 a. m., to consult with students about courses in Biology, Botany and Morphology. Laboratory work in Biology begins Thursday at 9:30, in room 25.

V. M. SPAULDING.
J. H. REIGHARD.

LATIN.—Course 1. Section V. Livy, will report to Prof. Rolfe. It will be limited to students who have shown exceptional proficiency. It is expected that this section will cover more ground than the other sections.

Course 3. Section IV will be given by Mr. Clement.

HYGIENE.—Students wishing to take the courses in Bacteriology will find Mr. Novy in Hygiene Laboratory every afternoon this week. An optional course in Water Analysis will be given this semester.

MR. NOVY.

ENGINEERING STUDENTS.—A course in Foundry Work will be given the first semester.

All engineering students wishing to take work in the Mechanical Laboratory must see me Wednesday or Thursday, at 11 a. m., at my office.

PROF. TAYLOR.

OUR RUGBY TEAM.

THE NEUCLEUS OF IT PRACTICING DAILY ON THE CAMPUS.

The Campus has taken on a home like look this past week. Every afternoon has seen some of our canvas backed Rugby players tossing the ball back and forth, or trying to kick goals. It has been cold and raw, but the spectators have had many a laugh as the boys would form an invincible V and split the wind with it, but if they have had nothing but the wind to buck against, they have at least been learning to stand shoulder to shoulder. And they are doing good work, these few who are back getting in condition by tossing the ball, tackling, breaking the line, trying the V or the gridiron, and learning the twist that gave Ames of Princeton his celebrated nick-name of "Snake Ames."

The boys are working under Malley, who has brought back a trunk full of new tricks and has already began to teach his men a few of them. Abbott, Trainer, Hatch, DuPont, Rathbone, Dygert, McAllaster, Stone, and Chadbourne take to them as naturally as any canvas-back does to water. Of course the boys are all "soft," and short winded as yet, but if they follow the liner laid down by Captain Malley it will be soiled meat and sand that Cornell runs up against this year.

It does one's heart good to hear Captain Malley talk. If he does one half the things he wants to do, he will do double of anything that has ever been thought of here

before, and there will be a game at Buffalo this year that will be marked by sandy playing, and a much closer score than Cornell will look for. To begin with, "Systematic Work" is to be the foundation of the Rugby eleven this year. At 4 P. M., every day, every man who wants to play on the team must show up on the [...]

(Oct. 2, 1890) All will welcome the revolution in college journalism which has taken place this fall. Heretofore, University news has been given to the college world through the medium of two weekly papers, which, to quote the remark of a prominent lawyer in town, have been "very weakly, indeed." They strove to be both newspapers and literary periodicals, and the result was that they were neither. Recognizing that the University was away behind the times in a most important feature of college life, and that the development of journalism was all in the way of specialization, the staff of the DAILY proposed to set the ball rolling by establishing a paper which should attempt to do but one thing--give the news--promptly and accurately. The DAILY pretends to do nothing else. Its action has had the effect of uniting the two weeklies in the publishing of a literary paper, which the combined board will easily succeed in making a far better paper than either of its predecessors.#

editor's introduction

First things first: If I'd included every story I wanted to include, this book would be 800 pages long.

For the last eight months I've done just about nothing else but read Michigan Dailies -- hauling the huge bound volumes around and swearing when I smeared printer's ink on my hands and face and clothes. (Would you believe it still comes off on your hands even when it's fifty years old?) I don't think I've ever worked this hard, or this intensely, in my life -- except for my four years on The Daily.

And over and over, I'd come to the end of a season, or a series, or a particularly great piece, and I'd think: Damn, we were good.

* * *

If your favorite story is missing, I apologize. Some of mine are, too. I had to make a lot of painful decisions, and I know that a great deal of fine work simply didn't make it into this anthology. In addition, some stories which were recommended, including some that I desperately wanted to run, I simply couldn't find, even after hours of searching. (One hundred years is a lot of newspapers.)

I had to make a decision very early on when I began this project -- the book would either be a relatively small number of long stories, or excerpts from a much larger number. I opted for the latter, for one primary reason -- I wanted, more than anything else, to capture the flavor of The Daily. (That's the reason why text styles change from article to article, too -- I have tried to copy the look and feel of the originals as closely as possible.)

This isn't a book about great writing, although there's a lot of it in these pages; rather, it's a book about down-and-dirty journalism, the day-to-day, assignment-sheet, race-the-deadline reality of getting a newspaper out on the streets every single morning, all of it done by a constantly changing group of eighteen-to-twenty-one-year-old kids. Getting the stories written and the papers out whether we had an exam or not; whether we had a date or not; whether we hadn't slept in 48 hours or not. And making it, when we had the time, the best Goddamn student newspaper in the world.

* * *

The decision I made meant, unfortunately, that I had to cut articles, and I did -- sometimes extensively (each deletion is clearly marked with an ellipsis.) Where appropriate, I took the basic journalistic approach and cut from the bottom; in long interpretive pieces I have tried to cut whole sections and focus on one aspect of the article, rather than hacking out bits and pieces.

To those writers whose work I have so cavalierly treated, I apologize and plead the old, hated and unanswerable editor's excuse of lack of space.

But please note -- I did not edit any article. The words you read here are the words as they were originally published, and in the original Daily style of the time (which is why, for instance, capitalization rules change from story to story.) Two exceptions -- first, I have corrected obvious typographic errors, on the grounds that no writer should be saddled into posterity with the errors of freshman proofreaders. Therefore, the responsibility for typos in this book is mine and mine alone. Second, I have in a few places been forced to edit headlines for space. (Occasionally, too I've inserted identifying text before a name when the original information was deleted; these inserts are placed inside brackets.)

* * *

The selection of articles may appear idiosyncratic, and to a certain extent it is -- any book, after all, can only be the single vision of the person who creates it, and obviously a different editor would have made different choices. But I have tried to include, most particularly, those articles which in some way illuminate something about what made, and makes, The Daily special.

In this I was aided immeasurably by an astonishingly generous cadre of alumni who wrote offering suggestions for articles and anecdotal reminiscences, many of which are included here; and who wracked their brains and searched their attics for more detail to help me find specific pieces.

One category of suggestion which I reluctantly decided against is the celebrity interview. Not because I couldn't find them, but simply because there were too many of them. There is hardly a celebrity -- political, theatrical, musical, international -- who didn't come through Ann Arbor at some time, to be interviewed or analyzed or skewered by The Daily. (This would, in fact, make a fascinating book all by itself.) But mostly, I was forced to omit them for, again, lack of space.

One other caveat -- you won't find the bad stuff here. Bad stuff, you ask? Of course there has been bad stuff. Find me a newspaper whose hundred-year history doesn't include the occasional lapse of judgment, the occasional rat bastard editor, the occasional byline-happy, integrity-short reporter. You'll find them in The Daily, too, once in a while. But no more often, I believe from my century of reading, than you'd find in, say, one hundred years of The Detroit Free Press.

This book is, most of all, a celebration of the first hundred years of a remarkable achievement -- generation after generation of college kids fighting off challenge after challenge from administrators, legislators, and pressure groups of every point in the spectrum, to maintain a press freedom unmatched on any college campus in the world.

This book is dedicated to them -- to us -- and to the determination that, for The Daily, there will unquestionably and absolutely be

--[more.]--

--Susan Holtzer, '60

Alumnus

Daily ghosts, we called them.

You used to see them all the time.

They stood in the doorway respectfully, tourists behind an invisible rope, afraid to step too hard on the floor. Wife behind, clutching her purse over her stomach. Son's eyes flitting around the barnlike room.

And the grey suit would talk in a low voice, his eyes wide, pointing here, there, gesturing with an art historian's rapture at the thoroughly pedestrian interior of The Michigan Daily.

He'd thrust them suddenly forward, waving his hand to unfurl a path through the center of the city room. She'd squeeze herself smaller and follow his clattering steps down the stairwell to the composing room.

They'd be gone. Maybe in a minute.

Sometimes the stranger just sat. Alone. Picked a desk top and chewed on a cigarette and watched.

And he'd be gone.

It never mattered. There was an edition to put out.

Sometimes a trainee, a freshman who didn't know any better, would take it upon himself to welcome the stranger.

"Can I help you with something?"

It was always a little weird. The face would gaze back at him incredulously, the mouth would start to form an answer, and the voice finally, from a great distance, reply: No. No, I used to work here... He'd think about it a minute and plunge on: Class of '61 I was city editor used to work with Harvey Clancy he's at CBS now but that used to be my desk right in that corner the place sure hasn't changed just thought I'd stop and have a look as long as I was in town.

Trainees are tolerant people. They'd smile politely before excusing themselves. Hadn't heard a word. Hell, somebody used to put out The Daily.

Daily ghosts, they were. As dead as yesterday's edition.

They all came back eventually, we said. They'd try to reach across the gap. Try to touch the present.

We, the living, ignored them. Daily ghosts. Curious phenomenon.

* * *

I arrived in time for the pm cycle, and bounded up the stairway past the Coke bottles and the fading notes stuck to the marble wall with library paste, the ends ripped off. Bundles of twined newspapers lay inert, as usual, on the bench. I slipped easily home, to this comfortable old shoe of a place: the typewriters, the desks, the hours and hours of talk, of time passing. The building wrapped itself around me with quiet familiarity.

4:20. A steady rhythm. The afternoon digest should be set by now. In the shop, Marion would be patting the galleys into place. Has anyone checked the wire lately? Some clown's left the photo cabinet unlocked again. Maybe --

But the faces. They'd all been replaced.

One of them looks up. Lord, so young to be in college.

"Can I help you with something?"

I used to live, for a time, at The Daily.

--Lisa Stephens, '68

chapter 1

getting the story

They used to call them scoops. I don't know what they call them now, but it's still, in the end, what newspapers are all about. Getting the story, whatever it takes — persistence, imagination, guts, sheer luck, and often, a sense of the ridiculous. Over the years, The Daily has shown them all.

UNDER FIRE, MOCKS WAR'S EXCITEMENT

S. B. Conger, '00, Journalist on
Battle-field, Writes Letter
to Homer Heath

PROUD OF GAME WITH HARVARD

(Jan. 14, 1915) S. B. Conger, '00, a newspaper man in Berlin, has written a letter to Homer L. Heath, '07, manager of the Michigan Union, which expresses his loyalty to Michigan, and at the same time throws sharp light on the true existing conditions of the present.

The letter was read at the meeting of the directors of the Union. It was dated December 11, and was addressed to Homer Heath, treasurer of the "M" club...

"Herewith please find check for $5.00 for my dues to the "M" club. I should have attended to the matter long ago, but we were so busy making war over here that it had slipped my mind until I came across Mr. Killein's letter this morning.

"Just got back yesterday from a visit to the trenches on the French front. I was right up in the front lines a good share of the time, but it is really not so exciting as it sounds, as even if one is not under fire, he is so well protected in the deep trenches and approaches that there is absolutely no sense of danger.

"Take it from me, nine-tenths of the stuff that is being written by correspondents about exciting scenes and experiences on the battlefield, charging infantry, riderless horses galloping about, bullets and shrapnel whistling about one's ears, etc., is pure bunk.

"I have been on battlefields a number of times, and have not yet seen anything so exciting as a game with Case. Best regards to all the boys you see. We certainly are proud of Michigan for that Harvard game.
Your friend,
S. B. Conger, '00"

An Interview With Gandhi

Bombay, India
April 14, 1923.

(May 25, 1924) Due to a rather unfortunate combination of circumstances I am able to give to the readers of The Daily an account of an interview with Mr. Gandhi which took place at Juliu beach on the afternoon of the thirteenth. Mr. Gandhi, who was recently released from prison by the British, is recuperating from an operation for appendicitis at a cottage on this beach, which is 14 miles from Bombay, and readily consented to visitors when informed that they were Americans.

...

Picture a slight figure, naked except for a loin cloth, his pale skin so tightly drawn over his body that one could almost count his ribs, his head clean shaven except for a tuft of hair on the top, indicating his Hindooism, rather a prominent nose under heavy eyebrows...

...

Naturally the first question was, "Mr. Gandhi, what do you stand by and what do you propose to do to reach your goal?" Gandhi's reply was a statement of the four cardinal points of the non-cooperative movement...

...

...First--Religious unity, Second--Freedom of the untouchables (the lower castes), Third--Total abstinence from liquor and drugs, Fourth--Industrial reconstruction.

"Since the above conditions are opposed to the policy of the British government the attainment of them necessarily involves a change in the present form of government in India. We hope, and believe that this change can he brought about without violence, for the progress that has been made shows beyond a doubt the power of Spiritual, even material force. However the Indian is not a coward and under certain circumstances might resort to physical force where it is necessary to gain his liberty or to establish and maintain organized government against foreign oppression or mob rule.

"We place Religious unity above our other aims because it is most desired by us and most misrepresented by those who are opposed to our purposes. The world is consistently informed that the moment that the present forces of occupation are withdrawn, the different religionists will fly at each others' throats and chaos will result. The text books in our schools have been deliberately falsified in order to make it appear to young Indian students of history what conditions in India previous to British occupation really were...

...

"The use of alcohol and drugs is rapidly increasing in India; women working in the cotton mills are giving opium to their babies to make them sleep while the mothers are working; the government forces the cultivation of opium...

...

"Industrial reconstruction does not mean a general reversion to primitive methods of manufacture or methods of tilling the soil. It merely means a denial of the gospel of speed, and the determination that every Indian shall have the time to develop spiritually as well as materially. It means that the farmer of India, is today weaving his own cloth rather than encouraging a system under which men and women become part of machines..."

...

Asked to state his attitude toward the British Government, Mr. Gandhi denied being anti-British per se but insisted on India for the Indians; not necessarily as a ruling force, but a freer partnership with England under which they will not be ruled by force; under which they will equal the English socially and which will concede their right to self determination at the proper time...#

--A. J. Diehl, ex '27.

Comstock Brands Ford Company
With Responsibility For Closure
Of Banks, Then Withdraws Charges

Governor's Early Statement Says Ford Group Would Not Subordinate Deposits To R. F. C.

BULLETIN

(Feb. 15, 1933) In a statement late last night, the governor said, "I misunderstood the facts in the Union Guardian Trust situation."

Harry Bennett, chief of service of the Ford Motor Company, reached at his home near Ann Arbor last night, denied that the Ford Motor Company was in any way responsible for the moratorium.

LANSING, Feb. 14--(Special)--Officials of the Ford Motor company were today termed responsible for the eight-day banking moratorium in Michigan by Gov. William A. Comstock.

He said that because the company refused to subordinate its deposits with the Union Guardian Trust Co. in favor of claims of smaller depositors and the R. F. C., the moratorium had been necessary to "protect small depositors and to save the state's banking structure."

"Here is the plain unvarnished story of the events which led to the declaration of the banking moratorium," Comstock said.

Would Leave Field

"The Union Guardian Trust Co. of Detroit has been doing banking business in Michigan under the laws of the state.

Like other financial houses it has suffered depreciation of its assets and was seeking to get out of the banking business, leaving that field to other units of the organization.

...

"The largest depositors of the company were the General Motors corporation, Chrysler corporation and the Ford Motor Co. Both G. M. C. and Chrysler had agreed to subordinate their deposits to the R. F. C., which was to have taken over the quick assets, and smaller depositors.

...

"The Ford company refused to make such an agreement and the result was necessity of a moratorium."..#

Spanish Letter Was Written By Ex-Student, Daily Reveals

Loyalist Letter Uncovered By Times Correspondent Found Work of Kahle

By ELLIOT MARANISS

(Copyright, 1938, by The Michigan Daily)

(March 15, 1938) A letter found by William P. Carney, of the New York Times, near the bodies of five dead, unidentified Loyalist volunteers at Belchite, Spain, was discovered by The Daily last night to have been written by Harland L. Kahle, former student at the University.

Mrs. W. H. Kahle, the student's mother, said last night in a telephone conversation from her home in Morenci, Mich., that "we haven't received any word from him at all recently." Friends of Kahle's in Ann Arbor had told her, she said, that her son was in Spain. "We think he has written letters and that they have been censored," she said.

The unfinished letter which Carney found began with "Dear Charles," and there was a reference to an apartment at 1003 East Huron Street, but no city was given. The writer of the letter also revealed that he had been in the medical corps "doing field first aid" and "for three days I was chief medical officer in the Lincoln-Washington Battalion."

Kahle resided at 1003 East Huron Street, Ann Arbor, all last year while he attended the University as a student.

...

There is no way of telling definitely from Carney's report, published in the Times Saturday, March 12, whether or not Kahle is dead. Carney's report reads:

"I found out from Insurgent officers that the five dead men included three Americans, a Greek and a Canadian."

...

In the unfinished letter starting "Dear Charles," the writer said his friends in the United States "seem to belong to a past and outgrown phase of my life."..#

TOM HARMON MISSING

Football Star Lost In Latin America

(April 15, 1943) Lieut. Thomas Dudley Harmon, football star at the University in 1938, 1939 and 1940 and the greatest scorer in gridiron history, is "missing in the South American area," but his shocked parents were clinging staunchly tonight to the hope that he is still alive.

Faced with a terse telegram from the War Department which expressed "deep regret" that their pilot son had not been heard from since April 8, Tom's parents waited in the house he built for them here and voiced their faith that he would bob up before long--"somewhere"--and safe.

"Tom is strong and knows how to take care of himself," said his father, Louis A. Harmon. "We can only pray now."

The 23-year-old former All-American of 1939 and 1940 entered the Army Air Forces a year ago. He received his silver wings as a twin-engine bomber pilot at Williams Field, Ariz., Oct. 30, 1942.

...

Harmon left the country in a plane which bore the legend, "Old 98--Little Butch" after the number he carried to fame on the gridiron.

"I'll get that first Jap for Michigan," he wrote a friend here recently...#

HARMON MISSING AGAIN

Wolverine Star Is Lost in China

By MARION FORD

(Nov. 5, 1943) The parents of 2nd Lt. Thomas D. Harmon were notified last night that the Michigan gridiron immortal has been reported missing for the second time since he entered training in the Air Corps March 31, 1942.

A telegram from the War Department yesterday said: "The Secretary of War desires me to express his regrets that your son, 2nd Lt. Thomas Dudley Harmon, has been reported missing in action over China since the 30th of October. If other information is received, you will be promptly notified. Signed, the Adjutant General."

His parents, Mr. and Mrs. Louis A. Harmon of 2200 Vinewood Blvd., last heard from their famous son a week ago Monday. His letter, dated October 13, said that he was in good health and promised them a Zero for Christmas.

In a letter to Coach Fritz Crisler dated one day later Harmon said that he was doing "a lot of flying" and described an engagement with the Japs. He said two of them had encountered 17 Jap planes, disposed of two and come through without a scratch.

"Jap pilots are not nearly so good as German ones," he said, comparing them to "mechanical fliers--you know every move they're going to make."..#

How Harmon Escaped from Enemy Fire

By LEONARD SCHLEIDER
--Special to The Daily--
WASHINGTON, Jan. 24 (1944)-- First Lt. Tom Harmon of the Army Air Forces, looking a little older and a lot wiser, came to Washington today to tell how he narrowly escaped being machine gunned by Japanese pilots after parachuting out of his Lightning fighter over China's Yangtze River...

...

Harmon related how a routine, every-day dive-bombing attack on Japanese docks and warehouses at Kiukiang on the Yangtze became a fierce dogfight, during which he shot down two Zeros, and then, when trapped from behind, was himself shot down.

...

To Harmon, an old safety man, fell the job of "Tail End Charlie." He was the last man in the formation, behind and above the dive-bombers.

They were almost over the target when things began to buzz. The top cover leader shouted "six Zeros at 3 o'clock" into the interphones. Harmon says he turned around and saw six more enemy ships at 6 o'clock.

...

To tell the story in Tom's own words: "I turned into the six Zeros behind me and busted right in between them. I got one in my sights, let go a burst of tracers that went into the cock-pit. Then I let go with my cannon. The Jap exploded and plunged straight into the ground."

...

"Suddenly," he says, "two shells hit into the armorplate behind me. A third shell went right between my legs."

Apparently that third shell was an incendiary for it started a gasoline fire in his cockpit. He turned the ship over and tried to beat out the flames with his hands.

He still bears the scars of that blaze on his hands and legs.

"I saw it was impossible," Harmon declared. He unfastened his cockpit cover and the suction tore him out of the cockpit, ripping off his trousers below the knees.

Harmon says he didn't know his altitude at the time he bailed out, so he pulled the ripcord immediately...

...

He played dead, hanging there in his chute. "I came down in a lake," Tom goes on, "but I didn't dare swim. The Japs continued circling. Every time they came over I ducked underneath my chute. They left after a while."

That was all he could tell. All we know is that Harmon was back at his base a month later. Presumably he was guided and fed by Chinese guerillas behind the Jap lines. "I can't say anything more," Harmon explained, "because reprisals on the Chinese people would be very heavy."..#

Exclusive: G.B. Shaw Gives Lowdown on Wallace

By NATALIE BAGROW
Daily Special Writer
Copyright 1948 by The Michigan Daily

George Bernard Shaw, who is never at a loss for an opinion about anything, has something to say about Henry A. Wallace and American liberals, too.

Looking at American politics from a British and Fabian view, Shaw asserts that Wallace must educate the liberals, "whose principles are flatly opposed to his (Wallace's)."

His views were set forth in a personal letter to an Ann Arbor couple recently. The Daily was given exclusive rights to publication of the letter upon receipt of Shaw's cabled permission to "give my answers all possible publicity."

High points in Shaw's letter are his comments that "no country is ready for a progressive party," that "all Presidents call themselves progressive," and that Wallace cannot restore amicable relations between Russia and the United States "unless Russia will let him, Congress or no Congress."

The letter was written by Shaw in response to a list of questions submitted to him by William Chase, a collector of Shaw and member of the Washtenaw County Wallace for President Committee...

...

The text of Shaw's letter follows:

Question: Is America ready for a progressive party?

Answer: No country is ready for a progressive party. Each citizen hates to be governed at all, though he wants to be protected against his fellow citizens. America is a geographical term, not a personal one. It takes all sorts to make a world, on both sides of the Atlantic as elsewhere. Ask me a sensible question.

Question: How can American Liberals accomplish the most to assure Mr. Wallace's election?

Answer: By giving up their obsolete Cobdenism, their exploded laisser-faire, and their anarchistic denunciations of what they call Totalitarianism. A law that is not totalitarian is no law at all.

Question: What is the practical value of a progressive president when the Congress is predominantly conservative?

Answer: All Presidents call themselves progressive. But as a Republican Congress can steal a horse when a Democratic one dare not, look over the hedge and neither of them will go very far unless and until circumstances drive them. Mr. Wallace, who is out to get a move on, need not stop to consider which Party wins if his new Party is defeated.

...

Question: Can Mr. Wallace, without full support of Congress, restore amicable relations between Russia and the United States?

Answer: Not unless Russia will let him, Congress or no Congress. But Mr. Wallace represents the people both of America and Russia as not wanting another war; and those who imagine that Stalin wants one or could afford one are nitwits two centuries out of date. Only army contractors and their financiers have any interest in war, not even soldiers as able as Montgomery and Eisenhower; but what both the U. S. A. and the British Commonwealth fear is the domination of the contractors backed by the popular association of national greatness with military glory and conquest instead of with deep political thinking. All Europe and America slandered Russia for twenty years, then slobbered over her when Hitler attacked her and she became our ally, and the moment the war was over began slandering her again. After that can you wonder that she mistrusts us? Wallace is the only candidate whose election would allay her suspicions.

Question: What is the American future, as you see it, if Mr. Wallace is not elected?

Answer: I don't see it; and neither does anyone else. I am not a prophet. Consult Old Moore's Almanac or Napoleon's Book of Fate, if you want the world's fortune told.

Question: What, in your opinion, would be the British reaction to Mr. Wallace's election?

Answer: What do you suppose England cares about Mr. Wallace? I might ask you what does American care about Churchill, Attlee, Bevin or Cripps? At election time one has to remember that the eyes of a fool are in the end of the earth. It is American votes that Mr. Wallace must win.

We are getting silly. Good morning.#

'U' Plans Research Project Near Huron River
Regents Yet To Approve Development

By CAL SAMRA and
HARLAND BRITZ

(Oct. 17, 1951) University officials are now working on plans for a gigantic new research and development center northeast of the Huron River, it became known last night.

The center, which might eventually house 14,000 people, is being planned on a long-range basis, and is destined to accommodate expansion of research facilities in future years.

‡ ‡ ‡

INITIAL PLANS call for erection of an Engineering Research Institute building at an early date, with a structure to house the multi-million dollar Phoenix Project scheduled to follow.

No specific details of the center have been announced and University administrators were reluctant to speak about it openly.

The plans are still in an unfinished stage and have not yet been approved by the Board of Regents. The Board will next meet Oct. 26, but is not expected to review the plans until its following meeting late in November.

‡ ‡ ‡

THE RESEARCH center would cover a 200 acre area bordering on Glazier Way and Plymouth Road, in the rolling hills overlooking the Huron River a short distance from campus.

Hints of the new project have been prevalent in recent weeks.

Speculation mounted when Dean Ralph A. Sawyer, of the graduate school, who is also a Phoenix director, published a progress report which said it was "likely the new Phoenix Project building would be erected in the area."..#

SAFE IN NEW ORLEANS:

'Riders' Flee Alabama Bomb Scare

By BEATRICE TEODORO

(May 16, 1961) Seventeen "Freedom Riders" flew to New Orleans last night following two bomb scares in the Birmingham, Ala. airport.

One of the 17, Walter Bergman, a former white professor at the University, said the group was testing the "speed of integration."

They had been forced to leave their first plane after the FBI received a telephone call warning a bomb had been concealed on the plane. The flight was cancelled, although no bomb was found.

A later call to a public insurance booth in the airport waiting room warned that a bomb had been hidden in the terminal itself. A man's voice said the bomb would go off in 18 minutes, but there was no explosion.

Safety Not Guaranteed

The group of nine whites and eight Negroes, members of the Congress of Racial Equality, decided to fly to New Orleans when Gov. John Patterson said he could not guarantee their safety.

...

The Freedom Riders first planned to continue the tour to Montgomery.

All Together

At the request of United States Attorney General Robert Kennedy, the CORE leaders decided to put their people on the bus. A highway patrol car was assigned to escort them, but Patterson later cancelled the escort.

"In view of the tenseness of the situation, it is impossible to guarantee the safety of these agitators. We will escort them to the nearest state line. However, we will not escort them to any other cities in Alabama to continue their rabble rousing."..#

INTEGRATION:

Freedom Ride-Hopes, Trials

(EDITOR'S NOTE: Following are paraphrased excerpts from letters written by Frances Bergman, a Congress of Racial Equality member from Michigan. Miss Bergman, whose husband is a former University professor, is currently participating in Freedom Ride, 1961--a massive "test case" of segregation bans on public facilities serving inter-state commerce.)

By IRIS BROWN
Daily Staff Writer

(May 17, 1961) MAY 9--We left the warm friendly atmosphere of Fellowship House in Washington completely spoiled, sure that the world is all sweetness and light. The possibilities of arrest or even of incidents seemed most remote...

* * *

AT THE OUTSET we divided into two groups. Group A started on Greyhound, but have since switched to Trailways and we shall be changing off and on as circumstances dictate.

Recently we have been forcing integration within the bus by having Negro members of the group sit toward the front alone so that white passengers boarding when the bus was full would be forced to sit with Negroes or stand. This has worked out very well.

Inside the rest-stops and at the terminal we operate in pairs, white and Negro, with one person as observer. In case of arrests the observer is ready to call the New York office, take the bags of the arrested person and then speed on by the next bus to catch up with the group.

When we are not traveling we are eating (often for the purposes of testing); when we are not eating, we are meeting. It takes time to get 17 people--this includes observers, cameramen, writers and reporters--sorted out each night for sleeping quarters. We finally fall into bed about one a.m.

...

* * *

MAY 10--When all the stores in Winnsboro, S.C. were closed to observe Memorial Day (Confederate) two of our members were arrested and I had an experience that will forever remain with me.

Hank (Henry Thomas of St. Augustine, Fla. and the Washington, D.C. Nonviolent Group) and Jim (Jim Peck, editor of the "CORE-lator") were seated at a counter. A woman, apparently the head waitress, went in back of the ticket window and kept saying, "Don't serve 'em." She then told Hank to "get over to the other side." Hank said he would not-- that he wished to be served. Immediately a man in plain clothes stepped up and said, "you're under arrest." When Hank asked what the charge was, he received no answer.

Then I asked why they were taking him to jail. "For being where he had no business to be," the plainclothesman said. I said that we were interstate passengers and court rulings say all facilities should be open to all such passengers. When Peck stepped forward and said, "I am with this young man. Are you taking us both?" the officer said yes.

After trying to locate a telephone, I found out where the police station was. I cleaned out my purse of "damaging notes"--names and addresses (oh, the land of the free) and deposited same in a trash can.

Later, I spoke with the police chief. He asked if I had been ordered out of the restaurant. "No, but my friends were and were arrested, and I'm concerned about them." He asked which one I was interested in. "Both," I said. When I then asked what they were charged with, he said he refused to talk to "my kind," and told me to "git outa town fast's you kin."

The atmosphere was hostile. A cab drove up. Instead of waiting four hours for a bus, I dashed out and made a deal to taxi to Columbia.

* * *

MAY 11 AND 12--Sumter is a different world and a sickening one. If Negroes picket or distribute leaflets or parade (ten people walking down the street is a parade) they are arrested. No people living in a totalitarian country could be more oppressed. I felt that we made a tremendous contribution here. We brought them home--unbelievable as it seems in the United States in 1961.

At a meeting in the evening at Paine College, Augusta, Ga. I was again impressed with the feeling that we represent new hope. The students' singing was the most thrilling part to me. A people who can sing after years of oppression. Amazing.#

Political Restrictions Spark Berkeley Riots

New Ruling Attacked by Student Mob

By JOHN KENNY
Assistant Managing Editor

(Oct. 2, 1964) A prohibition on student political activity sparked rioting yesterday at the University of California's Berkeley campus.

Over 2000 students protested an administrative ruling forbidding students to solicit funds or members for student political organizations on university property, Editor Susan Johnson of the Daily Californian reported by telephone last night.

Student leaders decided last night to break up a sit-in inside the university's administration building, Sproul Hall, "in good faith with the administration." About 100 students had been inside the building as crowds milled outside.

Miss Johnson said minor violence flared early last night when students attempted to bring food to the demonstrators inside Sproul Hall. University officials closed the hall doors, barring the students carrying food.

Several women attacked policemen. One policeman reportedly had his shoes torn off.

Eight student leaders were arrested Wednesday by university police for soliciting funds at a Student Nonviolent Coordinating Committee (SNCC) table on university property. These eight were later expelled from the university by Chancellor Edward Strong...#

1100 'Sit In' at Berkeley Administration Building

By ROBERT BENDELOW

(Dec. 3, 1964) Some 1100 students took over the administration building of the University of California at Berkeley last night in a sit-in demonstration against the threatened expulsion of four of their leaders.

Berkeley teaching assistants have mapped plans for a sympathy strike to take place in the near future. They threatened to strike immediately if any disciplinary action was taken against the demonstrators.

Protest leader Mario Savio told a rally which preceded the sit-in, "We're not going to break this up until we get what we want."

Inside the locked building, professors set up classes in such subjects as literature and Spanish. The classes were conducted by sympathetic teaching assistants. The fourth floor of the administration building, Sproul Hall, was set up as a study hall. For those who did not wish to study, a movie projector was in operation. Folk singer Joan Baez, who helped lead the protestors into the building, led singing in another room. Sympathizers sent food in to the students in the building.

A protest leader told The Daily by telephone that even full professors were inside the building, teaching impromptu sessions in "constitutional law, civil disobedience and non-violence."

The sit-in, following a noon rally, occupied the first four floors of Sproul Hall. The protestors did not obstruct traffic while the building was open, and left doorways and corridors open.

...

University officials warned the protestors early this morning that all were subject to arrest. Declaring themselves to be "the Free University of California in session," the protestors replied by vowing that they would have to be carried out of the building...#

801 Arrested at Berkeley On Orders from Governor

By ROBERT BENDELOW

(Dec. 4, 1964) California state troopers yesterday arrested 801 student demonstrators who Wednesday invaded the University of California at Berkeley administration building and staged an all-night sit-in.

The students were arrested amidst cries of police brutality, for what University of California President Clark Kerr termed "irresponsible and illegal action." Under orders from California Gov. Edmund G. Brown, the state troopers, augmented by local police, moved into the administration building at 3:45 a.m. yesterday and started to haul the limp demonstrators off to jail. Students who left voluntarily were not taken into custody.

Evacuation was completed by 3:15 p.m. yesterday afternoon. At one point, the number of sympathetic students climbing into the building was greater than the number police were removing.

In related actions, teaching assistants have gone on strike, and students are picketing all entrances to the campus and all major buildings. The teaching assistants not on strike refused to cross picket lines.

The action of the teaching assistants has thrown the campus into chaos, the Daily Californian, the Berkeley student newspaper, reported last night by telephone. "With the graduates on strike, more than 50 per cent of the classes have been cancelled, and mid-terms have likewise been cancelled," a spokesman for the paper said.

"Delirious as the non-demonstrating students are over this, the general consensus is that the Free Speech Movement has gone too far, and both the FSM and the administration are in the wrong," the spokesman claimed.

...

The protestors were jailed, with bail set at $250 to $3200 each. Mario Savio, the leader of the FSM and yesterday's demonstration was reportedly placed in solitary confinement...#

'We Pick, Sort and Send 'em'

By ROGER RAPOPORT
Special To The Daily

(Dec. 9, 1966) WASHINGTON -- Unlike most important buildings here, the nation's Selective Service Headquarters does not look like a mausoleum. Nor is it fronted by a circle driveway filled with doubled parked Cadillac limousines.

It's all business at the draft command post centered in a dumpy six story brick building just down F street from the Moonlight Cafe.

Working out of a top floor office is the world's largest personnel director, Lt. Gen. Lewis Blaine Hershey. He presides over 33 million American men registered with 4,088 draft boards across the country.

Hershey's office is furnished in contemporary American Legion--with flags from state militias, combat divisions, and Boy Scout troops surrounding the perimeter of the room.

Observers think that, with the possible exception of FBI Director J. Edgar Hoover, Hershey runs the biggest one man show in Washington.

...

Hershey has played the major role in boosting the nation's armed forces from 200,000 in 1936 to today's 3 million plus level.

Despite all this he runs an unpretentious office. One can call up the draft headquarters, ask for Gen. Hershey, and more than likely be speaking to him in 10 seconds...

...

Leaning back in his imposing executive chair Hershey scoffs at the notion that he is a draft czar. He points out that all induction decisions are made "by your friends and neighbors" at your local draft board.

"We've got 15,000 people running our local draft boards," he says, "and if you think all of them agree with me on anything you're crazy."

The general also contends that he doesn't change individual draft decisions.

"I got a call from a friend the other night. His son was set to be drafted in two days. The kid had been trying to enlist in the Air Force for months but was only able to move up from 68th to 36th on the waiting list.

"'It's pretty awful,' said the father, 'when a boy can't serve the country the way he wants.'

"But I just told him that this way his son is getting a chance to serve his country a lot sooner," says Hershey.

Since the draft law is up for renewal next year, many people have been firing off salvos at Gen. Hershey's system. They contend the draft penalizes the poor, lets students hide in college and disrupts the lives of young people.

But Hershey rejects such criticism as he lifts his feet off the fluffy lemon colored pile carpet onto his mammoth desk.

"We expect that 56 per cent of the 1.6 million college students we are now deferring will eventually serve. Only 40 per cent of all non-college students will ever serve."

He adds that about "40 per cent of all college graduates actually serve."

The General also contends that it's "nonsense to cry that you can't plan your life because of the draft. You can volunteer any time you want to."

The draft director hasn't been too happy about collegiate protests against his system.

"I've been pretty strong for the college student," says Hershey, "but I think he's only hurting himself with all this rebellion. That's not the way to get anywhere. The best way to get change is to work in a quiet manner, not an antagonistic one."

The General, who grew up on a farm near Angola, Ind., about 60 miles from Ann Arbor, shows little concern though about recent demonstrations at the University protesting the use of class rankings by Selective Service.

"The college kids in Ann Arbor have always been playful," he says. "I remember when I was a kid, the circuses wouldn't stop in Ann Arbor. The college students would always tear the tent down."

...

Despite the significance of his job Hershey prefers to discount his importance. Munching a take-out White Tower lunch of cheeseburger and tea, the General contends his office merely supplies the Pentagon's manpower needs.

"All we do is pick 'em, sort 'em, and send 'em."#

I haven't a clue how this story came about, or what a Daily reporter was doing in Vietnam. Sometimes it seems as though The Daily was **everywhere**.

Thieu bodyguard shoots aide
Calls for resignation spread in Saigon

By DAVID WHITING
Copyright 1975, The Michigan Daily

(April 4, 1975) Du Quoc Dong, Third Regent Commander of Saigon forces, was shot and killed last week by President of South Vietnam Nguyen Van Thieu's bodyguard after resigning his position, The Daily learned yestesrday.

Dong was killed in the Saigon palace while handing Thieu his uniform and gun, a source close to the United States government revealed.

HOWEVER, it remains unclear exactly why Dong was shot.

Thieu claimed Dong was a would-be assassin, it was reported, but Vietnamese sources close to the Saigon government contended, "Dong was going to the palace to resign...he was giving his gun to Thieu."

Within hours after the shooting Thieu announced the government had thwarted an attempted coup and arrested several persons but made no mention of Dong or the shooting.

However, those arrested were affiliated with former Vice President of South Vietnam Cao Ky, while Dong has been one of Thieu's key military aides for some years.

A YEAR AGO Dong was promoted from commanding Saigon's crack paratrooper unit--the elite of Thieu's forces, to a Regent Commander of South Vietnam.

In the past four months, Saigon-based military and Thieu have had a falling-out. The military has desired more input into Thieu's decisions...#

12 Special to The Daily

Chrysler stopped: Daily undaunted

(EDITOR'S NOTE: What follows is the first of a two-part account from three Daily staffers who covered this week's Chrysler plant shutdown in Detroit and braved much adversity to enter the plant and speak with striking workers.)

By DAN BIDDLE, KEN FINK and DEBRA THAL

(Aug. 17, 1973) To a trio of college journalists, it was Marx brought to life.

At Chrysler's sprawling Mack Ave. stamping plant in Detroit, the workers seized control of the means of production for some 40 hours and had both company and union officials tearing out their hair over what to do about it.

THE TROUBLE started with one Communist.

Bill Gilbreth had been fired from his job the previous Friday and decided over the weekend that the best way to take an insult like that was to take it sitting down.

So he came in Tuesday morning and sat down on top of his machine.

That stopped the assembly line and started the crisis.

...

WHEN THE Ann Arbor college press contingent arrived, the main gate looked like a popular booth at the Street Art Fair, except that the signs didn't advertise jewelry and no one was smiling. Channel 2 was looking for filmable people; Workers' Action Movement (WAM) agitators on the outside of the fence and true-to-life workers on the inside of the fence were harassing the security guards and looking for a fight.

The Daily had no interest in fighting anyone and was looking for a story.

...

BUT COMPANY officials were adamant in their refusal to let any press into the plant.

...

Reporter Biddle tried to talk over the fence to UAW Local President Hank Ghant, but Ghant seemed equally bereft of answers. "We don't support the strike," he said in a strained voice, "but we support their (the rebels) efforts to solve some of the problems here. What happens now? God only knows."

But He wasn't available for comment.

...

BUT THE DAILY was not to be stopped, and...finally a route to journalistic success emerged:

When in doubt, crawl under the fence.

So we did.

FRANK, who seemed to have no difficulty finding his way to either side of the fence, egged us on as we squirmed boldly beneath the cyclone fence delineating the main gate. The action had its drawbacks: it aroused the ire of security guards with gunbelts and swift-moving company officials with jackets and ties. Moreover it aroused the revolutionary fervor of demonstrators on both sides of the gate--something that WAM's people had been trying to arouse all afternoon.

They chanted "Hell, no, they won't go!" as officials moved toward us and tried to arrange our departure. One gentleman who had earlier been impressed with Biddle's politeness in seeking quotes remarked, "Look, friend, you're making my job awfully difficult. I wouldn't go in there if I were you. You're asking for trouble."

...

DEFYING WARNINGS from guards and incredibly hairy eyeballs from officials, we ran into the plant...#

Inside the bowels of Chrysler

By DAN BIDDLE, KEN FINK and DEBRA THAL

(Aug. 18, 1973) The demonstrators on the outside cheered; the officials on the inside shouted warnings and flailed their arms helplessly, and the unlikely band of nervous journalists and Afro-topped Chrysler workers trotted triumphantly into the bowels of the plants.

...

There, amidst vending machines, discarded paper cups and limp uneaten potato chips, sat the forces of revolution.

They stood up and cheered at our arrival; a dozen workers offered us chairs and started responding eagerly when we asked about the morning's events.

BILL GILBRETH, the man of the hour, overruled them.

His blond hair and shaggy mustache stood out in a room full of black men and women; his sense of planning was equally conspicuous. Gilbreth, a self-proclaimed Communist and member of the Marxian Progressive Labor Party, seemed to seek something more than the others: they were trying to shut down Chrysler, but Gilbreth was out to shut down the capitalist system.

...

FRANK LED US on a tour of the plant's conditions, pausing to point to huge grease puddles in working areas. He stopped longest at his own place on the assembly line, where, he said, he had to lift 300 K-frame engine mounts into and out of a stamping machine every hour.

The frames weighed more than 50 pounds each.

"Three, four guys have lost fingers in this machine," he said. Another worker added, "Down here, man, they don't run the fans or nothing. It's like workin' in hell. And upstairs, up there in the press room, that's double hell.

"OVER AT FORD, in their lunchroom, they got air conditioning, and good food. All we got is rats, roaches, and maggots."

If his word wasn't good enough, a pair of rats scurried across the floor as we walked beneath a long row of newly painted engine frames hung up to dry.

That was somewhat more impressive than Gilbreth's revolutionary theories.

OUR RETURN to the lunchroom was punctuated by a brief face-off with security guards. For a moment, push came to shove: Our worker escorts pushed the guards away and shoved us into a nearby staircase which led up to the lunchroom. Amid shouts of "Hands off, honkies!" we stumbled back to Gilbreth's group.

The blond Communist was still trying to "collectivize" his people; they huddled at a table and argued strategy. Further questions from the reporters proved fruitless, and we left the plant through a lightly guarded side gate with the help of our escort and some guards who apparently had little knowledge of our significance and no interest in arresting us.

The Daily got its story; we went and ate at Lafayette Coney Island somewhere in another part of Detroit.

AND THE next morning, Bill Gilbreth's revolution ended in jail.#

Reporter In Dreamland Makes "Sid" A Scalper

(Nov. 13, 1923) "Handling 40,000 tickets per football game over a stretch of 30 years and then to be pulled in for selling 20 pasteboards," sighed Sid Millard, so-called taxi-driver, yesterday in the office of Harry Tillotson, business manager of the athletic association.

Sid has been distributing tickets to Michigan football games in the athletic office for more than 30 years. "He handles every ticket that leaves the office for each game," said Mr. Tillotson, "and is one of the most loyal supporters of University athletics in Ann Arbor."

This is how Sid Millard, local printer, was arraigned before Judge John D. Thomas Saturday in justice court on the charge of ticket scalping. Poor Sid was home asleep at the time.

Reporter Evidently Asleep

A Daily reporter was assigned the cover Saturday night of ticket scalpers whose cases were to come up in Judge Thomas' court. He arrived at court, sat down, and apparently listened. "People fool you sometimes though," as Sid says, and we guess this reporter, over-stimulated by the afternoon's festivities, listened from the cool vale of slumber. After the cases of ticket scalping had been disposed of this reporter suddenly jumped from his seat and walked up to the judge.

"Have you tried any ticket scalpers yet, your honor?" he inquired.

The judge looked at him a moment and then sort of shook his head. The reporter walked to the back of the room. He ran into Harry Tillotson and Louis Burke, village lawyer. These fellows are filled with humor. The reporter stood near them waiting for the scalping cases.

"Sid Millard had twenty tickets that he sold for the game yesterday," said Harry. The reporter jotted something down. Louis Burke saw him.

"He's driving a taxi now, I understand," said Louis. The reporter jotted something else down. The reporter sat down again.

Hears Other Things

Two men...were brought before the court. The reporter suddenly arose again, jotted something down and left the court. Sunday brought this story on the front page of the Daily.

"Fines totaling $150 were doled out last night by Judge John D. Thomas to three men who pleaded guilty to ticket scalping at the game yesterday. Sid Millard, taxi driver, was fined $100 and costs and Peter Lamdo and Sam Mecero were let off with $25 and costs each."

Some men are born sleepy, some achieve sleepiness and others are naturally afflicted with sleeping sickness from birth. Still others are newspaper reporters but thank Morpheus there are not many of them.

"There will be no joy in Arborville tonight
For the star reporter has poohed out."#

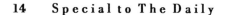

Alger Hiss Denies Delivering Secrets

(Editor's Note: Staffer Roma Lipsky is covering the Hiss Trial for The Daily. Miss Lipsky has been appointed Night Editor for the Fall term.)
By ROMA LIPSKY
(Special to The Daily)

(June 24, 1949) NEW YORK--Taking the stand in his own defense, Alger Hiss declared yesterday that he did not "ever transmit or deliver" any documents to "the man who calls himself Whittaker Chambers."

On trial for perjury, Hiss was calm and soft-spoken during an hour of questioning by his chief defense attorney, Lloyd P. Stryker.

SPECTATORS, who had been awaiting Hiss' testimony all week, were hushed as the former State Department official declared that he was not, and had never been, a member of the Communist Party.

During almost an hour of questioning, Stryker had Hiss review his career, tracing his life from Harvard Law School days to his work as Secretary-General of the San Francisco Conference which framed the United Nations Charter.

Stryker, attempting to prove Hiss' loyalty in contrast to Whittaker Chambers' statements that Hiss supplied secret government documents to Communists, stressed the integrity required in all positions held by Hiss.

He described his duties as secretary of the late Justice Oliver Wendell Holmes, assistant to Francis B. Sales, former Assistant Secretary of State, Executive Secretary of State at the Dumbarton Oaks Conference and advisor to President Roosevelt at the Yalta Conference.

Earlier in the day, the defense continued its attempt to prove that the battered old Woodstock typewriter on which the government claims the stolen documents were typed, was not in Hiss' possession in Jan. 1938. The government claims that it was during this time that the documents were stolen and retyped on the Woodstock.

Defense attorney Edward McLean carried the battered machine, introduced as evidence on Wednesday, to the witness stand several times as witnesses identified it.

* * *

RAYMOND AND Perry Catlett, brothers who had worked at odd jobs for the Hisses in Washington, both testified that the machine was the same one which the Hisses had given to them. The gift was made about the time the Hisses moved from 30th Street in Washington to Volta Place, they said.

Previous testimony showed that this move was made in December, 1937.

Raymond Catlett testified that an FBI agent named "Jones" offered him $200 earlier this year to locate the typewriter. Prosecuting Attorney Thomas Murphy jumped to his feet and angrily attempted to shake Catlett's story.

* * *

"WHO TOLD YOU to say that?" he asked. "They just asked me about it so I told the defense attorney here," Catlett said...#

Red Hearing Observed by Daily Editors

**By AL BLUMROSEN and
DON McNEIL**

(April 13, 1949) Judge Medina sat back in his chair, sad and resigned, defense attorneys pounded constant objections, Assistant Attorney General Frank Gordon doggedly threw question after question at star witness Herbert Philbrick while two Daily reporters looked on last week.

In the corridor leading to Room 110 of the New York Federal Court Building, three policemen stood legs spread, forming a barricade and checking all who tried to enter.

* * *

CROWDS FORMED to get into the courtroom two hours before the sessions began. A dozen people paced out front with signs condemning the "Trial of the Twelve." (Only eleven Communists are on trial since William Z. Foster was too ill to be in court).

A lone, ill-dressed man carried a sandwich board condemning the "red Fascists." Scattered city police watched impassively, kept people moving.

Inside the courtroom, government surprise witness Philbrick, New England advertising manager who had been in both the Communist Party and the FBI for nine years, elaborated on his earlier testimony.

Document after document, used by Philbrick in his teaching career with the party was passed into evidence over objections of defense attorneys.

* * *

THE JURY, tired after ten days of testimony, listened passively. As a result of eight weeks of defense haggling over the "Blue Ribbon" jury, it now numbers three men and nine women, including four Negroes.

Most of them followed the testimony closely, but a balding white haired man in the front row appeared to be asleep during part of the proceedings.

After each list of evidence was submitted, Judge Medina would summarize for the jury from careful notes. His summation invariably met with the defense's most usual phrase, "I object."

Usually the answer was a speedy "overruled."#

Judge revokes Dellinger bail

Surprise witness opens Panther trial

By JENNY STILLER
Special To The Daily

(February 5, 1970) CHICAGO -- A free-for-all between "The Conspiracy" and U.S. marshals broke out at the close of yesterday's session of the Chicago 7 trial as Judge Julius Hoffman revoked bail for defendant David T. Dellinger and ordered the 54-year-old pacifist to jail.

Hoffman cited Dellinger's "vile and insulting" interruptions of court proceedings, referring specifically to an outburst of "Oh, bullshit," aimed at a prosecution witness yesterday morning.

As defense lawyers attempted in vain to dispute Hoffman's ruling, U.S. marshals moving in to arrest Dellinger clashed with the defendants and their staff.

One staff member, press liaison Bob Lamb, was dragged out and handcuffed by four marshalls after he tried to protest other marshals' treatment of defendant Abbie Hoffman. Lamb remained in jail overnight awaiting arraignment this morning, probably on charges of assaulting a U.S. marshal.

Dellinger's "obscenity" was uttered yesterday morning during testimony by Deputy Police Chief James D. Riordan of the Chicago Police Dept.

Riordan was recalling alleged actions by Dellinger on the afternoon of Wed., Aug. 28, 1968, when the former co-chairman of the National Mobilization Committee to End the War in Vietnam interrupted him.

"Oh, bullshit," Dellinger laughed. "That's an absolute lie. Let's argue about what I stand for and what you stand for," he told the witness, "but let's not tell lies."

Judge Hoffman dismissed the jury and strictly admonished the defendant for his use of "profanity."

...

The trial continued peacefully until just after 5:30 p.m. when the Judge dismissed the jury for the evening before announcing his surprise ruling on Dellinger.

Hoffman cited cases to demonstrate that when a "trial is disturbed or impeded" by a defendant, the judge is within his rights to revoke bail.

Defense attorney William Kunstler attempted to condemn the Judge's action, but was cut off when Hoffman declared the court in recess.

As marshals moved toward Dellinger, defendant Abbie Hoffman stood in their way and said, "Don't take him."

The marshals then seized Hoffman and began pulling him away from the defense table. The defendant's wife Anita, sitting in the front row, tried to pull them away from him.

She was forced back into her seat by three marshals. Another marshal approached Abbie Hoffman while he was struggling with two others and threw him to the floor.

Lamb was arrested when he approached the marshals scuffling with Hoffman. Other members of the defense staff, as well as defendants Rennie Davis and Tom Hayden also joined in the melee.

As the uproar died down briefly, Davis yelled at the judge: "This court is bullshit! I say it too. Revoke my bail too. This court is the most obscene thing I have ever seen."

Jerry Rubin, standing near Dellinger, shouted: "You're not going to separate us! We're partners! Take us all!" The other defendants also took up the cry.

Rubin's wife yelled "Right on!" and was dragged from the room by the marshals. Fighting broke out again as Rubin attempted to get to her, screaming "Take your hands off my wife!" She was expelled from the courtroom but not arrested.

...

Kunstler, pleading with the judge to call off the marshals and reconsider his decision on Dellinger shouted, "Your honor, is their no decency left here?" He received no verbal answer.

...

Abbie Hoffman was livid as he screamed to his namesake on the bench, "You're a disgrace to the Jews, you runt! You're a fascist! Why don't you work for the Nazis?" #

By ALAN LENHOFF
Special To The Daily

(March 19, 1971) NEW HAVEN, Conn. -- The trial of Black Panther leaders Bobby Seale and Ericka Huggins opened here yesterday under tight security with the testimony of a surprise prosecution witness--Black Panther Margaret Hudgins.

Seale, party chairman, and Huggins, a local party leader, face charges of murder, kidnapping and conspiracy in connection with the May 17, 1969 slaying of alleged police informer and Black Panther Alex Rackley.

The pair, along with Hudgins, were among a group of 14 Panthers originally indicted last year by a New Haven grand jury on the charges. Hudgins was given a suspended sentence on a charge of aggravated assault after she agreed to plead guilty to the lesser charge.

Hudgins was served with the subpoena by state attorney's officers outside the courtroom of State Superior Court Judge Harold Mulvey while awaiting entrance to the trial.

Prosecuting Attorney Arnold Markle's motion to grant Hudgins immunity from further prosecution on the basis of her testimony brought a sharp accusation from defense attorney Catherine Roraback that Markle was engaging in a "grandstand play."

Far from serving the "public interest," as Markle claimed, Roraback said the granting of such a motion would deprive Hudgins of her constitutional rights to invoke the fifth amendment.

Roraback also pointed out that at the trial of Panther Lonnie McLucas a similar motion to grant immunity to Hudgins had been denied.

"The central issue is what is the public interest?" Roraback said.

Judge Mulvey recessed the trial for three hours and then granted Hudgins immunity from prosecution. She took the stand in the afternoon.

Hudgins was a defense witness last summer at the trial of McLucas, [who] was convicted of conspiracy to murder Rackley and was sentenced to 12 to 15 years in prison...#

8,000 protest at Harrisburg trial

by MARY KRAMER
Special To The Daily

(April 2, 1972) HARRISBURG, Pa. -- Holy week activities in support of the Berrigan conspiracy trial defendants came to a close here yesterday with a mass anti-war rally of over 8,000 people.

As the day progressed, it became doubtful that the jury would deliver its verdict during its second full day of deliberation.

The crowd marched in the early afternoon from an uptown rallying point to the state capitol grounds to hear a scheduled program of speeches.

Following an introduction and standing ovation, Rev. Daniel Berrigan read a letter from his brother Philip, a Harrisburg 7 defendant.

"Even if a conviction comes down, we are not convicted. It's the government's indictment. The real indictment is to be violent in any way," the letter stated.

Berrigan added that his brother and the other defendants thought of the children and the future "while they endured the kangaroos in the court."

The theme of the day was support for all political prisoners. Rep. Bella Abzug, D-N.Y., called for a "national committment to amnesty" for all war resisters, including the Harrisburg 7.

Rev. Ralph Abernathy added, "Richard Nixon should be the first to get down on his knees and ask the American people for amnesty."

Letters of support from foreign peace groups were read and Madame Binh, the head of the South Vietnam's Provisional Revolutionary Government, addressed the crowd by phone from Paris.

Although most of the week's activities were centered on religious or non-violent groups, a wide range of organizations participated in yesterday's rally.

At the head of the march to the Capitol grounds, was a contingent of Vietnam Veterans Against the War.

The remainder of the marchers were divided among Angela Davis supporters, Communist party members and a group called Federal Employes for Peace...#

Testimony conflicts in Plamondon case

By DAVID STOLL
Special To The Daily

(July 24, 1973) CADILLAC, Mi. -- In courtroom action yesterday which occasionally measured up to the standards of TV melodrama, prosecution witness Bruce Peterson took the stand in the trial of Rainbow People's Party members Pun Plamondon and Craig Blazier.

The two are being tried on charges of extortion, conspiracy and usury in connection with an incident which occurred last January near Traverse City.

AS ANTICIPATED, Peterson flatly contradicted major points of Uwe Wagner's testimony. Wagner is the man the two defendants allegedly threatened.

He has testified that the two brandished a knife and a derringer, threatened him with bodily harm and took his personal possessions as collateral on a $3500 drug debt.

Peterson, Wagner's roommate at the time, testified yesterday that he had not seen either a gun or a knife. He further testified that Wagner himself had suggested his possessions be taken as collateral.

ACCORDING TO Peterson, Plamondon and Blazier had warned off others who were planning to use "icepicks and battery acid" on Wagner if he did not pay up.

Threats made by the two, Peterson testified, included a vow to print Wagner's picture in the Ann Arbor Sun--a paper closely linked to the Rainbow People's Party--and a threat to tell immigration officials about Wagner's activities. Wagner is a German citizen.

The only time Plamondon became angry, Peterson added, was when "he discovered a syringe and three bottles containing morphine, methadone and Fidelin--a hard drug."

"HE TOOK THE syringe," Peterson testified, "and threw it on the floor and stomped on it with his foot. Then he took the bottles and flushed them down the toilet."

...

One particular bit of histrionics that occurred during this phase of the testimony came when defense counsel Buck Davis asked, "If I described Uwe Wagner as an egotistical, lying, slimy double-dealing little punk, would you agree with me?"

After a moment of reflection, Peterson cast his eyes upward and replied, "Yes."

In an unsuccessful motion asking that Peterson be declared "a hostile witness to the prosecution," a distraught Wilson pointed out to the court that Peterson has been "going with, sleeping with, eating at the expense of and being counseled by the defendants and their attorneys."..#

Plamondon guilty of extortion

By DAVID STOLL
Special To The Daily

(July 28, 1973) CADILLAC, Mi.-- A Wexford County circuit judge yesterday found Rainbow People's Party members Pun Plamondon and Craig Blazier guilty of extortion by threat of accusation.

However, Judge William Peterson found the two men innocent of three other related charges and criticized the state of Michigan for going to too much trouble in prosecuting the pair.

...

The judge called the extent of the prosecution's efforts "foolish" and told Plamondon and Blazier, "an inordinate amount of time and expense has been spent on you."..#

Plamondon, Blazier sentenced

By DAVID STOLL
Special To The Daily

(Sept. 29, 1973) CADILLAC -- Rainbow People's Party (RPP) members Pun Plamondon and Craig Blazier were sentenced to probation here yesterday in the wake of their convictions last month on the charge of extortion.

District Court Judge William Peterson sentenced Plamondon to five years probation and ordered him to pay $1,500 in court costs. Blazier drew two years probation and a $600 fine.

...

[Peterson] specifically directed the defendants to refrain from smoking marijuana, but imposed no restriction on RPP-related political activities...#

getting
the
story

**what
I did
for love**

...or, some of the weird
and wonderful things Daily
staffers have done in pursuit
of a story.

Certainly the biggest sports story during my year as Sports Editor was the naming of a new football coach. While the appointment of Bump Elliott as head coach was the headline, in many respects the real story was the "firing" of Benny Oosterbaan; except, of course, that Michigan does not fire coaches.

We had heard rumors for some time that Benny's style of coaching was too old fashioned, that we were in the era of the T-formation, and he was still using the single-wing. When we got word that the Board in Control of Intercollegiate Athletics was having a special meeting in the Union, we sensed that something unusual was up. One of our junior reporters was able to position himself at a heating duct outlet, through which he could hear everything being said at the Board meeting. About midevening he sent back word that Oosterbaan was being kicked upstairs, to some sort of assistant athletic director role, and Elliott was being named head coach.

I wrote the story, quoting a "reliable source." The story ran in The Daily the next morning, getting a half-day jump on all of the other media.

Perhaps that was the most fun. Throughout the evening, as we were getting our reports from our "source," we had to fend off questions from the local AP stringer (now a Detroit sportswriter), who spent most of his time hanging around The Daily. He sensed that something was up, and kept asking if there was any important news. We kept saying there wasn't, and he didn't have the story until the Daily was off the presses several hours later.

Alan H. Jones, '59

REPORT ELLIOTT COACH

By AL JONES
Daily Sports Editor

(Nov. 14, 1958) Chalmers 'Bump' Elliott will replace Bennie G. Oosterbaan as head football coach, reliable sources said last night.

The Daily learned last night that the Board in Control of Intercollegiate Athletics passed a resolution recommending that Elliott be named head football coach.

Submitted to Regents

It is reported that the resolution will be submitted to the Regents at their monthly meeting today. The resolution as reported reads: "The Board in Control of Intercollegiate Athletics recommends that Chalmers W. Elliott assume the duties of head football coach as of January 1, 1959, at a salary of $16,000 a year."

According to the source the Board has received a resignation from Oosterbaan. However, when he was contacted last night he had no comment to make. It was supposedly emphasized at the meeting that he had not resigned "under pressure."

...

"No Comment"

None of the members of the Board in Control would comment on the validity of the resolution. H. O. "Fritz" Crisler, Athletic Director, refused to either confirm or deny the existence of such a resolution.

The resolution, in any form, is not at present on the agenda of the Regents meeting. Lyle Nelson, Director of University Relations, said that something new could be put there by 'U' President Hatcher today.

...

At last night's meeting no other candidates were considered for the head coaching job, and Elliott was apparently a unanimous choice. Many other men had been rumored as possibilities in the past few years, but reportedly none were mentioned last night.

It is understood that Oosterbaan will remain with the Athletic Department in a new position, probably with a salary cut. The $16,000 in line for Elliott is the highest starting salary ever offered a head coach at Michigan.

...

Reportedly the members of the Board in Control decided last night that the resolution wasn't to be made public as yet. They were all sworn to secrecy, and the notes from the meeting have been suppressed.

...

When contacted before the meeting Marcus Plant, Faculty Representative to the Big Ten, and John Herrnstein, a student representative on the Board, both stated that such a resolution wasn't on the agenda for the evening...#

On the telephone

Daily Calls Moscow-- 'That's G-e-o-r-g-i, Operator'

(March 15, 1953) Can you call Georgi Malenkov?

The Daily tried to phone Russia's new premier early yesterday morning.

Result: 65 cents toll charge, three hours and forty-five minutes of time, a chaotic repartee with four operators on both sides of the Atlantic and a word of greeting from a famed correspondent behind the iron curtain.

❋ ❋ ❋ ❋

ALTHOUGH the call never got through to Malenkov, Russian major Jerry Wisniewski, '53, who handled the job for The Daily, cut his way through a series of brush-offs and wire tangles with a morning's worth of persistence...

7:59 a.m. (3:59 p.m. Moscow time)

Wisniewski: How do you do. I would like to place a call to Georgi Malenkov in the Kremlin, Moscow. I don't know the exact number. This is The Michigan Daily calling.

Operator: Just a minute...What is that city, sir? Is that in the United States?

Wis: In Moscow. This is in Russia,

---

not in the United States, please.

Op: What is your name and number?

Wis: This is The Michigan Daily, 2-3241, extension 33.

Op: Thank you. I'll call you back, sir.

...

Op: We have gotten through to Moscow. Apparently they're trying his home and it does not answer.

Wis: Thank you. Can you call to the Kremlin itself?

Op: The overseas operator doesn't feel we can call the Kremlin. Do you know what building he is located in?

Wis: Get the Kremlin and we can work from there. Or perhaps I could get through by way of the American Embassy. You see, this way we could get definite information.

...

Overseas Operator: He is not at the Embassy.

Wis: That I know. Why I want to call the Embassy is to get his number in the Kremlin (cut-off). Perhaps this will help. There is an American correspondent, Mr. Edward Gilmore of the Associated Press, who might know the number. Or if you can't get him Mr. Harrison Salisbury is the correspondent for The New York Times... I'm wondering why the secretary at the Embassy doesn't have the number of the Kremlin.

Op: Do they have a special line to the Kremlin?

Ov: That number is not listed at the Embassy.

Wis: I shold think you would have that number. It was published in an American magazine several months ago. I think it was an exchange and then four numbers. The first two, I think, are 7-3.

...

10:30 a.m. (6:30 p.m. Moscow time)
...Ov: We have Mr. Gilmore on the line. Do you want to speak with him?

Wis: This is The Michigan Daily calling. Couldn't you obtain the information from Mr. Gilmore?

Gilmore: Hello. (cut-off)

...

Op: If you want to speak to this correspondent, you might get the number of the Kremlin from him. It's a non-published number.

Wis: The reason I ask for this number from the Embassy is that it was published a couple of months ago in in a magazine. It would seem to me you could get this number. That's what I ask.

Ov: Hello, Moscow. Hello, Mr. Gilmore.

Moscow Op (aside): Nye anayu schto dyl (I don't know what to do)...#

EXCLUSIVE:
Daily Phone Call Fails to Find Benes

By AL BLUMROSEN

(March 12, 1948) From behind the Iron Curtain, four words slipped out to The Daily yesterday about President Eduard Benes.

"He is not expected."

In an attempt to give the campus complete coverage of the Czech coup and Masaryk's suicide, I tried to reach President Benes by transatlantic telephone Wednesday.

I called the local operator and asked to speak to President Benes in Prague. The local operator called the New York operator, who called the transatlantic operator who put through the call to an operator in Europe...

The scene at The Daily was tense with expectation Wednesday evening.

At 7 p.m., a report came in that Benes would call The Daily at 3 p.m. on Thursday. We waited with bated breaths.

At 9:45 a.m. I was dragged out of a political science class to talk to Czechoslovakia. (There is a five hour time difference between here and central Europe.)

Benes' assistant was willing to talk, but the president himself was not available. I told the operator to keep trying.

Tension mounted as the afternoon wore on. Whenever the telephone rang, furtive glances passed among the staff. If that was Benes, who would talk to him?

At 4:30 p.m. yesterday, the transatlantic operator called and said that Benes was not expected.

The call was cancelled.#

A Bunny philosophy: Getting paid for playing girl

By LISA STEPHENS

(EDITOR'S NOTE: Miss Stephens, '70, worked as a Bunny last summer at the Detroit Playboy Club.)

(April 13, 1969) **AND ON THE EIGHTH DAY,** God created the Bunny Mother to protect and shepherd all Playboy Bunnies.

For the Detroit Playboy Club he created Mrs. Lee Wozena, a University graduate who used to live in Stockwell and who watches over 31 Bunnies.

Not that Bunnies need a guardian angel. Contrary to delicious rumors, the Bunny world is a straight world, straight enough to warm the heart of the stuffiest mother superior.

...

Nor do Bunnies provide the center foldout for the magazine. In the entire history of Playboy, only three Bunnies have ever been found with a staple in their navel.

RATHER, YOUR function in the Club is that of a super stewardess or hostess. You serve drinks, smile, make pleasant conversation, smile, look pretty, smile, and make sure all the guests are having an enjoyable evening...

The first commandment of Bunnydom? "No Bunny may at any time and under any circumstances date a Playboy key-holder." No exceptions. You are fired on the spot; no questions asked.

...

You may not touch a Bunny, ever. Even a pat on the wrist. That may sound like a tall order for the average American male, but most men hold up amazingly well. Men who come to the club want to impress you with their sophistication, so they don't lunge at you...

...

A BUNNY may never sit down while on duty. She may "perch"--that is, lean up against a bar stool or railing if she's not busy--but never closer than three feet from a customer and then only if there's a chair arm, bar stool or table between them.

She may not drink in the club under any conditions, nor may she do so publicly if she is representing Playboy. She may not at any time be photographed with a drink or a cigarette in her hand, nor does she ever do anything in public to call attention to herself. In short, she follows all the rules taught in finishing schools.

...

BUNNIES ARE, in sum, projecting an image of an abstraction: the ideal pretty girl next door. They are the vestal virgins of the 20th century, made more attractive by their utter unavailability.

In a day when women decry their second-class citizenship and eschew femininity as an ever-present trap, it is surprising to hear some of the comments of guests in the club. Most men complain vehemently about wives who ignore them because they are too busy with their own careers or bridge clubs.

...

BUT WHAT about the girl inside the image? How does she get to be a Bunny? Does she become a toy or an object to be used? In an age of women's liberation, does she remain an unwitting slave? Bunnydom can be a rather spectacular way of beating men at their own game.

Look at it this way: I can't type. I went to look for a summer job, and the first thing a prospective employer asks a girl is: "Can you type?"

"No. But I speak four languages."

"That doesn't help. Can you type?"

"I'll be getting my B.A. in--"

"Sorry. I'm afraid the only place for women in our business is in the steno pool."

Or clerking. Or filing. Anything a trained monkey could do. Why bother?

Women get paid less in executive positions, too, if they are allowed to advance. Their salary can be as much as 40-60 per cent less than their male counterpart. Businessmen will pay you $100 a week because you're only a girl. But those same businessmen are willing to pay you more than twice that at the club--because you're a girl. There's much less selling out involved in wearing ears and a tail than in using your B.A. to correct bad diction on someone's office memos.

"I decided to come here," one fellow Bunny who quit her job as an engineer...said, "because I was tired of doing a man's work at a woman's pay and not getting any credit for it."..#

The Great Garbage Caper

One of the great challenges back then was to get stories, appointments, etc., in advance of their formal announcement at the Regents' meeting. One of my more audacious colleagues led a raid on the administration building to collect several bags of garbage from the basement. They lugged it back to The Daily and we sorted it out, discovering, among other things, discarded IBM typewriter ribbons on which you could read the text of letters announcing the appointment of two new University vice-presidents. Naturally we ran the story. Since then, IBM has changed its machines--and I'm confident the University has installed a shredder!

Sara Fitzgerald, '73

Overberger to be research VP

Chemistry chairman selected

By ROSE SUE BERSTEIN
Feature Editor

(April 15, 1972) Chemistry Prof. Charles Overberger has been selected University vice president for research, The Daily learned yesterday.

In a letter obtained by The Daily, President Robben Fleming indicated Overberger has been appointed to the research post.

Overberger declined to comment on the appointment last night, while Fleming could not be reached.

Vice President for Academic Affairs Allan Smith disclaimed knowledge of the appointment. "I haven't been to any meetings on it," he said.

Overberger is chairman of the chemistry department, director of the Macromolecular Research Center and an internationally recognized expert on polymer chemistry.

Like his predecessor, A. Geoffrey Norman, Overberger is believed by some observers to favor retention of classified research projects on campus...#

Police nab 14 in raids on two massage studios

By JONATHAN MILLER
Feature Editor

(Oct. 18, 1972) Squads of city police yesterday raided two local "massage studios," emerging with 14 prisoners, customer records and a quantity of marijuana.

After conducting a thorough search of the two establishments, they closed them down as "houses of prostitution."

...

The massage studios, described by one officer as the most extensive vice operations in the city's history, were simultaneously raided by the police shortly before 4 p.m...#

Ceasar's: Is the medium more than the massage?

By SARA FITZGERALD
Editor

(Oct. 18, 1972) The sign outside says "Ceasar's Retreat Health and Massage Studios, Inc."

But up the stairs at 212 W. Huron St., there was apparently more going on than just massage.

Early last month, The Daily received a telephone call from a female student who had answered a "Help Wanted" ad appearing in The Daily classified pages. The ad, which had run for about a week, read:

"YOUNG energetic people needed to work in health studio. Please call 769-XXXX for an appointment to be interviewed."

...

Using an assumed name, I called and made an appointment to be interviewed at 11:00 on the morning of Sept. 27.

...

I entered a waiting room with a couch and a sign that proclaimed "Girls, sauna, massage, pool, girls." A young woman met me at the entrance to the next room and immediately asked me, "Would you be willing to give a massage topless?"

When I replied "yes," she invited me in and gave me an application form to fill out.

...

She then rose to show me the layout of the place. The girls, she said, were expected to socialize with the members in the large carpeted room where we were standing. There would be pool tables installed in the room soon, she maintained.

...

She took me behind a partition and pointed out where the club's sauna would also eventually be installed. Then she led me into one of the club's three "massage" rooms.

The rooms were narrow, windowless, and equipped with a telephone, alarm clock and a narrow bed against one wall. Two of them had showers.

...

"Now when you massage a guy," she said, "he's likely to get horny. And he may want you to do anything from a hand job to a blow job to balling him. What's your reaction to that?" she asked.

I hesitated, then said, "Well, I guess it would depend on the guy."

She accepted that and went on. "What you make is between you and the guy. The rest of the girls don't have to know. However, we do have base rates as a guide. You see," she explained, "if one girl charges $10 for something and another girl charges $20, the customer's going to be mad. And we want the customer to be satisfied."

She paused, then continued. "Your practice session will probably be with the manager. He won't pull any punches--he'll want you to be prepared for anything!"

"Don't let your friends talk you out of it," she said. "I've had a lot of girls who said they'd do it, then went home and told their friends, 'You know that massage parlor I applied at...,' then their friends would convince them not to go ahead with it."

...

Two hours later, I called back and turned down the job.#

Marching with Stanford

By BETH NISSEN

(Sept. 25, 1973) Clad in a floppy white hat, cardinal-red jacket and goggles, I set out to get the inside story on the colorful Stanford Marching Band at last Saturday's Michigan-Stanford football game.

I turned my vintage 1973 Chablis wine bottle under the direction of their gypsy-clad drum major. All I had to do, I was assured, was follow the saxophone player in front of me.

WITH A GOOD supply of blind faith, I marched out in step (yes, they do all try to start on the same foot) and under the pressure of 80,000 pairs of eyes, ran to the correct positions guided by the shouts of cooperative band members.

Their sudden offer to let me march with them during half time had been no joke; it was just typical of their "have a good time" philosophy toward marching band.

"We like to do unrehearsed things on the field," explained bandsman Peter Boone, who enjoys the distinction of being the only acoustic guitar player in a Big Ten or Pacific Eight marching band.

"THE MICHIGAN band doesn't seem relaxed," he continued. "I had ROTC in high school and it wasn't that regimented." (A Stanford T-shirt read, "Free the Michigan 235.")

Despite a difference in philosophy between the two bands, the Stanford band members still held high respect for Michigan's military precision.

"For their kind of band they're the best," said Steve Burgert. "For our kind of band we're as good as can be expected."

...

"But I hate the sterile look of the band," he continued. "We prefer 1973 to 1810." (The band members agree that Michigan's style is outdated for them. They referred to Michigan's band leader as "Cadaver.")

Stanford band members passed a lighted joint around like a Michigan football, presumably to help them with the high notes.

"REALITY," philosophized Monty Bossard, "is 84 fools who drive 4,000 miles for an eight minute halftime."#

the political beat

Wire services are all well and good, but when major political events occur, The Daily just naturally has to be there, in person. Since the post-World War II years, Daily reporters have always considered Washington to be part of the beat.

One of the most famous Daily stories was the cover of the 1928 Presidential election. We supported Al Smith against Hoover, the only paper in Michigan to do so. George Tilley, one of the night editors, was writing strong pro-Smith editorials. I was supporting Smith in my Toasted Rolls column.

For election night Tilley and I had plans ready with a three-column cut of Smith and a one-column cut of Hoover. Tilley was to be night editor and I worked with him. When most of the night staff had left, we made up the front page with the cut of Smith at the top and the headline "Happy Warrior Vanquished." For a cutline there was "Glorious in Defeat" followed by about a five-inch double column strong pro-Smith editorial. At the bottom of the page in column seven, as I recall, was the one-column cut of Hoover with a noncommittal head "Next President."

--Lawrence Klein, '30

Anti-Red Bill Sent To Senate

Speaker Pro-Tem Rebukes Gallery Demonstrators For Disorder

By ARTHUR A. MILLER

(May 24, 1935) Before a gallery packed with more than 400 protestors to the Dunckel-Baldwin bill, some of whom were University students, the House passed the anti-violent overthrow measure while representatives on opposing sides nearly came to blows.

Figuring prominently among the bill's opponents was Rep. Redmond M. Burr of Ann Arbor.

Laws of parliamentary procedure were hard to enforce as cross debate filled the room with confusing noise. Immediately before the final count was taken, however, the assemblage quieted. An address by Rep. Joseph F. Martin, Jr., of Detroit, emphasized the "un-American" aspects of the measure, adding "when you suppress you condense and like gasoline, when it is condensed it explodes." He stated that the bill made possible the "raiding of any meeting, where your children or mine may be, if the wrong kind of handbills are being distributed -- and who is going to be sure of the people hiring the distributors?"

The gallery was conspicuously void of American Legionnaires who had been present at former sessions. The spectators were mostly opposed to the measure, many of them wearing tags with the slogan, "Don't pass 262," printed on them.

William Weinstone, Communist leader and the spearhead of the extra-official protestations, appeared at intervals in the gallery. In an interview, he stated that "despite the amendments, it remains the same bill in substance."

While the arguments were flying, the whole debate was termed "silly" by representatives, among whom were Martin, Burr and Clines. Immediately before its passage, the sponsors of the measure seemed to be acceding to the negative pressure since they offered arguments only spasmodically.#

Kelly, Hague Charged With "Steering" Convention

By BERNARD ROSENBERG
Special to The Daily

(July 23, 1944) CHICAGO STADIUM--July 22--With the cards stacked heavily against him, Henry Wallace went down to defeat Friday in the Chicago Stadium. But he did it in such a way as to enhance his immense popularity with the common man whom he has always championed.

Senator Harry S. Truman, new Democratic Vice-Presidential candidate, is a good man. That Henry Wallace is a better one is incidental to the forces behind each political figure.

American democracy was trampled underfoot at this convention in a manner that can but redound ill to the names of those involved. On the side of Truman was "Bossism;" on the side of Wallace were the people. Last week-end 64% of the rank and file of Democratic voters had expressed preference for Wallace above any aspirant. Dr. Gallup had revealed that but a meager 2% wanted Truman. How then did the Senator become the nominee?

For the answer, one needed but to look at the beaming features of "Big" Jim Farley, as he cast his half vote for Senator Barkley. Contentment that could probably be seen in the last tier of the stadium emanated from Farley's face. He and his fellow politicos had stopped Wallace cold.

Take genial Jim's hand, entwine it with Boss Hague's and Ed Kelly's and Tom Pendergrast's, put Henry Wallace in the middle; Squeeze. Then you have a pretty good picture of the way in which the people's will was flouted at this convention.

Time and again Chairman Jackson had to call for order in a gallery packed with Wallace boosters who kept chorusing their support for him throughout the crucifixion. Boss Kelly personally nominated Senator Lucas as a smoke-screen candidate behind whom he could hide until the second climactic ballot when Illinois, along with almost every state delegation, bolted to Truman.

Kelly started to say, "We want--" and the gallery shouted "Wallace." Five times Kelly started that sentence and five times the people finished it for him in their own way. That was the most heartwarming scene of a generally disgraceful charade.

...

...more than one hoot was audible when Truman rose to accept the position tendered him by conventioneers who hopped on the bandwagon with alacrity as soon as they saw who would win.

There was something pathetic about the good little Senator as he stood in the shadow of Boss Hannegan, his fellow Missourian, and went through the theatricality required by photographers...#

Truman Takes Helm; Daily Reporters in Capitol

Find City 'Somber, Waiting'

By MONROE FINK and
ALLAN ANDERSON
Special to The Daily

(April 14, 1945) WASHINGTON, D. C., 7:30 p.m., Friday, April 13--Arriving in Washington, D. C., at 7 p.m. we found quiet, somber Washington awaiting tonight the funeral services of Franklin D. Roosevelt, Thirty-Second President of the United States, to be held at four p.m. today in the East Room of the White House.

In the last twenty-three hours, by means of the thumb, we have traveled from Packard and Washtenaw to Pennsylvania Avenue in Washington, D. C. to witness the final honors that the nation's capital will pay to what a truck driver from Canton, a football coach from Belleview, Ohio, and a doctor from Wheeling, West Virginia all described as "the greatest President since Abraham Lincoln."

In all the 21 people who were responsible for our transportation from Ann Arbor to Washington, we found the same basic fears and emotions; a deep expression of reverence for the departed President and a distinct feeling of uncertainty as to the future.

...

"The best friend that the American workingman ever had," was how a coal miner who picked us up at 5:30 a.m. yesterday morning on his way to work at the colliery at Waynesburg, Ohio, put it...

"The President was sure working hard to see that we wouldn't ever again have to get involved in the mess we're mixed up in at present. What's going to become of those plans for a lasting peace is what I'm worried about," said a G.I. sergeant on the way to his camp just outside of Wheeling, West Virginia.

Washington is at present enjoying the momentary lull before the storm. As yet the great crowds which are expected to form along Pennsylvania Ave., the route which the funeral procession will take on its way to the White House from Union Station, have not yet arrived. The city has apparently recovered from its first shock on hearing the news. As the cab driver, whom we hailed upon reaching the outskirts of the city, expressed it, "By four o'clock this afternoon (Friday), I felt it would be alright if I took out my cab again and started to do a little business."#

Daily Extra To Uphold 'Latest Deadline' Tradition

(Nov. 2, 1948) Following its motto, "Latest Deadline in the State," The Daily will hold its presses until 6 a.m. tomorrow in order to bring readers the election results.

According to the best available estimates there should be fairly conclusive results at this time in the national elections.

WASHTENAW COUNTY returns should also be complete but the close Michigan gubernatorial race will probably not be resolved until later in the day.

...

Daily reporters will have special color articles capturing the election night flavor of a local party headquarters, interviews with candidates nervously awaiting returns, and impressions of a roving reporter. This "color" will supplement the straight news coverage of the local race.

Because of the late deadline the special election Daily will reach your residence slightly later than the normal delivery time. Extra copies will be sold during the morning at various spots on the campus.#

Truman No Longer Little Man In Big Job

By TOM WALSH
Special to The Daily

EDITOR'S NOTE: This is the first of a series of interpretive articles on political trends and personalities in Washington by a Daily staff correspondent.

(July 24, 1947) WASHINGTON-- Meeting the President of the United States is quite a thrill, but it is a far greater thrill to watch Harry Truman in action and to come away confident that, whatever his shortcomings when he first took office, he is now a competent chief executive in his own right.

That's the impression I got last week at a White House press conference at which the President announced his appointments to the National Labor Relations Board.

...

Falling in behind the regular Washington correspondents who charged into the circular, high-domed office, I jockeyed into a favorable position just as the President said, "I have several announcements for you this afternoon." Standing in front of his wide mahogany desk, the President seemed very much at ease as he read off his appointments in the slow monotonous voice that is familiar to millions of radio listeners.

As soon as Mr. Truman finished speaking, a barrage of questions followed.

...

A White House oldtimer tried to pin him down about a trip to Brazil. Laughing easily he parried with, "I've wanted to go for a long time. I haven't made any plans yet, Smitty, but I'll let you know in plenty of time to pack."

Most remarkable to me was not the answers he gave but the manner in which he gave them. No longer, at least, can Harry Truman be considered a "little man in too big a job" as he was so often labelled when he first took office. The President's self-assurance provided an enviable model and he was in complete command of the situation throughout the conference...#

Philadelphia Sound and Fury Reach Climax

Michigan Split

By JOHN CAMPBELL

(June 26, 1948) PHILADELPHIA, June 23--(Delayed) -- The once-solid Michigan delegation here at the GOP convention may not be able to stay together after all.

On the eve of the all-important balloting, it appears possible that a split will develop between the Dewey and stop-Dewey factions. Although the whole delegation has been plunking for Senator Vandenberg, it is known that many delegates actually prefer Dewey to Vandenberg and they have asked Governor Sigler to release them from their pledge early in the game if a Dewey landslide develops.

At the same time, the stop-Dewey forces have come out into the open in the form of a coalition including Governor Duff of Pennsylvania, Harold Stassen of Minnesota, Senator Taft of Ohio and Governor Sigler of Michigan. They asserted that they have made no "ticket deals" and only want to "give the delegates a fair chance to vote for the man they want." Nevertheless, Dewey supporters in Michigan may split the delegation wide open rather than join a move really aimed against their favorite...

Only avowed candidate who isn't sure (for public consumption at least) he's going to win is Gov. Earl Warren of California...#

Victory...

By HAROLD JACKSON
(Special to The Daily)

(June 26, 1948) CONVENTION HALL, Philadelphia, June 25--Thomas E. Dewey of the Class of '23 Lit tonight became the unanimous choice of the Republican Party for President of the United States.

Dewey rode to victory on an unnecessary third ballot taken shortly after the evening session convened at 8:00 p.m.

...

An almost unprecedented show of party unity preceded the taking of the ballot as every other candidate withdrew in favor of Dewey. Governor Bricker of Ohio led the parade to the rostrum by reading a letter from Senator Taft releasing his delegation and asking the unamimous election of Dewey. Next came Governor Warren's representative Senator Nolan and then Harold Stassen, tall and smiling, strode to the rostrum to withdraw himself from the race and pledge his support to Dewey.

...

On and on they came, Governor Sigler in shirt sleeves announced Senator Vandenberg's support of Dewey, next came Senator Baldwin, Connecticut's favorite son, and finally Harlan Kelly, blind Milwaukee veteran, and leader of the MacArthur for President campaign...#

(Nov. 5, 1948) ANYWAY, HERE IT IS--No, this isn't a picture of University alumnus Thomas E. Dewey glumly getting the latest election returns day before yesterday, but of the then future (now ex-) Presidential candidate as he appeared in a Union opera of the early '20's. This picture, exhumed from some musty files, would have run in yesterday's Daily if Dewey had won. He lost, but we're running it anyway because of its intrinsic interest and because we've already paid to have it engraved.

Stevenson Proper Leader
For The 'New America'

(Oct. 30, 1956) **WHETHER AMERICANS** desire it or not, the coming years will bring them face to face with a "New America." It promises to be more than a campaign slogan, no matter what the outcome of the election. It will be an America of unprecedented material prosperity as technological and economic science continue to advance. It will be an America with unprecedented proportions of its population made up of school age children as a result of higher birth rates and of retirement age adults as a result of increasing longevity. It will be an America of unprecedented urban decay, as the houses and apartments erected to support fantastic growth of our towns and villages into giant cities fall into ruin and blight. It will be an America faced with unprecedented--and almost daily--evolution in the strategy and structure of the Soviet empire.

...

THE QUESTION which has been placed before the voters in 1956 is not whether there shall be a New America but whether it shall be a Better America. For if the challenges which 1956 presents are lost--if the New America is smugly met with the Old Solutions--opportunity will degenerate into tragedy, and future generations will be forced to consider how the New America can be again made as good a place as the Old.

The New America will not become the Better America through the efforts of one man, or even one party. But in 1956, when the outlines of the last half of the Twentieth Century are beginning to emerge, Adlai Stevenson has emerged as a man uniquely aware of its challenges and determined to see our nation meet them.

Of all the characteristics which make Adlai Stevenson a proper leader of the New America--acute intelligence, refreshing candor, incisive articulation, sober judgment--perhaps none is more needed today than his keenly attuned perception of the problems of our times.

Perception, indeed, is one of the gaping inadequacies of our present leadership. It involves the ability to see change, to relate it to basic continuity, and to determine how much weight to give each in framing the nation's policies. It is the ability to tell the New America from the Old, and to give proper emphasis to the elements of change and those of continuity.

With acuteness of perception comes leadership to meet well-perceived needs and energy to awaken the New America to the changes it has experienced, as well as to go on meeting the continuing problems of the past. And with it also comes moderation, which is little more than such perception put into intelligent practice.

It would be misleading to attribute to Stevenson a monopoly on perception of the problems of the New America. The President's speeches sometimes hint at the same sort of problems the Democratic candidate has been discussing. But for a man of action so suspicious of "words" and "fine phrases," the President has shown himself woefully inadequate in the area of deeds.

...

The New Deal and the Truman Doctrine, however updated, are no longer sufficient to the problems of the New America, and while the "New Republicanism" of Dwight Eisenhower is far more relevant to our times than any brands of his party's doctrine within memory, it lacks the sensitivity, imagination and drive needed in 1956.

DURING recent months and years, Adlai Stevenson has described the problems of the New America and his prescription for meeting them. In his proposals for aid to education in the form of federal grants-in-aid, aid to students in the form of scholarships and fellowships, aid for hospital construction and increased grants for medical research, a voluntary but comprehensive health insurance program, aid to city planning and blight relief, lessening of Social Security and private restrictions on employment of older workers, and special low-cost housing for older people, he has offered practical solutions to some of the glaring and some of the subtle problems of today and the years ahead. It would be sheerest folly for a nation whose national income should grow by tens of billions of dollars in the next decade, which looks forward to spending billions on superhighways and color television, to ignore on economic grounds the growing challenges of the New America.

...

The question to be considered Nov. 6 is whether we are to view with Dwight Eisenhower a "happy" America and see it as an excuse for self-satisfied drift, or to view with Adlai Stevenson an anxious, imperiled and largely dormant America--in which complacency can mean disaster--and see it as an irresistible challenge to go forward into the New America with our eyes open, our objectives set clearly and loftily, and our full energies devoted to securing them.#

--PETER ECKSTEIN

Congratulations-- and Thank You...

(Nov. 21, 1956) ED. NOTE: The following letter was received from the Democratic nominee for President, Adlai Stevenson, in response to an editorial (Oct. 30) by Daily reporter Peter Eckstein.

Dear Mr. Eckstein,

I SHOULD have written you long before this to thank you for your letter and for that superb editorial. I am not exaggerating when I say it was the finest presentation of the Democratic position that I saw anywhere in the campaign.

I am, of course, profoundly grateful to you for all your help and encouragement and only regret that I didn't do better by you on Tuesday.

With warmest good wishes and my thanks to you and your associates at the Michigan Daily for the honor you did me, I am

Cordially,
--Adlai E. Stevenson

Kennedy Seen as Man To Beat
As Convention Patterns Emerge

Candidates Arrive, Prepare for Fray

(EDITOR'S NOTE: Daily Editor Thomas Hayden is currently in Los Angeles, attending the Democratic National Convention. Articles by him will appear daily throughout the duration of the convention.)

By THOMAS HAYDEN
Special to The Daily

(July 8, 1960) LOS ANGELES -- The Biltmore Hotel, convention headquarters, is a morass of suites and lobbies currently swarming with political beings and echoing dozens of Democratic refrains.

...

With the arrival of Sen. Lyndon Johnson (D-Tex.) yesterday, the party's major candidates began entering Los Angeles. Sens. John Kennedy (D-Mass.), Stuart Symington (D-Mo.) and Adlai E. Stevenson all arrive tomorrow. They will enter a political milieu already distorted by swollen claims of delegate strength from each of their camps, but despite those distortions several general trends are beginning to emerge.

Needs Early Victory

Almost everyone agrees that Kennedy must crash to the nomination within two ballots if he may be expected to win at all.

Two important Democrats, Michigan's Gov. G. Mennen Williams and New York's ex-Gov. Averill Harriman told reporters yesterday they expect the Massachusetts Senator's nomination, perhaps even on the first ballot.

Kennedy's hopes seem tied to the course of the large California and Pennsylvania delegations, where Gov. Edmund Brown and David Lawrence are still maintaining silence. The Kennedy supporters pressured both delegations for delivery of first-ballot votes in hopes of creating the needed bandwagon effect. But California may favor Stevenson and no one is quite sure of Pennsylvania's position.

If Kennedy cannot sweep to the nomination on an early ballot, many see Johnson as the next strongest possibility. But Johnson is likely to reach his ceiling at perhaps about 500 votes, 260 short of the necessary total, beyond which he will not be able to climb.

...

Just too many delegates from Northern and Western states are frigid to the Texas senator.

....

Stevenson's campaign has been precisely the inverse of Kennedy's. While Kennedy has clearly attempted a blitz, the former Illinois Governor is being plainly recessive, but nonetheless receptive.

An ambivalent attitude toward Stevenson seems to exist. One feeling, as summarized by a delegate I talked to in Utah last week, is that "Adlai is the greatest leader in the party--but dammit, Kennedy can win."

In other words, many are nostagically, or idealistically, for Stevenson, but realistically for Kennedy, or even Johnson...#

Military Repulses Protesters at Pentagon
After 100,000 Converge on Washington

Mass Arrests Begin; Tear Gas Employed To Disperse Crowd

By DANIEL OKRENT and GAIL SMILEY
Special To The Daily

(Oct. 22, 1967) ARLINGTON, Va. -- The Defense Department deployed over 2500 federal troops last night to repulse an anti-war demonstration from the doors of the Pentagon.

At least 200 persons had been arrested before midnight, when U.S. marshals began clearing the mall area in front of the main entrance by arresting some 500 hangers-on of a night-long sit-in.

Some 1500 "civil disobedients" stormed the Pentagon entrance last night at about 6:00 p.m. In clashes the demonstrators lurched at lines of marshals and military police, and threw vegetables and bottles at the troops.

(Sources informed The Daily that the troops' guns contained no bullets and at least one MP had put down his gun to join the protesters.)

About two dozen persons were reported injured in the initial clashes.

...

...From inside the Pentagon, spokesmen told The Daily that an aerial photo taken at 5:00 p.m. showed 30-35,000 people on the mall areas.

Tear Gas

At least one round of tear gas was fired during a wild melee in one of the Pentagon driveways. A defense department spokesman said "the other side"-- not the soldiers--had used the gas.

Several tear gas grenades were shot into the crowd on a bridge and the wind carried the gas across the whole north area of the Pentagon. The majority of the MPs on the north side wore gas masks the whole day. Demonstrators and pressmen hitched towels, handkerchiefs, anything across their faces to screen out the gas.

Bayonets fixed, the MPs had lined up shoulder to shoulder at the main entrance at 7:00 a.m. before the demonstrators arrived. They remained in their position facing the demonstrators throughout the whole confrontation.

The attempted storming, which followed a march from an earlier anti-war rally by over 100,000 persons at the Lincoln Memorial, first erupted into violence at approximately 4:05 p.m. when 1,500 demonstrators in the vanguard pressed into army lines at the head of the first level of steps on the Pentagon's north entrance. Another 30,000 protesters were on the Pentagon grounds at the time...#

During the 1968 election, Time Magazine announced that it was going to do a straw poll of college campuses to see how the students would vote. (Because the voting age was then 21, most undergraduates were too young to vote.)

Urban Lehner wrote an editorial suggesting that since the available choices were abysmal, everyone should vote for Harold Stassen as a means of voting "No."

The Time vote was scheduled to be conducted concurrently with the regular student government election. When the day came, someone found a large cache of unmarked Time ballots. A bunch of us gathered in the Senior Editors' office and spent a jolly couple of hours gleefully filling out extra Time ballots.

We got some green magic markers to validate them (this was done by marking a green 'X' in the upper right corner), and we filled out all the opinion questions more or less at random, so they wouldn't all look the same. But we all voted for Harold Stassen, dozens and dozens of times.

(I might add that no one did anything to affect the real SGA election, and we would have been shocked out of our minds had anyone suggested that we tamper with real ballots.)

Due to our ballot-box stuffing, Stassen carried UM by a landslide and got about 6% of the student 'vote' nationally, which was duly reported in Time, to much hilarity on Maynard Street.

--Jenny Stiller, '70

Harold Stassen: A Time-ly Choice

(March 12, 1968) **TIME MAGAZINE** has discovered a new gimmick in its indefatigible efforts to "tune-in" middle-aged businessmen on what's happening youthwise. Time is sponsoring "Choice, '68" mock elections to be held on this and other campuses along with student government elections.

Reflecting the acumen of Time's understanding of student opinion, "Choice '68" offer its campus electorate a most incoherent and illogical slate of candidates, presumably designed to thwart decisive action.

The Democratic anti-war vote will be split between active candidate Eugene McCarthy and adamant non-candidate Robert Kennedy.

Radicals have even a better choice. They can either vote for Trotskyite ideologue Fred Halstead or non-candidate Martin Luther King--a lost and bewildered civil rights leader.

Nonetheless, by voting for Harold Stassen, students can still effectively vent their feelings about Time Magazine while delivering a clear mandate of anti-war feeling.

STASSEN IS far more outspoken against the war than either McCarthy or Kennedy. Furthermore it would be a humanitarian gesture to give the former "boy wonder" Governor of Minnesota one final electoral victory.

Voters rarely have the opportunity to oppose both a war and a major cultural blight--Time Magazine. And one of the few blessings of today's election is the opportunity to confound Time's team of collegiate pulse-takers by voting for Harold Stassen in "Choice '68."#

--THE SENIOR EDITORS

Reagan makes his run as Nixon shows his cards

**By URBAN LEHNER
and WALTER SHAPIRO
Special to The Daily**

(Aug. 6, 1968) MIAMI BEACH -- California Gov. Ronald Reagan became an avowed candidate yesterday when he smilingly yielded to the urging of the unanimous resolution of the California delegation that he "declare his active candidacy for the Republican presidential nomination."

...

The rationale behind Reagan's moving forward by 48 hours the announcement of his active candidacy was explained by former Sen. William Knowland, speaking on behalf of the California delegation, who said, "There are delegates in all sections of the country who would support Reagan if they can be sure that he wouldn't drop out as a favorite son."

However, many observers interpreted the surprise Reagan announcement as a last-ditch attempt to offset the failure of the Reagan forces to pick up the delegates necessary to deny former Vice President Richard Nixon the nomination on the first ballot.

By announcing his active candidacy, Reagan will probably be forced to drop the low-key manner with which he has made a favorable impression on a large number of southern and western delegations.

The typical Reagan caucus meeting consists of the former actor explaining his favorite son candidacy, answering effectively a series of policy questions from interested delegates, and when before southern delegations, arguing forcefully that the nomination of Nixon would abandon the South to George Wallace.

But favorable impressions and promises of second-ballot support are of little value to Reagan, if he can't pry away enough votes to stop Nixon on the first ballot.

While there have been gains of a few delegates in some southern states Reagan has given no indication of the ability to make large scale breakthroughs in vital centers of Nixon strength...#

HUMPHREY NOMINATED ON FIRST BALLOT; POLICE, DEMONSTRATORS BATTLE IN LOOP

BULLETIN

Large crowds began gathering again outside the Conrad Hilton Hotel last night after Vice President Hubert Humphrey captured the Democratic presidential nomination. Heavily armed national guardsmen moved in, apparently replacing Chicago police forces at the downtown hotel.

By JOHN GRAY
Special to the Daily

(Aug. 29, 1968) CHICAGO -- An attempt by opponents of the Vietnam war and of Vice President Hubert Humphrey to stage a protest march on convention headquarters at the Hilton Hotel ended in a club swinging, tear-gas drenched melee yesterday.

No good estimate on injuries was immediately available, but witnesses said at least 300 were probably hurt.

The brawl between about 3000 demonstrators and Illinois National Guardsmen and police reached riot proportions. It began in the afternoon when demonstrators, mainly Yippies and members of the National Mobilization to End the War in Vietnam began congregating in Grant Park in preparation for the planned march.

...

Then the demonstrators, kept in line by Mobilization marshals, started to march out of the park eight abreast. They were met by a four-deep skirmish line of Chicago police, armed with clubs and tear gas grenades. The demonstrators were told that the march was illegal and that they would be arrested if they proceeded. March leaders began negotiations with police officials.

Meanwhile, groups of demonstrators began to drift away from the crowd toward the Hilton, which is located across the Illinois Central Railroad tracks and Michigan Avenue from the park. As they approached the tracks, they found all bridges over the railroad were blocked by recently moved-in National Guard troops.

What happened next is uncertain, but somehow demonstrators and police began clashing. Tear gas clouds began forming and some of the gas drifted across Michigan Avenue to the vicinity of the Hilton. Many demonstrators were beaten, several of them to unconsciousness.

Meanwhile, many demonstrators had gotten out of Grant Park and had begun to congregate at the Hilton, which was to become the scene of the bloodiest violence of four days of demonstrations. The crowd began to chant: "Peace now; Daley must go. We want Daley dead."

Then, without warning, police, with clubs swinging, charged into the ranks of the demonstrators. People on the sidewalk in front of the hotel were beaten indiscriminately. One man, dressed in a suit and tie, was beaten unconscious and two cops continued to beat him about the abdomen as he was carried from the scene...#

THIS WAS CHICAGO, U.S.A.

Daily photos on this page and the next by: Andy Sacks; Eric Pergeaux; Thomas R. Copi, and Jay L. Cassidy.

An indictment of 'objectivity'

By DANIEL OKRENT

(Sept. 1, 1968) **JOHN CONYERS** was telling the delegates about Chicago's storm troopers, telling about them in a manner sure to incense those managing the convention. But it was something crucial that he was telling them, something that most of the delegates either could not comprehend or did not even wish to attempt to comprehend.

I applauded Conyers' speech.

The woman seated in front of me in the Amphitheatre's press gallery turned slowly in her seat, glared at me full face, and hissed, "I resent that."

What do you resent? (said in earnest).

"This 'clap-clap' thing," she said, eyeing my sideburns and surely cognizant of the fact that I was probably the youngest reporter in the Amphitheatre...

...

FINE. The objectivity of the press in action. The most dangerous quality present in the American media. The false god of detachment that is primarily responsible for the current state of American newspapers, the too-often-quoted excuse for poor journalism.

I cannot swallow it, not at all.

Hopefully, after what transpired in Chicago last week the established media in America will begin to realize the same thing. To ask any sane human being who is functioning as a reporter not to have his own feeling is to emasculate him.

"Objectivity" serves to force him to become so detached that he cannot see what is happening because he is blinded by the glare of unreasonable isolation from people and events.

Why can't a reporter be asked merely to report things as he sees them? Of course he should be fair, he should be honest. But why can't the reporter be allowed to act his role of a person with very real feelings and emotions?

In Chicago last week, I think many, many members of the press began to see some of the light. All they had to do was stand there, and for five brutal nights in the

streets and four undemocratic days in the Amphitheatre, the press was shown certain realities that it could not turn its back on.

...

NO REPORTER in Grant Park could possibly have avoided the sting of the tear gas or the crush of a panicked crowd as it attempted to flee swinging billy clubs. No reporter in the Amphitheatre who was working on the floor of the convention could have avoided noticing the goons Mayor Daley had hired to follow the press around and monitor their words and actions.

...

THAT'S PROBABLY why so many reporters in Chicago stepped out of their normal behavior patterns. That's why, after the first few assaults, the first few nights, a good number of reporters found themselves facing the police, not staring at their backs.

That's why Sander Vanocur took time on the convention floor to explain to NBC viewers the harassment he was enduring.

That's why the Los Angeles Times' Ken Reich decided to file his convention

NOTE

Dan Biber, '71, was one of the casualties of tear gas attacks made by the Chicago police and the National Guard on Wednesday. In the sequence pictured on this page, Biber kneels before a guardsman on the approach to the Congress St. bridge which crosses the Illinois Central tracks in Grant Park. Because protesters were forbidden from crossing the bridge or standing on it, the guardsman released a spray of tear gas directly in Biber's face, sending him away choking and gagging. Biber later received medical attention from volunteer medics who had come to the Park to tend to casualties of police and National Guard action.

story in the first person, describing what he the individual had seen, not what he the reporter had seen.

That's why I felt like spitting in the face of the Secret Service man assigned to the press gallery when he took my picture because "we're supposed to photograph all subversive-looking people."

THE PRESS--particularly the national press, those with readership and influence--has responsibilities to the public. One of these is not to accept anything as dogma, no matter what the source. And that's why Hubert Humphrey, thank God, is going to have such a damn hard time getting elected.

...

Discarding the objectivity myth is simply a manner of honesty. The problem today is that the right to be falsely objective is in the hands of a small group of, if you will, "Establishment" publishers. Those who have a mind unlike that of the commercial press are particularly obligated to refute this ill objectivity by frankly stating that they are doing so. They have a duty to say "No, we are not 'objective,' we are merely trying to tell you what we see and what we know. What you do with it from there is your own choice."#

An indictment of 'objectivity'

OVER 350,000 STAGE PEACEFUL MARCH DESPITE MINOR CLASHES

LARGEST MARCH AGAINST WAR

By MARTIN HIRSCHMAN
and ROBERT KRAFTOWITZ
(Nov. 16, 1969) WASHINGTON --
The largest single anti-war protest in the nation's history ended yesterday with a massive, climactic march through the streets of the capital and a rally at the Washington Monument.

The crowd--estimated at over 350,000 people--sang, chanted and waved signs as it filled Pennsylvania Ave. and 15th St. from Capitol Hill to within a block of the White House.

Silent and unseen, behind the granite and marble facades of federal buildings, Marines and paratroopers waited, the government's insurance against violence. Guardsmen with machine guns manned an observation post at one point along the route.

Although well over 100,000 marched the 30-block parade route, at least 10,000 more had not completed the march when the parade permit expired at 12:30 p.m. Despite pushing and shouts at the parade marshals who tried to restrain them, they eventually turned back and walked across The Mall directly from the Capitol to the monument...#

10,000 ARRESTED IN ANTI-WAR PROTESTS

By LYNN WEINER
Special to the Daily
(May 5, 1971) WASHINGTON --
Over 2,700 more anti-war demonstrators were arrested here yesterday in the second day of planned civil disobedience to protest the Indochina war. The arrests swelled to over 10,000 persons, all apprehended during the last two weeks of continuous demonstrations in the nation's capital.

Some 2,200 people were arrested at the Justice Dept. yesterday afternoon after police declared a rally attended by almost 5,000 demonstrators an "illegal assembly" and ordered everyone in the area to disperse.

Late last night, Superior Court Judge Harold Green ruled that D.C. Police Chief Jerry Wilson was in contempt of court for not adhering to a court ruling that arrested demonstrators be given the option of being released upon posting $10 collateral payment.

Earlier in the day, police had said that those arrested at the Justice Department would be arraigned on charges of disorderly conduct and not released unless they post $250 bail.

Green's decision will mean immediate freedom for the approximately 400 protesters who Wilson ordered held until they posted the $250 bail...#

POLICE DISPERSE YIPPIE PROTEST

By STEVE NISSEN
and ROBERT KRAFTOWITZ
Special To The Daily
(Nov. 16, 1969) WASHINGTON --
An otherwise peaceful afternoon of protest was badly marred yesterday when more than 5,000 demonstrators--led by members of the Youth International Party (Yippies)--split away from the mass march and headed for the Justice Department Bldg.

The group had planned to protest the Justice Department's actions in the 'Chicago 8' conspiracy trial.

They were met by Metropolitan police from the special "civil disturbance unit." The demonstrators threw rocks and bottles at the officers, who retaliated with a barrage of tear gas and pepper fog.

The crowd gave ground, many of the group throwing rocks and bottles through windows of the Justice Department. Gas entered the building, sending Atty. Gen. John Mitchell and others running from his office choking.

The demonstrators attempted to regroup, but were routed by another barrage of gas.

In the meantime, a group of demonstrators gathered near Lafayette Park, perilously close to the White House. Worried police officials ordered a gas attack to disperse the group.

At the monument the swelling crowd heard speakers including Mrs. Coretta King, Sen. George McGovern (D-S.D.) and several folksingers...#

Protest ends with arrests

By TAMMY JACOBS
(Oct. 27, 1971) WASHINGTON --
"Phase One" of the People's Coalition for Peace and Justice's campaign to evict President Nixon ended on the streets near the White House yesterday with the arrest of 298 anti-war demonstrators, including movement leaders Rennie Davis, David Dellinger and Father James Groppi.

Those arrested, part of a group of about 1,000 demonstrators, were charged with disorderly conduct for staging a rush hour sit-in at the intersection of Pennsylvania Ave. and 15th Street, one block from the executive mansion.

Bail was set at $50 or personal recognizance for all those arrested, but most elected to remain in jail for the night, according to the Washington Police Department.

...

The demonstration came after a rally on the Monument grounds, during which PCPJ placed a telephone call to Paris and the crowd heard delegates from both the PRG and North Vietnam.

The rally and march were the culmination of "Phase One," which began over the weekend with the convening of what PCPJ calls its "People's Panel," a group of about 20 representatives of the anti-war movement.

The panel, which was set up in grand jury format, spent the weekend collecting "testimony" on such topics as the war in Indochina, economic and political repression in America and the American prison system...#

McGovern confident of victory in California

By ROBERT BARKIN
Special To The Daily

(June 3, 1972) SAN FRANCISCO -- An aura of victory surrounds the California campaign of Sen. George McGovern (D-S.D.) as it edges toward a conclusion next Tuesday.

The Field California Poll released Thursday shows that McGovern has a 20 per cent lead over his chief rival Sen. Hubert Humphrey in the battle for 271 convention delegates.

...

Especially satisfying for McGovern is that the polls are showing for the first time in any campaign "strength across the board."

"I am running equally well with whites, blacks, Mexican-Americans and other ethnic groups," he said. The final vote will "lay to rest the notion that my strength is confined to a few teenagers."

But McGovern is careful to note the importance of his youthful supporters. Referring to the large youth turnout at his rallies, he said, "I don't see how any politician can be unhappy to see thousands of young people in front of him."

...

McGovern has made a concerted effort to garner the vote of the minority groups in California. If these voters, once considered the private constituency of Humphrey, choose McGovern as polls indicated they will, the South Dakota senator will have a smashing victory...#

SGC MEMBER:
Taylor tells HISC about peace meeting

By LINDSAY CHANEY
Special To The Daily

(July 14, 1971) WASHINGTON -- Student Government Council (SGC) member Brad Taylor yesterday told the House Internal Securities Committee (HISC) that participants in the youth and student conference on a People's Peace, held in Ann Arbor last February, were "people who desired a North Vietnamese victory in Indochina."

HISC is holding hearings on the "radical nature" of groups which participated in the Washington anti-war demonstrations last April and May.

Taylor, a member of Young Americans for Freedom (YAF), testified on the individuals and groups which participated in the conference...

...

Taylor introduced as evidence a leaflet put out by the Mayday Tribe which showed, he testified, "the Washington Monument broken off at the top, indicating some type of violent activity." In the course of his testimony, he also introduced buttons, other leaflets, a supplement to the Argus, an edition of The Daily, and photographs of various speakers at the Feb. 5 plenary session of the conference.

In describing the Friday plenary session, Taylor identified...an SGC member as the person who placed a Viet Cong flag on the speaker's lectern. Taylor also recounted a telephone message to the conference from Madame Binh, head of the Provisional Revolutionary Government (PRG) of South Vietnam.

"No one had any doubt," Taylor said, "that the May demonstrations would occur regardless of whether the conference gave its stamp of approval."

The other witness at yesterday's hearing, Albert Forrester, an official of YAF, said that the National Student Association (NSA) had become a "clearing house organization for the left in the United States." He called NSA "unrepresentative" of U.S. students.

He cited widespread marijuana smoking at the 1970 NSA congress held at MacAlester College in St. Paul to illustrate his "unrepresentative" charge. "I didn't feel that the massive use of marijuana at the congress was representative of all students," he said. "I don't use marijuana and they certainly didn't represent me."..#

Split shows between staff, workers

By CHRIS PARKS
Special To The Daily

(July 14, 1972) MIAMI BEACH -- "I don't want to be a cog in a machine which just says 'Get out and vote for George'," Kirt West says, looking up from a cup of coffee in the basement of the Fontainebleu Hotel.

West is only one of hundreds of young McGovern volunteers who flocked down here last week, packing themselves deep in cheap hotel rooms to work for the Senator's nomination. "Two of us sleep in the beds and the other two on the floor," West says...

West's dedication, however, is not to a man but rather to ideals--an end to war in Indochina and social justice at home.

And like many of his fellow idealists he is very concerned lest his candidate compromise some of the stands which got him to Miami in the first place.

"If all McGovern gets is Dick Daley and George Meany on his back," West fears, "he will bow to their pressure."

This fear has been felt throughout the McGovern camp in the past few days. The result has been the formation of a group called Concerned McGovern Volunteers which is determined to prevent the Senator from "backsliding."

"We have to stay on his ass," West says. "He's making statements to test how far he can go. Then if he gets flak, he retracts them."

Two mass meetings and a number of regional caucuses of the group have been held, and West has been named midwest coordinator. The avowed goals of the group are to put heat on McGovern to stand firm on his committment to change, and to insure that the national campaign will be run as the primaries were -- on the grass roots level.

"Our organization has to mobilize people around issues at the local level," West says. "They (the national staff) have to realize that the only way to win is to run an issue-oriented campaign--that's the way we won the primaries."

...

Other things, too, bothered him about the game of big-time politics. "They did a lot of things to raise money like hiring attractive young women to flirt with rich old drunks," he says, shaking his head...#

Nixon agrees to release tapes in dramatic reversal of policy

By DAN BIDDLE
Special To The Daily

(Oct. 24, 1973) WASHINGTON -- President Nixon capitulated yesterday to an unprecedented groundswell of legal, Congressional, and public pressure by agreeing to surrender the Watergate tapes to U. S. District Judge John Sirica.

White House lawyer Charles Allen Wright stated in the surprise announcement to Sirica that Nixon would release nine pivotal, White House recordings and related Presidential papers for judicial review in belated compliance with an appeals court order.

AT AN AFTERNOON hearing Wright told a stunned courtroom that the President's decision came only two hours earlier on a day that saw a snowballing of popular and Congressional pressure for impeachment--in the wake of the stunning events of the weekend.

The White House announced later that Nixon will appear on nationwide television at nine p.m. tonight to defend the firing Saturday of Special Watergate Prosecutor Archibald Cox which prompted the protest resignation of Attorney General Elliot Richardson and his deputy William Ruckelshaus.

The firing of Cox was prompted by the former prosecutor's defiance of an order by Nixon to halt legal actions aimed at obtaining the tapes and related memoranda...

REFERRING TO THE president's ill-fated compromise attempt Wright told Sirica, "we had hopes that this kind of solution would end the constitutional crises.

"But events over the weekend," he continued, "made it very apparent that it would not."

After the hearing Wright told reporters "there would have been those who would have said the President was defying the law. But this President does not defy the law."

SIRICA PRONOUNCED himself "very happy" that Nixon had decided to comply with his original order to release the tapes.

...

Wright said it would be only "a matter of a few days" before Sirica could screen the tapes privately to decide if they should be presented to the Watergate Grand Jury.

SOME OBSERVERS HERE, however, expressed the sentiment that the tapes would not be particularly important. They suggested that Nixon had fired Cox to prevent the prosecutor from "putting the heat on in other directions."

They pointed to memos and documents dealing with the ITT and milk scandals of 1972. The White House yesterday gave no indication that it planned to release such materials to either the judge or the Senate Watergate Committee.

The announcement of Nixon's turnabout appeared to dampen but not drown growing efforts in the House of Representatives to prepare impeachment proceedings against the President...#

Note: The byline on the story below is reproduced exactly as it appeared in The Daily.

Nixon envisions 'era of peace'; 50,000 protest inauguration

By the Daily's Washington Bureau
Special To The Daily

(Jan. 21, 1973) WASHINGTON -- The second inauguration of President Richard Nixon went off as scheduled yesterday despite the loud protests of some 50,000 demonstrators.

The anti-Nixon demonstration, sponsored by the National Peace Action Coalition (NPAC) and the People's Coalition for Peace and Justice (PCPJ), was the biggest Washington has seen for several years.

But the massive rally was as peaceful as its organizers had predicted, as only 18 protesters were arrested.

A separate demonstration, by some 2500 members of Students for a Democratic Society (SDS) and the Youth International Party proved a bit more active. SDS and Yippies skirmished briefly with police on several different occasions, but no arrests were made.

The only real threat of a serious flareup in the demonstrations occurred late in the afternoon, when several hundred protesters attempted to join the end of the inaugural parade just before it passed the White House reviewing stand.

Police quickly contained the demonstrators, who had blocked a major intersection. Most of the 18 arrests were made at this point.

The official inaugural ceremonies, witnessed by 300,000 onlookers, went off with split second precision--such exactness in fact, that much attention was diverted to the more dramatic actions of the anti-Nixon protestors.

According to organizers of the Ann Arbor Counter-Inaugural Committee about 2500 Ann Arborites participated in the demonstration.

The procession was called a "March Against Death." Demonstrators carried coffins and signs depicting "atrocities committed by Nixon during his first four years as President."

Some tension momentarily flared as the demonstrators argued whether or not to burn fences, flags and whatever fuel was available at the base of the Monument. Only several campfire-like blazes were set, however...#

Reagan grabs for centrist support

By DAN BIDDLE and JIM TOBIN
Special To The Daily
Daily News Analysis

(Feb. 24, 1976) MANCHESTER, N.H. -- As Ronald Reagan's presidential campaign jet wheeled into take-off position at the airport here Sunday, Hugh Gregg, Reagan's tall, bristle-haired state campaign manager, stood by the runway with his hands on his hips and loudly promoted the candidate.

"If he goes out of here with anything better than 40 per cent, he'll go all the way," Gregg shouted over the engine's roar. "Better than 40," he repeated as reporters asked him to predict the outcome of today's Republican primary.

IT WAS windy and raining, but Gregg, formerly New Hampshire's governor, wore only a suit and did not seem to mind as water dripped down his face. An aide ran over and held an umbrella over his head.

Reagan's campaign here has shown clear signs of the same hard-line conservatism that split the GOP in 1964, but Gregg said this was no problem. "Not at all," he said. "I assume that all good Republicans will support the Republican nominee just as we will.

"We haven't been at all divisive...the Ford people have been very negative and distorted the truth but I wouldn't say they've been too divisive that they couldn't support us in November."

HE ALMOST barked his words, as if his listeners could readily accept the assumption that Reagan, not President Ford, is the voice of mainstream Republicanism.

But not so many people believe that yet, and Reagan and his aides here have struggled to put a gloss of acceptability on their conservative challenge to Ford.

Despite his claims to being a non-politician, the former movie actor has stumbled into the traditional problem faced by non-centrist candidates of both parties. He is trying to capture a portion of the middle without losing his natural loyalists on the right...#

(Oct. 13, 1973) **THE MAN PRESIDENT NIXON** nominated to be the next vice president, U. S. Rep. Gerald Ford (R-Mich.), strikes a classic football pose in this picture taken when Ford trod the gridiron for the Michigan Wolverines. Ford played for the University in 1932, '33 and '34.

Carter clings to slim edge

By ELAINE FLETCHER
and PAUL HASKINS
Special To The Daily

(Feb. 24, 1976) MANCHESTER, N. H. -- Ex-Georgia Governor Jimmy Carter established himself after Morris Udall in the New Hampshire primary, but now he appears to have gained a slight edge over former front-runner Udall in the race--one that is now only hours from its conclusion.

Carter has been heralded by his supporters as a new Kennedy, a political phenomenon; charismatic and competent.

AS CARTER'S popularity mounts, criticism directed towards him has intensified. For the first time in New Hampshire the national media has turned the spotlight towards the ex-governor, largely to scrutinize his proposals for reorganization of the executive branch of the federal government.

During his term as Georgia governor (1970 to 1974), Carter devised and implemented an overhaul of the state's executive branch that reduced the number of departments from 200 to less than a dozen.

Carter will propose a federal reform along similar lines, if he is elected. "Don't vote for me," he has said, "unless you want to reorganize the bureaucratic mess that we now have in Washington."..#

jailhouse
rock

Jails and prisons, from the inside or the outside, generally make good stories and sometimes great ones. The Daily has covered them from both sides, as well as having had at least its fair share of reporters being arrested in the course of doing their job.

Five Students Jailed In Demonstration With Strikers

(April 9, 1937) Five University students, one of whom is a reporter for The Daily, and an alumnus and a bystander were jailed last night on charges of disorderly conduct and disturbing the peace in the course of a bowling alley employees' strike against the Ann Arbor Recreation Center, 605 E. Huron Street.

...

With the exception of Edward Magdol, '39, a reporter for The Daily, all were held in the County Jail until this morning, when they were to be released on bail. Magdol's bail was supplied by The Daily.

Shortly before 8 p.m. [Ralph] Naefus...began to address the gathering but was warned by Sgt. Norman Cook of the Police Department that a license from the Mayor was required for a public address. When Naefus continued to speak he was taken into custody by Cook, and an onlooker who protested the action in terms which were reported by the police as "profane" also was taken.

A few minutes later [Tom] Downs addressed the group and was arrested for speaking without a license...#

Jailed Daily Reporter Tells How 'Hell' Spells Arrest

By EDWARD MAGDOL

(April 9, 1937) Last night as you approached Huron and State Street you could see the glaring electric sign of the Ann Arbor Recreational Center. Beneath it marched a picket line of striking pin boys, workers in the bowling alley, University students and citizens who sympathized with the strikers.

...

Student Workers Federation organizers attempted to explain the situation. One began to tell why the strike had been called, sketching the background of the management's negotiations with the pin boys.

...Because I was standing too far away, surrounded by police waiting for "trouble," as they put it, I was unable to hear exactly what the policeman was saying as he grabbed the workers' representative...

The next speaker for the union was arrested as he resumed the explanation of the strike -- of how the management of the Recreational Center had gone back on its agreement which it had signed with the boys last week.

...

I attempted to find out for my paper why the arrest was being made and to obtain other necessary information. I tapped the arrested man on the shoulder with my left hand, in which there was a large paper pad. In my right, quite naturally, there was a pencil. I asked the officer why the arrest was being made, on what specific charges.

Before I had a chance to hear any answer another officer dashed up behind me and grabbed me.

I asked him to release me since I was carrying out my duty as a reporter and not obstructing the duty of a police officer, as he charged.

Freedom Of Press

One of the bystanders asked me if I were a reporter for The Daily. I replied, "yes." He told me to give the police "hell" for preventing me from getting the news. I repeated, "I sure will give him hell." I understood him to mean "give him hell" in the columns of The Daily. I heard someone in the small group around us say something about freedom of the press. I asked the officer if he had ever heard of freedom of the press. He simply tightened his grip on my elbow and would not let me go home, as I then requested.

...I did not know on what charge I was being arrested until I had been seized and taken to the county jail with three of the arrested union members and the arrested bystander, who had said "hell" in the same manner.

Respectable Swearing

As a matter of fact one of the more prominent book store owners, in the presence of ladies, referred to one picketer on the steps of the Recreation Center as a "bastard." He has not yet been arrested on a disorderly conduct charge although he enjoyed the wild, approving laughter of two police officers...#

JACKSON RIOT QUELLED; INMATE DEAD

STATE POLICE COMMISSIONER ENTERS YARD

--Daily photos by Roger Reinke

NEW GYMNASIUM GUTTED BY FLAMES

Prisoners Still Hold Eleven Hostage

State Troopers Force Majority Of Convicts Back to Cell Blocks

By ZANDER HOLLANDER and SID KLAUS
Special To The Daily

JACKSON (April 22, 1952)--Violence swept Southern Michigan Prison for the second straight day yesterday leaving one convict dead, and ten persons wounded before state troopers and prison guards forced most of the convicts back to their cells.

Eleven guards were still being held hostage by some of Michigan's most dangerous criminals in detention block 15--known to the 6,500 convicts here as "The Hole."

Last night the defiant men in "15," led by robber and kidnapper Earl Ward, yelled down, "We are warning you again. If anybody is hurt, we'll cut off one of the 'screws' heads and throw it out to you!"...

The dead prisoner, 35 year old Darwin Millage, was the victim of a trooper slug late in the morning when guards cleared the prison yard to bring in a fire truck.

Four prisoners, two guards and two troopers were wounded later as more than 60 state policemen, pointing submachine guns and hurling tear-gas, drove the milling mob back to the cell blocks.

* * * *

ALMOST EVERY building within the 57 acre prison suffered damage in the melee, with the laundry, library, chapel, greenhouse, gymnasium, tailor shop, jute mill, barber shop and commissary gutted by fire... Nearly every knife and meat cleaver was missing when troopers recaptured the dining unit and officials feared that a resultant reign of stabbings and terror will last "for ten years." They believed that many of the criminals had already buried the weapons in the yard "for later use."

Early this morning four squads of eight troopers each were still patrolling the prison while 125 guards remained at vantage points on the walls. Two squads of troopers stood by as reserves...#

Rioters Cite Negligence, Brutalities

By BOB KEITH
Daily City Editor

JACKSON (April 22, 1952)--Complaints of brutality, negligent health care and bad management stood behind yesterday's explosive Southern Michigan Prison riot, reporters learned in a series of dramatic interviews with uprising inmates.

Rioters were glad to have someone to hear their grievances, and there was an indication from prison officials that several had some merit. Seven specific charges were made by riot ringleaders in Block 15.

Sex deviates are not segregated.

Beatings by guards with keys and key rings and iron chains are common, and prisoners are placed in dungeons for trifling rule infractions.

The cell block has poor ventilation.

Inmates are sent into disciplinary cells on the testimony of other convicts.

The counselor system is poor and psychiatric examinations inadequate.

Medical treatment is inadequate.

Epileptics and tubercular patients are mixed with other inmates.

* * *

IN REPLY, Vernon B. Fox, assistant deputy warden in charge of individual treatment, said "some changes will no doubt be made."

Fox admitted that an "occasional guard" has struck inmates with keys and other instruments, even though warned against it. "But we do everything in our power to prevent it," Fox said.

He expected to see the prison's "counseling" program improved...#

ROGER RAPOPORT:
Where the Draft Dodgers Lodge

(Sept. 20, 1967) MILAN--You're 1-A, against the war in Vietnam, and don't feel like moving to Canada. What should you do?

Consider jail.

A mere 13 miles south of Ann Arbor, Milan Federal Correctional Institution hosts 64 mid-western young men who have all been convicted of violating the U.S. Selective Service Act. They are serving out terms ranging from 2 to 5 years.

They are part of a growing number of men across the country who have opted for jail over military service. Federal officials estimate there are more than 500 men in federal prisons across the country--up from 256 a year ago.

At Milan the number of Selective Service violators has about doubled to 64 in the past year and now comprises about 11 per cent of the prison population of 590.

Milan has an unusually large contingent because it is designed for younger men (18-26) and primarily serves the Michigan, Indiana, Ohio, Illinois, and Western Pennsylvania regions which have many Amish and Jehovah's Witnesses.

Most of the Selective Service violators are here on religious grounds. There are 52 Jehovah's Witnesses, 4 Amish, 5 Black Muslims, and 3 non-religious. (One of the non-religious cases involves a young man who threw human excrement in his Minneapolis draft board file). Their fellow prisoners are largely multiple offense felons who have stolen cars and mail, forged money orders, sold narcotics, and violated parole.

PRISON COUNSELOR Dave Linder is quick to point out that "if you have any guys at the University thinking of going to prison as Selective Service violators, tell them they should be prepared for pretty much of a hum-drum existence. We don't have much for them to do."

Typically though, the Selective Service violators are admired. Says Protestant Chaplain Sam Vivens: "They are the best inmates you'll find anywhere. They work hard, never start any trouble and provide a model for the other prisoners to live by. I'd like to have a whole institution full of them." Adds Catholic Chaplain Ray Klauke, "I hate to subject these men to the low morals here."

And Warden Paul Sartwell says "I respect them, I do not view them as criminals." Mr. Sartwell currently has one Selective Service violator serving as gardener for the well-groomed lawn of his residence, located just outside the prison fence. And another Selective Service violator serves him as houseboy.

...

Rev. Vivens, who is the only Negro chaplain in the Federal prison system, sees most of the Selective Service violators and says that you "can generally tell where one of these guys is from by the length of his sentence. The men from Ohio and Indiana usually get two to three years. But the ones from Michigan usually get five."

ONE OF THEM is Marvin, a 24-year-old Jehovah's Witness from Grand Rapids who was sentenced to five years but was made eligible for parole after 20 months. He expects to be out of jail by November.

The tall, thin, blondish man works as a houseboy in his starched white uniform. He had been working at a laundry when the Selective Service ordered him to serve. He refused on religious grounds ("If I was in Russia I would have done the same thing") and went to Milan.

His wife also moved to this little town of 3,600 and now visits him "three times a week for three hours and fifteen minutes." Visits are permitted with inmates seven days a week.

Many of the prison inmates earn spending money by working eight hours a day manufacturing government metal beds and lockers in the prison industry. The noisy factory employes start at 14 cents an hour but "you can work up to the maximum 35 cents an hour in no time," explains a prison official.

BUT MARVIN PREFERS his housekeeping job at Warden Sartwell's house. After putting in six months at the job, he has qualified for a $19 monthly honorarium.

Marvin has taken bookkeeping at the prison high school, which has a staff of ten and can graduate a student with a degree from Milan High School. (The prison has 158 high school graduates, 54 functionally illiterates and 6 illiterates. More inmates have IQ's over 100 than below.)

He generally spends a good deal of time with his fellow Jehovah's Witnesses who worship jointly three times a week. Some of them are the children of men who served time at Milan for refusing to fight in World War II.

A number of responsible students who are taking a heavy high school load are given "preferred quarters" in the honors study unit. These are former cell blocks that have been converted to unlocked rooms. They are slightly smaller than East Quadrangle singles, and the fortunate inmates that have them are free to come and go on their own.

However, a prisoner with a college background wouldn't be eligible for the honors unit privileges since he wouldn't be attending high school.

MANY OF THE inmates are allowed to take jobs at factories in Toledo, Ann Arbor or Ypsilanti during the day and return to the prison after work. But Selective Service violators can't since Federal prison regulations prohibit it.

"Apparently the rationale," says counselor Linder, "is that by letting Selective Service violators work outside jobs more men would refuse to serve."

...

Still, the Selective Service violators don't seem to regret their decision to go to jail. "It's really not as bad a place as I expected," says Joe. "I'd do it over again if I had to."

AND THE PRISON officials expect to see more and more Selective Service violators. Says an official at the Federal Bureau of Prisons headquarters in Washington: "Unless the war in Vietnam stops, I expect there will be many more of these men."

But the prison officials aren't seeking more Selective Service violators. Says Protestant chaplain Vivens: "Don't tell everyone how good they'll have it here. We don't want them breaking down the doors to get in."#

The All-American Jail

In October, 1965 I was arrested along with 38 others for participating in a sit-in at the Ann Arbor draft board. Seven days later we were convicted by Municipal Court for violating a local trespassing ordinance and were given 10-day sentences. In November, 1965 our conviction was upheld by Washtenaw County Circuit Court, this time with a fifteen day sentence.

On December 18, eleven of us began to serve our sentences in the Washtenaw County Jail. The following is the first of a two part series of excerpts from some letters I wrote during and shortly after my fifteen day stay.

--BILL AYERS

(Jan. 7, 1968)...JAIL IS ABOUT the unhealthiest place possible. I'm sure it passes all the state regulations, etc., but that doesn't tell the real story...

...

We usually got undercooked oatmeal and boiled, black coffee for breakfast; baloney, bread, and tea for lunch; hotdogs, potatoes, and tea for supper. When we get something like vegetables, they're soggy and over-cooked (undoubtedly without vitamins). The hotdogs are falling apart (they look to be about 80 per cent corn-meal), and the potatoes are cold. I've never talked to anyone who could eat regularly in here, and most everyone loses weight. (I lost 20 pounds.)

There's absolutely no fresh fruit or vegetables. Sheriff Harvey told a group of local ministers that no fruit could be brought in because someone might inject dope or alcohol into it. This makes some kind of weird sense. But there's a commissary here from which prisoners can order food. The trouble is that they can only order candy bars and peanuts; no apples or tomatoes or oranges or bananas.

Also there's no place for exercise. I began feeling weak so I started doing push-ups a few days ago. Every day they get harder.

...

EVERYONE IN HERE is poor. There are young guys who've been in a number of times on petty offenses; older guys clearly on their way to Jackson; and old alcoholic-types who come in regularly when it's cold or someone feels like busting them. How can we pretend that prisons make any sense at all when the overwhelming majority of people are poor and are constantly returning?

EVERY YOUNG GUY I've met has been at Boys' Training School or Boys' Republic of Ionia. And it becomes clear that just as Harvard has Exeter and Andover, so Washtenaw County has these.

...

...A lot of the guys here are called "County Lifers"--they're in for 30 days, out for a week, in for 60 days, out for two, in for 10, out for a month. And it never ends.

...

(Jan. 9, 1968) THERE'S NO COMPARISON between my experience here and what most others are up against. I'm middle-class. I believe in what I did. I don't think my "crime" was wrong and neither do my friends or companions. I have financial, legal and moral support on the outside. I get constant visits from ministers and lawyers. I know my rights and when I'll be out. I decided when I'd drop my appeal and when I'd come in.

...

There's absolutely no stimulation. The colors are gray or light yellow or green. There's no music, no interesting tastes or smells or sights. Anyone in here for any period of time would become numb. When I get out I'll be enthused and excited by the sound of a radio (any music), the taste of real food, the smell of air.

ABOUT 2:00 on my birthday, one of the guys in my cell was melting a candy bar in a tin cup over some burning toilet paper. The turnkey came in and smelled the smoke. The kid who was doing it explained that he was trying to make hot chocolate. All eight of us were marched out and put into the "hole," a six by six black brick room with no toilet and an absolute minimum of ventilation...

...

We were in the hole until about 8:00 the next morning. There was no room to move and sleeping was practically impossible. A number of times we shouted to the guards that we needed to use the toilet. The response was always the same: "Do it in your pants," "Use the floor," etc.

...

The next day, after using the toilet and eating, we were put back in the hole. That afternoon a minister visited me, and, seeing our condition, put some pressure on the sheriff's office to get us out. He organized a meeting with Sheriff Harvey and a number of local ministers.

...

WE WERE TAKEN out of the hole the next day and put into a punishment cell for five days...

...

It was there that we met with the most harassment, partly because the turnkeys felt that we hadn't played fair in getting out of the hole the way we did. (We were supposed to stay four more days, but we had friends.)

I began to realize the ways humiliation and degradation are used in the jail, some as part of the system, others as the peculiar habits of the individual turnkeys. Some of the more common forms of harassment are: leaving lights on all night or turning them on and off at odd hours; no toilet seats on the toilets and construction of the sink directly over the toilet; turning the heat too high or too low; demanding that everyone have short hair and cutting off all mustaches and beards.

...

IN ALL-AMERICAN Ann Arbor it's odd that we have such an archaic institution. We're supposed to be progressive, forward-looking. Why aren't there ministers who make it their business to visit the jail periodically and find out what people's needs and problems are? Why aren't doctors volunteering to see prisoners on a weekly or bi-weekly basis to make sure they're healthy? Why couldn't others help organize an adequate library, sports program, or classes?

...

Even with reform, jails will be horrible places. Caging people up is a pretty extreme response to people's problems or needs. In a truly free, democratic society, jails would be smashed. The jails and the ghettos and the wars are the best measure of any society. And on this measure, our society as failed. Prison reform is a case of attacking the symptoms of a sick society. If we work to create a free society, Sheriff Harvey and his turnkeys and his jail will perhaps eventually all be thrown into the junkheap. #

Arrested Student Describes Jail Experience

EDITOR'S NOTE: Jeffrey Goodman was one of 30 students and faculty who were arrested Friday evening for sitting-in at the Ann Arbor Selective Service Office. These are his personal impressions of his experience in the County Jail.

By JEFFREY GOODMAN
Editorial Director

(Oct. 17, 1965) When the last load of sit-iners arrived at the Washtenaw County Jail after being carried out of the Ann Arbor Selective Service Office Friday evening, some of us in the paddy wagon decided we ought to be carried out of the wagon, too.

"Come on, now, we aren't the Ann Arbor police," a hefty County Sheriff's deputy barked.

We demurred a bit, and he slapped the nearest civil disobedient on the collar, dragging him from the truck. The rest of us began to move out on our own volition. I got a swift paw on the back of my neck while walking into the jailhouse.

...

ITEM: We were not allowed to make phone calls to our lawyer until after we were arraigned, though we asked the deputies continually. The law is that prisoners are allowed to make calls immediately after being arrested. One of us who insisted on this right by pounding on the cell door was put in solitary confinement.

...

ITEM: Among the possessions which were taken away from us at the booking ceremonies in the County Jail were glasses. That crippled about one quarter of us, and at least one person complained to Municipal Court Judge Francis O'Brien, when we were arraigned, that not having his glasses caused a painful headache.

O'Brien instructed Ann Arbor Detective Lieutenant Eugene Staudenmaier, who was standing right behind him at the arraignment, to see to it that our glasses were returned. We never saw Staudenmaier again, but while we were being filed back into the County Jail for the night we told our guard of O'Brien's directive.

"We run this jail. The judge doesn't run this jail. No glasses," he yelled. (The glasses were returned when we were released on bond.)

...

ITEM: The cell in which we 32 men were kept for the great majority of our stay in County jail was only about 18 feet square and "bugged." It had six hard-wooden "beds," virtually no ventilation, one sink and one toilet (without a seat or toilet paper, though we stole some of that from the city jail before and after arraignment). At two to a bed, there were 20 men who had to sleep on the floor. Like sardines.

ITEM: One of us who had to take a pill every four hours for an ulcer had his pills confiscated during the booking. He complained, but it wasn't until late Saturday morning, when he began feeling sick, that he got his pills...#

SHERIFF'S DEPUTIES ARREST DAILY EDITOR

By DANIEL OKRENT

(Sept. 5, 1968) Sheriff's deputies arrested Daily Managing Editor Stephen Wildstrom yesterday as he attempted to enter the County Bldg. to protest to Sheriff Douglas J. Harvey "harassment" of Daily reporters.

He was charged with assault and battery, a misdemeanor punishable by 90 days imprisonment, and later released on $25 bond.

Wildstrom was arrested immediately after a brief incident in which, several witnesses said, a small group of deputies knocked him to the ground and beat him "without provocation."

...

Witnesses to the incident denied that Wildstrom provoked the deputies in any way. One said that "Wildstrom was simply talking to the deputies when he was assaulted."

...

Wildstrom went to the County Bldg., on the corner of Huron and Main, after Daily reporter John Gray was denied permission to enter the public building to cover a meeting between county officials and welfare recipients protesting a cut in their allocations.

...

When Wildstrom arrived at the County Bldg., 30 minutes before the posted 5:30 p.m. closing time, he walked past a group of deputies and attempted to open the door, witnesses said.

At this point, they added, he was told he could not enter. Witnesses went on to quote Wildstrom as asking the deputies, "Isn't this a public building? Isn't it open until 5:30?" After the depu-

--Daily--Jay Cassidy

Deputies escort Wildstrom to jail

ties reiterated their refusal to allow Wildstrom to enter, he said, "I have business in there. I want to see the sheriff."

...

After declaring his intention to enter the building to the deputies, witnesses said, one of them replied: "You're the same kid who gave me lip yesterday. I'm not taking any more shit from you." (Wildstrom had also been at the County Bldg. Tuesday to protest earlier harassment of Daily reporters.)

Witnesses reported that when Wildstrom attempted to reply to the deputy's comment he was shoved backward, struck on the chin, and then knocked to the ground. Then, they said, several deputies proceeded to "knee him in the sides and back."#

Reporter jailed during demonstration in D.C.

EDITOR'S NOTE: Daily reporter Lindsay Chaney was arrested in Washington, D.C., Monday while covering an attempt by anti-war demonstrators to march toward the Pentagon. In the following article he relates his experiences, shared to some extent by the thousands of arrested protesters.

by LINDSAY CHANEY
Special To The Daily

(May 5, 1971) WASHINGTON -- Cell 39 at the D.C. police headquarters was five feet by seven feet and there were ten people in it. It was hot, humid, stuffy, and the tear gas which stuck to their clothing was still burning their eyes and making them cough.

Even so, they were luckier than those in the cell across the aisle which was crammed with 16 prisoners.

The group in Cell 39 had been arrested at 6:30 a.m. in the vicinity of the 14th Street Bridge, which spans the Potomac River connecting suburban Virginia to the capital.

Most of those arrested were remnants of a group which had earlier assembled near the Washington Monument for a march to the Pentagon.

When the original crowd of 700 marched down 14th St. toward the bridge, it was stopped at the first intersection by lines of riot-equipped police. Many of the demonstrators ran around the police lines, and a few slipped through, but further down the street there were more police who began making arrests.

A small group which reassembled about half a block from the bridge was attacked by a whooping band of metropolitan police, who grabbed every demonstrator they could and herded them together by the street to wait for a prison bus.

I was observing the arrests when I was apprehended.

Many journalists were also arrested, mostly those from the college press or with long hair. These included Paul Travis of The Daily, as well as reporters from the New York Times and the Washington Evening Star.

...

Under normal police procedures for mass arrests, those arrested are informed of their rights, told the exact charges against them and photographed at the scene of the arrest. This procedure was not generally followed Monday, although it was reinstated during arrests yesterday.

Shortly after arresting me, Officer Mike Mood, badge number 2544, pointed to a long haired photographer and said to another policeman, "There's another one of them, get him."

Mood was tired, but he seemed happy about overtime pay because of this week's demonstrations. "Let's see," he said to a policeman standing next to him. "This has been 25, 26, 27 hours, at $9 an hour that makes..."

"You guys knock it off," warned an officer who appeared to be in charge at the scene. Mood became silent.

When the prison bus arrived, the arrested group consisting of about 25 people boarded it for a 20 minute ride to the lock-up at the Municipal Bldg. On the way, the bus stopped to pick up another group which was arrested on the bridge itself.

This second group of demonstrators had been victims of tear gas before being arrested, and the gas filled the whole bus, causing considerable discomfort.

...

Cell 39 was allowed to leave at 8:30 p.m. As we marched out of the cellblock, a smiling sergeant reminded us, "You had it good. This could have been Chicago."#

OBSERVED 'BILLBOARD BANDITS'

Photographer, Daily reporter arrested

(April 17, 1971) A staff reporter of The Daily and a free-lance photographer were charged yesterday with committing a felony while observing a group of youths engaged in cutting down billboards on a road about 10 miles north of Jackson.

The Daily reporter, Jonathan Miller, and the photographer, Andy Sacks, had accompanied the group with the intention of observing their activities and publishing an illustrated account.

Both were apprehended by three armed residents of Rives township and turned over to the State Police. Late yesterday afternoon, Miller and Sacks were arraigned in Jackson County District Court, and released on bail.

The charges were that each had "aided and abetted the malicious destruction of property in excess of $100"--a felony. The two were also charged with damage to property--a misdemeanor.

Miller had been authorized by the Senior Editors of The Daily to accept an invitation by members of the "billboard bandits" to accompany them as a reporter on a billboard raid Thursday night.

Both he and Sacks followed the bandits for several hours, taking notes and pictures, but not participating in the bandits' activities, they said.

Shortly after 11 p.m., while the bandits were engaged in cutting down a billboard, three members of the family that owned the land on which the billboard was located approached the scene armed with rifles.

While the bandits immediately scattered, Miller and Sacks said they stayed where they were, believing that in their role as reporters, they would not face difficulties if apprehended.

The trio took Miller and Sacks to their home and held them at gunpoint until State Police arrived.

After spending the night in the Jackson County Jail, the two were arraigned yesterday afternoon. Both stood mute to the charges and a plea of "not guilty" was entered by the court...

"We have nothing to do with the destruction of the billboards," Miller said. "We specifically kept our distance from the participants, merely observing the situation with the intention of writing something about it."..#

Daily reporter case dropped

(May 5, 1971) The Jackson County Prosecutor's office has dropped felony charges against a staff reporter of The Daily and a free lance photographer who were arrested last month while observing a group of youths engaged in cutting down billboards near Jackson...#

**taking
it on
the road**

It's never easy for Daily reporters to get travel money out of whoever holds the purse strings in any given year. All the more amazing, then, to see the far-flung datelines they've managed to insert into the paper over the years.

Rehabilitation Is Begun
In Louisville, Cincinnati

(EDITOR'S NOTE: Bonth Williams, special Daily correspondent, returned to Ann Arbor yesterday after a survey of the flood districts.)

By BONTH WILLIAMS

(Jan. 31, 1937) The most gallant heroism mixed with the most stupid inefficiency--that is the picture of the relief progress in the inundated Ohio Valley as the three cities of New Albany, Jeffersonville and Louisville flounder dazedly in the wake of very slowly decreasing flood waters.

...

Peculiar Attitude Noticed

There on the banks of the fast-rushing Ohio, the only plot of ground in the entire city still above the water is half an acre surrounding the Rose Hill School. On that half acre are clustered all that is left of the once thriving community. Every dog that could make the high ground stayed there yesterday, and we watched as they were shot down to make room for the human beings who were crowded in the same area. A cow was shoved into the water while giving birth to a calf.

People in these cities are assuming a peculiar attitude. Every third person has a badge of some sort or other, and a great many of the less directly hit residents seem to be enjoying the whole ghastly mess.

Youth National Guardsmen with smiling, unknowing faces patrol the streets and stalk everywhere. In some instances they are very useful, but in others are a constant feeding and housing problem.

Food Is Plentiful

The number of dead in Louisville has been greatly overestimated, however, as have many of the horror stories of the flood. Friday evening the correct count stood at 169, and indications were that it would mount, but not reach staggering figures. Many of the deaths were from natural causes.

Food is plentiful and good in all relief centers and we enjoyed excellent meals at the relief kitchen where everything is free and of the best. Most of the poorer element in town are eating more and better than they ever have before in their lives.

The indispensible items necessary for fighting flood are a pair of rubber boots, dry warm clothing and a bottle of whiskey. Profiteering has been practically eliminated by drastic action of the authorities, who made an example of one merchant who charged $16 for a pair of boots.#

Martial Law Prevented 'Vigilante Violence'

EDITOR'S NOTE: Edward Magdol, a member of The Daily staff, rode with Norman Thomas, three-time Socialist candidate for President, from Ann Arbor to Anderson, Ind...

By EDWARD MAGDOL

(Feb. 16, 1937) A "Wild-West" barroom incident in the modest industrial city of Anderson, Ind., early Saturday morning promised to embroil that community in vigilante attacks on auto workers had not the Indiana National Guard proclaimed martial law.

Accompanying Norman Thomas, three times candidate for President on the Socialist Party ticket, who drove from Ann Arbor to Anderson to see for himself, he said, what conditions prevailed there, this correspondent was informed of a series of events which indicated the probability of "vigilante violence."

Threaten Reuther

The immediate cause for the proclamation of martial law in Madison County was a shooting of several union workers at about 12:30 a.m. Saturday by a barkeeper who, it is said, is a company policeman of the Guide Lamp plant. The actual details of the shooting, for which the wounded men were arrested and the shooter released by Chief of Police Joseph Carney, were still unverified.

Previous to this incident, it was learned, threats had been made by a mob of vigilantes on the life of Victor Reuther, U.A.W. organizer in the Anderson area...#

General Motors Officials
And Union Heads Parley
With Gov. Murphy Today

By FRED WARNER NEAL

(Jan. 14, 1937) FLINT, Jan. 13--(Special to The Daily)--The first real negotiations between officials of General Motors and the United Automobile Workers were awaited eagerly by this strike-bound city tonight as the presence of nearly 2,000 national guardsmen made more rioting extremely unlikely.

The negotiations will take place in Governor Murphy's office in Lansing at 11 a.m. tomorrow between William S. Knudsen, General Motors executive vice-president, Homer Martin, U.A.W. president, and other officials of both sides.

...

The parley, however, it is felt in both union and management circles, would only be a start toward settlement of the sit-down strike, which is tying up America's automobile industry. Strikers here are still indignant over the riot Monday night, and members of the strike committee, in an exclusive interview, firmly asserted that they will not budge until a settlement is reached "or until Roosevelt says move." This was the 15th day of the sit-down strike.

No More Violence Seen

Meanwhile the possibilities of a recurrence of Monday's violence are exceedingly slim. The strike committee representatives maintain that violence is the one thing they do not want, and any move which might have precipitated rioting anew--the serving of warrants on directors of the strikers' counter-offensive--failed to materialize. Sheriff Thomas Woolcott, to whom the warrants had been issued for serving, said he had been "given to understand that Governor Murphy had advised against it."

While General Motors officials in the city expressed the hope that Governor Murphy would not be antagonistic to their cause, strikers frankly proclaimed the belief that "Murphy is definitely on our side."

"We at first thought the Governor had let us down when he called the National Guard," John Manley, acting head of the strikers' committee, said. "But I guess they are here as much for our protection as anything else," he added.

There is little chance that martial law will be proclaimed, or, for that matter, that the soldiers will leave their quarters at all. Lieut. Col. Joseph Lewis of the 119th field artillery, commandant of military forces on the scene, said that it was within his authority to act whenever he wanted to, with or without proclaiming martial law, but he indicated that he considered it very unlikely.

Lieut. Col. George L. Olson is in direct command of western Michigan's 120th Infantry, the more than 1000 men of which constitute the largest unit in the field.

Warrants Issued

Warrants for the arrest of Victor and Roy Reuther and Robert Travis, sit-down strikers who directed movements against Flint police in Monday's riot, were issued today by Prosecutor George Joseph. Governor Murphy's "advice" against their serving came after it was felt in some circles that because of the popularity of the men, such action might stir up the strikers...#

Rain, Hash, Straw -- National Guard Settles In Flint School

By RALPH W. HURD

(Jan. 14, 1937) FLINT, Jan. 13--(Special to The Daily)--Smoke from hash-cooking fires pushing into rain-darkened air; youthful National Guardsmen digging in mud around company mess tents; the 126th infantry, more than 1,000 strong, quartered since this morning in a straw-littered school house, long condemned as unsafe; pretty librarians in a rickety building next door wonderingly looking on; across the street, a bustling police headquarters.

Along the street comes a union "sound car" broadcasting distinctly and loudly for all the guardians of law and property to hear. "Mass meeting at 8:30 p.m. in Pengelly building to protest the actions of city police during the riot Monday night at the Fisher Body plant against innocent workers who were only asking for food."

Inside the now-militarized school house, army discipline slowly creating order out of confusion. Straw and blankets prepared for beds, with cots expected. Privates traipsing around, bulgy sandwiches in one hand and steaming tin cups of coffee in the other. Intelligence officers already operating a field communication system capable of connecting with Bell Telephone in emergencies such as a proclamation of martial law.

Rations planned out of a 70-cent per day per man budget, and mostly out of cans at that. Around a small table, set with gleaming tin, regimental officers prepare to eat a dinner of hash, bread, butter, jam and coffee; at the head Lieut. Col. George Olson, in private life an insurance man; his executive officer, Maj. Louis J. Donovan, county clerk of Kent County; also a vocational school teacher, a superintendent of hatcheries, a county chief deputy treasurer, two high school principals and a band leader and all hoping fervently that "there won't be any trouble," and that the 15-ton bell in an "insecure" loft above them "won't fall on us."#

Daily Finds City Tense

Reporter's Eyewitness Description

By JAMES ELSMAN, JR.
Daily Editorial Director
Special to The Daily

(Sept. 26, 1957) LITTLE ROCK, Ark. -- As this day begins, Little Rock maintains a quietness that is nearly as heavy, close and suspenseful as its weather.

Law has come in the form of at least 1,000 combat-ready troops of the 101st Airborne Division bivouacked on or near Central High School.

These stern soldiers yesterday set the pattern in citizen-soldier relations when they rifle-butted one man in the head and pricked a bayonet cut into another's shoulder.

Both men had challenged the 101st picket line.

No Interference

In the Central High School auditorium, Major General Edwin A. Walker told pupils, "Those who interfere...with the proper administration of the school will be removed..."

Pupils reported "there were federal troops all over in the halls," and that "three or four guards followed every nigger to class."

Inside the school, a pupil who called himself Joe Doaks said that if federal troops had not been inside the building, "They (the Negroes) would have been hurt bad."

Got Up and Left

Asked if he had seen any of the Negro pupils, the same pupil said, "Yeah, one of them sat near me in lunch. I got up and left."

The only incident in school came in the morning when classes were held up for more than an hour by a bomb scare. The building was emptied while troops searched for the alleged bomb.

No bomb was found and classes were resumed at 9:22 a.m. The Negro students went back into the school under the protection of bayonet-armed soldiers.

...

The only troops now on guard around the high school are Arkansas National Guardsmen. Although some Negro soldiers arrived in Little Rock, none are on duty around the school...#

DAILY ENTERS CENTRAL HIGH

(EDITOR'S NOTE: The following is the personal account of Jim Elsman's experience as the only newspaperman to get inside the newly-integrated Central High School.)

By JAMES ELSMAN, JR.
Daily Editorial Director
Special to The Daily

(Sept. 27, 1957) I was in my seat at 8:45 for my first class at Little Rock Central High School.

Ironically, this was a history class. But while these students were studying history, they were also making it. Two seats to my left sat Jefferson Thomas, one of the Brave Nine. When I told him I was an imposter--a reporter from the North-- he smiled like any adolescent when someone is putting something over on the teacher.

He answered two questions with a good-willed patness; well-coached by the NAACP.

"Have any trouble today?"

"No sir."

"Expect any trouble any more?"

"I don't expect any."

Sold Picture

Jefferson then bored into his textbook and I proceeded to snap his picture with a borrowed $15 camera. (TIME-LIFE later bought this shot--sight unseen--after bidding a top price of $200 on condition that they mail The Daily a print immediately.)

A click of my shutter set the class buzzing over my presence, a situation which caught the teacher's attention when she walked into class. This time I answered two questions:

"Do I have a new student today?" (Looking at me.)

"No ma'am."

"Do you belong here?"

"No ma'am."

Whereupon followed a beckon and a reminiscence-filled trip to the principal's office. The woman asked four soldiers--there were between 50 and 80 in the school's corridors--to guard the integrated class during her absence. We chatted, and she told me she had once worked in Ann Arbor for Survey Research Center.

Irate Words

After irate words from the principal, I was escorted casually outside by a soldier, to be dressed down by an officer. Not willing to let me go, he harangued me about how I had endangered the lives of all involved and had further jeopardized press privileges--the privilege of standing outside the school.

My entrance to the school began in Ann Arbor Tuesday when my editor and I discussed such a move.

After being repulsed at one entrance by a soldier for not having an identifying library card, I moved on to a corner drugstore where I made arrangements with a hookey-playing girl--Katherine Thornton--to borrow her card.#

Soldiers Replace Student Monitors

Special to The Daily

LITTLE ROCK, Ark. -- Football and dances--not studies or even integration--were on the minds of the students of Little Rock's Central High School yesterday.

More than 50 soldiers guard its halls in place of the usual student monitors, a grim reminder of what has gone before and what may come. But the atmosphere isn't military. Most of the soldiers are under 21 years of age, and they readily exchange smiles, small talk and laughter with the only slightly-younger students.

Throughout homeroom period the school's cheerleaders were darting from room to room, rousing the spirits of all in preparation for today's football game. Although it may not have been planned that way, the pep rally had the effect of turning what barbaric feelings exist away from the Negroes and toward the Istrouma High "Indians."

Attendance was somewhat higher yesterday than the day before. About 1400 students came to school, as against the 2000 who normally converse in the halls...

...

But the students now staying home are apt to be the potential trouble-makers. If the troops were to leave the inside of the school, given the present student body, there might not be trouble. But if the troops were to leave and the trouble-makers were to return, what then?..#

Two Daily Reporters Jailed in Strife-Torn Cuba

(Daily reporters Huthwaite and Elsman spent their Spring vacation in Cuba attempting to get an interview with rebel leader Fidel Castro. Before they could travel to contact Castro in the Sierra Maestra mountains they were the first reporters arrested by the Cuban government as it attempted to deny privileges to all newspapermen in Santiago. The following is an account of their activities.)

By BARTON HUTHWAITE and JAMES ELSMAN, JR.

(April 15, 1958) "Vive siempre las ideas de Fidel Castro y movimiento del 26 de julio."

These words were found scrawled on the wall of a Cuban military prison in Santiago de Cuba. Their author was among the thousands of Cuban rebels who have given their lives in an effort to overthrow the regime of dictator-president Fulgencio Batista.

Translated they mean: Long live the ideals of Fidel Castro and the movement of July 26.

Fear Spreads in Cuba

A wave of fear engulfs the Republic of Cuba. Havana, once crowded with American tourists, is strangely silent. In Santiago de Cuba, the rebel hotspot, Batista's troops prowl the streets with pistols and automatic rifles at their sides.

Constitutional guarantees are a memory. Suspected Castro sympathizers are dragged from their homes and imprisoned without being told why.

Captured Castro rebels are machinegunned without even a trial and their bodies left where they fall.

Americans Grow Worried

American property owners in Cuba, prospering under Batista, are becoming worried. A part-owner of several hotels in Havana offered us $100 a day to act as bodyguards and carry guns while he inspected his holdings in the Cuban capital.

The plane from Miami to Havana carried only six passengers with a capacity load of 60. When we arrived in the city, we took a room in a hotel located on the Prado, the city's main street.

Four days later, a bomb was thrown into the lobby of this same hotel and also a fierce gun battle raged a short distance

POLICE--Elsman talks with one of the many National police stationed in Havana. This friendly policeman's smile turned to a frown and he motioned Huthwaite to stop taking pictures. The police in Santiago de Cuba confiscated several rolels of the reporters' exposed film.

down the street.

It was in this outwardly calm city of Havana that we obtained the names of several Castro sympathizers. Our cab driver insisted on taking us to the numerous lower class bars that abound in Havana and we seized the opportunity to obtain the names of contacts that would take us to Castro when we arrived in Santiago de Cuba.

Castro Captain Spoken To

One contact was a captain in Castro's army hiding out in Santiago de Cuba. The other was a family known to be Castro sympathizers.

Cubana Airlines, the only company still flying into the city, had at least one of their planes shot at during recent trips. We booked passage into the strife-torn province of Oriente and the city of Santiago de Cuba.

The airport at Santiago bustled with government troops, several planes stood by in case of rebel attacks.

We were stopped, our papers checked, and our names recorded at the airport. One soldier quickly grabbed a Cuban newspaper we had brought from Havana. No attempt was made to stop us except for "security purposes."

Informer Suspected

Later, while relaxing in our hotel room in the city, the Cuban soldiers had a change of heart. Apparently an informer had reported we looked like suspicious Americans to the police.

Three armed men took us to the much-feared Moncodo barracks in the heart of Santiago de Cuba for an "investigation." The "investigation" was to last 20 hours--incommunicado in a prison cell.

Our baggage was taken, our papers and also our personal belongings. Only our money was allowed to remain with us.

After a fitful night on concrete benches, we were served a breakfast of a crusty bread and something that bore a faint resemblance to coffee.

The armed guards still refused to tell us why they were keeping us. Lunch consisted of a sandy rice and a coagulated gravy sauce. They also refused to allow us to call the American counsul.

We finally bribed the guards to bring us some fruit juice and candy bars from the camp canteen. Rattling the cell bars, and calling out for the commanding officer brought no reply from our guards.

Finally after 12 hours in the 90 degree heat of the cell, we started to sing the "Star Spangled Banner." A machinegun-bearing guard ordered us to be quiet or he would "separate us."

That afternoon, the American consul arranged for our release.#

Slippery Rock Legend Continues

(Nov. 10, 1957) Slippery Rock has no idea where or when it became a legend.

It is not sure, either, what particular fascination it holds; why some of the largest colleges in the country faithfully follow the activities of its football team.

It doesn't know any of these things, but it is perfectly delighted with the whole idea.

Officially, State Teachers College, Slippery Rock, is an accredited institution of the state of Pennsylvania, one of 14 such education schools in the state, and placing its emphasis on physical education.

But there is something special about it that can only become evident by being there.

Students Very Close

There is about Slippery Rock an air of exuberance that is almost tangible. It is a feeling so strong that it is evident in the day-to-day life on campus, so infectious that even breakfast at 6:45 a.m. is a gay affair.

This is due, in large part, to the close-knit character of the student body. This is inevitable in a school whose entire population of 1,027 is housed in two dormitories, with one cafeteria between them.

Furthermore, the campus itself is completely intrinsic. There is so little need for the tiny town which surrounds it that girls must sign out if they leave campus during the day.

For everything they need is at their fingertips. There is a bookstore in the administration building; there is a small movie theatre below the library for entertainment, and there is "The Hut," a student-built snack bar and recreation building, for relaxation.

But the enthusiasm comes, mostly, from the curriculum. They are physical education majors, and they delight in their skills. Practice, working out, and criticism of each other's peformances play a large part in their lives.

...

This, perhaps, is what creates the magic in their football team. They play to win, yes. But they play also just for the sheer joy of playing.#

STUDENTS ENJOY FOOTBALL FAME:

Slippery Rock Legend Continues

Slippery Rock has no idea where or when it became a legend.

It is not sure, either, what particular fascination it holds; why some of the largest colleges in the country faithfully follow the activities of its football team.

It doesn't know any of these things, but it is perfectly delighted with the whole idea.

Officially, State Teachers College, Slippery Rock, is an accredited institution of the state of Pennsylvania, one of 14 such education schools in the state, and placing its emphasis on physical education.

But there is something special about it that can only become evident by being there.

Students Very Close

There is about Slippery Rock an air of exuberance that is almost tangible. It is a feeling so strong that it is evident in the day-to-day life on campus, so infectious that even breakfast at 6:45 a.m. is a gay affair.

This is due, in large part, to the close-knit character of the student body. This is inevitable in a school whose entire population of 1,027 is housed in two dormitories, with one cafeteria between them.

Furthermore, the campus itself is completely intrinsic. There is so little need for the tiny town which surrounds it that girls must sign out if they leave campus during the day.

Everything Right There

For everything they need is at their fingertips. There is a bookstore in the administration building; there is a small movie theatre below the library for entertainment, and there is "The Hut," a student-built snack bar and recreation building, for relaxation.

But the enthusiasm comes, mostly, from the curriculum. They are physical education majors, and they delight in their skills. Practice, working out, and criticism of each other's performances play a large part in their lives.

They get athletic training, of course, in their classes, but they do not stop there. Individuals and teams hold practice sessions during spare hours, strictly on their own.

This, perhaps, is what creates the magic in their football team. They play to win, yes. But they play also just for the sheer joy of playing.

HANGING OUT ITS SHINGLE—Slippery Rock has friendly greeting for visitors. "Hi! Tradition" dictates a greeting for everyone, is observed scrupulously. Porch of East Gym is to right, tower of Old Main (administration building) is silhouetted against sky. Tower clock is currently out of order.

"SCASH 'EM"—Slippery Rock cheerleader yells favorite cheer as the "Rockets" scramble for the football. Cheerleader squad is divided into Varsity and Junior Varsity, always have more candidates than they can use. Students are enthusiastic about football team, cheer even when they fall behind.

☆ ☆

DAILY PHOTO FEATURE

Pictures by
CHARLES CURTISS
Story by
SUSAN HOLTZER

☆ ☆

SLIPPERY ROCKS—Creek for which school was christened shows obvious reason for name. Legend says it was so called by an Indian who went fishing and slipped into the water. Students use it now for occasional wading, study stretched out on some of the large, flat rocks that dot the water.

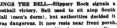

RINGS THE BELL—Slippery Rock signals a football victory. Bell used to sit atop South Hall (men's dorm), but authorities decided it was dangerous. It now rests near front porch, and must be rung with clapper manually.

LEARNING THE FUNDAMENTALS — Combination of seriousness and gaiety characterize students' attitude toward athletics. Soccer class divides into teams, "rehearses" games. Building in background is North Hall, women's residence hall.

Apartheid Protests Grow

COLUMBIA:
Alumni recall '68 protest

By KERY MURAKAMI
Special to the Daily

(April 14, 1985) NEW YORK -- When students at Columbia University began their anti-apartheid blockade of Hamilton Hall last week the obvious comparisons were made between them and their activist predecessors of the 1960s.

But yesterday, the two generations of protesters stood side by side as 50 Columbia alumni who participated in the 1968 anti-war protests returned to the scene of their civil disobedience to support the students.

"WE'RE NOT here for nostalgia," Helen Meyers, a 1969 graduate told the 300 person human blockade of Hamilton Hall. "We've never stopped our commitment," she said. "We're still looking for places to take our stance. This is the time and the place."

The alumni, carrying a banner reading "Alumni of '68 supports you," sat down with the students on the building's front steps.

ELEVEN DAYS ago, 20 students chained the main entrance to the building and started a sit-in in front of its doors. The protesters are attempting to pressure the university into divesting its stocks in companies that do business in South Africa. The crowd has since grown to as many as 500.

"You teach us and continue to be our backbone," Tony Glover, a Columbia senior involved in the protest, told the alumni. "The issues are different but we have the same degree of commitment. We fight with the same passion you fought with. We're doing things with your lessons in mind."

While the alumni may provide the history for the protests, "they're certainly not our role models," said Daniel Fass, a Columbia junior. "We're more focused on our goals. We want the university to divest. We're not trying to tear down the institution."

"But there is certainly a link in terms of student activism," he added.

...

THE ALUMNI members were welcomed warmly by the students but one alumnus who advocated violence was greeted with boos after forcing his way to the microphone.

"You have to understand the nonviolent, passive protest did not work," said Larry Dicks, a 1968 protestor. "You're not going to win until you elevate the struggle and shut this campus down.

"You have to get a little angry and get a little more militant," Dicks said. "Let's fight for a better world, power to the working class."

After Dick's speech, Glover rushed to the microphone and said "we want ours to be a non-violent message." The students cheered and began changing "Peace."..#

BERKELEY:
Weekend slows Cal. protest

By PETE WILLIAMS
Special to the Daily

(April 14, 1985) BERKELEY, Calif. -- After three days of intensive anti-apartheid protests, student demonstrators at the University of California-Berkeley yesterday used their fourth consecutive day on the campus for reorganization and workshops on civil disobedience and non-violent protests.

But the more than 100 people who have remained on the front steps of Berkeley's Sproul Hall were not disappointed with the decreased turnout yesterday. Many attributed it to the fact that the majority of the student population is not on campus on weekends.

"THIS IS really our turning point because it is the weekend period. Thre are a few people who come to study or go to the library, but there are not many people on campus," said Ian Elfenbaum, a senior in economics who is participating in the protest. "When school starts again on Monday, we'll know whether we have peaked out or whether more people will join in."

"Weekends are always hard; you just have to cross your fingers and really hope," said protester Lorenzo Sadun. "The support you get is from the people going by."

Sadun is involved with the campus chapter of the College Democrats--one of the many groups who have formally pledged support to the action.

"I DON'T know of anyone who doesn't support the protest," Sadun said. "This is something everyone--outside of the College Republicans--is in support of."

Sadun was unsure how many groups had actually pledged support, but he said it was "only a matter of calling them and asking them for support."

The original protest was organized by a group called the UC Divestment Coalition. That protest, held last Wednesday, started the sit-in which has now lasted four days.

"WEDNESDAY'S protest was sort of spontaneous. . .and then a group of about 50 people said, 'Fuck it, let's just stay here'," said one demonstrator who would only be identified as Steve.

Brendan Cummings, a freshman who has remained on the steps of Sproul since Wednesday, said the protest originally had little to do with a similar protest at Columbia University in New York.

"Wednesday was planned way before anything at Columbia," Cummings said. "It was to be a protest for divestment on all the UC campuses."

ACCORDING TO Cummings, the organizers had not planned a sit-in to follow the protest, but instead planned a phone-in campaign in an attempt to tie up university phone lines.

"But people just didn't want to leave," he said. "So we actually planned the sit-in at the protest -- not before."..#

---

the
Big
Story

There are some stories that fall into the "Do you remember where you were when..." category. They're the ones the participants remember with crystalline clarity, and others ask about particularly -- "how did The Daily cover that?" Often, they're the stories that defined a Daily generation.

A sensational event over which we editors toiled like metropolitan reporters, was a battle between a company of State Militia (out serenading a newly married member, with volleys of blank cartridges) and students. The militia attacked with clubbed muskets, resulting in the death of a student. Eight soldiers were arrested for murder but the case was repeatedly postponed and finally noll prossed in May, 1891 for lack of identification of the murderer.

--Ralph Stone, '92L
(from The Daily, Nov. 16, 1940
Fiftieth Anniversary Edition)

MURDER!

AN ENCOUNTER BETWEEN STUDENTS AND MILITIA.

(Nov. 13, 1890) Last night about 9 o'clock, the students were alarmed by sharp firing in the most thickly populated part of the city....

...

...it was found that the firing came from a portion of Company A, who were celebrating the marriage of a member of the company. Students to the number of several hundreds were soon assembled. After the company had fired several volleys, they passed into the house, carrying their guns with them. The students gave the University yell, and called for a speech. Some one came out of the house and the boys were quiet, to hear what he had to say. His speech was a single sentence: "This is the biggest crowd of ignorant people I ever saw."

...

...After a little time the speaker again came out, and leaning against the gatepost with threats ordered the students to disperse. Soon the militia filed out and marched down the street to the intersection of Division and Liberty. Here Sergt. Granger, who was nominally in command of the company, made some remarks, stirring up the militiamen to resist the students, who were following the soldiers and guying them. The "soldiers" by this time were extremely angry, and seemed determined to have their revenge on the students. At the command of Granger the militia made a determined charge. They used their muskets as clubs, and chased the students about, following them individually, and bent on doing serious harm. Still the students made no resistance. It was in this charge that I. J. Denison, a Freshman, was struck on the head by the butt of a musket.

Finally, the students rallied and supplied themselves with sticks and stones as means of resistance. Some one struck Sergeant Granger on the head with a missile. This disabled him, but he still urged the militiamen to go on. This led to a second charge, in which several students were injured...

...

...Finally comparative quiet reigned, several policemen appeared on the scene, and the soldiers were persuaded to go down town. Prof. Thompson came and asked the students to proceed to the campus. Before long the boys were all gathered about the Law Building. Prof. Thompson then made a speech from the steps, thanking the students for their self-restraint under the circumstances, and asking them to go quietly home. In obedience to his request, the crowd dispersed...#

The press down in the hole on Maynard Street was all set to roll a little past midnight on Friday, August 3, 1923 when the AP flashed the news that Warren G. Harding was dead in San Francisco. The boys had torn the forms apart in a flash and by the time someone pulled me out of my upper deck...the whole story was being set.

"No sense in your coming down," Bob Ramsay told me on the phone. "We are not going EXTRA." -- so I went back to bed.

Then something hit me like a thunderbolt. Half our editorial space was criticism leveled at the presidential tour -- and who was I to quarrel with the dead? Pulling pants and sweater over pajamas I made The Daily in four minutes flat -- intent on switching to some other copy. I found the press already rolling.

"You're too late, but what do you want? These editorials couldn't be more timely. Might as well go back to bed," they told me.

...at 2 a.m...someone ran in with word that the Ann Arbor News was going EXTRA and would be out on the streets by 6 a.m. Nothing could have settled things more quickly. If anyone was going to take the town we would. We corralled the skeleton Summer editorial and business staff as fast as we could and by 3 a.m. six or eight of us were out on the streets, each with a bundle of papers under his arm to cover a given district before the News came out.

--Paul L. Einstein, '25
(From The Daily, Nov. 16, 1940
Fiftieth Anniversary edition)

The President's Job-- He Has One

(Aug. 3, 1923) Washington breathes once more with the news that President Harding has passed the crisis and is gaining health. The anxiety of the whole capital has been aroused by the last two days reports concerning the chief executive's condition. Politics were forgotten, animosities set aside, differences over policies ignored while not only Washington but the whole nation stretched forth a hand of sympathy to the President.

There is scarcely any doubt that President Harding's breakdown was due directly to the severe strain of his trip. The number of speeches he has been called upon to deliver and his lengthy itinerary have been a constant drain upon his vitality. Those who believe the position of chief executive is an easy job need only to examine the lives of former presidents. Most of them went into office strong and hard working men. They came out physically weakened. The job of President seems hard enough without the additional strain of Presidential tours.#

FLAMES GUT HAVEN HALL; DAMAGE HITS $3,000,000

By DAVE THOMAS

(June 7, 1950) The University's 87-year-old Haven Hall was completely gutted by a fire of undetermined origin yesterday despite the efforts of firemen, police, and swarms of students and faculty members who battled the blaze for more than four hours before finally bringing it under control at 9 p.m.

Officials tentatively placed the loss at $3,000,000. The building and its contents were completely covered by fire insurance, they said.

...

Six Ann Arbor fire trucks poured an estimated 700,000 gallons of water into the flaming building which housed the departments of history, sociology, and journalism and the University's extensive Bureau of Government Library.

...

The building was completely gutted down to the ground floor. Walls, floors and stairways were completely destroyed.

...

The first trucks and police cars arrived five minutes after the call was put in. As they drew up, students, many of whom had been writing final examinations only minutes before, were filing out of the building in an orderly fashion.

Others who had snatched fire extinguishers and pushed to the upper floors, were being forced down the stairways by smoke and heat.

Several faculty members and graduate students attempted to re-enter the building to save research work and documents.

Students from a gathering crowd which grew to immense proportions -- almost 20,000 at one time according to police estimate--rushed to help on the undermanned fire trucks.

...

Meanwhile the fire was racing the entire length of the attic and breaking through the roof of the three-story structure at both ends.

Students from the journalism department lugged a score of typewriters and the Associated Press Teletype machine out onto the lawn in front of Haven Hall. A few books and files were dumped from the windows.

Angell Hall was emptied and locked so that no one would be caught should the fire spread. Heavy streams of water were concentrated on the southwest corner of Haven Hall where the 50,000 documents and books of the government library were going up in smoke, to save the literary college structure.

...

During the four and one-half hours at which the fight was at its peak, three powerful fire engines sat idly in the fire department garage for lack of enough trained men to man them.

...

Fire Chief Zahn said "if it hadn't been for the students there's no telling how far the fire might have gone."..#

It was a beautiful spring day in 1950, and in dormitories and rooming houses all over Ann Arbor, students were outside, sitting on benches, sprawled on lawns, busily studying for final exams. The Daily had closed down for the semester, and at the Student Publications Building, Superintendent Ken Chatters was overseeing a major project: the replacement of our old flat bed press with a spanking new rotary press. Part of a wall facing Maynard Street had already been torn down to provide entry for the rotary press, the flat bed press was covered with a tarpaulin, and the building was in shambles.

In the billiards room at the Michigan Union, two solitary figures hovered over a table, cues in hand. "Seven ball in the side pocket," declared Phil Dawson, the Daily's Editorial Director. "Do you smell smoke?" I asked. "Someone with a bad cigar," Phil answered, suspecting that I was trying to distract him.

Now the smoke was quite thick, and Phil looked up from the table, his nose wrinkling. "Must be a fire," he said. "Yep," I answered, missing an easy angle shot. The two intrepid journalists played on, vaguely conscious of the sound of approaching sirens. Finally Phil ambled over to the window, looked right, then left and gasped, "My God, it's on campus!"

Across the street, at the end of the block, a huge throng had gathered. Fire engines were pulling up to the curb. All attention was focused on venerable old Haven Hall, enveloped in billowing clouds of dark smoke and leaping tongues of flame. We looked at each other. "Let's get to The Daily!" I yelled. We raced down the stairs, past the administration building, down Maynard Street and burst into the Daily building, shouting "Ken!" "Lauren!" (Ken's assistant). Chatters emerged from the press room, wiping grease from his hands. "We have to get out an extra!" Phil shouted. "Haven Hall is burning down."

We each grabbed a phone and began calling staffers in to work. Some staff members, with keener journalistic instincts than mine or Phil's, were already at the scene. City Editor Al Blumrosen and Associate Editor Don McNeil were among the first on the scene, jotting down notes, interviewing bystanders, and directing photographers Wally Barth and Alex Lmanian. Soon most of the staff was at work. We handed out assignments, made a rough layout of a six-page paper and helped Ken and Lauren pull the tarpaulin off the old press.

By 9 p.m., exhausted and disheveled, we gathered in the press room, watching in triumph as our extra edition rolled off the old press. Distribution was no problem. Each staff member took a stack of papers and headed for a section of campus or town. Up and down the streets we walked, hawking our papers until well after midnight, yelling "Extra! Extra! Haven Hall Burns Down!"

It was a heady, rewarding experience, and for the senior staff a fitting climax to four tumultous years on what undoubtedly was, and still is, the nation's best college newspaper.

Leon Jaroff, '50

Spectators Help, Hinder Firemen

By LEON JAROFF
(Daily Managing Editor)

(June 7, 1950) A huge crowd, estimated at 20,000, watched, helped, and hindered Ann Arbor firemen as they fought yesterday's disastrous Haven Hall fire.

Minutes after the billowing white smoke began to pour from the roof of Haven Hall, thousands of students and townspeople had completely ringed the burning building, hindering firemen and volunteers as they struggled to bring hoses within effective range.

* * *

SOON AFTER city and state police had roped off the danger areas, burning sections of ledges and roofing began to fall where, only a few minutes before, crowds of onlookers had stood.

Scores of students immediately volunteered their services to Ann Arbor's undermanned fire department.

One of the first hoses to reach the second floor of the building was dragged up a front fire escape by 15 students, some in suits and ties. Later, this same group narrowly escaped injury when a mass of blazing wreckage slid from the roof, missing them by only a few feet.

* * *

SMALL GROUPS of students and an occasional faculty member plunged into the building repeatedly to rescue records, typewriters, and stacks of newly-written bluebooks. Prof. Arthur Bromage, a city councilman, vainly urged them to stay out of danger as the flames closed in.

But some, faculty and students alike, faced with the loss of unfinished doctoral theses and documents representing years of grueling work, remained in the building until flames made further search

impossible.

An occasional bit of com-ic relief brought cheers and laughter from the crowd. Three students on the second floor of the blazing building threw stacks of uncorrected final bluebooks to "safety" below.

Fire hose couplings came loose occasionally in the midst of the crowd, drenching hundreds of students to the skin. Very few left to dry off, however.

Many journalism students, who had been in the midst of final examinations when the fire routed them from Haven Hall, stood among the crowd, their unfinished bluebooks clutched in their hands.

One student finished his final on the steps of Angell Hall and searched through the crowd until he found his professor. The bluebook was accepted by the surprised professor who commented that it was "a little late but permissible in the light of present circumstances."..#

THREE ON FACULTY SUSPENDED

Suspension Surprises Witnesses

By ALICE B. SILVER
Associate Editorial Director

(May 11, 1954) The three faculty members who were suspended after their appearance before the Clardy committee in Lansing yesterday expressed surprise last night at President Harlan Hatcher's action.

...

＊ ＊ ＊

THE THREE faculty members explained their surprise on the basis that their teaching qualifications were not called into consideration by the suspension statement.

They agreed that the "suspension in absence of any questioning of our teaching competency is unfair to our students."

...

The three men also pointed to what they consider a contradiction in the President's statement. In the concluding sentence of that statement the President said, "...it is the University's policy that members of its family be given the protection to which they are entitled under our laws and traditions."

＊ ＊ ＊

HOWEVER, the three explained, the President's letter to them said their refusal to answer questions of the committee "raises serious question as to your relationship to the University and to your colleagues and places upon you the duty to go forward to explain your actions."

The three men raised the question of why "the exercise of rights which the President apparently concedes should place our University status in question."

...

Davis, who invoked only the First Amendment before the Committee, on the grounds that the Committee's questions constituted a violation of his freedom of speech, press and assembly, said that he was aware of the danger of a contempt citation. He added, "I do not believe I was in fact guilty of contempt."

He maintained that the committee "spent quite a bit of time on my political opinions. These questions were clearly violations of the First Amendment."..#

No Action Taken On Two Students

By JIM DYGERT

(May 11, 1954) University President Harlan H. Hatcher ordered late yesterday the immediate suspension of the three faculty members who appeared before the House un-American Activities subcommittee yesterday in Lansing.

No statement was issued in regard to University action concerning the two graduate students...who also appeared before the committee

‡ ‡ ‡ ‡

THE THREE faculty men, Prof. Mark Nickerson of the pharmacology department, Prof. Clement L. Markert of the zoology department, and H. Chandler Davis, an instructor in the mathematics department, were notified of their suspension in letters from President Hatcher.

...

According to Arthur L. Brandon, Director of University Relations, the suspensions mean that "they will not be permitted to carry on their work at the University." He emphasized, however, that the suspensions were "without loss of pay."

The investigations, said Brandon, will be initiated by President Hatcher, who will ask the deans of the colleges concerned to conduct the investigations...

...

When the investigations have been completed (no time limit has been set), recommendations will be made to President Hatcher upon the consideration of which he will decide either to initiate dismissal action or reinstate the faculty men...#

SALK POLIO VACCINE EFFECTIVE

Report It Works 8-9 Times in 10

By LEE MARKS

(April 12, 1955) Salk vaccine works.

After months of anticipation, an anxious world today heard Dr. Thomas Francis, Jr. report that the vaccine is between 80 and 90 per cent effective.

It is absolutely safe.

Speaking at a meeting of more than 500 scientists and physicians, Dr. Francis claimed the vaccine had produced "an extremely successful effect" among bulbar patients in areas where vaccine and a harmless substitute had been used interchangeably.

There is now no doubt that the fight against polio is nearing an end. Children can definitely be inoculated successfully against the crippling effects of paralytic polio, Dr. Francis' report proved.

Dr. Francis delivered his historic 113 page report at a meeting at Rackham Lecture Hall, sponsored jointly by the National Foundation for Infantile Paralysis and the University of Michigan.

Financed by close to one million dollars in March of Dimes funds, Dr. Francis' report brought to an end months of speculation and anxiety.

'Incredibly Safe'

One fear voiced by some scientists turned out to be unfounded. The vaccine was termed "incredibly safe."

Reactions were nearly negligible with only 0.4 per cent of the vaccinated children suffering minor reactions. An amazingly small per cent (0.004-0.006) suffered major reactions...#

JFK KILLED

... ...

JOHNSON TO TAKE OFFICE

DALLAS (AP)—President John F. Kennedy, thirty-sixth President of The United States, was shot to death today by a hidden assassin armed with a high-powered rifle.

Kennedy, 46, lived about an hour after a sniper cut him down as his limousine left downtown Dallas.

Automatically, the mantle of the presidency fell to Vice-President Lyndon B. Johnson, a native Texan who had been riding two cars behind the chief executive.

Kennedy died at Parkland Hospital, where his bullet-pierced body had been taken in a frantic but futile effort to save his life.

Lying wounded at the same hospital was Gov. John Connally of Texas, who was cut down in the spray of bullets that ended the life of the same fusillade that ended to the presidency.

Connally and his wife had been riding with the President and Mrs. Kennedy.

The first lady cradled her dying husband's bloodstained head in her arms as the presidential limousine raced to the hospital.

Connally slumped in his seat beside the President.

Police ordered an unprecedented dragnet of the city, hunting for the assassin.

They believed the fatal shots were fired by a white man about 30, slender of build, weighing about 165 pounds, and standing 5 feet 10 inches tall.

The murder weapon reportedly was a $30.00 rifle.

Shortly before Kennedy's death became known, he was administered the last rites of the rifle.

Roman Catholic Church. He had been the first Roman Catholic President in American history.

Even as two clergymen hovered over the fallen President in the hospital emergency room, doctors and nurses administered blood transfusions.

[Continued on Back Page]

President Lyndon B. Johnson

SEN. KENNEDY DIES

President declares mourning

Loses 24 hour fight for life

LOS ANGELES—Sen. Robert F. Kennedy, 42, died today at 1:44 a.m. PDT (4:44 a.m. EDT), slightly more than 24 hours after being shot in the head on a savage attack in a downtown Los Angeles hotel.

The death was announced of 42 a.m. PDT by Frank Mankiewicz, the senator's press secretary. Mankiewicz had made an unscheduled walk to Good Samaritan Hospital's press room after advising newsmen earlier that there would be no further medical bulletins on the senator's condition unless there was a significant change.

With Kennedy at the time of his death were his wife, Ethel, now expecting her eleventh child; his brother Sen. Edward M. Kennedy, and his sister-in-law, Mrs. John F. Kennedy. Three of the Kennedy's ten children were at the hospital, but not in the room.

A Roman Catholic priest was also in attendance at the time of death.

Kennedy the leader: A moral imperative

Killer foretold murder

RFK on his campaign in Detroit

Alleged assassin Sirhan Sirhan

REV. KING SLAIN

LBJ Confers With U Thant, Delays Hawaii Conference

Riots Hit U.S. Cities

Nobel Laureate Shot By Memphis Sniper

MEMPHIS, Tenn.—A sniper's bullet struck down Martin Luther King Jr. tonight at man standing on the balcony of a motel here and the hate-scorn of a sniper here the dead here than in hope to love hate upon to Joseph Hospital.

The Late Rev. Martin Luther King

Non-violence Brought World Fame to King

Hanoi Reduces Khe Sanh Attack

State Senate Passes Open Housing Statute

Violence Erupts In N.Y.C.

Nation Mourns Tragedy

DEPUTIES ARREST 52 AT SIT-IN; 900 STUDENTS PROTEST ON DIAG

28 'U' students jailed at protest

Street confrontation with the Tactical Mobile Pigs

By MARTIN HIRSCHMAN
(Sept. 7, 1968) **WHEN THEY MOVED** on the Washtenaw County Bldg. at 5:30 p.m. yesterday, the Tactical Mobile Pigs were carrying rifles and shotguns--all too long it looked like they were going to use them

These specially trained pigs--clad in their blue uniforms and spaceman helmets--were part of the force which kept demonstrators outside the building away from the other pigs who were carrying, pushing and dragging the protesters out from inside.

So when a group of people drew close to the building's entrance and Sheriff Douglas J. Harvey yelled at them to get back, it was the Tactical Mobile Pigs who moved in.

(I was in that crowd.)

The pigs pointed their rifles and shotguns towards the faces and bodies, yelled to get back, and started walking forward.

The people in front of the crowd started inching back and some turned around, ducked down low and pushed the people behind them to move back.

(I was terrified.)

...

Finally, the group managed to put some space cautiously between them and the tactical pigs, but when they did, there was no very safe way to turn.

ALL AROUND, hundreds of pigs-- tactical pigs still pointing their rifles straight ahead, regular pigs with riot sticks maintaining a no-man's land on Huron St. and attacking pigs who were "escorting" their prey into the waiting pigmobile.

(While his mother was conferring with newsmen, a small boy, tired of playing marshall with his red armband, took out a well-hidden capgun and began firing. He was remonstrated immediately, "Don't do that!" He looked up

with a question on his face and I could see one of the marchers pointing to the rifles on the roof of the county jail.)

Yes sir, there"'s been a good deal of talk about the ring-a-ding pig state we're living in. Lots of talk.

But there it was, an organic pig state on Huron St. And it was pushing people around and penning them in and twisting their arms and gobbling them up.

(I was incensed.)

And there were people who watched calmly from the windows of the Ann Arbor Bank across from the County Building.

But not being down on that street, all they saw was worth exactly nothing.#

28 'U' students jailed at protest

By PHILIP BLOCK and STEVE NISSEN
(Sept. 6, 1968) Fifty-two people were dragged from the second floor of the County Bldg. yesterday by more than 100 law enforcement officers under the direction of Sheriff Douglas Harvey.

The group was protesting what they termed insufficient county welfare aid. Twenty-eight of those arrested are University students. Most of the others were welfare mothers receiving Aid To Dependent Children (ADC) funds.

The police raid took place at 5:50 p.m. after negotiations between the welfare recipients and the WMC reached a deadlock. The sit-in demonstration had begun at 5:15 p.m. just before the building was scheduled to close...#

THIS IS ANN ARBOR, USA

By DAVID WEIR and
ALISON SYMROSKI

Photographed by:
Jay Cassidy
Thomas R. Copi
Eric Pergeaux
Andrew Sacks

THIS IS ANN ARBOR, USA

**By DAVID WEIR and
ALISON SYMROSKI**

(Sept. 7, 1968) ...During the long march to the County Building; during the four-hour sit-in; during the bus ride to City Hall; we kept remembering that we were trying to do something for the welfare mothers whose children need clothes for school.

But there were times when we didn't think about much but ourselves and the cops. When the first battery of cops came hurtling into the County Building lobby with their riot clubs held high, it was hard to remember that we were doing something for the welfare mothers.

And when the cops slammed us into the doors of the County Building as we were "escorted" out it was hard to remember that we were doing something for the welfare mothers.

And when the cops ripped our shirts and threw us into the door of the bus and we screamed "pigs, pigs, pigs" it was hard to remember that we were doing something for the welfare mothers.

And when we were huddling in the damp cold rooms in the basement of City Hall, waiting to be arraigned upstairs, it was hard to remember that we were doing something for the welfare mothers.

But it was at these times that we found out what it is like to be a welfare mother.

It hadn't been very difficult to carry signs around the County Building Thursday afternoon, or to verbally support the welfare mothers when talking among ourselves. We knew that we supported their demands and were sympathetic to their problems.

It wasn't until we saw the cops' faces and felt their grip and smelled their breath that we understood how it feels to be black and poor and hated. We saw police not with the rosy cheeks and Pepsodent smiles of our grade school readers, but with faces filled with barely restrained anger and hate.

...

...getting arrested doesn't get raincoats for children.

But we made a commitment. It wasn't raincoats and it wasn't shoes. Rather, it was a repudiation of the "freedom" guaranteed us but denied others by the American System.

And that's the beginning.#

POLICEMEN USE TEARGAS, CLUBS
TO ROUT 1500 NEAR SOUTH U.

45 ARRESTED; MANY INJURED

(June 18, 1969) Some 300 state, county and city police used riot sticks, tear gas, and Pepper Fog to clear 1500 people from a ten-block area near South University Ave. last night, arresting about 45 persons.

The series of confrontations between 8:30 p.m. and 2 a.m. left at least 15 police and many others injured. An estimated 15 were reportedly treated and released at St. Joseph's Hospital. University Hospital reportedly treated nine persons, none of them police. Another person was treated and released at Health Service.

...

The police action came on the second night large crowds gathered in the South University area. Monday night, however, some 700 persons were allowed to dance, drink wine, set off fireworks, and perform motorcycle stunts in the area.

Ann Arbor Police Chief Walter Krasny said last night that he expects further disturbances and vowed, "We are going to control the streets of Ann Arbor and not give it to a bunch of people who think they own it."

He said that the National Guard had been alerted but was not called in.

Krasny also explained that he did not enter the area Monday night because of "limited manpower."

...

The main crowd at East University and South University was dispersed at about 1 a.m. by police who gave the crowd a 10-minute warning

before moving in to disperse them. When the crowd did not break up, police began chasing them down East University toward East Quad.

One of the policeman injured was struck by what appeared to be a firebomb at 1:20 a.m. The policeman, who was part of a contingent charging up

East University near East Quad was momentarily enveloped by flames when an object thrown by one of the fleeing students hit him.

The fire was put out quickly by others of the contingent and the injured policeman was taken away. His condition is unknown...#

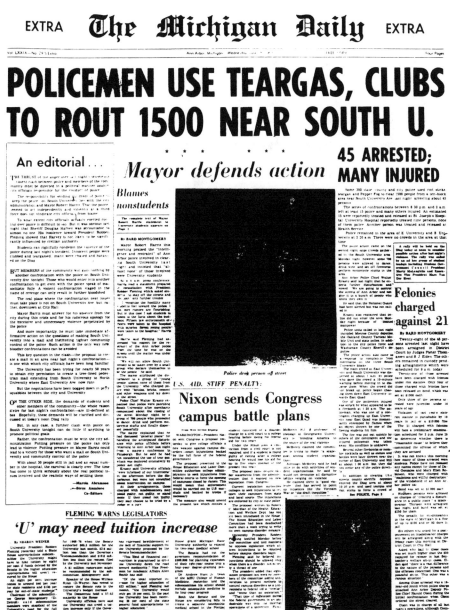

SOUTH U. CLEARED AGAIN
Police make 30 arrests

(June 19, 1969) Some 400 Ann Arbor police, Washtenaw County Deputies and Michigan State Police cleared a ten-block area around South University Ave. early this morning, arresting at least 30 people.

Hospitals reported treating at least four persons.

Dr. Edward Pierce, a former chairman of the Ann Arbor Democratic Party and a one-time mayoral candidate, was arrested by two Washtenaw County deputies who dragged him about 5 yards with the seat of his pants on the cement.

...

The police action at 12:45 a.m. began as two groups of 300 police each moved in on South University, one group coming from South Forest and the other moving in from the direction of South State St.

...

Those coming from the direction of South State were mostly state police, but included some Ann Arbor police. At about 1 a.m. about 200 people remained at the corner of South University and East University.

Ann Arbor Deputy Chief Harold Olson gave the crowd a five minute warning. Many of the people cried out "Where can we go?" Most of the people left by going down East University.

After five minutes, the police coming up from State Street divided the remaining people into two groups and forced them in opposite directions along East University.

...

Sheriff's deputies later turned down Church, arresting several people. Meanwhile, the state and Ann Arbor police continued to push down East University in both directions.

At approximately 1:45 a detachment of about 30 Washtenaw County deputies swept down Church St. They searched alley ways and small side streets for stragglers. They made about four more arrests...#

Diag rally rejects demand

By BARD MONTGOMERY

(June 19, 1969) More than 1000 people gathered on the Diag for a noon rally yesterday and voted down a proposed demand for the immediate closing of South University Ave. last night.

The crowd heard President Robben Fleming, student and community leaders and other speakers, most of whom urged them not to return to South University last night for another confrontation.

Student Government Council President Marty McLaughlin warned, "If we go out there tonight, we will have to face an armed struggle for control of the city, for which we are not prepared, or we will get creamed. The city will not act in a responsible manner."

...

Leaders had prepared four demands to be presented to the city. These were discussed at the beginning of the rally. But the first demand--closing of South University--was rejected and some of the leaders then began to argue that only people who had been involved in the confrontation should be allowed to vote.

An argument began and no further votes were taken...

President Fleming promised that he would "work in every way to protect students" from police intervention on campus but admitted he had no authority to prevent them from acting on campus...#

'No Furniture Store Done Me No Favors'

(July 25, 1967) DETROIT -- On the northwest side of this city, "free, white and 21" wasn't quite good enough last night. Having wandered into the heart of the worst Detroit riot since 1943, we considered ourselves lucky to have gotten out alive.

You could blame it on mid-summer madness: the riots and our going into Detroit Sunday night to cover them. But that wouldn't be right. The riots were a long time coming and we went scared, wanting to see and learn.

...

We drove northeast on Clairmount, other cars both in front and behind, still feeling safe. There was a fire to our left about two-and-a-half blocks past Woodward, a fire truck parked on the right... The flames were rising three stories high and leaning wildly over the sidewalk. As we got closer we realized that the fire was out of control and that the fire truck had been abandoned. There were crowds of black people milling about on both sides of the street, maybe 200 to one side of a block. The first rock hit us a moment later as we passed John R Street. Within a few seconds, we heard five or six thuds, glass shattering, and our photographer, Bill Copi, crying, "I've been hit!" We sped ahead and then turned right onto Bush, about 15 or 20 blacks chasing after us for a block.

...

Turning onto Grand Boulevard we thought we had reached safety. There were well-kept apartment houses, whites as well as blacks on the street, and lots of traffic. But within a few blocks of Henry Ford Hospital, we saw our first National Guard. We parked between Lawton and Linwood and walked over to the nine guardsmen stationed at the corner of Linwood and Grand. Some were sitting on the grass, some standing around, and two were searching and questioning a Negro man and his wife. All had rifles, bayonets fixed.

We showed them our press cards. The corporal, who seemed to be in charge, looked the cards over, looked at us, and fulminated, "The University of Michigan don't eat shit around here. There's a 9:00 curfew. It applies to white and black."

We tried to talk to several people on our way back to the car. The whites didn't want to stop. We did manage to talk to several Negroes.

...

[A man] dressed in work clothes, looking haggard, came over to us... We were standing in front of our car, the shattered window clearly visible from the sidewalk. It was that, we think, that attracted him. He was 27, had worked at Ford, and admitted with some pride that he'd been looting that afternoon. He explained the riots this way: "We done had enough. If whitey don't give us what's ours right now, we goin' to take it or leave it burnin'....I can't stand the layoffs, the heat, the rats, the fuzz cussin' us out anymo'. ...I saw my brothers throwin' rocks and bustin' up stores and I saw my chance. ...No furniture store ever done me no favors."

WE GOT BACK into the car and continued west on Grand... There were five Negro youths at the corner as we made a right onto Livernois. One shouted, "Hey, look at that!" as the others began to move toward our car. We stepped down hard on the accelerator...#

—MICHAEL DAVIS
—HENRY COSTONY

EXTRA **The Michigan Daily** EXTRA

JOHNSON WILL NOT SEEK NEW TERM AS PRESIDENT

An Editorial

Orders Immediate Halt in Bombing Of North Vietnam Except DMZ Area

Asks for Session Of Geneva Parley

Election Thrown in Turmoil: Nixon Sees Humphrey Entry

'Greatest Thing Since V-E Day'

University Students Celebrate Announcement on Diag

In the late winter of 1968, on a Sunday night, Lyndon Johnson announced that he would not seek re-election as President. Ann Arbor exploded with delirium; everyone thought it meant the Vietnam War was over. It was reported (orally) that all the beer in Washtenaw County was sold out.

--Jenny Stiller, '70

It was always very painful when major news occurred when we were on a break from our publishing schedule. One such time was in April 1972, when the United States bombed Hanoi.

Arch Gamm, then the printing superintendent, refused to call in the printers from their vacation because they had just put in so much overtime on the Summer Sublet Supplement. Someone hit upon the idea of using the facilities of the Rainbow People's Party to put out a quick tabloid. So we used The Daily's wires, wrote an editorial, announced the inevitable demonstration the next day, and produced a Daily that looked nothing like The Daily. Getting into the spirit of things, we even added an exclamation point on the headline. Then, after staying up all night working on our paper, several of us passed it out on the Diag and left copies at the dorms.

--Sara Fitzgerald, '73

The Michigan Daily

Special Issue · Ann Arbor, Michigan · Monday April 17, 1972 · Four Pages

U.S. BOMBS HANOI!

Ann Arbor protest set

by CHRIS PARKS

HUNDREDS OF U.S. WARPLANES yesterday caused heavy damage around Hanoi and Haiphong. Meanwhile, in the South, Communist rockets and mortar shells slammed into Da Nang and U.S. positions 70 miles northeast of Saigon

See BOMBINGS, Page 4

See PROTESTS, Page 4

SUSPECT HELD IN BURSLEY SHOOTINGS

Alleged gunman to be arraigned today

(April 18, 1981) Leo Kelly, a 22-year-old Bursley Hall resident described by many as a loner, is scheduled to be arraigned tonight on charges that he shot and killed two fellow residents during a fire scare early yesterday morning.

Ann Arbor police arrested Kelly in his sixth-floor Bursley room shortly after the 6 a.m. shooting, which left University students Edward Siwik, 19, of Detroit, and Douglas McGreaham, 21, of Caspian, dead of shotgun wounds.

As of late yesterday, police said they had established no motive for the attack, which shocked and baffled residents of the North Campus dorm, the University's largest. Police Chief William Corbett said Kelly was calm and coherent when police found him sitting on his bed with a sawed-off, 12-gauge shotgun.

University rules prohibit possession of firearms in residence halls.

According to student witnesses and police, the Good Friday morning tragedy started when Kelly allegedly tossed one or more Molotov cocktail firebombs down a Douglas Wing corridor, starting several small fires.

In the confusion that followed a fire alarm, the suspect apparently went into his single room and reappeared in the corridor wielding a shotgun. Between two and five shotgun blasts were heard, felling Siwik and McGreaham, who were at point-blank range.

Siwik, who lived only a few doors away from Kelly, was shot in the upper right chest and died shortly after being taken to University Hospital.

McGreaham, shot in the back, died at nearby St. Joseph Hospital following emergency surgery. He was a resident adviser living on the fifth floor of a different wing of the building and had gone to investigate the fire alarm and help evacuate students.

Randy Moon, an RA who ran up to the sixth floor with McGreaham, said last night, "Doug hit the floor and I hit the floor. We all assumed at the time it was firecrackers." He added, "to me it seems as if it was a random shooting."

ONE STUDENT who lived two doors from Siwik said "Kelly went sort of berserk." After the firebombs exploded, the resident said, "he just stepped out of his room and fired a couple of shots at the nearest people to him, and went back in his room."

...

Students reported that several dorm residents who were gathered outside the building jeered at Kelly as he was led from the scene. According to witnesses, some students shouted to Kelly, "Why'd you do it?"

"He just smirked and walked on by," said a Bursley resident.

...

Students in the dorm were "numb" after the incident; many were afraid to return to their rooms for several hours after the shootings.

...

[A freshman] said he felt "anger that something like this could happen. The people who died were doing their damndest to get everybody out. They had no concern for their personal safety.

"People are dazed," he continued. "They keep saying, 'This isn't real. When are we all going to wake up'?"

Some residents mentioned that the early morning fire alarm was at first ignored by many students. "Some people were ignoring the fire alarm until the RA's started to clear out the halls," one student said. "We get them all the time on weekends."..#

EXTRA The Michigan Daily **EXTRA**

Vol. XCI No. 157   Saturday April 18, 1981   Twelve Pages

SUSPECT HELD IN BURSLEY SHOOTINGS

Alleged gunman to be arraigned today

Leo Kelly, a 22-year-old Bursley Hall resident described by many as a loner, is scheduled to be arraigned tonight on charges that he shot and killed two fellow residents during a fire scare early yesterday morning.

Ann Arbor police arrested Kelly in his sixth-floor Bursley room shortly after the 6 a.m. shooting, which left University students Edward Siwik, 19, of Detroit, and Douglas McGreaham, 21, of Caspian, dead of shotgun wounds.

As of late yesterday, police said they had established no motive for the attack, which shocked and baffled residents of the North Campus dorm, the University's largest. Police Chief William Corbett said Kelly was calm and coherent when police found him sitting on his bed with a sawed-off, 12-guage shotgun.

University rules prohibit possession of firearms in residence halls.

Daily staff writers David Meyer, Janet Rae, Howard Witt, and Tim Yagle filed reports for this story. The story was written by Howard Witt.

According to student witnesses and police, the Good Friday morning tragedy started when Kelly allegedly tossed one or more Molotov cocktail firebombs down a Douglas Wing corridor, starting several small fires.

In the confusion that followed a fire alarm, the suspect apparently went into his single room and reappeared in the corridor wielding a shotgun. Between two and five shotgun blasts were heard, felling Siwik and McGreaham, who were at point-blank range.

SIWIK, WHO lived only a few doors away from Kelly, was shot in the upper right chest and died shortly after being taken to University Hospital.

McGreaham, shot in the back, died at nearby St. Joseph Hospital following emergency surgery. He was a resident adviser living on the fifth floor of a different wing of the building and had gone to investigate the fire alarm and help evacuate students.

Randy Moon, an RA who ran up to the sixth floor with McGreaham, said last night, "Doug hit the floor and I hit the floor. We all assumed at the time it was firecrackers." He added, "to me it seems as if it was a random shooting."

ONE STUDENT who lived two doors from Siwik said "Kelly went sort of berserk." After the firebombs exploded, the resident said, "he just stepped out of his room and fired a couple of shots at the nearest people to him, and went back in his room."

Jim Bonevich, a freshman who lives

See TWO, Page 2

ABOVE LEFT—Ann Arbor Police lead suspect Leo Kelly away from Bursley Hall. The brand of Omega Psi Phi fraternity is visible on Kelly's right arm. Below left—Freshman Ed Siwik is wheeled into an ambulance. He died shortly after arriving at University hospital.

AP photos by Daily photographer Brian Masck

Virile Male, Dainty Gal Explode Sex Test Theory

By GAYLE GREENE

(Oct. 19, 1951)Three gentle kicks and a graceful bend by a tall, strong, young architecture student in the act of picking up a spoon, put a big dent in some carefully ironed-out psychological theories on masculine and feminine behavior.

Would-be psychologists claim that the manner in which a person stoops to pick up an object on the floor, as well as their way of lighting a match, taking off a sweater, catching an object in their lap, and other minor mannerisms may be used to determine male and female differences.

...

A recent Daily survey revealed, however, that these traits do vary.

A trip to Ferry Field found hemen football players kneeling to pick up the ball in a graceful fashion although the theory holds that men lean over from the waist to pick up an object while a woman kneels gracefully.

* * *

ALMOST 90% who took the match test struck the match away from themselves although the theory holds that this is the feminine way and that a man should strike a match toward himself.

This behaviorism is one that has been strengthened by childhood safety training. "Also it's a good way to avoid having one's necktie catch on fire," Sam Davis, '53, said.

...

MAN'S DESIRE to prove his athletic ability was the uncontrolled variable in a test dating back to "Tom Sawyer" in which an object is thrown into the subject's lap. The man, by instinct, according to the theory snaps his legs together while a woman, used to skirts, spreads hers to catch the object.

Yet, instinctively, in all the tests made this weekend in The Daily Survey, each male subject reached out to spear the object as though it were a forward pass, while the coed, too, made a feeble attempt to prove her own athletic ability.

All the fuss over tests and surveys was deplored by Roger Brown, psychology instructor, who said, "These tests are an elaboration of the obvious. All one has to do to determine male and female differences is to look."#

Pooh's Ultimate Significance

(EDITOR'S NOTE: The following is an accurate report of a public lecture sponsored by a little-seen University group yesterday.)

BY FAITH DIXON HUNT

(May 20, 1960) "To consider Winnie the Pooh merely a Bear, as certain critics such as Marvin Felheim have, is to completely miss the true significance of the work," Prof. R. C. Fnnes-Southerby declared last night.

Prof. Fnnes-Southerby, described as noted teacher and critic who has contributed several definitions to the Oxford English Dictionary (specifically "polytechnic" and "pornography"), spoke at the decennial Aardvark award lecture of the John Barton Wolgamot society on "The Morphological and Allegorical Purpose of Pooh."

...

The theme of the Pooh books is Pooh's endless and futile search for his own identity, according to Prof. Fnnes-Southerby. "The point of view that Heath-

Stubbs takes in his recent book 'Of Winnie the Pooh and Other Fugitive Essays,' where he sees Pooh as Richard III, is entirely untenable."

Fnnes-Southerby sees Pooh as the middle-class man, searching for identity, "unable to carve for himself an enclave in society in which he can practice his art." Eeyore he sees as the poet manque, the disillusioned intellectual, Piglet as the ineffectual lower classes, and Kanga as the American Matriarch, "obviously with a Boston accent."

...Discussing the river scene, in which Roo, Kanga's daughter, nearly drowns, he pointed out that the crisis shows each character as a real character.

Piglet, the helpless proletarian, jumps up and down shouting, "I say, I say." Owl, the Jungian wiseman archetype, delivers grave statements. But Eeyore, "the critic who is not a critic, the philosopher who is not a philosopher, becomes practical in an emergency," and offers his tail to save Roo...#

chapter 2

home turf

For The Daily, the University is the equivalent of Capitol Hill for the Washington press corps — the place where decisions are made that directly affect the lives of every one of its readers. And like the D.C. press, The Daily too has cultivated "high-placed sources" to bring its readers high-impact news — insider journalism at its best.

covering
the
university

In '94-'96...we were not only pressed for funds but an unscrupulous Business Manager had pledged future advertising for all sorts of merchandise. The paper was distinctly "in the hole."

The Law School was getting a new dean and shifting from a two-year to a three-year course. The new dean was responsible for the new law curriculum and while proposing to give it to the press at four o'clock in the afternoon, pledged them not to use any portion before that hour.

George Harrison, business manager, took the pressmen of the Washtenaw Times, which did our printing, and filled them with "red eye" while I, with the aid of the printer's devil, got the paper out at noon, with the new three-year course entire. The Daily was out at noon. Did it stir the animals up? Dean Hutchins swore he would have our blood.

Years later when as President he visited Pasadena he said that he knew me, but when pressed as to what it was he knew, answered: "Nothing good, I assure you, so let us forget it."

--William A. Spill, '96L
From The Daily, Nov. 16, 1940
Fiftieth Anniversary Edition

LAW FACULTY MEETING.

A SCHEDULE OF HOURS ADOPTED FOR THE LAW DEPARTMENT.

Lectures to be Doubled--Fourteen Hours Will be Required--The Laws' Lives Will be a Burden--Classes to be Known as "First Year" "Second Year" and "Third Year" Men.

(April 5, 1895) The faculty of the law department was in session yesterday and this morning completing the changes necessitated by the inception of the three years' law course next fall. In the lengthening of the course the work of the law school has not been made easier, but, on the contrary, it has been augmented by the change.

All students in the "third year," "second year" and "first year" classes, as they will be designated, will have fourteen hours of required work a week, including two hours in section quizzes. The year will be divided into two semesters, as in the literary department, and examinations will be given at the close of each semester...

...

Lectures will be one hour in length, but the number in a course will be increased 50 per cent, so that the same amount of instruction will be given. In certain subjects the amount of instruction given will amount to much more than heretofore...

...

The work in the first year will be mainly by means of textbook instruction, which will be in charge of Prof. Hutchins and Prof. Knowlton. The third year men, or senior laws, will receive no material changes in their work...

...

All instruction to be given by the resident professors will be arranged at regular hours. A schedule showing the time of recitations, lectures and quizzes has been prepared and will be published with the annual announcement...#

The C. C. Little Years

I have been searching my memory to recall those exciting and turbulent Little years. A few facts and a lot of impressions. I was fond of C. C. His press conferences were a joy to reporters because of his wit and his fund of dirty jokes--and his willingness to open up on an off-the-record basis.

Of course we all knew he would have to resign in time. The affair with the lady dean would have been overlooked if he had not antagonized with impartial force the DAR, the Catholic Church, and the faculty. And of course a large section of the student body because of the auto ban.

He castigated the DAR for its pecksniffian and disdainful attitude toward immigrants and foreign-sounding names. The Daughters seethed. He enraged the Church with his uncompromising stand on birth control (Margaret Sanger was not a polite name in those days). He by-passed the faculty in making appointments. A special infringement was the appointment of Peter Munro Jack as head of the Rhetoric Department, and announcing it from England where he had interviewed Jack upon recommendation of T. S. Eliot who had been Little's classmate at Harvard. Jack lasted three years of his contract but in that span brought contemporary literature to the campus--from Virginia Woolf to Eliot to I. A. Richards, and a new and lively approach to literary criticism. The auto ban was forced because of a number of fatal and near-fatal accidents to students, and given the plethora of prohibition hootch on campus, he did his duty and vigorously defended his action.

He took a courageously unpopular stand on almost everything, and in the end this had evoked too much displeasure in the Legislature, so much that the University appropriation was threatened, and out he had to go.

--Lawrence Klein, '30

(July 3, 1925) If he is elected by the Board of Regents, Dr. Clarence C. Little, who, until his resignation yesterday, was president of the University of Maine, will be the sixth President of the University.

1925

...

It was understood yesterday, from reliable sources, that a committee representing the Board of Regents went east shortly before Commencement to confer with Dr. Little, and to determine further his fitness for the position. The committee is said to have consisted of Regent William L. Clements, chairman, Professors Jesse S. Reeves and Herbert C. Sadler, and Dr. Frank E. Robbins.

...

Dr. Little is well known as a scholar and public speaker, and is said to be unusually well liked by the students at the University of Maine. An athlete of no mean ability during his undergraduate days, having been a Varsity track man at Harvard, Dr. Little has always retained an active interest in athletics and athletic affairs. He is said to be over six feet tall. The following is an excerpt from a letter received by one of the Regents from a prominent eastern man, "Dr. Little comes from sound New England stock with a long tradition of culture."..#

LITTLE NOT YET ELECTED PRESIDENT, CLEMENTS SAYS

(July 3, 1925) "Though it looks very much as though Dr. Little will be President of the University, he does not yet hold that office," according to Regent William L. Clements, chairman of the Regent-Faculty Committee for the selection of a new President, in a long distant telephone conversation last night.

"The University does not offer positions until it knows that they will be accepted. The significance of the stories from Maine is merely that Dr. Little will accept the post if it is offered to him."..#

USE OF LEISURE TIME IS OF VITAL INTEREST TO EDUCATOR--LITTLE

THEY SHOULD KNOW STUDENTS' ACTION AT ALL TIMES STATES PRESIDENT

(April 30, 1927) "The educators of the country, as the overseers of the dispensation of the money of the tax-payers, have the right to,

---

CHURCH GROUP CRITICIZES PRESIDENT LITTLE'S STAND

(Dec. 10, 1925) Communications criticizing the stand taken by President Clarence Cook Little in advocating birth control have been received by the members of the Board of Regents from the League of Catholic Women, which convened in Detroit last week, it was learned yesterday.

It is not known at the present time whether the Regents will discuss the content of the letter at their next meeting, nor has the content of the communication been made public.#

---

and must in the near future, enter the lives of the students during their leisure hours as well as school hours," was the statement of President Clarence Cook Little in his address on "The High School from the Viewpoint of the University" before the Michigan Schoolmasters' club last night in Hill Auditorium.

"Because of the complexity of our civilization," he continued, "we cannot allow students whose parents are bearing only a small part of the cost of educating them, to be pirates in their leisure time. It is our right and duty to know what our students are doing in the time outside of school, both after hours and during the summer vacations. We must get away from the idea that schools are only a convenience."

High School Needs Shown

President Little then went on to outline some of the ways in which the high schools must advance to the place where they are meeting the requirements that the advance of the modern universities demand. He stressed the point that the universities must interest themselves in, and must consider more than the "subject matter learning" of the prospective entrant...#

PRESIDENT LITTLE ASSERTS DORMITORY IS NOT NEW

(Feb. 10, 1928) Expressing surprise at the unfavorable reaction which his advocacy of dormitories had caused among Ann Arbor residents, President Clarence Cook Little yesterday explained that the dormitory project was not a new idea, but that it has been an integral part of the University policy. "The University has always accepted every dormitory that was offered without cost and I merely propose the addition of others without cost to the University," he said.

...

The President also pointed out that even in the event dormitories are built, there is no need for excessive alarm on the part of the landladies, since the early plans call for the housing of only 1,000 students in the dormitories, probably freshmen, and this number will not completely cripple the rooming business in Ann Arbor.

President Little met Tuesday afternoon with a committee of the Women's Housing league at which time several decisions were reached at the close of a considerable discussion. The committee decided that it would urge members of its league to do their best in fulfilling the requirements of the University, and President Little agreed not to over-emphasize the bad conditions of the rooming houses to the exclusion of their good features. In conclusion a statement was given out by the landladies' committee declaring that the "whole conference was extremely good natured" and scoring the "contrary utterances in the press by landladies who are not members of the Women's Housing league."#

REGENTS RATIFY UNIVERSITY COLLEGE

NEW EDUCATIONAL PLAN ADOPTED AT SPECIAL MEETING

(April 26, 1928) Definite approval of all phases of the University college proposal was voiced yesterday by the Board of Regents in a special meeting called for that purpose. The action of the board, surprising to many members of the faculties who had expressed their disapproval of the plan, formed the last step in a process begun more than a year ago.

The resolutions adopted by the Regents yesterday morning, covered the principal points of contention over the University college issue. Believing the plan to be beneficial to the students of the University the board directed the President to appoint as early as possible an executive committee, and that this body should work out the details of the plan, including the appointment of a single responsible head. The University college is to go into effect Sept. 1, 1929, and is to be effective for all schools and colleges which admit their students directly from high school, with the exception of the School of Nursing and the College of Pharmacy.

President Clarence Cook Little, who has led the movement for the University college adoption, yesterday issued the following statement: "I hope and believe that in the 17 months which intervene before the opening of the University college it may be possible to enlist in the various phases of the problem the enthusiastic support of more and more members of the various college faculties."

...

The University college proposition received its first valid form from the hands of the committee appointed by the President, and this was reported Feb. 14 of this year. It was then taken up by the faculties of the College of Engineering and Architecture, and after three meetings was defeated by a heavy majority. This marked the first open opposition to the plan.

...

After four successive sessions had been held by the faculty of the literary college, resolutions were finally adopted which amounted to rejection of the University college plan on the grounds of inadequate finances and consequent danger to the interests of the students now in school...#

LITTLE SENDS REPLY TO CAUSTIC LETTER OF D.A.R. PRESIDENT

(July 18, 1928) A reply to the letter of Mrs. Alfred Brosseau, national president of the D. A. R. which she wrote following an address of President Little at Wayne recently, was issued from the president's office yesterday.

The text of the letter is as follows:

July 17, 1928

My dear Mrs. Brosseau:

...may I express my appreciation of the fact that you clearly distinguish between the University of Michigan of which as you state I "happen at the moment to be President" and my personal views. Fortunately for me those who are the governors of this institution give me the right to personal opinions even though they may not agree with them and I am glad that these opinions will not be confused by you with the University which so greatly appreciates what you and your husband are doing to aid needy students. Of course that fact cannot for a moment be desired by either of us to influence me in stating what I believe to be right.

To some Americans of Revolutionary descent and to some equally American citizens whose ancestry in this country is more recent the present situation appears menacing... We believe that organizations should exist for the use of mankind, not for his enslavement. We believe also...that we have not only the right but the duty when we see a society--no matter how fair be its name--standing as a menace in the path of such relationships between our country and its citizens to say so in no uncertain terms.

In these days life is very complicated. It is very probable that neither you nor I are entirely right in our point of view... Why not agree to disagree without personal bitterness or slurs as to one anothers personalities or positions. The world will probably go on just the same.

Very truly yours,
C. C. LITTLE

The letter from Mrs. Brosseau was sent as an answer to an address delivered by Dr. Little in which he criticized the D. A. R. black list, intimating that the alleged tendency of the D. A. R. to supress certain speakers was un-American.#

STUDENTS TO INVESTIGATE FACULTY

PRESIDENT SUPPORTS STUDENT INQUIRY OF YOUNGER FACULTY

(Nov. 1, 1928) President Clarence Cook Little will give his unqualified cooperation to the Student council on a plan now being completed to conduct a student investigation of the younger members of the University faculty, according to an announcement last night by Paul J. Kern, '29, before the regular meeting of the council.

...

The plan of procedure...will be secretly to nominate student investigators, each of whom will be provided with form questionnaires which they will fill out and hand in anonymously. The grade received by the student under the instructor will be included in the form questionnaire.

It is understood that only faculty men up to the rank of assistant professor will be reported on the questionnaires.

...

This plan originated from a need on the part of the administration to act upon reports more definite than rumor and hearsay in promoting younger men on the faculty to professorships. At present there exists no adequate means of discovering the various capabilities and defects of the newer men and their eligibility for promotion...#

LITTLE SURRENDERS POST

PRESIDENT'S RESIGNATION GIVEN UNANIMOUS VOTE BY BOARD OF REGENTS; REGRET IS EXPRESSED

(Jan. 22, 1929) Unanimously accepting the resignation of President Clarence Cook Little under the terms included in his letter of resignation to each regent last Saturday, the Board of Regents of the University last night passed the following resolution:

"In accepting the resignation of President Little the Board of Regents expresses the most profound regret.

"His high ideals of educational standards, his initiative, his constructive aspirations, his frankness, courage, and sincerity have made the severing of relationships a heartfelt loss to us all.

"We trust that the future may have for him the richest rewards."

In his letter to the regents, President Little gave as his reasons for his resignation his belief that his "methods of handling situations dealing with the interests of private donors, political interest, local interest, and alumnae interests, are not consistent with policies which the Board of Regents deems wise," and that he hopes "to be more effective in scientific research and teaching than in administration."

...

Dr. Little aroused strong antagonism and equally vigorous support soon after he came to the University of Michigan in 1925 to take the place of Marion Leroy Burton who died while in office. Little advocated several new forms of educational methods, a sane form of birth control, a ban on the student use of automobiles, denouncement of the D. A. R. blacklist, closer contact with alumni by means of an Alumni college, a University college, and other things...#

MICHIGAN TURNS ITS BACK ON A GENIUS

(Jan. 22, 1929) Out of the not-too-unruffled quiet of the administrative sanctum has come the final decision that President Clarence Cook Little will retire. He passes into private life with no immediate prospects of employment, but with the satisfaction of having kept to an ideal despite the demands of dictatorial legislators, or of so-called independent students. Michigan loses, with his passing, a man who had greater potentialities as one of the foremost educators of the world, than any man at present in the educational field in the United States.

The University of Michigan and the Board of Regents have failed to recognize the genius inherent in the man. In his entire career he has been harrassed by petty interferences, has been stalled and halted by petty class feelings, and has always been the victim of middle west narrowness and prejudice. Yet he remained always intelligently aloof from his detractors; he pursued the course as he wished; he accomplished many great things in his brief tenancy; and as he leaves, those who believed in him and saw in his ideas the future greatness of the University of Michigan are genuinely sorry that the middle class minds of the Middle West are not yet enough developed to understand a man with vision, with aspirations, and with a genuine grasp of educational affairs.

Those few who rejoice at his going are the few ho will not relinquish their petty control to the hands of a visionary. They are the few who impede progress by their stolidness and their pseudo-conservatism. But for these few the passing of President Little is more a direct criticism of them than a victory for their cause...#

LITTLE FILES FOR DIVORCE

By Associated Press

ANN ARBOR, Mich. June 24 (1929) - Suit for divorce from his wife, Mrs. Katherine Day Little, was filed in Washtenaw County Circuit Court last week by Dr. Clarence Cook Little, resigned president of the University of Michigan, it was learned today.

Papers connected with the suit were withdrawn after being recorded and it was impossible to assert what grounds were to be made the basis of the action...

Apparently not even intimate friends of Dr. and Mrs. Little have been appraised of the action... No intimation that a separation was contemplated by either Dr. or Mrs. Little had reached the University campus and acquaintances of the couple hesitate even to speculate as to the basis of the suit.

Dr. and Mrs. Little were married May 27, 1911. They have three children, all of school age...#

Faculty Plans 'Teach-In'

By ROBERT MOORE

(March 19, 1965) Faced with widespread criticism and "irrevelant" argument, the faculty group that six days ago announced a walkout in protest of U.S. policy in Viet Nam has cancelled its plans to call off classes.

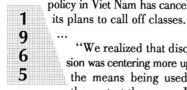

...

"We realized that discussion was centering more upon the means being used in the protest than upon Viet Nam. The group decided it needed to change its tactics," said Prof. William Gamson, chairman of the group.

...

The "teach-in" would last from 8 p.m. Wednesday night until 8 a.m. Thursday morning. It would include lectures by critics of American policy in Viet Nam and seminars considering the alternatives to the Asian commitment...#

Protest, Learning, Heckling Spark Viet Rally

By ROGER RAPOPORT

(March 26, 1965) "Get The Daily out of Viet Nam, Defoliate the Arb, Deflower the Thetas, Stop the senseless waste of human beings, Close the Union Pool."

The sign stood high above a midnight Diag throng at Wednesday night's teach-in. But aside from the few sarcastic onlookers most of the shivering crowd of over 2000 listened closely to Prof. Kenneth Boulding of the Economics Department saying, "The poorest peasant in Viet Nam should have as much right as the richest American. The world has become much too small and crowded for what we are doing."

...

Nearly 3000 students came to hear one or more of the lectures or take part in the seminars held in Auditoriums A, B, C, and D of Angell Hall as well as six Mason Hall classrooms.

"We only expected 500 students," said Prof. Arnold Kaufman of the Philosophy Department, one of the 200 faculty members who planned the event.

Women were allowed all night permission to attend the teach-in and as Jared Stammel, '68, remarked, "This undoubtedly gave a big stimulus to the event."

...

Three bomb scares forced evacuation of Angell Hall and an early start for the midnight Diag rally. Hecklers abounded in the crowd, like the one athlete who came dressed in an Alabama football shirt (No. 55). A group of 75 students marched through the crowd chanting "Better dead than Red."...

Nearby a student said "this thing isn't fair at all. They aren't presenting the other side. These people want another Munich." One of the faculty leaders quipped to a friend, "That guy is going to enlist tomorrow."

One student remarked, "Just look at who is leading this thing--the philosophy and psychology department. You don't see any political science people here--do you?"

...

Chairman Albert Gamson of the psychology department noted that many sign-carrying hecklers "came into our seminars and engaged in intelligent debate. This was our purpose: to promote serious examination of United States policy."

Gamson said, "I learned something I should have known, how bright and serious our students are. The closeness between faculty and students was most moving."..#

An Editorial...

(March 26, 1965) **THE USUALLY UNORGANIZED** and ineffective intellectual community is beginning to stir. With the phenomenal success of yesterday's Viet Nam protest and the burgeoning plans for similar activities on campuses across the country, it is clear that at least some faculty and students are seeking a greater role in shaping American policies.

...

BUT THE SUCCESS of yesterday's protest should not preclude more radical actions in the future. Faculty and students at the University should not forget the issue which originally confronted them when they were planning a teaching strike instead of a "teach-in." That issue is whether teachers have the de facto as well as de juris right to make final judgments on the relative value of different educational activities and whether the right extends, without legislative or administrative sanctions, to political protests which require class time.

Given the original faculty group's deeper immediate concern for Viet Nam, however, we feel the decision to cancel the teaching strike is tactically justified. The faculty group would not have been able to present as large and effective a program as it did yesterday if it had had to fight on a second front at the same time...#

--THE ACTING SENIOR EDITORS

Heyns May Leave 'U', Become Chancellor of Berkeley

Reported Acceptable To All U-C Factions

By ROBERT JOHNSTON

(July 17, 1965) Roger W. Heyns, vice-president for academic affairs since 1962, may leave his post at the University to become chancellor of the University of California's troubled Berkeley campus, according to unofficial sources close to the California regents.

While there was no announcement that an offer had been made following the California regents' monthly meeting yesterday afternoon, there have been several indications in the past two days that the regents, as well as faculty and administrators at California, could agree on Heyns as the next chancellor if he would accept the position.

Attempts to find a chancellor to replace Acting Chancellor Martin Meyerson have been plagued until now by a conservative faction of the California regents which has refused to accept candidates acceptable to liberal faculty and students at Berkeley. Making Meyerson's appointment permanent has apparently been ruled out by the conservative Regents.

...

Meanwhile, Heyns was the guest of regents and administrators at a private party at President Clark Kerr's home Thursday night. In addition, it was learned from Kerr's office that Heyns spent yesterday morning with the California president prior to the regents meeting. He also conferred with California administrators a week ago Thursday.

The next California Regents meeting is scheduled for the middle of August and...a new chancellor will probably be appointed at that time.

If Heyns has, in fact, been offered the job, he will apparently have to make a decision on it soon, thus allowing time for the regents to find another man before their next meeting, if Heyns refuses...#

'U' Presidency Interests Heyns, Source Says

By BRUCE WASSERSTEIN
Executive Editor
Special To The Daily
Copyright 1967, The Michigan Daily

(Jan. 31, 1967) BERKELEY--Chancellor Roger W. Heyns is "very interested" in becoming the next President of the University of Michigan if the job is offered to him according to an authoritative source.

But, the source stressed, Heyns is very wary of leaving Berkeley in the midst of a crisis. He said "Heyns would undergo considerable mental anguish over the problem of leaving a sinking ship."

However, despite many job offers, the source said that "Heyns would consider the University presidency the most desirable academic position if he left Berkeley."

Harlan Hatcher will be retiring this summer after having served as University President for 15 years. Heyns was the University's vice-president for academic affairs until he accepted the Berkeley chancellorship, in the summer of 1965.

As yet, he said, there has been no formal contact between Heyns and the Regents about the presidency. It is known that several informal contacts between Heyns and University officials have been made.

...

Heyns views his job at Berkeley as that of a leader uniting the various campus factions and guiding them toward educational excellence, he added.

But the events of the past week have seriously disillusioned Heyns about his effectiveness in the California political climate.

"Much of what he has worked for has gone down the drain," the source said, pointing out that "the polarization between faculty and the regents which Heyns sought to diminish has re-emerged stronger than ever before."

For example, the source said, "Heyns is bitter about both the Kerr firing and the faculty's reaction to it. As he pointed out in a public speech, Kerr was one of the reasons he came to Berkeley, and he believes that the firing was both ill-timed and unwarranted."

...

He pointed out that the current atmosphere in California requires that Heyns fulfill a basically political role in maintaining Berkeley's autonomy from external political pressures.

...

"Heyns is afraid that if Reagan continues on his present course the University of California will be ruined. The chancellor under these circumstances is not interested in becoming president of the University of California, nor does he think it likely that he will be offered the job. At California, the job he wants is the job he has--the Berkeley chancellorship.

"But if the budget is cut substantially, Heyns will have had enough of California. He is interested in education and not in politics."#

Charge Article Damages Heyns' Chances at 'U'

By ROBERT KLIVANS

(Feb. 1, 1967) A Daily report yesterday that Roger W. Heyns is "very interested" in becoming the next President of the University if the job is offered him may damage his chances for the position, a Regent and several faculty members said yesterday.

Regent Robert P. Briggs (R-Jackson), chairman of the Presidential selection committee said yesterday that, by trying to promote Heyns, now chancellor of the University of California's Berkeley campus, as the replacement for President Harlan Hatcher, some supporters may be doing him "more harm than good."

Briggs said that Heyns "is too smart a man" to say that he is interested in the University presidency before being offered the post.

Several faculty members also voiced dismay at the article, emphasizing that the statements had placed Heyns in an embarrassing situation at Berkeley.

...

A report by James Reston in Sunday's New York Times stated that "the University of Michigan is already pressing Chancellor Roger W. Heyns of the Berkeley campus to accept the presidency of that university."..#

Five Men Remain as Candidates for 'U' Presidency

By ROGER RAPOPORT
Editor

(March 24, 1967) After months of searching and screening for a new University President, the Regents have narrowed down a list of 200 prospects to about five serious contenders.

Formally, about ten men are still in the running to replace President Harlan Hatcher, who retires in December. But top University sources indicate only five men are now serious contenders. "We may have something definite moving within the next week," says one Regent.

Sources indicate five men now being intensively considered are: Franklin Murphy and Roger Heyns, respective chancellors of the University of California's Los Angeles and Berkeley campuses; John Lederle, president of the University of Massachusetts; Robben Fleming, chancellor of the University of Wisconsin's Madison campus, and John Gardner, U.S. Secretary of Health, Education and Welfare.

Chairman of the Presidential Selection Committee Regent Robert P. Briggs (R-Jackson) says that the Regents have not made their final decision and that no one has been offered the job yet.

This week Fleming was offered the presidency of the University of Minnesota, and Gardner and Lederle have publicly denied any interest in taking a new job.

Minnesota Regents Chairman Charles W. Mayo said Sunday that Fleming has been given two weeks to decide if he wants to take that school's top post.

Most think Gardner was serious when he announced recently that he wasn't interested in becoming a college president this year. "He's committed to President Johnson for another year," said one top University official.

...

Both California Chancellors Murphy and Heyns have been considered potential successors to University of California President Clark Kerr who was fired in January.

After a published report in January that Heyns was "interested" in the job here, Briggs says "the roof caved in on us."

California papers played up the story which reportedly prompted some pressure on Heyns not to desert Berkeley. Heyns is known to be concerned about seeing through his job on the strife-ridden California campus.

Heyns, who was vice-president for academic affairs here until September of 1965, has been perhaps the most controversial presidential prospect here.

Heyns is the top choice of both the student and faculty advisory committees to the Regents on presidential selection.

He was also given a top ranking by the alumni advisory committee which gave group rankings.

A University graduate who was at the school for 25 years prior to going to California, Heyns is enjoying wide faculty support here. However, he has been facing some stiff faculty opposition too.

...

Some of the opposition reportedly stems from his handling of budgeting as a vice-president here.

...

The Regents remain confident they can get the "right" man for the post. "After all," says one Regent, "it's not a bad job and it pays pretty well."..#

REGENTS TO VOTE TODAY ON FLEMING FOR NEW PRESIDENT

Consider Choice In Closed Session

By ROGER RAPOPORT
Editor

(March 28, 1967) The University Regents are holding a special closed meeting at 9 a.m. today to vote on Robben Wright Fleming, chancellor of the University of Wisconsin's Madison campus, as successor to University President Harlan Hatcher.

The decision to hold the special meeting today was made over the weekend after another prime presidential prospect, U.S. Secretary of Health, Education and Welfare John Gardner, told the Regents he would not take the job here if offered it.

Sources indicate that today's meeting was called because the Regents fear their list of top presidential prospects will narrow further if they do not act quickly.

...

Sources indicate Fleming stands a good chance of being voted the offer by the Regents today. They have scheduled a special public meeting at 10 a.m. today, followed by a press conference.

The Regents had originally planned to hold off on their presidential vote for another one to two months. However, the Minnesota offer to Fleming has apparently forced the sudden vote.

If offered the presidency here, Fleming is expected to accept today or Wednesday, sources indicate.

Asked about the possibility of deciding between the Michigan and Minnesota offers, Fleming said in a phone interview at his house in Madison last night, "It would be a tough decision for me to make. I've had the advantage of talking to the Regents of both schools and I think if the (Michigan) offer was made, I expect my answer would come quickly."

...

Fleming said he planned to call a news conference for late today or Wednesday to announce his decision on the Minnesota offer.

Fleming added that "it's conceivable" that he would make an announcement simultaneously about both jobs if offered the Michigan post.

Fleming's nearest competitor, Roger Heyns, Chancellor of the University of California at Berkeley, reportedly poses no serious threat to the chances of the Wisconsin chancellor in today's vote.

Heyns' chances were squelched by some faculty opposition and his "too controversial" status, sources indicate...#

Black woman to be LSA dean

Jewel Cobb to assume position

By SARA RIMER and JUDY RUSKIN

(Jan. 19, 1975) A black woman educator, Jewel Plummer Cobb, will be appointed as the new literary college (LSA) dean, several high University sources told The Daily yesterday.

Cobb, dean of Connecticut College, was selected by the Regents to fill the vacancy created by the appointment of former LSA Dean Frank Rhodes to the post of academic vice president in early 1974, sources said yesterday.

Zoology Prof. Billy Frye has been serving as acting LSA dean since July, 1974.

COBB AND two other candidates for the position were interviewed earlier this week by the Regents at their monthly board meeting. Frye and David Danielski, the ombudsman at Cornell University, were also considered for the post.

University president Robben Fleming last night refused to comment on the appointment. Fleming is expected to formally announce the Regents' decision sometime later this week.

...

COBB COULD not be reached for comment at her home in New London, Conn., last night.

One University official said Cobb was "quite impressive...She's a good person. She seems to be extremely articulate, thoughtful and deliberate in her thinking."..#

Cobb choice causes controversy

By SARA RIMER

(Jan. 21, 1975) Speculation and reaction to the naming of a black woman as literary college (LSA) dean rippled through the University yesterday, but the administration refused to provide confirmation of the already-controversial choice.

From several well-placed University officials, The Daily learned Saturday that the Regents had selected Jewel Plummer Cobb, dean of Connecticut College, to fill the position vacated when former LSA Dean Frank Rhodes was appointed vice president for academic affairs in early 1974.

Cobb, who returned to Connecticut after being interviewed by the Regents here last week, declined comment Sunday evening "until it's official." However, she conceded she "had some indication" about the appointment.

...

THE LSA FACULTY, which had rallied behind Frye for the position, reacted with amazement yesterday to the Regents' choice of an outsider over the man widely lauded for his skill in coping with the present economic crunch.

Several officials expressed skepticism about an outsider's ability to step smoothly into a big university hit by major cutbacks. One official warned, "She better be damned good."

Unenlightened by the administration, which remained mute yesterday, high-level officials groped for a rationale behind the Regents' choice.

ONE SOURCE who affirmed the LSA faculty's overwhelming support for Frye asserted that "it was strictly a regental appointment. They bypassed the administration's choice."

The source contended that both Rhodes and President Robben Fleming had favored Frye for the deanship, and that this accounts for the administration's three-day silence on the appointment, which the Regents voted Friday in a tightly closed session.

...

The Regents, University President Robben Fleming and Rhodes all kept a tight clamp on information yesterday, refusing to comment on the Daily's report.

Several high officials said the fact Cobb was a black woman was the double-edged key to her selection. One source claimed, "Because the University was having trouble with affirmative action, they picked the ideal person--a woman who is black. It's perfect."..#

Fleming hedges on appointment
Regents choice reaffirmed

By SARA RIMER and DAN BIDDLE

(Jan. 22, 1975) President Robben Fleming last night insisted that "a couple of weeks" may pass before the University names a new literary college (LSA) dean--but the Daily's high-level sources reaffirmed that the Regents picked a black woman, Jewel Cobb, for the position late last week.

Two well-placed sources reiterated last night that the Regents chose to offer the deanship to Cobb, a 51-year-old Connecticut educator, after reviewing the three final candidates last week. One of the sources confirmed that the Regental vote for the present dean of Connecticut College was unanimous.

BUT LAST night, during the question-and-answer period of a local radio talk show, Fleming indicated the decision was yet to come.

Fleming's comments appeared to flatly contradict the Regents' decision. He told the Daily a short time later: "In due course, the decision will be made." He then repeatedly refused to comment when asked if any decision--or reversal--had already taken place.

...

One of the Daily's sources reported that the Regents had voted "right down the line"--unanimously--for Cobb.

THE SOURCE told the Daily last night that the Regents had discussed the Daily's Sunday announcement of Cobb's selection at a meeting in Lansing Monday night. According to the source, the Board was "irate" that the choice had been reported before official confirmation.

Since Saturday, when the Daily learned that Cobb had been selected in a tightly closed Regents meeting, Fleming, Vice President Rhodes, and the Regents all refused comment on the decision. But when asked if they were denying reports of Cobb's selection they repeated, "No comment."

The administration appeared to be making strong efforts to close off information leaks. One source reported being told "not to talk" by other officials...#

Cobb rejects initial 2-year, no-tenure deanship offer

By SARA RIMER, DAN BIDDLE and JUDY RUSKIN

(Jan. 28, 1975) The administration last week offered a two-year, no-tenure contract to Jewel Cobb, the Regents' unanimous choice for the literary college (LSA) deanship, The Daily has learned.

Cobb rejected the offer Friday and demanded a reconvening of the Regents to revise her proposed contract, two well-placed sources affirmed last night.

AFTER ARGUING over the contract items in a six-hour Sunday meeting, the Regents gave President Robben Fleming and Vice President for Academic Affairs Frank Rhodes a carte blanche to present Cobb with whatever terms the two officers deemed acceptable, the sources said.

...

BOTH SOURCES contended Fleming and Rhodes made the original offer with no intention of persuading Cobb to accept it.

A source close to Cobb said the deanship candidate was disappointed by the no-tenure offer and believed that the administration--Fleming and Rhodes--"must not have ever seriously considered her, or they would have cleared it (tenure) with the zoology department beforehand."

Cobb, a prominent biologist and cancer researcher, had expected to receive tenure in the zoology department, according to the source, who said that department has refused to guarantee her tenure as part of the deanship contract.

SEVERAL high-level sources in LSA and elsewhere have affirmed that the two-year, no-tenure offer given Cobb varies greatly from the standard five-year-plus-tenure proposal given to earlier LSA deans.

The source close to Cobb suggested the zoology department had denied her to protect "its own man"--Acting LSA Dean Billy Frye--who was one of the three final deanship candidates considered by the Regents ten days ago.

...

EARLIER in the day, Fleming refused to disclose the outcome of the Regents' Sunday meeting, despite a flurry of reports describing a growing rift between the administration and the board's more liberal members.

...

A source close to the Regents said the board member described the six-hour, highly secretive meeting as "the roughest one I've been in." At least one Regent, the source contended, came from the meeting convinced that Fleming and Rhodes made a "manipulative" effort to get Regental approval of carte blanche negotiations with Cobb...#

'U' refused Cobb on tenure issue

By DAN BIDDLE, SARA RIMER and JUDY RUSKIN

(Feb. 6, 1975) The University administration last week flatly rejected Jewel Cobb for the literary college (LSA) deanship and told the Connecticut educator that the decision was based on the zoology department's refusal to grant Cobb tenure, The Daily has learned.

Three well-placed sources have affirmed that President Robben Fleming informed Cobb on January 28 that she could not fill the post offered her by the Board of Regents in a unanimous decision more than two weeks ago.

THE BLACK woman biologist told Fleming she was willing to accept the controversial no-tenure deanship offer, according to two sources close to Cobb, but Fleming replied that the University could not allow that in light of the zoology department decision.

Fleming told the LSA faculty's Monday meeting that the University failed to reach "mutually satisfactory terms" with Cobb because an unnamed department had refused to grant her a guarantee of tenured professorship as part of her contract.

...

But The Daily's sources said the final step in the Cobb negotiations was an outright refusal to accept the Regentally selected candidate--despite her expressed willingness to accept a no-tenure contract if the term could be extended to five years...#

FRYE NAMED DEAN

By ANN MARIE LIPINSKI and KEN PARSIGIAN

(Feb. 13, 1976) University Vice President for Academic Affairs Frank Rhodes announced yesterday that acting LSA Dean Billy Frye has been appointed dean of that college for a five-year term.

...

THE CHOICE of Frye as dean has already been labeled by some as a move to "maintain the status quo" in the college of LSA. At least one member of the deanship search committee has also questioned whether the affirmative action guidelines established last year by the University administration for filling the position were observed in choosing Frye...#

Cobb not among 10 dean finalists

By ANN MARIE LIPINSKI and KEN PARSIGIAN

(Feb. 14, 1976) Jewel Cobb...was again a candidate for [LSA dean] this year, The Daily has learned.

Cobb, however, failed to make the deanship search committee's list of ten finalists.

IT WAS ALSO learned that former acting LSA Dean Billy Frye...was supplied with information concerning the position which the other candidates were not given.

Frye, [Vice President for Academic Affairs Frank] Rhodes confirmed last night, knew the names of the other two candidates which the search committee offered to the Regents, along with Frye's name, as their list of three finalists for the deanship.

...

"It seems rather logical now that Frye was chosen as dean," said Cobb...

When asked if she knew of any reason why she was not selected as a finalist this year, in light of last year's unanimous regental approval she replied: "No. I have no thoughts one way or the other."..#

Regents to name Shapiro University president today

By JULIE ENGEBRECHT

(July 27, 1979) Harold Shapiro, currently University Vice-President for Academic Affairs, will be named University president this morning, many reliable sources indicated yesterday.

A meeting of the University's Board of Regents was scheduled yesterday for 10 a.m. today...

...

SOURCES, INCLUDING some administration officials, those close to Shapiro, and other University sources indicated Shapiro would be the name announced by the Regents today.

...

Shapiro was one of the final two candidates discussed by the Regents at Inglis House Monday night, according to Regent James Waters (D-Muskegon)... He would not name the other finalist, although he said the candidate is not currently employed by this University.

...

Waters also said the Board began Monday night's closed meeting with only six candidates left, of which "only about four were seriously discussed." Waters also disclosed that his vote went to Shapiro.

WHILE THERE has been speculation about other University administrators being considered for the post, Waters said Shapiro was the only finalist within the University.

...

A source close to one of the candidates indicated the new president was to be chosen from within the University, and that it would be Shapiro.

LSA DEAN Billy Frye was "around the top 18," according to Waters. He added that the Board reduced its list of candidates from about 18 to six within the last two weeks.

Of the final six candidates, "the majority of them were on all three advisory committee lists," according to Waters. The three advisory groups were comprised of students, faculty, and alumni.

None of those contacted, including Waters, said they knew when the new president would take office.

...

Some University officials would not even say whether the new president would be named today, but several Regents said the meeting's purpose is to announce the new president...#

Princeton considers Shapiro

By REBECCA BLUMENSTEIN

(April 9, 1987) University President Harold Shapiro may be under consideration as a potential candidate for the presidency of Princeton University.

Although the selection process is secret, several Princeton faculty and administrators have speculated that Shapiro--a highly respected Princeton graduate of 1964--is a likely successor.

"We are conducting a wide-open and nationwide search for a successor to our current president," said John Kenefick, head of the search process and vice-chair of Princeton's executive officers.

ACCORDING to the Daily Princetonian, Princeton's alumni who are top academic officials at other universities are prime candidates in the presidential search. In modern history, all Princeton presidents have been selected from the alumni ranks.

...

Shapiro has not announced any interest in pursuing the presidency of another university, but his sabbatical at the beginning of the year indicated that he may be growing restless with his current position.

In addition, when interim president James Duderstadt announced several major initiatives during Shapiro's absence, speculation arose that Duderstadt is being groomed to inherit Shapiro's position...#

Two named as presidential contenders

By JULIE ENGEBRECHT

(Aug. 10, 1979) Secretary of Health, Education, and Welfare (HEW) Patricia Harris and Indiana University (IU) Vice-President Robert O'Neil both were considered for the University presidency, several sources said this week. O'Neil was among the candidates interviewed for the post, according to the president of IU's Board of Trustees.

Few details about the University's presidential selection process have been revealed... The Board and search committee members still are reluctant to discuss the names of those considered during the search, and the number of presidential contenders who were interviewed has not been made public.

...

Harris knew her name had been on a list of candidates for the University presidency, Harris's secretary said Wednesday. The secretary added that while someone had recommended Harris for the post, the recently-named HEW chief was not interested in the job.

...

STUDENT SEARCH committee member Carolyn Rosenberg confirmed that Harris had been placed on search committee lists, but added that committee members expected that the Cabinet official would not be interested in the University presidency.

IU's O'Neil, 44, has been vice-president of the Bloomington, Ind. university 1976.

"I knew he was being considered, and I knew he was interviewed for the job," IU Board of Trustees President Donald Danielson said yesterday.

...

Sources in O'Neil's office and IU students said several months ago O'Neil was interested in the University post...

...

Staff members of the [Indiana] Daily Student [the IU student newspaper] say O'Neil has little chance for advancement at IU because its president, John Ryan, has been there only a few years...#

Profs charged with sexual harassment

By JANET COHEN
Copyright 1983, The Michigan Daily

(April 16, 1983) Charges of sexual harassment this year have led to the resignations of two University faculty members and formal disciplinary hearings for two other professors, according to University officials.

Virginia Nordby, director of the Office of Affirmative Action, said her office also is looking into about 10 other cases of harassment which she terms "serious."

IN ONE CASE pending in Rackham Graduate School, a medical school professor "did in the laboratory sometimes refer to women as cunts and did on occasion grab or twist the arms of (a female student), did make sexually suggestive gestures, and did write instructions to the student on a notepad pictur-

ing female genitalia," according to the confidential report of a faculty review committee.

The professor admitted, according to the report, that he "twice caused the release of potentially dangerous nitrogen tetroxide, once squirted (the student) in the eyes with acetone and on one or more occasions left radioactive materials about in ways that were potentially dangerous."

The three-member Rackham Appeals Board concluded that the medical school professor who was advising the female student on her doctoral dissertation when the alleged incidents occurred, "should be removed from the rolls of the graduate faculty for five years," which would keep him off research committees and ban him from working with Rackham students.

...

A SECOND professor involved in a sexual harassment case faces possible dismissal for his actions. His case currently is being heard by the faculty's Committee on Tenure under "Section 5.09" of Regents' bylaws for cases involving dismissal.

This is the first time in the University's history that such dismissal hearings have been held, said Charles Allmand, assistant to the vice-president for academic affairs.

...

In the two cases that led to resignations, Nordby said, the deans took action promptly once the facts--which she labeled "rather outrageous"--became clear. The deans told the faculty members involved that it would be wisest for them to resign, she said...#

But was he the top choice?

BY RYAN TUTAK

(Sept. 8, 1988) The University's Board of Regents settled on James Duderstadt as the University's 11th president this summer--but only after the four other finalists were out of the picture.

After sifting through almost 300 names, the regents appointed Duderstadt, the University provost and vice president for academic affairs, to the post in a special meeting June 10.

They announced the meeting June 9, three days after the top candidate, New York Public Library President Vartan Gregorian, pulled out. Three sources close to Gregorian said he rejected a private offer June 6 from the regents to take the post.

...

Walter Massey, the only Black finalist and University of Chicago's vice president for research, was second in line. The exact date of his withdrawal is unknown, but after the search he told The Maroon, Chicago's student newspaper, that he had no plans to leave Chicago to come to Ann Arbor...#

home turf

taking on athletics

Within just a few weeks of the first issue, The Daily was already making it's position clear. No one, at least, can accuse them of not starting as they meant to go on...

(Oct. 6, 1890) The policy of our college press heretofore, has generally been to bestow unstinted praise upon our athletic teams, regardless of their actual merit. For instance the nine last spring were told that they were a match for any American college--yet were beaten by a small college on the eastern trip and on the home grounds by Oberlin.

The eleven of last year had no idea of any defeats in training or of the existence of such a thing as defeat--until after the Cornell game. This will not be the policy of the DAILY. We believe that a spirit of mild criticism will do more to help our athletics than promiscuous adulation.

Let us look at things as they are. We cannot expect to send out an eleven equal to that of Princeton or Yale, because we do not receive the same trained athletes from the preparatory schools. We are always behind in methods of training and coaching. We have but little athletic enthusiasm here and for that reason the necessary funds are hard to raise. These are the facts. Now for the remedy.

We must put ourselves in as close connection as possible with the athletic centres in the East. The DAILY will aid very much in this respect.

Then we must develop enthusiasm and college athletic pride by having some good games played here. It is a selfish and a short-sighted policy that arranges all the games away from home, and one that deprives the team of college support, moral and financial. There is no reason whatever why Cornell cannot be induced to come here this fall in return for our game there last year. Games can doubtless be arranged at Ann Arbor with Oberlin, U. of Wisconsin, Northwestern and Notre Dame. Good games like these played here will serve the double purpose of arousing college enthusiasm and raising a fund towards paying the expenses of the eleven.

Lastly every man who can play football at all must come out and try for the new team. The men who have shown up so far are by no means, let us hope, all the good men in college. The best men will get on the team.#

ticket wars

One of the ongoing battles in which The Daily engaged was (and is) over tickets to athletic events – how they're distributed, what they cost, and especially, who gets which seats where.

CRITICISES METHODS OF ASSOCIATION

Writer Thinks Athletic Association Members Did Not Get Fair Chance to Secure Good Seats for Penn Game

(The Daily assumes no responsibility for sentiments expressed in communications.)

Editor, The Michigan Daily:
(Nov. 9, 1911) Far be it from me or any other "scrub" underclassman to criticise the doings of the high and mighty Athletic Association...
...

...It was advertised by this Association early in the year that a great advantage in purchasing a membership ticket was that the members were to receive first choice in the sale of tickets to the Pennsy game. On the morning of November 7 when these seats were put on sale for members I arose a trifle early (4:30 a.m.) and took my place as 53rd man in line,...
...

...of course I could not have expected that there were seats left any nearer the center of the field than the forty yard line. When I was given a chance to take my choice, however, I found that I was limited to a space between the twenty and thirty yard lines....
...

The chart was well marked up with red pencil and from what I could tell from these markings at least two-thirds of all the bleachers on Ferry Field were already sold. Now I contend first, that all those seats then marked off with red pencil were not sold and that these early and eager buyers are being handed out less favorable seats--contrary to the rights which this Association pretends to extend to them. And Secondly, I contend that even if it were true that a rushing mail order business has taken two-thirds of these bleacher seats already, (which I do not believe,) they have been given out in derogation of the rights of the Association members to first choice...#

--A MEMBER

WOULD TAKE ANOTHER RAP AT ATHLETIC ASSOCIATION.

Mathematician Copes With Seat Sale Situation and Discovers Interesting Data

(The Daily assumes no responsibility for sentiments expressed in communications.)

Editor, The Michigan Daily:
(Nov. 11, 1911) Where O where are the verdant freshmen, and the gay young sophomores, and the jolly juniors, and the grave old seniors? They are in the cold wild world waiting for their tickets to the Pennsy game.

Far be it from us to...criticise the Athletic Association; but we trust that they will make allowances for the thermostatic paradox (see Reed & Guthe, page 1728) that as the temperature of one's toes is reduced, that one's feelings rise by the law of Divine Compensation...
...

But a few data with your pardon:
Average number of students in line --89.307.
Line lasts, daily average--10.25 hrs.
Time spent actually buying tickets--5 hrs. 47 min.
Time wasted daily, total average--905 hrs. 2 min. 48 7-8 sec.
Time each student wastes, average--2 hrs. 47 min. 11 1-4 sec.
Time spent actually buying tickets, average--1 min. 7 1-8 sec.
Time wasted per student, average--2 hrs. 46 min. 4 1-8 sec.
Number of students per day, average--327.
Total time wasted per day, average--905 hrs. 2 min. 48 7-8 sec.

Thus we may conclude that any way we look at it, there is wasted in the ten days of the sale, precisely 9050 hrs. 28 min. 8 3-4 sec.

This enormous lapse, you will note, would allow one student to perform any one of the following combinations of stunts:
Prepare 1,247,887.2 lessons in various snap courses.
2 lessons in S & R.
Consult the Dean (X) times.
...

This appalling waste of humanity should be utilized.

Is there no hope, no respite? Are the Association officers deaf to the promptings of "Noblesse Oblige?"
...

Yours in relief,
GOODEN TYRED.

Ticket Sale
By Preference

Our Faulty Distribution System

Editor's Note: From the following article it can readily be seen that something is seriously wrong with the present system of ticket distribution at Michigan. It is a pretty well known fact that tickets sold for as high as fifteen and twenty dollars at the Detroit Board of Trade on the day of the Wisconsin game this year...)

(D. Byron Ayres)
(Dec. 3, 1922) Confirmation of the rumor that favoritism is shown in the distribution of football tickets was established last week in an interview with Harry A. Tillotson, Assistant Director of Intercollegiate Athletics, and by a study of the 1922 distribution of seats to students for the Illinois and Wisconsin games.

When asked if perhaps the so-called "class preference" system of distribution contained a preference within a preference, Mr. Tillotson said, "There are, of course, certain groups, clubs, and organizations which have sections reserved for them in advance and whose applications are filled before those of the general student body. Around these especially reserved sections the student body receives its seats by our class system of distribution."

Mr. Tillotson admitted when questioned further that there are also some bodies of alumni who receive blocks of seats in recognition of their good work in boosting Michigan, and in being instrumental in sending athletes to this University. He also admitted that athletes are given preference over all students in general, they being able, on some technicality, to dodge the rule forbidding any person from receiving more than four tickets to any one game and to obtain an almost unlimited number of tickets to their friends and others.

...

Further questioning brought out confirmation of the fact that the Palestine Lodge of Detroit had received a block of 500 seats to one of the games this year and that they had done so for the past ten years.

...

In an interview in Detroit last Sunday, Mr. George Nedweg, Manager of the Palestine Lodge, pointed out...that each year Mr. John Ablard, proprietor of a small cigar store in Detroit, was appointed chairman of the lodge football committee, because of his former intimate relations and friendship with Coach Fielding H. Yost...

* * *

"As to certain alumni bodies," said Mr. Tillotson, "we do reserve groups of seats for a few. But there are a great many more who are and have for a long time been disappointed in this regard. I will admit that the alumni at Holland received about 150 seats in a block for the games this year, and they have for some time past. The former president of the "M" Club lives in Holland and has done great work in the way of boosting Michigan. It was he who was instrumental in getting Roby and Cappon to come here."

...

A very high percentage of... "mistakes" was brought to light as a result of a canvass of ten fairly representative fraternities on the campus, with regard to the Illinois and Wisconsin games...

...

In one fraternity six juniors, rated as such by the Athletic Association, received much better seats than the average senior in this same house at both the Illinois and Wisconsin games.

In another house where two seniors sent in with two juniors, the tickets received were better than those of the average senior.

...

Out of the ten fraternities reporting, 88 seniors were listed, of whom twenty occupied seats back of the ten-yard line, due to "mistakes" on the part of the Athletic Association.

...

Another interesting feature of the situation is the admission by Mr. Tillotson that players get as many as forty-five or fifty tickets to a game for their friends...#

Tickets For
Gopher Tilt
Bring Distress
Students Criticize
Method Of Distribution

By HOMER SWANDER and
HALE CHAMPION

(Oct. 21, 1941) Thousands of perspiring, exhausted students literally fell out of the packed Administration building yesterday bitterly condemning a system of ticket distribution which forced them to fight for hours for what they felt were inferior tickets.

The struggle began at 8 a.m., five hours before the ticket office was scheduled to open, and reached a climax early in the afternoon when the near-riot became so intense that at least two women fainted and others who had waited for hours gave up in disgust.

Maintaining that there was no justification for such an unprecedented rush, Harry Tillotson, ticket manager, emphasized that there were enough tickets to satisfy all student demands and that three additional tickets could still be purchased with each coupon. He added that student tickets would be available all through the week...

However, faced with a recurrence of the same situation when Ohio State tickets are distributed, Mr. Tillotson said that the system now in use would be altered in some respects.

This statement was made as the shoving, pushing, sweating throng continued to mill around both the inside and the outside of the building, while four policemen attempted to keep only a semblance of order...

...

Not only was there objection to the handling of the job, but many criticized the seats that were being given out. Of the 25,000 seats between the two goal lines, only 8,000 were alloted to students and almost all of those to seniors and their guests.

Each sweat-soaked student who limped home to send his suit to the cleaners (very few women lasted out the initial stampede) was thoroughly convinced that he was just one seat out of the end zone...#

Percy Jones G.I.'s Denied Game Tickets

(Oct. 10, 1946) The University Athletic Board turned thumbs down on a request yesterday that amputees at Percy Jones General Hospital in Battle Creek who had been alloted tickets to other Michigan home games be allowed to use student tickets at the Army game Saturday.

Andrew S. Baker, ticket manager, said that transfer of student tickets is unlawful, since they are tax-exempt.

"That's the rule," Baker told The Daily, "and I don't know where we can get authority to change it."

The Daily appealed yesterday to people who don't plan to see the Army game to turn in their tickets for distribution to wounded soldiers at Battle Creek.

...

Prof. Ralph W. Aigler of the Law School, faculty member of the Athletic Board, said that the University "just couldn't take the risk" of allowing student tickets to change hands--even in the case of the soldiers.

"Tax authorities have insisted that these special tax-free tickets be placed in a unit by themselves. The danger we would run would be the tax authorities asking us to pay a tax on all of the student spectators if we allowed any transfer of tickets," he said.#

'U' Athletic Board Reverses Decision

(Oct. 11, 1946) The University Athletic Board last night put its stamp of approval on transfer of student tickets for the Army game to World War II amputees at Percy Jones Hospital in Battle Creek.

Acting swiftly on renewed appeals by The Daily and the University chapter of the American Veterans Committee, the board reversed yesterday's decision against the transfer after learning that the Bureau of Internal Revenue would permit such action.

An official of the bureau's Detroit office told The Daily that tax exempt tickets could be transferred... provided the tickets were free...#

Ticket Foul Up Forces Change In Distribution

By ART HIGBEE and FRED SCHOTT

(Feb. 27, 1948) Five thousand student preferential basketball tickets for tomorrow's Ohio State game underwent a strange odyssey around campus Wednesday--and consequently a few of them failed to show up at University Hall yesterday when official distribution got underway.

...

The overhauled distribution set-up means that no one applying for tickets will get more than two of them, and each ticket handed out will be accounted for by a punched ID card.

The ticket-journey began Wednesday afternoon when Chuck Lewis, chairman of the Student Legislature's Varsity Committee, picked up the 5,000 Ohio State ducats from University ticket manager Don Weir. Lewis carried the 5,000 tickets to his room at 1429 Hill and left them there while he had dinner at his fraternity house, Sigma Alpha Mu, at 1800 Lincoln.

After dinner Lewis went back to his room, gathered up the tickets, and took them to the League, where he turned them over to Wolverine Club officers. Exit Lewis.

...

At 9 a.m. yesterday the tickets were passed out to students who jammed U Hall even before the scheduled distribution time.

But somewhere along the line somebody got to the tickets. Jim Barie and Hugh Miller of Tyler House, East Quad, phoned The Daily at 1 a.m. yesterday--eight hours before official distribution time--and reported that [a student] who lives down the hall, had flashed two of the tickets.

They questioned [him] further. He said that his roommate...had talked about picking them up that evening during rushing. So they pressed [the roommate] for a few answers, but [he] clammed up.

When The Daily tried to reach [him] yesterday for comment, he could not be found, not even by the anonymous fraternity men who kept knocking on his door all evening.

...

[The roommate], who claims he has never been to a basketball game, said that two tickets had been given to him during a Sigma Alpha Mu rushing party Wednesday evening, but that he hadn't seen any other tickets.

Mark Abend, SAM president, had long since admitted that [the roommate] had been present at the SAM house that night, but flatly denied knowledge of any bootleg tickets.#

QUEUE IN THE GRAY:
Students Line Up for Tickets Again, Undaunted

By JACK MARTIN
Daily Special Writer

(Feb. 28, 1948) Students were queuing up again this morning--this time in the gray dawn down at Ferry Field--for another attempt at those elusive Iowa preference tickets.

A near-riot broke up the business yesterday when lines that extended to University Hall's third floor dissolved under the pressure of over 5,000 ticket-hungry individuals.

Nothing that the Deans or the Ann Arbor police could do would make order prevail, so after twenty minutes of confusion the ticket booth was closed and the announcement made that no ducats would be forthcoming until the next morning.

First Arrival

Yesterday morning's distribution, handled by the Wolverine Club and the Student Legislature, was scheduled to get under way at 9 a.m., but the first ambitious fan arrived before the booth at 7.

...

Two policemen arrived at 9--and immediately the tickets began to flow. This condition maintained for five minutes.

At that point classes began to change, and chaos resulted. In the words of Greenfield, "The lines exploded. When they saw the newcomers hurrying down the hall they thought the people were rushing the cage. So they rushed, too, and in a second there was a solid jam in front of the booth."#

B-Ball seats infuriate 'M' fans

By TOM KEANEY

Where are my seats? In a parking lot in Ypsilanti.

(Nov. 6, 1985) ...While almost everyone is looking forward to the upcoming basketball season, not everyone is pleased with their assigned position for viewing the games.

"I've been going for 12 years, and these are the worst seats I've ever had," said music school sophomore Brady Flower just after opening his envelope.

That sentiment seemed to be prevalent among season ticket holders as they came away from the ticket office yesterday. Many students have worse seats this year than they did last year. Why? The answer is fairly simple--the numbers have changed.

LAST YEAR about 1,700 students purchased season tickets for basketball. This year the figure is at almost 5,000. With this in mind, the mathematics is not too difficult to figure. More people are competing for the same number of good seats; thus, more people are coming away unhappy.

...

The reason for the sudden rise in ticket demand is obvious. Michigan looks to have one of the best basketball teams in the country this year. The Wolverines have been ranked no lower than fifth in pre-season polls and are number one in many.

...

THE BEST seats in Crisler Arena, which holds 13,609, are generally considered to be those in the "blue" section, right around the perimeter of the court. Students are eligible for about one-fourth of the blue section. The remaining three-fourths goes to alumni and other people who have been buying season tickets for years....

...

Ray Macika, an engineering student, said that students should have priority over alumni. "They should put the students down in the blue since they're the ones that are active."..#

WILD RUMORS OF INFIDELITY OF COACH YOST ARE SPIKED IN EMPHATIC ANNOUNCEMENT

WILDCAT JOURNALISM IS CHARGED WITH RESPONSIBILITY FOR FIASCO

(Oct. 17, 1928) Speculation was rife on campus yesterday over the sudden announcement that Coach Fielding H. Yost, "grand old man" of Michigan football, had left for an indefinite stay in Nashville, Tenn., where his brother-in-law, Dan McGugan, is coach of the Vanderbilt university team. Rumors at once began to circulate that the Michigan Yostmen were in danger of losing their leader to Vanderbilt. Yost, in a special announcement last night, however, branded the rumors as without foundation, stating that he had gone to Nashville on a business trip of a few days' duration and to join his wife, nee Eunice Fite, a former Nashville girl.

...

Coming on the heels of his recent announcement that his coaching activities would be confined to the development of passers and kickers, Coach Yost's departure for Vanderbilt at a crucial moment in the 1928 football season is interpreted by many alumni and students as significant of a desire to sever athletic relations with Michigan, whose teams he has coached and whose prestige he has extended for more than 25 years. Whether his action is due to disappointment at the poor showing the Wolverines have made so far this season is problematical, but his "probable" return in time to see the Columbus game indicates that the squad will not be without his leadership.

...

Wild rumors of Yost's immediate resignation to accept a big job at Vanderbilt which spread yesterday were based on yesterday afternoon's Detroit Times' false inferences from an article published in yesterday morning's Chicago Tribune, which stated merely that the veteran mentor had left Ann Arbor for Vanderbilt where he would aid, as he did last year, his brother-in-law in coaching the Commodores during his stay.#

HAS ANY ONE HERE SEEN YOST?

"THE LOST LEADER"

To L. A. McG.

Now where the hell's Professor
 Yost,
Despair of the West, and Michi-
 gan's boast?
He coached our point-a-minute
 teams,
Made football history--now it
 seems,
When Michigan's hopes are begin-
 ning to wilt,
He'd rather coach at Vanderbilt.

Or can't they tell on Ferry Field
Who is king--who's to wield
The ultimate power, have final
 choice--
In gridiron pow-wows raise his
 voice--
Pick the men to play the game--
And if he loses, take the blame?
                              Yellit.

* * *

Isn't it a shame that Mr. Yost's vacations always come during football season?

* * *

If Vanderbilt university, where Yost has gone, needs his coaching any more than Michigan, they surely must be terrible.#

PRESS ANGLE

By GEORGE J. ANDROS
(Daily Sports Editor)

(Nov. 29, 1936) **ALEX LOIKO** has gone back to Hamtramck.

There is a story in that. It is a story that Grantland Rice or Damon Runyon could write--or maybe Bud Shaver. It is a story that I do not like to write, but one that should be written.

If you are among the many who saw Loiko's picture in the Detroit papers several times a week before the Michigan-Michigan State game, you may very well have made some sarcastic remark when you read the brief bulletins last Thursday telling of Loiko's dropping out of school.

Because Alex did not exactly live up to the reams of publicity that were turned out in his favor early last fall. Kip soon found out that his prospective triple-threat backfield star did not have the necessary speed.

...

But that is not why Alex went home. He went home because the struggle was more than he or any other fellow in his position could go through. One might even say that Alex went home for dinner. Because it was true that one of the "swellest fellows" ever to play on the Michigan Varsity team was not getting all the food a hard working athlete should have. And, naturally, his financial difficulties handicapped him in other ways as well.

...

Alex's case happens to be just one of several nearly identical ones among the members of the football squad--that's the tragedy of the story.

It is definitely known to those on the inside that several members of the squad were not getting enough to eat during the season--and that very few if any were getting the proper type of food for an athlete in training.

Some of the boys cook their own meals. Nothing wrong in that, but one can hardly expect the results to be beneficial to the health of a football player--especially when a minimum amount of money is expended for groceries...#

Note – This is a story from an April Fool's edition, traditionally an occasion for satire, but revealing nonetheless.

GLOOM DESCENDS ON GRIDIRON GIANTS

By Sheldon C. O'Brien

(April 1, 1932) Grave fears that the recent tax legislation with regard to amusement receipts would cause drastic salary cuts for the football players was expressed here last night. A cloud of gloom hung over the camp of Kipke's mentors as the news came in, although the coach declared there was no need for alarm.

"The boys are willing to do their bit to help Uncle Sam along," stated Kipke in an exclusive interview to the Daily. "We understand there have been recent rumors of depression, and I am sure that they would all be ready to play for love of the game and one-half of one per cent pay cut...#

Officials Defeat Reynolds' Plan; Second Gridder Quits Michigan

By FRED H. DE LANO

(Dec. 6, 1936) While the faculty representatives of the Western Conference were rejecting the proposal to give financial aid to athletes in the Big Ten, Don Paquette, one of Michigan's most promising sophomore football players, announced yesterday his withdrawal from school because of conditions which a training table would have remedied.

Paquette is the second Wolverine gridder to leave the University within a week, Alex Loiko having withdrawn last week because of alleged failure to obtain enough food. Paquette, forced to work evenings for his board, said that he found the task of keeping up with his school

14 Gridders Support Plan

By CARL GERSTACKER

(Dec. 1, 1936) Unanimously 14 members of the Varsity football squad last night approved The Daily's move to initiate training tables in the Big Ten Conference.

...

"Abe" Lincoln, veteran right tackle, voiced the sentiments of the whole team when he said in reply to the question, "Do you believe that training tables would be beneficial to the Michigan football squad?" "Say, set that to music. I'm for it 100 per cent--no, I'm for it 200 per cent. Write an article--lots of articles--on it. It will help all the way round--morally, physically, spiritually. I'm for it all the way."

Players Favor Change

Every one of the 14 Varsity players contacted, 10 of whom are working for either their board or room or both, agreed that eating at a training table would give them more time for study and would provide them with a more wholesome and better balanced diet.

...

Four of the Varsity players have been cooking their own meals; one had to borrow money to buy his clothes and have enough to eat three meals a day; one lost his job because he was unable to report for work on the week ends that the team was playing away from Ann Arbor; and another lost his job because of an injury suffered in a Varsity game.

Bill Barclay supported a plan given to him by "Germany" Schultz, famed Michigan lineman, under which the players would contribute any money that they made in their board jobs to the training table and eat there instead of at the places where they were working.

...

It is generally true that at least half of the football players' courses are in bad shape by the end of the regular season. A typical example would be George Marzonie, fiery guard, who spent three hours a day washing dishes during the past football season. After attending classes until 3 p.m., practicing from 3 p.m. to 6 p.m. and then washing dishes from 7 p.m. until 10 p.m., George had little time to devote to his engineering studies...#

Tulane Admits Bid For Star Freshman In Reply By Coach

Scholarship Was Offered Harmon For Services, Press Statement Reveals

(Nov. 16, 1937) Latest developments in Tulane University's attempt to lure away Tom Harmon, freshman footballer enrolled here, brought a candid admission yesterday from the southern school that it sought his services because "we had heard that he planned to transfer of his own volition to another school."

...

As regards a reported "offer," Bevan commented: "The only offer made to him was that of an athletic scholarship which is perfectly legal in the Southeastern Conference."

Harmon released the telegram to The Daily in an effort to absolve himself of any allegations that he might have been subsidized by the University. These allegations grew out of an announced investigation by the local athletic board into rumored charges of subsidization.

One of the outstanding prep athletes in the nation last year, the Gary, Ind., youth was the recipient of numerous bids from large universities. He chose to enter Michigan, he said, "because I don't believe in that kind of stuff (subsidization). Besides I came to school for an education, and Michigan answered that purpose. I expect to go to law school."

Asked whether he needed a board job--as reported in yesterday's Daily--he replied, "You bet I do. If I don't get one, I may have to leave school."..#

ASIDE LINES

By IRVIN LISAGOR

(Nov. 16, 1937) **RAMIFICATIONS,** indeed, will develop from The Daily's publication of a telegram to Freshman Tom Harmon, of Gary, Ind., from Tulane University in New Orleans.

...

Does this, one wonders, portend the future of college grid sports? Will universities openly bid for another school's ivory in much the same manner as is now practiced in organized baseball? What will happen when large stadia have been paid for and huge gate receipts keep pouring into University coffers? Whither college football anyhow?

TOM HARMON has attained more than a modicum of fame for his high school athletic prowess, and consequently was snowed under by invitational offers from various schools throughout the nation. He decided to enter one which made no overtures whatsoever, which shelled out exactly nothing in the way of pecuniary inducement, simply because he was level-headed and wise enough to weigh a school's qualities for something more than its ability to "buy" his football talents. His coach, Douglas Kerr, was a Michigan man and interested in getting his protege in here. Michigan alumni in Gary admittedly encouraged him by pointing out the educational advantages of Michigan. That's the story of the Gary alumni, and Harmon himself. Until disproved -- and the athletic board's recently announced investigations evidently fails to do so -- we accept it.

...

THE BOARD will undoubtedly appreciate the fact Tulane, at least, considers Michigan "simon-pure." With football developing such queer angles we may someday protest with indignant insistence that we are not tainted by rank amateurism, that our players possess as high a standard of living as the next...

We reiterate, someone with an ulterior motive forced the board into its alleged action, and that ulterior motive was the removal of Harry Kipke. It was the wrong approach, and may boomerang to defeat that purpose, especially if Ohio State succumbs to Kipke's Wolverine advances. But whatever the eventuality, Tulane has started something. Or perhaps the credit belongs to our own athletic board.#

Football Star Whitewashed

MSC Is Revealed As Making Offer

By IRVIN LISAGOR
(Copyright, 1937, The Michigan Daily)

(Nov. 17, 1937) Openly flaunting investigations of Michigan's rumored subsidization of athletes, a representative of Tulane University has reiterated an "offer" made to Tom Harmon, brilliant freshman back enrolled here, according to a telegram released exclusively to The Michigan Daily last night.

The wire was signed by Bill Bevan, former All-American guard at Minnesota and present line coach at the southern school, and was evidently prompted by Michigan's athletic board's recent statement to the effect that certain freshman gridders were under suspicion of being subsidized by alumni groups.

...

Labelling Michigan a "simon pure school," Bevan's wire suggested that Harmon may be completely exonerated of the charges leveled at him by covert whisperers. The Gary youth has been vehement in his denials of aid, pecuniary or otherwise... He admitted being encouraged to enter Michigan by his high school coach, Douglas Kerr, a former Wolverine athlete, and alumni in Gary whose only overtures consisted of a lecture on the educational advantages of the local institution.

...

Reliable informers told The Daily last night that Tulane's offer, as is the custom among southern schools which abide by this proselyting practice, probably included allowances for board, room, tuition, laundry, books, clothes, and from $10 to $20 spending money a month. Exceptional athletes are further proffered a flat sum to tide them over the idle summer months, these informers reported.

...

Although Harmon was reluctant to reveal other bids which he received, he did name five Western Conference schools... These included Purdue, Illinois, Indiana, Chicago and Northwestern. Among other well-known universities that sought him were Alabama, Louisiana State, Yale, Princeton, Michigan State, Southern California, Pittsburgh, Cornell and Washington...#

Stadium Rule Bars Patient From Game

(Oct. 10, 1952) A University Hospital polio patient was refused permission yesterday to attend Saturday's Michigan-Indiana football game because of a Stadium policy against wheelchair patients.

The policy exists because of the difficulty of getting a wheelchair into the stadium, according to ticket manager Don Weir.

* * *

THE PATIENT concerned is Dicky Brink, 9 years old, who has been at the respiratory center for three years.

Although he is completely paralyzed and requires a respirator, he was considered well enough this summer to attend a baseball game in Briggs Stadium.

Hospital officials tried several weeks ago to purchase a box seat so that the boy, an avid sports fan, could see the game. They were told at first that they might get the ticket. However, Athletics Director Prof. Herbert O. Crisler later reversed this, clarifying the stadium policy.

Prof. Crisler could not be reached last night for comment. #

Stadium May Be Opened To Patient

(Oct. 12, 1952) Dicky Brink didn't make it to the football game yesterday-- but he may yet see a game this season if "conditions are favorable."

...

...Athletic Director H. O. Crisler announced on a radio broadcast during halftime yesterday that the boy "will be able to see some game under conditions which will be favorable to him without any risk either to him or to any of the players."

The policy against wheelchairs exists, Crisler explained, because of the lack of facilities within the stadium. He said that any wheelchair would have to be brought in through the tunnel, but that this was impossible yesterday because of the congestion caused by the high school students participating in "Band Day."..#

BEHIND THE LINES
● The Case of Dicky Brink

By CAL SAMRA
Daily Editorial Director

(Oct. 12, 1952) FEW WRITERS like to truckle to sentimentalities; ordinarily, they're too absorbed in pell-mell verbiage about politics, war, and women to take note of the banal day-to-day struggles of people trying to gather a bit of happiness out of an often brutal life.

One sweep of a callous pen can add or subtract millions of humans without capturing the heart-break of one individual. The case of Dicky Brink does not provide this writer with such an easy way out.

Nine-year-old Dicky, who has been confined at University Hospital three years with a bad case of polio, will probably never be able to use his limbs. He is completely paralyzed.

For weeks, Dicky, an avid sports fan, had his heart set on seeing the Michigan-Indiana game. He'd never seen a football game before. Since his health chart had shown improvement after the youngster was taken to a Detroit baseball game last summer, several orderlies and nurses tried to make the necessary arrangements-- indicated that they would assume all responsibility for him.

But an icy matter of policy stood in the way. The athletic department refused permission. Reason: "the difficulty of getting a wheel-chair into the stadium."

On Friday, Dicky cried throughout the night.

On Saturday, there was room for 30,000 additional fans.

On Saturday, 6,000 other kids got in free on the basis of their musical talents.

On Saturday, the turnstiles clicked out a merry tune, and everyone was happy.

On Saturday, the sun beat down majestically, the bands played, and the Wolverines went on to wallop Indiana, 28-13.

It was a highly-enjoyable afternoon; it would have delighted Dicky Brink.

A sad commentary it is that Dicky had to learn so early in life that some people are more important than others.

It's getting cold outside for Dicky Brink. #

Patients Get To View Game

By CAL SAMRA
Editorial Director

(Oct. 26, 1952) Pennant-waving alumni, descending on Ann Arbor in nostalgic droves, had their day yesterday, and the public relations couldn't have been any better.

Temperatures were pleasant, the Wolverines trounced Minnesota 21-0, the Michigan band deserved the usual superlatives, and the many homecoming displays, the later housewarmings and receptions added a sentimental touch to "dear old Michigan."

* * *

BUT THERE was something else which a lot of students noticed. Dicky Brink, 10 year old respiratory patient who was denied admission to the Michigan-Indiana game two weeks ago, was sitting comfortably in Athletic Director Fritz Crisler's personal box on the 50-yard line. Hospital officials made the necessary arrangements, which included a chest respirator.

Dicky and 12 year old Patricia O'Brien, another polio patient at the University Hospital, were having a great time with a score of dignitaries and celebrities around them. They even got Gov. G. Mennen Williams' autograph...#

'Tie-In Sales' At Game Protested

Student's Letter...

To the Editor:

(Oct. 1, 1946) ...During the intense heat of the [Indiana] football game, many of the fans wanted to enjoy a "coke" or some other non-intoxicating beverage. But most of us learned that if we wanted "pop" it was also necessary for us to purchase a very unappetizing looking frankfurter at the exorbitant rate of fifteen cents. Another favorite racket of the shyster concessionaires working at the University of Michigan Stadium was to sell the unsuspecting student a warm soda, and a minute later charge him or her ten cents for ice to cool the soda.

What is this University coming to when it allows such illegal practices to take place on their premises?...

...

...we here at this institution of higher education would surely learn better business practices than those used by the petty crooks operating in our football stadium.

There is a great possibility that the University officials have no inkling of these practices, as this was the first game of the season. But, if these unscrupulous acts are tried again, then I urge the University officials, to throw (bodily or otherwise) the owners and workers of these concessions off of the university grounds, and at the same time bring suit against them for this "tie-in" sale racket they are perpetuating on our campus.

Preston R. Tisch

Crisler's Reply...

Dear Mr. Tisch:

The copy of your letter addressed to...[The] Michigan Daily...was received and carefully read.

Information had previously come to me about the so-called "tie-in" sales and an investigation was made immediately. Unfortunately, several sales had already been made before the Concession Supervisors were informed of this practice.

...

...the practice which existed at the Indiana game will not be tolerated. The Concessionaires have been informed that if there is their contract will be cancelled immediately...

H. O. Crisler, Director

(EDITOR'S NOTE: The following is a copy of the telegram Director Herbert Crisler sent to the concessionaires.)
Charles Jacobs
Sportservice
Hurst Building
Buffalo, New York
"So called tie-in sales were made by some of your concession personnel in the Michigan Stadium at the Indiana game. A dime was charged for cup of water or piece of ice. Undoubtedly this was done without your knowledge. Please take steps immediately to stop these practices or contract will have to be cancelled."

H. O. Crisler

Cazzie in Politics

(March 4, 1964) ATTACKING Cazzie Russell is roughly equivalent to attacking God, motherhood and the flag.

But Cazzie has ventured into the world of politics, and in doing so he is making a great mistake. He should not, under any circumstances, be elected today as the next student representative to the Board in Control of Intercollegiate Athletics.

THERE ARE A VARIETY of boards on this campus--the Union board, the League board, the Board in Control of Student Publications and the athletic board. All of them have student, faculty, alumni and administrative representation--the theory being that all elements of the community should be involved in the decision-making processes for which these boards are responsible.

The athletic board already makes a sham of this practice. Women, for no reason, aren't allowed to vote for the student representative.

BUT MORE IMPORTANTLY, Athletic Director H. O. (Fritz) Crisler has the nominating system rigged so that an athlete has repeatedly been named to fill the post. If any non-athlete wants to run for the board, he has to bring in a petition with 250 male signatures.

An actual Regents bylaw stipulates, however, that "a board consisting of the student managers of the several athletic teams and the intramural managers" has the automatic power to place two candidates on the ballot. Why they should have this power is again beyond reason, but they don't even exercise it.

No managers council met to pick the two athletes running in today's election. Managers will readily admit that the candidates were picked by Crisler and announced in the managers' names.

THERE IS NO REASON why the students of this campus should stand for such a system, and they can vote their dissent by voting today for one of the non-Crisler candidates.

Two students--Tom Weinberg and Charles Pascal--are legitimate candidates. Of the two, Weinberg is by far the most qualified.

He has covered both sports and the athletic board for two years as a Daily reporter. If elected he has promised to do all he can to clean up dubious practices of the board.

Indeed, Weinberg is so obviously qualified that Crisler, at the last minute, decided he needed Cazzie Russell in order to maintain the athletic department's monopoly on the board.

CAZZIE CAME HERE for one reason--to play basketball. He's great. But it is patently unfair for Crisler to use Cazzie's name in order to keep the athletic board stacked.

--H. NEIL BERKSON

Athletic Seat To Weinberg In Close Vote

By JOHN WEILER

(March 5, 1964) Thomas Weinberg, '66, scored an upset victory yesterday as he became the first non-athlete elected to the Board in Control of Intercollegiate Athletics within memory.

Weinberg polled 1,182 votes in defeating basketball star Cazzie Russell, '66Ed, 962; Charles Pascal, '66, 280, and Stephen Smith, '66, 167, for a two-year term...#

The Daily vs Crisler Arena

IM Program Endangered by Events Building

By LEONARD PRATT

(May 11, 1966) The University's intramural sports and physical education programs are facing a long period of lean financial years just when they need the money most, according to authoritative sources.

A long-range decline in the athletic revenues which have supported them in the past, plus a large long-term drain-- the University Events Building now under construction--are the crux of the problem, the sources say.

IM sports are administered by the Department of Physical Education and Athletics under a Regents by-law which gives the department jurisdiction over "the required work in physical education for men and women, intramural sports, recreational activities..."

These activities are financed by the department which, in turn, obtains its money from the Board in Control of Intercollegiate Athletics...

...

Over the years, the IM program at the University--unlike any other Big Ten IM program--has...become entirely dependent upon the University's intercollegiate sports.

The problem now is that the University's intercollegiate sports are becoming less and less able to support it. As one member of the athletics board put it, "We're in a tight belt situation for the forseeable future." There are two basic reasons for the board's sudden demise as a money-maker for the department.

First, intercollegiate athletics are becoming more and more expensive. Coaching salaries are rising, travel costs are on the way up and athletic scholarships are also subject to a certain degree of inflation. Yet at the same time the revenue they bring in is fairly constant.

Second, the department has committed itself to the construction of the new $6.7 million Events Building. $5.8 million of this was bonded, but the department still has to pay the extra $900 thousand plus the interest on the bonds, which run for a period of 25 years. No help is available from the University's $55 Million Fund Drive; only some $67 thousand has been pledged to the Events Building, and half of that is earmarked for the furnishing of a special alumni reception room.

...

Both these factors mean the board's operating reserve has been reduced to a very low level. Administrators stress that it is in no real sense in trouble with either the Events Building or intercollegiate sports. But its finances for expansion are nonexistent.

Yet the IM program has needed additional money for a long time. As enrollment has risen, and as the trimester has become a reality, more facilities have been needed to accommodate the crush of users.

IM administrators cite the need for a new IM building, more fields for the Central Campus and IM facilities on North Campus which, despite the completion of Cedar Bend dormitories scheduled for the fall, has none. At the same time they stress they cannot move at all without athletic board money.

While board members say they can finance the IM program at its present level, all deny their ability to expand it at all.

The athletic board has recently been sending out appeals to find help in supporting the IM program. Prof. Stuart Churchill, a faculty member on the board, spoke to the April meeting of the Senate Advisory Committee on University Affairs--then the central body of the Faculty Senate--and reportedly urged them to consider the problem. A SACUA member says the meeting questioned whether the athletic board should in fact still be charged with supporting the IM program.

H. O. Crisler, department director, says simply that the department has made "University people aware of the situation" and can do little else than wait for someone to come up with an answer.

Other department officials say openly that the University's central administration has been asked to take over the IM program directly--for example, to support it with student fees, instead of gate receipts, as is done at other colleges--to free athletic department money.

No administrators report the existence of any concrete plans for a solution.#

Pool Ceiling Signifies Collapse

By FRED LaBOUR
Daily News Analysis

(Sept. 15, 1967) The creaky roof that has attempted to shelter the University's weakened intramural program from the problems of neglect, lack of planning, lack of funds and an amazing lack of communication, has literally begun to crumble.

On Tuesday night a section of the IM pool ceiling collapsed and crashed down into the pool area. The pool was not in use at the time and there were no casualties. It appears, however, that it will not reo-

Arena Rental Fees Hit

By DANIEL OKRENT

(Nov. 15, 1967) A conflict concerning projected use of the nearly-completed University Events Bldg. has precipitated a special meeting for the ironing out of remaining problems.

The antagonists, H. O. "Fritz" Crisler, Athletic Director and ex-officio chairman of the Board in Control of Intercollegiate Athletics, and Don Tucker, '68, president of the University Activities Center (UAC), will discuss a pre-stated Board in Control policy concerning rental fees for the plush new arena, scheduled to open by Dec. 1.

...

As currently outlined, the Board in Control policy sets up criteria for determination of use priorities for the building, and also establishes a rental scale for student organizations. This is the bone that Tucker hopes to pick.

Cost Too Much

"At $1500 and labor costs nightly guarantee, or ten per cent of the gross income less taxes, whichever is greater, the fee for using the building is just too much for a student organization to spend," Tucker said. He added that he hoped the 15,000-seat arena would provide adequate facilities for large-scale concerts sponsored by UAC, featuring particularly expensive entertainers.

...

"The building was paid for out of student fees at a rate of $10 per student per academic year. It only follows that students should be able to use the building at a price that is not prohibitive."..#

pen for what associate director of intramurals Dr. Rodney Grambeau calls "an indefinite period of time." According to Grambeau, the collapse was apparently caused by rain and melted snow seeping through the decrepit roof and weakening the beam structure.

Theoretically, the IM building was due for a new roof five years ago but a frustrating maze of bureaucratic red tape and an administration that appears to be deaf to the entire IM problem have prevented any constructive work from being accomplished.

This story of delayed action because of administrative bungling is repeated again and again by Grambeau as he reflects on the current IM situation. "There is absolutely no coordination between projects or plans on campus," he says. "We are not even in communication with the people who are supposed to be working on our recommendations. Our hands are tied."

...

Another worrisome problem for the IM department is the critical situation involving the hundreds of students living in recently completed housing on North Campus. "There is," says Grambeau, "no plan whatsoever for organized recreation on North Campus. The administration failed to make any allowance for recreation in the plans for the residence halls."

...

With the IM situation shifting from the merely ludicrous to the physically dangerous, as evidenced by the roof collapse, Grambeau senses the need for a drastic change in University policy.

"We're usually ranked about fifth in the country on most things," he says. "But on IM's we'd be lucky if we were in the top 500. The other schools in the Big Ten, especially Michigan State, Ohio State and Wisconsin, are making tremendous progress in these areas...

...

"What we need at this point is a campus director of recreation. Somebody to coordinate and oversee everything that is going on. Somebody who will take responsibility for the mistakes. somebody who has lines of communication open to him so he can plan in a more than haphazard manner."..#

Renting the Events Building: Will the Price Ever Be Right?

(Nov. 17, 1967) **THE ATHLETIC DEPARTMENT** has had little experience in show business. The 101,000 seat football stadium is too big for Greek Theatre, and too drafty for Arthur Rubenstein. Yost Field House is so smelly that about its only non-athletic use is rained-out commencement ceremonies. The baseball stadium isn't much of a drive-in movie theater.

But now the athletic department has a fine new 15,000 seat Events building that will lend itself to far more than a dozen basketball games a year. Student sponsored concerts, shows and lectures are a natural for the new building.

...

Unfortunately a Presidential committee has established a fee of $1,50 against ten percent of the gross income, whichever is greater, for all profitmaking events.

On a per seat basis this is at least 55

per cent higher than the $265 plus labor charged for 4,100 seat Hill Auditorium.

THIS SPELLS TROUBLE for both student groups and the Events buildings. Organizations will be forced to charge higher rates for concerts in the Events building. Or, the groups will shy away from financial risk and stay with Hill Auditorium, depriving the new building of needed revenue.

...

THE REGENTS WOULD do well to defer final approval of the fee schedule until [student organizations auditor Maurice] Rinkel and the student officials can determine if campus organizations can afford the events building price.

For it appears the new rates should be revised downward so students can enjoy the new building they are paying for.

–ROGER RAPOPORT
Editor

The Whistle-Blowers

'U' Athletes Get More for Their Money

By CLARK NORTON
Sports Editor
and HOWARD KOHN

Copyright, 1968, The Michigan Daily

(Feb. 9, 1968) In the fiercely competitive world of intercollegiate athletics, major universities often go to great lengths to keep their players happy.

But to give all schools an equal competitive opportunity, the Big Ten has enacted stiff rules that prohibit financial aid to tendered athletes above and beyond their normal scholarships.

In 1957 the Big Ten established a ban on special outside aid to tendered athletes. Part two, Rule seven, Section two of the Big Ten Code says that athletes can't receive special aid beyond their scholarship simply because of their athletic achievements.

Is the rule working?

An independent Daily investigation shows some evidence that it is not.

One local restaurant, a men's shop, and two theaters admit giving discounts and free merchandise to varsity athletes at the University. In addition, one former pharmacy owner admits giving discounts, free meals and part-time jobs to athletes in a nine-year period from 1958-1967.

Francis Tice of Tice's Men's Shop admitted he had been giving "10 per cent discounts to players since before World War II when Al Wistert and some of the other boys worked in the store." He added that he would give discounts to any athlete with an 'M' Club card. (The 'M' Club is made up of varsity letter winners from all sports.)

Pat Paron of The Brown Jug restaurant says "I have a policy of giving 10 per cent discounts to players and have on occasion given free meals to the basketball players when the coach has sent them over."

G. H. Hoag, manager of the Michigan Theater, admits giving 3,000 free theater passes annually, worth $1.50 each, to players after games....

...

Roy Snyder, former owner-manager of the Michigan Pharmacy, said he had "given discounts to players, especially to married ones."

All five businessmen said that Michigan's coaches know and approve of the discount practice. Coaches mentioned were head football coach Bump Elliott, assistant football coach Tony Mason, former assistant coach Bob Hollway, and head basketball coach Dave Strack.

John D. Dewey, Big Ten Assistant Commissioner and Examiner, told The Daily that he would consider the discount practice a violation of conference rules. "If they (discounts) are given only to athletes to the exclusion of other students, then they are illegal."

Athletic Director H. O. (Fritz) Crisler expressed surprise when asked about the discounts yesterday, adding "I will conduct an immediate investigation and clamp down on anything uncovered."

However, Crisler later admitted to The Daily that he had distributed a memorandum on Wednesday advising all coaches that The Daily was conducting an investigation into the discounts.

When asked about the discount policy, Strack said, "I didn't realize they were such a common practice, but I knew of course that they weren't an uucommon practice. I've never thought about their legality, and I am frankly surprised that they are considered illegal aid."

Hollway categorically denied that anything illegal was going on.

Elliott and Mason could not be reached for comment.

Crisler said he knew Hoag had been giving tickets away, but had understood they were limited to certain Friday nights and had not received widespread distribution...

...

A number of athletes interviewed by The Daily admitted they had taken advantage of the tickets (referred to as "Victory Passes"), the discounts and the free merchandise.

Football player Paul Johnson, '68, said the "entire football team that makes training table starts the season off by going to Tice's for $10 worth of free clothing, usually a pair of slacks."

Other past and present Michigan athletes who admitted to The Daily that they had received both discounts and free gifts from local merchants included [four students], all football players. #

(Feb. 11, 1968) Printing stories that embarrass a lot of people poses problems. First, it alienates advertisers who finance the paper. Second, it alienates officials who reporters "have to work with." Third, editors and reporters have to live in the same town with people they are exposing. Finally, if you do enough muckraking you can alienate so many readers that you may wind up with few friends.

So if you do your job and report everything that should be known, you're likely to wind up with a deficit, lots of enemies, harassed reporters, and broken windows.

MOST PAPERS SOLVE the problem with an expedient solution--they understaff. Not only does it save money but it keeps the reporters so busy they don't have time to work on in-depth exposes.

...

So as a result, a college daily with a young staff of part-time, underpaid reporters has been left the muckraking job. The Daily does it not because it revels in making enemies but because it feels that a free press is worthless unless it is used to try to keep everyone honest.

This poses problems, for while everyone pays lip service to the concept of a free press, most people don't really want one.

The sad truth is that people want a free press only as long as it doesn't hurt them or their friends. The library director enjoys reading about the latest troubles at Willow Run and Willow Run people get a kick out of finding out about troubles in the library. The English department is grateful for a scoop on the resignation of the vice-president for students, and the vice-president for students is glad to know ahead of time who the new English department chairman is.

EVERYONE IS ALWAYS begging us to leave stories out about themselves. The library director tells us that printing a certain story will "only bring down the state legislature to investigate--and they don't understand." The English faculty asks us to wait "until the appointment is official."

The only way to handle such requests is to simply ignore all of them equally...

Correction boxes and Letters to the Editor are the antidote for mistakes, but most papers seldom err on major investigative pieces. For example, no one has accused the paper of any factual errors in Friday's sports discount story.

Besides, if everyone's request to hold stories was honored, you wouldn't have any reason to read this paper. You pay $8 a year for The Daily because you expect us to tell you ahead of everyone else that Robben Fleming is the new president, that Vice-Presidents Cutler, Niehuss and Stirton are leaving, etc.

Generally, our readership is sympathetic toward our exposes because the stories usually involve relatively few administrators on complicated issues like conflict-of-interest, bidding, discrimina-

'Lest Ye Be Free of Sin, Cast Ye Not the First Brick'

tory practices, and classified research.

But it's relatively easy to take on conflict-of-interest, discrimination, and secrecy. What takes real courage is to question a sacred cow central to the lives of the average student--athletics.

IN THE BEST journalistic tradition, Sports Editor Clark Norton and reporter Howard Kohn wrote a story Friday which pointed out that local merchants have been giving discounts to football players in violation of Big Ten rules.

There seems to be little dispute about the issues involved. As soon as Athletic Director Fritz Crisler found out, he asked every store owner to stop the discounts and went on to launch an investigation into the entire business.

But predictably, Michigan sports fans were up in arms. Local sportscasters

lambasted the paper. In Detroit, toupeed Channel 2 commentator Van Patrick chided them as "would be Pulitzer Prize winners." (Actually, The Daily already has been nominated for a Pulitzer Prize in local investigative reporting for last fall's series on military research.)

Patrick went on to charge that Norton and Kohn were "purists...naive journalists who apparently had nothing better to do with their time than dig up things that have been going on for years." Patrick even joked with weatherman Jerry Hodak about the brick that went through The Daily's window Friday night (narrowly missing innocent girl reporters.)

...

MUCH OF THIS is to be expected from the adults. But the depressing fact is that many students reflect an even more narrow-minded attitude.

...

"The Daily really did it this time," said a sorority girl. "Why did you pick on your own school?"

"What's the matter, don't you support the team?"

Sure, Kohn and Norton are among the most ardent sports fans on campus, cheering over victory and anguishing over defeat. And they were dismayed by what they found.

...

All the paper did was print the story. The Daily didn't give any athletes discounts on subscriptions or write the Big Ten rules.

But then The Daily's windows make a much better target for two halves of a brick (thrown in Friday night) than any local theatre or the Big Ten office in faraway Chicago. Someone has to take the blame.

ASSUMING WE ALL live through this affair--and certainly there are more weighty campus issues than athletic rule infraction--we hope you're convinced that The Daily is serious enough about its job to print any legitimate story.

...

The Daily doesn't want your love, but we do hope you understand that one permanent risk of a free press is that you may get caught by it. We think this risk is far outweighed by the advantages of having an honest interpretation of what is going on.#

'The $porting Life'
at Michigan State

By JOEL BLOCK
Second of a Series

Copyright, 1968, The Michigan Daily
(Feb. 11, 1968) EAST LANSING --
Trying to make a long-distance phone
call from Michigan State University's
South Case Hall here can be time-con-
suming.

...

About 1 a.m. Friday morning I was
waiting for a student to finish his call on
a first floor pay phone at South Case.

"Don't wait for that guy to get off the
phone," a baseball player standing nearby
told me.

..."He's a football player and he
gets all his long distance calls paid by his
coach. It's a slush fund, you know."

So I went upstairs to the third floor
and made my call. As I was getting off the
phone a hefty MSU freshman football
player walked up to an adjacent pay
telephone, flipped a dime into the slot
and dialed the operator.

"I'd like to make a long distance call
to Chicago and charge it to 355-XXXX.
You'll have to verify the call at 10 a.m.
tomorrow, it's my coach's number."

A check of the MSU faculty and staff
telephone book showed that 355-XXXX
is the phone number of [the] Spartan offensive line coach.

Assistant Coach Al Dorow qualified
the charging of phone calls to coach's
telephones. "The players can charge
their calls to us only in a case where they
have troubles at home with their parents
or something like that," he said.

Michigan State's practice of giving
football players free phone calls is apparently only one of several practices which
may violate Big Ten rules.

Michigan State football players also
get discounts at the four major movie
theaters near the campus. Warren
Wardwell, city manager of the Butterfield theater chain in East Lansing explained how the discount process works.

"All four theaters (the State, Michigan, Campus, and the Gladmer) have
lists of players on the varsity and freshman football teams. A player has to show
his ID card and pays a $.25 service
charge to get into the theater.

...

"We also try to give passes to visiting
teams if we can catch the manager to give
the tickets to him. We only gave discounts during the football season."

Wardwell was asked where he got
the football lists from. "I can only tell you
that I get the lists from someone, but I
can't tell you who," he replied.

...

The football staff also takes care of
the hearty appetites of their hard-work-
ing athletes. The players are handed
"grill passes" which provide them with
tasty bedtime eating at the snack bars
located in the dormitories (including Case
Hall) and the campus Union. One freshman football player--turned wrestler--la-
mented to me that the coaches wouldn't
give him any more passes because he was
struggling to make his wrestling weight.

Dorow denied the existence of the
grill passes. "The only thing the athletes
have are their regular meal tickets to use
in the dorms. You're not supposed to do
those things," he said.

In a letter dated "6 Mar. '67"
MSU's offensive backfield coach wrote a
boy who is now a freshman football
player, "The opportunity for a summer
job is yours plus MSU will do anything in
its power to assist you in working."

Big Ten rules prohibit recruiters
from promising summer jobs to prospective athletes.

MSU players get plenty of free tickets. A freshman told me he got two tickets
to every home game. Sophomores get
four tickets, juniors got six and seniors
got eight tickets to home games.

The Big Ten rules say that the athletic department can give a maximum of
four tickets to juniors and seniors and
two to sophomores. Freshman players
aren't supposed to get any tickets.

Head Coach Duffy Daugherty has
an unlisted telephone number and couldn't
be reached for comment. Neither Athletic Director Clarence (Biggie) Munn or
Assistant Athletic Director Bert Smith
could be reached either.

Dorow had the following comment:
"There's nothing wrong at MSU, it's all
in Ann Arbor. You don't have the right
to investigate Michigan State, that's the
job for the Big Ten and the NCAA."#

Big Ten, Athletic Board To Probe Irregularities

By DAVE WEIR

(Feb. 10, 1968) The Big Ten will
launch an immediate investigation of
apparent violations of conference rules
by University athletes.

John D. Dewey, Assistant Big Ten
Commissioner and Examiner, told The
Daily that he will personally visit Ann Arbor early next week to investigate allegations listed in a Daily article yesterday.

...

In addition to the Big Ten inquiry,
University Athletic Director H. O. (Fritz)
Crisler announced late last night that the
University Board in Control of Intercol-
legiate Athletics has already started an
investigation into the matter.

During last night's monthly meeting, the Board "gave extended consideration to the allegations appearing in the
article in The Daily yesterday morning."

* ...All merchants alleged to have
extended special discount or merchandise privileges that might jeopardize the
eligibility of members of athletic teams
have been requested to discontinue any
such practices immediately...

* The Board has directed that any
athlete who has received merchandise
free of charge or at a discount must make
restitution immediately to the merchant
or face the loss of his eligibility and his
grant-in-aid...#

Investigation clears 'U' of charges

By DAVID WEIR
Sports Editor

(Oct. 4, 1968) The Big Ten yesterday cleared University athletics of alleged rule violations.

In a 21-page report of its investigation, the conference absolved University
athletes and coaches with the single
exception of a loan transaction between
football player Cecil Pryor and ex-assis-
tant coach Y. C. McNease.

In the report, Big Ten Commissioner Bill Reed said, "With the exception of the loan transaction, it is my
considered judgment that with respect to
the allegations...either there is not sufficient grounds for believing a violation
occurred; or that remedial action taken
(by Michigan) is adequate."..#

BROAD-SIDE

by robin wright

You've come a long way baby, but...

(Oct. 15, 1969) **WE'RE STILL FIGHTING.**

Yep, the age old struggle for emancipation of the woman has not stopped yet. One of the latest causes is to obtain the right for female journalists to grace the premises of athletic press boxes, playing fields and locker rooms (hum-m-m-m).

...

It all began at the end of the football season last year when the junior Daily sports staffers traditionally...were allowed to sit in the press box to get the hang of writing covers, side-bars, columns, etc. about the game.

One of the juniors was a seriously committeed female sports writer. When it came for her to sit with her colleagues, the unspoken rule of no women in the press box arose.

Although the first response was a flat "no," things looked a little more like compromise after the chiefs of the athletic department were alerted to the 14th amendment of the federal constitution which states:

"No state...shall...deny to any person within its jurisdiction the equal protection of the laws."

THE SPORTS EDITOR of the Daily then knocked heads with the publicity department and the new athletic director and reached an agreement with only minor fuss and a one game delay: the young lady would be allowed on the premises if she agreed to remain inconspicuous.

The matter seemed completely resolved with all sides content that justice had been done -- until the question of a female photographer on the field arose at the Vanderbilt game this year.

...

ALTHOUGH REFUSED press box facilities by a patrolman at the game, she garnered up enough nerve to insist upon her right to stay on the field. After being on the sideline less than five minutes she was approached by a field checker who requested that she leave.

Deciding to consult her fellow Daily photographers before taking a stand, she promised to return and let the checker know her answer. She naturally obtained backing from her peers, along with promises that should she be bodily thrown off they would cover the event in the paper.

Thus she returned with a negative reply to the checker, who was so startled that she would deny his request that he simply slithered away stammering...

THE NEXT STEP was a confrontation with a Sanford security field guard who threatened involuntary bodily removal if the lady photographer refused to leave the field. Shaking, and with tears in her eyes she stood firm, fearing a serious encounter with other armed guards.

As it turned out, the security guard had no more desire than the field checker to abuse the young lady, so she remained on the field for the rest of the game. (You see, we can make them back down once in awhile!)

But the story keeps going for the tradition is not one exclusively at Michigan... The challenge will again be taken on as the Daily attempts to integrate the press box at Michigan State during the game this Saturday.

LIKE OTHER press tags, MSU's state "no women, children or dogs (as if they are all in the same category) allowed in the press box."

Although MSU has a new liberal acting president who is sympathetic to students' efforts, and despite MSU's desire to at least match Michigan's accomplishments in the field of athletics, it looks like there may be a challenge to a female's right to sit with her equals again.

But let's hope not. Civil rights suits are so messy, in addition to the bad name they give an institution these days...#

Board denies discrimination by sex

By ANITA CRONE

(Oct. 28, 1970) Before each home football game, the athletic department holds a cocktail and dinner party for the visiting press and coaches of the visiting team. The Regents, vice-presidents of the University, and the Daily senior sports editor are among those traditionally invited.

The exceptions to this tradition have been Regent Gertrude Huebner, former Vice President for Student Affairs Barbara Newell and Daily executive sports editor Pat Atkins. These women have never been invited to the "smokers."

The athletic department has denied the policy is discriminatory, claiming the "smokers" are private parties.

However, the Regents bylaws state the University will work to eliminate discrimination in "private organizations recognized by the University" and by "non-University sources where students and employes of the University are involved."

Atkins recently filed a statement with the student organizations office citing the athletic department's failure to extend an invitation to her.

Contacted last night, Atkins said, "I consider myself a professional member of the press, and I feel I should receive the same courtesies extended to other members of the press."

The complaint is being investigated by Claire Rumelhart, the women's advocate in the office. At the conclusion of her investigation, Rumelhart will report to Vice-President of Student Services Robert Knauss.

...

William Mazer, president of the "M" Graduate Club, said a recent executive meeting of his club, which discussed inviting women to the smokers, unanimously decided "not to invite women."

Mazer continued, "We don't invite women for their own protection. When a group of men get together and drink, the language gets a bit rough. Women should feel honored not to be invited."

Commenting on the situation, Huebner said last night, "I personally don't feel left out by not being invited.#

Irate Schembechler shoves Daily reporter

By GEOFF LARCOM

(Oct. 2, 1979) Michigan football coach Bo Schembechler shoved a Michigan Daily reporter yesterday afternoon after the writer asked him a question regarding the Wolverines' kicking problems this season.

Dan Perrin, one of the four senior editors covering football for the Daily, had been interviewing Schembechler alone with a tape recorder for about five minutes when the outburst occurred.

ON THE TAPE, Perrin is heard asking: "Would you emphasize the kicking game more when recruiting from now on, after what's happened so far this season?"

Schembechler started to answer, but suddenly became angry with the reporter.

"We emphasize...you guys are way out of base asking me that damn question, anyway..." Schembechler shouted. "What the hell do you ask me for, when you know it's not true?"

AT THAT POINT Schembechler threw Perrin's microphone down, poked him in the chest, and then put his hand on Perrin's throat and pushed him backward.

"Don't try to make me look bad, you understand, son, or I'll throw you the hell out of Michigan football," Schembechler could still be heard saying on the tape.

Later, when asked what it was Perrin had said to anger him, Schembechler laughed and said, "I don't even remember, you know these kids."

THE SHOVING took place at around 1:30 in a hallway outside the press luncheon room at Weber's Inn on Jackson Rd., where Schembechler is interviewed by the broadcast media following his weekly luncheon with the working press.

Perrin was somewhat shaken after the incident.

"I was confused," he said. "At first, I didn't understand why he lost his temper. In retrospect, I think Bo was just frustrated with his kicking game, not necessarily angry with me as an individual..." Perrin said.

Michigan's place kickers have converted on one of ten field goal attempts this season.#

Letter from 'U' icers confirms hazing incident

By LORENZO BENET
and GARY LEVY
(Oct. 16, 1980) Members of the Michigan hockey team released a statement yesterday revealing their version of

Exclusive

the hazing of five freshmen members of the squad Sunday night. The statement was signed by all 29 members of the team, incuding the freshmen that were hazed.

The statement said "we do not condone our actions but feel the facts around the incident have been grossly distorted."

It said, "the freshmen hockey players were brought to a house off campus and given alcohol. No physical force was used but peer pressure was evident. The intent of the drinking was not to force the freshmen to become sick."

ONE FRESHMAN player involved, who has asked to remain unidentified, did not have his entire body shaved and does "drink," according to the release. The statement said the player was outside for the shaving, but was brought inside after the shaving to be warmed. When he became sick he was led outside to vomit, and then was brought back inside, the account read...

...

The letter said that after it was apparent that he had become sick, he was placed into "the back of a fully-heated Plymouth Duster hatchback." He was taken straight to Markley Dormitory, a seven-minute ride, and was not driven around campus for more than an hour.

When the three players and the freshman arrived at the dorm, the release said, the player was taken into the lobby by the players where they were met by some twenty members of Markley Reeves hall. It said the players were told to leave and also said the player was not "dumped on the hall doorsteps, incoherent and unable to walk." The player was coherent and able to walk to his room on his own. Markley residents confirmed this statement.

The statement said the players attempted to check on the freshman, but were turned back by Markley residents. Phone calls later in the evening to check on him were not answered...

THE HAZED freshman continued to remain silent about the incident.

"I don't want to talk about it. It's over now; I want to forget it," said the hockey player, who asked to remain anonymous. He refused to comment any further.

"He told me he did not want to prosecute the players involved because he 'has to play hockey with them for the rest of the season'," said Steve Krahnke, a resident adviser in Markley Hall where the player lives.

MEANWHILE, University Athletic Director Don Canham said the three team captains sent a letter of apology to the University, the athletic department, and to the players who were hazed.

"The letter said there would never be any hazings again and the players involved were considering some type of community service to make up for their act," he said.

...

Canham also said the disciplinary action taken against the players involved in the incident has remained private "to protect the players from further embarrassment."

...

He also said the public has no business knowing how the athletic department disciplines University athletes.#

...and what Canham did say

(Nov. 8, 1980) *The following communique was sent to the Daily by a University alumnus. According to Athletic Director Don Canham's office, the letter was sent to several people who had written Canham about the hockey team hazing incident of October 12, 1980. The words set in italics were underscored in the original.*

October 31, 1980
MEMORANDUM
FROM: Don Canham
SUBJECT: Hockey Hazing

I have heard from a number of people concerning the story that appeared in the Detroit Free Press and The Michigan Daily about the hockey hazing at an initiation party. I am not only amazed, but greatly disturbed that, *to date, we have seen no clarification or an accurate presentation of what actually occurred.* I guess it is the age old story of the first falsehood never being correctly retracted. Frankly, the situation as reported in the Free Press and The Michigan Daily was not what actually happened. The hockey team itself has tried to set the record straight with very little success. All players, including the hazed athletes, signed the correct version.

...

...While the hazing or initiation is uncalled for, it did not take place as it appeared in the newspapers. The athlete himself has signed a statement attesting to that.

...

No one is trying to defend hazing or initiations or things of that nature. *Virtually all of the players were wrong, and the hazing got out of hand as it often does.* I know of no institution in the United States that has not had problems with initiations and hazing, and I know of no institution that has not expressed distaste and dissatisfaction in the practice. I thought that young people today had more maturity than they have shown in this particular case. We knew nothing about hazings that have evidently been going on for several years or we would have done something about it.

...

The brilliant solutions that I find in my mail are that they (the players) should all be expelled from school *immediately;* they should all be held up to *public ridicule and be listed by name;* we should cancel the hockey season and if not that, bar the offending athletes forever from playing hockey at The University of Michigan. Whatever became of fair play and due process?

I assure you that we will take none of these actions. Instead we are making every effort to straighten out the matter and to help and guide the young people who were involved and who, *incidentally, are absolutely crushed by the hostile reaction of their own student newspaper, and who see me almost every day searching for a way to right their wrong.*#

Editors arrested outside athletic board meeting

**By MAUREEN FLEMING
and TOM MIRGA**

(Oct. 29, 1980) The editor-in-chief and an editorial page editor of The Michigan Daily were arrested last night following an attempt to gain admittance to a closed meeting of the University's athletic department board in Crisler Arena.

Mark Parrent, editor-in-chief, and Joshua Peck, editorial page editor, were arrested by Ann Arbor police for allegedly trespassing on University property. They were released last night on personal recognizance...

PARRENT, PECK, and several other members of the Daily staff tried to attend the University Board in Control of Intercollegiate Athletics meeting, which was held in the Hospitality Room in Crisler Arena. The Daily contends the meeting should have been open because the newspaper feels the board falls under the jurisdiction of the state's Open Meetings Act of 1976, according to Parrent.

...

POLICE WARNED the Daily staff members they would be charged with trespassing if they persisted in their attempts to enter the meeting. "It's not trespassing if you're attending a meeting that should be open," Parrent told police.

University Athletic Director Don Canham said following the meeting that the board does not come under the jurisdiction of the Open Meetings Act. "We make policy on our own department," he said. "We don't make decisions on tax dollars because we don't use tax dollars."

Canham also said the meetings historically have been closed because the board discusses personnel matters and other "sensitive issues."

"WE TALK ABOUT a lot of things that we're not ready to publicize," he said. For instance, Canham explained, the board last night "was toying" with the idea of constructing handball courts beneath Crisler Arena.

Canham said that depending on the agenda, future meetings could be open. He explained that at the next meeting the board would be discussing the "bowl bid."

"You can come down and listen to that one," he told reporters.

PARRENT SAID he has asked Canham, through the Freedom of Information Act, for the minutes of all Board meetings dating back to March 31, 1977. Parrent said he also asked Canham earlier in the week for the agenda for the meeting held last night.

"The Daily has never asked me for an agenda," Canham said. All the paper has to do is to call, Canham explained, and he will mail one. But Parrent claims Canham told him in person last Friday that an agenda did not even exist.

The Daily believes last night's meeting was particularly important, Parrent said, because staff members anticipated discussion of the recent hazing incident involving members of the hockey team and the current Title IX investigation.

A COPY OF the agenda obtained after the meeting showed both items were scheduled for discussion.

...

Parrent and Peck were arrested shortly after police officers read to the group of editors and reporters the state trespass act and told them that attempts to enter any other part of the building would constitute a violation of the trespass act. Parrent replied that the group's only reason for being in the building was to get into the meeting...

Peck then headed toward a partition that some meeting participants had entered earlier. Police Sgt. Arthur Hughes asked the group to leave.

"WE DON'T WANT to leave," Parrent replied.

"You don't want to leave, then we're going to escort you out," Hughes said. He then grabbed Parrent's arm and began dragging him away. Parrent asked whether he was under arrest. "I am escorting you out," Hughes replied.

After a few moments of debate, Hughes placed Parrent under arrest. Soon afterward, Peck was also placed under arrest and led out of the building.#

Hey, Canham! Open up!

(Oct. 28, 1980) **THE MEETINGS** are closed--in fact, even the time and location are kept secret. The minutes are never released. Even the agendas are private.

Some Nixon-era security council? Almost. These are the meetings of the Board in Control of Intercollegiate Athletics--the ruling body of Don Canham's athletic department.

...

Athletic Director Canham's reticence about any controversial athletic department issue is well known. For years, he has cloaked the well-oiled, profit-making athletic department in virtually complete secrecy.

That secrecy, however, is absolutely intolerable at a public university. Not even the Senate Advisory Committee on University Affairs--the executive body of the entire faculty--completely closes all of its meetings. Yet Don Canham and the Board in Control persist in their audacity.

We urge Canham to open today's--and any future--board meeting to the public and the press, for we believe he stands in violation of the state's Open Meetings Act.

Essentially, the Open Meetings Act requires most meetings of any public policy-making group to be open. The spirit of the law is clear--it is intended to open the decision-making process to public scrutiny.

The University's attorneys, however, have claimed that the Board in Control of Intercollegiate Athletics is not a policy-making body because it derives its authority from the Regents, and therefore is not compelled to open its meetings.

That claim would certainly appear to represent a violation of the spirit of the Open Meetings Act. The board, by the powers vested in it by the Regents, controls the finances of the athletic department. Further, the board is responsible for making and enforcing most rules in the department. Finally, it serves as a check on Don Canham, questioning him on all facts of Michigan athletics.

...

Any way you look at it, those details add up to a policy-making body.

...

Open the meeting, Mr. Canham. If the athletic department has nothing to hide, you have nothing to fear.#

'M' athletics: Out of control

Ex-Big Ten rep. assails Canham

By BILL SPINDLE

(Feb. 8, 1983) ...Champaign, Ill., and its campus -- more than 300 miles from Ann Arbor -- may seem a long way off, but according to some people close to Michigan athletics, Illinois' problems in 1980 may hit closer to home than many people think.

Several months after his term expired as the University's faculty representative to the Big Ten, Prof. Thomas Anton now is talking about the sad shape of Michigan athletics and its domination by one man--Don Canham.

After six years of working on the Board in Control of Intercollegiate Athletics--three as a member and three as the Big Ten representative--Anton says that control of athletics has slipped from the hands of the faculty into the lap of Athletic Director Canham.

"We tend to put all our eggs in one basket," Anton says. "I don't think our board has much control.

AND ANTON isn't the only insider who feels that way. "The board in control is really a board of advisors to Canham," says Prof. Morton Brown, who began his term on the board last fall. "They may provide helpful advice on some issues, but they are not controlling athletics. The operation has become too big and too complicated for boards to run."

...

The Board in Control of Intercollegiate Athletics, made up of faculty, administrators, alumni, and students, has a reputation of being so impotent it is jokingly referred to as "The Board Out of Control of Intercollegiate Athletics" by many faculty members.

PART OF THE problem comes from the board members themselves, says Anton.

"The fundamental problem with faculty is they are not interested in athletics," he says. "The attendance record is not very good, and when they go, they can't do much because they are so uninformed. Most are quite content to let the director have his way on policy matters.

"The notion of being a part of a very successful program is very attractive," Anton says. "You go to one meeting a year and if the football team is successful you go to the Rose Bowl. That is a perk most other committees don't have."

ALUMNI ON the board have an even worse reputation among the University's faculty members for backing Canham on almost every issue.

"Alumni generally don't do much more than support the director," says Anton.

...

Canham scoffs at the criticism of the board.

"I control those guys (board members)? You've got to be kidding," he said. "I'm (surprised) at the knowledge on that board. I'll say one thing--the board is in control of athletics."

...

THE EXAMPLE of Dave Wilson's eligibility at Illinois may be an extreme one, but Anton says the loss of control has led to some troubles at this University.

For several years the University has been accepting five or six students each year who would not have been admitted if they were not athletes, Anton says.

Those admitted sometimes had below a 2.0 high school average when "cake courses" were thrown out. Some athletes were admitted with SAT scores below 700 (out of 1600).

...

Board members were not condoning those admissions, says Anton. They were not even aware it was going on.

Other issues--including the abuse of a hockey player in a hazing incident in 1980 and the suspension of five football players for the use of narcotics the same year--were never given a full discussion, apparently because Canham didn't want to and the board would not challenge him on the issue, Anton says.

ANTON SAW those incidents as a chance to come up with a uniform policy for incidents in the future. That chance was not used, he says.

...

Despite Anton's view, several veteran board members feel the board has enough control over the department to ensure that problems such as those at Illinois do not surface in Ann Arbor.

...

SITTING IN his office tucked into the top corner of the Frieze Building, Social Work Prof. Howard Brabson says his experience with athletics has taught him the board's relationship to the department--something he says many members have not learned.

"Some of (the board members) want to be personal advisors to the director of athletics, when the Regents bylaws don't say that," says the second-year Board member.

He says he has become involved with many aspects of the athletic department in his term on the board, especially with the academics of some athletes.

Leaning in his chair, he points to the pictures hanging on his office walls of some of the University's greatest basketball players. He has followed their careers after graduation closely enough to know where each is now working.

The board's job is to set general policy under which the athletic department can operate, says Brabson. The board members who have trouble are the ones who want to become too involved in the details of the operation, he says.

But Canham won't even give the board members access to those details they want, says Anton.

THE ATHLETIC director "is very protective of activities of his own department and regards any information that gets out as dangerous. So he doesn't want to release information unless he can control its form," Anton says.

Early in his term on the board, Anton proposed that Canham mail out information when the board was asked to consider budget issues. "Canham made it clear to the members that (the suggestion) was an outrage," says Anton. The proposal received only two supporting votes because the board was intimidated, he says.

...

Canham says he does not mail out information early because he often does not receive information early enough and because "if you mail it out they will forget to bring it.

"That has never been an issue of any kind," Canham says. "If anybody wants something mailed out they can have it mailed out."

BOARD MEMBER Brown, however, says that sometimes it is a problem.

"The issues, with the documents, are passed out at the meetings. There is no time to look at it carefully, there is no time to find out if there are other impor-

[More]

tant documents that would be helpful," he says.

Several board members complain that they were asked to raise football ticket prices at the January meeting without enough information to make a reasonable decision.

BOARD MEMBER Lawrence says that Canham pressured the board to raise ticket prices without providing information on ticket sales, total department revenue figures, or a "rationale" for why they needed the raise.

Canham passed out a summary of what other Big Ten schools are going to charge next year. He claimed the decision should be made at that meeting to meet upcoming publicity deadlines.

Although several members thought that inadequate information was supplied, no one asked for more complete financial data, Lawrence said.

Although the Board is supposed to be in control of the department, Anton says that at the meetings the opposite is true -- Canham controls the board.

"Members learn very quickly that you either support the director or you oppose him," says Anton. "And you don't find opposition very often.

"He controls the agenda. The board talks about what the director wants to talk about and if there is something he doesn't want to talk about ithen it won't be discussed."

But Canham and other board members claim that members can put anything they want to on the agenda.

"Anyone can put something on the agenda," says present Big Ten Faculty Representative Gikas, who also served as a board member for three years.

The one glimmer of hope Anton sees after eight years working in athletics is the more aggressive attitude University President Harold Shapiro seems to be taking toward the University's problems in athletics.

Shapiro was one of the more active university presidents in the NCAA's recent drive to raise academic standards.

"What I see is his becoming more and more positive," says Anton. "I see his activities being designed to impose...the higher standards of the University...on the (athletic department), which hasn't lived up to our higher standards..."#

Alumni upset with regents, Fleming over AD search

By STEVE BLONDER

(March 10, 1988) The University's Board of Regents have offered the athletic director job to Michigan football coach Bo Schembechler without the stipulation that he retire from coaching after this year, according to both alumni and administration sources who requested anonymity.

Interim University President Robben Fleming denied this information, and regents refused comment.

...

The regents and Fleming have been the recipients of a letter writing campaign by alumni who favor allowing Schembechler to serve both as athletic director and head football coach.

...

"With all of the letters and calls, don't the regents understand when they have made a mistake?" asked former Michigan and NFL great Ron Kramer.

Several regents said they had received letters, but that they had not altered their position that serving as both athletic director and football coach is too much for one person.

"The Alumni and the M club are important members of the Michigan community. I take their views to heart," said Regent Philip Power (D-Ann Arbor). "However, no one person should hold the jobs of both athletic director and coach."

...

Schembechler was offered the athletic director job last week, but turned it down because of the stipulation that he retire from coaching.

Other alumni feel that Schembechler was not really offered the job because conditions were placed on him that the regents knew he would not accept.

...

Kramer expressed the alumni's displeasure with the tight-lipped attitude which has overtaken the regents said Fleming.

"We're liable to have a 1965 uprising (the civil rights marches). We have an interim president who has to give the answers, and doesn't have the answers... He's got to take the lead," Kramer said.

[Alumnus Richard] Caldarazzo said many alumni are particularly bothered by the secrecy surrounding the search.

"We're fearful that sometimes regents make decisions behind closed doors and then try to slip out the back door. It's our school. All around the country right now, our school is a joke," he said.#

Regents name Bo as new AD

By STEVE BLONDER

(April 20, 1988) Michigan football coach Bo Schembechler this morning will be named to replace retiring athletic director Don Canham, according to a source in the office of Interim University President Robben Fleming.

The source also said that Jack Weidenbach, the University's Director of Business Operations, will be appointed associate athletic director. Weidenbach will be in charge of running the day-to-day operations.

Both Schembechler and Weidenbach were unavailable for comment...

...

Several members of the University's Board of Regents, along with Fleming, have maintained that serving as both football coach and athletic director is too much work for one person. Contacted last night, Regent Philip Power (D-Ann Arbor) said that the regents had not budged on this position.

"I think it was the feeling of the Board that Bo was extremely well-qualified to be athletic director. However, serving in both jobs poses terrible risks for any human to be in," he said.

...

SEARCH committee member Sarah McCue said, "I'm glad the regents decided to go with the search committee's expectation rather than their own." The committee recommended three finalists to the regents--Schembechler, North Carolina Athletic director John Swofford, and St. Louis advertising executive Clayton Wilhite...#

By BUD BENJAMIN

The Banshee Howls...

(Oct. 8, 1938) **CLARK SHAUGHNESSY** is the head football coach of Chicago University. This position might aptly be compared to playing traps in Guy Lombardo's so-called orchestra or to being Mussolini's barber. All are peculiar.

As football coach of Chicago University, Mr. Shaughnessy has several unusual functions. The most strenuous, nerve-wracking and ghastly of these is watching his team play each Saturday. Humane societies and women's clubs have long objected to submitting one man to such pure and unadulterated punishment, but the hardy Irishman can take it. His second duty is that of coaching his team, but this, as we shall see, is a relatively unimportant function. Thirdly, he must satisfy the whims of the members of the press. It was the latter that he attacked with a waning vim at 4 p.m. yesterday in front of the Stadium dressing rooms. As he talked, his squad of 33 dressed quietly in preparation for an hour's workout on today's battlefield.

Shaughnessy wore a jet black coat, which compared rather unfavorably to Francis Schmidt's plaid reversible and Fritz Crisler's natty camel's hair job. Yet it was entirely appropriate. Pensive and glum, Mr. S. kept his head down and his voice low as he answered the questions.

One of the reporters asked him what veterans would be in the starting line.

"What veterans in what line?" he cracked. "We only have six veterans on the whole squad. Pink will be the only one on the line."

How did things look for the impending game?

"Well," mused the downcast one, "maybe I shouldn't say it, but we're not in Michigan's class. There's no use kidding ourselves about it. We're too young, too green. We've got kids on this team--18 and 19 years old."

"They're willing kids," he continued, his voice and face rising simultaneously. "They'll pitch in. They've got great spirit. But what the devil, how can you beat age and experience?"

...

"We had no spring practice to speak of, " he continued. "What we had consisted of an average of 12 boys working nine hours--not days, mind you, but nine hours for the entire spring.

"Sure," he added wryly, "they try hard. They have to work too fast though. Faster than any team in the Conference. And what difference does that make with no subs and not time."

Shaughnessy spoke with a crisp sincerity that impressed even the hardened gang of the fourth estate. He seemed hopelessly and impossibly buried in the rut. Someone asked him how he thought the game would end.

He looked up. "If we play a good game tomorrow," he snapped, "I'll be more surprised than you fellows. Sure they'll try, they'll fight, but what the devil."

...

"We brought 33 fellows on the trip," he mused, "but some of them we carried as a reward for attending practice. Only 16 or 17 are fit to play."

"Gee," he whispered--his head really buried now, "gee, I'd hate like the devil to get a bad licking tomorrow."

The players were ready, and he unloosed on last morsel of morbidity.

"You know," he said, "we had a good end by the name of Howard this year. He got hurt. Naw, not in a game. He never saw a minute of scrimmage. He got hurt scuffling in the Field House the first day of practice, and today's his first game. Can you imagine that? Scuffling! So there you have it, boys. Anything's possible on this team."

He turned and bid us a solemn farewell. I started the trip back, and all the way that "anything's possible" kept drumming through my head. It was only a year ago, you know, and there were only four minutes to play, and. . .#

Varsity Squad Proves To Be 'Melting Pot'

By MYRON DANN

(Oct. 16, 1941) Notre Dame has long been noted for its "Fighting Irish," the fame of Minnesota's tow-headed Swedes has spread to every corner of the gridiron kingdom; while the football history of Fordham's great team has invariably been written by its long named Polish lads. But an attempt yesterday to find a predominant race on the 1941 Michigan football team proved merely to be another indication of the great American "melting pot."

A poll among the Michigan gridders revealed that no less than eighteen different racial stocks are represented, the enumeration of which sounds like the roll-call of the old League of Nations.

The Germans head the list with five members: Bill Mazlow, Tippy Lockard, Walt Freihofer, George Hildebrandt and Bob Stenberg. Tied for second place come the English with Ted Kennedy, Paul White, Don Robinson and Chuck Haslam; and the Czechs with George Ceithami, Bob Kolesar, Rudy Smeja and Elmer Madar.

"When Irish Eyes Are Smiling" is the theme song of Bob Ingalls, Phil Sharpe and Leo Cunningham; while Dave Nelson claims Scotch ancestry.

The Scandinavian delegation consists solely of Harry Anderson, who springs from Norwegian parents. The closest you can come to being a pure blooded Lithuanian is to be like Al Wistert and Jack Harwales.

No Michigan team would be complete without a couple of Finns so this year's representatives are Rube Kelto and John Laine. The pride of Holland is rested on the sturdy shoulders of Harlin Fraumann and Don Boor. Flop Flora's folks hail from Italy. Husky guard Marv Pregulman is of Russian-Jewish descent while Bill Pritula's parents came from the neighboring region of the Ukraine.

There was difficulty in finding a full-blooded Pole on the team this year, so the closest we could come was Al Thomas who had great grandparents from that country. Ralph Amstus takes Ed Frutig's place as Switzerland's representative on the team...#

Schembechler enters Michigan tradition

By ROBIN WRIGHT

(Jan. 9, 1969) There's been Fielding, Fritz, Bennie, Bump. . .

. . .And now there's Bo.

Glenn Edward Schembechler-- who compensated for his last name with the nickname 'Bo' -- has succeeded Bump Elliott as Michigan's head football coach.

Schembechler's appointment was announced December 27 after Elliott resigned to accept the long vacant job as associate director of intercollegiate athletics.

...

Schembechler described his coaching personality as "semi-conservative. I don't like the odds on risk plays. I like to rely on what I know is successful.

"And I'm a tough and unyielding coach if I think I'm right," he added.

Despite his tough-guy attitude toward coaching, Schembechler feels he is equally devoted to the players as to the game.

He explained, "I like a close association with the players. I don't want to know them just between four and six each day at practice.

"My players take precedence over anything if they have a problem and need my counsel. I'll be available at all times.

"I don't want them to feel all I give a damn about is their knocking around the football."

Schembechler also feels that the player in turn has an obligation to be a good representative of the team, and to obey the subsequent restrictions.

"When there are 75 people together, there must be restrictions on them in order to be successful -- it's not unlike a military situation.

"Football requires more concentration than any other sport, and therefore I don't want a self-centered player on my team.

"For example, I despise long hair. It shows that someone is worried too much about himself.

"Football dominates a player's life during the season. He needs to think about the game and his physical condition, and not about his hair."

Schembechler practices what he preaches.

Devoted to the game twelve months a year, Michigan's new coach "feels guilty if I don't do something about my job every day -- Sundays too."

Although he is a fan of most other sports, especially baseball, Schembechler has no hobbies, except playing handball at noon to keep in shape.

He explained that "since I don't smoke, and I don't have any hobbies, I eat when I'm nervous. I eat and go to bed to work off nervous energy. I sleep until ten the next day and then go over to see the game films. I like to get at it right away."..#

the carrots test

I was assigned to write a feature article on the "raw carrots/cooked carrots" test that was administered to all incoming freshmen in the late 1950's and early 60's. The test was part of a research program of Prof. Benno G. Fricke of the Psychology Depart-ment. It contained forced pairs, and asked which you would rather do or have. The most famous was: "Do you like raw carrots/Do you like cooked carrots – which would you like more?" (measured creativity). Another pairs asked if you preferred going to a masquerade party or a bonfire (measured presentation of self).

Prof. Fricke pulled out my scores in order to better explain the findings and asked if I remembered taking it. I most certainly did because I refused to finish the test – I would rather watch Maverick than go to either a masquerade party or a bonfire. The result was that I had a very high motivation for success (99+) and very low social adaptability (02). But Prof. Fricke consoled me by saying that he had pulled the scores of other Michigan Daily staffers and we were all in the lowest ten percen-tile in social adaptability. Needless to say, while that tidbit didn't fit in print, it went around The Daily and soon several people had obtained their own low scores.

—Harry Perlstadt, '63

Test Analyzes Success Potential

By HARRY PERLSTADT

(March 18, 1961) A University professor is currently analyzing the results of a test which "may make a major contribution to higher education and campus counseling by predicting success in college and aiding in vocational guidance."

The test, which was devised by Prof. Benno G. Fricke of the psychology department, indicates a student's motivation for success. "By contrasting the responses of students who did very well academically with those who did poorly and comparing their motivation for success we are pretty confident that the resulting correlation is not chance," Prof. Fricke said.

The opinion, attitude and interest survey, which entering University freshmen take during orientation week, contains diverse statements with which students are asked to agree or disagree.

From their replies percentile rankings are obtained on a variety of traits.

Prof. Fricke found that students who do well academically usually obtain a higher motivation for success ranking than students of the same tested ability with low grade point averages.

...

In addition to the high correlation between motivation for success and academic achievement, the test score on intellectual quality is very similar to the results obtained by the traditional intelligent tests. The new test can also be used for vocational guidance.

During orientation week, Prof. Fricke, who is also a freshman-sophomore counselor, had the freshmen list their preferences for different fields of endeavor. The opinion, attitude and interest survey compares the student to those who have already entered these fields...#

Originator defends 'raw carrots' test

By ELLEN BRESLOW

(March 26, 1975) The author of the infamous Opinion, Attitude and Interest Survey (OAIS), nicknamed the "raw carrots" test by freshpersons who plod through it during orientation each year, last night defended the exam's validity.

While Benno Fricke claimed his exam assists the University in evaluating students, he told the small handful of people who assembled in East Quad last night that because of growing controversy surrounding the test incoming freshpersons will no longer have to suffer through it.

He complained, "Students always lose when a few radicals cause trouble."

...

Fricke, director of the examinations and evaluations office here, argued last night that much of what the test reveals should not be openly discussed with the student. "Most of the test," he said "can be used to help the University make better decisions about the students, rather than the student making specific decisions about himself."

He said the tests are available to "academic counselors, have continually been provided for Health Service use, and now, of course, are completely open to those students who care to see them."

However, Fricke admitted under continued questioning that the test results are often misused. He argued that all test results of this sort, including SAT and Achievements are often misused and misinterpreted.

...

Masculine orientation is the most controversial evaluation area of the test. Fricke said the scale might be better termed "psychological sex."

HE ASSERTED, "Men tend to be more aggressive, inconsiderate and sportsminded, while women tend to not like swearing, enjoy books more and be more considerate of others."

Fricke admitted after...prodding that the masculine orientation scale, built on a "normal college population," may be used in determining careers and could "inbreed specific occupational qualities."#

Presenting... The 1969 Edgars

(Feb. 15, 1970) In keeping with a long standing tradition, The Daily today announces its selection of the 1969 Edgar winners. The Edgars are awarded to those public personalities who last year best approximated the virtues of our nation's foremost Edgar, Mr. Hoover of the FBI. A few are given to those who have earned their own unique brand of distinction.

* * *

The Richard Nixon Policy Cannot be Made in The Streets Edgar to Vice President for Academic Affairs Allan Smith who said he didn't care if students voted overwhelmingly not to use student fees for the proposed IM Bldg. "We're going to make up our own minds," said Smith.

* * *

The U.S. Army Engineer Corps Edgar to Sec. of Interior Walter Hickel of Alaska for designing an Alaskan highway now under five feet of water.

* * *

The Dr. Henrik Verwoerd Memorial Edgar to William F. Buckley for saying in a Detroit Free Press interview that Eldridge Cleaver "couldn't possibly" have written Soul on Ice.

* * *

The Playmate of the Month Edgar to the Ann Arbor News for its front page, 8-column cheesecake of Spiro Agnew floating in the pool of the Jakharta Holiday Inn.

* * *

The Newton Minow - Spiro Agnew Edgar for Good Taste in Television to CBS for dropping the Smothers Brothers Comedy Hour and substituting "Hee-Haw."

* * *

The Carl Parsell "Support Your Local Police" Edgar to Ann Arbor Police Chief Walter Krasny for explaining that a "blow to the face does not constitute assault."

* * *

The Profiles in Courage Edgar to Mayor Robert Harris for commending the Ann Arbor Police for its restraint on South U on June 16 and 17.

* * *

The Richard Nixon "Priorities" Edgar to EMU President Harold Sponberg who welcomed the EMU '73 freshman class with "Here at Eastern we

consider students one of our most valuable assets."

* * *

The Clement Haynsworth Achievement Edgar to New Mobe for leading the anti-war protest at the Rose Bowl that never materialized. "It's a tremendous opportunity for football fans to express their opinions in a non-violent manner," Mobe said.

* * *

The Pacemaker Edgar to the Michigan State News for incorrectly naming their new presidency in the story that broke the news.

* * *

The Kelly Girl of the Year Edgar to Acting Vice-President for Student Affairs Barbara Newell who has been acting in that capacity for 1-1/2 years.

* * *

The Right to a Fair Trial Edgar to Detroit Recorder's Judge Robert Colombo for sentencing John Sinclair to 10 years in jail for possession of two joints of marijuana, and for explaining, "John Sinclair is out to show that he and his ilk can violate the law with impunity. Well, his time has come. You may laugh, but you will have a long time to laugh."

* * *

The Roger Rapoport Conflict of Interest Edgar to the Regents for asking Fred Ulrich to testify on the feasibility of a student bookstore.

* * *

The Jeane Dixon Edgar to WWJ sports reporter Al Ackerman for declaring that "Michigan doesn't stand a chance against Ohio State."

* * *

The George McClellan Tactical Excellence Edgar to Moby Benedict, Michigan's baseball coach, for playing Dodger second baseman Ted Sizemore, last year's Rookie of the Year, as a catcher while he was here at Michigan.

* * *

The Cassius Clay Modesty Edgar to the Regents for attempting to change the name of People's Plaza to Regents Plaza.

* * *

The Julie and Tricia Nixon Edgar to the Miss America contest chaperones who refused to let their charges discuss a Women's Liberation protest because it was "too controversial" for nice American girls...#

chapter 3

the investigators

"Investigative reporting" is a recent phrase but an old concept. The Daily, at least, was doing it as far back as 1912. Not every investigative piece is a blockbuster; sometimes the real gems are the small stories that don't look like much. Until they hit the fan, that is.

BOOKS SHOW OWNERS OF WATERWORKS

Men to Whom Money Will Go if City Votes To Buy Out Company, Revealed By Secretary Of State's Records

(March 31, 1912) Advices from the state capital have disclosed the identity of the stockholders of the Ann Arbor Water Company. The books of the Secretary of State contain the list of the men who are financially interested in the outcome of the present proposal to purchase the privately owned water works. These are the parties to whom the money will go if the proposed plan of purchase receives a favorable vote tomorrow.

Ann Arbor citizens will have an opportunity tomorrow to vote on the proposed purchases of the water company's holdings by the municipality for a consideration of about $450,000. It has been a debatable question for some time as to just what persons hold stock in the water corporation, and to clear up the matter, the names of the fifteen stockholders, together with the number of shares held by each, are appended:

Titus Hutzel, 133; W. J. Booth, 11 3-7; E. D. Hiscock, 47 5-7; Thos Kearney, 80; M. J. Cavanaugh, 80 47; A. R. Hale, 693 493-1050; C. E. Greene Estate, 91; J. V. Sheehan, 11 3-7; J. F. Lawrence, 280 407-1050; Arthur Brown, 90; W. J. Herdman Estate, 154; B. Spokes, 23; O. E. Butterfield, 84; Walter Mack, 16; Wm. Wagner estate, 34.#

TURN DOWN WATER PLANT PURCHASE

Ann Arbor Citizens Go Against the Proposition by Margin of Two Votes.

(April 2, 1912) By the close margin of two votes, Ann Arbor citizens yesterday turned down the proposition of the municipality purchasing the water plant. Out of a total of 2,386 votes cast, 1,429 favored the acquisition, but as these did not constitute the necessary three-fifths, the water plant will probably remain in private control for some time to come...#

"Brown Jug" Thief Detected Solving Mystery Of 19 Years

(Nov. 24, 1922) Discovered! For years the statement has appeared in The Daily prior to every Minnesota game concerning the little Brown Jug that "it had undoubtedly been stolen by someone from the enemy camp," and so it had. But it is only recently, after two weeks of investigation, that it is possible to tell exactly who stole the now famous five gallon brown water jug.

Oscar Munson was his name! He had been in the employ of the University of Minnesota for 24 years. At the time he disappeared with Michigan's historic water bottle he was janitor of the University armory. Since that time has has served in many capacities, though the football team has always been his chief interest, and only last summer he was created custodian of athletic equipment. And now Oscar is after that same little jug which he eloped with way back in 1903 hoping to "custode" it with the other athletic property in the Gopher camp.

In 1903, after the game, it was noticed that the Wolverine water jug had disappeared. The invaders hunted high and low all over Minneapolis for their container, but nowhere could it be found. As soon as they left for Ann Arbor, Oscar bore it out from the armory basement as a trophy of battle. The student body and the athletic association took the suggestion and draped it with Minnesota colors, placing it in their trophy case, as a challenge to all future Michigan elevens.

Slightly wrought up over the happening, Michigan was led to see the joke but insisted that the jug should be returned with due glory the next time they defeated the Gophers. And since then the tradition has grown up that the Jug should be present at every Michigan-Minnesota football game, to be borne home by the victors and placed in their trophy case until the following year.#

WORKERS MADE TO BUY HOUSES IN SUBDIVISION

Claim MacNamee Sold Homes by Threats of Dismissal

Six of Seven Places in Plot Owned by B & G Men.

By Carl S. Forsythe.
(Oct. 1, 1931) An alleged Ann Arbor "racket" was charged last night when it was asserted that Homer B. MacNamee, recently resigned foreman of labor in the buildings and grounds department, quit last week after charges were made against him that he forced his workmen to purchase homes in a subdivision which he owns and operates.

Evidence was furnished by Cy Potter, an employee, who said he was mistreated by MacNamee and who was told that he would be fired. Potter, when interviewed at his home in the MacNamee subdivision last night, stated that he went to Shirley Smith, vice-president and secretary of the University, and informed him of MacNamee's activities.

An investigation followed which terminated in MacNamee's resignation.

Seven families are now living in the subdivision, six of the houses being owned by men who worked under MacNamee in the buildings and grounds department, Potter said.

He further stated that Cad Waite and Frank Paddock, both of Cadillac, were "fired" for not purchasing lots.#

TRAGEDY IN FLAMES:
Apartment Fire Is Fatal to Student Bride

(April 4, 1943) Funeral arrangements are being made today for Agnes Day Gilson, 19-year-old bride of two weeks who was fatally burned yesterday when a spot fire raced through her two-room apartment which only 24 hours before had been the scene of a gala housewarming party.

And in the meantime, her husband, Dr. Charles Mark Gilson, 24-year-old Health Service dentist, is lying in St. Joseph's Mercy Hospital, severely burned...

...

The young bride, who was a junior in the literary school, and her husband were trapped in their basement apartment when fire broke out in the basement of the Doric Apartments, 331 E. Liberty, early yesterday morning.

The most apparent means of escape from the apartment was a rear staircase. The young married couple dashed up the flaming steps racing through 13 feet of solid flames, and two hours later the young bride was dead, her severely-injured husband grief-stricken by the news...#

Burned Apartment Violated Building Code

By MONROE FINK
(April 7, 1943) Although the building code of Ann Arbor distinctly provides that there shall be two separate exits from every floor in an apartment building, the basement apartment at 331 E. Liberty in which Agnes Day Gilson was burned to death and her husband critically injured Monday, had but one.

This fact was brought to light by Mrs. Charles Noble of Ann Arbor, who is "conducting a private investigation of my own." Mrs. Noble is a member of the Health and Welfare Committee of Ann Arbor Citizen's Council.

...

The exact provisions of the code pointed to by Mrs. Noble were Section 3, Sub class F 1 and 2 which provides that there shall be two and distinct exits from every floor regardless of height of building, and more exits if necessary...#

No Building Permit Issued For Firetrap

(April 8, 1943) The basement apartment at 331 E. Liberty St. in which Agnes Day Gilson...was burned to death Monday operated as a dwelling without the knowledge of city building officials, George H. Sandenburgh, City Engineer, told The Daily last night.

The building was converted into an apartment house in 1929 after a permit for three first and second floor dwellings but not for a basement apartment was granted, he said.

Walter P. Staebler, chairman of the City Building Code Board of Appeals, said last night that "to my knowledge no request for utilization of the basement apartment has been made in the last eight years."

Only One Exit
Investigation by a Daily reporter showed that there was but one stairway exit from the apartment. Three small windows measuring approximately 18 by 30 inches, about three square feet, were in the bedroom of the burned dwelling and these opened inward like conventional basement windows.

The State Housing Code provides that windows may be classified as auxiliary exits if they are 12 or more square feet in area exclusive of the frame...#

NO 'COCOANUT GROVES'!
Dangers of Majestic Exposed by Professor

(April 8, 1943) (Editor's Note: The following article was submitted to The Daily as an open letter to Daily readers by Prof. George B. Brigham, Jr., of the architecture college...)

THE Cocoanut Grove disaster in Boston has caused many people to question fire hazards in Ann Arbor.

Many will remember the old wooden Arcade Theatre on North University Avenue, Ann Arbor, which burned to the ground one night, very fortunately after the closing hour.

Hazards still exist here as has been disclosed by local and state inspection.

How many Ann Arbor citizens know that the Majestic is built entirely of wood with only a thin veneer of brick on the exterior to make it look safe; that this wood construction is not protected with fire stops; that the heating plant is not sufficiently segregated; that the aisles and lobby are too narrow, and that the exits, which may be adequate in width, are poorly placed, with dangerous steps at the main entrances?

How many know that the Whitney is a close second to the Majestic and that even though the exterior walls are solid brick, the interior is wood, and the exits are as questionable as those of the Majestic?

Both of these theatres were declared dangerous several years ago, and were given five years by the City Council to liquidate and close—five years in which a public disaster might have happened. The Majestic is closed and the Whitney should have closed at the end of the five-year period on January first of this year, but is still open to the public. This is not the fault of the City Engineer's Building Inspector, who has been overridden by the City Council.

...

If you were a Councilman, would you be willing to shoulder responsibility for a possible second Cocoanut Grove catastrophe?

...

As a citizen of Ann Arbor, can you sit by and allow these Councilmen to legislate fire hazards?

—George B. Brigham, Jr.
Professor, School of Architecture

Vets Satisfied, Daily Survey Reveals

Questions Prepared By Newcomb, Tibbitts Use Scientific Selection

(June 9, 1946) The overwhelming majority of the University's male veterans are satisfied with the education they are receiving here, a Daily survey of veterans' opinion reveals.

Designed to gain an accurate picture of veterans' views and plans, the survey reached 100 of the campus' 5,155 veterans enrolled this semester.

The questions were prepared by Prof. Theodore Newcomb, of the sociology department, a public opinion expert who assisted in a public opinion survey for the U. S. Army in Germany, and by Clark Tibbitts, director of the Veterans Service Bureau.

Members of The Daily staff polled the veterans, who were scattered through every part of Ann Arbor, Willow Village, Ypsilanti and other outlying sections.

The veterans to be polled were selected by Prof. Newcomb by means of a formula which guarantees a scientific sampling.

Upsetting previous predictions that most veterans want a full-length summer semester, less than half the veterans polled said that the University should go back to the three-semester year.

Slightly more than half of the 100 veterans were at least fairly well satisfied with campus social life, but nearly one-third said it had aspects which were undesirable.

...

More than half of those polled indicated they will use all of the time in college to which they are entitled under the G.I. Bill of Rights, while they were almost unanimous in the intention to complete a degree program. More than four-fifths of the veterans intend to complete their education at the University.#

Move To Lift League House OPA Ceilings

(Nov. 4, 1945) Whether league houses are "part of the University" and thus exempted from OPA price regulations has been the subject of a six months' controversy between the Office of Price Administration and University officials, The Daily learned last night.

"The league houses of the University of Michigan are a part of the University housing system and as such are specifically exempt from OPA control," Marvin L. Niehuss, University vice-president pointed out.

...

Meanwhile, complaints have been filed with the OPA by University women against operators of several University league houses charging violations of price ceilings for board, an OPA official revealed.

The most recent complaint charged that one league house raised the prices for breakfast and lunch 20 per cent over the one dollar per day OPA ceiling this term.

The University is petitioning the OPA in Washington, according to a local OPA official, in an attempt to lift the ceiling on league house board...

...

OPA has requested students charged above ceiling prices to file complaints, anonymously if they wish, with the Price Administration. Complaints may be filed by calling 24464.#

Ruthven Protests OPA's Seeking Complaint

(Nov. 6, 1945) ...In a strongly-worded telegram to Chester Bowles, Director of the Office of Price Administration, President Alexander G. Ruthven yesterday stepped into the current controversy over whether or not Ann Arbor league houses are subject to OPA regulation.

Quoting an article in Sunday's Daily in which the OPA requested students to file complaints, anonymously if they wished, against overcharging by league houses, Dr. Ruthven protested "vigorously the OPA's solicitation of anonymous complaints from students respecting matters primarily under University supervision." He maintained that league houses were an "integral part" of the University housing system and that "reckless and irresponsible public solicitation of anonymous complaints among the student body" would only make more difficult the solution of the University's complex housing problem.#

Excessive Housing Profits Revealed By Daily Survey

By JACK DAVIS

(Nov. 10, 1937) Notoriously high rents in Ann Arbor's approved rooming houses assumed new meaning today as a survey by The Daily disclosed landlords' profits last year averaged 10 per cent and in some cases skyrocketed to an 18 per cent return upon the capital investment. The average rate of profit on single houses outside the University area is estimated by city real estate experts to be between two and three per cent.

These figures mean that students could obtain rooms in the 22 houses considered for slightly more than half their present rents and still allow rooming house proprietors a six per cent return. Moreover such a return would be from two to three times that obtained upon property in any other section of the city.

The following results were bared by The Daily's investigation: The total revenue earned during eight months by the 22 houses selected at random for the test was $29,923.50; total expenses for 12 months were estimated at $13,200; the total value of these properties according to corrected city assessments is $166,688. On the basis of these figures the annual return is 10 per cent.

...

The figures for expenses, while only estimates, have been checked by the economics department and by experts in Ann Arbor real estate.

Income alone is calculated upon an eight-months basis, all expenses are for the full year. No account has been taken of the returns from summer students...#

One-Third of Vets Receive Checks

(Nov. 22, 1946) Less than one-third of the University's 11,098 veterans have received subsistence checks this month--although the Veterans Administration reported that the Cleveland finance office had mailed checks to more than 80 per cent of the 62,000 veteran students in Michigan--according to a Daily poll of campus post offices yesterday.

J. F. Campbell, Chief of the regional VA Rehabilitation and Education Division, said Wednesday the Treasury Department's disbursing office at Cleveland had mailed checks to 52,000 veterans on Michigan campuses last week.

The estimates from the quadrangles and West Lodge ran between 20 and 25 per cent, while Vaughan House reported less than 15 per cent.

"The fellows just haunt this place waiting for their checks," one post office clerk said.

...

Previous statements gave assurance that every eligible student veteran should have received his first check within 10 days to two weeks, the Free Press said.#

STUDENTS SUBPOENAED
Called To Appear At Clardy Probe

By ALICE B. SILVER
Associate Editorial Director

(April 15, 1954) Two University graduate students have been subpoenaed by the House Un-American Activities Committee to appear at the hearings of Rep. Kit Clardy (R-Mich.) May 10 in Lansing, it was revealed last night.

Mike Sharpe, chairman of the local Labor Youth League and a doctoral candidate in economics, told The Daily last night he received a subpoena on March 31.

The other student, also a Ph.D. candidate in economics, said he was subpoenaed March 26 but refused to make public his name "to avoid losing my job."

∗ ∗ ∗

THE REVELATIONS by the two students were unexpected. In February Rep. Clardy told The Daily that "under present plans no University students will be called to testify."

Contacted last night in Washington, Rep. Clardy said he was not thinking of graduate students when he made the February statement. To his knowledge,

he said, no undergraduates will be called.

(Reports that four to six University professors received subpoenas have neither been confirmed nor denied by the University administration.)

Rep. Clardy, who was stricken with a heart attack in March, explained that because of his illness he is not able to recall when the decision was made to call the graduate students.

"The two were identified as persons who need to be brought before the Committee; it doesn't matter if they are students," he added. He said he remembered the two names but not the details of their cases.

...

SHARPE, a 25-year-old resident of Chester, Pa., said emphatically, "I will not cooperate with the Committee in any way. To cooperate with the Committee would be to contribute to the destruction of our Constitutional rights."

...

The other student also said he will be "an unfriendly witness. I will refuse to cooperate in discussing other persons," he added. The student said he has not decided yet if he will answer questions about himself. In previous years he has publicly acknowledged membership in the Communist Party.#

Juvenile System Probed

'Understandings' Rule Children in Detention

By MILT FREUDENHEIM and CLAYTON DICKEY

(June 6, 1946) Unwritten "understandings" form the basis of Washtenaw County's juvenile correction procedure, an investigation by two Daily reporters revealed.

Asked what provision is made for notifying the County Probate Court of children apprehended by officers and placed in detention, Judge J. G. Pray explained that there was an "understanding."

"Police and matron notify us at once," the judge said, "or report the next morning."

Asked what provision is made for placing children in the detention home at night, Judge Pray said that the "understanding" was that police take offenders

to the Detention Home and report to him the next morning. "They sometimes miss," he added, "but not very often."

The "understanding" for holding children when the Detention Home is completely filled is to place those aged 15 and over in the County Jail, the judge said. The attendant told The Daily that when the home is filled to capacity (six children), she places a notice on the door.

Asked if there is a state code for procedure in juvenile court cases, Judge Pray said he thought there was but that it was not used by his court.

An average of 60 to 70 youngsters a year come under the jurisdiction of the County Probate Court's "understandings." There is no legal maximum on the time children may be held in the Detention Home. They spend an average of two weeks there, Judge Pray said, "sometimes as much as three months."

In an investigation of the home, reported yesterday, The Daily found that children held there are locked in narrow bare rooms with only secondhand books to break the monotony.

...

Asked what preventive measures are taken with children who have come under the court's jurisdiction, Judge Pray said he talks to them and their parents. Social workers from state agencies are consulted in "not more than 10 per cent" of the cases, he said.

"One in 20 repeat," Judge Pray stated, attributing repeat offenses to home conditions. "We try to get them into good homes," he said...

Commenting on the county's Detention Home, Judge Pray said that it would be better if the county had a separate, larger home, but that such facilities would be "awfully expensive."..#

Probe Of Football Pool Control Seen; 'Bookie' Is Arrested

Losses Estimated To Reach $9,000

By NORMAN A. SCHORR

(Nov. 23, 1938) A general investigation of football pools and other gambling devices in Ann Arbor, which have "taken" students and townspeople for about $9,000, was seen in the offing last night with the arrest and arraignment of John R. Pieters, of Kalamazoo, charged with the operation of one of these pools. ...

Students Not Paid

Action by the student was instigated when Pieters, graduate of the University in 1922 and owner of the City Cigar Store at 106 E. Huron St., did not pay off students and townspeople an estimated $3600 in winnings. [One student] "won" $80 and other students reported unpaid winnings ranging from $1.75 to $200.

The bookmaker's offer to pay five cents for every $1 bet was rejected by a crowd of 100 students Monday at the downtown cigar store. Pieters said that his backers had "skipped" on him, and he too had been victimized.

Students were also involved in three other pools which operated from Detroit and Chicago, and whose operators also left town this past weekend, without meeting obligations estimated to reach more than $9,000, it was learned last night...#

Operators of Local Pool Also Swindled Detroit Bettors

By NORMAN A. SCHORR

DETROIT, Nov. 24 (1938) (Special to The Daily) --Detroiters were swindled out of at least $15,000 by the two men who operated the "green ticket" football pool in Ann Arbor through personal representatives on the University campus, Lieut. John McCarthy of the Detroit Police Department said late last night.

The two men named in The Daily Tuesday...are being hunted here. [One] was the Ann Arbor agent, students said.

This duo, however, are not the real backers of the pool, Lieutenant McCarthy said. Police believe that two other men whom McCarthy described as "petty larceny thieves and cheap hangers-on" are the men who are behind the pool. Another pool, the National Daily, which also operated in Ann Arbor was also under the control of these men, he said.

Intended To Run Out

"These men didn't have more than a few hundred dollars behind them and had no intentions of paying off this week," McCarthy said.

Police are holding [the] owner of [a Detroit recreation hall]. He was arrested Tuesday when detectives found that a telephone number appearing on the pool ticket with the caption "Call Julie between two and six" was that of a public booth at the recreation hall...#

Dice Racket Uncovered By Students

Evidence Unearthed By Daily Reporter

(Nov. 24, 1938) Evidence gathered by two University students resulted in the arrest yesterday of [the] alleged operator of a dice game in the United Cigar Store at 118 E. Huron. ...

The students, Thomas Keppelman, '38E, and Harry L. Sonneborn, '40, a Daily reporter, had familiarized themselves with the dice game, which was played on a counter in the rear of the store.

They played the dice game from 4 to 4:30 p.m. yesterday, when Keppelman left and met Mayor Walter C. Sadler and William M. Laird, city attorney, at Justice Reading's office. Keppelman swore out a John Doe warrant for [the man's] arrest...#

Grid Pools Run By 'U' Students

Campus Authorities, Police Deny Knowledge of Gambling Set Up

(EDITOR'S NOTE -- This is the first of a series of interpretive articles dealing with student-run football pools here on campus.)

By DAVIS CRIPPEN

(Nov. 9, 1950) Unnoticed by both city and University officials, student-run football pools have taken firm root on campus this fall.

Because the pools are largely student-run locally, it is hard to get definite facts on their operations, since those who know the facts are unwilling to "squeal" on their friends. However, it is probable that:

1. There are at least two different pools and that they come from national syndicates.

2. The take of the pools each week is probably somewhere between $1500 and $2000 a week.

3. The campus pool organizations, right up to the top, are student-run, with the heads acting as the contacts with the national organizations.

At least one of the top student bookies--who said he had retired because he wasn't clearing enough for the risk involved--denied the national tieup. He went on to say he'd heard that his rival had lost $1,000 the week before on a particularly easy card.

He explained his competitor's ability to pay off by saying he probably had built up enough reserves in the earlier part of the season. No one, by the way, has accused any of the operators of welching.

It is probable, however, that such a loss could not be met without outside aid. Adding strength to the theory of outside tieups is the fact that the cards are not printed in Ann Arbor but are flown in each week.

Just who the local agents are tied in with is an even murkier subject than their local operations. A student who has studied the operations as closely as anyone on the outside could, thinks that one of the cards comes out of St. Louis while the other originates in Chicago.

But these aren't the only possibilities. Names bandied about in campus rumors on the subject have included the Capone Gang and nationally known financier Frankie Costello.

But wherever they come from, legally they should not be in Ann Arbor. City ordinance 121 -- An Ordinance Relative To Disorderly Persons and Conduct -- says in Section 6, that "No person shall keep, carry on or maintain or aid in keeping, carrying on or maintaining any lottery, policy, pool, bucket shop or any like scheme."

Yet when Capt. Albert Heisel of the Ann Arbor Police was asked about the situation, he replied shortly, "We don't know anything about it."

Heisel heads the department's Plainclothes Division which is supposed to check gambling in the town.

However, Heisel did add, "If you find anything out, we'd like to know about it."

University administrators, when questioned on the problem, were equally in the dark. Dean of Students Erich A. Walter, who heads the Office of Student Affairs which is entrusted with maintaining student discipline, knew nothing of the gambling activities, but declared, "We obviously disapprove."

He went on to say that the policy followed in previous affairs of this kind was for the local police to apprehend the offenders and then turn them over to the University for punishment or, if the offense was more serious, to try them in the regular courts. #

Police Nab Two Student Bookies

By DAVIS CRIPPEN

(Nov. 29, 1950) Police yesterday arrested two students as the brains behind the football pools which operated on campus for five weeks this fall.

Assistant County Prosecutor Edmund DeVine said that [the two] had admitted that they were the leaders of the campus bookies. At times they had distributed up to 1500 cards a week, DeVine said.

But they lost money even though they handled $2500 a week, he added. They stopped their operations, it was revealed, shortly after The Daily published a series of articles exposing campus gambling.

DeVINE SAID the only tieup with the outside discovered so far was a Chicago printing firm, the Arcadia Sales and Publishing Co., from which [they] are said to have purchased the cards.

Devine declared, however, that the police were continuing their investigations by checking on those who worked under them.

He also said that the police would check further on the printing firm and possible connections it might have with the rackets...

YESTERDAY afternoon The Daily had The Associated Press check in Chicago on the firm. The AP got this statement from ...the company's owner: "We are printing brokers, who do job printing. We have our own shop and we don't print betting football cards."

Last night The Daily sent a communication to The Daily Northwestern asking them for any information they might have on the printing firm.

Devine was not sure whether or not the Chicago firm or the two students had violated any federal laws in handling the cards... #

Authorities Charge Students With Campus-Wide Gambling

By BARTON HUTHWAITE and PHILIP MUNCK

(Jan. 29, 1958) Seven students, including a first-string football player and the captain of the basketball team, are being arraigned this morning for their part in a campus-wide football gambling card syndicate.

The crackdown came after five weeks of investigation by the Ann Arbor detective bureau and The Daily with the cooperation of the University.

...

Police indicated that the students were working separately and that some students were not involved as deeply as others.

...

H. O. (Fritz) Crisler, director of athletics, said yesterday in a prepared statement, "We are removing from their respective athletic squads...both athletes involved in these charges until their cases are decided."

...

The gambling cards have been passed since the beginning of the football season this fall with an average weekly take estimated at about $3,500 per week.

Both football coach Bennie Oosterbaan and basketball coach Bill Perigo expressed shock at the disclosures and said that they were not aware of the athletes' participation.

Remove Athletes

"We don't wish to pre-judge a case of this kind before all the facts are known and to date we know only what has appeared in the press," Crisler said.

"However, the University expects its athletes to remain above suspicion, necessarily maintaining even higher standards of conduct than expected of students generally," he continued...#

Daily Reporters Hanged in Effigy

—Daily—David Arnold

(Oct. 31, 1958) DIAG DISPLAY--...two Daily reporters were hanged in effigy on the Diagonal. One figure carried a sign reading "Barton (I led two lives) Huthwaite." The other was divided in half. "Munck" was written on one side of the "body" while the other half was labeled "Huthwaite" with the further appellation, "Quisling."

STUDY AIRS CRITICISM OF QUADS
Staff Document Seeks Revisions

By THE SENIOR EDITORS

(March 16, 1961) The University does not provide an adequate living experience for men in residence halls, nor is it satisfactorily studying residence hall problems, an East Quadrangle resident advisor charged last night--and he provided an unpublished, 181-page report to support his claims.

Herbert C. Sigman, Grad, said the report, which is highly critical of many conditions in the residence halls, has not been taken seriously by top-level administrators responsible for policy-making.

A critical response to Sigman's statements came promptly from John Hale, assistant dean of men in charge of residence halls, who said the lengthy report "might have some truth in it," but is based on invalid survey methods. The report...has not been used as a working document because of its "poor" research.

...

The report, based on interviews with a sample of 40 undergraduates, was prepared and issued last spring by staff men in East Quadrangle under direction of Harold Scheub, who was then resident advisor of Strauss House.

...

Describing himself as a "constructive, but very definite, critic," Sigman asserted that students in the residence halls, particularly freshmen, too often derive a negative experience from their time in the quadrangle.

...

Students, Scheub declares, feel "no identification with the quadrangle and the house. It is institutional, they claim...

The staffs, Scheub continues, tend to regard the students as "children; then warming to the role of the protective parent, the staffs wrap the students not in swaddling clothes but rather in numerous restrictions--perhaps all designed to make life more convenient and comfortable for the student, but many of them boomerang and leave the student feeling guarded, unhappy and limp."

Scheub noted that students do not have enough to say about the running of the residence halls, and that the administration "is quite pleased with student opinion so long as student opinion does not cross administrative opinion."

As an example of how student opinion may prove helpful, he pointed out that of the 40 students interviewed only one frequently used Benzinger Library, and 29 have never used it. "One may be caused to wonder about the wisdom of pouring $10,000 into that enterprise in the next three years."..#

IQC Establishes Group to Study Criticisms of Quad Conditions
Council to Distribute 'Confidential' Report

By MICHAEL OLINICK

(March 17, 1961) Inter-Quadrangle Council last night unanimously decided to set up a committee to study comprehensively and in detail the unpublished report of conditions in the mens residence halls.

...

IQC's action came as the possibility of administrative use of the report grew stronger.

Council members questioned John Hale, assistant dean of men in charge of residence halls, on the "confidential" nature of the report and why it was not given to IQC for study and discussion.

...

The report was not made available to IQC members until yesterday afternoon. Hale refused to release it to them until he conferred with other University administrators.

Hale claimed the report was not released to any student government bodies last spring because it was "an internal administrative study distributed as a strictly confidential report."

Hale said the report was based on an invalid survey and had "poor" research methods behind it. "There was no attempt to hush it up, but it was not best to use it to institute discussion."#

The Theatre Affair

An Editorial...

(Sept. 23, 1965) **THERE IS A GOOD CHANCE** that a $1 million gift from University Regent Eugene Power for the construction of a theatre will be announced tonight at the President's Premiere for this fall's Association of Producing Artists season.

We recognize the University's need for a modern repertory theatre. But there are implications in this gift which clearly call for public consideration of its effects on the University.

The specific issue raised is where the additional money to build the theatre can be obtained. Planners have set a $3 million price tag as a minimum. The University will have to supply at least $2 million to complete the project.

BUT WHERE CAN THE MONEY be obtained? Administrative officials have ruled out the possibility of federal or state money, since these sources are usually reserved for academic or research structures. A third alternative, private money, seems unlikely. The theatre's name will already be reserved for Power, and hence donors will prefer to look for other projects on which they can inscribe their own names.

The final and ultimate source is University money, the funds which are used to pay salaries, to stock the library and to establish new academic departments.

...

We are particularly concerned that the residential college, a small liberal arts institution that could restore the feeling of personalized instruction here, may well never get off the ground because of this diversion of funds. And the Legislature will never foot the entire bill for the college.

In fact, the residential college is in danger of being shelved, administrative representations at the last Regents' meeting notwithstanding.

HERE WE MUST BLAME President Hatcher.

It is he who has encouraged the commitment of $2 million in precious educational dollars to the theatre. It is President Hatcher's responsibility, thus far neglected, to point out to Power the desperate need of funds for a residential college instead of offering generalities on how well plans for the program are progressing when they are stalled for lack of funds.

The University community should also be concerned with the feelings of other academic officers who represent the faculty. Vice-President for Academic Affairs Roger W. Heyns strongly regretted the allocation of University funds for a theatre, even though he was a leading proponent of the repertory company in Ann Arbor. Heyns' reason: this money belongs to the faculty and to the students (since it comes from their research and their tuition.)

...

SO IT IS TO YOU, Regent Power, that we appeal. Your gift tonight, no matter how well intended, will only be detrimental to the academic growth of this institution.

...

Do not commit this institution, always hard-pressed for financial resources, to an allotment of several million dollars that are simply not available for a cultural project.

WE APPRECIATE your generosity, but we ask you to reconsider your judgment.#

--THE SENIOR EDITORS

Hatcher Fails To Unveil Plans For Theatre Gift From Power

President Angered, Disturbed by Daily's Critical Editorial

By MERLE JACOB

(Sept. 29, 1965) In a surprise move last night, University President Harlan Hatcher did not announce plans for the construction of a repertory theatre at the President's Premiere of this fall's Association of Producing Artists series.

There had been official indication to Daily reporters that an announcement would be forthcoming...

Power did not attend any of the festivities of opening night and declined to comment afterward.

Puzzling Day

Hatcher's failure to announce the theatre capped a day in which these events transpired:

--In the morning, Hatcher denied reports that he would reveal plans for the theatre, which will be named after Power. The President did, however, reiterate the community's need for a modern theatre;

--In the afternoon, Power was described by a close friend as "taking it very hard," a reference to an editorial appearing in yesterday's Daily that criticized the Regent's intention of committing the University to construct a theatre.

--In the evening, Hatcher was characterized as "extremely upset" about the editorial and angered that the theatre had been unveiled in the press.

Other University officials remained in the dark as to the timing of the announcement. However, they reiterated earlier statements that plans for a theatre have been approved, and that architects for the project have been consulted.

Power has been known for many years as a strong supporter of excellent theatre and an interested patron in building a modern structure with his name here...#

Regent's Letter Discloses Power's Anonymous Gift

Xerox Stock Given To 'U' For Building

By LEONARD PRATT

(Oct. 1, 1965) Regent Eugene B. Power of Ann Arbor gave 2000 shares of stock in the Xerox Corp. to the University anonymously in January of 1964.

Information on the worth of the gift was unavailable at press time this morning. However, Power confirmed reports in the Detroit News yesterday that his gift is to be $1 million.

In that report he reiterated his intention of making the gift. However, when asked last night if he intended to withdraw the gift, he replied:

"I'm sure as hell thinking about it."

At the time of his gift, Power was president of University Microfilms Inc., a subsidiary of Xerox.

The facts of the gift were disclosed yesterday by Regent Irene Murphy of Birmingham in a letter criticizing the front page editorial that appeared Tuesday in The Daily.

Regent Emeritus Donald M.D. Thurber also charged The Daily with "questionable practice" in a letter received last night.

Thurber later said that the origin of the gift was a "very carefully-guarded secret" and that many of the Regents only learned that the gift was Power's "later and by accident."

The gift's entry in the minutes of the January Regents meeting reflected the hush which surrounded its acceptance. It is one line of type saying, "Anonymous donor, 2000 shares of securities to establish a special fund."

...

Mrs. Murphy also mentioned that, despite what The Daily had been told, there may well have been no intentions to announce the theatre's construction Tuesday night, but rather to simply go ahead and build it quietly.

This would presumably explain University President Harlan Hatcher's denials that he was to unveil the theatre Tuesday night on the one hand and the fact that plans for such a theatre have been approved on the other.

...

Power himself reacted very adversely to the front-page editorial running in Tuesday's Daily, saying that the editorial had upset him very much.

Power denied that a rumored dispute over the naming of the proposed theatre had held up the gift announcement...

Displaying his resentment against The Daily's editorial, Power said that he told Daily Editor Robert Johnston that "a gift of a million dollars is probably more than you will make in a lifetime."#

Officials Remain Silent on Theatre Dispute

By BRUCE WASSERSTEIN

(Oct. 2, 1965) The controversy over Regent Eugene Power's anonymous donation to the University for a theatre continued to rage yesterday as Regents and administrators refused to break a self imposed silence barrier.

...

Despite the unclear statements by University officials on the subject, Security and Exchange Commission and University records attest to the fact that Power has already donated stock for the purpose of building a theatre.

The theatre for which Power is donating money will cost an estimated three million dollars. So far Power has donated the equivalent of 11,000 shares of Xerox corporation for a special fund set aside to finance the theatre.

On December 27, 1963 Power gave the University 2000 shares of Xerox whose market price that day was $413. As of January 6, 1965 Xerox stock underwent a 5-1 split which gave the University 10,000 shares of stock worth about $830,000.

On December 22, 1964 Power gave anonymously 1000 shares of Xerox to the University whose market price that day was $101 per share.

...

One of the prime points of confusion in the controversy is why the Regents have gone about recognizing the donations for the theatre so secretively. For example, one faculty critic said last night, even if the donor wanted to remain anonymous, there was no reason why the gift should have remained unpublicized.

Another example of the hush-hush atmosphere surrounding the gifts is the fact that the Regents set up a special committee headed by music school dean James Wallace to study the need for a new theatre soon after the first Power gift. However, Regent Irene Murphy indicated that "many distinguished architects and stage directors" have been at work on the theatre while Wallace said this week that none of these people had contacted his committee about the theatre.#

Theatre Gift

To the Editor:

(Oct. 2, 1965) I WISH to protest the casual Philistinism of your front-page editorial on Tuesday. Like good gay burghers you divide the world into necessities (a Power building for the Residential College; funds for the Center for Research on Learning and Teaching) and luxuries (the arts; here a theater described unforgettably as "a cultural project.")

Apparently "Culture" is decorative and useless; it belongs with sports cars and electric carving knives among the pleasant superfluities of a comfortable life. On the other hand are the realities, for which in the prose of the editorial we must spend our "educational dollars."

YOU ARE complacent in accepting as self-evident this bourgeois division, and you are condescending when you suggest that Regent Power give his name to a more practical structure. There are people... who think a living theater more urgent and requisite than any number of Centers for Research on This and That.

--Prof. Donald Hall
Department of English

'U' Plans To Use Student Fees for Campus Theatre

By ROGER RAPOPORT

(Jan. 10, 1967) The administration has proposed a "tentative financial plan" that would pledge up to $4.3 million of operational budget money--to be taken from student fees--to finance the construction of a new University theatre, The Daily has learned.

Under the plan, now being considered by the Regents, the school would pledge annual payment of $175,000 worth of student fees out of the University's general fund over the next 25 years to repay a $2 million loan (at 5 per cent interest) on the theatre.

The move is contrary to administration plans announced this summer which indicated the theatre would be financed entirely through gifts.

It also runs counter to the traditional University policy of spending student monies on student-oriented buildings such as the Michigan Union and North Campus Commons.

...

The theatre, which is now budgeted at $4.5 to $5 million will be paid for with the $2 million loan, a $1.3 million gift from Regent-emeritus Eugene B. Power, and $1.2 to $1.7 million worth of undesignated gifts from the school's current $55 Million fund drive, according to the tentative plan.

In August administrators assured reporters that the theatre would be financed exclusively with Mr. Power's donation and other gifts from the school's $55 million fund drive.

In addition to the theatre, the Regents are looking at an administration plan to spend $4.1 to $5.4 million worth of student fees to build a new faculty center and $7.2 to $14.4 million worth of student fees to build new campus recreational facilities...#

An Editorial...

(Jan. 11, 1967) **AS DISCLOSED YESTERDAY**, the University administration appears ready to approve a plan to dip into the General Fund and spend up to $4.3 million of the student tuition fees and from $1.2 to $1.7 million from the $55-M Fund Drive for a University theatre.

...

Good faith has been abused. In formally announcing a $1.3 million gift toward the theatre from former Regent Eugene Power, the administration gave assurances that the remainder of the cost of the building would be paid for by gifts, but that has now changed. Moreover, the cost of the building has soared from the first estimate of $2.5 million (March, 1965) to $3.5 million (August, 1966) to its present range of $4.5-5 million.

THE STRUCTURAL PROCESS of decision-making on the theatre plan has also been highly unsatisfactory. Indeed, one might even question how the decision was made within "the administration." For "the administration" seems, in this case, to mean primarily President Hatcher. At least three vice-presidents are known to have had doubts about the theatre's financial plan.

Moreover, little effort has been made to consult the deans of the schools and colleges on a question of priorities obviously vital to them. While a faculty planning committee for the theatre has been at work since 1964, its efforts have largely been confined to establishing architectural and stage requirements.

Furthermore, although students are paying for over half its costs via tuition, there has been absolutely no formal consultation with any students--as individuals or as groups--on the theatre.

...

A DECISION TO FINANCE a University theatre with up to $7 million in funds vitally needed elsewhere bears very clear implications for the University community as a whole. Only when such problems are considered--and only when the views of the whole community are sought and heeded--will such a decision be a just one.#

--THE SENIOR EDITORS

New theatre assured by second Power gift

By PHILIP BLOCK

(Jan. 9, 1969) An additional gift of $1.4 million to the University from former Regent Eugene Power and his family has assured construction of a new University theatre beginning this March.

The theatre will provide facilities for both dramatic and musical productions and will seat over 1400 persons.

The theatre, named by the Regents the Power Center for the Performing Arts, will be located in Felch Park, east of the Rackham Bldg.

The gift brings the Power family contributions for the center to a total of $3 million. The Regents have authorized the use of up to $500,000 in undesignated gifts to meet the remaining costs of the project.

Because of the absence of sufficient gifts to cover the cost of the center as originally planned, the University has broken the project down to two separate phases. Phase one will include the construction of a combination theatre-concert hall-auditorium with backstage facilities and dressing rooms. Phase two will consist of additional dressing rooms, offices, rehearsal facilities, and set construction facilities.

The Power family gifts along with the $500,000 in undesignated gifts allocated by the Regents will be used to cover the cost of phase one of the project. Phase two financing plans have not been drawn yet but the University has told Power that he second part of the project would be built within ten years.

Power originally gave $1 million for the construction of the center in December, 1963, in the hope that additional private gifts would complete the financing of the center. However, the University has not been able to obtain enough private gifts to cover the remaining costs.

...

The current financing plans for Phase one do not include the use of any student fees.#

The Microfilm Affair

UNIVERSITY MICROFILMS, INC.

UMI and the 'U' Library: A Long History

By ROGER RAPOPORT

(Oct. 23, 1965) In 1938 Eugene Power acquired space in a former Ann Arbor undertaker's parlor, invested $1,500 and thus brought to life University Microfilms.

Since that modest start 27 years ago University Microfilms has attained international stature in the library world and become a profitable and respected multi-million dollar enterprise.

...

Eugene Power, the President of University Microfilms, is also a Regent of the University...

An examination of the current relationship between University Microfilms and the University reveals the following:

* University Microfilms is selling copies of University of Michigan doctoral theses. This apparently violates a student-University "agreement" signed by virtually all University of Michigan doctoral candidates. The agreement gives the University the right to microfilm, store, and sell copies of students' theses. In fact, microfilms of University doctoral theses are actually stored at University Microfilms. The company sells copies at a commercial profit. As a result University Microfilms may be violating the terms of copyright on many of the theses written at the University of Michigan since 1957.

* In 1958 after the University spent about $50,000 to develop a shelflist of books for the undergraduate library, University Microfilms microfilmed the entire set of catalogue cards at no charge. The company now sells the set of 57,000 cards to new libraries for $1,900.

* University Microfilms uses the name of the University to advertise the product, calling it "The University of Michigan Undergraduate Shelflist." According to the University attorney consent must be obtained from the University for the use of its name in advertising a commercial product. According to Power, University Microfilms did not obtain consent.

* For the past year University Microfilms has had microfilming cameras in a small room on the third floor of the Undergraduate Library to microfilm University books for commercial sale. The company pays no rent for the privilege.

All four of these developments have occurred since 1956 when Power became a Regent.

In 1956 Power wrote the State Attorney General for a legal opinion on his company's relationship with the University.

The Attorney General's 1956 letter stipulated that Regent Power could sell nothing to the University. A state law forbids Regents to sell anything to a University. Prior to 1956 University of Michigan dissertations were microfilmed by the company at a charge of $25. However, the attorney general's letter stipulated that this practice had to be suspended.

However, the Attorney General said University Microfilms could buy University of Michigan dissertations from the library and reproduce them for commercial sale. It also stated that University Microfilms could continue to microfilm University books.

Since that opinion was rendered nine years ago, the four previously mentioned developments have evolved. What is the nature of these four relationships?

The "agreement" for publication of doctoral theses signed by most doctoral students states specifically, "The manuscript is to be microfilmed and returned to the graduate school, the negative (or microfilm) being kept on file at the University of Michigan Library where positive film copies (printed copies made from the negative) will be made on request at the announced rates."

According to John Gantt, head of the library's photoduplication service, "We (the library) do the filming and then we let University Microfilms have the negative. They store the film and sell copies."

University Microfilms pays no charge for getting the negative and stores it in a special vault along with those from many other universities. University Microfilms prints and distributes abstracts (brief summaries) of these at no charge.

...

A prominent local attorney...believes that this business arrangement appears to be a violation of the written "agreement." Hence, several thousand graduate students in the past ten years may well have had their agreements violated by the University.

Moreover he points out, "If the student copyrighted his thesis no one could sell it without his permission."

The attorney also commented that this verbal agreement between the University and the microfilm company for transfer and publication of the student's thesis could be construed as a contract.

According to an informed source, the University's legal office has suggested to Vice-President for Business and Finance Wilbur K. Pierpont that the relationship could possibly be in violation of a state law.

...

Power says, however, that to the best of his knowledge he has never been informed by the University of any possible violation of this law.

Asked about getting actual written permission to sell copyrighted manuscripts Power said, "Well I didn't get permission, but I know that Vice-President Pierpont is very sensitive to these matters and this (arrangement) was all cleared through him when I was elected a Regent."

...

The second new development between the microfilming company and the library is the undergraduate shelflist, which was basically the work of the Assistant Director and Bibliographer of the Library R.C. Stewart... Stewart and several assistants went through approximately 400,000 prospective titles to aid in the selection of 40,000 books for the original Undergraduate Library collection.

Upon completion the University's Undergraduate Library shelflist of books was recognized as one of the finest in the
[more]

nation. In 1958 University Microfilms copied the shelflist.

...

The shelflist can be purchased in card catalogue form for $1,900, in a book form for $875 and on microfilm for $100.

Save Expenses

New libraries desiring to save the research and expense involved in developing their own shelflist can save money by buying the University of Michigan shelflist for their own use.

By way of comparison, the G.K. Hall Company in Boston also copies library shelflists in specific fields. The shelflist is sold to clients in book form.

A royalty on books sold is paid by the Hall Company to the library involved. University Microfilms pays no royalties.

According to a spokesman at the Library of Congress, microfilming companies may copy catalogue cards from the Library of Congress. However, all the work is done by the Library of Congress at a fee of one and one-half cent per card.

When Harvard University completed its Lamont shelflist, the project was reprinted by the Harvard Press.

With respect to the royalty question, Power contends that, "If we (University Microfilms) paid a royalty we would have to enter into a contractual agreement with the University." He indicated that he felt this could be in violation of the state law prohibiting Regents from entering into contracts with the University.

Advertisement

A University Microfilms advertisement that has appeared in many magazines and brochures advertises the product as the "University of Michigan Shelflist."

According to University Attorney E. A. Cummiskey the name of the University cannot be used without the prior consent of the University. In the academic area this would necessitate the consent of the vice-president for academic affairs.

...

University Permission

As of now the company has not even requested University permission to advertise the product as "The University of Michigan Shelflist."

Moreover, the same advertisement fails to give proper credit for financing the shelflist project. An advertisement which has appeared in many magazines and pamphlets says the shelflist was developed "with funds provided by a foundation grant."

...

While Power did not obtain consent for the use of the University's name in the advertisements, he did obtain permission to place University Microfilm cameras in the Undergraduate Library.

Before Power became a Regent he had several cameras in the basement of the Graduate Library which were used to microfilm University books. University Microfilms also let the library use the cameras at no charge to microfilm library materials.

When Power became a Regent he did not mention these cameras in his letter to the Attorney General but on his own volition he removed the cameras from the library. In the place the cameras once occupied, the University established its own library photoduplication service.

Cameras Removed

Why did Regent Power remove his cameras?

"Because," Wagman explained, "in 1956 when Power was elected a Regent we decided our relationship with Power would become much more formal.

"At the same time Regent Power, because of the attorney general's opinion could no longer film University of Michigan dissertations for a fee. We (the library) decided to build our own laboratory (to film dissertations and other materials). It kept things nice and clean and above board."

Then why did Wagman invite Power to return his cameras to a place in the library in 1964?

"My thinking varied," Wagman explained.

Service to Others

"The reason the camera was put in was because I suggested to Regent Power that since our shelflist (the University of Michigan shelflist sold by University Microfilms) was used as an acquisition tool and since a lot of libraries would want copies of books in our library that were listed in the shelflist it would be a service to him and other libraries if he could produce wanted copies of out-of-print books.

"At the same time it would be worthwhile for him to do this from a business point of view. In order to do this he had to use the UGLI and it would be a lot simpler to stick cameras in the UGLI," Wagman added.

...

Wagman said that he would be happy to let any other microfilming company enjoy the privilege enjoyed by University Microfilms. If they wanted to put cameras in the library for the same purpose he would let them.

Experience and Equipment

Regent Power said the microfilm company had two cameras in the library before 1956 because, "We were doing filming for the University for which they paid us. University Microfilms had the experience and the equipment to do the job.

"Now as I recall we took the cameras out when I became a Regent because the library couldn't pay for work done by University Microfilms. This would have been a violation of the state law on conflict of interest."

...

How does library director Wagman regard the University's relationship with University Microfilms?

Speaking frankly, he said, "We get much more from University Microfilms than we give them."

He estimated that University Microfilms has donated about $150,000 worth of microfilming services over the past 10 years.

"Regent Power has never said no to any of our requests."

...

"The whole idea is to make books widely available." He explained that University Microfilms' many projects, such as preserving decaying books and making out of print books readily available, have been a valuable service.

Praise for Company

Wagman is full of praise for University Microfilms, calling the company "exceedingly progressive," and adding that "they have made great contributions to scholarly research."

Wagman's viewpoint is shared by an executive at University Microfilms who describes his firm as "A commercial enterprise active in the field of education."

"The University of Michigan has a very progressive library, and has shared much with us."

According to Power "...We recognize that the University must have the benefit of the services we offer and we must make them available. We make them available often at very substantial sacrifices in order that the University not be penalized because I am a Regent," Power concluded.#

REGENT POWER RESIGNS

Attorney General's Statement Result of UMI Investigation

By ROGER RAPOPORT

(March 12, 1966) Eugene Power resigned from the Board of Regents after ten years of service to the University yesterday shortly after Michigan Attorney General Frank Kelley said there was a "substantial conflict of interest" in his business dealings with the University.

University President Harlan Hatcher, commenting on the ruling and the resignation, said, "It is indeed a harsh choice that deprives the state of Mr. Power's direct service to the University and to higher education."

In his statement of resignation Power,

'U' Family?

To the Editor:

(Oct. 29, 1965) HAVING HAD seventeen years of experience in raising funds for a college, perhaps I am qualified to observe that the best way to launch a campaign for $55,000,000 to get money for a badly needed theatre and other resources for the benefit of students is for one portion of the University family to cultivate its best friends while simultaneously another member of the family kicks those friends in the teeth.

--Algo D. Henderson

Answers To Give?

To the Editor:

(Oct. 29, 1965) CONGRATULATIONS on Roger Rapoport's recent article and editorial on the relationship between UMI and the University. Seemingly, Rapoport has researched thoroughly and offered the results of that research with commendable clarity and restraint.

I hope that he and The Daily will pursue this matter to the end and will not be frightened or discouraged from such pursuit. This University has some answers to give, and The Daily should keep prodding until such answers are forthcoming.

--Prof. Edward Shafter
College of Engineering

the president of University Microfilms, Inc., noted that "Under the present situation it becomes impossible to serve both as regent of the University and as an officer of University Microfilms Inc., especially in view of the plans for increased participation in the field of education by both University Microfilms and Xerox Corp., of which I am a director."

Three Questions

Kelley concluded in his opinion that three basic questions exist in Power's business relationship with the University.

"--Microfilm cameras owned by the company have been placed in the University library without rental;

"--The undergraduate shelf list was sold without royalty payments to the University;

"--Copies of doctoral dissertations were sold by University Microfilms and microfilms of doctoral dissertations were stored in the company's vaults rather than in the vaults of the University library."

All three matters were originally raised in The Daily story last October 23 that touched off the investigation.

Affirms Integrity

Kelley said that, "There is no question of Mr. Power's motives, his integrity or his devotion to the interest of the University...it is clear that serving without compensation, Mr. Power has made invaluable contributions to the welfare of the University and to the cause of education and scholarship in the state and indeed, the nation..."#

An Editorial...

(March 12, 1966) EUGENE B. POWER announced yesterday he is submitting a letter of resignation to the Board of Regents. This has caused as much dismay to The Daily as it has to the rest of the University community. Though we originally disclosed the business transactions which raised questions about his relations with the University, we have never felt that the best way to improve those relations was to sever them and we emphasize today that his resignation has simply been offered, not accepted.

We felt, and still feel, that The Daily had an obligation as a newspaper to print the facts about the business transactions between Mr. Power's concern and the University. At the time they were reported, as now, they suggested the possibility of a technical conflict of interest. The questions about such business relationships were substantive and serious, and they had to be answered.

...

Regent Power, demonstrating his conviction that a public man's affairs and his business relationships must be beyond all legal reproach, submitted his letter of resignation yesterday. But the future of the University suggests that decision--which President Hatcher characterized correctly as a "harsh" one--ought not to remain standing.

Power has served the University in a distinguished manner for 10 years, during which he has displayed an unusually enlightened leadership among the Regents. His devotion to academic freedom is unquestioned. His support of the proposed University Residential College is strong. His contribution to higher education throughout the nation and the world through his microfilming services is remarkable.

Moreover, the University will shortly make major decisions affecting its future: the Residential College and the selection of its next president. Regent Power's value to the community is such that his loss in these critical times would be a severe blow to the University and its future progress.

HAVING SOUGHT IN THE PAST to ensure that his activities met with full sanction of the laws, and having yesterday resigned as Regent when an admittedly unclear clause appeared to preclude his joint role as Regent and businessman, Eugene Power is indeed above moral reproach...#

--THE ACTING SENIOR EDITORS

Pentagon Charges 'U' Is for 'Rich White Students,' Asks Opportunities for Negroes

More Negro Faculty, Students Urged Here; Better Image Asked

By MARK R. KILLINGSWORTH
Editor

Copyright 1966, The Michigan Daily

(Nov. 11, 1966) Charging that the University is known as a school "basically for 'rich white students'," a Defense Department document disclosed yesterday makes 25 recommendations for "broadening equal opportunities" here.

The confidential document--the result of an intensive Pentagon study made during July--says the University should do more to ensure equal employment opportunities in Ann Arbor, start special programs to recruit qualified Negro students and appoint Negro faculty members to University policy-making committees.

It also urges the creation of an office of equal opportunities with a professional staff reporting directly to President Hatcher.

The report itself--described by a Pentagon spokesman as "routine"--was undertaken to investigate the University's compliance with Title VI of the 1964 Civil Rights Act...

First Investigated

The University is believed to be the first university to be investigated for compliance with the Act. Studies will be made of other schools receiving federal aid--hence the designation of the study here as "routine"--but there was no indication as to why the University was studied first.

...

Employment Also Studied

The Detroit area Contracts Compliance Office of the Defense Department, which made the study, also made an investigation in October of the University's employment practices under an Executive Order by President Johnson banning discrimination in employment in Federally-supported programs. Qualified sources indicate no recommendations have yet been made in this area, however.

...

There are presently less than 25 Negro faculty and administrative staff members and less than 350 Negro students on campus.#

Clash Over Status of Recommendations

By ROGER RAPOPORT

(Nov. 12, 1966) University officials said yesterday that Defense Department recommendations stating that the school is known as "basically for rich, white students," are "confidential...should not have been made public" ...and are "not a report to the Defense Department."

...

Walter R. Greene, chief of the Detroit branch of the Contracts Compliance Office of the Defense Department, which made the survey, said in a telephone interview last night, "We simultaneously sent the recommendations to the University, for further discussion, and to our office in Washington, to inform them of our activities."

Greene said it is "standard operating procedure to give our recommendations to the parties involved."

He added, however, that University officials had specifically asked him to provide them with recommendations if they could be made available.

...

Executive Vice-President Marvin L. Niehuss said in a statement yesterday that the recommendations were "a set of confidential suggestions made to the University at its request in order to expand and broaden its existing equal opportunity programs" and "were sought by the University in advance of any formal report in an effort to broaden programs already under way."

Niehuss added that the recommendations are "not a report to the Defense Department and its release was not authorized by that department nor by the University."#

DOD Report Hits MSU Discrimination

By JIM HECK

Copyright 1968, The Michigan Daily

(March 15, 1968) A Department of Defense report attacking Michigan State University for racial discriminatory practices and recommending methods by which they should be eliminated has been filed with the Office for Civil Rights of the Department of Health, Education and Welfare, federal officials confirmed yesterday.

The 20-page document specifically attacks MSU's hiring procedures in non-academic minor job classifications.

Walter Greene, past director of the Detroit Contract Compliance Office of the defense department, said Michigan State "has failed to engage in affirmative action as specified under government contracts to seek Negroes to fill certain job areas."

...

The study, conducted under Executive Order 11114, says hiring procedures for academic and major job classifications were better than at the University of Michigan, but that hiring procedures for minor job classifications showed definite discrimination in every area except food service.

The confidential document asks MSU to establish an office of equal opportunities with a staff responsible directly to MSU President John Hannah. (Hannah is director of the United States Civil Rights Commission.)

Greene said the report's recommendations "were similar to those issued for the University of Michigan, but written for MSU's particular structure."

The document urges an educational program be set up to inform minority groups in Michigan of the vocational opportunities and on-the-job training offered at MSU.

It suggests the institution seek Negro faculty members from Negro colleges. Although not attacking explicitly MSU's academic hiring procedures, the report suggests improvement could be made.

...

Federal officials indicated that other schools in Michigan are also involved in similar reviews...#

MSU: Land Grab at Land Grant

By MARK LEVIN
Copyright, 1967, The Michigan Daily
(Nov. 8, 1967) EAST LANSING. In 1941, when John Hannah succeeded his father-in-law, Robert S. Shaw, as president of the Michigan State College, land here was cheap and plentiful.

As the renamed Michigan State University has blossomed into an educational institution of international reputation, many changes have come to pass.

...

And as enrollment soared and the campus mushroomed, so did land prices. For example, land adjacent to campus evaluated in 1941 at $200 an acre is today worth $5,000.

Rising property values have indeed proved profitable for local real estate dealers. University administrators have shared in the benefits.

* From 1940 to as recently as 1963, Hannah accumulated some 180 acres of land adjacent to the campus. He says he purchased the land for retirement purposes, but sold the parcel this past July for nearly $1 million to the Walter Neller Real Estate Company of Lansing. MSU Vice-President for Business and Finance and Treasurer Philip S. May is on the board of the Neller Company.

* Vice-President May himself and the Philip Jesse Company, a holding company whose secretary-treasurer is May's wife, purchased land from the Whiteley Foundation on Michigan Avenue, opposite the MSU campus last year. After securing a $1.1 million mortgage from Michigan National Bank (MSU's chief fiscal agent), the Philip Jesse Company contracted to build an office building on the site. The building was completed this past summer. A portion of the building is leased to the International Business Machines, Inc. IBM does a substantial amount of business with MSU.

* The secretary of the Whiteley Foundation is Harry Hubbard, a Lansing attorney. One of Hubbard's clients is Heatherwood Farms Dairy, which was recently awarded a $545,000 contract to supply MSU with dairy products.

What is the propriety of these activities?

Article IV, section 10 of the 1963 Michigan Constitution states:

"No member of the legislature nor any state officer shall be interested directly or indirectly in any contract with the state or any political subdivision thereof which shall cause a substantial conflict of interest. The legislature shall further implement this provision by appropriate legislation."

...

In 1940, while still a specialist in poultry science at MSU, Hannah began to acquire land in neighboring Meridian Township, across the street from the MSU outer boundary on Hagadorn Road. Steadily increasing his holdings until as late as 1963, Hannah reportedly hoped one day to retire there and continued his agricultural research.

However, this past summer, Hannah sold his 180 acre nest-egg to the Neller Company for an estimated $5000 an acre, according to an August Detroit News article.

In an interview with The Daily, Richard Neller, a director of the Neller realty firm, confirmed the purchase of the property, but would not comment on the reported sale price.

...

MSU Vice-President for Business and Finance and Treasurer since 1947 Philip J. May is one of the five directors of the Neller Company, according to the firm's annual report filed with the Attorney General in May, 1967.

...

However, a spokesman for the Neller Company says May was at one time on the board but has since resigned his post.

Holding Company

The Neller Company rents an office building at 1111 Michigan Ave. An agent for the Neller Company says the building is owned by Philip May. However, according to records in the Ingham County Register of Deeds Office, the property is owned by the Philip Jesse Company.

The directors of the Philip Jesse Company are Mrs. Viola May, wife of Vice-President Philip Jesse May, Robert G. May of Sioux Falls, South Dakota, and Warren May of Pierre, South Dakota.

In order to construct the 45,000 square-foot office building, the Philip Jesse Company secured a $1.1 million mortgage from the Michigan National Bank. According to MSU controller Paul Rampsa, Michigan National Bank serves as the chief financial agent for MSU.

...

May purchased the land on which the building is situated from the John and Elizabeth Whiteley Foundation, a charitable trust... May bought two parcels of land from the foundation, one in the name of Philip J. and Viola May and the other in the name of the Philip Jesse Company. May sold part of the first parcel to Alan Ginsburg and Steven Annas...

...

Harry Hubbard, secretary of the Whiteley Foundation, is according to Martindale and Hubbell Law Directory, the legal representative for Heatherwood Farms Dairy. Heatherwood Farms was recently awarded a $545,000 contract to supply MSU with dairy products. MSU closed down its own dairy because they said it was inadequate to meet growing needs. Heatherwood Farms submitted the lowest of seven bids, according to an official at the MSU Food Stores Office...#

Kelley rules MSU VP in conflict of interest

By STEVE NISSEN
Special To The Daily
(June 19, 1968) LANSING--The private business activities of Michigan State University Vice President Philip May represent a conflict of interest, State Atty. Gen. Frank Kelley ruled yesterday.

A member of MSU's Board of Trustees called for May's resignation last night at a hastily called news conference.

"The day in which Phil can be of any value to the university...is behind us," said Trustee C. Allen Harlan.

Rep. Jack Faxon (D-Detroit), who requested Kelley's opinion last November following a story in The Daily revealing May's relationship with International Business Machines, predicted, "May is going to have to resign or face a major challenge in the courts."..#

Diana Oughton, 1942-70: Portrait of a radical

By JIM NEUBACHER
News Editor

1970, The Michigan Daily

(March 21, 1970) Diana Oughton died March 6, her body and her dreams of a better world shattered by a dynamite blast in a Greenwich Village townhouse.

How she got to New York, the long, evolutionary process that took Diana from a quiet upbringing in a rural midwestern town to revolutionary bomb-building in the nation's largest city involves a chain of events and mental decisions not well understood by those who knew her less than intimately.

...

Diana was the daughter of the most prestigious man in town, a bank vice president and candidate for the state legislature who was wealthy, popular, and philanthropic. She had lived in the conservative atmosphere of Dwight [Illinois] through her first year of high school, making straight A's and sitting on the student council. Then she went off to private, exclusive schools in the East.

A classmate, John Kresi, who has remained in Dwight and now coaches and teaches at the junior high school there, remembers Diana this way:

"She was real nice, popular, by far the smartest kid in the class. You'd never know she had a lot of money in her family because she was interested in people, she cared about them, and she was active in things."

Kresi agrees with the assessment of another close friend of the family who says Diana made a "complete reversal from the way she was years ago." Kresi was one of the few people in Dwight who knew of Diana's membership in Students for a Democratic Society, and he was still shocked at the news of her death in what police have described as a "bomb factory."

Diana left Dwight to attend her last three years of high school at the Madeira School in Greenway, Virginia, and then went to study at fashionable Bryn Mawr, from which she graduated in 1963.

It was at this juncture in her life that Diana made her first great commitment to a cause in an attempt to help those who needed it. She went to Guatemala for the American Friends Service Committee to

--Daily--Thomas R. Copi

A leader in the James Gang

teach reading, staying there for two years and returning in late 1965. According to friends, this is where Diana began to get "radicalized."

"The thing that happened to Diana is what happened to a whole lot of people in our generation," says a friend who knew her well in Ann Arbor. "It was the Kennedy thing. After he was killed in '63, she went to Guatemala for two years, and tried to do something. When she came back, she understood a lot. She understood America's imperialism first hand, and began to develop a good class analysis."

Yet Diana was far from being a full-fledged radical when she returned. She came to Ann Arbor in 1966 to enroll in the University as a master's candidate in elementary education. It was then she became involved in the Ann Arbor Community School, an experimental innovative project in elementary education. At the community school, free education was provided to young children in the Summerhill tradition of unfettered, curiosity-stimulating education.

And it was at the community school where she fell in love with Bill Ayers, son of a prominent, rich corporation head in

Chicago, a concerned young man who was one of the prime movers of the community school project.

For the next three years, until her death two weeks ago, she and Ayers progressed on parallel courses, loving, counseling, and influencing each other politically and socially.

...

It was a bad experience at the community school that provided the launching point for both Ayers and Diana to become active in SDS. State building inspectors threatened to close the school unless large amounts of money were invested to bring the building up to code. Rather than do that the school moved, moved again when the state officials repeated their demands and finally, faced with the prospect of spending nearly $50,000 for a new building, closed for good.

"Bill became disillusioned when the city and the state stepped on him and the community school," says a friend who now lives in New York.

Soon after, in the summer of '68, Ayers and Diana went with Eric Chester, a local SDS leader at the time, to the SDS national convention in East Lansing.

Fresh from a struggle with the system over the school, they found appeal in the words of the SDS leaders there. Both became active, and began what was to become a lightning-fast radical evolution.

Back in Ann Arbor in the fall of '68, Ayers and Diana emerged as members of the militant Jesse James Gang, which managed to oust Chester and his campus-oriented followers from the local SDS chapter. From there, Diana and Ayers moved quickly into first the regional, and then national ranks of SDS. By December '68, at a national SDS convention in Ann Arbor, Ayers was being talked about as a potential national officer of the organization.

Diana moved with Bill during this period, prompting the uninformed to say that she was "duped" by Ayers, that she was led into radicalism while blinded by love. But both close friends and detached observers who knew her during this period are emphatic in their insistence that Diana knew what she was doing, that she thought for herself.

"She was Bill's sidekick, but she wasn't an ideologue of any kind," says one of the observers. Not a radical himself, this observer said Diana thought for herself, and argued rationally about politics. "She was definitely political but never strident," he says.

Student Government Council president Marty McLaughlin, as a leader of the Radical Caucus during the SDS power struggle with the Jesse James Gang, faced Diana across the semantic firing lines. He makes the same point:

"She was one of the few on their side you could talk to without wanting to punch in the nose," he says.

And a local police detective whose job it is to keep an eye on student radicals says, "She was a radical, but you could communicate with her."

...

That Diana was an independent radical thinker rather than "Bill's girl" following blindly in his political footsteps is further evidenced by the change which took place in their relationship around the time of the December '68 SDS national convention here in Ann Arbor. To the outside observer, it looked as if they were "breaking up." But that isn't what happened.

"What happened," says an Ann Arbor radical who knew Diana as well as anybody, "is that their relationship got more revolutionary. They moved beyond monogamy."

A radical young woman who knew Diana well puts it even more succinctly.

"Diana understood what Women's Liberation meant far better than anyone I ever knew," she says. "And she lived it. She wasn't just concerned with the pill, or abortion, or equal employment. She knew those were just symptoms."

Diana, she explained, believed that a liberated woman must take her place as a radical thinker and doer in the realm of the international struggle, relating to her primarily male colleagues as a revolutionary, not as a woman. Doing this, the friend asserts, proved that Diana was not a slave to Ayers' intellect.

...

It was during that summer [1969] that the "Weatherman" was born, child of the long-festering, three-way split in SDS between the campus-oriented student power advocates, the socialists interested in a worker-student alliance, and the militant revolutionaries led by Mark Rudd of Columbia. It was this last faction which became the Weatherman, and which claimed 10,000 members six months later--among them Bill Ayers and Diana Oughton.

In the fall, Diana and Ayers went their separate ways for a while. She moved to Flint in September, where, in a house on E. Fourth St. she set up regional Weatherman headquarters with two other members...

In October, she came to Ann Arbor "on business" and a friend recalls that he noticed that she had become more militant. She went to a meeting at Canterbury House, he says, where she tried to persuade people to join in a "Weatheraction" scheduled for the following week in Chicago. The majority of the audience, the observer remembers, turned on Diana, condemning the militancy of Weatherman, and accusing her of attempting to lead sheep to the slaughter.

She went to Chicago herself, and was arrested Oct. 9 along with 16 other women during a bloody, window-smashing, police-fighting march by over 300 of the militants.

Released on bail, she went back to Flint, where she remained until November, planning for action at the Nov. 15 moratorium action in Washington...

Diana left Flint at the end of November, and never returned... Little is known about her activities between then and her death March 6 in New York, except that she helped to organize and participated in the first national Weatherman conference in Flint in late December, '69. At that conference, police and FBI officials believe, plans were laid for a series of violent actions in the spring of 1970.

"The fact that they kept quiet and didn't talk about what they were doing is the reason they were able to do what they did," says a radical who had some limited contact with her during the last three months of her life. He describes how Diana, and her circle of close friends, grew more and more radical:

"A whole new collective consciousness came out of the internal struggle of SDS," he says. "They were becoming more organized, more sure of themselves, more revolutionary. They were the Americong. The government drops bombs on the people in Vietnam, so they felt someone should put bombs in buildings in New York City. They adopted an analysis on an international warfare level, and they lived it.

"The group she was with, they moved so fast in their heads and in their actions that it's hard to speculate where she was going or where she would have wound up," he continues. "And now we'll never know."..#

Sheriff boycotts firm for refusing election posters
Tow service loses business

By JONATHAN MILLER
Feature Editor

(Sept. 24, 1972) County Sheriff Douglas Harvey has ordered his men to boycott an Ann Arbor towing company which refused to display Harvey campaign posters on its property, The Daily learned yesterday.

In a memorandum directed to all sheriff's department personnel yesterday, Harvey told his officers to call on an alternative towing company in cases where wrecker service is needed by the department.

The sheriff is presently seeking his third four-year term of office.

...

The memo did not cite a reason for the change, but highly reliable sources within the Sheriff's Department said it was because the manager of Northside [Towing Company] had last week ordered Harvey campaign posters removed from his company's yard at 3127 S. Wagner Rd.

Neither Harvey nor Capt. Wilson could be reached for comment on the memo last night.

Undersheriff Harold Owings, who is Harvey's Republican opponent in the Nov 7 general election, said that Northside offered the department "very good service.

"They're very competent people as far as I know," he added. "The indication I get is that the memo was issued because they won't support him."

Democratic candidate Frederick Postill, a former deputy fired by Harvey for "insubordination," said that the memo was, "a typical Harvey stunt."

"I've talked with drivers from other towing companies who told me they were unable to get sheriff's department business because they didn't do the sheriff personal favors," Postill said.#

Huge scalping racket hits Dylan concert

By DAN BIDDLE
and JEFF DAY

Copyright 1974, The Michigan Daily

(Feb. 1, 1974) Hundreds of choice main floor tickets for tomorrow night's Bob Dylan concert at Crisler Arena have been systematically rerouted and sold at exorbitant prices in violation of the concert contract.

A Daily investigation has produced evidence that employes and associates of the Dylan tour's Detroit promotional agency... have been directly involved in a huge ticket-scalping operation.

REPRESENTATIVES of [a Detroit promoter] cooperated with the concert's bonded Detroit agent in a scheme to remove at least 300 and possibly as many as 1000 choice seats from the concert's contract-designated ticket distribution plan.

The abducted tickets were then passed out to a group of at least five scalpers who offered the tickets wholesale to other sellers or sold the seats themselves at prices ranging from $25 to $75 for seats on the main floor.

Bill Graham, one of the nation's foremost rock impresarios and promoter of Dylan's tour, reacted with anxiety when contacted last night at Madison Square Garden, where Dylan was performing.

"THE ONE THING we're not is scalpers or ripoffs," said Graham when told of the Detroit scalping network. "If this thing (scalping) has actually taken place, I assure you, I'll take action before we have an Ann Arbor show."

Graham emphasized that the show would go on. "What do you think I am, crazy? We'll have a show. But so far we haven't encountered a single goddamn scalping incident on this tour, and I'll see to it that the conditions (in Ann Arbor) will change before the show goes on.

"The main concern of (Dylan and his backup group, The Band) is for the audience. We aren't doing this thing for these smucks that wave $100 bills and rip off tickets," he said...

...

A CHECK run by The Daily on high-priced ticket offers produced several near-identical accounts of the ticket racket from its lower-echelon scalpers.

...

THE TICKET SCALPING network described by The Daily's sources violates the Dylan concert contract as well as state statutes barring conspiracy to "establish an agency or suboffice for the sale of seat tickets of admission...to a place of public entertainment, at a price greater than the sale of seats at the box office."

...

The scalping ring violates the contract's provisions stating "no bulk ticket sales" and barring promoters...from purchasing their own seats in front of row 18 of the main floor.

One Ann Arbor scalper who has been peddling main floor seats at $50 each said he could supply "any amount" of tickets...

...

Another local scalper said "...two whole sections" [were held back].

A SOURCE CLOSE to the ticket racket described a meeting held early this month... 10 to 15 "middlemen" gave them blocks of choice tickets, and arranged seat prices and percentages for each "middleman."

The source, who joined the three scalpers in refusing to be identified, said the "middlemen" then distributed the tickets to scalpers for sale in Ann Arbor and Detroit.

...

UAC-Daystar collected money orders for Crisler Arena's 13,600 available seats from a long line of Dylan fans at the Hill Auditorium box office Dec. 16. ...the ticket orders [were delivered] in 100-envelope bundles, along with the tickets to the Cobo Hall box office in Detroit on Dec. 31.

Cobo's ticket agent had been previously designated as the "single bonded ticket agent" required by the Dylan concert. His assistant received the ticket order bundles... UAC staffers vigorously maintain that "every precaution was taken" to keep envelopes in the same order as the buyers who placed orders at Hill.

But most of the best-in-the-house $8.50 tickets--in Crisler's main floor A-B-C sections--were removed from the bundles at the Cobo box office sometime between Dec. 31...and late January, when the scalpers began advertising in area newspapers.

The first ads--offering "top quality seats" for prices ranging from $25 to $75--appeared in mid-January, pre-dating the official ticket mailings by several days.

HENCE THE scalpers' large blocs of tickets could not have been obtained through purchase of the Hill Aud. box office. None of these tickets reached buyers until Jan. 21--one day after the official Cobo mailing.

UAC first became concerned with the possibility of ticket fraud when dozens of irate Dylan fans called to complain about receiving low-quality seats despite the buyers' high position in the line at Hil. Other callers said they had held positions higher than 2,000 in the Hill line, but received refunds rather than seats.

The planned ticket-ordering procedure would have covered a maximum of 8,000 seats--four to a person--before reaching the two thousandth position in line. Hence, Crisler's 13,600-seat capacity could not have been filled by the time "customer 2,000" reached the Hill ticket window.

A DAILY SURVEY of ticket holders and UAC complaints has shown that no more than 50 of the Hill customers received seats on the main floor. That figure leaves more than 700 of the choice seats unaccounted for.#

UAC secures ticket refund

By JEFF DAY

(May 21, 1974) National rock promoter Bill Graham came through late last week on a promise made after February's Bob Dylan concert to reimburse local concert-goers who lost money because of ticket scalping.

Graham made the promise in an unscheduled appearance at the end of Dylan's Crisler arena concert, after a Daily investigation revealed that a Detroit... scalping ring sold choice seats for as much as $100 each.

On the basis of his promise, Graham sent a check to Ann Arbor promoter UAC-Daystar to help cover cost overruns as well as additional expenses caused by the ticket problems.

According to UAC-Daystar coordinator Sue Young... "Bill Graham made good on every promise he made."..#

Inefficiency at 'U' Hospital leads to neglect of patients

By AMY SALTZMAN

(Jan. 31, 1979) Behind the University Hospital's reputation as a top-flight medical center lies a stark reality of patient neglect, confusion, and endless delays, according to patients, nurses, and doctors.

...

THE CRITICISMS of 'U' Hospital, the first university-owned and operated teaching hospital in the country and a recognized leader in research among medical facilities nation-wide, have primarily focused on the overwhelming inefficiency of the system that powers the hospital.

Dr. Richard Fiddian-Green, an associate professor of surgery at the Medical Center, was so outraged by this inefficiency and its effect on the treatment of his seriously ill daughter that he wrote a letter of complaint to top hospital administrators. The following is a summary of that letter:

Last October, Fiddian-Green's daughter developed meningitis. On Saturday, Oct. 7, she was brought to the Pediatric Walk-in Clinic where she was given a lumbar puncture. Performing the analysis of such spinal fluid should take approximately five minutes. In this case, the doctor and his daughter waited for over three hours.

...

IT TOOK an all-out effort on Fiddian-Green's part to find the specimen and have it analyzed. During the search for the missing spinal fluid, the doctor discovered that the machine used to examine the fluid was broken and that no arrangements appeared to have been made to have the machine repaired or to examine the fluid by hand.

Fiddian-Green next went to the Biochemical Division where he found that its staff had "not received" the specimen, even though it had been sent hours before. The doctor was then told that the specimen had "just arrived" and the short analysis was finally performed--more than three hours after the lumbar puncture had been taken.

...

[Hospital] Director [Jeptha] Dalston said that problems of this kind are, in part, inherent to an institution like 'U'

Hospital. "There are hundreds of thousands of lab tests taken every day, and we simply don't have the modern systems that we need to handle all of them," he said.

...

IN THE Fiddian-Green case, a lack of coordination was a major reason for the delay. "In this particular instance, the medical technologist did not recognize that it was a priority specimen and consequently, there was a substantial delay," said Bruce Goldstrom, the assistant in clinical affairs.

...

According to Dalston, many of the problems involved in the Fiddian-Green case were a direct result of the ancient hospital structure. By virtue of design the new building will be more efficient, he added.

...

CONTINUOUS aggravation... even led one frustrated doctor to comment that 'U' Hospital "is not a real hospital. The system is terrible. The place is a mess," he said.

The doctor, a two-year resident of the hospital, said that he spends an average of 120 hours a week at 'U' Hospital and that 50-60 per cent of that time is devoted to "secretarial work."

...

And a reporter's tour of the hospital revealed that doctors are performing tasks generally assigned to nurses or other employees...

A major problem frequently voiced by doctors and patients involves the amount of time that patients spend waiting around as a result of frequent bureaucratic mix-ups.

Waiting around for extended periods of time is particularly prevalent for patients moved for testing, according to [House Officers Association president Dr. Harry]Colfer...

...

DALSTON SAID that the combination of a shortage of personnel and the enormous size of the hospital often necessitates leaving one patient to retrieve another. The hospital director stated, however, that the Hospital Replacement Project will solve some of these difficulties. Because the new hospital will be

structurally more efficient, it will be easier to reach patients, he said.

In the meantime, however, the hospital's obvious personnel shortages have severely restricted the staff's ability to attend to the patients' basic needs, according to staff members.

...

According to one nurse, the staff shortage is the result of the hospital's high turnover rate. The two main reasons she cited for this high turnover rate were that the hospital's wages are not competitive with other hospitals in the area and that the hospital's "tense" atmosphere makes it an unpleasant place to work.

...

Another area of patient dissatisfaction centered around the overall maintenance of the hospital. Patients repeatedly showed concern over the lack of cleanliness in the wards or rooms and in the toilet and washing facilities.

DIANE HAITHMAN, a student volunteer at the hospital last summer who distributed patient attitude surveys, said that patients were worried about the disease that could spread as a result of all the filth. "The bathrooms were a mess," said Haithman. "Old patients who were given enemas often couldn't control their bowels and the results would make the situation even more unpleasant."

...

INSPECTIONS made regularly by the State Department of Public Health further confirm these maintenance problems. The last inspection was performed on November 17, 1978 and pinpoints the sixth and eighth floors of the main hospital as being particularly poorly maintained.

...

Many of these maintenance problems can, in part, be attributed to the outdated structure that houses the main hospital. The main hospital is over fifty years old--10 years older than the normal maximum life for a hospital of its kind--and, consequently is hampered in providing relatively modern comforts.

...

THEY ARE problems which presumably will be rectified by the new hospital--scheduled to begin construction in 1980. But the question that still remains in the minds of many doctors and staff is whether the extreme inefficiency currently hampering patient care can be solved by a shiny new hospital.#

Back door admissions: Lying to get in

By GEORGEA KOVANIS

(April 24, 1985) Ask Caroline how she managed to get herself into the University and she'll candidly admit that she lied her way in.

After being told by her high school counselor that her grade point average didn't meet admissions requirements for LSA, Carolina decided upon another approach. She fibbed to University admissions counselors, feigning interest in a career in parks and recreation, and enrolled in the phys-ed program. She transferred into LSA the next year.

...

The procedure is simple.

ALL STUDENTS have to do is enter a back door, a program such as physical education or natural resources that has lower entrance standards or is in less demand than LSA. If these students are able to keep their cumulative GPA above 2.0 for a year, they can then move over to LSA.

"I just really had to feed them a lot of BS because I was lying to get in," said Caroline. "I told them I wanted to be a forest ranger because I didn't know what you could be with a physical education degree.

"I knew somebody who had done it before. I knew it was so easy to transfer out once you get in," she said of her decision to enter LSA through a back door.

...

Most administrators say back dooring isn't a problem. Some say it's not happening at all. But talk to students, and they'll admit that it occurs a great deal.

How frequently? No one knows. Admissions department officials say they don't keep statistics on the number of students participating in cross-campus transfers. And in any case, they reason, it would be impossible to find out whether or not a student is using a program as a back door.

"A STUDENT who might consider doing such a thing is unlikely to announce it," said Robert Holbrook, associate vice president for academic affairs.

"You face a real problem when you're trying to second-guess a student who says their life long dream has always been a career in natural resources."

...

"WE'VE HAD incidents where students are in a program just to get to Michigan," Erickson said. "There's absolutely no reason for a student to choose a program they don't have an interest in.

"I would say any student who contemplated doing this would be in for a great deal of grief," Erickson said.

But according to John Bassett, natural resources school associate dean, students aren't being deterred by stern warnings like Erickson's.

"I'd say 45 of our 80 freshmen (transferred) if I had to make a guess," Bassett said. The majority of these students who made up the freshman class of 1984 transferred because they were using natural resources as a back door into LSA, he added.

...

"There's no question they have used us...as a way to get into the University," he said. "We've been used as a back door. You tell me how to prevent it."

...

The school is, however, taking some steps to cut down on the number of students using natural resources as a back door, Bassett said. And although he would not detail the plan, he said the school's new freshman curriculum which requires calculus and chemistry courses is helping to ease backdooring.

...

THE SITUATION Bassett described is similar to that in the Division of Physical Education where program chair Dee Edington estimates that half of the members of 1984's freshman class will transfer out of the program by the time they are juniors.

Edington, however, said that this transfer rate is not unusually high. "If as a high school senior you had to choose geology or English, you'd have 50 or 60 percent transfer," Edington said. "You come into LSA, you have an option of 30 departments, or whatever they have."

But in any case, Edington admits that at least some of those transfers are the result of backdooring.

WHY DO students single out physical education and natural resources for use as backdoors?

In phys-ed there are no minimum admissions standards. "We don't have any cut-offs. It's whatever admissions can give us," Edington said, adding that the school simply asks the admissions office for students to fill its freshman class.

...

In natural resources, students with high school grade points of 3.0 are likely to be admitted because the school's applicant pool is so small. There are simply fewer qualified students from which to choose.

CAROLINE SAID she doesn't regret her decision to back door her way into the University.

"I feel I should have my opportunity to get the best education I can."

"I don't feel bad about (backdooring) because just as I'm cheating someone out of a school they want to be in, I'm being cheated of the opportunity to succeed here," she said.

"I CAN'T be so altruistic and cheat myself out of my education."

Despite Caroline's reasoning, Erickson maintains that back door students are indeed cheating others of a chance to succeed in physical education or natural resources.

"A student who goes into a program simply to get into that institution is denying another student," Erickson said. "They are deliberately excluding another student" who wants to be in that program.

...

Sometimes, [Natural Resources Prof. Charles] Olson said, he is able to interest back door students in natural resources.

John, who would speak only on the condition that his real name not be used, is one of those students.

"I had too much fun in high school and you can't get into Michigan engineering school with what I had," he said. "I applied to LSA and they turned me down."

After being turned down by LSA, John applied to the School of Natural Resources with the intention of transferring into LSA. And unlike most back door students, John decided to stay in the school.

"I PERSONALLY don't think (back dooring) is bad because a lot of people like me had too much fun in high school," John said... "Getting into the University is just like a job. If you can get into a corporation, you're golden."#

Series To Unveil Red Fronts
Communists Still Active on Campus;
LYL Seen as Leading Party Link

(EDITOR'S NOTE: This is the first in a series of interpretive articles dealing with the activities of the Communist Party and Communist-front organizations in Ann Arbor and at the University...)

By ZANDER HOLLANDER
Daily Feature Editor

(Jan. 7, 1953) This will not be a pleasant story.

In the course of its telling it will reveal that Communists have been and are now active at the University, that they carry on as Party groups and covertly as front organizations, that their number, although small, is greater than is generally assumed and that the number of fellow travelers -- both willing and duped -- is greater still.

...

THE EMPHASIS on Communist Party "Front" groups and fellow travelers cannot be overdone when discussing the local scene. The Party, in Ann Arbor and at the University, conducts most of its "public" activities through one such front, the Labor Youth League.

These are "public" only in that the League's name is openly associated with some ventures.

An example is the leaflet slipped under student doors of the East Quadrangle between 4 and 5 a.m. on December 3, 1950, exhorting students to "Silence the war mongers! Demand an end to the bloodshed in Korea! Stop World War III!"

This mimeographed propaganda sheet, titled "13 Steps to World Suicide," was typical of LYL moves in its surreptitious distribution. It was attributed only to "the Labor Youth League of Michigan."

* * *

THIS PATTERN has persisted since the League's local inception, revealed in The Daily on March 23, 1950. When Daily editors Leon Jaroff and Don McNeil charged LYL with being "hopelessly Russophile" and with adopting "cloak and dagger methods" of secrecy, its local chairman... retorted in the letters columns:

The initial basis for the series was a secret report of the LYL -- at that time a CP affiliate -- detailing its action plan for the coming year in working into sundry liberal organizations. The report -- whose authenticity was not disputed -- was leaked to The Daily by a disaffected member (or was he an FBI plant? In retrospect one can never be sure).

...the Woodward-style investigative reporting by Zander Hollander; midnight rendezvous in deserted rail yards, furtive encounters with CP representatives, and a Daily raid on the LYL communications weapon -- of all things, a mimeograph machine.

M. Crawford Young, '52

"The League is not a secretive organization -- we invite and welcome the participation of all interested persons in our group discussions and meetings. We intend to apply for recognition as a campus organization this semester."

The Labor Youth League made no effort to gain recognition as a campus organization that semester or afterward. In any case, it is doubtful whether the University would have accorded recognized status to LYL at the time.

...

Certainly the League hasn't a glimmer of a chance of securing recognition today. For it should be noted here that the University of Michigan has not been easy pickings for the Communists or their front. Its faculty and administration, all fully aware of the danger from this direction, and University authorities, have consistently held Communist activities under surveillance.

LYL's obsession with secrecy has not abated either. The League refuses to make public its membership lists, the number of members, time or place of meetings, local structure and leadership, sources of income other than dues or activities.

...

Locally, the League's position as the leading Communist front is well established. Almost all of Ann Arbor's Communists are members of, or are associated with, the League. Its activities are determined by a core of students and townspeople who are members of the Ralph Naefus club, Washtenaw County's Party cell...#

By CRAWFORD YOUNG
Daily Managing Editor

(Jan. 7, 1953) **THE BEGINNING** today of a Daily series of articles describing the activities of the Communist Party and its front organizations in Ann Arbor and on the campus merits a few words of explanation.

... we wish to make it clear that we do not in any way subscribe to hysteria as a method of dealing with the Communist problem which confronts our society today... To make political capital out of the real need for information and awareness in this sphere is to become a party to as despicable a transgression of the American ideals of freedom and democracy as the invidious subversion of the Communists themselves.

...

The University has always been aware of this situation, and is on the whole to be commended for its handling of it. Despite several serious missteps, the administration has walked the tightrope of rational academic freedom which must be their traverse across the chasm of hysteria and consequent dangers of thought control and regimentation.

...

The sole purpose of this series is to raise the informational level and awareness in an area where knowing your enemy is half the battle.#

SL Debates Censuring Daily

By HARRY LUNN

(Jan. 15, 1953) Parliamentary entanglements prevented a vote on a motion to censure The Daily for its series of articles on campus Communist activities in the final minutes of last night's Student Legislature meeting.

...

INTRODUCED by Paula Levin, '55, the proposal read, in part: "We feel that the methods of journalism used in the recent series on Communist activity on this campus were those which stifle discussion rather than facilitating the free discussion of ideas.

"Therefore, in the interests of preserving a free and objective atmosphere, the SL expresses its disapproval of the recent series of articles."..#

Details of LYL Report Told
Stalinist Document Lauds Group
For Infiltration, Urges Expansion

(EDITOR'S NOTE: This is the third in a series of interpretive articles dealing with the Communist Party and Communist front organizations in Ann Arbor and at the University.)

By ZANDER HOLLANDER
Daily Feature Editor

(Jan. 9, 1953) The dog-eared sheaf of Daily bond stationery is a verbatim copy of a secret directive and report of the Labor Youth League, Ann Arbor's major Communist-front group.

The original, written by a key figure in the Ralph Naefus Club, local Communist Party cell, passed through The Daily's hands for several hours last spring.

* * *

TITLED "Report on the Evaluation of Last Semester's Work and Perspectives for the Future," the confidential document looks back on the LYL's operations from September to January, 1952, and exhorts the local workers to do better in the future.

Highlights of the report:

1. Its claim that the League has organized fronts on campus.

The report back-pats members for successful establishment of two recognized student groups at the University. Subsequent events indicate that LYL is organizing a projected third group.

2. Its emphasis on agitation among Negroes.

...

3. Its call for an immediate expansion of membership.

Declaring that "no attention has been paid to recruiting until the beginning of this semester (spring, 1952)," the tract demands that "our work... include the perspective of expanding the League, of training students in the science of Marxism. The National Student Commission of the League recommends that membership be doubled by the end of the semester."

Here, and elsewhere, the document orders "special attention... to the recruiting of Negro students."

* * *

INTERLARDED LIBERALLY with quotes from Lenin, Stalin and Gus Hall, Communist Party brass hat now serving a term for conviction under the Smith Act, the document opens with a plea that the League's "main aim is to be more effective in mass work." A "united front," it goes on, is essential.

"The high road to achieving peace and socialism is through the successful application of the united front in mass work."

But, the report chides, "the prerequisite . . . is the mastery of Marxism-Leninism. We are weak in many aspects of Marxist-Leninist theory and practice. In order to achieve our goals, we ourselves have to go through a transformation, ridding ourselves of capitalist ideology and values (such as hurt feelings in the face of criticism) and remaking ourselves into the kind of people who can carry on Leninist work."

* * *

THE REPORT goes on to lash the group's members for the "low quality" of "our methods in collective work." Scoring "individualism" which "perpetuates onesidedness, and handicaps our struggles," the document claims "the membership and the leadership did not get the advantage of enough collective discussion."

What is even more heinous, group members have been too sensitive to criticism from their leaders and comrades, as well as "frequently taking it in the wrong way."

...

Written in the pedantic, rhetorical style of Stalin himself, the LYL's report and evaluation bristles with the Soviet Premier's "obvious question -- obvious answer" technique and parrots his passion for sloganizing abstract material for easy memorization...#

Coed Reveals Herself as FBI Informant

By ALICE B. SILVER
Associate Editorial Director

(April 20, 1954) "This is to certify that I, ..., have been giving information on my fellow students to the Federal Bureau of Investigation."

So reads the first sentence of a notarized affidavit. It is signed by a 19 year old coed at the University.

The two principal characters are the coed and a male graduate student -- the same unnamed student who has been subpoenaed by the Un-American Activities Committee to appear in Lansing May 10. He has in the past avowed membership in the Communist Party.

The coed, who withdrew from the University a week ago, was a junior majoring in political science. She is a Canadian citizen.

* * *

THE STORY HAS an ordinary beginning. The graduate student asked the coed for a date. "I had heard of him and was interested in his ideas," she explained in a telephone interview between here and a Canadian city.

...

"Because I am an alien and my parents are employed in Ann Arbor, I wondered whether my association with him would be dangerous," she said.

* * *

FOR ADVICE ON the matter she went to Robert Klinger, Assistant Counsellor of the International Center. At this point the facts become blurred.

The affidavit states: "I contacted the FBI after being strongly urged to do so by Mr. Robert Klinger..."

Klinger told The Daily she "asked me if her association with persons of known left tendencies would endanger her immigration status. I told her the current law (McCarran Act) does frown upon anything that would appear Communistic on the part of an alien and is a deportable offense.

"She asked me what she should do and I said I couldn't counsel her on that matter. She then asked me if she should take information to the FBI and I told her to do what she felt in her heart was her duty."

* * *

"KLINGER'S STATEMENT shocks me," the coed commented. "I trusted him.

"Klinger told me there was no danger in dating the student. However, he did strongly urge me to contact the FBI about the matter.

"It was something he said as I left his office that gave me the idea to do what I did.

"He asked me to try and get information for him on two questions: 1. Who has been placing 'Communist' literature on the magazine racks of the International Center? and 2. Who wrote the pseudonymous letter to The Daily attacking the International Center?"

"Of course I would like to know the answers to those two questions," Klinger commented.

"I may have asked her to get me such information, but I don't remember. I have asked others for similar information. But this is not the kind of information I would pass on to a Federal agency."

* * *

"I WENT TO the local FBI office," she said.

According to the coed she told the FBI agents she was dating the graduate student. She said she asked "whether my position would be better if I gave them information on the activities of this and other students. They said 'yes' but did not urge me to do anything against my will.

"I left the FBI office with a new sense of security."

...

"The FBI offered to pay me on three occasions but I refused," she said.

* * *

EXACTLY WHAT happened from the moment the coed says she left the FBI office in December to April 1, when she signed the affidavit in the presence of the graduate student, is not clear.

"She took down the names of people who came into my apartment," the graduate student claims. "This is what incensed me. People dropped in for all sorts of reasons. Now innocent people may get hurt."

"I assure you that is not true," she said. "That was not my job. I took down information on only a small group of people... mostly just on their conversations. I told the FBI only that which I thought would be interesting to them."

...

"I SPENT MOST of my time on a character study of the graduate student," said the coed. "I know it sounds rather weird but this is what the FBI led me to believe they wanted. No, I did not turn in information solely on him."

...

How often she reported to the FBI she could not say. "From what I gathered it was once every two weeks in the beginning and then less later," the graduate said.

"I phoned or wrote in my information. They do not like to be seen with a student.

"They gave me no specific instructions," she said. "Only the usual about telling no one and leaving no traces. And when I raised doubts about what I was doing, they gave me three stock answers so I could rationalize my doubts away. I've tried again and again to remember what those three answers were but I can't."

...

"They never said anything about it, of course, but I am pretty sure there are other student informers. I don't know their names or how many. I do know for a definite fact that there is one other." She wouldn't say how she knew this.

* * *

"HOW DID I feel during those four months?

"Well, you develop a sort of mental insulation. Your self-evaluation and self-judgment become dull.

"But insulation can only last so long."

* * *

ON THE afternoon of April 1 her "insulation," which had been gradually wearing away, disappeared.

"I became aware of exactly what I was doing."

In a scene they both called "hysterical" she told the graduate student the whole story. They went at once to a notary public to write and sign the affidavit.

"He was extremely decent about the whole thing."

"I don't entirely blame her -- the people who put her up to this are the ones responsible. It's a shame they would pick on someone her age. This shows how desperate they are for informers."..#

Hatcher Affirms Cooperation Policy

By ALICE B. SILVER
Associate Editorial Director

(April 21, 1954) A policy of cooperation with governmental investigating agencies was affirmed by University President Harlan Hatcher last night.

The President made his statement following the revelation [a] coed worked as an FBI informant.

...

* * *

PRESIDENT Hatcher said the University will answer for any "duly constituted governmental agency their questions pertaining to security or criminal actions."

The general reaction to the story of Miss Price was one of uneasiness and surprise.

"There is something basically wrong when in an educational institution there is an atmosphere of suspicion," commented Prof. Theodore Newcomb, chairman of the Social Psychology Program.

Prof. Philip Taylor of the political science department explained he does not think "this kind of thing imposes an atmosphere of fear except when an individual is in a government job or plans to seek such employment."

Student Legislature president Bob Neary, '54 BAd., said he would hope "the FBI does not take the kind of information Miss Price gave at face value but has someone more experienced check on it."

* * *

"**THIS KIND** of story makes us all feel uneasy," Prof. Arthur Carr of the English department said. "We begin to wonder what the FBI is doing, whom they are watching and why."

...

"I think it is a disgrace that legal minors should be encouraged to do that kind of thing," Prof. Marvin Felheim of the English department maintained.#

Rifled ROTC files contained clippings on radicals

By MARTIN HIRSCHMAN
Editor

(Oct. 18, 1970) Rifling ROTC files during the 33-hour takeover of North Hall last May, some demonstrators came upon an unpleasant surprise--a huge file on themselves.

The file, about two feet thick, was filled mostly with newspaper clippings of the activities of Students for a Democratic Society and other radical groups.

It also included dozens of glossy photographs with the faces of many radicals identified, and a series of communications from military and University officials on procedures for handling disruption of the military officers training program.

The file was stolen by some of the demonstrators and sources say most of its contents were destroyed when it became known late in the summer that the Federal Bureau of Investigation was probing the May 7-8 takeover.

But ROTC officers, who freely admit they were keeping the file, say they have again begun saving clippings and other information about anti-ROTC and left-wing activities.

Navy ROTC Cmdr. Russell E. Hurd says the file is kept solely to keep officers informed about and prepared for potential demonstrations and confrontations.

"It's just for our own information on which way SDS and other groups are going in regard to ROTC," Hurd says. He denies that information from the file is being transmitted to Naval Intelligence or to the FBI.

"We're not keeping an intelligence or subversives file," he says.

Hurd explains pictures in the files were taken both by ROTC personnel and University officials. ROTC officers took pictures at the specific request of the University, he says. "The University asked us to take some of those pictures," Hurd says. "We did so for a while until we ran out of film." He says the University request that pictures be taken was made by Chief Security Officer Rolland Gainsley, and University Photo Service cameraman Stuart Abbey, who has testified against many demonstrators involved in the 1969 bookstore sit-in concerning his bodily ejection from the LSA Bldg. by protesters who did not want their pictures taken.

In line with what he calls an attempt to "know our enemy," Hurd says clippings kept on file may include articles on University faculty members who express opposition to ROTC.

...

While Hurd claims the main purpose of the file is to keep up with anti-ROTC actions, much of the clipped material in parts of the file removed in May had little to do with military officers training program.

One folder labelled "SDS, etc." contained no mention of ROTC at all. Two articles concerned [an SDS member's] alleged assault of a professor during a recruiter demonstration last February.

Another clipping was a two-paragraph letter to the editor of The Daily from the Radical College, a group of left-wing faculty members and students which formed last year. The letter argued that those involved in disruptions during the strike for increased black admissions last spring should be granted amnesty. It made no mention of ROTC.

...

Another folder in the ROTC file was labelled "Student Demonstrations (Guidance)" and contained a series of communications with University and military officials.

One set of communications concerns several meetings between ROTC and University officials in September 1968. At these meetings, procedures for dealing with disruptions were agreed to and it was decided to increase off-hour security precautions for North Hall, the ROTC classroom and office building...#

Local SDS leader may have been U.S. undercover agent

By DAN BIDDLE
Copyright 1973, The Michigan Daily

(June 1, 1973) A Daily investigation has produced evidence that a former local activist and co-founder of Weatherman, the violence-prone offspring of Students for a Democratic Society (SDS), may have been a government agent.

Sources formerly close to SDS-Weatherman activities in Detroit, Ann Arbor, and several other cities, have linked ex-Weatherman [John Doe] to a confessed FBI informer and several bizarre SDS-related events in the late 1960's and early 70's.

THE SOURCES, who have asked to remain unidentified, have told reporters from The Daily and the Fifth Estate, a radical Detroit weekly, of a further possible connection between [Doe] and at least one secret federal grand jury hearing to probe SDS activities.

The sources further suggest that [Doe] may have been in contact with Guy Goodwin, a top official in the Justice Department's Internal Security Division. Goodwin headed government prosecution of radical figures in 1970 and 1971.

...

The Daily's sources have described "fairly clear" connections between [Doe] and Larry Grathwohl, a confessed FBI informer who is currently testifying before a grand jury probe of SDS in San Francisco.

...

An investigation last week of Grathwohl's activities in Ann Arbor and Detroit produced numerous accounts of events in 1968-70 which led many activists to believe that high-level SDS figures were on FBI or CIA payrolls.

Suspicion in each incident centered around [John Doe], one Ann Arbor source said. "If Grathwohl was the lieutenant pig, [Doe] was the general."

AFTER COMING to Ann Arbor "out of nowhere" in the fall of 1968, [Doe] almost immediately moved to the top of a split group within the local SDS chapter. While most local radicals continued to support much or all of SDS' complex ideological line, [Doe's] faction called for vaguely defined "militant street action" and repeatedly attempted to break up SDS meetings here.

...

[Doe] was one of several SDS leaders who founded Weatherman in the spring of 1969.

In the fall of that year, he was one of more than a dozen top-level "Weathermen" arrested in Chicago. According to The Daily's sources, the entire group spent several days in jail and underwent intense police questioning.

But [Doe] was released immediately.

...

SOURCES SAY suspicion around [Doe] intensified when the local office of the Radical Education Project (REP) was burglarized in early 1969.

REP, an umbrella group including teachers and students, shared its office with Ann Arbor SDS. The burglars removed an extensive list of SDS regional contacts and an entire documentation of REP's people.

A REP source says the break-in was "clearly an inside job," and that suspicion immediately pointed to [Doe], who was one of only a handful of people who were highly familiar with the office layout.

...

DETROIT SOURCES say [Doe] mysteriously reappeared after other "Weatherpeople" had vanished in 1970 and 71.

His reappearance coincided precisely with a Detroit secret grand jury hearing where Grathwohl testified. One source states that he saw [Doe] in Detroit with a large man closely resembling Grathwohl at the time of the hearings.

[Doe] apparently made a similar coincidental reappearance several months later in Cleveland during another secret federal probe of Weatherman's activities.

A CHECK into Congressional hearings on SDS in early 1969 may add credibility to some charges of agent provocateur aimed at [Doe]: the House Committee on Internal Security outlined a massive list of persons involved at every level of the radical group.

Sources here and elsewhere say that [Doe's] name was the only important one omitted.

In early 1970 a long list of Weather-

man leadership figures received federal indictments for conspiracy to destroy public buildings and attack police. [Doe], who was by then widely known for his Weatherman activities in Michigan, Illinois, Ohio, New York, and other states, is described by sources as the only "leader" who was not indicted...#

Probe points to SDS informant

By DAN BIDDLE
Copyright 1973, The Michigan Daily

(June 2, 1973) A continuing investigation by The Daily has revealed further evidence that a former local radical leader and co-founder of Weatherman may have in fact been a federal undercover agent.

...

Detroit sources say that in early 1969 [John Doe], then the leader of SDS' statewide Detroit-based organization, joined with activists from Chicago, Cleveland and New York in the formation of the Jesse James Gang, a network which soon became known as Weatherman.

LATER THE SAME year [Doe] became one of a small group of Weatherman's national operatives.

In that capacity, sources say, [Doe] was in direct and continuous contact with Larry Grathwohl, a confessed FBI informer who was then a key figure in the Detroit Weatherman collective.

...

One former non-Weatherman SDS activist was "shocked" to encounter [Doe] at a November 1971 conference... [Doe], the activist recalls, gave no explanation of his public presence months after other Weatherman leaders had vanished to escape the FBI. #

> I've used the "John Doe" alias to make it absolutely clear that the name in this expose has been changed – but not, let me emphasize, to protect the undercover agent himself.

'U' faculty members secretly recruit for CIA on campus

By RENEE BECKER
Copyright 1978, The Michigan Daily

(This article is first in a series detailing CIA links to the University.)

(April 14, 1978) The Central Intelligence Agency (CIA) and a small group of professors at the University of Michigan have been secretly working together to recruit students since the mid-'60s, according to documents recently released by the CIA.

The documents, received by the Daily as a result of a Freedom of Information Act (FOIA) request, include correspondence between the CIA and various units within the University, including the Center for Chinese Studies, Political Science, History, Economics and Geography departments.

...

CIA documents the Daily has received indicate the Agency has used University professors as covert recruiters of select and talented students for CIA employment.

One of the clearest examples of the CIA using University faculty for covert recruiting exists in a letter dated December 1, 1972, written on University of Michigan-Center for Chinese Studies stationery, addressed to then-CIA Coordinator for Academic Relations (CAR) Harold Ford.

IN THE LETTER, the University professor, whose name was deleted, asks Ford if, despite budget cuts at the CIA, "you are still interested in forthcoming graduates, and if so in what categories."

The letter continues: "I could not fill another agency's request for a woman (preferably) who could read Chinese and handle military analysis, both personnel and strategic, this fall, so I am not pushing people out willy-nilly."

...

When asked if the CIA used professors at universities for recruiting without the knowledge of college officials, CIA spokesman Bill Peterson maintained that there was a fine distinction between "individual" efforts to aid the CIA and official CIA campus recruitment.

"First of all, any individual who wanted to help the CIA of their own volition, voluntarily, is certainly not going to be turned away by the CIA," said Peterson.

The Agency does not believe that all contact a professor might have with the CIA need be reported to university officials, according to Peterson.

...

BUT SECRET CIA recruiting on college campuses did not begin or end with Ford. In 1966, the CIA began a Summer Intern Program in foreign studies. The program, which was open to anyone interested, gave students an opportunity to do "substantive scholarly research in their fields of academic research."

The program, which is still in operation, is geared toward graduate students, and allows individuals to work with "professional analysts." An explicit goal of the program was CIA recruitment--about half of the summer interns become permanent CIA employees, according to the Agency.

While Summer Intern Program literature was made available to more than a hundred colleges and universities, including Michigan, a letter from the CIA to one University professor shows that the actual recruiting did not occur in the "official" manner, that is, through the Career Planning and Placement office.

THE LETTER, dated February 10, 1967, states: "Because it (the Summer Intern Program) is to be a very small and somewhat experimental effort on our part, we hope to develop a list of candidates through personal contacts.

"Our regular Recruiting Officers," the letter continues, "know of the program and are prepared to discuss it with any student who may be interested in this kind of summer activity. I would, of course, appreciate your calling this program to the attention of any serious and mature student whom you think would be a likely candidate."

...

On December 20, 1974, Gary Foster, at that time coordinator for Academic Relations for the CIA, mailed 28 letters, including one to an unidentified contact at this University, asking for "help in spotting candidates for an intensified minority hiring program we are currently conducting."

In the letter Foster said the CIA was "primarily looking for analysts, and researchers in international politics, international economic systems and related disciplines. We also need linguists, particularly in the rare European and Asian languages, especially Russian and Chinese."

In closing, Foster pledged anonymity. "Your contact with us on this subject will be treated informally and confidentially. We will appreciate any help you can give us and I look forward to hearing from you."

UNIVERSITY President Robben Fleming yesterday said he found nothing wrong with the content of any of the...letters.

"There isn't anything surprising about this," he said. This type of recruiting is "done by all employers."

...

When asked why the CIA keeps this kind of search for talent a secret, Fleming said, "the only reason that I can see is that they may have told those people (professors) that their recommendations would be held confidential."

Fleming said not all professors are secretive about this kind of contact with the CIA. "Some are very open about it and wouldn't hesitate to tell you that it is their patriotic duty to make these recommendations," he said.

But in The Daily's investigation there were no professors who would admit to the kind of recruiting referred to in the CIA documents.

"I would bet you that 60 per cent of the recruiting (government and corporate) doesn't go on in the placement office," said Fleming. The problem, he said, is whether the agency "departs from what many of us consider normal ethical standards." Fleming said he saw no such departure in the latest documents.

The Campaign to Stop Government Spying, headed by Morton Halpern, former Deputy Assistant Secretary of Defense and one-time Senior Staff member of the National Security Council, is now urging the University to adopt guidelines which would force professors to make public any contact with the CIA. #

Reports link CIA to 'U' China Center

By RENEE BECKER
Copyright 1978 The Michigan Daily

(April 15, 1978) --"The University of Michigan at Ann Arbor is clearly in the forefront of the Centers on Communist China."

--"At the Harvard/Stanford level?"

--"It's above Stanford."

So began a conversation between employees of the Central Intelligence Agency (CIA) on December 3, 1965. The transcript of that dialogue begins an extensive documentation of the CIA's secret ties to the University's Center for Chinese Studies.

...

Approximately 75 per cent of these documents directly concern the Center for Chinese Studies and reveal the CIA's various ties to individuals from the Center which date back to the mid-sixties.

In the spring of 1966, the CIA conducted a series of field trips to China studies centers at 25 universities. The purpose of these trips "was to assess the facilities, faculty, curriculum, and faculty research interests in order to develop some feel for the China study activity in the country."

THE FIELD TRIP report on Ann Arbor offers nothing but praise for the University's Center for Chinese Studies.

"As one of the nation's outstanding centers for Far Eastern studies...whether as a source of qualified graduates or a location for training agency personnel, Michigan belongs in the top rank," the report states.

...

THE CIA, in several cases, provided research aid to University professors. In one well documented case beginning in October of 1967, the CIA arranged interviews, provided research materials, and had Agency analysts cooperate with a University professor.

"I have decided to try to do an interview project focusing on problems of political communication within the Chinese political system," wrote the unnamed professor. This would involve interviewing "between twenty and thirty ex-cadres from the party or government..." A cadre is a Chinese Communist party or government official.

...

The professor asked if twenty to thirty ex-cadres would be available for an interview and whether he could gain access to them...

...

The CIA response to the professor's inquiry discounted the possibility of finding 20 to 30 Chinese ex-cadres anywhere. But the CIA agent promised to arrange interviews with a few ex-cadres who live in the Washington area...

...

The documents indicate the professor met with CIA personnel on several occasions. He met with a top CIA China analyst and with at least one ex-cadre before going overseas to complete the project.

WHEN THE PROFESSOR returned, the Agency offered him a job. A letter dated May 1, 1970 refers to an informal meeting the professor had with the CIA agent and his wife.

"I appreciated the chance to talk over with you in some detail the employment possibility with your group," wrote the unnamed professor. "There is much that is very attractive about the position you suggest."

...

While the CIA was offering them jobs, professors sometimes returned the favor by clearing the way for Agency personnel to get University jobs when those agents were laid off because of CIA budget cuts.

In a letter dated April 6, 1973, a University faculty member, also connected with the Center for Chinese Studies, wrote Hal Ford, CIA Coordinator for Academic Relations, expressing his concern for those at the CIA who might be laid off.

THE LETTER continues: "Would you convey my feelings to any involved with whom I have had a personal or professional relationship? Is there anything I might do to help elsewhere in town? Should any of my friends on the Hill be alerted?"

...On Christmas Eve 1968 a professor connected to the Center for Chinese Studies sent a letter to a CIA employee.

"Regarding (deleted), I am quite interested in having him join us here as a resource person for a year or two...I am having a bit more trouble mobilizing support for him around the Center than anticipated, but I hope we can work out a mutually satisfactory arrangement,"

wrote the unnamed professor.

In the 1966 CIA field trip report, the CIA agents made the following recommendation: "Rather than having CIA engage in competition with the universities for the relatively few products of the China centers, it seems more profitable to use the idle capacity of such schools as Michigan for training of agency personnel already on duty in CIA."#

Don't delay on CIA guidelines

(April 16, 1978) ALL SPECULATION ended last week with regards to possible University-Central Intelligence Agency connections. For the first time, significant details were made available under the Freedom of Information Act (FOIA) about previously secret relationships between University faculty and the CIA which existed as long ago as the mid-1960's.

...

The detailing of University-CIA ties brings up again the question of whether there should be formal restrictions on what a member of the University community can or cannot do in cooperation with the nation's intelligence agencies...

...

...guidelines have been considered at this University, but have been given low priority by some officials because there has previously been no documented proof of secret relationships with the CIA.

There is proof enough now to satisfy even the most skeptical of community members. We suggest that the Regents and the Senate Advisory Committee on University Affairs (SACUA) examine once more the merits of the so-called Harvard Guidelines.

In light of the recent disclosures-- and of possible future disclosures of even greater magnitude--the University should adopt restrictions which guarantee students an education free of government manipulation.#

FBI spied on local gays

By DAN OBERDORFER

(May 11, 1978) The FBI monitored activities of the University chapter of the Gay Liberation Front (GLF) during the early 1970s but called off its watchdogs after determining that the group was more social than political in orientation, according to FBI documents released last week.

The heavily-censored documents were obtained through a Freedom of Information Act request by [a] GLF member, a University employee. The documents show the FBI employed at least two informants to gather information about the group.

...

IN A MEMO to former FBI Director J. Edgar Hoover on June 17, 1970, the Detroit field office of the FBI said it would, "through sources, follow activities of this group (GLF) to determine whether it becomes a viable 'new left' organization at the University of Michigan."

A few weeks later FBI headquarters ordered Detroit to "continue to obtain information" about GLF because it "is a self-described New-Left type student organization at the University of Michigan."

Another document says GLF "worked with SDS and other campus groups in recent disorders."

ONE INFORMANT WHOM the FBI said "furnished reliable information in the past" and whose name was deleted from the documents, said GLF was "working towards legalization of homosexuality."

The FBI seemed most concerned with a regional convention GLF planned for Ann Arbor in the summer of 1970. Because University President Robben Fleming refused to permit the use of campus facilities, the convention was postponed until the next summer, according to the document.

GLF claimed Fleming had originally authorized the convention to be held in December 1970, "but subsequently cancelled his approval. . .out of fear of embarrassment to the U-M."

The eight-page document concluded: "The contents (of this memo) are not to be distributed outside your agency." The letter was not declassified until May 1977.

It also details attempts by GLF to obtain permission for the conventoin, especially a demonstration held outside Fleming's home. According to one FBI source, 30 students carried signs in front of the house until "several representatives of the group entered the home of the U-M president disrupting a social event under way in the president's home at that time."

The document continues: "Source advised that the demonstrating group was clearly using the GLF banner and slogan as a political weapon of the 'new left' in general agitation against the U-M administration."

THE SOURCE said he knew this because many people active in the demonstration had also participated in other campus protests. Because the sources saw a heterosexual former chairman of the University Students for a Democratic Society chapter and his girlfriend at the demonstration, the informant determined the pair "uses GLF as a device to further 'new left' agitation."

The FBI ended its surveillance of GLF in July 1971 when it determined the gay group was not "a viable New Left-oriented group."

"It appears...that this group is mainly interested in social and campus acceptance of homosexuals rather than being a politically-orientated (sic) organization of the New Left," wrote one Detroit-based FBI agent.

The agent continued, "(GLF) is small in number and ineffectual as an independent group... They, as a group, have not taken any independent, aggressive action..."#

SEVERAL CONTACTED IN RECENT WEEKS

Students are target of FBI questioning

By LEONARD BERNSTEIN

(Jan. 28, 1979) The Federal Bureau of Investigation (FBI) has increased its intelligence-gathering activities at the University in recent weeks, according to student sources.

The students, who requested anonymity, said the FBI contacted at least three University students--some of them foreign--in the weeks following political demonstrations on this campus and outside the home of the Shah of Iran's mother in Beverly Hills, California.

THE STUDENTS confirmed that some of those contacted were connected with a demonstration staged at the Rackham Building during a speech here by former Israeli Foreign Minister Yigal Allon on December 17 of last year.

But the sources said it is unclear if the FBI's actions are part of an investigation into the Allon incident. They said the questions could be part of the government's response to an Iranian student demonstration in Beverly Hills, or the result of a general increase in intelligence activity.

"We don't have enough evidence to state conclusively at this point that, yes, this is because of the Allon incident," said MSA Vice-President Kate Rubin,

who is working with a group of students attempting to halt the intelligence activity. "Either way, we don't expect this to stop."

...

Ben Brewer, a spokesman for the FBI office in Detroit, said he could not comment on whether any investigation was being conducted at the University.

The student sources refused to reveal the names or nationalities of those contacted because, they said, some of these students feared retaliation against relatives in foreign countries. They also refused to identify the campus groups with which the students are connected because they fear that negative publicity might discourage University students from working with those organizations.

...

Some students said they were unsure how many people had been contacted. They explained that persons contacted are often afraid to tell anyone else they have been approached.

But one member of the group organized to fight the actions speculated that others had been approached.

"My guess is that it's more than three people, but it's hard to substantiate," she said. ..#

FBI asks 'U' library for records on scholar

By PERRY CLARK

(Feb. 18, 1982) Agents of the FBI visited the University's Engineering Transportation Library last week in an attempt to ascertain what materials a visiting Russian scholar was reading, library employees said.

FBI officials would only acknowledge that the incident occurred and that two agents were involved. They refused to issue any further comment.

ACCORDING TO John Walters, stacks supervisor at the Engineering Transportation Library, FBI agents came to the library and spoke with Head Librarian Maurita Holland. He said they asked her about a visiting mathematics scholar from the U.S.S.R. and, specifically, about what library materials he was using.

Holland would not comment on the incident, but did read a library policy statement which said, "The library will not reveal the names of individual borrowers nor reveal what books are charged to any individual."

Associate Library Director Jane Flener said the library was investigating the incident. "We don't keep a record of who reads what," she said.

...

Employees of the Undergraduate Library, where the Engineering Transportation Library is housed, said they heard that the visiting scholar... was photocopying sensitive documents on computer technology and mailing them to the Soviet Union. Flener said, "That's a presumption. I don't think anyone knows what he was doing with them."

Flener added that, "We have nothing in our library that is not public knowledge. It is in the public domain."

ENGINEERING library employee Joe Badics said the claims of the Undergraduate Library employees had been "blown all out of proportion."

The incident is similar to others which have occurred at universities throughout the nation in the past year. At the University of Minnesota last fall, the State Department sent a letter to Prof. W.R. Franta of the computer science department, asking for information on a Chinese exchange student, and telling the university to restrict the student's activities in certain academic areas.

Franta showed the letter to the university's president, C. Peter MaGrath, who called it "appalling." MaGrath wrote back to the State Department, saying he would have nothing to do with such a request.

STATE DEPARTMENT representative Keith Powell called the Minnesota situation a misunderstanding. He said it was a routine affair that had been handled clumsily. #

the investigators

The Daily discovers dope

Discover Widespread Use of Marijuana on Campus

By JAMES SCHUTZE

(Oct. 20, 1965) When Ann Arbor police recently arrested five young Ann Arbor residents for sale and use of marijuana, they struck the first blow of a crackdown on the sale and use of the narcotic.

Whether they know it or not, the authorities have barely begun the fight. Reliable sources indicate that there is currently a hard-core ring of 200 users operating in Ann Arbor. They are all in violation of federal statutes prohibiting "possession and sale" of the narcotic. Moreover, their influence, by example and by actual distribution of drugs, affects an estimated several thousand young people here, including University students, non-student hangers-on and high schoolers as young as 15 years old.

Although the police thus far have revealed few ideas about the origin of the marijuana sold in this city, informants with personal knowledge of the operation of the ring indicate that most of the drug is raised by students in a field outside Chicago. Some persons are also known to be locally growing the plant from which the drug is cured.

Whatever the source, some 200 students in the "hard-core" marijuana ring are "turning on" several times a week. For the uninitiated, "turning on" is the process by which the user becomes narcotically inebriated through deep inhalations of the smoke from marijuana cigarettes.

Often, the hard-core users "turn on" together at a special party by passing a marijuana cigarette, called a "reefer," around a circle like a peace pipe.

Parties are not the only places which attract marijuana users, however, the informants report. "Just go sit in the MUG (Michigan Union Grill) any one night and you'll see a minimum of a hundred pot-heads (users) walk by," declares one co-ed familiar with the inner core of users.

One of the persons recently arrested by police scoffs at the figure "200" as a hard-core estimate. He explains that one building alone in Ann Arbor has 35 tenants smoking the drug.

Perhaps the most serious ramification of the marijuana epidemic here is the effect on high school students.

A prominent local attorney was not surprised to hear of 15-year-old "baby hippies" in Ann Arbor. He told of one case where a local youth had confessed long-time use of marijuana. "That kid came from a family as good as any other," the lawyer stormed. "He admitted that he had been using marijuana since he was 15. Now, how the hell do you get at the guy who was giving him marijuana when he was 15 years old?"

A graduate student and teaching fellow here concurs with the lawyer's analysis. During a recent visit to the MUG, he observed, "The teeny-bops (high school users) were right over there selling to each other. They think it's twice as cool now as it was before the arrests."

...

The distribution of marijuana is a complicated task, involving, the informants disclose, the procural of the narcotic from big urban areas like Chicago and Detroit.

One informant named Chicago as the central source for the drug. Her reason: "I think a lot of people, well, uh, shall we say our most famous buyer, you know, has been known to make a couple of trips to Chicago..."

The police, although determined to clear up the marijuana racket in Ann Arbor, are still investigating the local situation. "Talk is cheap," declares Detective Captain Harold Olson of the Ann Arbor Police Department. "You show me a list of 200 names of users, and I'll do something about it. Right now we're doing everything we can to follow through what we have. You make one arrest and that leads to two more, and that leads to a fourth. We are in very close contact, by the way, with the University whenever a student becomes involved with us."

Duncan Sells, director of student activities, confirms that communication on this issue between student and local authorities is excellent. He notes that "we were all ready to chip in and pay the bail of one of the students recently arrested, but we discovered at the last minute that he wasn't a student."..#

Crime on Campus: Maryjane Makes the Scene

EDITOR'S NOTE: This is the second of a three-part series on the various forms of crime on the University campus.

By DANIEL OKRENT

(Feb. 1, 1968) Three years ago, when this year's current crop of seniors were freshmen, the greenish cuttings of Cannabis sativa were as rare as demonstrations supporting the Dow Chemical Co. are today. However, with the changing of times and what some sociologists consider to be an outgrowth of rapidly-increasing youth alienation, marijuana has found its way onto campus in unprecedented quantities.

That "the weed" has made its presence known is indisputable. Students, who two years ago saw it to be a mysterious untouchable, include it in their weekend diets regularly. Police officials, once surprised at its presence and skeptical of its influence, now pass it off as another item on their beat. University housing officials who might once have said that pot is for social outcasts are now

not surprised to find its distinct odor slipping out of the best students' rooms.

Whereas past records indicate that the number of drug arrests in one year could practically be counted on Police Chief Walter Krasny's fingers, mushrooming importation, distribution and use of marijuana carried last year's arrest figures well past 40. The bulk of these arrests, Krasny says, occurred in the last four months of the year.

The extent to which illegal stimulants--many medical authorities do not classify marijuana as a "drug"--have penetrated the campus has reached the point where Krasny can refer to drinking parties and pot parties in the same sentence.

"It's a problem we can't hide from. There is a far higher percentage of users than we would like to think," he says. He is not willing to make a numerical estimate, but does say the figure is much higher than the 200 quoted by Detective Lt. Eugene Staudenmeier last year.

He maintains, though, that it is considerably lower than the 3000 regu-

lar users and 10,000 "who have tried it" that Ann Arbor author John Rosevear claimed in September at the time of the publication of his book, "Pot: A Handbook of Marijuana."

Enforcement of narcotics laws is one of the Ann Arbor police department's most difficult tasks. To admissably prove "possession," the drug must be on the person, or in a person's house. In other words, it is often difficult to establish possession when a person is in the residence of another individual...

...

As a result of courtroom difficulties in prosecution, only 15 actual charges came out of all arrests the Ann Arbor police made during 1967. The remainder of the cases were dismissed.

...

The cost of Ann Arbor grass varies with the supply on the market. Now readily available at $10 per one ounce bag, prices had jumped to $15-$20 immediately after the current semester started.

The previous rise in the sale price was due to the December arrest of a young Detroiter who was seized by federal agents while trying to pick up a shipment of over 200 pounds of suitcase-packed marijuana at Metropolitan Airport...#

Police stand by, crowd gets high at Wisconsin marijuana festival

**By GREG DOUKAS
and DOUG JACOBS**
Special To The Daily

(Sept. 26, 1971) MADISON, Wis. -- "Free dope, free dope," chanted almost 1,000 demonstrators yesterday, as they smoked marijuana and marched in drizzling rain from a lakeside park near the University of Wisconsin to the State Capitol, about a half mile away.

Under the watchful eye of state police, participants in the "first annual marijuana harvest festival" held a smoke-in and march to protest the jailing of Dana Beal, organizer of the 1970 and 1971 July 4 smoke-ins in Washington, D.C. Beal is now awaiting trial in Madison for possession of marijuana.

Police, both at the demonstration and later last night, refused comment as

to why members of the crowd were not arrested for possession and use of marijuana.

Despite the open smoking of marijuana and taunting of police, there were no arrests until after the demonstration ended. At that time, about a dozen people were picked up for throwing rocks and breaking street lights.

For the most part, however, the festival and march was orderly. "We're too wrecked to even antagonize the police," said one participant.

...

Participants threw handfuls of joints into the air throughout the festival, and although the source of the illegal intoxicant was unknown, one observer noted that "all the joints were wrapped in Zig-Zag papers the same way--it all must have come from the same place."

After two hours of smoking and

speeches, the group left to march to the capitol. A permit for the march had been granted to the "First Annual Marijuana Harvest Festival and Dana Beal Anti-Heroin Movement," a few weeks earlier.

"Man, this crowd is so zonked, we can't even sing straight," said one University of Wisconsin junior on the way to the capitol. Others in the crowd expressed similar sentiments.

...

Speakers read off several demands of the group, including: legalization of marijuana, a free one-ounce per week allowance of marijuana, freedom for all "political and psychedelic prisoners," and an end to the Vietnam war, with peace treaty provision that the United States buy $100 million worth of marijuana a year from Vietnamese farmers...#

Pot convicts 'elated' with sudden freedom

By JONATHAN MILLER
Special To The Daily

(April 11, 1972) JACKSON -- For four hours they came, dressed in prison blue pants, looking young and somewhat stunned--their confinement ended by order of the state Supreme Court.

James Griffin was in the fourth year of a 20-40 year sentence for possession of marijuana, his third offense, when the Jackson County circuit judge, sitting in a library on the second floor of Jackson's visitors wing, told him he was free.

"I'm elated," he said.

On Friday, the state Supreme Court issued writs of habeus corpus for 128 persons imprisoned on marijuana charges.

"It's far out," grinned Larry George, 18, as he ran into the glare of the television cameras, the flashes of photographers, free to return to his home in Benton Harbor.

George had been inside for five months of his 1-1/2 to 10 year sentence for possession of two joints of marijuana.

The prisoners were paraded before a three-judge panel of Jackson County circuit court judges, who verified each individual's eligibility for release.

Many of them said they'd smoke pot again, and many more of them expressed bitterness at their long confinement under what is now an obsolete felony statute.

They all seemed delighted at their sudden release.

One prison warden, however, was not so delighted.

"They'll all be back here again when they're five years older. I know so. I've seen too many of 'em," he said.

Released today were 80 prisoners who had been serving varying sentences for possession of marijuana, among them two women.#

Dope famine? Not likely, but prices may rise

By JONATHAN MILLER

(March 15, 1973) In February it was 14,000 lbs. of marijuana confiscated in Los Angeles. Two weeks ago the government picked up nine tons of pot in Florida. Last week in Ann Arbor 400 pounds of reefer was nabbed by the cops. Tuesday, the government grabbed 25 tons of the stuff on the Arizona-Mexican border.

Does all this mean that American pot heads will face a dope shortage this year?

The answer to that is: Probably not.

Almost everyone, from a spokesman for the Bureau of Narcotics and Dangerous Drugs (BNDD) to street dealers in Ann Arbor, agrees that the size of the marijuana market is now so great that a few random busts, however large, will likely have no great impact on the traffic.

At most, these experts say, these big seizures will merely drive even higher the already inflated price of weed.

Accurate statistics on the marijuana industry are hard to come by, but an educated guess by the city police department here is that upwards of 1,000 lbs. of marijuana a week are imported and sold in Ann Arbor.

If the figure is correct, and dealers interviewed by this reporter concur with the police estimate--even last week's haul of 400 pounds cannot be expected to have more than a temporary impact on the local market--and that seizure was the biggest in Ann Arbor history.

Explains Lt. Calvin Hicks, head of the drug squad of the city police department:

"These sizeable confiscations have a tendency to create a cooling off period whereby the smuggling and transportation end drop off for a while. The dealers back off and try to read how much heat law enforcement is putting on."

But even Hicks concedes that the effects of the raids are at best temporary, and unless more seizures are made the traffic soon gets back to normal.

The attitude of the BNDD is somewhat similar.

Hank Price, a spokesman for BNDD, told The Daily that no one at his agency was under any pretensions that even the big raids announced recently would have a marked effect on the overall traffic.

"It's going to take time," Price said. "But we are starting to get closer to the sources."..#

Pot, alcohol on campus as prevalent as ever

Cocaine gaining popularity fast

By MITCH CANTOR
First in a four-part series

(Oct. 11, 1979) In the 1960s, the rise in student activism and unrest was accompanied by an unprecedented boom in drug use on college campuses. A decade later, while activism has faded into apathy and unrest into calm, drugs have maintained their status as a part of everyday life in Ann Arbor.

1979

...

"TEN YEARS AGO it was all much newer to us, and we were all sort of overwhelmed by any and all drug use. Since then, we've come to see that it's here, and it's here to stay..." said Jim Asberry, Couzens Hall building director, who has worked in college housing for 11 years.

Marijuana, alcohol and cocaine are the three most popular drugs on campus today, and the first two are probably at least as popular as they were 10 years ago. But sources disagree about which substance is more widely-used.

"I'd say pot is more popular (with University students) only because a lot of people I know smoke and go to classes, smoke and do other things. And it's not that easy to perceive when people are high, whereas when you're drunk, it is," said Anne, a University junior.

JOHN, A University junior who sold pot and cocaine last year, claims pot is very popular, but still second to drinking because stereotypes about marijuana smokers seem to persevere.

"Alcohol is viewed in a much different sense than smoking pot. It's just 'cause people go out and have a beer, and they see nothing wrong with it. When you start talking about weed, they start thinking about communism, hippy-freaks, ya know," he said.

AT THE SAME time, however, there seems to be some opposition to the view that alcohol is more socially acceptable.

"Despite the illegality of pot, I think the general population can easily see that alcohol is worse (than pot) 'cause it's so much worse for you physically. A lot more people get messed up on alcohol," said Jill, a pot smoker and University student.

...

Those interviewed agreed that no other drug is used by more than half the student population. But they said the third most widely-used drug--cocaine--is skyrocketing to new popularity.

"I THINK coke has gotten a lot more popular in the last few years. It's a lot more available," said Carol, a University student.

...

"It's the accepted thing. It's the three-martini lunch of the younger generation.

"People aren't as afraid of cocaine as they are of acid (LSD)," Carol explained. "Every once in a while there'll be someone who comes to the dorms to lay out lines (of cocaine to be sniffed), and everybody will come in to try it. Not that many people would eat part of a hit of acid."..#

A2 drug dealers: profit hunters or benefactors?

By MITCH CANTOR
Third in a four-part series

(Editor's note: All those identified by first name only requested anonymity.)

(Oct. 13, 1979) "Before I came to U-M my picture of the drug dealer was that (which) was purported by the movies they showed in grade school. You know, someone saying 'Hey, kid' on the playground. Every drug dealer I know I consider quite bright. Most people I know who sell acid are very involved in the philosophy of selling acid, the fact that they would like to enlighten people."

--an LSD user at the University

For all drug users, regardless of which substance is being sought, a general rule of thumb seems to be, "Only buy from someone you know and trust."

"I ALWAYS buy acid from a friend, and I never do acid that somebody hasn't already done..." said Anne, a University junior.

...

Similarly, drug merchants like to protect themselves by only selling to people they know and trust. In general, said John, buyers are all usually part of "a circle of a few close friends, particularly when you're dealing with a substance that carries as heavy a penalty for getting caught as it (cocaine) does. It pays best not to deal with anyone you don't know personally."

WHERE A dealer gets his product depends on what drug he/she sells. Marijuana is grown in many parts of the U.S. (particularly Oregon and Hawaii) as well as being imported. Most dealers and users, however, say that imported marijuana (which is usually superior to "home-grown") doesn't often make it to the city.

...

THE DRUG merchants themselves are for the most part University students who have contacts in higher levels of the drug world. "If you're not inside a circle of people who would have easy access to the substance then you wouldn't be dealing," John said.

According to Lieutenant Patric Little of the Washtenaw County Sheriff's Office, "A drug dealer's a guy who's in it to make money. He's not in it to free anybody's spirit. he doesn't care what he sells you."

BUT USERS and dealers discount that allegation to some extent.

"I wasn't into only selling drugs for the money. There's definitely a plus to it in knowing that you're giving people the best you can buy and the best they can buy..." said John, who sold cocaine and hashish last year.

...

A primary concern among drug buyers is quality of the product. Among popular drugs, cocaine is quite often cut (diluted) down to about 20 per cent before it reaches the buyer...

...

Generally purity is too difficult to determine without purchase of the drugs, due to "bootleg" manufacturing and uncertain origins of different drugs. Purity is usually a matter on which the buyer must trust his/her source.

"...I don't think they're gonna try and screw you, cause if they do, well, that's how they lose their business," said Dan, a University sophomore and pot smoker.#

entr'acte

"Hello! Is Marion At Home?" Or "Fresh Is As Fresh Does"

(Oct. 3, 1922) About once in 20 years there appears a new joke. There are said to be about seven different ones in existence, and this is probably a sport by-product, or some other offspring of one of them. Maybe it isn't a new joke at all, but it has at least proven fresh and alluring to the dates verdant increment to our campus population, and to the funny boys, who sit around figuring out some new one all the while, it seems to be real hot stuff.

All you need to play this joke on your favorite freshman butt is a piece of paper and a pencil. Take the latter and grasping it firmly in the right hand or the left if you are a southpaw, and moistening the lead on your tongue if you like that sort of thing, take also the piece of paper and write on it "Call 2249 and ask for Marion." Leave this on Mr. Frosh's desk. Then all you have to do is to wait. Your freshman victim comes in, sees the little note on his desk where you have put it, has visions of golden hair and eyes that are brimming with blue, and dashes for the phone and calls 2249. This being a popular number he may

have to call again, but when he gets it he will find that this is the President's house and that "Marion" is none other than the President of the University, who tacks various degrees on the end of his name, wields a wicked horseshoe, and cannot under any circumstances be considered a fair substitution for a flapper.

The fact of the matter is that the favorite joke this year is that outlined above, and it has been played so many times that there is a groove in the presidential rug leading up to the telephone, and the inhabitants of 815 South University avenue are finding it just a wee bit less funny than it was the first time the phone rang... There are symptoms that perhaps something may be developed along some other line. Only today a blushing freshman appeared in the President's office and asked whether he could have permission to take the course in Philanthrophy.

Aren't they cute, though, those freshmen? And isn't it a shame that they will grow up and get sophisticated and then you can't play these humorous little jokes on them?...#

Tan, Blue, Brown Mice? Sure, The University Owns Hundreds

By ARTHUR A. MILLER

(Oct. 12, 1935) White mice, tan mice, pink, brown, and jumping mice, even blue mice, hundreds of them living side by side in a rather new building that looks like an ice cube and which you can hardly notice from a distance of 25 yards.

No, it isn't an hallucination. It is a hard brick building called the Laboratory of Vertebrate Genetics and it stands in a clearing near the University coal yard.

...

Dr. Frank H. Clark, who conducts research in heredity there, says that before students began to get FERA assignments in the laboratory, hardly anyone walked in or about except himself and a small staff.

But it is an interesting place even though it contains those same rodents

traps are made for.

Dr. Clark, who knows more about mice than most people do about themselves, tells of many novel facts which an anti-mouse world seems content to forget. The geneticist tells, for one, of a peculiar characteristic of a certain type of field mouse. He says that "If you cage a field mouse of this type, and rattle a bunch of keys in front of it or jingle a bell near it, it develops epileptic fits immediately." Tobacco smoke or incense burning near it will have the same effect and as soon as the stimulus is applied the animals run about in their cages, hitting the walls with their heads and after a while just turn over and are overcome with convulsions.

Deer mice, said Dr. Clark, are the most numerous mammals in North America. And upon entering the isolated laboratory, one would think that they had

all been herded into one building.

...

Yet mice do not occupy the complete attention of the laboratory. For outside the main building is a small wooden coop. It is unpainted and faded but one's spirits will rise upon entering it, for on a ledge which circles the room, one will see two very surprised owls. One will also leave immediately if one's acquaintance with owls has been limited, since the birds are unchained and they have a habit of clacking their bills and looking unfed. But the geneticists maintain that they are harmless, so one will probably leave anyway.

...

The place, on the whole, is not unpleasant. It is a little quiet out there at times, but there are always the chirps of the white, the tan, and the pink mice to break the silence.#

chapter

4

the crusades

The thing about crusades is that they almost never come to a neat, satisfying conclusion. Individual parts may come to an end, but usually the underlying issue remains to rise again. The odds are that The Daily will be writing stories about police activities, University investment policies and faculty library use on into the twenty-first century.

the
crusades

groves
of
academe

(March 4, 1911) Two or three years ago something of a row was precipitated by the protestations of a student against faculty "misuse" of their library privileges. The members of the teaching force of the university hotly responded with communications and signed interviews, and the matter was let drop.

The defense of the faculty was based upon the supposition that the books drawn, even though numbering in individual cases into the hundreds, were highly technical, and not in demand with the "common peepul." At that time the DAILY took no sides in the controversy.

Recently a member of the staff had an opportunity to con the book shelves of a member of the literary faculty. There were over seventy-five volumes belonging to the university library in this collection. A few were highly technical; a great many were books in common use among students; and a considerable number, dealt with subjects entirely outside the range of this particular instructor's labors. Further, many of the books had not been opened for weeks or perhaps even months.

The library, at stated intervals, notifies the members of the faculty to bring in and check up the books drawn out by them. It is a matter of common knowledge to many that this law is oftentimes ignored absolutely, or evaded...

...

Whether this treatment of the privileges accorded instructors constitutes an abuse we leave to the individual conscience, but it does at times savor of the inconsiderate. Certainly it hampers the efforts of many a student; and it is hard to see where it works any great good.#

Faculty abuse 'U' libraries

By JUDY SARASOHN
(Sept. 14, 1969) A graduate student, John Wilhelm, went to the General Library recently to obtain the only volume there of a journal he needed for his dissertation work. However, Wilhelm was unsuccessful because the journal was being held, although it was far beyond the proper time limit, by a University professor.

Wilhelm was not the first person to ask for the journal--library staff had called for it several times before but the professor informed them not to bother him because he would return it when he wanted to.

The head of the circulation department of the General Library, Anne Okey, checked her files and discovered that the professor had at least 34 overdue books in his possession.

The library staff insists that only a small minority of the faculty is irresponsible and "totally contemptuous" of other users of the library. But, this small minority is responsible for over 3,500 books that have been overdue for at least two months. This accounts for from one-sixth to one-tenth of the General Library circulation.

The hard core abuser is quite different from the occasional absent-minded professor, teaching fellow, or research assistant, notes Miss Okey and Wilhelm.

Many swear at Miss Okey and her staff when they are requested to allow others the use of the overdue books. Although some--but not all--cooperate with other professors, students invariably receive a worse response, Wilhelm says.

"Most students now believe it's a hopeless situation and don't try to pursue the books," says Wilhelm.

But, as the situation stands now, there are no sanctions against faculty members who have overdue books. And library director Frederick Wagman and Miss Okey believe the situation is critical.

Wagman went before SRC to request the committee to recommend to the Senate Advisory Committee on University Affairs that sanctions be created.

Wagman says he does not have the authority to require faculty members to pay fines if they refuse to return books after the eight-week loan period. Wagman does not have the authority to require a professor to simply return 10 or so books--as in one case--before he goes on sabbatical.

...

If a particular unidentified department was fined for the overdue books held by its faculty, the bill would be $2,760. But the money is unimportant to Wagman: "We don't want to sell books; we want them back."#

INSTRUCTOR GIVEN ABRUPT DISMISSAL

(Feb. 26, 1924) J. A. Sallade of the mathematics department of the engineering college will not be appointed to the faculty next year and according to his declaration has been refused a statement of the reasons for his dismissal by the head of the mathematics department in this college, Prof. Alexander Ziwet...

Popularity of his classes is given by Mr. Sallade as the cause of the trouble which gave rise to the present situation. Enrollment in his classes grew so large that Prof. T. R. Running, also of the mathematics department, who is in charge of the routine of the class enrollment in-

FEELING RUNS HIGH AS SALLADE PLANS TO RESIST ACTION

STUDENTS PROTEST DISMISSAL WITH PETITIONS, BIG MEETING TODAY

(Feb. 27, 1924) Interest in the case of J. A. Sallade of the mathematics department of the engineering school, centered yesterday upon statements and refusals to speak by the principals and petitions among the student body...

Petitions were in circulation among the students yesterday, addressed to President Burton, requesting that Mr. Sallade be retained in his present capacity. Arrangements are being made to have a meeting of all student engineers today.

Professor Ziwet refuses to make any statement whatsoever in regard to the matter. When asked to deny or affirm statements of Mr. Sallade, he refused.

Cooley Makes Statement

The following statement was issued by Dean Mortimer E. Cooley of the engineering school, late yesterday afternoon:

"The case of Mr. Sallade is one of more or less routine in the Dean's office... It is not an unusual case except in its publicity. It is not the policy of the Dean's office to discuss such matters publicly. It is believed more exact justice to all can be accomplished better in some other way. Suffice to say the interests of the College of Engineering and Architecture, or its students and faculty, will be of first consideration."..#

formed Sallade that it would be necessary to send some of the men out.

Mr. Sallade, believing that the size of his classes would in no way interfere with his teaching did not comply with the order, whereupon Professor Ziwet went into both sections of the instructor's class and attempted to send part of the students to another section under a different instructor. The students refused to leave.

Last Thursday, according to the statement of Mr. Sallade, he was called to Professor Ziwet's office. "You will not be reappointed to the faculty," declared the head of the mathematics department. "You are impossible!" Later in the week, Mr. Sallade said he requested a statement of the reasons for his dismissal from Professor Ziwet who answered his request by declaring, "You will get no such statement!"

Such action is looked upon by Mr. Sallade as a "gross injustice" to himself as he will find it difficult to make any satisfactory explanation to future employers. He declared that all good colleges demand at least a statement of reasons for leaving a previous position. Students in his classes have assured him of their backing in his demand, he declares.#

LIGHT ON THE QUESTION

(Feb. 27, 1924) A poisonous weed is best nipped in the bud. It is always good policy for either an institution or an individual to investigate, explain or deny ugly rumours. All explanations from a source that is authoritative, like a thunderstorm on a sultry evening generally serve to clear the air.

At present several significant questions seem to be troubling the campus. Can Michigan keep her leading professors and instructors? Are men in any department of the University discharged because of their popularity with the student body? Is it customary to discharge men of high standing without first giving such men a complete explanation for such action?

Questions such as these deserve attention from authoritative sources. Truth makes for an atmosphere of wholesome cleanliness, whereas ugly rumours infest the air with germs of corruption and confusion.#

Nervous Collapse of Sallade Forces Suspension Of Teaching

(March 1, 1924) As a result of a complete nervous collapse last night, J. A. Sallade, of the mathematics department of the engineering college, is confined to his bed and will be unable to teach again this semester. When Mr. Sallade has sufficiently recovered he will leave town for an indefinite rest. He was notified last week that his services in the University would no longer be required after this semester and to the subsequent actions proposing his reinstatement is attributed the breakdown.

The investigating committee was told of Mr. Sallade's illness while in session and after expressing their extreme regret and sumpathy, adjourned until it was found whether further inquiries would be of any use.

...

Mr. Sallade endeavored to present his case to at least two classes in the literary college yesterday. He also challenged the students to leave one class of Prof. T. H. Hildenbrandt of the engineering college...

A meeting which was to have been private between Dean Cooley and Mr. Sallade yesterday afternoon became a discussion group when many students in the classes of Mr. Sallade packed the large office and entrance to Dean Cooley's office...

...

Greatly depressed, yet apparently with indomitable courage, Mr. Sallade defended his action, stating that the whole matter was crushing his spirit and breaking up his whole life which had been devoted to teaching his high ideals to others.

Dean Cooley declared his admiration for the spirit of Mr. Sallade and his ability to enthuse his students but in summing up the situation declared that the rules of the college must be carried out regardless of everything else. The classes must have a limited number of students and if Mr. Sallade is willing to teach to this number his position is still open to him, he said. Dean Cooley expressed his willingness to receive a petition requesting that the faculty change this ruling as to sizes of classes, saying it would be given their careful consideration...#

ONE OF HOPWOOD PRIZES ELIMINATED

(March 13, 1932) Four prizes of $2,500 each will be given as major awards in this year's Hopwood prize contest, instead of five, as was stated in The Daily.

In the announcement which has been an official source for information pertaining to the contest, five awards of this denomination are listed but because of a depreciation in the original principal from which the yearly amounts are taken, the committee has found it impossible to award more than four major prizes, making the total amount of prize awards this year $12,000 instead of $14,500...#

STUDENTS RESENT HOPWOOD RULES

(March 11, 1932) Resentment against the Avery and Jule Hopwood Prizes committee by students intending to enter the annual literary contest this year reached a peak yesterday as a result of the appearance Wednesday and Thursday mornings of a D.O.B. notice to the effect that all recipients of prize money would be required to file a statement with the committee that the money would be spent for the furtherance of creative literary activity only.

...

...it was expressly stated that "each recipient of a major award shall be required to submit to the committee...a statement showing that he intends to spend his award according to some plan calculated to further his literary activity in accordance with the spirit of the bequest" and goes on to say that the committee shall determine whether the statement of the plan submitted is satisfactory to the terms stated above.

...

By many it was felt that the committee was intent upon subsidizing English courses at Michigan by making the further study of English composition practically a requirement to win an award.

Upon being interviewed on the question last night, Assistant Professor Bennett Weaver, of the English department, director of the Hopwood awards, stated that "...The committee, in drafting this rule, interpreted the spirit of the bequest to the effect that the money was to be used for making proficient writers out of young students interested in this field."#

Through the Hoop For Hopwoods

(Sept. 27, 1961) ...University students seeking to get their hands on the generous Hopwood stipends to further their writing careers...must be carrying 12 hours of credit (graduate students need only nine) to compete. They must also achieve a C average this semester. Grads, with a lighter load, are obligated to amass a 3.0 mark.

...

...Somewhere in his schedule of academic elections, he must squeeze in one course in composition in the English language and literature department or in the journalism department.

...

...There are many students on the campus who are not majoring in English or creative writing or journalism, but who write. Their regularly elected field of concentration may not afford enough time to complete the work of a regular course in composition or they may not desire the requirements of writing on a schedule. (In the manner of C.P. Snow and Winston Churchill.)

IT IS TRUE that Hopwood's will specifies students in the rhetoric department, and that the present rules may be a liberal interpretation of his language. It would be no stretch of his interpretation to include those electing any course in the English department....#

--MICHAEL OLINICK

Hopwood Award Salaries

(April 7, 1932) APPARENTLY the Board of Regents shut its eyes, went wild with so much money on its hands, or wasn't thinking at all when it passed, on June 30, 1931, a resolution giving to Assistant Professor Bennett C. Weaver $3,000 for administering the Hopwood Prize contest and $1,000 to Associate Professor Roy W. Cowden for being his assistant.

According to the will left by Avery Hopwood, the money is to be used for awards to those students "who perform the best creative work in the fields of dramatic writing, fiction, poetry, and the essay." The Regents, thus, are clearly overstepping their bounds when they give a $3,000 salary to a member of the faculty who is already being paid the customary assistant professor's salary. Cowden is receiving $1,000 but at the same time is having the like amount deducted from his regular compensation.

...It is a fair call to think that Avery Hopwood intended that a man, already receiving a livable salary, should not receive an additional one for taking charge of a literary contest, especially at the expense of a major award.

...Weaver's duties are not sufficiently arduous to make the amount he is receiving a fair compensation. In a two month's investigation, it was found that his duties consist of advising students (shared with other members of the committee), presiding over committee meetings and executing decisions of the committee, and handling correspondence.

The payment of a $3,000 salary to one man is especially to be condemned since it has necessitated dropping one major award consisting of $2,500 which might have gone to some student well-deserving of it...

...

Whether Professor Weaver is aware of the circumstances, it is hard to tell. In frequent interviews, he has repeatedly denied that any member of the committee was getting a salary... In this he has been sincere, but it is hard to believe that one who is to receive $3,000 should be unaware of it.#

Negro Scholar, Almost Blind, May Quit 'U'

By MORTON MINTZ

(March 7, 1942) Herman C. Hudson, '44--the shy Negro boy who has translated the blurred images of his nearly-blind eyes into eloquent speech and amazing accomplishment--may soon be just another one of those students forced to leave school because he couldn't meet expenses.

He fought the toughest obstacles in his search for knowledge. Now, after a year in college, his scholarships are uncertain. They provide only the barest necessities, and not a cent for clothing or spending money. But they mean everything to him.

Herman Hudson can hardly see.

Attacked by spinal meningitis at the age of four, the nerves of both eyes were largely deadened, injured beyond repair. This did not dull his ambition: he was determined to be a scholar whatever the effort.

One of five children in a poor Detroit family, Herman graduated from Northwestern high school with an all "A" record, greatly aided by various devices for the near-blind.

While in high school he was awarded by student and faculty vote the National Honor Society pin for "scholarship, character, leadership and service to the school." In addition to holding the captaincy of the debate team in one of its most successful years, he participated in a number of oratorical and extemporaneous speech contests, winning all but one.

'Vaguely Outlined Mass'

Though gifted with outstanding public speaking ability, he was handicapped even in this by his eyes. He overcame research difficulties adequately but could not take advantage of audience reaction. He does not experience changes in facial expression at all, only a few heads in the first few rows and behind them a vaguely outlined mass. His glasses merely tone up his vision and are not corrective.

His lifelong hope of attending the University of Michigan was realized through one of these speech contests. He delivered a talk before the Detroit Lions Club which inspired a spontaneous offer to pay his room and board if he came here.

Encouraged by the offer, Herman obtained a tuition and text book scholarship from the State Rehabilitation Division and came to school here in February, 1941.

Cannot Read Print

Since then "life," as Herman puts it, "has been no picnic." It has been scarred by helpless frustration and marked by achievement. His heart set on the legal profession, with history his major, Herman attained an all "A" record in everything but history. For in this subject the required reading has been too much for Herman, since he cannot read print.

Herman has no way of studying except that of employing a person to read him the assignments aloud. This has worked well so far. Herman made his scholastic record during the first year with only 12 or 13 hours of "sound readings" a week. A shortage of NYA funds, which pay the readers, reduced this form of study to an insufficient 10 hours this semester. And Herman, who believes he needs a minimum of 16 hours weekly, is convinced his education is being seriously obstructed for this reason.

Keen Memory

His memory is so keen that he studies extremely little for final exams. Not having been able to take many notes, he

Aid Arouses Hopes Of Blind Scholar

(March 10, 1942) Herman C. Hudson, '44, is a happier and more optimistic student today.

The nearly-blind scholar who only three days ago thought he might have to leave school in June has received many offers of help from persons who read of his plight in Saturday's Daily.

The Abe Lincoln cooperative house offered Herman room and board free of charge if his present funds expired. Numerous persons have offered to read aloud to Herman for a total of approximately 30 hours per week--more than he had dreamed he would get of this, his only form of study. And Herman hopes a University tuition and textbook scholarship is in the offing.#

painfully developed the facility of making one reading session impress the material firmly upon his mind.

When Herman writes a speech or a paper for his English composition course, he uses a special typewriter with letters nearly one-quarter of an inch high.

...

Pessimistic Future

Herman's desire to learn will never burn out. But today, with no money from family or other sources, he is pessimistic about his future. The scholarship for tuition and textbooks may be cut off in June because the State Rehabilitation Division is getting constantly smaller appropriations from the Federal Government. Likewise, the Lions Club may feel too pinched to continue providing his room and board.

He is doing all he can to get University scholarships and stay in school. He has little but his courage to back him. He would gladly work but his eyes render him unfit for any ordinary jobs. If Herman Hudson leaves the University next June, his loss will not be the greatest.#

SCHOLAR—Herman C. Hudson, '44 took first place in the district contest of the National Extempore-Discussion held last night.

University records show a Herman Hudson, '44, received B.A., M.A. and Ph.D. degrees from the University, and went on to become a college faculty member.

Prof relieved of duties after classroom slide show

By PAUL TRAVIS
Associate Managing Editor

(Oct 10, 1972) Mark Green, a 35-year-old assistant chemistry professor, yesterday was relieved of his teaching duties for showing an anti-war slide show to his Chemistry 227 class last week.

In a move which could precipitate a major dispute over the academic freedom of faculty members, Thomas Dunn, acting chemistry department chairman, suspended Green, with salary, "pending a review in the near future."

Students in the class are presently conducting a petition drive to have Green reinstated.

Although Dunn could not be reached for direct comment last night, he reportedly felt the slide show was "irrelevant" to the subject matter of Green's course in chemistry lab techniques, according to Vice President for Academic Affairs Allan Smith.

Green maintained, however, that the show was relevant because "it demonstrated the misuse that is possible of the technology taught at the University."

In notifying Green of the suspension, Dunn cited Green's "actions beginning October 5."

On that date, Green permitted the Interfaith Council for Peace to show a 30-minute anti-war slide show to his organic chemistry classes.

The slide show, according to Green, "showed the manner in which the current air war is conducted. It also showed ads where large science-based corporations advertised with pride how they had turned their technological strengths to serve the military needs of our country in Vietnam."

He said he wanted his students to know that "the material we teach, in part, is used by those corporations to produce the weapons shown on the slides."

About 10 other University professors have already shown the slide show to their classes, said slide show sponsors.

After the first showing... Green placed a note in the mailboxes of all department personnel, publicizing the next show...#

Prof's suspension stirs protest

By EUGENE ROBINSON

(Oct. 11, 1972) While chemistry Prof. Mark Green is the only faculty member thus far to be censured for using class time to show the Interfaith Council for Peace's antiwar slide show, he is far from the only one to have shown the exhibit.

Approximately ten other professors from a range of departments have also shown the slides during class time, all with apparent impunity.

...

[Green] is only one of a number of University professors who use unusual approaches or unusual material to present their subjects.

Geography Prof. John Kolars, for example, often reads poetry to his introductory classes, as well as frequently discussing seemingly unrelated current affairs.

Kolars yesterday maintained, "Part of teaching anything is making people think of the possible effects of what they are learning." He said he has occasionally lectured on the Vietnam War from a geographical point of view.

...

Occasional lectures given by some professors seem to have an even more strained relationship to the actual information the course is designed to discuss.

History Prof. John Bowditch's class on European history from 1850-1870, for example, reportedly spent its first session last term discussing the high cost of plumbing and the ten most important persons in the 20th century.

...

Each year journalism Prof. John Stevens, in the midst of his course on the history of the media in America, devotes a class meeting to a film of the 30 best rated TV commercials of the year.

And psychology Prof. Robert Bjork teaches his students how to swing a golf club as part of a class session on skill learning.#

Assault on freedom

(Oct. 11, 1972) ...[Thomas]Dunn's suspension of [Mark] Green is reprehensible in a community of scholars which values the right of an instructor to teach his students free from the shackles of administrative or governmental control.

...

If class time can be deemed "misused," who can really make that decision? The department chairman? The vice president for academic affairs? Why not the professor?

Further, how is the distinction to be made between class time that is used appropriately and that which is not? As Green himself points out, the issue would not have been raised if he had shown a promotional film put out by a chemical company. Is he suddenly guilty for demonstrating some of the more negative applications of the same science?

IT IS EXTREMELY narrow-minded to view the educational process as a series of facts to be memorized, a series of skills to be learned...

...

In commenting on the Green case, Vice President for Academic Affairs Allen Smith told The Daily, "It's only a cause celebre if you make it one."

Smith, however, is wrong. Students and faculty haven't made it into a controversy. Dunn, and the administration which backs him, have.

--THE SENIOR EDITORS

GREEN TO TEACH PENDING REVIEW

By ERIC SCHOCH
and BETH ECNATER

(Oct. 14, 1972) Acting Chemistry Department Chairman Thomas Dunn yesterday reversed his own order and reinstated Prof. Mark Green to teaching Chemistry 227 "effective immediately."

Although Dunn indicated Thursday to The Daily that it was "purely speculative" whether or not Green might be reinstated soon, he said last night he had intended all along to reinstate him when the student-faculty committee had been formed...#

Ex-prof questions tenure denial

(Sept. 26, 1980) Editor's note: Every year, dozens of assistant and associate professors face an important question: Has their scholarly work been good enough to warrant a permanent assignment as a University professor? Only about half of the aspirants are granted the cherished tenure.

...

Most of the professors who are denied tenure leave silently, and seek employment elsewhere. The entire tenure selection procedure is characteristically quiet. Those who grant tenure and affected professors generally do not make revealing public comments.

Occasionally, however, a particular case sheds light on the mysterious tenure procedure.

...

The case of Clement Henry, a former associate professor of political science, is unusual because of the number of people either directly involved in, or close to, the decision-making who have been willing to discuss the reasons Henry was denied tenure.

Together, their comments provide a revealing look into the tenure procedure.

* * *

By LORENZO BENET

Clement Henry, a former associate professor of political science, suspects he was denied tenure last March by the LSA executive committee because of his personal political beliefs and his area of specialization.

Many of his colleagues believe his suspicions may be well-founded.

TWO MEMBERS of the executive committee, in a rare break in the silence usually surrounding such decisions, say the committee refused to promote him because his latest book was not of a high enough quality.

Committee members say his personal beliefs were never at issue in the tenure deliberations.

Henry, who sought a promotion from a non-tenured associate professorship to a full professorship, is only the second faculty member in the history of the political science department to be denied tenure after receiving a unanimous recommendation for promotion by the department's faculty members, according to Sam Eldersveld, a professor of political science.

...

Henry, Eldersveld, History Prof. Dick Mitchell, and former Director of the Center for Near Eastern and North African Studies William Schorger have hypothesized that Henry was denied tenure because he specializes in an area (Near Eastern and North African Studies) of minor importance to the University and supports the Arabs in the Arab-Israeli conflict.

...

Five of six executive committee members reached by phone vehemently denied that politics entered into the deliberations over Henry or any other faculty member who received a tenure review last year.

"Budgetary issues and the degree of specialization of a faculty member's field are not part of the tenure review process," explained Associate Dean of Academic Appointments Robert Holbrook. "Tenure decisions are based on scholarly record, teaching, and service."

WORD OF HENRY'S tenure denial was received with dismay and disapproval from the political science department and scholars worldwide, Eldersveld said.

"The whole thing is a mystery to me..."

...

"But let's face it," said history Prof. Mitchell, "The University is under financial seige and it has to make priorities around where to make cuts. If you're in a peripheral area, like Clement (Henry), you may be sacrificed. Faculty members in area studies could be squeezed out in the coming year, but my colleagues and I don't think the University should operate that way."

"SOME ZIONISTS who were students in Henry's class (Arab-Israeli conflict) may have sent letters to the executive committee saying he didn't teach his class objectively," said Schorger, who directed the center for Near-Eastern and North African Studies for 16 years. "Some committee members may have similar feelings, although the political science department and Henry himself insist he was evenhanded in the classroom."

According to Executive Committee member Edna Coffin and then-Executive Committee member Albert Feuer-

werker, Henry was denied tenure because his most recent book, "Images of Development: Egyptian Engineers in search of Industry," which is being published by MIT Press, did not meet the standards of the committee and did not measure up to Henry's previous publications. His other publications include two other solo books; three books written in conjunction with other area scholars, and more than 25 articles and papers that have been published by political science journals and presented at national conferences.

"He also had not published much over the last few years," Coffin added.

...

"If my most recent book and other publications were the basis of my tenure denial," said Henry, who has spent 10 years teaching and conducting research in the Middle East with several grants from major foundations, "then the Executive Committee and the social sciences promotion sub-committee were not qualified to review my material."

...

IN LSA, ONCE a faculty member has been recommended for promotion by his department, his publication material is reviewed by a humanities, natural sciences, or social sciences promotion sub-committee comprised of six faculty members. For example, since Henry was recommended for promotion by the political science department, his material was reviewed by six professors from the social sciences: Psychology Prof. Elizabeth Douvan, History Prof. Albert Feuerwerker, Anthropology Prof. Kent Flannery, Economics Prof. Peter Steiner, Sociology Prof. Charles Tilly, and Political Science Prof. Warren Miller, according to a document from the LSA dean's office. Miller had to exclude himself from the deliberations concerning Henry because of a possible conflict of interest.

...

"To the best of my recollection," said Eldersveld, "The department was told Henry received an unfavorable review from the social sciences sub-committee. It's incomprehensible to me that the college turned him down on the basis of his publishing record. His publishing record is internationally renowned and for his age bracket, he's at the top of his group."#

Students can sample about 25 'cake' courses

By MARIANNE EGRI

(April 1, 1979) One student's "cake" can be another's headache.

But undergraduates say in conversations that truly easy courses share some characteristics: light homework assignments, straightforward exams, lenient grades, and minimal required attendance.

STUDENTS WILL have the chance to sign up for at least 25 "cake" courses at registration this week--some will use them to balance heavy schedules, others to fulfill distribution requirements painlessly, still more to improve grade points, and, of course, most to be able to relax a little in the fall.

"We have an informal list (of easy classes) that we recommend to people," said Matt Rohr, a coordinator at Student Counseling Office. "We know from previous experience, or we've heard it from friends, so we file the information away and pass it on. But we keep our eyes on the department to make sure the classes haven't changed and the same professor is teaching it."

Here are some opinions from students and professors on some of the easier courses around:

SPEECH 100 (Fundamentals of Public Speaking). Engineering sophomore Kipton Moravec said, "The material is easy, it all depends on how you present it." Prof. Bill Colburn said, "How easy the course is depends on the student's natural ability for public speaking, but we work hard to present a good course."

...

PSYCHOLOGY 474 (Introduction to Behavior Modification). LSA junior Ellen Finegoth said, "Everyone in the class has an opportunity to get an A because everything is laid out on the table in a contract. It works; everyone learns the material because they know they can get an 'A', and it's interesting.

Prof. James McConnell said, "A lot of students take the course because it's perceived as having limited intellectual content, but this is true only for those students to whom learning is memorization. We don't give 'A's, students earn them. We specify what they're to learn and we reward them for doing exactly what we ask them to do."

JOURNALISM 201 (Social Role of Mass Media). LSA freshman Greg Thomas said, "It's kind of a blow-off course because you don't have to go to any lectures. Ninety per cent of the tests are on the book which is clear-cut." Prof. Marion Marzolf said, "I don't think it's a very hard course, but it's definitely not a course where we give all 'A's. The concepts are not difficult but it's very important because it teaches students to be critical media consumers."

...

GEOGRAPHY 101 (Intro). An LSA sophomore said, "It's a great class because there isn't much reading, the tests are multiple choice, and the prof. is interesting." Prof. John Kolars said, "I don't think it's a tough class, but it's not a gut 'A'. I work hard to make it entertaining and one reason students take it is they've heard it's easy. It comes down to the puritanical ethic--if something is dull, then students think it's worthwhile, if it's entertaining they think it's easy."

...

NATURAL RESOURCES 303 (Outdoor Recreation). Freshperson nursing student Sarah Newton said, "There's no required reading and there are two take-home midterms. I looked the answer up in the encyclopedia and that was more than sufficient. I feel like I'm totally wasting my time, the class is for athletes." Prof. Ross Tocher said, "It's an easy course because there's no memorization, no math, and no assignments. It's essay oriented and the reading is almost recreational reading because it is whatever area the student would like to read about."..#

-Daily--Bill Hampton

" . . . and then, before they've had time to recover from that, we hit 'em again on Wednesday morning!"

Let them eat, er, take cake

By PAMELA KRAMER

(April 2, 1981) Imagine a class that meets from 11 a.m. to noon on Mondays, Wednesdays, and Fridays, requires minimal attendance and few study hours, and guarantees four credits along with an A.

That sort of class is the quintessential "blow-off" course, according to many students passing through the peer academic counseling office. And, costing several hundred dollars, it is one of the most expensive pieces of cake they'll ever have the pleasure of tasting.

WHILE SOME people spend their entire college careers and a great deal of energy seeking out cake courses, others take an easier approach.

"We have one guy who comes in every semester for us to plan his schedule," said Dave Friedman, a peer academic counselor. "He wants easy four-credit classes, with nothing on Friday, and a 4.0 grade point at the end of the semester."

But, Friedman added, "I don't want people to think this office is the center for cake courses."

...

But, Friedman and other counselors point out, what one person considers a blow-off could be "harder than hell" for someone else. The seemingly simple definition of a cake course is actually elusive.

"I'd say a cake course is one that allows you to devote most of your time to other classes," said LSA sophomore Jill Schultz.

Social Behavior of Human Primates (Biological Anthropology 368) is a good example, according to Schultz. The course requires two objective exams, more than 500 pages of reading and for some students, a paper.

"It's probably one of the easiest courses I've ever had, but I've learned from it," Schultz said, adding that Prof. Hugh Gilmore who teaches the class makes the material easy to learn.

GILMORE, WHO HAS built up his class "from nothing to 500 students," said he doesn't mind at all that someone might call it a piece of cake.

"The way academia is, I'm supposed to be ashamed that someone would call my class a cake course," he said. "I'm supposed to say, 'I'm so smart, carrying the banner for Western Civilization, and I failed 90 percent of my class.'

"But it's meant to edify and enlighten people, to get them interested in it, and I know I've done that."

...

Peer counselors shake their heads sympathetically when speaking of students who heard a course was a blow-off, CRISPed into it and found out too late they were wrong.

"We get course evaluations here (at the peer counseling office)," said Friedman. "And you wouldn't believe some of them. Here. Econ 408, huge letters "Blow-off." Consumer Economics is not a blow-off."

BUT AN economics major might think it is, tell an English major about the class, and the result would be a very unhappy student.

"You have to be interested in a course, whether you heard it was difficult or easy," Friedman said. "An unchallenging course can cause stagnation, and that can mean a lower grade."..#

The ABCs of the G.P.A.
Gradeflation hits humanities, but sciences may be immune

By PAMELA KRAMER
and LINDA RUECKERT

(April 3, 1981) Are science courses tougher than the social sciences and humanities courses? Or are liberal arts professors grading easier to draw more interest to an area increasingly threatened by today's society?

Whatever the answers, data from the University's Office of the Registrar show that grade-point averages of "hard science courses" were often lower than those of social sciences and humanities courses.

THERE ARE A NUMBER of speculations about why this difference exists.

"It's not too surprising in a chemistry course or a physics course to have a lower grade point average than, say, a Psych course," said Prof. Charles Rulfs, who teaches Chem 123. The Chemistry division's total grade point was 2.677, while the Psychology Department's was 3.271.

Prof. David Shappio of the Department of Biological Sciences said he was surprised by some of the lower grade point averages, but that "in some of these big science courses, the students are taking several at once." The Biology Division's total GPA is 2.961.

"A STUDENT MAY BE taking Biology with Organic Chemistry, and sometimes even Physics on top of that," he explained. "Having done that myself, I know it's a heavy load, and that might have some effect (on the grades)."

Also, many professors say, students often take introductory level courses only to fulfill prerequisites, and although passing the class is important, the grade is not.

Another possible reason for the discrepancy between natural sciences and many other disciplines is that "often what is learned per se (in the humanities) is not easily quantifiable," according to one English professor.

"In a discipline like English one learns not so much a testable body of material, but rather, one acquires a gradual facility for literary interpretation," he explained.

...

MANY UNIVERSITY officials and faculty members cite "grade-flation" as a major problem in evaluating grade point averages.

"It's an appropriate matter for concern," said Macklin Smith, chairman of the undergraduate English program. "It makes things difficult for the individual professors. When you're faced with only three 'acceptable' grades, meaning A, A- and B+, evaluation is not as effective."

...

A CLOUD OF speculation hovers around the possible causes of grade inflation. One theory is that during the Vietnam War many professors on campuses across the country were more lenient in grading so that more students would be eligible for academic deferment.

"I think it was more because in the sixties and early seventies a different philosophy of education permeated college campuses," Judge said. "The emphasis was more on the positive side (than in the past), and I think the change in grading was part of that change in philosophy."..#

the crusades

the auto ban

The auto ban was resented by the students and by The Daily (in editorials and undertone) more for the method of enforcement, via the Dean of Students Joseph A. Bursley, than for the ban per se. Bursley hired a motorcycle cop to patrol the streets at night to seek out violators. The cop had a receding chin and immediately became known as Andy Gump, after the chinless comic character.

The cop would snoop around locations of campus dances and other local dance halls to write down license numbers.

By the way, married students could drive, as could any student who needed a car on a job during those hours when on the job. Of course, those of us who were correspondents naturally needed a car at all hours.

—Larry Klein, '30

AUTOMOBILE REGULATIONS

(April 23, 1927) Several automobile accidents of rather serious consequence recently have once more brought the regulations concerning the use of cars by students to the fore. It is rumored that the University authorities believe the present ruling to be a failure and contemplate a change this summer--that change probably to be the complete abolition of student-owned cars, following the example of Illinois, Princeton and other colleges.

It is admitted that the rulings this year have not been successful. The trouble, however, lies not in the regulations, which are the sanest treatment of the problem yet advanced in the United States, but in the prescribed means of enforcement...

The regulations at present provide that freshmen and sophomores shall not own or operate automobiles at Ann Arbor, that students who fail to maintain a "C" average, no matter what class, shall be denied permission, that students under 21 years of age must obtain the written consent of their parents, and that all cars must be registered in the office of the Dean of Students. That is an ideal arrangement; change is unnecessary.

The regulations further provide that enforcement be left to a committee, appointed by the President of the Student Council, consisting of six students and two members of the faculty... The Daily recommends that the Board of Regents change this one action, creating a committee of three, to be composed of the Dean of Students, a representative of the office of the dean of women, and one other member of the faculty to be appointed by the President of the University...

...

...Strict enforcement after the laxity of this year will undoubtedly be temporarily unpopular, but in the long run such action would be far more satisfactory to all concerned that the unreasonable abolition of all cars, with no regard whatever for the rights of those students who are perfectly capable of operating cars in a sane manner, with no danger either to themselves or the community.

Above all, Michigan does not want complete abolition of student owned cars!#

Value Of Rolling Stock Soars When Students Take To Skates

By Timothy Hay

(April 24, 1927) "If we can't ride, we'll roll," seems to be the philosophy of students seen yesterday on campus rushing along on roller skates, evidently in protest of the proposed ruling of the Regents banning student autos.

The stadium on the diagonal was a favorite skating rink, and students welcomed the move that found some use for the white benches. Edward C. Pardon, superintendent of the buildings and grounds department, said last night that as far as he knows there is no rule against skating on the campus walks, although bicycles are barred.

Hardware stores reported last night that they were completely sold out of skates and were ordering additional supplies by express. One store reported that in one hour they sold more than a dozen pair, and that one fraternity bought six pairs in a single lot.

...

Perhaps the R. O. T. C. will be called out to handle the traffic tangles that are sure to result at the intersections of the walks...

Athletic officials have not as yet announced intramural skating races, but they ought to have them. No ruling has been made as to whether students who get a speed equal to that of an auto out of their skates will be hailed up for driving without one of these student auto permits...#

FIRST ACCIDENTS FROM ROLLER SKATING OCCUR

(April 29, 1927) First casualties due to the roller skating fad were reported yesterday. Amos Smith, senior in the Ann Arbor high school, suffered a fractured leg late Wednesday night and William Stevens, '30A, received cuts about the head. Both were treated at the University hospital...#

LITTLE WILL TEST NEED OF AUTO BAN BY RIGID ACTION

President Grants Request Of The Daily; Failure Means Ban Of All Student Autos

(April 26, 1927) Rigid enforcement of the present automobile regulations, backed financially by the University and resulting in drastic punishment for offenders convicted, will be tried in Ann Arbor the remainder of this semester. This action, decided upon by Present Clarence Cook Little after a conference with the editors of The Daily yesterday afternoon, is intended to give the present regulations a real test, and if it becomes evident that they can be enforced, a general ban on student cars will not be considered necessary.

The President, although believing the best procedure to be the abolition of all student cars with the idea of eventually reinstating them gradually if such action is ever deemed feasible, is willing to cooperate with The Daily in giving students a last chance to prove themselves worthy of keeping their cars. He agrees that the present regulations constitute the ideal settlement of the situation provided they can be enforced without the expenditure of an unreasonable amount of money for policing. The Daily has maintained that the regulations, because of their lax enforcement thus far, have never been given a chance, and with the aid and cooperation of the student body, will attempt to prove to the administration that the present rules, having gained the respect of the students, can be enforced.

If the experiment succeeds, the present rules will be continued; if it fails it will have been definitely proved that abolition of all cars is the only way out of the situation at Michigan, and neither students nor The Daily will have any justification to further opposition to the ban...#

PATERNALISM

(May 1, 1927) A strict ban on automobiles..possible night hours for fraternities and men's rooming houses..an espionage system for the detection and the analysis of the student during his leisure time and during the summer vacation..courses in concentrated judgment and wisdom.. in short, absolute paternalism in American colleges. All these are the pictures painted by President Little in his speeches of the past week before the students and organizations of educators in convention here.

Even granting that the University has the right to do all of these things and that the moves might further the cause of actual education, it would seem that the natural obstacles to the plan make it impractical and almost impossible of realization. There is, in the first place, the question of administration and expense. The force required and the expenses involved in the enforcement and execution would cost many thousands of dollars. And it would be difficult to get away from the reformatory side of life, the danger of moralizing and idealizing, and the painting of fanciful castles in the air. Once started there would forever by wrangling about the actual results of the work being done because of its intangible nature and because of the impossibility of ascertaining its success.

...

On the whole it seems that the circle of prohibitions that would be drawn around education would, in the first place, be almost impossible of enforcement, and would, in the second place, lose the cause of higher education in a maze of technical police work. To place too many restrictions on education and make it not only selective, but also paternal, will have the effect on the majority of making the University an advanced grammar school, and a diploma the reward for those who have the spinelessness required to accept a vast amount of supervision while an education is forced on them.#

TO THE STUDENTS:

(April 26, 1927) The President of the University, after a conference with the editors of The Daily, has consented to give students of Michigan another chance to prove their ability to handle the automobile situation without the necessity of a ban on all student owned cars. The final decision in the case, after three days of debate, now rests squarely with the student body.

If the present regulations are rigidly enforced until the close of school in June, there will be no general abolition. If the students, with all the facts clearly before them, prefer to continue to disregard the reasonable laws now in effect, there can be no excuse whatever for any opposition to the more drastic rules. Complete abolition will then be, obviously, the only possible remaining procedure.

The punishment meted out to students who continue to drive without permits will be severe. An effective effort to bring guilty students before the committee will be made...

The drastic punishment of offenders is to be preferred to laxity that can lead only to the prohibition of cars to the hundreds of students who use them sensibly and appreciate them as one of the greatest of modern conveniences.

The Daily has opposed the general ban because of the conviction of its editors that students, when they appreciate the situation, will aid wholeheartedly in the enforcement of the present laws. The President has generously offered the student body another chance despite the total failure of the regulations up to this time. Cooperation will mean the continuance of the restrictions: non-cooperation will mean the complete ban on all cars at the close of this semester. The decision rests with the campus.

THE EDITORS OF THE DAILY

STUDENT CARS BANNED

H. C. Emery Will Enforce Auto Ruling
In New Position As Assistant
Dean of Students

(June 20, 1927) Appointment of Dr. G. Carl Huber to succeed the late Dean Alfred H. Lloyd as head of the graduate school, acceptance of the resignations of Dean Mortimer E. Cooley of the College of Engineering and Architecture, and Prof. J. E. Reighard of the zoology department, and the complete ban of all student automobiles for next year were the principal measures taken by the Board of Regents in its annual meeting Friday night.

...

Drastic Action Taken On Autos

The announcement that "no student in attendance at the University from and after the first of the semester this coming fall shall operate any motor vehicle, except in exceptional and extraordinary cases, when at the discretion of the Dean of Students this rule may be relaxed," came as the culmination of several months of debate and the trial of a compromise plan of partial limitations.

Harvey C. Emery, instructor in physical education, was appointed assistant dean of students, to be in charge of the enforcement of the new regulation. Michigan is the third large university in the country to take such drastic steps regarding student driven cars.#

DISCIPLINE OR PROHIBITION

(June 20, 1927) The Regents, after months of arguing, and after putting into effect for a few weeks the compromise advocated by The Daily, have decided to ban student automobiles except "in exceptional and extraordinary cases."

The Daily respects the Regents for their careful consideration and their interest in student welfare. It notes their discretion in delaying their action until after most of the students had left town. The Daily pledges itself, as an institution supporting the voice of authority in the University, to further the enforcement of whatever regulations are in effect to such an extent as it deems logical and compatible with the best interest of the University community.

However, the editors respectfully maintain their opinion on automobile regulations as stated in previous editorials. They do not feel that the compromise plan has been in operation long enough to judge wisely its success. They do not feel that evidence so far indicates that the plan has been anything but successful. They do not consider a complete restriction feasible.

...

However, the ban is to be accepted as passed. Now it only remains to hope for a liberal interpretation of the provisions for special permits. In accordance with its opinion that a majority of the students are perfectly capable and competent to operate cars without harm or destruction, The Daily trusts that the administration will allow these people to continue driving. The difficulties to enforcement will be endless, and in order to avoid such complete failure as would result in disregard of the ban, the only possible means of maintaining control, admittedly desirable if not too drastic, appears to be to employ considerable lenience in granting special permits.#

• • •

(June 20, 1927) The Regents certainly added a note of joy to Commencement. All we seniors are rejoicing now that we are graduating while this is still a University, and not a kindergarten.

• • •

DOWN THE DIAGONAL

(June 20, 1927) "Now that the Regents are taking so much interest in the life and safety of students," remarked the Cynical Senior yesterday, "maybe they will tear down some of the fire-traps and tumble-down shacks in which they hold classes."

Maybe it was just a coincidence, but: June 16--last of students leave town; June 17--Regents place ban on autos, after delaying it two months.

AS ONE ALUMNUS TO ANOTHER

After a year of panning the alumni, we sort of hate to have the stigma attached to our own name, but all the professors seemed anxious to thus curse us, so here we are. And since we're here, we might as well make the best of it.#

--Timothy Hay, A.B.

Dean Rea Frowns at 'Canoe Ban' Rumors; Too Hard for 'Andy' to Enforce, He Says

(May 22, 1930) Telephone calls came in thick and fast at The Daily office yesterday because someone had spread an insidious rumor that the Board of Regents was contemplating a ban on student use of canoes. Indignant undergraduates, and gleeful members of the present graduating class, who were delighted to hear that their younger classmates would be forced to suffer even more than they had suffered under the present auto regulation, were calling up frantically to secure definite information.

Walter B. Rea, assistant to the dean, was immediately interviewed but the news was quite as much of a surprise to him as to those seeking the confirmation.

"We would have a tough time," said Rea, "attempting to regulate such a ban, even if it were contemplated..."

...

Rea suggested that such an enforcement would lead to other difficulties as well. The University rule of parking without lights or operating a vehicle without a license would be hard to enforce in the event of a "canoe ban."..#

---

city matters

The Taxicab Wars

TAXI RATE RAISE OBJECT OF STRONG STUDENTS' ATTACK

FRATERNITIES AND SORORITIES WILL FIGHT COMPANIES TO FINAL SHOW-DOWN

CITY COUNCIL BALKS RAILROADING EFFORT

(Nov. 7, 1917) Investigation of the proposed increase in taxicab fares was begun Tuesday by the ordinance committee of the city council, according to one of its members.

Some of the committee look favorably upon a system of meter taxing for fares. They feel that the plan proposed by the taxicab companies is one which would be unfair and making a class discrimination against students.

...

Raise Unconstitutional

It is thought probable that the new schedule of rates may not be constitutional... for, according to a council member, the new scale of prices would affect University students more than any other class.

...

"We most certainly will place our every effort to prevent the increase," said one fraternity president. Another declared that the rates would be accompanied by the falling off in patronage of about 60 men that he knew were convinced of the unfairness of the plan.

"Most girls will no doubt feel as we do," stated a sorority president. "We will help the men combat the so-called 'gouge prices' of the taxi companies. We can walk and we will. I am sure there are other girls who will be ready to co-operate."#

RAPS TAXICAB COMPANIES

STUDENT BELIEVES RECKLESS "PROFITEERING" AT PRESENT TIME SHOULD BE STOPPED

Editor, The Michigan Daily:

(Nov. 8, 1917) An issue has been raised by the faculty and students of the University of Michigan relative to the action of the city taxicab companies in raising their rates...

...

...Now when every patriotic student in the University is endeavoring to the best of his ability to economize, it would be a rank injustice to impose any extra burdens upon him either directly or indirectly.

...

Many students and members of the faculty are buying Liberty bonds, many are subscribing to the Y. M. C. A. army fund, many are helping the Red Cross. Many students are working their way through school and buying Liberty bonds at the same time... Should these men be imposed upon? Why can't this issue be put up to the taxi companies in this light? Surely, they are expected to get onto the band wagon and do their patriotic bit.

...

...They must not expect to make the profit they did formerly especially now that their patrons are undergoing extra burdens imposed by the war. It is ludicrous to even think of meatless, wheatless and sweetless days if we allow such a palpable injustice as this one proposed by the taxi companies.#

A JUNIOR LAW

THE PARTY RATE

(Nov. 8, 1917) How is the actual cost of service which the taxicab companies deliver worth the exorbitant rate they demand for parties? Why should they charge 25 cents for the average run during the day, and two dollars per couple for a round trip some special evenings?

...

The companies more than once have failed to live up to the present ordinance in regard to parties. Last winter one wanted three dollars the round trip for a certain dance. Those in charge knew the limit was two dollars and immediately secured another company. This is only one instance in which a company was perfectly willing to break the present ordinance provided it could do it.#

ATTACK EXORBITANT TAXICAB RATES

DAILY TO OPEN FIRE ON LOCAL PRICE RACKETS

By BARTON KANE

(Sept. 20, 1931) An effort to eliminate exorbitant charges by taxicab drivers in Ann Arbor which in the last few years have cost students thousands of dollars, will be made this fall by The Daily. Within a few days, prices of all companies will be published.

Free lance drivers are operating on Ann Arbor streets, and it is they in particular who fleece the students each week end and especially on football days. Each year with the opening of the football season the various cab companies

---

COMPLAINTS

Students are asked to send all complaints of overcharging on the part of cab drivers to the editorial director of The Daily together with the name and number of the cab which attempts to jump prices.

---

go up in their prices without notice to patrons, and, as a result, many are charged as much as $1 per person for transportation to the stadium. If companies do that this year, students will be asked to form a boycott against such companies, and to patronize only those that give them regular prices.

Failure of students to complain has afforded the chance for the drivers to evolve into a class of petty racketeers, according to one driver who wishes his name withheld.

"Our prices depend on the passengers we are carrying," he said. "If we know them, we charge the regular price, but if we don't know them, the price is raised."

"I guess about the only way to give the students a break is to make meter cabs compulsory. Unless the city council does that, the racket will go on as in the past. Still, it's the students' fault--they seem willing enough to pay."#

PROBE BARES RACKETS

STUDENTS, FACULTY COMPLAIN OF EXORBITANT TAXI CHARGES

By BARTON KANE

(Oct. 1, 1931) Additional rackets practiced by Ann Arbor taxicab drivers which are used to fleece students were revealed today through The Daily's investigation of cab rates. Complaints were received from students and faculty members concerning exorbitant charges, and Wilford "Punchy" La Beau was identified as a wildcat driver who has charged abusive rates.

Harry McCain, owner of the Buick Taxi company, told investigators that drivers often take company signs from their cabs just before the close of campus social functions on Friday and Saturday nights, in order that they may jump the usual company rates and overcharge the students...

...

Wilford J. "Punchy" La Beau, operator of a wildcat cab, was definitely identified by The Daily as one of the local racketeers who is charging 35 cents for each passenger and an additional ten cents for each stop, no matter how short the run may be. La Beau has a sign on the front of his Plymouth sedan which says "35 cents Flat Rate."

...

...The head of one of the legitimate companies told The Daily that "Punchy" said last summer he would re-paint his car if necessary in order to fool the students.

...

Within a few weeks, the Ann Arbor city council will consider the taxicab situation, it was understood last night, and at that time The Daily will send representatives to ask for low meter rates or a set rate for all cabs operating in Ann Arbor...#

Students and The Taxi Cabs

(Oct. 1, 1931) THE recent demands for revision of taxicab rates so as to eliminate the independent wildcat operator, or else bring him under control so that the student or citizen who uses Ann Arbor cabs will not be overcharged, call for nothing less than a revision of section 10 of the city ordinance to regulate taxicabs and similar vehicles in the town of Ann Arbor.

This part of the municipal code sets forth the maximum rates that may be charged by Ann Arbor cab drivers, to be determined by taximeter. If no such meters are used, the ordinance continues, the cabs shall display a sign stating "Flat Rate 35c." But whether that flat rate shall apply regardless of the number of passengers, is not stated. And many drivers have ruthlessly overcharged their passengers either because they were ignorant of the legal provisions, or because they were accompanied by women and felt they could not argue with the drivers.

...

Compulsory meters on all cabs, charging on a basis somewhat nearer the figures charged by metropolitan cab companies would be much fairer than the present rates.

...

It is high time the council took action, or else people will start to believe that the taxicab interests constitute such a vested interest that no one dares to attempt to control or regulate them.#

STANDARD RATE IS AGREED UPON BY CAB OWNERS

(Nov. 5, 1931) ...Agreeing on a standard rate for the first time in history, the Ann Arbor taxicab owners met yesterday and drew up a schedule of prices to be effective beginning next Friday.

This ends the brief taxi war, in which three companies reduced their charges to 25 cents a trip for five passengers. The new rates represent a slight increase over those in force at the beginning of the present semester.

"We feel that this schedule, which will be rigidly adhered to, will afford owners a fair margin of profit and will not be too high for students to pay," a representative of the operators told The Daily last night...#

Storm of Protest Follows Campaign On Parking Lights

BY BARTON KANE

(Aug. 5, 1932) Tagging of students' cars by the Ann Arbor police department for parking without lights has necessitated a general warning to Summer Session students to avoid leaving their cars in front of dormitories, rooming and fraternity houses. A notice posted recently in the office of Chief O'Brien stated that the force should also watch for stop-street violators.

Mayor W. Wirt Newkirk criticized the method used by the department, and stated that he did not feel that it was just to tag some and permit others to go. "If they would get them all," he said, "they would have a thousand every day."

He intimated that the police have zoned the city, and are picking up "a few cars each night to keep the ordinance alive."

Judging, however, from the number of complaints which have been made to

---

Police 'Get 'Em All,' But Release Big Ones

Investigators for The Daily going through files of traffic violations last night found one marked Albert Rapp. "Yes," explained the policeman, "it doesn't matter whether he's prosecuting attorney or not. We get 'em all."

Further investigation, however, revealed that "Released" had been marked across the card. After first stating he did not know what the inscription meant, the policeman admitted it meant just that, hurriedly grabbed it and thrust it in another file.

O tempora, O Mores!

The Daily the police are more than "picking up a few each night."

...

Women at Mosher-Jordan dormitory stated that they had been leaving their cars out all summer, and that they had never been warned or tagged before. Two women, Miss Bernice Francis of Standish and Mrs. Sally M. Brown of Saginaw, who live in Betsy Barbour dormitory, received tags last night for "no lights."

...

Officers at the department stated last night that they saw no reason why special courtesy should be shown out-of-state and out-of-town violators.

...

Police last night maintained that there is no drive on at present to tag violators. It is a thing that goes on all year long, they said...#

An Editorial

(Feb. 17, 1933) Prices are down. The buying power of the dollar has increased. Food is cheaper; rent is cheaper; taxis are cheaper; movies are cheaper.

But it still costs a half a dollar to get a haircut in Ann Arbor.

College boys are suckers. They don't know the value of money.

This seems to be the slogan that barbers in the campus area have adopted. In every other town in the state haircuts have come down to 35, 25, and 15 cents. Evidently these prices allow fair profits.

...

There is one way to bring the price down to normal. That is for students to have their tonsorial work done in their home towns.

The loss of business to local shops would cause price competition. And the barbers would be forced to change their slogan about the college boys and suckers.#

Barbers Differ Over Price Cut

(Feb. 17, 1933) Although several boss barbers around the campus claim that there will be no reduction in the price of haircuts, others indicated yesterday that a lowering of rates in inevitable.

At a recent meeting of the boss barbers, it was agreed upon that the price of haircuts for adults would remain at fifty cents, while children under 12 would be charged only twenty-five.

...

The recent damaging of barber shops in Detroit as a result of price wars was mentioned by some as the reason why they would not act in violation of the barbers agreement to keep prices up, although they admitted that they were too high.

Haircuts at the Union, although the cash price is fifty-cents, can be obtained at forty-one cents, if coupons are used...#

Haircut Rate Reduced

(Feb. 18, 1933) Boss barbers in Ann Arbor held a meeting last night and reduced the prices of haircuts to 35 cents.

The action was taken after it was learned that students were protesting the high rate and intended to have their hair cut out of town unless prices were forced down. It was also learned that law students were thinking of installing a barber shop in the Law Club.

The new price level is in accord with that of other cities surrounding Ann Arbor.

Although the possibility of a "price war" was termed absurd by the boss barbers last night, nevertheless, they announced that, in the event that individual shops, not in harmony with the action taken last night, cut prices to a still lower level, they would be ready to meet competition...#

Police Open Drive; Daily Investigators Seized

By BARTON KANE

(Aug. 6, 1932) Ann Arbor police yesterday arrested three editors of The Daily staff who were investigating traffic law enforcement activities and taking pictures and held them at the police station nearly two hours for investigation.

Upon the arrival of police commissioner W. L. Dawson, however, they were released. He admitted that Casper C. Michelsen, the patrolman who took the three men to the police station had no right to arrest them.

The incident occurred shortly after noon yesterday when it was discovered that patrolman in plain clothes had been stationed at six corners to catch traffic violators. Commissioner Dawson later admitted that a drive had been started in all parts of the city on violators. Yesterday's activities were confined to drivers who failed to stop at stop streets.

Between 11 and 1 o'clock, members of the force were placed at the corners of North University and State streets, South University and State streets, Liberty and State streets, Packard and Main streets, and Huron and Fourth avenue...#

Police Refuse To Release Data On Traffic Arrests

By BARTON KANE

(Aug. 7, 1932) Refusing to divulge any information concerning the "holding for investigation" of three Daily Editors Friday, Sergeant Louis W. Fohey, acting Chief of Police of Ann Arbor, yesterday profanely dismissed two Daily reporters from the Police Station before they had any opportunity to investigate further arrests of traffic violators.

Sergeant Fohey, who complained about some of the words used in articles that appeared in The Daily pertaining to enforcement of automobile regulations, was asked exactly what terms he thought objectionable.

"I'm not answerin' any question," he shouted. "Get the hell of here!"

...

When requested to give the reason for the arrest of the Editors, he replied that the police could arrest anyone that they wanted and could hold them 48 hours for investigation.

He told The Daily reporters that he could arrest them, if he desired, on a charge of murder.

When asked, "What murder?" he replied, "Oh, any murder. There are lots of them."

Traffic Violations Mount

The number of arrests for traffic violations mounted yesterday and, although the picket of plain-clothes spotters that had been stationed at street intersections in the University area was removed, regular officers continued to hand out tickets.

...

Chief of Police Thomas O'Brien, long known as the "friend of the students" returned from his vacation yesterday and will be interviewed this morning. He stated last night that he had nothing to do with the Police force at this time, that the squad during his vacation was under the direction of Sergeant Fohey and the commissioners alone.#

Mayor Orders Quiz in Police Methods Here

By BARTON KANE

(Aug. 9, 1932) An investigation was ordered yesterday by Mayor H. Wirt Newkirk into the practices of the Ann Arbor police.

The session is scheduled for 7:30 o'clock tonight in the City Hall when the police commissioners, Mayor Newkirk, Daily investigators and witnesses will consider charges of "discourtesy" and "false arrest" on the part of the local department.

Witnesses of the Michelsen episode in front of the Union last Friday afternoon with whom The Daily has not been in touch are requested to call or see the city editor or his assistant today. Anyone who wishes to register complaints against the police should also call or visit The Daily offices...

The group will also consider the case of Patrolman Michelsen who is alleged to have called state educators who are enrolled in the Summer Session abusive names.

Continue Drive

The drive continued yesterday with the tagging of many motorists. Regulations which the local department are attempting to enforce are printed on page four of this paper...#

Why The Daily Crusades

(Aug. 7, 1932) NOT to fight the Ann Arbor police. NOT to make news. NOT to seek abuses from the local department. But to bring courtesy to 3,800 students who are guests of the University and the city of Ann Arbor during the Summer Session. Further to warn the students that they must not violate the city ordinances, and to assist them in avoiding the necessity of paying cash for fines.

The issue was opened by The Daily as a friendly means of calling to the attention of the students that a drive had been opened. Early the next day, however, the first rift was made when the police picketed the campus area with four plain-clothes officers besides the regular allotment of bluecoats. The other special police officers carried on the campaign for the whole city area.

...

Despite the overwhelming abuses The Daily does not wish to "fight" the department. We WANT courtesy for the students. We WANT the civil rights of citizens regarded in the making of arrests.

These we want because we do not feel that the citizens of Ann Arbor desire to harbor an arrogant police system. The police are the servants of organized society. They are at the disposal of orderly citizens. And The Daily feels that Ann Arbor honestly desires friendliness from these visitors who come for two months each summer with thousands of dollars to deposit in local coffers...#

Brutal Beating Case Brought Against Police

Five Witnesses Charge Suma With Inexcusable Manhandling Of Victim

(May 7, 1937) Accusations of extreme brutality in arresting Fred Chase, 33-year-old University custodian, on a drunk and disorderly charge were levied yesterday against Patrolman Herman Suma of the Ann Arbor police force by five eyewitnesses.

Chase, who is still confined to Dr. Gates' private hospital, claimed that he was struck in the eye with either a billy or

> Other witnesses to the arrest of Fred Chase at 12:40 p.m. last Saturday on the corner of State and North University Avenues are asked to communicate with The Daily.

blackjack at the time of his arrest last Saturday afternoon. He is also suffering from a badly bruised neck and lacerated lip.

Chase was arrested at the corner of State and N. University Avenues at 12:40 p.m. Saturday on a street crowded with visitors to the Michigan Schoolmasters' Convention.

...

Admits Drinking

Admitting that he had been drinking, Chase stated he was waiting to cross State Street by the Quarry Drug Store when Patrolman Suma noticed that he was staggering and ordered him to "Come on!" Chase moved back a step and Suma smashed him across the face. He was semi-conscious from then on and has no recollection of further events until he came to in a cell at the county jail, he stated.

Police hit Chase "So hard I could see his eyes roll," after he was in the police car and sitting between two policemen according to Edna Steeb, an employee of a State Street book store who was passing by in a car. "It was completely unjustified," she said.

Betty Gillen, a clerk at The Quarry, said: "The man wasn't causing any trouble. There didn't seem to be any excuse for hitting him. He made no resistance."

...

Still another witness called it "The most disgusting thing I ever saw."..#

Junior Levies Third Charge Against Police

(May 9, 1937) Edward J. Slezak, '38Ed. yesterday accused police and the prosecutor's office of refusing to issue a warrant for the arrest of a truck driver who, he said, had assaulted him Feb. 27. It was the third charge aimed at police in as many days.

Slezak said that police overrode his insistence to swear out a warrant with orders to "Go on home." The truck driver, whose name Slezak said was Crow, was greeted by his first name by police the night of the arrest, Slezak stated.

Slezak charged he suffered a slight concussion of the brain as a result of the beating.

Accuses Truck Driver

He said he had called police when the truck driver began roughing him. Police made Slezak go with them, he charged, and allowed his attacker to proceed to the station by himself in his own car.

...

"They held a conference in the office and were just coming out when Crow came in. A policeman greeted him by his first name. He went inside and stayed there about five minutes. When he came out he was allowed to leave freely. They told me to go home.

"I stated I wanted to swear out a warrant and they again told me to go home. One policeman said, 'You students should stay on the campus.' They continued to refuse either to swear out a warrant or take me back to the place I was arrested. I had to walk home," Slezak continued...#

Maedchen In Uniform...

(May 13, 1937)...We still believe that the police have been very decent on many occasions when they might have been more severe. But this makes only the more embarrassing the series of incidents which have recently arisen in which the police have apparently acted with inexcusable brutality.

This is not a feud between The Daily and the Police Department. It is not a crusade. It is not even primarily the concern of students. It is a matter for the citizens of Ann Arbor, and we shall consider our part in the matter closed when the citizens have caused the case to be heard in public and have been informed whether brutality has been used in the past and whether it will be a part of police tactics in the future.

Above all, in this instance, The Daily is functioning, not as a student newspaper, but as a community newspaper... It is not a question of the treatment which student offenders receive from the police. It is a question of the treatment which the police accord to underprivileged, defenseless citizens of Ann Arbor...#

2 Patrolmen Suspended For Brutality

(May 14, 1937) Patrolman Herman Suma and Casper Enkemann were suspended yesterday from the police force for four days without pay for "unnecessary brutality" during the arrest of Fred Chase, University custodian, on May 1 for drunk and disorderly conduct.

Punishment of the two climaxed an investigation which began last Monday at the instigation of citizens who witnessed the arrest. Each of the officers will lose $20 in pay as a result of his suspension.

...

Mayor Walter C. Sadler said last night that he would be personally responsible for the elimination of such police actions in the future...#

The Incorrigible Cell:
Harvey's Ace-in-the-Hole

By STEPHEN FIRSHEIN
Associate Managing Editor
and URBAN LEHNER

(Feb. 23, 1968) "The 'hole' has been used for 40 years," says Washtenaw County Sheriff Douglas J. Harvey, "and it will be used when I'm gone."

The county jail's "hole," or "incorrigible cell" is a nearly pitch-black 6-by-7-foot room with a solid metal door, no bed, no toilet facilities, no floor drain, and subminimal ventilation. It is employed according to the portly first-term sheriff "for prisoners who assault an officer, fight with or sexually attack other prisoners, destroy county property within the jail regulations."

...

Indeed, the hole has been used for a variety of other offenses.

- About a year ago, a Negro man, in jail for alimony payment delinquency, was thrown into the "hole" for several hours because he refused to shave off his beard.

- Over the past Christmas holidays, in separate incidents, two groups of antiwar protesters incarcerated on a 1965 trespass charge were thrown into the incorrigible cell after guards discovered the inmates making hot chocolate over toilet paper fires on the cement floor. In both cases, according to witnesses, the same person--a "regular" at the jail, and not a draft protester--made the fires...

- A law student at the University spent a night in the hole because he made a gibe when the deputy sheriff was filling out the arrest information card. He had originally been picked up because he had warned a boy at the scene of an automobile accident of his "constitutional right to remain silent" when being questioned by a policeman.

The protesters' treatment in the county jail has stirred a controversy which became heated last week when Gus Harrison, director of the State Department of Corrections wrote Harvey a letter requesting that he close down the hole because it has no sanitary facilities.

"I of course had no idea the cell was there," Harrison said in a phone interview last week. "My inspector did, but he had no reason to think it was being used." Apparently the cell's use came to Harrison's attention recently.

"Wasn't there some commotion up there about some draft protestors? I guess that's what led us to believe the cell had been in use," he said.

Harvey declines to estimate how often the hole is used but does claim that "there was one stretch of eight months when it was never used."

The sheriff said last week that Harrison's "recommendation" that the incorrigible cell no longer be used is officially received and noted. But, he continued, "Recommendation refused."

"As a police officer, I'm naturally suspicious," says Harvey.

He continues, "I can't help but wonder if Mr. Harrison isn't suddenly starting to wilt from a little heat applied by some of the local subversive minorities."

...

Whether the department of corrections is aware the hole existed or not, Sheriff Harvey's incorrigible cell fails to meet the state standards required by the "Rules for County Jails," issued by Harrison's office. According to R 791.23 Rule 3(c), housing facilities for jail inmates shall consist of "One or more incorrigible cells of a minimum size of 8 feet by 8 feet with plain walls with vertical bars in front, and the front lined on the inside with security screen. These cells shall be equipped with a concrete bunk 18 inches high and 24 inches wide and a 4-inch floor drain."

Yet one former inmate who measured the cell by counting out paces, claims the cell is 88 inches by 66 inches, well below the specifications, even allowing a few inches leeway. Eric Chester, Grad, who was among the protesters, says that "When I slept on the floor of the cell my feet and head were touching the opposite walls and I'm not eight feet tall." (Chester measures 5-feet, 10-inches.) Instead of vertical bars there is a solid steel door. The cell lacks a bunk or a floor drain. "The only thing in that cell is two pipes across the ceiling," says one jail trustee. Trustees are well-behaved prisoners permitted to spend several days a month out of the jail.

The incorrigible cell finds more sympathy among county officials than Lansing prison authorities. County supervisors on the six-man sheriff's committee generally support Harvey's use of the hole. The committee meets regularly to discuss questions relation to the county police force, conducts irregular tours of the jail, and reports to the entire board on the sheriff's budget -- some $750,000 this year...#

Incorrigible Cell Closed After Second Order

By MICHAEL DOVER

(March 6, 1968) Washtenaw County Sheriff Douglas Harvey closed the controversial "incorrigible cell" yesterday after being asked to do so for the second time by the State Department of Corrections.

However, according to Undersheriff Harold Owings, "We're going to make two new incorrigible cells out of another cell."

The old incorrigible cell became a center of controversy recently when two groups of persons arrested at the Octiber, 1965 Ann Arbor Draft Board sit-in were put in it for allegedly trying to melt candy bars into hot chocolate.

The cell broke a number of state regulations including the requirement that it have toilet facilities and a bunk, as well as being smaller than the size for single-person incorrigible cells required by the state.

The new cells will be properly constructed, according to Owings.

...

Undersheriff Owings said yesterday the cell was not closed earlier "due to the fact that the letter was only a recommendation. Someone can tell me to jump off a bridge and I won't do it," Owings added.

Apparently, yesterday's visit by the Jail Inspector cleared up the matter. "He showed us why the cell didn't comply," Owings said. In addition, Russell "ordered" the cell closed...#

the crusades

free speech

1
9
2
3

WICKERSHAM DENIED RIGHT TO SPEAK IN CAMPUS BUILDINGS

(Oct. 11, 1923) Action of the Regents in barring George W. Wickersham, former attorney general of the United States, from speaking November 2 in Hill auditorium on the League of Nations was extended yesterday when Shirley W. Smith, secretary of the University, ruled that Mr. Wickersham would not be allowed to speak in any University building, because his speech dealt with an issue of partisan politics...

...

The present situation arose when the newly-organized local division of the League of Nations Non-Partisan association invited Mr. Wickersham to speak in Hill auditorium November 2. Mr. Wickersham is now president of the council of the League of Nations Non-Partisan association of which Justice John H. Clarke, formerly of the United States Supreme court, is the leader. When the matter was brought before the Board of Regents at their session September 28 permission for Mr. Wickersham to speak was denied on the grounds that it would be unwise for University buildings to become forums for the dissemination of partisan political opinions. It was further stated that the will of Regent Hill, donor of the auditorium, specifically requested that political speeches be prohibited from its platform.

Faculty Committee Protests

A faculty memorial committee is now preparing to draw up a resolution to be signed by faculty members who believe Mr. Wickersham should be permitted to deliver his speech...

...

Despite the fact that his appearance in Hill auditorium has been prohibited by University authorities, Mr. Wickersham will speak here on the date originally set, November 2. It is not yet known what auditorium will be available, but it is stated definitely by members of the League association that the Regents' action will in no way interfere with their program.#

More Disapprovals Of Action Barring Wickersham Voiced

(Oct. 13, 1923) Three more members of the University faculty yesterday expressed their disapproval of the action of the Board of Regents in barring George W. Wickersham, former attorney general of the United States, from speaking in Hill auditorium under the auspices of the League of Nations Non-partisan association. All feel that in the application of the University ruling upon which the action was based, more careful consideration of the merits of the speaker would be wise.

Van Tyne Against

Prof. C. H. Van Tyne, head of the history department, stated last night that he is not in sympathy with the action of the Regents. "I believe that opportunity should be given for the discussion of both sides of questions of such importance. The rule should be used only in case the speaker is not qualified to speak authoritatively on the subject."

Practically the same attitude is taken by Prof. O. J. Campbell of the English department. "I favor action on each individual speaker, according to his qualifications," he declared. "No sweeping rule against speeches of a partisan nature is fair to the speakers or to the University audience. I do not consider Wickersham's address to be of a sufficiently partisan character to be banned."

Dean Alfred H. Lloyd of the Graduate school believes that an action such as that of the Regents "breeds more partisanship than any sane statement of a public question by a man such as Wickersham possibly could." He considers the ruling unapplicable in the case under consideration...#

Regents Uphold Ban on Political Speakers

Ruling Will Limit Partisan Talks to Closed Meetings

By DICK MALOY

(April 14, 1948) The Board of Regents have closed the door to full-scale political activity on the University campus.

Public meetings featuring partisan political speeches will not be permitted on University property, Regents announced yesterday. However, political speeches may be presented at closed meetings of the various approved student political clubs.

The Regents ruling followed a Student Affairs Committee request for clarification and possible liberalization of University by-laws banning political speakers from the campus.

The SAC, top student-faculty policy group at the University, asked that the "speakers ban" be erased following approval of Young Democrat, Republican and Wallace student clubs. The newly-formed political clubs sought to bring top-flight speakers from the various parties to the University campus during the coming presidential campaign.

The SAC learned that its request had been turned down yesterday during its regular meeting. A Daily representative on the SAC suggested that a resolution expressing disapproval of the Regents action be passed but members of the committee felt that such a resolution would accomplish nothing.

Under the Regents ruling any political speaker appearing in Ann Arbor will be forced to appear in public parks or in downtown halls. This procedure was followed during presidential campaigns in the last few decades when political speakers appeared in theatres, public halls and parks.

The SAC request for lifting the "speaker's ban" follows similar requests in other colleges around the nation. Authorities at the University of Washington recently revised previous rulings and permitted political speeches on campus. However, other colleges have reaffirmed previous stands prohibiting political speeches on their property.#

Speeches Ban 'Unrealistic,' Groups Say

(April 14, 1948) Campus political leaders showed a rare unanimity yesterday when they branded as "unrealistic" the Regents' interpretation of the political speeches ban.

Chairmen of the three newly recognized political clubs -- student Democrats, Republicans and Progressives -- agreed that they would strive to have the ruling liberalized...

Max Dean, chairman of the Wallace Progressives, called on the organizations to work together to have the ban rescinded.

"The purpose of a political organization," he said, "is to convince people that its platform and candidates are the best. Under the Regents ruling, we can only convince ourselves..."

Anthony Cotes, chairman of the Young Democrats, called the Regents' action an "example of the University's paternalistic attitude.

"The benevolent permission granted to partisan groups to organize," he said, "has been counterbalanced. Those same organizations are now impotent."

Stifling of "a very necessary education in politics" was seen as an outgrowth of the ban by James Shoener, chairman of the Young Republicans...#

An Editorial...

(April 14, 1948) **UNIVERSITY** students have been taught another lesson in the "proper" isolation of academic life.

The Board of Regents has refused to allow speeches advocating political candidates at open campus meetings.

Just so students won't get the wrong idea, however, the Regents re-affirm their desire "to encourage student interest in and discussion of public issues as a part of the educational process."

But the Board's action on political speakers doesn't quite match its words. The biggest public issue right now, and for some time to come, is elections. In rejecting the Student Affairs Committee's request for a more intelligent policy on political speakers, the Regents didn't explain how students are supposed to become well-informed about candidates and platforms in a political vacuum.

The Regents carefully state that speeches supporting particular candidates can be heard in meetings open solely to members of the sponsoring student group. But how many students belong to the campus political groups? And what about the students who are still trying to make up their minds?

Main reason for the Regents' decision apparently lies in their concluding statement: "The Board does not favor the use of the name, prestige or property of the University in connection with the promotion of the platforms or candidates of partisan political groups at political meetings."

It is hard to see how the bugaboo of disrepute which seems to dog the University at every turn can apply here. Various members of the faculty often sound off on all manner of subjects political without jeopardizing the University. Surely a parade of political candidates of all parties speaking here would obviate any charge of partisanship.

The Regents, acting for the people of this state, took the easy way out. They decided that education and politics don't mix very well, at least not in public. Ironically enough, it is the people of this state who suffer most as a result of this shortsighted policy. By "playing it safe," the Regents have put one more obstacle in the way of an educated electorate.

In an earlier editorial The Daily senior editors pointed out that revision of the By-Laws by the Regents would take "vision and courage."

Their bid fell short.#

--The Senior Editors

SAC Stymies SL 'Meet Regents' Plan

(Feb. 24, 1949) Student Legislature's "Meet Your Regents" get-together ran afoul of the Student Affairs Committee, but Legislators last night mapped a new course to get approval for the meeting to be held on campus--or off campus, as an alternative.

After SL president Jim Jans reported the SAC unfavorable to the proposed Regents meeting and declared that he believed they would oppose-- even more strongly--holding the meeting off campus, the Legislature moved to take the matter directly to the Regents.

President Jans was authorized to contact today, by telephone, all members of the Board of Regents and ask them point blank to attend the meeting on campus or at the Masonic Temple.

They also planned to attempt to put the issue onto the agenda of the Regents meeting this weekend if possible.

...

JANS REPORTED THAT SAC had denied the use of Rackham lecture hall for the student-Regent meeting, although he commented that they were "exceedingly cooperative and willing to offer alternatives." They said the meeting would tend to put the Regents "on display" and would be "inappropriate" before the spring election, according to Jans.

He also told Legislators that the SAC's Lecture Committee ruled that all present members of the board could attend, but that challenging candidates could not attend an open meeting on the basis of the political speakers' ban.

THE SAC suggested a closed meeting including all Regents and SL members, which Jans felt would allow the attendance of all four candidates. #

REGENTS END SPEECH BAN

By DICK MALOY
(Daily City Editor)

(Feb. 27, 1949) The controversial "speakers ban" was removed yesterday by the University Board of Regents.

The "ban" has prohibited political speeches at open meetings on the University campus. It was imposed last April in a University by-law.

* * *

REGENTS killed the by-law and gave the University Lecture Committee full power to pass on the merits of any person wishing to speak on the campus...

...

Yesterday's relaxation followed the appearance of committees from the Student Legislature and the Faculty Senate before the Regents last month. The Senate group presented arguments against the ruling.

* * *

THE LEGISLATORS argued against the ban and presented an alternative proposal asking that the lecture committee be given power to pass on all speakers.

It was this alternative proposal which the Regents accepted yesterday.

In relaxing the ban the Regents said:

"These regulations shall be administered by the Committee on University Lectures with the understanding that they are designed to serve the educational interests of the academic community rather than the political interests of one party or candidate."

In passing on the merits of persons wishing to speak here the lecture committee will have to work within the framework of this qualification.

President Alexander Ruthven called the move a wise one which "will be administered and accepted in the spirit in which the Regents have acted.

"It shows the Board's confidence in the lecture committee and in the good judgment of the students," Ruthven added.

Passed last April, the original ban on political speeches here touched off a storm of criticism. Several alternative proposals were presented to the Regents prior to last month's move by the SL and the Faculty Senate.

Political interest ran high on the campus during the life of the ban because of the recent presidential campaign. At one time spontaneous gatherings for political discussion took place on the diagonal.

These were later forbidden by Dean Erich Walter in an interpretation of the "ban."..#

An Editorial

(Feb. 27, 1949) The Board of Regents has demonstrated an understanding of a great University's purpose.

The rescinding of the ten-month old political speakers' ban has again united the Administration and student body on one concept of education.

* * *

To the Regents must go credit for realizing the sincerity and conviction of the body of students they serve.

To the students and faculty--congratulations for pushing their conviction, as individuals and as a group, until the point was driven home.

The University Lecture Committee will administer the liberal new regulations. It will need courage and wisdom in carrying out its vital duties.

We join President Ruthven in the hope that "the by-law will be administered and accepted in the spirit in which the Regents acted."#

--The Senior Editors.

SPEAKERS HALTED BY `U'

Committee Fears Talks 'Subversive'

By BOB KEITH
Daily City Editor

(March 4, 1952) Two men associated with allegedly subversive organizations were temporarily banned from speaking on campus yesterday in an apparently unprecedented move by the University Lecture Committee.

1952

The speakers, proposed by two student organizations, were denied permission to appear "until sufficient evidence is produced" to satisfy the committee that the speeches would not be subversive.

Permission was withheld from:

1) Abner Greene, executive secretary of the American Committee for the Protection of the Foreign Born, branded as a subversive organization by the Attorney General. Greene was released from jail a month ago following a six month sentence for contempt of Congress in last summer's much publicized Civil Rights Congress bail fund case. He had been scheduled to speak at last night's meeting of the campus Civil Liberties Committee.

2) Arthur McPhaul, executive secretary of the Michigan Chapter of the Civil Rights Congress, also branded subversive. McPhaul, who spoke on campus last year, was scheduled to address the campus Young Progressives Thursday night.

McPhaul was an unco-operative witness at last week's Communist probe in Detroit.

* * *

IF THE BAN against the men becomes permanent, it will mark the first action of its kind in recent University history. Only three other speakers... have been barred as subversives since the Lecture Committee was set up... and all were avowed Communists. As far as anyone on campus has been able to determine, Greene and McPhaul are not...#

An Editorial...

(March 4, 1952) Abner Greene is an authority on the question of foreign born deportees. Last week, the Civil Liberties Committee on this campus asked him to come here and speak to them about this subject.

...

Greene, despite his background, and close association with so-called "Communist front" groups, is not an avowed Communist... This puts him in a somewhat different category than the three avowed Communist speakers previously banned by the Lecture Committee.

...

In acting as they did, the Lecture Committee has entered into an entirely new phase of interpretation, going beyond existing rules to the extent that they may now not only ban persons who are openly Communists (in the Lecture Committee's terms, those advocating overthrow of the government) but also those who are suspected of being Communists (suspected of advocating overthrow of the government). In short, until a man can prove he is innocent of being a Communist, he is guilty, and should not be allowed to speak for fear he might slip over the line.

All of this focuses directly back on the rule which the Lecture Committee is bound to enforce, and the virtual impossibility surrounding their commission. We feel that the rule itself is a very poor one, the concept of a lecture committee worse, and by examples such as this both are showing themselves inoperable in practice. The Lecture Committee cannot determine what a man is going to say: they can only find out who he is, and conjecture on what he will say.

That is what the Lecture Committee tried to do in this case. In treating it as they did, they showed tendencies even more deplorable than the actual rule which they must enforce. They were willing to require proof of innocence, rather than of guilt. They should give the whole matter, and that of Arthur McPhaul, who received the same handling, positive reconsideration.#

--The Senior Editors

Academic Freedom And The Speakers' Ban

(May 20, 1952) The Lecture Committee Saturday added another encroachment on academic freedom to a list which has been growing rapidly since the March banning of Abner Greene and Arthur McPhaul.

...In defending its previous decisions, the Lecture Committee made a great point of the "temporary" nature of the prohibition. It based its need for more information on the claim that there were some grounds for suspicion that Greene and McPhaul, since they belonged to organizations branded subversive by the Attorney-General, might advocate overthrow of the government.

In the latest decision, however, the mere label of "subversive" attached to Mrs. Shore by virtue of her membership in a blacklisted organization and her recent expulsion from the CIO were considered sufficient grounds for a definitive, permanent quietus.

Thus the lines of interpretation harden. Another nibble has been made at academic freedom. The by-law stating "no addresses shall be allowed which urge the destruction or modification of government by violence or other unlawful methods..." now covers not only died-in-the-wool Communists who advocate force but also all those who can by association, be conceivably suspected of this intent.

...

We feel this represents a curtailment of academic freedom which cannot go unchallenged. We feel that the whole concept and principle of the Lecture Committee is wrong; however, there seems to be little indication that the Regents will see fit at present to abolish the Committee. Perhaps a practical alternative at this moment is to seek liberalized interpretations of the by-law through whatever channels available...#

Crawford Young   **Barnes Connable**
Cal Samra   **Zander Hollander**
Sid Klaus   **Harland Britz**
                            Donna Handleman

The Lecture Committee's Power

(EDITOR'S NOTE: This is the first in a series of editorials on the current infringements on student rights.)

DURING THE past two months a series of speaker bans and investigations have set a precedent dangerous to the future well-being of this University. Both the bans and the investigations could be aptly labeled an amateur witch-hunt, amateur insofar as the methods used were blatantly illegal and the procedures tinged with melodramatic secrecy and sloppiness.

...

Because the administrative groups have chosen to act in secret and to hinder honest attempts to clarify the situation, the atmosphere is thick with suspicion and doubt. The University has been accused of violating the rights of many of its students. The available facts bear the accusation out.

...

IT WAS THEREFORE small surprise that the Lecture Committee banned Arthur McPhaul and Abner Greene from speaking on campus. Both men are officials of groups on the Attorney General's subversive list. Both are accused of being Communists. This latter charge carries deep meaning to the Lecture Committee which regards violent overthrow of the government a fundamental concept held by all Communists despite an individual's record or writings to the contrary.

...

Seemingly encouraged by the success of its ban, the Lecture Committee went even further when it arbitrarily suspended the privilege of the Young Progressives to have speakers, and asked that they be investigated to see if they are a "responsible group." It is reasonable to expect that the actions of student organizations be open to review. It is also reasonable that requests for such an inspection be allowed. However, there should be reasons given for such a request, and to date the Lecture Committee has failed to do so.

...

The extent to which the Lecture Committee is becoming the campus watchdog over "Communism," both by its own choosing and by the power being gradually vested in it, was re-demonstrated several weeks ago. Professor Dirk Struik of MIT, who is accused of advocat-

ing the violent overthrow of the government, visited an informal faculty group. When the faculty members inquired whether they could use University property they were told to clear it with the Lecture Committee. Never before have faculty members been required to submit their guests to a screening. The group refused to do so and met off campus.

It is unfortunate that the off-campus movement is the only recourse left to students. For a price they can secure most any hall in town, and one or two free

of charge. Any time, however, that students must leave the University to hear differing points of view, there is sickness in the academic halls.

...

As it proceeds unchecked the Lecture Committee presents a dangerous threat not just to the freedom of speech but to the freedom of living in a democratic society ruled by laws and not by superstition.#

--Leonard Greenbaum

Speakers Ban Fight Doomed

By BARNES CONNABLE
Daily City Editor

(Dec. 18, 1952) A five-year struggle to overhaul University policies on outside speakers has been stopped cold, it was revealed last night.

At an unusually quiet Student Legislature meeting, SL President Howard Willens, '53, told the group that recent talks with the Lecture Committee on liberalizing speakers regulations had broken down.

* * * *

THE ANNOUNCEMENT dashed hopes for eventual approval by the Board of Regents of SL's plan for restricting the University's power to ban "subversive" speakers from campus appearances.

The Legislature's resolution, first passed last May, was designed to elimi-

nate a University body's previously determining whether a speaker was likely to violate a Regents' by-law prohibiting subversive talks.

The new plan would have called for a guarantee by the sponsoring student group that the lecturer would obey the regulation. Joint Judiciary, with the approval of the University Sub-committee on Discipline, would have acquired the power to determine whether the guarantees had been fulfilled and mete out penalties accordingly.

...

The majority of the Committee was described by Willens as viewing the barring of members of subversive groups from campus speeches as justifiable for the duration of the cold war...#

An Editorial...

(Dec. 18, 1952) This is an epitaph.

Hopes for liberalizing the present outside speaker restrictions were buried as the Lecture Committee this week rejected the Student Legislature plan for a compromise on the issue.

Thus an apparently insurmountable barrier now blocks further student efforts toward improving what is an unsatisfactory situation for students, faculty and administration alike. A dead end in a five-year era of struggle to protect academic freedom in its real sense on this campus has been reached.

...

It cannot be denied that the exigencies of the cold war and the Korean conflict place our democratic ideals under

a peacetime stress which they have never before faced.

But our system is also endangered by allowing the sphere of free activity and inquiry to constantly shrink under the impact of demagoguery and hysteria.

...

It is discouraging to note that another student effort to improve a vital area of the University has been blocked. A great university should encourage a vigorous interest by the students in its policies and decisions...#

--The Senior Editors: Crawford Young, Barnes Connable, Cal Samra, Zander Hollander, Sid Klaus, Harland Britz and Donna Hendleman

Freedom Limits Here Analyzed

"Redbook" writer Andre Fontaine visited the University on his tour of the nation's educational institutions and reported "Fear on the Campus" after talking to student leaders and administrators.

A survey of 50 Illinois colleges and universities turned up six areas of infringement on academic freedom.

These two studies are the latest in an ever growing series of investigations which reveal a startling picture of the nation's campuses.

They raise the question of how this University looks against the background of infringement of student freedom.

This interpretive article has been prepared to analyze University regulations and authorities having the power from which alleged infringements could arise. It is not all-inclusive in its scope but primarily covers those powers over student sponsored lectures and formation of student groups which were attacked in the Illinois survey.

By HARRY LUNN
Daily Managing Editor

(March 28, 1954) Two University groups, the Lecture Committee and the Student Affairs Committee, are in a unique position of control over the political life of the campus and have been charged with placing undue limits on student activity in this area.

...

THE STUDENT Affairs Committee, which dates back to 1904 in one form or another, has the potential authority to severely curtail all student activity including political life and expression.

A series of SAC requirements embodied in the handbook "University Regulations Concerning Student Affairs, Conduct and Discipline" regulate all aspects of student organizations including recognition, approval of activities and denial of recognition.

The handbook's introduction declares "It is the ideal of the University that virtually every aspect of life in the University community should contribute to the education and development of the student."

...

And later it adds "Each proposed rule is evaluated by two standards--will it promote the general welfare? and will it promote the educational process?"

* * * *

SOME STUDENTS, studying the handbook and the record of SAC decisions, believe that the general objective stated at the outset has been perverted by interpretation of how each rule should be applied.

Comments of "How will this look in the press?" are not uncommon in SAC meetings when a program such as the SL-sponsored Academic Freedom Week is up for discussion.

...

SAC restrictions on last fall's Academic Freedom Week drew criticism from some quarters for their supposed harshness. Some provisions of the SAC regulation on the Week were relaxed after SL assured sponsorship, and the balance were defended as being necessary for proper conduct of the meetings.

Within the SAC rule book, certain sections could be invoked which would limit student activity. A brief survey turns up rules which:

1) Enable SAC to abolish student sponsored functions "at which conditions arise which are injurious to the prestige of the University."

2) Prevent class or student boycotts by making participants in such action liable to University discipline.

3) Prevent off-campus affiliation by a student organization without SAC approval.

4) Make all organization activities subject to SAC approval.

5) Prevent student conferences or similar group meetings without SAC sanction.

6) Make solicitation of funds, clothing, books, votes, signatures, memberships or subscriptions; or sale of tags, tokens or literature, or similar group meetings without or in University buildings subject to SAC approval.

Rules of this type, held by SAC to be necessary for proper administration of student affairs, are open to interpretations which can bring charges of wrongful curtailment of student freedom.

* * *

THE LECTURE Committee, a center of controversy several years ago when it banned a series of speakers, holds control over use of University property for meetings.

A five-member faculty group, the committee had two non-voting student members from Student Legislature added in May, 1952.

Set up in 1935, the group was empowered to administer Regents' policies "with the understanding that (the policies) are designed to serve the educational interests of the academic community rather than the political interests of any party or group."

Chief point in the Regents' policy statement was the provision that "timely and rational discussion of topics" would be encouraged "under guarantee that... there shall be no violation of the recognized rules of hospitality and no advocacy of the subversion of the government of the United States..."

* * *

FROM 1935 to 1947 the committee issued no bans and made no policy statements, but in December of the latter year, it set a precedent of banning openly avowed Communists from talking on campus. Two bannings in 1948 and one in 1950 reinforced this policy.

...

In the spring of 1952 the committee widened its conception of objectionable speakers to include those associated with groups named "subversive" on the Attorney General's list, whether or not they were openly avowed Communists.

...

To most students the emerging policy set a continually limited area for political activity and drastically curtailed freedom to hear unpopular views.

...

In a 1952 all-campus referendum students recorded a two-to-one disapproval of the committee. Twenty-seven faculty members protested its existence on a petition made public in April, 1952, and the literary college faculty went on record against the lecture group that summer...#

Speaker Policy Leaves Option:
Court Test or Disobedience

(March 15, 1961) **A LETTER RECENTLY** sent to Student Government Council from the University Committee on Lectures is interesting enough to reprint in full, with comments interspersed:

 1961 March 7, 1961
Student Government Council
The University of Michigan
Student Affairs Building
Ann Arbor, Michigan
Gentlemen:
Near the end of last semester, you wrote a letter to the faculty members of the Committee on University Lectures in which you asked numerous questions about Sec. 8.10 of the Regents' Bylaw, concerning the use of lecture rooms and auditoriums.
...
The character of the questions included in your questionnaire and the detail sought in the answers to them suggest to us that your inquiry is based on an erroneous assumption. You seem to assume that the Committee undertakes to determine the acceptability of the political views of speakers invited to the campus by student organizations.

THE ASSUMPTION is not erroneous. The committee has concerned itself with "acceptability" at least five times in the last eight years. The total would be higher had not many student groups, fearing trouble from the Lecture Committee, preferred to schedule their speakers in off-campus facilities.

This is not so. The policy of the committee has been for some time to grant permission for the use of University property to any recognized student organization willing to assume responsibility for assuring that any outside speaker invited to address a public meeting will comply with the provisions of the Regents' Bylaws. The principal role of the Committee with regard to outside speakers for student organizations is to see that the organizations are advised of the need to comply with the Bylaws and that the proper officers acknowledge this responsibility.

BUT THE BYLAW itself undertakes to determine the acceptability of a speaker's political views, and the Lecture Committee administers the bylaw--hence there is no sense to the argument that the Committee does not judge acceptability. Complying with the bylaw means permitting the University, through the Lecture Committee, to prejudge the acceptability of speeches to be held in campus facilities. Such prejudgment, in addition to the complete emasculation of the spirit of a university, seems to be unconstitutional, since it violates the First Amendment.
...
The faculty members of the Committee are puzzled by the formality and timing, as well as the subject matter

of the questions submitted, because we know of no case in many years in which the question of compliance with the bylaw has been raised.

See the case of John Gates, 1957. And is it really so puzzling to see a student questioning compliance with a bylaw which is intellectually dishonest, and which, if history is any indication, will be enforced again? If anyone should be puzzled, it is the students who hear their University leaders talk of truth and idealism and noble democratic purposes, but see no such talk reflected in deeds.

The bylaw clearly expresses the policy of the Regents. The first paragraph reads: 1) Use of Lecture Rooms and Auditoriums. The policy of the Board of Regents is to encourage the timely and rational discussion of topics whereby the ethical and intellectual development of the student body and the general welfare of the public be promoted and a due respect inculcated in the society at large and for the constituted government of the state and union.
...
The tone of your letter seems to place the emphasis on a restrictive interpretation of the bylaw.

Permissiveness, when referring to speakers' policy, sounds strangely regulatory. The University should not simply permit but actually promote the development and articulation of thought.

...Recognized student organizations are, by the very fact of their university recognition, assumed to be responsible agencies of the Regents. When a student organization requests the use of an auditorium for a public meeting, the committee assumes that the student organization is entitled to the privilege and that it will meet its responsibility for such a meeting in a manner which, in the language of the Regents, would be "in spirit and expression worthy of the University." The responsibility for a fair interpretation of the bylaw rests with the sponsoring student organization.

Very truly yours,
Carl H. Fischer, Chairman
University Committee on Lectures

STUDENT organizations are legally responsible to the Regents. Ethically, they are responsible to themselves. If these responsibilities conflict, and they should conflict over Sec. 8.11(1), then it is the individual's conscience which must be primarily served, not the Regents' request, nor the constituent's whim.

Student Government Council, if true to the ideal of a free university, will further negotiate with the Lecture Committee and seek elimination of the potential and actual restrictive features of its bylaw and operation. If there is no success, two choices are left.

THE FIRST is a court test of the bylaw. The second is conscientious disobedience.#

--THOMAS HAYDEN
Editor

REGENTS REVISE SPEAKER RULE

Board Constructs 'Liberal' Ruling

By DENISE WACKER

(Sept. 22, 1962) The Regents yesterday adopted a policy on non-University speakers with the stated intention of liberalizing standing regulations "to foster a spirit of free inquiry of a wide variety of issues."

The new speaker policy eliminates pre-censorship of off-campus speakers' addresses, provides that no speeches may be given which advocate action contrary to law, and establishes a committee to enforce this policy and carry out a "public education program."

It will not go into effect until final Regents action is taken next month...

...

Timely Discussion

The policy statement encourages "timely discussion," but points out that necessary restrictions must be placed on certain topics.

It goes on to say that recognized student organizations are encouraged to invite speakers to lecture here, subject to certain provisions:

"The speaker must not advocate or urge the audience to take action which is prohibited by the rules of the University or which is illegal under federal or state law. Advocacy of the subversion of the government of the United States or of the State of Michigan, or the urging of the modification of our form of government by violence are specifically included in the above restriction."

7-Man Board

To insure that this policy be upheld, the Regents acted to establish the Public Discussion Committee--a seven-man board composed of three students and three faculty members including the Vice-President for Academic Affairs, who will chair the body. The Vice-President for Student Affairs will act as PDC secretary...#

An Editorial...

(Sept. 22, 1962) **CONCERNED PEOPLE** have awaited the changes in the University's policy toward outside speakers with hope that this institution would establish a truly free forum for inquiry and expression.

The Regents, however, perpetuated the masquerade yesterday with their newly announced policy on Bylaw 8.11.

...

The Regents claim that the new policy eliminates prior censorship entirely--certainly a commendable step forward. Under the proposal, however, the Vice-President for Student Affairs has the power "to certify that all appropriate steps have been taken before the event is offically scheduled." This could give him the power to deny use of facilities on any expedient ground. This is certainly an exercise of prior censorship.

...

PRIOR CENSORSHIP is already included in the proposed bylaw. The range of speech topics would be more restricted than under the present bylaw where speakers could not advocate the subversion of the state by violence or unlawful means. Under the new policy, they could not advocate or urge any action which is illegal under federal or state law or which is prohibited by any University regulation. The policy, avowedly adopted to enlarge the scope of expression, actually imposes a stricter perimeter.

For example, the policy makes it impossible for a speaker to reach a positive answer to the question of whether or not someone else should advocate destruction or modification of our government by violence or illegal means.

It prevents a speaker from advocating a constitutional test case involving violation of a state or federal law. And finally, a Panhellenic national officer cannot come to campus and encourage the sorority presidents not to comply with the Student Government Council regulations requiring submission of adequate membership statements.

The new bylaw thus would ban legitimate discussion by non-University personnel of the desirability of protesting any University regulations by a nonviolent resistance.

...

The administration's policy on outside speakers is but another example of the hypocrisy which has marked the University's approach to major issues in the last few years. A fine statement of progressive principles should not be used as a preface to an essentially regressive policy. A philosophy has no meaning if it is ignored when specific action is taken...#

--THE SENIOR EDITORS

Suggest Violation Of Rule

By DENISE WACKER and RONALD WILTON

(Nov. 6, 1962) There is speculation that a statement made by the Rev. Martin Luther King last night, during an informal discussion at the Michigan Union, represents a violation of the recently-passed Regents By-Law 8.11, pertaining to the University's policy on off-campus speakers.

Responding to a question concerning participation in civil disobedience and direct action projects held against existing state laws, Rev. King said: "yes, I would certainly advocate civil disobedience if there are state laws that are unjust and morally wrong, and are used to preserve a system which is wrong.

"Then, one has a moral responsibility to take a stand against these laws. It's civil disobedience on a local scale, but civil disobedience on the federal scale," Rev. King added.

Regents Bylaw 8.11 states that "The speaker must not advocate or urge the audience to take action which is prohibited by the rules of the University or which is illegal under federal or state law."

...

However, several University officials have expressed the opinion that Bylaw 8.11 refers only to Michigan law, and in this case, Rev. King has violated no portion of the rule...#

the
crusades

the
bookstore
battle

SBS denied booklists

By CHRIS STEELE

(Jan. 10, 1969) Student Book Service, the little cold-water flat bookstore on South University, would like very much to join five major campus bookstores in their co-operative University-wide course text listings, but they can't get in.

The Textbook Reporting Service, an organization composed of Ulrich's, Overbeck's, Follett's, Wahr's and Slater's bookstores, collects lists of books for most courses each semester through mailings to each professor.

The joint effort by the five saves professors and departments duplication of effort in supplying the information and saves the administrative costs to the stores, which they share.

SBS has asked to join the group every semester for three years and has been unsuccessful, manager Ned Shure reports.

"We have asked to be included and we are willing to pay any price for the service," he says. Shure says the other stores have refused to allow SBS to join the Textbook Reporting Service because they object to SBS's generally lower prices.

...

In order to obtain complete booklists, SBS has had to send out separate forms to faculty members. "It costs a lot to get the information," Shure says, "three years and a few thousand dollars."..#

Faculty vow to order texts only at SBS

By SHARON WEINER

(Jan. 16, 1969) Twenty faculty members of the economics department have pledged to order textbooks only from the Student Book Service (SBS) until the store gains access to the Textbook Reporting Service used by five major bookstores.

A petition, drawn up by Prof. Michael Manoff to force "the big stores to let SBS join the group," was signed by the faculty members, including the department chairman, Prof. Harvey Brazer.

...

Signing the petition "seemed like a good way to exert pressure... to let the SBS into the organization," explained Prof. Robert Holbrook of the economics department.

Cites Inconvenience

"It's an inconvenience to fill out a form ordering books for both the textbook service and the SBS," he added. "Many professors now don't bother with the SBS, since the other list is sent to five stores.

"Hopefully," said Holbrooke, "the mere existence of such a petition will lead to acceptance of the Student Book Service into the group. Until then, I will send my book list only to the SBS."..#

SBS admitted to book listing service

By CHRIS STEELE

(Feb. 7, 1969) Student Book Service has been admitted to the Textbook Reporting Service, an organization of local book merchants, reversing a long standing policy.

In an open letter to faculty members, dated Feb. 3, the reporting service announced that the textbook lists they compile will be supplied to Student Book Service.

...

In the letter to the faculty the bookstores gave their reason for including SBS as an attempt to save the faculty "additional work" of filling out forms for both the service and SBS. The letter also expressed a desire to give the faculty the "most reliable, competent and complete system of ordering textbooks."

The letter does not mention the faculty petitions but does "thank" faculty members for "bringing the matter to our attention."

...

Explaining the reason for the move, SBS manager Shure said "they were up against the wall because of The Daily and the faculty petitions, but they didn't complain."..#

STUDENTS SEIZE LSA BUILDING AS OVER 1000 MASS IN SUPPORT

DEMAND REGENTS MEET ON BOOKSTORE

(Sept. 26, 1969) Over 100 of the 600 demonstrators who occupied the LSA Bldg. yesterday afternoon remained inside as of 4:45 a.m. this morning protesting the refusal of the Regents to create a student-run discount bookstore.

Nearly 1,000 persons remained outside in support of the demonstrators.

Meanwhile, University and city offi-cials conferred early into the morning concerning possible action.

At 9:10 p.m. the University obtained a temporary restraining order enjoining the demonstrators from continuing the sit-in, but attempts to serve the order were thwarted when those outside blocked all entrances to the building.

...

Meanwhile, Sheriff Douglas J. Harvey, who said he had mobilized from 500 to 1,000 deputies earlier in the night, later indicated he was withdrawing his men because police and University officials could not agree on removing the demonstrators.

"I have had it with that type of appeasement. If they want police action, all they have to do is ask for it," Harvey said. "I'm not standing by all night with 100 men, most of them on overtime, while Fleming plays footsie with some radicals."#

POLICE ARREST 107 IN LSA BLDG. ON ORDERS FROM PRES. FLEMING

7 INJURED IN POLICE CHARGE

(Sept. 26, 1969) One hundred and seven students were arrested between 3:35 and 5:00 this morning in the LSA Bldg. by about 250 Ann Arbor and State Police at the request of University President Robben Fleming.

At least eight persons were injured moments later as police, perhaps Washtenaw County Sheriff's deputies, swept the State St. side of the building and staged one charge toward Angell Hall.

State Police also reportedly injured a number of people when they rushed students in front of the building only seconds after reading an order that they move in two minutes. About 250 students were sitting-in in front of the building at the time.

...

At least two students who were arrested and released early--Eric Chester and Mark Hodax--said the city police who made the arrests inside the LSA Bldg. used excessive force, including making the students "run a gauntlet" between a line of officers, jabbing them with nightsticks as they ran.

...

Don Koster, an attorney representing a number of the arrested persons, was temporarily not allowed to see any of his clients early this morning. Others attempting to bail students out were also not allowed into City Hall until about 8 a.m.

...

The students first entered the building around 3 p.m. yesterday afternoon protesting the refusal of Fleming and the Regents to reconsider the structuring of a University discount bookstore.

...

At 9:30 p.m. those sitting-in on the second floor of the LSA Bldg. received word that Fleming had agreed to meet with one representative of the protesters.

The group discussed the offer and agreed to send Eric Chester as their representative. They mandated to him to agree that the sit-in would end if Fleming agreed to call a meeting of the Regents within 24 hours with the clear understanding that there would be favorable action on the SGC bookstore proposal. Fleming would not agree...#

An Editorial...

(Sept. 26, 1969) **LAST NIGHT'S** takeover of the LSA Bldg. and the subsequent police action ordered by the University administration must be seen as a great tragedy for all members of the University community.

We believe the responsibility of this tragedy lies squarely on the shoulders of Robben Fleming.

Through his reliance on police action, his unwillingness to seriously negotiate student demands and his blatant, baseless threats to students and faculty, he has destroyed the peace that this campus has lived in for the past three years.

FLEMING HAS forced this confrontation, and Fleming has asked for a fight. The fight isn't over the bookstore, and it isn't over ROTC. Fleming has created a confrontation over the issue that the students are best prepared to fight for and the issue students have the most right to win: student control over student affairs.

...

The bookstore issue is just one more in the long, long list of examples of administrative rejection of legitimate student demands for equitable participation in this process.

...

We feel that appropriate action for the students to take would be a call for an immediate and unmistakable indication from Fleming that he is willing to change the way he has been running the University or that he is willing to make way for a president who will. We also feel it would be appropriate, if support can be established, to call for a general student-faculty strike in support of demands for immediate reforms in the University decision-making process...#

--THE SENIOR EDITORS

POLICE ARREST 107 IN LSA BLDG. ON ORDERS FROM PRES. FLEMING

An Editorial . . .

7 INJURED IN POLICE CHARGE

State Police escort arrested protestors from LSA Bldg.

Group plans Diag protest rally

Police line blocks off State St.   *State Police break demonstrators*

Survey shows 37% of 'U' students smoke pot

𝕿𝔥𝔢 𝕸𝔦𝔠𝔥𝔦𝔤𝔞𝔫 𝕯𝔞𝔦𝔩𝔶

STUDENTS SEIZE LSA BUILDING AS OVER 1000 MASS IN SUPPORT; 'U' OBTAINS INJUNCTION

Report to ask no ROTC tie

DEMAND 'U' REGENTS MEET ON BOOKSTORE

Angell Hall fire blamed on arsonist

Strikers negotiate large rent cuts

Jury set for 'Chicago 8'

On Strike! Shut It Down!

(Sept. 27, 1969) **STUDENT LEADERS** have called for a general strike Monday to protest the decision by President Fleming to order mass arrests of students peacefully occupying the LSA Bldg. and his continued refusal to engage in meaningful negotiations over the establishment of a University bookstore.

But recognizing that the administrative decision on the bookstore is only symptomatic of the lack of democracy in University decision-making, strike leaders have called for a wide-spread student struggle for greater participation in University affairs.

We applaud this effort.

STUDENTS HAVE demonstrated unequivocally that they will not be suppressed by threats and intimidation from Fleming and his police. They must show the University that it cannot deal with student pressure by harrassing student leaders and ordering mass arrests.

To back down now would be to condone Fleming's decision to break with 150 years of University tradition by employing police--rather than dialogue--to deal with student protest.

...

The issue is one that does not lend itself easily to calm discussion. It is a question of power, and few people give away their power calmly. Students are clearly justified in demanding more than a mere advisory role in this University.

STUDENTS MUST strike to demonstrate that they will no longer allow the central administration and Regents to make decisions unilaterally for 35,000 students.

For the Regents and administration have demonstrated time and again--the bookstore is only one example--that they represent interests wholly alien to those of students.

This oligarchy cannot be tolerated any longer.#

--LESLIE WAYNE
Arts Editor
--RON LANDSMAN
Managing Editor
--MARCIA ABRAMSON
Associate Managing Editor
--STEVE ANZALONE
Editorial Page Editor
--JIM FORRESTER
Associate Sports Editor

--STEVE NISSEN
City Editor
--JOHN GRAY
Literary Editor
--PHIL BLOCK
Associate Managing Editor
--CHRIS STEELE
Associate City Editor
--JOEL BLOCK
Sports Editor

--DANIEL ZWERDLING
--MARTIN HIRSCHMAN
--LORNA CHEROT
--HAROLD ROSENTHAL
--RUSS GARLAND
--LAURIE HARRIS
--DAVID SODERQUIST
--WILLIAM DINNER No. 654
--JIM McFERSON

--JIM BEATTIE
--MARTY SCOTT
--ALEXA CANADY
--DAVID CHUDWIN
--CAROL HILDEBRAND
--ERIKA HOFF
--JUDY SARASOHN
--AL SHACKELFORD

Note - The list of signers of the above editorial is reprinted <u>exactly</u> as it appeared in The Daily.

EXTRA **The Michigan Daily** EXTRA

STRIKE SUPPORTERS PREPARE FINAL PLANS

Proposals for negotiations fail; 'U' withdraws injunction effort

SGC VOTES 6-1 TO BACK STRIKE TODAY

Strikers hit refusal to convene Regents

McLaughlin attacks 'U' coercion

Today's events

Defense may launch legal attack despite drop of court injunction

Survey of faculty indicates scattered support for strike

Protesters discuss legal plans

State officials eye 'U' situation

Bookstore negotiations may begin

By PAT MAHONEY

(Oct. 1, 1969) Action on the bookstore issue slowed yesterday as both sides recuperated from the strike Monday and planned new action.

President Robben Fleming said yesterday he had not met with students or faculty on the bookstore issue. He explained that he would undoubtedly "pursue the SACUA resolution" beginning today.

The resolution, adopted Monday by Senate Assembly, called for the Senate Advisory Committee on University Affairs to meet with students and administrators to negotiate the bookstore question.

Meanwhile, education Prof. Joseph Payne, SACUA chairman, said that SACUA had not met yesterday and has not planned any immediate meeting with students. SACUA will have a noon meeting today to make arrangements for negotiations on the bookstore issue.

At the meeting today, SACUA will consider a proposal for an ad hoc student-faculty-administration committee on the bookstore issue. The proposal was approved unanimously yesterday by Assembly's Student Relations Committee.

...

SRC recommended that the committee include President Robben Fleming, one or two administrators, members of SACUA, three faculty members of SRC and seven to eight students chosen by SGC "representing the various alternate proposals" on the bookstore...#

REGENTS PASS BOOKSTORE PLAN

BACK STUDENT CONTROL SETUP

By DAVID CHUDWIN and ALAN SHACKELFORD

(Oct. 18, 1969) The long-standing controversy over creation of a University discount bookstore was apparently resolved yesterday as the Regents accepted in principle a plan allowing for student-faculty control of the store.

By a 5-3 vote, the Regents agreed to modify the bookstore plan they approved last month to make it conform with the proposal recently developed by student and faculty representatives.

Regental approval of the plan was based on the condition that the proposed bookstore corporation would qualify for exemption from the state sales tax, and that the University would be isolated from liability for any debts the store might incur.

"The whole proposal is built on the assumption you can do those two things," said President Robben Fleming. "If something doesn't work out we'll have to look at this thing again."

Under the plan approved yesterday, the bookstore would be funded through a fee assessment against all students and faculty members and refunded when they leave the University. The funding plan must be approved in a student referendum before the money will be assessed.

Control of the bookstore would be delegated to a policy board composed of six students and three faculty members.

The bookstore would be set up as a non-profit corporation and would run on a break-even basis.

First year savings are not expected to exceed one per cent, including the four per cent sales tax exemption. The policy board would appoint a professional manager to run the operation.

"There are some unresolved problems," said Fleming. Among those he mentioned were defining who is a student for the purpose of the assessment, freeing the University from liability, and assuring the sales tax exemption.

"A majority of the Regents continue to support a bookstore," said Regent Otis Smith (D-Detroit). "We're adopting the proposal but we're making it very clear certain points have to be ironed out."

Groundwork for yesterday's agreement was laid at an open meeting Thursday between the Regents and members of the Senate Advisory Committee on University Affairs (SACUA), Student Government Council, the Bookstore Coordinating Committee and other groups...#

University Cellar may be forced out of Union

By JANET RAE

(Oct. 14, 1981) The University Cellar may be forced to move out of the Michigan Union if negotiations between bookstore officials and the director of the Union do not result in a settlement by day's end tomorrow.

Student government leaders staged emergency meetings with U Cellar personnel Monday night and yesterday in a last ditch effort to form counter-proposals to those prepared by Michigan Union Director Frank Cianciola. Cianciola, who has declared certain key points as no longer negotiable, has given the U-Cellar board of directors until tomorrow to make a legal commitment to remain in the Union.

ACCORDING TO Mary Anne Caballero, president of the U-Cellar board of directors, the provisions demanded by Cianciola for a new lease would make it financially impossible for the bookstore to remain in the Union without substantially increasing prices.

"The administrators (Cianciola and Vice President for Student Services Henry Johnson) are telling us to raise our prices in order to stay alive," Caballero said. "We feel as students that that would be stabbing our fellow students in the back."

...

Under Cianciola's proposals, the bookstore's square foot rental rate would rise from $5.48 to $9.07, an increase amounting to $85,000 annually. Board members said that when they originally agreed to foot most of the bill for renovation of the new site they were unaware the rent increase would be so high.

"We didn't expect both costs to be dumped on us at the same time," Caballero said. "Even (Johnson) thought we wouldn't have to start paying the $9.07 figure until we moved into the new location."

CIANCIOLA SAID he imposed the deadline for an agreement when U-Cellar officials first told him they were considering relocating to a site outside the Union. He said the schedule for the overall Union renovation project had been largely planned around U-Cellar needs. If U-Cellar decides to move out of the Union, he said, that could place the project behind schedule, a situation that would affect the entire University.

"If they're not going to be there, we need to know that," he said. "It's just not fair to the campus community not to meet the deadline.

"There is an extremely favorable bidding situation right now," he said of other merchants' interest in the space. "We're talking about the entire Union renovation project."

CABALLERO SAID that, under Cianciola's present proposals, U-Cellar would have to find other sources of revenue in order to remain in the Union. Board members believe that insignia items--the popular 'M' and 'Go Blue' souvenir items sold in other stores--could provide enough profit for U-Cellar to stay afloat. But Cianciola will not allow a change in the store's 12-year agreement not to sell such items, maintaining the Union store's monopoly on the popular souvenirs.

"This income from the sale of insignia souvenirs is a significant portion of the Union's current operation, and is expected to increase in amount and importance in the future,"

Cianciola told the board members in a memo outlining what he considered "negotiable" and "not negotiable." "These revenues are necessary for the overall operation of the Union, including providing services to the student body as a whole."

...

Caballero said one advantage the U-Cellar would enjoy by moving out of the Union would be the ability to sell insignia items and make the bookstore more of a general retail store. Under the U-Cellar's current agreement with Cianciola, the Union director personally maintains control of what the U-Cellar may and may not sell.

"We have to give him a laundry list," Caballero said. "Then Frank must tell us whether or not we can sell all the items on the list. But we have no guarantee against someone else in the Union selling the items he has approved for us."

...

U-CELLAR officials say they are also concerned by Cianciola's refusal thus far to renew their guarantee of use of the Union ballroom during fall and winter book rush.

"The ballroom question is a real dilemma for me," Cianciola said. "It is in the interest of the Union and in the interest of students to have accessibility to that facility at the beginning of the academic terms for programming activities."

Caballero said denial of the use of the ballroom would be financially devastating for the U-Cellar...#

New Union bookstore gets rights 'U' Cellar sought

By THOMAS HRACH

(Sept. 15, 1984) Come January, there will be a new textbook store in town geared up and ready to do battle with Ulrich's and the University Cellar--two well established heavyweights in the campus bookselling business.

Barnes and Noble, a New York firm, is scheduled to move into the ground floor of the Michigan Union by the time winter book rush rolls around, according to Frank Cianciola, Union director. It will occupy the same space one of its rivals--the 'U' Cellar--once leased before it moved out two years ago because of high rent costs and a rule barring it from selling any memorabilia bearing the University insignia.

...

The Union would not give up its exclusive right to sell insignia items within the building two years ago, but under a tentative agreement with Barnes and Noble the Union will turn those rights over to the New York firm and close the Union-run retail outlets in the building.

...

Under the agreement with Barnes and Noble, the Union has closed its first-floor General Store and the Candy Counter on the ground floor and plans to shut down the Emblem Shop. The new bookstore will have the exclusive right to sell the products once offered by the Union's stores...#

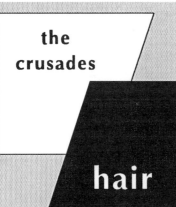

Job Aid Denied Bearded Men

By IRIS BROWN

(May 2, 1961) Summer Placement Service Director Ward D. Peterson admitted last night he has discouraged several bearded students from full use of the service's facilities.

Peterson said he does not like to send people with beards out on summer jobs as representatives of the University. Evart Ardis, director of the Bureau of Appointments, said last night that the anti-beard policies are not those of his bureau. He promised to examine the situation.

Peterson said the policies originated with himself.

In several cases, Peterson has not given students the service's normal application forms, from which their names would be given to visiting employer's representatives. The students have also not been allowed to have employment resumes duplicated, another regular service...

...

Camp Job

Bearded Richard Rice, '62, went to Placement Service yesterday and expressed interest in a summer camp job. Peterson replied that the service did not send out people with beards...

...

When Peterson asked Rice about his previous camp experience, he said, "Did you have the beard then?" Finally Peterson told Rice that he could use the files; however he did not give him an application blank to fill out nor did he ask him to sign a list kept of all students who come to the Bureau.

...

Two weeks ago Steven Shaw, '63, requested application for a national park job. Peterson asked him if he were wearing his beard for a joke, and then said that he could not sign up. #

SUMMER PLACEMENT SERVICE:
Give These Men a Chance!

(May 3, 1961) **REGARDLESS** of the policies set by university summer placement bureaus, many bearded men of the past have been able to secure jobs.

A short sampling includes:

ABRAHAM LINCOLN--President of the United States (1860-65) whose first

Abraham Lincoln

James B. Angell

Charles Darwin

Uncle Sam

jobs consisted of grocery store chores, rail-splitting and cabin building. Several of his employers later wrote about his honesty.

JAMES B. ANGELL--President of the University (1871-1909) got an early professional start as a private tutor and assistant librarian. Later the Michigan Union was dedicated to his memory...

...

CHARLES DARWIN--Spent his early years in study and travel. "My summer vacations...were wholly given up to amusements," says Darwin. Although he later wrote a fine book on the "Origin of Species," he was an "incorrigible" student who was known to skip classes.

UNCLE SAM--Made his debut in the War of 1812...

...Luckily, today he represents only the United States of America, leaving the University's clean-shaven image intact.

SANTA CLAUS--Started out as a "do-gooder" in the sociology department. He switched the site of his operations to the North Pole when... a tightening of regulations by the Lecture Committee required that someone "well-versed in the other side" be allowed to speak concurrently. #

BEARD PREJUDICE
Ultimatum: Shave or Go

(Feb. 19, 1965) An instance of the world's ambivalent attitude toward beards displayed itself yesterday in the Lawyer's Club kitchen in an apparently discriminatory act against beard wearers.

Aaron Grossman, '66L, formerly employed in the Lawyer's Club kitchen and proud possessor of a full reddish-brown beard, got his whiskers caught in an administrative meat cutter yesterday when Mrs. Margaret Langer, director of the Lawyer's Club, laid down an ultimatum.

She asked Grossman to shave his beard or else--the "else" being the removal of his time card from the rack and subsequent discharge.

Grossman, considering it a matter of principle, refused and was "discharged." However, when asked to comment on the matter, Mrs. Langer said, "Aaron was not discharged."

When it was investigated further by Grossman, Mrs. Langer revealed that she "did not sit here and say you were fired."

Because the Lawyer's Club is not under the supervision of University housing, Mrs. Langer was well within her rule against beards.

"My discharge," Grossman said, "is an unreasonable, arbitrary and capricious abuse of administrative discretion, having no reasonable relationship to the quality of my work. It demonstrates an overt prejudice to the wearing of beards in violation of the traditions set by such great men as Jesus Christ, Abraham Lincoln, former University President James B. Angell and many others."

Grossman, recently married, said he enjoyed working in the kitchen and would like to be able to continue to work there. He will not, however, shave his beard. He said he felt that a satisfactory compromise might be reached if he agreed to wear a hair net. Mrs. Langer has refused to consider the proposal. #

Long-hair workers face firing

By JONATHAN MILLER

(Feb. 12, 1971) Five employes of the Great Atlantic and Pacific Food Company (A&P) store on East Huron have been given until noon today to get their hair cut or lose their jobs.

Mike Palid, one of the workers faced with the deadline, said last night he would not cut his hair, and several other long-haired employes also said they will refuse to comply with the order.

Student Government Council at their meeting Wednesday night called for a boycott of the A&P because of their "insidious attempt to force the cultural values of the company on their employes." Council also asked members of the community to personally protest the policy to the manager of the store, Warren Hartman.

Hartman declined to comment on the situation last night but A&P Regional Supervisor Ray Rutter said, "This has always been our policy. It's nothing against anyone with any type of hair as far as hiring is concerned, it's just so we can have things uniform, we want our people neat and uniformed."

...

A store clerk in Seattle, Wash., who was fired by a Tradewell supermarket because of what the company called excessively long hair, failed recently in a bid to get his firing ruled illegal by an arbitrator on the grounds that it violated Title VII of the 1964 Civil Rights Act... #

Protesting the A&P firings

(Feb. 13, 1971) TWO YEARS AGO, the A&P store on Huron was forced to stop selling California grapes when a boycott of the store reduced its total sales 20 per cent. Today, as the store attempts to oppress long-haired young people, a similar action is needed.

...

The store's managers say enforcement of the dress code is necessary because those currently violating it are driving away customers. But the facts show quite clearly that this argument is false, and that the actual motive of the store management is a prejudice against the employes' appearance and the life style that appearance represents.

...

THE ONLY way to end the store's discriminatory policy is therefore to fight it economically, as was done during the grape boycott. This could be done in many ways. Most obviously, students could cease to buy food at the A&P on Huron St.

...

In addition, students have been urged by the workers under attack to picket the store and to encourage customers to shop elsewhere. Finally, and most immediately, the workers have called for a peaceful protest at the store beginning at 1 p.m. today.

THE WORKERS suggest that the protest might involve filling shopping carts, joining check-out lines, but walking out without actually buying the groceries. Although this should be executed peacefully, the store must be convinced to end its discriminatory policies. The A&P should not make money from those whom it will not employ. #

--JIM BEATTIE

Boycott of A&P ends; hair policy unchanged

By JIM McFERSON

(March 11, 1971) The three-week-old boycott of the E. Huron St. A&P has ended with no change in the store's policy of barring long-haired men from employment.

According to A&P employes, business was reduced by as much as 30 per cent during the first week of the boycott, but the store's current intake is only a little less than normal.

...

Suspended employes attribute the boycott's end to the University's recent spring vacation which interrupted strike activities and to their own feeling that the store will simply not rehire them.

"I'm disappointed that the boycott ended--not because of my job, but because the store shouldn't be able to get away with shit like that," said Bob Quiroz, one of the suspended employes... #

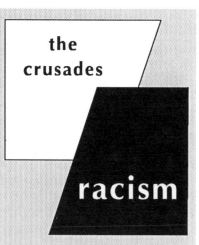

the
crusades

racism

Exclusion Of Ward Protested

Demand Cancellation of Georgia Tech Game If Ward Is Benched

(Oct. 17, 1934) Latest developments in the Willis Ward controversy last night were:

1. The claim by the united front committee on Ward that more than 1,000 students have signed a petition which urges, in part, "Either Ward plays or the game must be cancelled."

2. The addition of eight more faculty members to the list.

3. Denial by the committee that any "march in the Stadium" was planned for Saturday.

4. Receipt of a letter from Herbert F. Wilson, secretary of the University of Michigan Club of Indianapolis and prosecuting attorney of Marion County, Ind., stating that "it is poor sportsmanship (on the part of Georgia Tech) to ask the Michigan coaches to not play Ward."

...

Plans are being made to present the signed petitions to Athletic Director Fielding H. Yost and Coach Harry Kipke. The petitions read: "We, the undersigned, declare ourselves unalterably opposed to the racial discrimination evidenced in the proposed exclusion of Willis Ward from the Georgia Tech game. We support the slogan: Either Ward plays or the game must be cancelled."

...

The committee denied that any plans had been made for a demonstration in the Stadium in the event that Ward did not start the Georgia Tech game, but individual members of organizations represented on the committee have implied that some "action" might be taken if Ward were injured during the course of the game.

Mr. Wilson's letter further said that "Ward is a splendid athlete, a good student, and a good sportsman in every sense of the word. These characteristics ...and not his color should be the basis for Georgia Tech's determining whether or not they should play against him."..#

THE RACE PROBLEM.

Hon. Frederick A. Douglas Discussed it Last Night Before a Large Audience

(Oct. 20, 1893) University hall was little more than two-thirds filled last night to hear the well known colored statesman and orator, Frederick Douglas. The audience was, however, an enthusiastic one...

Fifty years of hard and unrelenting toil for his people and race have left their mark on Mr. Douglas, but in spite of his feebleness he would at times, wrapped in enthusiasm, break forth with an eloquence which completely held his audience.

The subject of the lecture was "The Race Problem," commonly miscalled as Mr. Douglas pointed out "The Negro problem." This latter name, he felt, was unjust and had a tendency to prejudice innocent people. In treating the problem he spoke of the recent outrages and lynching in the south, at some length pointing out the great injustice done, and the anarchy that must and does exist in a country where its citizens are not allowed any trial whatever.

...

Toward the close of his lecture Mr. Douglas left his manuscript and told of an interesting experience he had, when before the war he went around lecturing in behalf of the slaves. He came to a small town in New Hampshire, on Saturday, and was going to speak three times the next day in the town hall. The hotels were, of course, closed to him on account of his color, but on inquiry he found that a certain Mr. G. was an abolitionist, and would probably entertain him. But Mr. G. was a distant abolitionist and though he housed Mr. Douglas, he did not eat with his guest. Sunday morning Mr. G. drove his wife down to the hall in a four seated carriage, and it so happened that they started just as Mr. Douglas came out of the house. Thereupon the abolitionist called out: "I suppose you can find your way down to the hall."...

...

"Had it not been for a Mr. Morris, a senator from that district, I would not have had anything to eat that day, and as it was, did not, till after my talk in the afternoon."#

Ward Sympathizers Rally Tonight

(Oct. 19, 1934) A declaration of gratitude to those students, faculty members, and organizations that have aided in the campaign for his participation in the Georgia Tech game Saturday was made last night by Willis Ward.

Meanwhile, plans were completed for the student rally to be held at 8 p.m. tonight in the Natural Science Auditorium for the purpose of crystallizing sentiment on the Ward affair.

In response to an invitation to present their views on the matter, Athletic Director Fielding H. Yost declined, but Head Coach Harry Kipke could not be reached at a late hour last night for a statement as to whether he will appear at the meeting.

C.B. Fisk Bangs, secretary of the Charlotte chapter of the Michigan Alumni Association, yesterday wrote in answer to a letter from the Ward United Front Committee that "It has long been the policy of the State of Michigan and the University that there will be no racial discrimination, and I feel that Mr. Ward should be permitted to play if he is otherwise qualified, regardless of his color.

Win Over Georgia Tech Eleven

By ARTHUR W. CARSTENS

(Oct. 21, 1934) Tiny, dynamic Ferris Jennings, sophomore quarterback starting his second game for Michigan, provided the Wolverines' margin of victory over Georgia Tech here yesterday when he returned a punt 68 yards for a touchdown.

Hildebrand kicked the point after touchdown and both teams later scored safeties when the rain made ball-handling extremely hazardous to make the final score 9 to 2, but it was the 140-pound youngster's spring for Michigan's first score of the year that put Kipke's men back in the winning column.

...

Ward In Press Box

Willis Ward and Frank Lett did not appear in uniform; instead they watched the game from the press box. In reciprocation Coach Bill Alexander benched E. H. Gibson, Tech end and one of their outstanding players, before the game started, using Boulware in his place. There was no demonstration of any sort either before or during the game...#

Willis Ward Summary...

(Oct. 23, 1934) **IT WAS THE PECULIAR** characteristic of the Ward-Georgia Tech matter that everyone who touched it did so only to lose in respect and esteem. The athletic department, responsible first for scheduling the contest and then for a willingness to risk serious campus disorder rather than cancel it, was guilty of placing the University and the student body in a very difficult position. The National Student League, which used the affair as a means of causing as much embarrassment and gaining as much publicity as possible, achieved neither its professed purpose of putting Ward in the game nor the greater purpose of lessening discrimination against negroes -- both in the North and the South. The Tory group of the Ward protest meeting Friday night, led by almost all the prominent extra-curricular men on campus, did not convince one single person, despite the soundness of its arguments, because the group insisted upon an appalling exhibition of bad manners, bad taste, and bad sense.

It will be unfortunate if the Michigan coaching staff, as well as the coaching staffs of other northern universities, concludes that the manner to avoid situa-tions of this type in the future is to refrain from coaching and playing promising Negro athletic material. That is certainly a possibility, and if it is one which the ra-bid pro-Ward group overlooked it is only another indication of the shortsightedness of the faction. But the easier and more decent way both for the students who comprise the University and the people of the State who support that Uni-versity, is not to schedule games with institutions below the Mason-Dixon line.

Michigan is democratic. Its history, its tradition, its honor is founded on a bed rock of education for all those who are capable of getting it, regardless of race, or color, or social and financial position. Let Michigan of the future play with those who are of her own eminently worthwhile type.#

Critique

To the Editor:

(Oct. 23, 1934) ...We do not charge that The Daily has murdered our citizens and destroyed our towns. We do charge that in the Ward affair may be seen the efforts of The Daily to avoid discontent by a masterly sidestepping of the real issue editorially and by a suppression of the real facts or deliberate failure to obtain credible information...

We ask why no attempt was made to discover whether the Board in Control of Athletics scheduled the Georgia Tech game oblivious of Ward. We ask why no thought was given to the reasonable inference that the game was accepted on the express condition that Ward would not play. We ask why no effort was made to ascertain at what time Ward had been informed of this matter...

The Daily could have attempted a publication as news of what actually transpired even if it did not have the courage to condemn the treatment of Ward as a negro rather than a Michigan man in its editorials...#

Cyril F. Heiske, '36L.
Morris Weller, '35L.
Robert E. Acherburg, Jr., '35L.
Wm. Babcock, Jr., '35L.
A. D. Kennedy, Jr., '36L.

Capable Negroes Fail To Get Teaching Jobs

By JIM CONANT

(April 8, 1943) Highly qualified Negroes have failed to obtain positions on the faculty of the University because of their race, it was indicated by a Daily investigation completed yesterday.

There have been competent Negro graduate students at the University, notably in the fields of mathematics and sociology; but no Negro has ever received a final recommendation to a teaching position.

The reason given by faculty members for this situation varied from fear of student reactions to a conviction that the appointment of a Negro would never be approved by the authorities.

Case of William Claytor

The case of one man was outlined to The Daily yesterday by Prof. Harry C. Carver of the mathematics department. William Claytor, one of the most brilliant men in his specialty ever to come to Michigan, missed out on a faculty job solely because of his race, Prof. Carver said.

"I'm not interested in stirring up trouble," said Prof. Carver. "But no one has a right to say that a Negro should not teach at a state university. Claytor is now a lieutenant in the Coast Artillery; in view of the shortage in the mathematics department, I wish he were here to help us out."

Approximately three years ago Claytor, a Ph.D. from Pennsylvania, was the most promising man for a vacancy in the mathematics department. At that time, Prof. Carver said, he failed to receive an appointment because no one would take the responsibility of saying "yes" or "no" to the appointment of a Negro.

"Claytor had the stuff," Prof. Carver pointed out. "He was a perfect gentleman, a good mathematician by any standards, Negro or white, and had the personality for a teacher."

Never Reached Administration

In spite of the fact that several members of the mathematics department endorsed his candidacy for an instructorship, Prof. Carver continued, the recommendation for the appointment never reached the desk of the President or the Board of Regents.

"I believe," Prof. Carver emphasized, "that if Claytor's appointment had gone through, it would have met with no opposition from the Administration. I am confident that neither the President nor the Board of Regents would turn the application down for racial reasons."

Claytor's abilities were also highly praised by Prof. Raymond L. Wilder, with whom he worked here. "Claytor is one of the outstanding Negro mathematicians in the country. As a scholar and a teacher, he was good."

Others Hire Negroes

Universities which, at the present time, hire Negro instructors include Harvard University, the University of Chicago, New York University, and the City College of New York.

Negroes here have been employed as technical assistants and readers. The reasons for faculty hesitancy in recommending them for teaching positions were indicated yesterday by Prof. DeWitt H. Parker, chairman of the philosophy department.

"This particular problem has never confronted our department. If it had, however, there might have been some feeling that students would be embarrassed by a Negro instructor, and that the appointment would not go through the authorities. With regard to graduate students, of course, Negroes have always been on an equal footing with every other student."#

5 Per Cent of Students Resent Negro Instructors

By JIM CONANT

(April 9, 1943) Only five per cent of literary school students would raise any objection to a Negro instructor, a Daily poll indicated yesterday. At the same time President Alexander G. Ruthven stated squarely that the University has never made racial distinctions in considering applicants for teaching jobs.

Students in ten classes answered, by secret ballot, the question: "Would you object to a Negro instructor?"

Out of 215 students questioned, only 11 answered "yes" while 202 stated that they would have no objection. Two blank ballots were also recorded.

...

The least objection came from the 67 philosophy students polled. Included among the 64 "no's" were 14 highly emphatic replies. In these classes there was a strong preponderance of girls. As in the others polled, there were no Negroes present.

...

The only strong "yes" statement read, "About the time we get Negro instructors, so long Michigan."

President Ruthven, interviewed in connection with yesterday's Daily story, said: "In considering applications for teaching positions, the University has never made distinctions of race, color, and creed, and never will."

Dean Edward H. Kraus of the Literary College commented, "The general opinion is that Negroes can serve to greater advantage in the institutions of their own people. In the case of a Negro applicant here, sympathetic consideration would naturally be given, involving his record and ability."

Campus leaders expressed opinions similar to those of the students polled.

Dick Ford, president of the Union, said: "I feel that everyone ought to have an equal break -- that's what we're fighting for. A Negro instructor would certainly be all right by me. Incidentally, I've spent thirteen years in the South."

Dave Matthews, captain of Michigan's championship track team, said, "I have no prejudices. When it comes to eating, shows, entertainment, there should be no barriers, and that goes for education and teaching, too. After all, education's supposed to be a process of learning to be broadminded and fair; and if you can't do that, you might as well stop being educated."

Bob Ufer, champion quartermiler, commented, "Anyone who is qualified and meets the requirements should be allowed to teach. After all, that's what we're fighting for."..#

NISEI, NEGROES NOT WANTED:
Prejudice Explanation For Plant Labor Lack

By STAN WALLACE
Special to The Daily

(July 16, 1944) SOUTH LYON, July 15--Two racial prejudices--one against Negroes and the other against Nisei Japanese--have divided this Michigan community into two hostile camps and have tied war production at the Michigan Seamless Tube Co. into a knot for the past month.

William McHattie, president of the company, reported production off more than 35 per cent and attributed it directly to a shortage of more than 150 laborers.

The War Manpower Commission (WMC) offered to send 150 Nisei--American citizens of Japanese descent--to alleviate the situation and the announcement brought hostile reaction from the United Steelworkers Union Local 1900 (CIO).

Cries of "I wouldn't work with any kind of Jap" and "we'll walk out the minute a Jap comes in" sent the management into hurried consultation with the Union grievance committee which voted solidly against any such move.

This crisis occurred about a month or more ago and a substitute program involving the importation of Negro workers into the plant sent the townspeople of this otherwise peaceful community into a furor of discussion.

...

Union Takes Stand Against Nisei

The men in the plant -- all union members -- consist of loyal citizens who have made this their home for many years with a strong element of Southern whites from Kentucky and Alabama. They have made it clear that they would "walk off the job if squint-eyes" were brought in.

...

The management of the Michigan Seamless Tube-- winner of three Army-Navy E's for production achievements in the past--found itself pressed by the War Production Board to meet production quotas while at the same time they faced the seemingly impossible task of placating all interests here in an attempt to recruit workers.

Mayor J. B. Calhoun said he thought the community would accept Nisei for they feel that they won't remain here after the war, but that they wouldn't consider Negroes because of what they called "the permanency of their settlement."

One irate citizen aired his opinions in the local drug store yesterday for all who would listen:

"What do we want niggers here for? They will only make trouble and want to go everywhere us white folks go. They will stay around and just think of my kid sittin' next to one of those ** !!! in the schoolhouse. No sir, no niggers for this town."

One union member, hot and tired perhaps from working ten hours in the rolling department because of the shortage, belligerently asked, "Aren't we fighting those yellow Japs? We don't want to work with any of them."

...

Plant Strives to Increase Production

"We aren't interested one way or another who works in the plant," McHattie stated. "All we want to do is produce at full capacity and get on with the war.

"The only thing that we can do is bring Negroes into the plant and that will be done as soon as the U. S. Employment Service can recruit them," he said.

Last week one Negro signed up in Ann Arbor to work in the plant but when he arrived in South Lyon Friday and saw that he would be the only Negro in the entire city he turned around and came home.

The weekly newspaper here, The South Lyon Herald, reported a statement this week by Robert M. Cullum, area supervisor for WRA discussing the withdrawal of approval for Nisei here.

"We found the officials and grievance committee of the local steelworkers union solidly opposed, and when William Miller, president of the union, said that while he would oppose it, the possibility of violence was very serious, we had no alternative but to withdraw approval."

Cullum's statement did not entirely remove the possibility that Nisei may not apply and be employed by Michigan Seamless, but he said efforts to recruit them from relocation centers would be stopped.

Since October part of the deficiency in manpower has been made up by importing Kentucky and Arkansas "hillbillies" and they are being housed in a Federal Housing Project a quarter of a mile from the plant.

These Southerners lined up solidly with the Union and rumors in the project indicated that half of them would move out if either Nisei or Negroes were brought in.

...

As matters now stand, the Union is solidly opposed to importation of Nisei, would walk out if they came, and reluctantly agreed to Negro workers; the townspeople oppose entrance of both racial groups into the community, would prefer the Nisei, and would have to stretch their tolerance a long way to admit Negroes.

The management's only interest is the war production it must complete. It would follow the WMC directive of "no discrimination in war plants."

When reminded of article three of their constitution which prohibits any acts of discrimination on the part of members, Union officials said "we don't hate the Japs, we just don't want them."

South Lyon -- a typical American "war town" -- is now quiet, awaiting the arrival of Negro workers. No one here would care to predict the consequences of their coming.

Then somebody in the barbershop flipped on a radio that brought news of the war -- a war some people here seem to have forgotten about.#

Daily Makes Survey of Barbers' Discrimination

Majority of Local Proprietors Admit They Are Unwilling to Serve Negro Patrons

(May 25, 1947) Twenty-two of Ann Arbor's 26 barber shops will not serve Negro patrons, according to a Daily survey, and the reason given is that "our customers wouldn't like it."

Checking an allegation by Carroll Little, president of Inter-Racial Association, that the Ann Arbor Barbers' Association has an agreement whereby Negroes are not served, The Daily interviewed proprietors of every barber shop in the city...

Only two shops whose barbers belong to the Ann Arbor Barbers' Association will serve Negro patrons, it was found.

Michigan State Law specifies, "All persons within the jurisdiction of this state shall be entitled to full and equal accommodations, advantages, facilities and privileges of...barber shops..."

Two Negro-operated shops, in the downtown area, will serve any customer, their proprietors said. These are not members of the barbers' association.

...

The two barbers' association members who have no policy against serving Negroes are:

Michigan Union Barber Shop: Union business manager Franklin Kuenzel said, "The Union Barber Shop has no policy regarding service as to race, color or creed." Asked if the Union Barber Shop has ever served a Negro, he replied, "I don't know."

Lee's Barber Shop, E. University (opposite University High School): Lee Mulhollen, proprietor, said, "We don't want to serve Negroes. We have served dark-skinned boys. We would serve Negroes, since we can't refuse by law."

The two Negro-operated shops are:

Easley's Barber Shop, 115 E. Ann: John Easley, proprietor, said "I'll wait on anyone, white or Negro."

Wolverine Barber Shop, 209 N. Fourth Ave.: Udoles G. Collins, barber, said: "We serve anyone."

...additional barber shops surveyed in the campus area are:

Dascola Barbers, 615 E. Liberty: Dominic Dascola, proprietor, said, "We have nothing definite as to policy. We have given some service to Negroes, e.g., shoe shines, but not in the past year. If a Negro came in, whether we would service him would depend on whether the barbers would. On the basis of the present situation, it would be poor business to serve Negroes."

Moe's Barber Shop, basement, 320 S. State: James George, barber, said, "We never intend to serve Negroes. We never had a Negro come in and ask. No further comment."

Ferry Field Barbers: 806 S. State: W. A. Miller, proprietor, said, "Negroes have been served here. I think you're going at this from the wrong end. As soon as the public is educated, I think the barbers will cooperate, that is, when the public is willing to give Negroes equal rights."..#

Election Reveals Students Against Barbers' Tactics

(Dec. 12, 1947) A total of 4,383 students cast a decisive 5 to 1 vote against barber shop racial discrimination in Wednesday's IRA survey.

The vote was divided as follows: White male, 2,214; White female, 1,122; Negro, 70.

The first of three questions asked, "Do you believe that private establishments which serve the public should refuse service to a customer on the basis of race?" received a "yes" vote of 556; "no," 3,375; and "no answer," 132.

The second question, "Would you continue to patronize your barber if he were to serve both Negroes and White?", was answered "yes" by 3,293; "no," 645; and "no answer," 125.

...

The poll was sponsored and formulated by the Inter-Racial Association but was conducted by the Student Legislature to insure impartiality.

...

Many of the ballots, bearing notations, expressed dissatisfaction with IRA's method of handling the current Operation Haircut although they agreed with the principle, they said.#

Discrimination To Be Fought By Committee

(Dec. 12, 1947) Positive steps to combat racial discrimination were taken yesterday by the Coordinating Committee on Racial Discrimination in its provi

> A Negro student, who was refused service in an E. Liberty St. barbershop yesterday said he would file a complaint against the proprietor, who is violating the Diggs Act by his discriminatory policy.
>
> The incident, which was witnessed by two University professors, a clergyman and a student, will be the basis for the court case being promoted as part of "Operation Haircut."

sions for immediate consultations with the barbers and important civic organizations on the issue of a boycott against the barbershops.

The committee endorsed a plan of action embracing the continuance of the boycott, work in committees to promote community support and a publicity campaign to inform students about the boycott.

Meanwhile, the Student Directors' Association, representing the Protestant student counselors on the campus, had unanimously passed the following resolution at a meeting Wednesday: "Discrimination among the races is contrary to the Gospel. We would urge the support of those barber shops which do not practice discrimination. We would urge an educational program to eliminate discrimination in other fields in our community. We feel there are more desirable means of education than picketing."#

SAC APPROVES ANTI-BIAS RULE

Disputed Motion Gains Passage by One-Vote Margin

By HARRIET FRIEDMAN

(May 4, 1949) A hotly-debated motion denying University recognition to any future organization which prohibits membership because of race, creed or color passed the Student Affairs Committee yesterday by a one-vote margin.

...

* * *

ORIGINALLY PASSED last month by the Student Legislature, which then recommended SAC action, the ruling sets up new criteria for barring groups which apply in the future with discriminatory clauses in their constitutions. It does not affect organizations already recognized.

A second SL-sponsored motion calling for filing of constitutions by all campus organizations was passed by SAC in revised form.

After affiliated students on the committee pointed to difficulties in removing secret rituals from fraternity constitutions, the motion was changed to allow filing of "constitutional forms" which provide the essential information demanded for recognizing groups.

* * *

TWO OTHER moves against discrimination proposed by the affiliated groups themselves were outlined during the testimony on the motions.

Pan-Hellenic President Mary Stierer revealed a ruling passed by sorority presidents which requires all sororities to abolish discriminatory clauses.

IFC Vice-President Dick Morrison, speaking agsinst the SL motions, proposed an alternate plan used by the University of Minnesota IFC which is educating against discrimination through social contact, discussion, noted speakers and printed leaflets...#

An Editorial...

(May 4, 1949) No student organization can ever again expect University recognition if its constitution contains a discriminatory clause. This is the effect of yesterday's Student Affairs Committee decision.

The action is the first result of several months effort on the part of student leaders in IFC, Pan Hel and the Student Legislature to determine the extent of discrimination here and do something about it.

All deserve credit for realizing that unreasoning prejudice can have no permanent place in a democratic community.

But yesterday's action should bring hope, not contentment.

IFC and Pan Hel have pledged themselves to a campaign of education and action against existing discriminatory practices.

The next move is up to them.#

The Senior Editors.

No Prejudice In 'U' Halls, Officials Say

(EDITOR'S NOTE: This is the first in a series of six articles dealing with student housing facilities, with particular reference to racial and religious factors.)

By BUDDY ARONSON

(May 8, 1949) "There are no considerations made of race, religion or color in accepting residents in Men's Residence Halls."

Such is the stated policy of all University housing units.

As evidence of its policy, the statement issued by the University points out that all freshmen are guaranteed acceptance in a residence hall, and that as many upperclassmen will be accepted as space permits.

* * *

HOWEVER, IN requesting a room in the Men's Residence Halls, the applicant is required in the application form to indicate his religious preference and to include his photograph.

Miss Edith Gowans, Administrative Assistant in charge of men's room assignments, said that the question of religion is included in order to help her form an accurate overall view of the student.

She cited other questions on the application form pertaining to such factors as age, occupational objective, military experience and personal habits...

...

Miss Gowans admitted, however, that an incoming student who does not indicate by name a preference for a particular roommate is almost invariably assigned one of his own religion.

* * *

(A PROTESTANT student living in the East Quad reported to me that he was astonished when his housemother told him, "I'm terribly sorry but a mistake has been made and you have been assigned a roommate of a different religion than yours.")..#

Discrimination in Fraternities

(EDITOR'S NOTE: Following is the first in a series of seven articles discussing discrimination in fraternities at the University. The study is based on research, conferences with Interfraternity Council members, fraternity presidents and members, and editors of other college newspapers.)

The social fraternity defends the individual's right to liberty and equality of opportunity.

--From "Principles of Democracy," statement of the National Interfraternity Council, 1941
By THOMAS HAYDEN

(May 2, 1959) The declaration of principles quoted above can be found on the walls of a vast number of fraternity houses across America.

But whether or not the social fraternity does in practice defend the principle of "liberty and equality of opportunity" is a complex, controversial, and perhaps imponderable question.

Particularly in this decade, there has been expression of a strong and heated feeling, both nationally and locally, regarding the existence within fraternities of membership policies restricting individuals because of religion and ancestry.

...

Four fraternities on this campus--Acacia, Alpha Tau Omega, Sigma Chi, and Sigma Nu--contain constitutional clauses barring individuals because of race or religion.

Opinions on the subject fall generally into two broad divisions.

One side in the debate holds that a private, predominantly-social group, such as a fraternity, has the right to set its own admissions requirements.

...

Those opposed to discrimination claim it is not compatible with democratic principles. They say judgment of an individual should be based on his character rather than the color of his skin or his religious beliefs.

...

Finally, and of serious concern to the University, is the argument that the fraternity's right to discriminate should not be allowed to exist in an educational community which theoretically fosters beliefs and practices free from prejudice...#

In our time the Fraternity will have to decide whether we want Negroes and non-Christians as brothers...
David R. Rood, former chairman of Alpha Tau Omega Committee on the Study of Selectivity Clauses
By THOMAS HAYDEN

(May 4, 1959) The future of the fraternity system may depend on an effective solution to the problem of racial and religious discrimination in membership policies.

Some fraternity men, many of them alumni, will insist like one Tampa attorney, "the words 'white Christian' should never be deleted from the membership requirements of our fraternity."

But his type is fading away, local fraternity men explain. There has been a gradual trend against discrimination which stretches over the past century.

...

But the trend away from discrimination has been anything but "gradual" in some areas outside the fraternity world. A large number of colleges and universities across the nation have taken steps to speed up the "gradual" pace of the fraternities.

...

All the various forms of pressure have been suggested, at one time or another, as solutions to the problem at the University. The local administration, however, has consistently supported the fraternity policy of education as a means of eventual solution.

...

Presidents Ruthven and Hatcher, in their statements in 1951 and 1952, both claimed the educational approach was the only fair means of handling the problem.

...

No Threat

The Interfraternity Council's written philosophy since 1953 has been that the "most desirable and effective method for the removal of these clauses is the action of the individual fraternity without any coercive threat."

However, some parties maintain that fraternity progress has been nil; that fraternities have removed their clauses, only to bury them in their secret rituals or elsewhere...#

A NOTE TO RUSHEES:
The Bias Clause Fraternities

(Feb. 15, 1954) **TODAY MARKS** the beginning of fraternity rushing and Brotherhood Week, both of which bring to mind the subject of Greek bias clauses.

...

...many prospective rushees, particularly freshmen and sophomores, are probably unaware that 13 University fraternities have various types of bias clauses in their constitutions barring certain racial and religious students from affiliation.

Therefore, it seems only fair that the names of these fraternities be printed, along with the particular religious and/or racial groups discriminated against.

The information below was obtained Friday from house presidents and members of the respective fraternities via telephone conversation.

As revealed, the clauses of the following fraternities are:

1--Alpha Tau Omega. A clause barring Negroes.

2--Delta Tau Delta. Accepts only Caucasians.

3--Kappa Sigma. Accepts only persons of Caucasian race who profess a belief in the Bible.

4--Lambda Chi Alpha. A clause barring Jews and non-Caucasians.

5--Phi Delta Theta. Open only to white Christians.

6--Sigma Alpha Mu. Limited to Jews.

The following fraternities possess bias clauses, the nature of which are not known:

1--Acacia.

2--Delta Chi.

3--Sigma Chi.

4--Sigma Nu.

5--Sigma Phi Epsilon.

6--Theta Chi.

7--Trigon#

--**Mark Reader**

Blacks present demands

Ask more recruitment, 'U' financial support

By SHARON WEINER
and W. E. SCHROCK

(Feb. 6, 1970) Black students presented demands last night to President Robben Fleming and Student Government Council for increased recruitment of black students and faculty, increased financial aid and supportive services, and expansion of the black studies program and center.

Specifically, the demands, which were drawn up at a mass meeting of black students Wednesday night, call for:

--The admission of at least 900 new black students next fall, including 450 freshmen, 150 transfers and 300 graduate students;

--An increase in the proportion of blacks in the University to ten per cent by 1973-74;

--Additional annual increases in this percentage until the proportion of blacks "shall approach, if not exceed" the proportion of blacks in the total state population;

--The hiring of several full-time recruiters to aid this increased enrollment;

--The establishment of "an intensive supportive services program" to serve the new black students;

--An increase in University financial aid to black students;

--The establishment of a University-wide appeal board to deal with financial aids;

--The revamping of the parents' confidential statement to allow for "hidden costs;"

--The granting of tuition waivers to in-state black students to be admitted under special programs...#

The case for minority admissions

(Feb. 24, 1970) THE DEMANDS of the Black Action Movement (BAM) for increased minority admissions certainly merit the support of the University community.

Although the black student community at the University has increased dramatically during the last few years, the overriding impression of the University is still one of a school for rich white students as the Green report characterized it in 1965.

The BAM proposal for changing this condition is reasonable if not a bit conservative. In a University of more than 30 thousand students, it demands that only 900 black students be admitted next fall--450 freshmen, 150 transfer students and 300 graduate students. The demands also give the University three years to increase the proportion of blacks in the University to 10 per cent--more than enough time.

...

UNFORTUNATELY, it is becoming increasingly apparent that the administration and the University community-at-large are unwilling to give enthusiastic support to the program. The administration argues that although the proposals are theoretically desirable, the necessary financing is not available.

It is noteworthy that the same administration has proposed that students be assessed $15 per term for 30 years to finance the construction of two IM buildings. They considered that this request would be reasonable, yet they are unwilling to consider seriously a similar proposal to finance minority admissions submitted by Students for Effective Action (SEA).

...

TWO OTHER arguments, that the quality of the University will suffer and that it is unfair to lower admissions standards are merely examples of academic elitism.

The only real question in admission should be whether or not the students can succeed at the University, not what type of credentials he has to get in. The innate ability of the students that would be admitted under the minority admissions program is no less than that of the majority of students already here. With the help of supportive services to fill in the gaps that were caused by poor academic backgrounds, not lack of intelligence, the majority of the students should be able to succeed.#

--ALEXA CANADY
Editorial Page Editor

Black students enter classes, read demands

By ROB BIER

(Feb. 26, 1970) Disruptions occurred in several classes yesterday when black students attempted to read a list of demands for increased minority admissions.

A few later scuffles broke out and classes were cancelled in at least four cases when the instructors refused to let the blacks speak. Other classes were more peaceful when the students were allowed to present their demands. Most left after about ten minutes.

It was unclear last night what group, if any, organized the actions of the black students. Walter Lewis, of the Black Students Union, said last night that the actions were unconnected with a teach-in sponsored at the Union yesterday by the Black Action Movement (BAM).

...

Several of the classes which were visited by groups of 10 to 20 black students were in the Angell Hall auditoriums. Classrooms were entered as early as 8:30 a.m. and the blacks continued their actions late into the afternoon.

One of the less peaceful incidents occurred in the anthropology 428 class of Prof. Robert Eckhardt when the blacks were refused permission to speak. Eckhardt said he asked a student to call the campus security police, but added that when a girl left to do that, she was stopped by some blacks.

According to campus security chief Rolland Gainsley, a boy who went to her aid was knocked down in the ensuing scuffle.

Eckhardt later said that such attempts to pre-empt class time were "absolutely intolerable." "The University can't operate if at any given time a group can come in and disrupt," he said.

The scene was somewhat different in Prof. Klaus Riegal's psychology 451 class where the blacks were allowed to speak. Riegal said last night that several students in the class told him the presentation had "opened their eyes.

"I think we didn't help them (the blacks) enough," Riegal added. "I don't know how much good this will do."..#

Racism and Repression: Offspring of the 'U'

(March 20, 1970) **THE REGENTS' ACTIONS** yesterday--passing paper platitudes which refuse to deal seriously with the minority admission crisis, and calling squads of riot police to secure the administration fortress against a peaceful demonstration--show that a serious battle to substantially increase minority admissions is just beginning.

The Regents' compromise proposal, which endorses 10 per cent black enrollment by 1973-74, but without adequate mechanisms for funding it, isn't worth the paper it's printed on in bringing black and other minority students to campus.

...

The administration does not intend to open the University to admit the minority students who have the right to enroll here. It will commit no resources, it will not commit the funds because minority admissions do not rank among the administration's highest priorities.

The University administration no longer maintains an aloof, "liberal" distance from the police it uses, but has allied with them.

...

THE FIRST STEP every student and faculty member should take now is to strike and close the University: halt the functions of an institution which refuses to serve minorities and which refuses to listen to its own students. Strikers should rove through dorms, fraternities and sororities, knock on apartment doors, explain the issues--and make it clear that the minority admissions crisis affects not only black students and Chicanos and other minorities, but every white person as well who lives under the University and must ultimately bear responsibility for its policies.

Such responsibility is material, not only idealistic. Institutions--like nations--are never spared internally the effects of their policies and attitudes toward externals. Nations which become chauvinistically aggressive against neighbors go through parallel transformations within their borders. National discipline is rigidified, criticism suppressed, police forces strengthened.

SIMILARLY, institutions which act in an elitist fashion toward the surrounding society find the effects of that elitism corrupting every facet of its internal life. In the case of the University one can easily detect the effects of elitism in the curriculum, the power distribution among the various constituencies, the growing brutality of the administration toward upstart students.

The campus must strike--and show the Regents and administration that this University will not continue operating until it begins turning its interests toward the disadvantaged groups who have every right to an education.#

--DANIEL ZWERDLING
Magazine Editor
--ALEXA CANADY
Editorial Page Editor
--BRUCE LEVINE
Editorial Page Editor

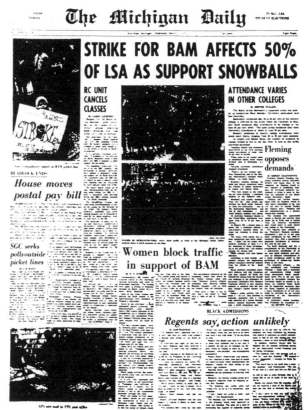

Open it up or shut it down

(March 24, 1970) **THE COMING** days are crucial to the success of the strike called by the Black Action Movement for substantial increases in black enrollment. All members of the University community should actively participate.

With a state college age black population of 18 per cent, the BAM demand for 10 per cent black enrollment by fall 1973 must be seen as minimal, reasonable and obtainable. But it can only be obtained with an adequate financial commitment from the University administration.

...

The strike tactic speaks directly to the question of priorities. There is so much wrong with the way the University is run that it would best be shut down rather than continue on a path that is socially meaningless if not destructive.

SUPPORT FOR the strike appears to be growing in all corners. Hundreds of teaching fellows and faculty members are either cancelling their classes or holding discussions on the black demands. Thousands of students are on strike.

If support for the strike continues to grow, it will force the Regents and administration to face their responsibility to the black community directly and meaningfully. Widespread participation in this effort is essential.#

--THE SENIOR EDITORS

Food service, LSA Bldg. blocked as strike grows

By ART LERNER
and BOB SCHREINER

(March 28, 1970) The strike called by the Black Action Movement reached a new stage yesterday as dorm food service virtually ceased and students kept the LSA Bldg. closed.

Classroom attendance remained low and operations at numerous central campus buildings ended.

At a mass meeting in Rackham Aud. an overflow crowd heard BAM leaders say that the strike will continue until BAM believes an adequate agreement has been reached with University officials.

Food service was discontinued in almost all University dormitories yesterday when University employes respected student picket lines. It was unclear yesterday whether workers who stayed away from their jobs would lose their pay.

At both South and West Quads a vast majority of workers voluntarily refused to cross student picket lines and no meals were served all day long.

...

Picket lines were set up at all possible entrances to the dorms by 4:45 a.m. When a dorm worker arrived, he was asked to support the strike and handed a leaflet explaining the BAM demands.

Most workers seemed to be observing the picket lines. A handful of workers, however, told the students that they were sympathetic to the demands but were forced to work from necessity. They passed through the picket lines without incident.

...

Early in the morning, strikers formed picket lines around the LSA Bldg. The interior of the office building remained deserted throughout the day, as the pickets maintained their presence around all the entrances.

Meanwhile, class attendance at the University remained at a low level yesterday as the strike moved through its sixth full day...#

BAM ENDS CLASS STRIKE
Accepts regental statement

By DAVE CHUDWIN

(April 2, 1970) The class strike in support of Black Action Movement proposals for increased minority admissions ended last night as BAM members overwhelmingly approved a regental proposal in a euphoric mass meeting in the Union Ballroom.

After 16 hours of discussions with President Robben Fleming, the Regents released a statement which said that 10 per cent black enrollment by 1973-74 was assured along with necessary financial aid, recruiting and other supportive services.

The Regents rejected, however, Bam demands for no reprisals against strikers, a black student center, tuition waivers and University collection of student fees for the Martin Luther King Fund. They also expressed support for Fleming's handling of the situation.

Despite BAM's endorsement of the Regents' plan, some members of the white Coalition to Support BAM were not satisfied with the agreement. "If they want to call it a victory, because they saw that the strike couldn't continue, let them--I don't," one Coalition member said after the meeting.

"This wasn't the best agreement we could have settled on but it was a first step, a first substantial step," BAM leader Dave Lewis told the crowd of about 1,200 people in the ballroom.

...

Receiving a standing ovation from the enthusiastic crowd, each member of BAM's 11-man negotiating team expressed support for the regental proposal last night but emphasized that BAM would continue its efforts.

"We say there can be no total victory until the racist malignancy either consumes this country or we cut it out," anthropology Prof. Gloria Marshall told the gathering. "We will fight on, because like all mankind we hope, and because we're arrogant enough to know we'll win."..#

BAM ENDS CLASS STRIKE
Regents act on demands
Accepts regental statement
Prof charges two students with classroom disruption

Racist jokes aired over 'U' radio

Students protest WJJX broadcast

By EUGENE PAK

(Feb. 19, 1987) More than 30 students descended upon the studio of campus radio station WJJX to demand the cancellation of racist and sexist broadcasts on one student disc jockey's program.

The disc jockey, Ted Sevransky, an LSA sophomore who uses the name "Tenacious Slack" on his weekly show, hosted a program containing a series of racist and sexist jokes on Feb. 4, including "Who are the two most famous black women in history? ...Aunt Jemima and motherfucker," and "Why do black people smell? ...so blind people can hate them too."

After listening to the tape, LSA senior Ernie Robinson shook his head and said, "I don't even want to hear that tape anymore."

According to students who had taped the program off the radio, Sevransky had two other people, "Miami Mike" and "Shamalama Asbuhi" (a derogatory slur against West Quad's minority council) call in with these jokes.

The students had hoped to protest as Sevransky began his program, but when they arrived neither Sevransky nor any WJJX staff member was present. A note was found at the office warning the station manager that students would be protesting the program. The station did not broadcast anything.

The student protestors had prepared a typed statement against the program, part of which stated: "We view this as another example of the increasing upsurge of racist incidents on this campus..."

Over the phone, LSA senior Jim Lamb, WJJX's program manager, said Sevransky "likes to talk a great deal on the air," and he had only learned about the content of Sevransky's program Tuesday night.

WHEN LAMB arrived at the station and heard the tape of the program, he immediately fired Sevransky, stating that "he is no longer a part of WJJX, and will never be."..#

Racism pervades black student life

By EUGENE PAK

First in a five-part series

(March 9, 1987) In dormitory cafeterias the separation is visually striking: Black students sit with black students, white students sit with white students.

Laws relegating blacks to separate, often inferior, public facilities and institutions were repealed more than 20 years ago, but a separation along racial lines is still evident today--both nationwide and at the University.

Many say the separation occurs not because of racism, but merely because students stick with friends who share common interests.

Marvin Woods, president of the Black Student Union, said, "People get together based on their common interests and not so much phsyical similarity, even though that does play a part in it."

The separation of black and white students "is a combination of a little bit of negative feeling against the other group and each group having its own set of interests and cultural values," Woods said. "It's more cultural interest than racial animosity."

Nevertheless, it is clear that many black students feel alienated from the rest of the University community, both socially and academically.

...

Part of the problem stems from a cutural clash. Many of the black undergraduate students on campus are from Detroit, while many white students are from the surrounding suburbs or northern areas of Michigan...

...

Thus, even before they arrive on campus, many white and black students have not interacted with students of other backgrounds.

Rejection

Black students who have tried to interact with other students have faced resistance, rejection, and even fear.

At a racism teach-in held last month at Alice Lloyd, Francis Matthews, an LSA sophomore from Detroit, said sometimes people seem afraid of him. "Sometimes I'm walking and people look back, and they start to walk faster or duck out of the way.

"I love being black. I'm proud of it, but at times it makes you feel negative about yourself. It tends to make you think for no good reason at all about who you are. I'm thinking, 'Do I have to keep on taking things like this'?"

Another student recalled an incident last year, when someone threw a full beer can at her from his dormitory window. The assailant yelled "nigger" at her as the can just missed her head.

Such overt racist incidents, coupled with cultural and social obstacles can make campus life unbearable for many students.

Race and academia

Many black students also face alienation in the classroom. Attending a large lecture hall can be intimidating for any first-year student, but for a black student, who may be the only black in the entire class, the experience can be even more problematic.

"Whenever we talk about black people or black issues in my biology class, everyone would turn around and look at me... I felt a little awkward," said LSA sophomore Felicia Jernigan. Jernigan is the only black student in her class.

...

In a 1980 study on black University students, sociology Prof. Walter Allen found that most enter the University with high academic credentials--67 percent were ranked in the top 10 percent of their graduating class.

However, these students may not be accustomed to the University's predominantly white culture. Few attended high schools where black enrollment was less than 10 percent, as it is here.

Not surprisingly then, nearly half the students in Allen's study reported that they did not feel as if they were a part of general campus life.

Such dilemmas create a sense of isolation for students. Many black students see the University mainly as a place to study, and frequently go back home on the weekends.

[Eunice] Royster said she sees many black students "getting away from it, going somewhere where they are comfortable, where how they look isn't being questioned; where they aren't going into a store and being inspected more severely. Who wants to live that way?"..#

LIVING WITH
RACISM

(March 6, 1987) EDITOR'S NOTE: It took several bold acts of racism to get the state's media, the University administration, and many students to focus attention on a serious problem that has never come close to being resolved.

The state of Michigan is 12.9 percent black. Its foremost educational institution is just 5.3 percent black--16 years after the University administration promised to raise black enrollment to ten percent. The situation is so bad that last year, when black enrollment increased by just 24 students, the University hailed the gain as a significant step forward. But two dozen people in an undergraduate population of 23,000 hardly causes a ripple.

...

Unfortunately, what's happening at the University is not just a reflection of larger, social currents. It is here, in this often tense environment, that our attitudes and expectations about the races are cemented. We will carry those views into the "real world." In other words, we don't simply react to contemporary race relations--we help to determine them.

With this issue of Weekend Magazine, the Daily begins a week-long series of articles on campus race issues.

ROB EARLE

The Daily, like the rest of campus, is no example of integration

ON THE THURSDAY BEFORE spring break, the Daily ran a story about a disc jockey at WJJX who had his friends call in and tell racist jokes on the air. In our story, we printed the jokes. I was wary about doing that, but the reporter insisted that several black leaders wanted the jokes printed, to show just how bad racism is at the University. So, despite my misgivings, we printed the slurs.

When I saw students reading the paper the next morning, I knew I had been steered right. Nobody was laughing at those jokes. Most people just couldn't believe that it actually happened, that something like that was allowed on a University radio station. Printing the jokes brought home to the readers just how bad the situation at WJJX was.

Still, I was not surprised to find a letter Friday from a University employee who disagreed with our decision.

"What possible purpose in the public interest can be served by perpetuating jokes that have as their basis the slurring of a person's racial or ethnic characteristics?" this reader asked, and went on to say to print the jokes was "racist and certainly irresponsible journalism."

Two weeks ago I would have agreed. Ever since a cartoon we ran last term brought a response more enraged than anything in recent memory, the staff has been on egg shells about racism. We worry that the Daily is seen as racist by the University community and what we can do about it... But this problem of printing the jokes has shown me one thing--the Daily staff does not understand racism.

If you've ever been in the Daily office around 4 p.m., when the business staff is starting to wind down their operation and the editorial staff is preparing for the night shift, you will notice that minorities in all aspects of our operation are few and far between. The staff is overwhelmingly white.

How can these people really understand racism?... How can anyone understand racism when all they've ever done is seen racism, and never experienced it?

That, I believe, is the major problem with the Daily and racism. Until very recently, we understood racism only on an intellectual level. Not running those jokes seemed like the logical thing to do--it would have avoided perpetuating them and made the Daily seem sensitive to the feelings of our black readers. As it turned out, this was totally wrong. If racism could be dealt with logically, it wouldn't exist at all...

MICHAEL JAY WALKER

Campus life for blacks is marked by alienation and frustration

Many of us have found the recent rash of racist incidents on campus to be especially repugnant. My own personal values seem to have been challenged ever since I arrived at the University in 1982. Nothing I've seen here is new or unprecedented.

....

When I graduated from [a boarding school in Colorado] and came to the University of Michigan I was hoping to find something different. I had assumed that the greater number of blacks here would make a difference. What I found was only a testament to the law of relative proportions: the relatively small numbers of blacks here suffered from the same problems.

There are apparently three choices for the new black student: 1) to be confined to a separate minority community, 2) to assimilate to the larger white culture, or 3) to make an effort to find a balance between the two. For students with my background the easiest choice is to assimilate and to continue to passively ac-cept the ignorance I experienced in those predominantly white schools. Because of the University's insufficient recruitment efforts the majority of black students have very similar backgrounds. Lack of diversity means coming into the black community as an outsider for an out-of-state minority student, making the first choice difficult. The most intimidating alternative is trying to assimilate with the larger white community while turning to the smaller black community for your cultural identity...#

Student Movements: Common Goal

By THOMAS HAYDEN
Special to The Daily

(July 9, 1960) LOS ANGELES -- Despite the absorbing turmoil of the Democratic Convention here, more than a few persons are carefully observing a related and highly significant event, the so-called march on the convention for a stronger civil rights plank.

Not only are they interested in the powerful demands for Negro rights, but also in the mysterious student movement at the base of the civil rights drive.

...The American student is suddenly responsive to, and often critical of, his social environment. No one seems to understand either the motivation or the ultimate direction of the student movement, but there is no escaping the fact that the movement does exist, that it is developing potency and momentum, and that it has the ability to sometimes change a social situation.

...

The question one must ask is simple, yet no one has quite been able to answer it: What, precisely, is the nature of the movement? Or, it may be stated otherwise: What happened to the so-called Silent Generation of the Fifties?

...

Its general nature, I believe, may be defined by its common purpose which winds through its whole fabric. The assertion that human beings must be free, functioning as components in a society equal to all the other components of that society. Further, that society, which is in many ways institutionalized and bureaucratic, must be humanized.

...

* * *

ALL THIS STILL leaves the basic question of motivation. What inspired the American student to begin the campaign, to defy authority, to jeopardize his present place in society in hopes of building a sounder future?

One reason is simple. Many of the students involved are older than the average American student. Some leaders at the University of California, for example, are 25 to 28 years old...

A more important, and a more general, reason may be found by defining the student's position in society. The four years of college education have been likened to a parenthesis. That parenthesis interrupts the otherwise straight line of a student's life development.

* * *

IT IS A PERIOD regarded by many students as superfluous to their course in that it has no strictly definable effect on the rest of their lives. In other words, the college student is suspended. He has no demanding attachments--no job ties, no family, no property, no investments. He is free in a sense that no older person in the economy is free.

In this atmosphere the student has the opportunity to make a detached analysis of his society and its trends. Quite naturally, he asks questions like the question presently being asked: Since in theory the Negro must have equal rights, why does he not have them in fact?

...

One historical fact helps explain the movement's recent development. That is the apparent passing of McCarthyism and its intolerance of "rebellious attitudes." Prior to the McCarthy days, the student movement was definitely under way, inspired to an extent by returning war veterans who had been exposed to the realities of this world beyond the college parenthesis.

* * *

VIEWED IN THIS way then, today's student movement is the regeneration of something not quite killed by the McCarthy era. One may also see it as an objective response to the society from which the student is somewhat detached.

I suspect, however, that this analytic approach fails and that somewhere there exist other reasons for the current student renaissance.

...

If a fear of the profound complexity of modern life forces the majority of students to withdraw into conservatism, what is it in life which magnetizes the minority of students into quite fearless rebellion?

The student seems to have reached a point where it is so self-humiliating not to assert himself that he is impelled to cry out at any material cost so that he may somehow preserve the integrity of his personality. I do not profess to know if this is the final answer. In fact, no one seems to know at the moment. But 500 students will picket the Democratic Convention today.#

the women's pages

When responses came in from Daily alumnae to our announcement of this anthology, I was surprised at some of the bitterness that still remained after twenty or thirty or even more years. And then I was surprised at my own surprise, because it remains in me, too. Only in bits and pieces, of course, but still...

I suppose I was the first woman managing editor of The Daily, and of course it happened only because of World War I. In the fall of 1918 there wasn't an experienced male Daily staffer who could take the job. They were all either already in France, or drilling at Battle Creek, or would be fast asleep in SATC barracks in the new Union building at the hour The Daily went to press. (I note that the Daily staffers of 1944 were almost all women, for the same reason no doubt -- World War II.) I had been Women's Editor my senior year, so I, a three-months graduate working on my home town paper, was called back to Ann Arbor. The generous salary was $25 a week.

—Mildred Mighell (Blake), '18

What was life like working for The Daily in 1927-31? It was tough! Back in those days, the days of the auto-ban, co-eds had a long, hard day. We ALWAYS wore high heels, hat and gloves on campus and our stories were strictly limited to the 'Women's Page,' which I hope you no longer have. We weren't really supposed to be on the paper, were never ever spoken to by the male staff -- just tolerated. I know things are different now, and while I don't regret a minute of my Ann Arbor days, I'm glad Michigan has joined the 20th century.

—Helen Domine (Barnes), '31

My memories of The Daily are mostly of the editorial office on the top floor of the old building on Maynard Street, with School of Music students practicing in the basement -- and the second-class status of women reporters!

—Ruth Gallmeyer, '32

I was the culprit of a well-kept secret regarding an s-line on a story about Dean of Women Alice Lloyd, who banned slacks on campus for women. The s-line read 'Born Thirty Years Too Soon.' I really had in mind that in 30 years no one would care (proved true), but Miss Lloyd took it personally and called the City Editor to find out the guilty party. He refused to say so Miss Lloyd had to be satisfied with scolding him for the insult heaped upon her by an inept (or probably malicious?) headline writer.

I wonder if the men's dean dictated attire for male students?

—Claire Sherman (Thomas), '44

ELSIE A. PIERCE ·

Elsie Pierce Edits Daily

(May 17, 1936) For the first time in The Daily's history, a woman student, Elsie A. Pierce, '37, was named its managing editor.

Although Miss Pierce is the first woman student to reach the managing editor's position, a woman who was not a student, Mildred C. Mighell, held the post in 1918. There was no man eligible because of the World War, according to Prof. Edson R. Sunderland of the Law School, secretary of the Board in Control, and Miss Mighell, who had graduated the previous June, and had already obtained a position on a newspaper, was selected for the job.

Miss Pierce was the first woman night editor of The Daily...#

'U' Coeds Shirk Local War Responsibilities

By MAVIS KENNEDY

(Dec. 1, 1943) Many Michigan women have not heard that this is an all-out war, that there is a job for everyone. A poll taken recently in Stockwell Hall revealed that 118 out of 250 women are doing nothing but going to classes, and studying now and then.

1943

These 188 women are representative of hundreds of other University women who are failing to do their part.

...

THE REAL REASON WHY UNIVERSITY WOMEN ARE SHIRKING RESPONSIBILITY IS THAT THEY ARE TOO STEEPED IN NOSTALGIC LONGING FOR THE GOOD OLD DAYS TO REALIZE THAT THEY ARE LETTING THEIR COUNTRY AND THEIR COLLEGE DOWN.

They spend hours in bull-sessions talking about the days when a coed's biggest worry was about her dress for this week's ball, whether or not the letter-man in chem lab was going to date her, and if a particular sorority was going to give her a bid--*days when Guadalcanal, Mindanao, and the Aleutians were just names on a map that had to be learned the night before a geography final...*

THEY MISS THE PROLONGED ADOLESCENCE OF FORMER COLLEGE LIFE AND DISLIKE BEING REMINDED THAT THE WORLD IS FULL OF UNPLEASANT PROBLEMS.

...

It took a war to swing colleges into the world of the living. Unless the parasitic females of the University wake up to their responsibility and see each one has a job that no one else can do, then peace will mean the return of the stagnant lethargy of the good old days. And the 118 can crawl back into their ivory towers.#

WOMEN TAKE OVER:

Marion Ford Heads Daily's First All-Girl Senior Staff

(Nov. 4, 1943) Petite feminine feet are filling the shoes of the senior editors on The Daily this fall as four girls carry on in the top positions of the paper's editorial staff.

History was made as Marion Ford became managing editor; Jane Farrant, editorial director; Claire Sherman, city editor; and Marjorie Borradaile, associate editor.

When the Board in Control of Student Publications announced the recent appointments, The Daily acquired its first staff composed entirely of girls with the traditional printers' ink in their blood.

During the summer months Miss Ford also acted as managing editor of The Daily, so the post of top man--pardon us--top woman, is not new to her. A resident of Miami, Fla., Miss Ford, '44, is a member of Alpha Omicron Pi...#

Student Blames Coed Apathy on University

Editor's Note:

The following letter was written to The Daily in answer to the editorial on coed apathy in war work which ran yesterday. We feel that the writer, who wishes to remain anonymous for obvious reasons, has hit the root of the problem.

(Dec. 2, 1943) **PERHAPS** Miss Kennedy has almost hit the nail on the head when she finally gets down to offering "adolescence" as an explanation of the co-ed's failure to take on war-time responsibilities.

It is not, however, the escapist's adolescence, which she implies, but rather it is the same kind of adolescence that resulted in India's refusal to cooperate with Great Britain in fighting the war--*and the Michigan co-ed has not even had the promise of better treatment after the war! ...*

...

A BACKWARD GLANCE REVEALS WOMEN ON THE MICHIGAN CAMPUS OCCUPYING AN INFERIOR POSITION. THEY HAVE BEEN HERE MAINLY FOR THE DATING PLEASURE OF THE MEN, NOT TO OCCUPY AN EQUAL PLACE WITH THEM...

...

Of course she THINKS she has no time for war work when she has been taught that poor little co-eds cannot absorb any education if there are any distractions whatsoever and so there must be "captains" on each corridor, racing up and down, seeing that a strict military silence is observed for the benefit of the "students."

Her every move is supervised. Even her room is inspected every week. House mother, assistant house mothers, social directors, night chaperones, house officers, corridor leaders, ad infinitum, all cooperate to see that the co-ed never has occasion to do any independent thinking, to learn initiative, or to transfer any of the knowledge gained from education to practical living.

NOW SHE IS, OVERNIGHT, ASKED TO STAND INDEPENDENTLY ON HER OWN TWO FEET. NEVER HAVING HAD EVEN THE RESPONSIBILITY OF DECIDING WHAT TIME TO RETURN HOME AT NIGHT, SHE IS SUDDENLY SUPPOSED TO AWAKEN WITH THE ABILITY TO DO STUDIES, CAMPUS ACTIVITIES, AND WAR WORK--ALL AT ONCE.

...

They find something ludicrous in the constant exhortations to "volunteer" when they are living under a system of rules, the bare essentials of which take from 10:30 to 11:30 to read, the listener knowing that unwittingly she will probably break three just returning to her room...

...It is too much to ask that they emerge from their sheltered cocoons of a policy of mid-Victorian supervision and behave immediately as members of twentieth century society. If Michigan co-eds are to do their duty, we are afraid it will only be accomplished through a long process of gradual maturing, or else through the same methods that direct their other activities--compulsion.#

Cinderellas

(Jan. 26, 1946) Once upon a time there were 5,000 coeds attending a large midwestern university. Oddly enough, every one of them was named Cinderella. There was an ugly rumor going around that if anyone of these lasses was not safely tucked in her trundle bed by 10:30, a certain group of fairy godmothers would transform her into a pumpkin!

But all American coeds are not named Cinderella. Far from it. Take Northwestern for example. There the flower of feminine youth stays out until 2 a.m. Friday and Saturday nights, and seniors have six 12:30 permissions a month on week nights! Imagine!

At Barnard College of Columbia University in a town nearly as encouraging to wickedness as Ann Arbor, women get 10:30 hours every night. If they stay out till 1:30 ANY NIGHT, they must telephone for permission, earlier in the evening. ...

One can't help wondering:

If a young lady old enough to get married legally is not old enough to take care of herself.

If seniors who are four years older than freshmen are not four years more mature.

If weekday nights preceeding classless days are not as good date nights as Fridays or Saturdays.

If the administration of some universities do not under-rate the discretion of their feminine charges.#

--Milt Freudenheim

Woman's Place

(May 11, 1949) **STUDENT LEGISLATURE** President Jim Jans can't remember the last time the Legislature finished the evening's business in one of the bi-monthly meetings.

And former SL Vice-President Bill Miller can vouch for it. Bill has had a motion under consideration since last fall which has been consistently postponed because of SL's inability to act.

The major difficulty, a rather simple one, lies in the fact that no legislative body can complete its business without the legislators.

At least one-third of the student body's elected representatives are caught between their duty to their constituents and a natural physical condition--they are women--which requires them, according to University regulations, to be in their dorms by 10:30 p.m.

For "Hamlet," the coeds can stay out until 11:30 p.m. For the IFC Ball, J-Hop, Pan-Hel and any number of other social functions they are given according time extensions. Women on The Daily's editorial staff are allowed to stay and finish their jobs. But for the job of learning and practicing self-government and democracy they can't be given a single minute beyond their regular time.

How is this to be interpreted, but as an expression of the administration's opinion that there is no place in politics for the female sex?

If the University believes otherwise, an OK from the Dean of Women's office will clarify the situation. Permission to attend these sessions until midnight, where they'll get into less trouble than elsewhere, could easily be given. It would indicate a vote of confidence by the administration in the praiseworthy efforts of the student government--men and women.#

--Don McNeil

This miniscule extension of women's curfew was granted, finally, not because the University was suddenly converted to a belief in the right of women students to control their own lives, but, oddly enough, because of the new Undergraduate Library, which remained open until midnight. When women students, who had to be locked away by 10:30 p.m., realized that men had the library -- and its precious reserve books -- all to themselves for an hour and a half every night, the outcry was so great that even the Dean of Women had to give in.

New Midnight Closing Hours Set for Upper-class Women
Freshman Curfew Extended to 11 P. M.

By JANE McCARTHY
(Dec. 4, 1958) The Women's Senate yesterday passed a revision of women's hours providing for a 12 midnight closing for upperclassmen and an 11 p.m. closing for freshmen Sunday through Thursday.

The new hours may go into effect next semester.

The plan for the revision, drafted by Women's Judiciary Council, approved by the Dean of Women's office and passed by a 68 to five vote in the Senate, also makes two other changes in the present women's hours.

Freshmen will be granted eight Automatic Late Permissions per semester and housing units will be closed to visitors at 10:55 p.m. Sunday through Thursday. ...

Originally, a 12 midnight closing had been planned for all women, Miss Drasin said. However, the house directors, the Dean of Women's office and the girls themselves felt that an earlier closing was desirable for freshmen who are being oriented to the University...#

Cold War on the Hill: Dress Regulations

(March 16, 1961) **A FEW WEEKS** ago, Alice Lloyd's council wanted to change its regulations and permit slacks at breakfast and lunch every day, on Saturday evenings and in one of the public lounges.

1961 The next week, having established a philosophy which stressed the importance of neatness and consideration for other residents and guests, the council modified its proposal somewhat. The house presidents met again with the assistant deans and resident directors. In an extremely mature, co-operative session, they worked out a plan for permitting slacks to be worn to breakfast and to Sunday night suppers, because these are times when there are few if any guests. Slacks were also to be innovated in one of the main floor lounges so that girls who wear them on dates will have a place to sit and talk with their escorts.

The next big issue to be solved concerns one of Markley's main lounges. Since September, the Markley Council has been trying, with remarkably little success, to have its lounge 3 made into an official "Bermuda Lounge" where girls could study, visit, or bring guests in slacks.

The need for such a lounge is painfully obvious. After costing an astronomical sum, the Markley lounges are virtually empty at all times except Friday and Saturday nights and Sunday afternoon. The reasons are twofold. Firstly, smoking is forbidden in these lounges, although other dormitories permit smoking in their main lounges and it would be an easy matter to obtain a few ash trays. Secondly, and more important, it is strictly taboo to wear slacks or bermudas in these lounges. It is such a great offense, as a matter of fact, that any girls caught in one of the lounges in slacks is subject to one half hour's worth of late minutes, a dormitory's most effective weapon.

...

What I want to know is, what is there in the physical and philosophical makeup of slacks which makes them unacceptable for young ladies according to the absolute moral laws of the universe? Looking at it objectively, slacks are made of the same material as skirts; they have the same patterns as skirts; they serve the same function as any clothes, and they are more comfortable, serviceable, and practical to boot. As to whether they LOOK better than skirts, that is a question of aesthetics on which, I believe, it is only fair to admit that people may hold differing opinions without one view or the other being right or wrong.

...

A pair of slacks, well pressed and worn with a neat blouse and sweater, are infinitely prettier, and yes, even more ladylike, than the standard cotton "dinner dress" unwashed and unironed, which hundreds of girls throw on in a rush for meals and take off immediately afterward when they change into the clothes they wear for attending class, studying, going to the library, or even meeting a date for coffee...#

--JUDITH OPPENHEIM

overtime: Parents, Morals and Wisdom

By FAITH WEINSTEIN, Editorial Director

(March 15, 1962) "I don't think the rules here are too harsh and I don't think a majority of the girls think they are being put upon. As a matter of fact, there is some astonishment at the small minority doing all the current squealing. They mean to deny that our parents might have a little bit of wisdom."

This is the opinion of Peggy Shaw, vice-president of Panhellenic and clearly a satisfied co-ed. Miss Shaw's statement, originally run in the Detroit Free Press, was picked up by the Michigan Alumnus in this month's issue, and used to counter criticism of current rules and regulations by members of The Daily staff.

As a member of the squealing minority, I may have no right to say anything; but I think Miss Shaw is wrong. There are plenty of women in the dorms and even in the sororities who are very unhappy with women's rules and the atmosphere of constraint which they breed.

...

Women's hours are outdated and in most cases unnecessary. Parents of this generation are generally moderate people, imbued with at least smatterings of the ideal of teaching the child to take care of himself. If there were no women's hours, few girls would go careening wildly down the paths of sin in rebellion against parental rigidity. Many of today's co-eds have been setting their own hours since they were 16 or 17, and have learned moderation and self-control in the home, where such training belongs.

...

Regulations designed to keep girls morally pure are simply ludicrous. They range from the rules prohibiting freshmen women from going to apartment parties to the regulation which effectively prevents a father from seeing the room he pays for his daughter to live in, except in "exceptional" circumstances. (Interestingly enough, these old rules are not extended to mothers in the quads--I suppose men are intrinsically more dangerous than women.)

Essentially the situation boils down to this: morals are instilled in the home or they aren't instilled at all. No number of University regulations will stop any girl from doing anything she wants unless they keep her chained to the wall.

I think the angry alumna who writes that she is "horrified by the extent to which student licentiousness has been growing for the past few years" is wrong. I don't think students are any more licentious than they have ever been. But if they are, it is not the University's role to instill in them the morals the parents neglected.

In the first place it can't. The University is too big and too impersonal to offer more than inadequate restraints; it has neither the responsibility nor the ability to provide a moral code.

In the second place, it shouldn't. To repeat the tired old arguments, the parent, not the University is responsible for the undergraduate, and the University should control the underage student only to the degree the individual parent requests...#

ASK STUDENT AFFAIRS SHAKEUP

Faculty Criticizes Staff, Structure

By JOHN ROBERTS
Acting Editor

(May 30, 1961) "Re-assignment of present personnel" and "sweeping structural changes" in the Office of Student Affairs were recommended yesterday by the University Senate's Committee on Student Relations.

In a report sent to Vice-President for Student Affairs James A. Lewis, the committee also requested a positive program for implementation of the Regents' bylaw on discrimination, a thorough review of student housing arrangements and establishment of an orderly grievance mechanism for students.

...

The complete report, which has not yet been released, capped a three-month study of the organization and policies of the Office of Student Affairs, particularly the Dean of Women's Office.

...

The student relations committee, headed by Prof. Charles Lehmann of the education school, began its study late in February after receiving a documented complaint from a group of students.

The 1960-61 Daily senior staff was the nucleus of the group, which also included James Seder, '61, Mary Wheeler, '61 and Barton Burkhalter, '62 of the Human Relations Board.

Protesting the orientation and practices of Dean of Women Deborah Bacon and her office, the students' document reported several incidents indicating irregularities in the conduct of her functions.

...

Miss Bacon had no comment.

The examination of policies and practices in the Office of Student Affairs grew out of widespread but unorganized complaints against the Dean of Women's Office. These came to the attention of the student group, which began collecting and ordering information relating to the office's attitudes and practices.

Women's complaints and allegedly objectionable letters to parents were collected and the relationship of the dean's office to women's judicial and legislative bodies investigated.

The findings, presented to Lewis and the committee Feb. 21, were in the form of a 40-page confidential document divided in two parts. The first was a general discussion of the relationship of the dean's office and residence halls staffs with the undergraduate women. It detailed four specific charges. The second part consisted of accounts of specific incidents...intended to substantiate the general charges of part one.

The first of the four charges protested Miss Bacon's conception of her role in the University community. Her position, the document alleged, favors "transmission of 'home and church' customs of American society to the student without allowing enough latitude for experiment and inquiry..." and enforces an essentially conservative pattern of behavior on youths who are not trusted to think for themselves.

Several Instances

To support this charge, the report listed several instances in which Miss Bacon had allegedly interfered with democratic student government and judicial proceedings, as well as transcripts of interviews with her.

The second complaint alleged that actions by the dean's office have the effect of segregating individuals of differing racial, religious or national character, and cited two letters sent to parents of white girls who had been dating Negro or foreign students.

"Her interference suggests that a Negro-white relationship is indicative of instability on the part of one or both of the individuals involved," the document stated. "It also suggests that interracial contacts would bring a damaging protest from a midwestern community like Ann Arbor, a midwestern school like the University, and a constituency such as the University has."

...

When the student relations committee agreed to study this document, it made clear that this in no way meant prior acceptance of the validity of the evidence or conclusions. Miss Bacon had access to the report during the course of the inquiry...#

An Editorial...

(May 30, 1961) **LONG-STANDING CONCERN** over the paternal orientation of the Office of Student Affairs, particularly that of the Dean of Women, has now received analytic attention from the Committee on Student Relations.

...

Our involvement speaks not only of a discontent with existing conditions, but more important, of a persuasion that the University can and should constantly seek institutional improvement.

We seek fundamental changes in the Office of Student Affairs which, in protective and sometimes arbitrary ways, discourages fluid interchange of mores, beliefs and customs. Beyond the necessary "sweeping structural changes" and "reassignment of present personnel" proposed by the faculty committee, changes of a deeper character are needed -- structural change must be accompanied by meaningful University-wide commitment to student freedom of action, association, thought and development.

...

A COMMUNITY which is educational in spirit and statement should not simply tolerate interaction among individuals of all ages, experiences, faiths, races and cultures, but should positively oppose any barriers to dynamic association among its members...

...

...The Office of Student Affairs--particularly the office of Dean Deborah Bacon-- has too often neglected or violated such university spirit.

We congratulate the faculty committee for its interest, its efforts and its conclusions. Its members have responded forthrightly to the first issue ever brought to them by students--and this perhaps indicates the birth of a relationship between groups too often unconnected...#

--THE SENIOR EDITORS
1960-61, 1961-62

BACON QUITS

By ROBERT FARRELL

(Sept. 30, 1961) Dean of Women Deborah Bacon has resigned.

The Regents yesterday accepted the resignation from her administrative post, to be effective at the end of this semester.

Miss Bacon will, however, retain her present appointment as an assistant professor in the English department.

In a statement released by University President Harlan Hatcher, Miss Bacon called her 11 years as dean of women "thrilling, exciting and satisfying."

'Not in Tune'

"The burden, however, grows heavier year by year, especially inasmuch as I personally am not in tune with some of the changes which seem inevitable in the years ahead," she added.

...

The resignation followed on the heels of severe criticism of the Office of Student Affairs and the Dean of Women leveled last spring by student and faculty groups..#

An Editorial...

(Sept. 30, 1961) **DEAN DEBORAH BACON** has resigned. Her resignation marks a significant step in a process which must radically change the role of the student at this University.

...

Even her critics have frequently respected and liked Miss Bacon. But we feel strongly that her resignation as Dean of Women is in the best interests of the University.

For as Dean of Women, Miss Bacon has represented policies which are no longer acceptable in the University community--extreme paternalism, the stifling of individual expression, the restriction of open associations.

...

Hopefully, Dean Bacon's resignation means her policies will be discontinued. This is not enough. Ahead must be the shaping of a philosophy and the creation of a structure for the Office of Student Affairs which will minimize arbitrary control and maximize individual responsibility...#

--THE SENIOR EDITORS

Alumnae Council Seeks To Retain Dean's Office

By DAVID MARCUS

(Nov. 19, 1961) The Alumnae Council--women's branch of the Alumni Association--has requested a conference with the Office of Student Affairs Study Committee to ask retention of the position of Dean of Women in a revamped OSA structure, Mrs. Lola Hanavan, a Council member, said yesterday.

At their national meeting in September, the council passed a resolution calling upon "the President and Board of Regents to maintain the position of Dean of Women with all its dignity, prestige and responsibility for maintaining standards of conduct among women students and of providing assistance to them."

...

The motion passed by the Council cites the expectations of parents that the Dean of Women will maintain standards of conduct and her function in interpreting the role of women at the University...#

overtime:
Deans and Alumnae

By FAITH WEINSTEIN
Magazine Editor

(Nov. 21, 1961) **THE ALUMNAE COUNCIL** wants a dean of women. They want one very badly--badly enough to send delegations to President Hatcher and try for conferences with the Office of Student Affairs Study Committee.

But the strength of their desire is unfortunately not matched by intelligent insight into the policy they are advocating. Judging from their motion, only the shallowest and most obvious factors are being considered.

...

The alumnae suffer from an unavoidable lack of information and contemporary insight. They can bring their suggestions and their pleas to the OSA study committee, but the final decision is rightly in the hands of the students and faculty members of the committee, who are in the best position to know what changes are needed.

The alumnae are a tradition-bonded group. This is not really their fault--women's groups and alumni associations are not ordinarily known for their revolutionary stands.

But the time has come for a revolutionary stand. Now, while the OSA is in a flexible position, it is time for the University to examine its entire relationship with students.

...

Girls who used to stay at home under the watchful parental eye now get jobs, get married, get out of the house as soon as they leave high school.

But as soon as a girl decides to go to college, she must give up all hope of freedom for four years. Instead of being an adult in an adult community, she becomes a child of unwanted parents. At the moment when the non-students are beginning to break the parental ties, the student is forced to accept a new set of paternal restrictions from an unknown and overpowering "local parent."

The woman student suffers most intensely from these restrictions. The discontented man can get out of the quads after his first year if he wishes; the woman is trapped in the dorms for three or four years (depending on the apartment permission whims of the Dean of Women's Office).

But the woman student is herded, cajoled, has her conduct graded by her housemother, her hours regulated by the University. The Dean of Women's Office casts a long and constricting shadow.

A dean's office has its uses. It can handle student loans, scholarships, the functional administration of housing and perhaps a voluntary counseling bureau for students with personal problems. And if it is to serve these functions, there need be no differentiation of sexes by deans' offices.

But it should have no arbitrary authority over the lives of the students of the University--they are here for an academic, not a moral education.#

Women's Judic, or The Student Always Loses

((April 3, 1962) Women's judiciaries are probably the greatest single tribute to the tyranny of the administrative forces on this campus.

On the surface, nothing could be more democratic than student bodies interpreting and implementing student-made regulations governing students. On the surface, the judicial system functions speedily and harmoniously, and there is really no way to view the set-up but from the surface anyway.

Below the surface there is nothing but a jumble of unwritten law, unestablished precedent, unrecognized authority and the incredible, invisible sleight of hand which insures that under the most kosher of appearances, the student always loses.

A good case in point is a recent event in Alice Lloyd Hall. A resident, making up "late minutes," was caught studying in the lounge with her boy friend rather than repenting in her boudoir.

When confronted with her crime, she was told she would have to make the late minutes up the following week and was again caught studying in a public area instead of making up her debt to society in solitary.

...

Lloyd Judic assigned the defendant one hour's worth of late minutes and admonished her for not checking on the rules governing makeup of late minutes before she violated them for the second time. The girl protested that nowhere in either the Alice Lloyd handbook or in the all-campus Women's Roles and Rules, is it specified that late minutes must be made up away from public areas of the building.

...

Judic members, when blamed for prosecuting infractions of non-existent laws have a standard line of protest:

All regulations should not have to be spelled out. The girls know the rules and should abide by them even when they are only informally stated.

...

What this rationale means in practice is that:

When a girl appears before judic she often has no knowledge of what regulation she has supposedly violated.

When informed of the nature of the infraction, she is not immune to punishment even if she can prove the rule does not exist. Judic, since it believes the rule exists or ought to exist, assumes that everyone else has the same basic understanding.

Therefore, even if judic cannot find a girl guilty of a stipulated, hard and fast law, it can punish her for a "hostile or uncooperative attitude," since she has violated a "tacit understanding."

...

It is time the hocus-pocus with women's rules is ended, and the responsibility fixed firmly with its source instead of juggled dextrously from judic to dean and back again over the head of the hapless student, who has no defense anywhere, since technical right is no defense in a "moral" violation and moral right is no defense in a technical violation.

Perhaps open and recognized tyranny poses less of a threat to justice than the anarchy of sham democracy.#

--JUDITH OPPENHEIM

REGENTS ABOLISH CURFEW
Houses To Set Visitation Policy

By STEVE NISSEN

(Jan. 20, 1968) The Regents yesterday approved the elimination of curfew requirements on a one-year experimental basis for all women students in University residence halls who obtain written parental permission.

The Regents also agreed to policy changes which will allow each University housing unit to determine by a democratic process the hours of visitation by members of the opposite sex.

Both rule changes apply to all types of University-affiliated housing including fraternities and sororities.

...

Regent Paul Goebel was the sole dissenter in the decision to liberalize residence hall regulations. "I want to go on record as opposing the resolution," he said...

"The Regents wish to continue to foster a climate within which personal freedom and responsibility contribute to educational and social development," the resolution stated...#

AHCCTPFDNMW?

By JAN BENEDETTI

(May 24, 1972) The intriguing hypothesis that sexism at the University flourishes partly because President Robben Fleming does not meet officially with enough women recently underwent an exhaustive test.

A group of women, the Ad Hoc Committee Concerned that President Fleming Does Not Meet With Women (in short, the AHCCTPFDNMW) stationed themselves outside Fleming's office for a week, recording and observing all his visitors.

The AHCCTPFDNMW discovered that during the study week:

--Fleming met with 145 persons, including only 21 women (13.1 per cent).

--The overwhelming majority of the women he met with arrived in groups with a majority of men. These groups were typically not concerned with women's issues.

--None of the women saw Fleming without an appointment or without first checking with the secretary, practices that many of the male visitors were not obliged to observe.

The group submitted these findings to Fleming, who "could not deny" the conclusions, according to a published report.

The AHCCTPFDNMW suggested that Fleming "begin interchanges with women at an informal level, to familiarize himself with women's activities and arguments." The group also recommended that more women should occupy high-level positions to exercise influence on decision-making...#

'U' band marches on--minus women

By PAT BAUER

(Sept. 17, 1971) "And now ladies and gentlemen, the Marching Men of Michigan." The loudspeaker blares the familiar words at halftime of each football game, while the fans watch the University's marching band high-step onto the field.

The marching band, now in its 59th year, is still composed totally of men, despite claims by director George Cavender that action has been taken to rescind its no-women rule.

The regulation barring women was officially revoked last July 1, making it possible for women to audition for band positions.

However, Claire Rumelhart, University women's advocate, claims that women who have inquired about marching band membership since then have been repeatedly told that "the band can have no women members."

She also cites a one-page memo currently being circulated within the music school as evidence of the band's policy.

The memo states, "Marching band is required of all male students unless assigned to the alternate section..." The memo goes on to explain that the alternate section includes "those men with physical problems which preclude their participation in the marching band, and women." It was signed by Cavender.

Cavender says the memo was released before the no-women rule was rescinded, although the memo is undated.

When asked why the memo was still being circulated, he replied, "It's all a question of loot. We couldn't afford to put out a new memo, so the old one was circulated. After all, 99 per cent of the memo was correct; only one per cent was incorrect."

And although the rule prohibiting women from marching band membership was eliminated from the 1971-72 School of Music catalog, counselors were not notified of the policy change. "I saw no reason to have done that," Cavender says.

All of the problems began this summer, says freshman orientation leader Phil Chornor, when freshman women expressed an interest in joining the band.

"The Orientation Office kept calling the Band Office, and they told us first one thing and then another. Some days they would say girls were allowed in the band, and some days they would say that they weren't," he says.

This ambivalent attitude, he says, was so discouraging that few freshman girls bothered trying out for the marching band.

One girl, however, was more persistent in trying to get into the band. Gail Peters, '75, called in August for a band audition and was told that "there are no spaces open."

When she persisted, Peters says, she was told that "auditions ended Sept. 5th, before school even opened. Of course I couldn't come and they knew it."

The marching band's official publication said auditions began Sept. 5th.

...

Although Cavender has changed official music school policy in order to allow women to join the band, he is still adamant that the marching band is no place for a woman.

"It's more violent physical activity than would be proper for a lady. It would be too hard--we couldn't excuse a woman from rehearsals if she had 'female problems.' I certainly don't excuse any of my boys from practice."

He also suggests that a woman might become bored with the marching band, saying that many a woman "had fun with her band" in high school, but "now there are other activities which should be her main interest.

"After all," Cavender says, "most girls play with dolls when they are young and nobody makes them stop doing it. They join Girl Scouts and nobody makes them quit. Why should they stay with a marching band?"

And, he adds, the band only has one locker room. "I wouldn't invite a young lady into those conditions."

Many of the "Marching Men of Michigan" are similarly convinced that women could not perform on the field as well as them. "A girl would just never make it," a clarinet player stated. "It's just too strenuous.

"They'd never be able to lift their legs as high as we do for any period of time. On the first day of practice, the guys couldn't even take it. Four guys threw up right there on the field."..#

Women take the field

By JAN BENEDETTI

(Sept. 16, 1971) ...When the University Marching Band performs its half-time show today, it will mark the opening of the ranks of the "Marching Men of Michigan" to women.

And though Director of Bands George Cavender still refers to the band members in practice as "gentlemen," the women seem to be adjusting to their new role.

"I joined the band because it's a great organization and because I like to march," says one woman member. "We're treated just like everyone else." However, another woman disagrees. "It seems like Cavender didn't want us in the band. He has been giving some girls a rough time. He makes a special point of yelling at some of the girls in front of everyone."

A male adds, "Cavender definitely did not want the girls in the band, but now that they're in he's trying to make the best of it."

Cavender himself refused to speak to reporters yesterday. According to several band members, the director told them he wanted no publicity until after today's game...

...

This year, a vestige of disapproval of the break with "tradition" still lingers in the minds of some male members. "It just seems that things are not the same," says one male.

But the performance of the women this year seems to have changed many opinions.

"It doesn't make any difference having women in the band," says one member. "They're better than a lot of the guys."

And another adds, "Everyone watches the girls in formation to see if they keep up with the rest.

"They do."#

'U' Justifies Submission Of Student Lists to HUAC

By MICHAEL HEFFER

(Aug. 29, 1966) Despite mounting protests from some student groups and faculty members, the University has reemphasized the justification for its Aug. 11 decision to send membership lists of three campus political organizations to the House Un-American Activities Committee.

1966

The decision was reached after several days of consultation among University vice-presidents following the receipt of a subpoena from the House Committee, which was about to hold a series of hearings on proposed legislation to halt left-wing interference with troops and equipment shipments bound for Viet Nam.

The re-emphasis came yesterday as University President Harlan Hatcher stated that the University's position is that as given by... Vice-President for Student Affairs Richard Cutler on Aug. 17.

Balancing

At that time Cutler said the University had reached its decision after "balancing" the fate of the individuals involved with the good of the University...#

EXPAND CUTLER'S POWER

Responsibilities Include Complete Disciplinary Control

By ROGER RAPOPORT

(Oct. 22, 1966) The Regents voted Vice-President for Student Affairs Richard L. Cutler sweeping new powers over the non-academic conduct of the student body at their regular monthly meeting yesterday.

The move shifts all disciplinary authority for student conduct from what Cutler called "diverse and often conflicting sources of authority" to the Office of Student Affairs.

New Power

Effective immediately, Vice-President Cutler now has:

--"Ultimate authority" over non-academic conduct of students and student groups;

--The power to establish standards for non-academic student conduct, and

--All non-academic disciplinary powers formerly spread out between President Hatcher, the other vice-presidents, academic deans and the faculty.

The Regents also directed Cutler to:

--conduct an "immediate and comprehensive review" of present regulations "with a view to...furthering the goal of personal, social and moral development of individual students and student groups."

--"review the existing regulations and procedures of Student Government Council," particularly regarding student organizations; and

--"establish such interim regulations and enforcement procedures as are necessary" during his review of present rules.

...

The new regulations were based on recommendations made by Cutler...#

An Editorial...

(Aug. 29, 1966) **THE UNIVERSITY'S** response to the House Un-American Activities Committee's subpoena demanding membership lists of three campus political organizations reflects serious errors of judgment. Despite the legal and political complexities of the situation, we deplore the University's compliance with the subpoena...

While we understand the Administration's case concerning the legal issues involved, we feel that under ideal circumstances the University should have filed suit in Federal court seeking to have the subpoena declared void for violating the First Amendment.

...

The administration, in complying with the subpoena... defaulted on a major responsibility to the University community. This abdication is made more appalling by the complete absence of President Hatcher from the discussions and final decision and the evident failure of his vice-presidents to attempt to persuade him to participate in them...

YET perhaps the most serious error of all was the University's failure to make public its receipt of the subpoena. Here the philosophy that the decision-making process should be open to the widest possible number of individuals under the circumstances was dealt a serious blow. Public discussion would have focused the attention of the entire University community, including the Regents, on the whole range of possible responses to the subpoena--among them those the administration now admits it should have considered but did not.

Moreover, a public announcement of the receipt of the subpoena would have enabled the individuals on the membership lists to file suit to enjoin the University from complying with the subpoena. This course--which at least one high administrator now thinks would probably have been the best under the circumstances--would have avoided the need for the University to risk political capital in a suit of its own on allegedly weak legal grounds. But at the same time it would have given the students involved the right to judicial scrutiny of the committee's request...#

--THE SENIOR EDITORS

Dr. Cutler, What Happens to Students Next?

By MARK R. KILLINGSWORTH

(Oct. 25, 1966) ...Viewed in the context of recent weeks and recent decisions, the Regents' approval of near-dictatorial powers for Vice-President Richard L. Cutler presents some profoundly disturbing questions.

The major one is: What's going to happen to students? The answer: Nobody knows yet.

The next issue is: Who decides what happens to students? The answer is the same.

CUTLER NOW HAS all non-academic disciplinary powers formerly spread out between President Hatcher, the other vice-presidents, academic deans and the faculty.

He has all the non-academic disciplinary powers which Intra-Fraternity Council, Panhellenic Association and Inter-Housing Association used to have.

...

In short, if he wanted to, Cutler could easily institute a one-man control over every aspect of non-academic student life at the University.

...

The record suggests that, when the University bothers to ask students what's on their minds, it usually gets some fairly intelligent answers.

President Hatcher, for example, said Friday he had found students were "perceptive and mature in understanding what the proposal (for vice-presidential advisory boards) is about"--not surprising, since students proposed the idea to Hatcher themselves.

THE RECORD also suggests that, when the University takes the time to explain its workings to students, the students get a better understanding of University goals and problems--and are that much better at offering advice.

...

And, finally, the record suggests that, when the University ignores students, a crisis erupts. The University ignored the thoughts of the students involved when it complied with the House Un-American Activities Committee's subpoena in August. The result, as the Faculty Senate Assembly put it, was "regrettable" and a nightmare of administrative bumbling. The University ignored students on the police-on-campus issue. The result was a sit-in.

* * *

SO, WHAT IS particularly alarming about Cutler's assumption of dictatorial powers over students is this recent trend in University policy--away from the Reed Report, away from the idea of asking students' opinions, away from the belief that people who live under rules should help make them...#

Appeal Role Assumed by V-P Cutler

By NEIL SHISTER

(Nov. 4, 1966) Exercising power granted him at the last Regents meeting, Vice-President for Student Affairs Richard Cutler has set up an "interim" judiciary system with his own office serving in the principal appellate capacity.

The new system, which was outlined in a letter sent yesterday to the chairman of Joint Judiciary Council, has abolished the Committee on Standards and Conduct as an appellate body and replaced it with the Vice-President for Student Affairs.

...

Temporary Set-Up

The new system Cutler has created is in effect until an over-all review of judicial procedure at the University is completed and final recommendations for a permanent system are made...

...

In his letter Cutler said he "wishes the interim structures and procedures to depart as little as possible from existing ones." Thus he has granted to JJC power to "continue to serve in its present capacity as the campus-wide student judiciary body."..#

Letters: Weiler's Resignation Notice

To the Editor:

(Oct. 26, 1966) This is a copy of the letter I sent yesterday to Dick Zuckerman, chairman of Joint Judiciary Council.

THIS LETTER is to serve as notification of my desire not to actively participate in any further activities of the Joint Judiciary Council.

In light of the Regents' meeting of Friday, Oct. 23, 1966, where Dr. Richard Cutler, vice-president for Student Affairs, was granted (as he had requested) sweeping powers in the area of non-academic discipline, I fail to see the possibility of the Joint Judiciary Council having any meaningful role in the future.

Although it is true that the Council can work with Dr. Cutler to set up what he considers is an "equitable" judiciary system, the final proposal must still pass Dr. Cutler's approval, and I sincerely doubt if I could agree with anything that would be necessary to pass this final approval.

...

Very simply I do not feel that as an individual or as a member of the Joint Judiciary Council, I am interested in working with Dr. Cutler to set up what he considers is an equitable system for handling non-academic discipline.

...It seems to me that this move precludes many of the precepts of student participation in University affairs and makes what I believe is due process totally impossible. It gives the man who has power to make all the rules, virtually all the power to enforce them and this is truly a bad situation. It gives one man the incredible power to do anything he desires in the area of non-academic discipline.

...

...I fail to see the possibility of a meaningful and equitable solution. I cannot in good conscience serve in a totally meaningless capacity. I therefore respectfully submit my resignation to the Joint Judiciary Council of the University of Michigan.

--**John Weiler, Executive Secretary Joint Judiciary Council**

Cutler Creates New Rule
Banning Student Sit-Ins

Surprise Step Made Over Weekend

By ROGER RAPOPORT

(Nov. 13, 1966) In a surprise weekend move Vice-President for Student Affairs Richard L. Cutler banned student sit-ins "which interfere with the normal and orderly operations of the University."

In a new regulation released yesterday, Cutler specifically outlawed "by way of illustration but not limitation, unauthorized occupancy of the private office, conference rooms, or reception rooms of any University staff member, blocking ways of access to such areas, unauthorized occupancy of University buildings beyond normal closing hours and disrupting by other means the necessary operations of the University."

Cutler said that students who violate the new regulation, established under interim powers granted him by the Regents last month, will be judged by Joint Judiciary Council. "Penalties may include warning, probation, reasonable monetary fines, or suspension or expulsion from the University."#

1,500 STUDENTS STAGE SIT-IN

By SUSAN ELAN

(Nov. 30, 1966) Charging that the University administration refused to meet their demands, 1,500 students packed three floors of the campus Administration Bldg. yesterday in the largest sit-in in the school's history.

The students demonstrated in response to President Harlan Hatcher's refusal to accede to their demands that the school cease compilation of class rankings for the Selective Service and rescind a controversial new sit-in ban.

At a noon rally on the diag students rejected Hatcher's conciliatory offer Monday to resolve the dispute by establishing three new committees as "sweet talk."

The students at the rally marched on the Administration Bldg. after Student Government Council President Ed Robinson told them, "Last Monday's teach-in asked for a yes or no answer from the administration on our demands. I would interpret President Hatcher's statements yesterday as not meeting that ultimatum."

As the students marched off to the sit-in, SGC members Robert Smith, '67, and Jay Zulaff, '67, pleaded with them not to go. About 200 students stayed on to hear Zulaff say, "The administration has started to work with us. . .We must continue to work with the administration."

The students filled the lobbies, foyers, and some corridors of the first, second and third floors starting at about 12:20. Access to offices was largely blocked for University employes.

Technically the protest did not violate the controversial new sit-in ban which has been the focal point of the two week old dispute here.

Robinson spoke to a wide cross-section of students in short talks on all three floors. He thanked the students for attending and said their numbers showed "a real committment to student decision-making."

...

Robinson received frequent applause as he told the students they were doing "the best thing that has ever been done for education anywhere."..#

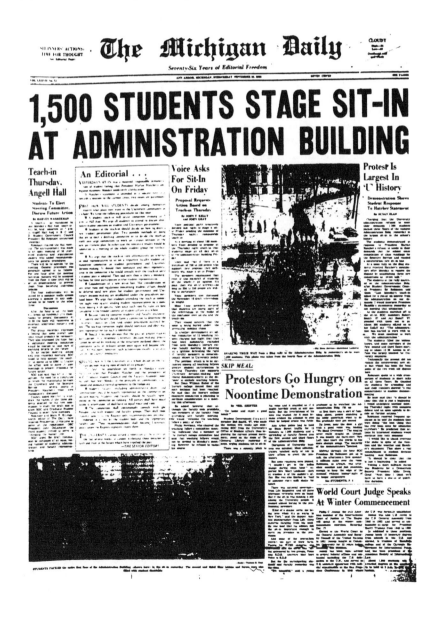

SGC Replaces 'U' Code

By URBAN LEHNER

(Sept. 15, 1967) Student Government Council abolished the "University Regulations" code for students and replaced it with a code written by SGC at its meeting last night.

While including sections of the University's rules in its own, Council unanimously enacted major changes in the regulations dealing with men and women living in University housing, speakers at public lectures, demonstrations, and intoxicants.

The "University Regulations" code was written by the administration. Although students were consulted on some of the rules, "the University did not consider itself deterred from making a rule whatever students thought of it," claimed SGC President Bruce Kahn.

The regulations are enforced by Joint Judiciary Council. JJC members are appointed by Council. The decision to rewrite the rules was made last spring when a majority of the newly appointed JJC members pledged to enforce "only those rules made or approved by students."..#

JJC Acquits Two Students In Landmark Judgment

Vows to Uphold Only Regulations Written and Approved by Students

By PAT O'DONOHUE

(Oct. 4, 1967) Joint Judiciary Council last night acquitted two students charged with violating University regulations on grounds that "It would not enforce any rule that had not been passed by an autonomous student legislative body."

In the landmark decision, JJC held that it would not recognize the validity of two University regulations because they had been set by the school administration rather than the student government.

...

In both cases the students filled out a new JJC-supplied mimeographed "Motion for summary judgment of acquittal on grounds of nonstudent influence upon the legislation creating the rule sought to be enforced."

In one case, a graduate sociology student was charged with not registering an automobile in compliance with University regulations. The student freely admitted that the charge was true.

However, he contended, and JJC upheld, that he was innocent because the driving regulation was not a student-made rule at the time of the offense last spring.

...

The JJC decisions may mark a vast change in campus judiciary procedures. Under existing University rules, a student acquitted by JJC cannot be punished by any other University agency...#

Regents Say Rules Action Exceeds SGC Jurisdiction

By PAT O'DONOHUE

(Nov. 18, 1967) Student Government Council has "exceeded its jurisdiction by purporting to abolish existing University rules and regulations," the Regents said yesterday.

In a prepared statement presented at their monthly meeting, the Regents claimed, "Without Regental approval, such legislation is totally without effect. Previously existing regulations therefore remain in force."

...

The Regents' statement contended that "There need be no breach between Student Government and the Regents. The Regents will sympathetically consider proposals for revision of the present system. They have established proper administrative channels for this purpose. The Regents cannot abandon their constitutional authority and responsibility."

The Regents asked SGC to provide them with a "full written report of the basis on which unilateral actions have been taken and for which Regental approval has not been sought. Representatives of Student Government Council should be prepared to confer with the Regents at an appropriate time."

[SGC President Bruce]Kahn said, "I'm glad to see that the Regents are interested enough to want to talk with members of SGC about the problem."..#

SGC Abolishes Vehicle Rules

By URBAN LEHNER

(Nov. 10, 1967) Student Government Council last night by a 7-5 vote abolished all Student Vehicle Regulations except those pertaining to bicycles. SGC Administrative Vice-President Mike Davis, Grad, said, "This means that any student--regardless of class year--may keep and drive an automobile in the Ann Arbor area without fear of punishment."

Vice-President for Student Affairs Richard L. Cutler said, "The Student Government Council does not wipe out a Regents bylaw. I guess we'll have to wait for the Regents to do that before it's official."

However, Davis and at-large member Judy Greenberg, '68, commented that "it is extremely doubtful that the Regents' constitutional authority to govern the internal affairs of the University can be extended to infringe upon the legislative right to tax and license. Therefore we are not doing away with Regental authority," they continued. "Rather, we are refusing to join an almost certainly illegal extension of it."

Sources indicate that state Attorney General Frank Kelley will render an opinion on the issue in the near future.

And Ken Mogill, '68, head of the Student Traffic Court (STC) observed, "STC will only recognize rules made by the proper student authority. In this case, SGC is the proper student authority."

STC, a lower court of Joint Judiciary Council, hears all cases of alleged infractions of student vehicle regulations.

At-large Council member Janis Sorkin, '69, said "It is illegal according to a state attorney general's opinion for the University to regulate traffic on streets it doesn't own. The only way they can get around this is by saying they're regulating student conduct."

Neither Mogill nor Miss Sorkin expects the number of cars on campus to increase dramatically as a result of the SGC move. Both admit that a parking problem will ensue, although they feel the University will be able to solve it...#

Student Protesters Break Up Meeting
Allege Talk On Contract

By SUSAN ELAN
Associate Managing Editor

(Oct. 12, 1967) A group of 40 student activists sailed into a secret meeting between a top Navy admiral and University administrators on North Campus yesterday, and broke up a planned three hour presentation.

The students charged that Rear Admiral S. R. Brown, director of the command control and electronic division of the Office of Naval Operations in Washington, was in Ann Arbor to sign a $2 million military ordnance research contract. University officials flatly denied the charge.

The confrontation began when 15 students surrounded Adm. Brown and top research and engineering school officials as they lunched at North Campus Commons during the noon hour. The students fired questions at the officials about the alleged research contract.

After lunch, the students, joined by 25 pickets who had remained outside, followed Adm. Brown, Vice-President for Research A. Geoffrey Norman and others to the electrical engineering department's Cooley Laboratories a block away. Parked at the front of the laboratory was Vietnam Fall's "Peacemobile," a large yellow trailer.

The students hurried into the second floor meeting room reserved for a film showing and settled into the back rows. University officials had scheduled a three hour series of technical presentations and briefings for the admiral, as well as discussions.

University officials asked the students to leave the secret session but they refused and demanded "to see the movies."

...

When the students refused to leave, the University officials called off the meetings at Cooley...#

LSA Board Rejects Cutler Move To Punish Daenzer
May Consider Future Non-Academic Cases

By STEVE NISSEN

(Dec. 1, 1967) The administrative board of the literary college has rejected a request from Vice-President for Student Affairs Richard L. Cutler that VOICE-SDS Chairman Karen Daenzer, '70, be disciplined for participating in an Oct. 11 protest against visiting Navy Rear Admiral S. N. Brown. The discipline reportedly involved suspension of Mrs. Daenzer.

Associate Dean James Shaw, who heads the college board said last night, "The administrative board has declined to involve itself in disciplinary action involving students in the North Campus incident."

Cutler made a formal request to the board after receiving a complaint from the engineering college about the protest by 40 students on North Campus.

...

According to Jack Mannning, administrative assistant to Shaw, the board has refrained from considering Cutler's request to expel Mrs. Daenzer as a specific case. In fact most of the members of the board did not know that Mrs. Daenzer was involved.

...

Mrs. Daenzer Unaware

Mrs. Daenzer was unaware last night of Cutler's letter about her which was sent to the board nearly a month ago. Manning voiced surprise that Cutler had not informed Daenzer of the charges against her. "I'm amazed he didn't tell her, that's the very first thing you should do," he said.

When reached for comment last night Cutler refused to discuss his letter. "I guess if you have a letter in your hands which has my signature on it, I wrote it," he said...#

Cutler Asks Grad School To Punish Navy Protesters
'U' Releases OSA Letter Requesting Disciplinary Action Against Daenzer

By KEN KELLEY and JIM HECK

(Dec. 2, 1967) Vice-President for Student Affairs Richard L. Cutler disclosed yesterday that he asked the administrative board of the graduate school to take disciplinary action against VOICE-SDS members Eric Chester and Sam Friedman for participating in an Oct. 11 demonstration against visiting Navy Rear Admiral S. N. Brown.

Cutler also confirmed a Daily story yesterday that he sought the literary college administrative board to take disciplinary action against SDS Chairman Karen Daenzer, '70, who was one of 40 other students in the October demonstration.

...

Cutler said a second letter identical to the one sent the literary college board "was sent to the dean of the Rackham School except that reference was made to other individuals." (Chester and Friedman)

Both Chester and Friedman learned Cutler had asked the graduate school to take disciplinary action during a discussion with the Vice-President yesterday afternoon. Dean Stephen Spurr of the graduate school said last night, however, that he has not told the administrative board of the graduate school the names of the two students.

Spurr said the board is currently only considering whether or not it wants to start disciplinary proceedings against students who participated in the demonstration...#

An Administrative Disgrace

(Dec. 2, 1967) **IN THE WANING** months of the Hatcher administration, no principle seems so sacred that it cannot be sacrificed at the altar of student punishment. But the latest action--requests to undergraduate and graduate college boards by Vice President for Student Affairs Richard Cutler that academic punishment be used for an alleged non-academic violation--is simply intolerable.

...

ONE CAN SHOUT police-state tactics and administrative negligence, but these are not the issues. Rather, the whole case reflects the desperation and vindictiveness the administration now has toward punishing alleged violations in the non-academic sphere.

...

THE SCORN with which the administration was once viewed has now turned to shame. It is unbelievable that the University's leaders have a conception of a University as a free and open arena for controversy and yet clandestinely manipulate to have war protesters thrown out of school.

It is now less than a month till the new President, Robben Fleming, assumes office. With revelation of the latest administration conspiracy, it seems one month is much too long. Whether or not President-designate Fleming was involved in this latest fiasco is unknown, but the hope persists that as the old administration leaves, its warped ideas, devious tactics, and tired personalities will exit also.#

--ROBERT KLIVANS
Editorial Director

REGENTS END DRIVING BAN
Rescind OSA's discipline power

By STEVE NISSEN

(July 20, 1968) The Regents [yesterday] rescinded the sweeping disciplinary powers delegated in 1966 to the Office of Student Affairs.

Through a resolution introduced by Regent Gertrude Huebner, the board agreed to postpone action "in deference to the request of both faculty and student members of the academic community."

...

One faculty member last night called the stripping of disciplinary power from OSA "the end of an era."..#

REGENTS SET NEW CONDUCT RULES

By ROB BIER

(April 18, 1970) In a surprise move yesterday, the Regents unanimously passed a set of "interim" conduct rules and disciplinary procedures for dealing with cases of disruption. Their action met with immediate expressions of outrage and dismay from students and faculty representatives.

A key provision of the procedures calls for adjudication of disruption cases by a hearing officer appointed by the president. The officer is empowered both to determine guilt and to specify punishment.

...

"When a decision like this is made without involving the people it affects, we are moving toward something totalitarian," said SGC member Bruce Wilson...#

The Regents' declaration of tyranny

(April 18, 1970) **THE ESTABLISHMENT** of new tyrannical disciplinary procedures by the Regents yesterday is intolerable both in form and content. The Regents and the administration should be condemned, and implementation of the procedures opposed by all members of the University community.

...

Furthermore, students and faculty members were never apprised of the imminence of the regental action, nor were the specific steps they took ever discussed with members of SGC or the Senate Advisory Committee on University Affairs, the top faculty body.

THE MOST odious portion of the statement adopted by the Regents involved the creation of a new disciplinary mechanism to adjudicate rules which the board also enacted.

Under the procedure, President Robben Fleming would appoint an outside hearing officer who would act as a judge, jury and executioner for accused members of the University community.

As it is written, this section is obviously designed to produce the conviction and expulsion of anyone whose continued presence at the University is undesirable to the administration.

...

The rules adopted by the Regents, and the arbitrary manner in which they were formulated, constitute an obvious notice to the University community that dissent will not be tolerated. They were a declaration of tyranny that must not go unchallenged.#

--THE SENIOR EDITORS

'U' to stiffen student conduct policy

By CLAUDIA GREEN
and BILL SPINDLE

(Jan. 19, 1984) In a move some say will "help protect the safety of the campus," and others insist will simply be used to "stifle dissent," the University is seriously considering adopting a new code of student conduct.

The code, and a University judicial system that would be created along with it, would allow the University to punish students who vandalize campus or another student's property, sexually harass students or staff, or sell illegal drugs, among other violations of the code.

...

With this new system, many say, the University would be able to keep its own house clean, rather than relying on the civil courts to handle discipline. Incidents between students, or between the University and a student would be handled through an internal court headed by either a professor or an administrator.

The system would let the University deal with problem students more quickly and efficiently, administrators say. It would also allow the University to expel dangerous students and keep them off campus.

"WHAT happens if someone sets a dorm on fire?" said Tom Easthope, an associate vice president for Student Services. "You send him to civil court where he gets off on a technicality. Then we have an arsonist going to school. There are situations in which we can set rules, where in fact we have the obligation."

The code would not replace civil or criminal charges. Charges could be brought against students in criminal court as well as from within the University.

The proposal, however, is not lacking opponents. Jonathan Rose, an attorney at Student Legal Services, is one of the strongest.

THE CODE is not aimed at stemming campus crime, but rather at containing student protests of University policies, Rose said. The code could be used to punish students who hold sit-ins, rallies, or class strikes to protest policies, he said.

The code forbids students from interfering with University activities such as class attendance or research.

...

WHILE MARY Rowland, the Michigan Student Assembly's president, agrees with Rose that the code could be used to quell dissent, she also opposes it on broader grounds. She called it a "regressive move for the University to go back to making parental type decisions for students," like it did in the late 1950s and early '60s.

She also said that the code allows the University to punish students twice--once within the University and a second time in the courts...#

'U' leaps at the chance to babysit

By DAVID SPAK

(Jan. 25, 1984) If I had any doubt that the overwhelming majority of students couldn't give a damn about what happens at this University, those doubts were all thoroughly obliterated in the past two weeks. In that time, students have been getting into the swing of a new term, worrying about the chemistry problems due Monday, and trying to stay warm in underheated apartments. But the University has moved to make major changes in students' lives.

The students have hardly uttered a whimper in protest.

What happened that is so terrible that this lack of reaction should upset me? Why is this different from the apathetic (but somehow understandable) response to a handgun control rally?

THE UNIVERSITY took two leaps toward returning to its role as parent and two leaps away from its role as educator.

The first leap was the establishment of stricter dormitory alcohol policies...

...

Leap number two is potentially more important and more dangerous. It is--or more correctly, might become--the imposition of a non-academic code of student conduct. The University, to protect you from yourself, wants to force you to behave. And they are going to give you the rules to obey as well.

...

WHO WOULD decide when you have been naughty or nice? Not Santa, but a hearing officer or hearing board. Most of the time, this hearing officer would hand down a ruling, except when the punishment could include suspension or expulsion. Then the board, consisting of a student, a professor, and an administrator, would rule. (By the way, in this court it's the University's two votes to the student's one.)

University administrators say this code is long overdue. According to Tom Easthope, an associate vice president for student services, the code was designed as a middle ground between doing nothing if a student did something wrong or taking that student to court (the one the government provides us). "In the last several years there were some types of things you don't want to bring to criminal court, that you want to handle internally," he said. "I'm not sure everything should be brought through criminal courts."

That's so nice--I wish I believed him. What Easthope really is saying is that the University doesn't want to get a lot of bad publicity for prosecuting a bunch of Progressive Student Network members for trespassing if they decide to take over another research lab. Instead, the University would quietly suspend or expel the miserable gatecrashers.

...

In developing the code of conduct, the University also wants to tell students that society's rules don't apply. "We're going to give you the rules of how it should be," administrators want to say. That isn't what the University is here for. It's supposed to be here as an educational institution--a place where a full spectrum of ideas are scrutinized and individuals have the opportunity to freely choose among those ideas. Those ideas include civil disobedience, and free speech. They also include facing the consequences of your actions, as any other member of society would.

Are any students listening?#

U. Council drafts code alternative

By ERIC MATTSON

(Sept. 5, 1985) The code--a proposal to govern students' behavior outside the classroom--is dead, at least for now.

A year ago, students and administrators were gearing up for a battle over the code. Students said the code was an attempt to control students' private and political lives, while administrators said the code was necessary to protect the University community from a few troublemakers.

THE STUDENTS pasted "NO CODE" stickers around campus, held demonstrations and forums, and hired an airplane to fly around Michigan Stadium on a football Saturday with the message, "Students Unite--Dump the Code."

But suddenly, in November, 1984, the fight recessed to a room on the third floor of the Michigan Union. University President Harold Shapiro, after months of "talking about whether to talk," had had enough, so he returned the code to its original promulgators, the University Council.

The council, a nine-member panel consisting of three students, three faculty members, and three administrators, is authorized by a Board of Regents bylaw to formulate rules to govern the University community.

NOW, SEVEN months after the council's first meeting, it is unclear what type of document will emerge, but a comprehensive code seems to be out of the question.

...

Exactly what the council can do to satisfy students, faculty, and administrators is unclear. The council seems to be moving toward consensus on emergency procedures for dealing with violent behavior, but less serious offenses, such as vandalism, haven't even been discussed.

...

Social work Prof. Ann Hartman, a faculty representative on the council, said, "The whole point of our system is to protect the University community, not punish the accused." The original code was designed to punish the offender.

UNDER THE new plan, a central coordinator would decide whether "emergency restrictions"--on class attendance or presence in certain buildings, for example--should be imposed upon someone accused of a violent offense pending a formal hearing...#

No code

(Sept. 5, 1985) **THIS TIME** last year, the University was trying to push something called the code for non-academic conduct on the students. A set of rules to try to control students outside the classroom, the code was blasted by the University community--students and faculty alike--as being totally inappropriate.

...

Now, a year later, the situation seems much brighter. The University Council, after months of deliberations, seems to be heading towards a code which protects, not punishes.

Under a new council idea, students could still be barred from a classroom if, for example, they attacked the teaching assistant, but a hearing would have to be held within two weeks to continue the sanction.

But the main difference is that these sanctions--so far--are only for life-threatening situations. Before, similar sanctions could be applied for any action the University deemed unsatisfactory, such as protests that disrupt normal University activity.

...

Although the situation seems better, students must not become apathetic. The University Council has not considered how to deal with civil disobedience. Students must be ready to fight any attempt by the administration to limit students' freedom of expression...#

Racial incidents lead to code speculation

By REBECCA BLUMENSTEIN

(March 12, 1987) As the University administration searches for a response to recent racial attacks, speculation has arisen that a code to control student behavior outside the classroom has become more imminent.

"Since the University administration is feeling a lot of pressure to do something about racism, the executive officers have split on whether or not to use a code to try to prevent future racial attacks," said Kurt Muenchow, president of the Michigan Student Assembly.

"Although there was speculation it was going to be brought up at the next Board of Regents meeting, I was promised that any code action would be tabled until September," he said.

Although none of the University's executive officers confirmed a timetable for future code discussion, Robin Jacoby, assistant to the vice president of academic affairs, confirmed that the controversial issue has been discussed often within the administration this week.

Recent racial attacks at the University have sparked discussion of the code as a way to handle racism. The broadcasting of racial jokes on WJJX student-run radio station and the distribution of a racist flier at Couzens have prompted the creation of two ad-hoc committees to consider the possible expulsion of the students responsible for the incidents.

"These recent events have certainly brought the question of the code to the forefront," said Jacoby.

Although the University can currently expel students only with a presidential order, a code would give the administration the power to use academic sanctions to regulate unwanted non-academic student behavior.

"I can't say it wouldn't be nice to handle such incidents with a consistent policy, rather than having to form an ad-hoc committee each time such an incident occurs," said Richard Kennedy, vice president of government relations and head of the committee investigating both the Couzens and WJJX incident...#

Fleming drafts code
Proposal imposes sanctions on discriminatory acts

By STEVE KNOPPER

(Jan. 11, 1988) A week after assuming office, Interim University President Robben Fleming has drafted a policy to deter, through academic punishments, student harassment and discrimination.

1988 Several students said yesterday that Fleming's draft is similar to, if not harsher than, the proposed code of non-academic conduct that has been the subject of intense debate the past four years.

...

A BOARD of Regents' bylaw states that any change in the rules of non-academic conduct must be approved by the University Council, a nine-member committee of students, faculty, and administrators. It must also be ratified by MSA and the faculty's Senate Advisory Committee on University Affairs.

But Fleming, in the draft, said he proposes "to establish a system for handling complaints of discriminatory behavior on the part of students" through another regental bylaw that grants the president power to promote the "maintenance of health, diligence, and order among the students."

...

Fleming's draft, in bypassing the council process, has enraged David Newblatt, an LSA senior and council co-chair. "As a University Council member, I think it's an outrage that they're totally ignoring the University Council process and bylaw process," he said.

The proposed rules, which would apply "everywhere on the entire campus," imposes different penalties for three levels of harassment:

- Written or spoken harassment would be punishable by "probation" if a student refuses to apologize;

- Physical contact would be punishable by a one-semester suspension after a second offense.

- Assault would be punishable by a one-year suspension.

Panels set up by the respective schools and colleges would judge whether students are guilty.

MANY student leaders say Fleming's statement might suppress Constitutional freedoms of speech and demonstration and unjustly regulates non-academic behavior. But Fleming, in his document, argued that the University is justified in having control over students' behavior outside of classes.

...

LAW STUDENT Eric Schnaufer, who helped organize the original "No Code" movement in 1984, said, "This is the vaguest, nastiest, most obnoxious code proposed to date. Fleming's statement on discrimination is the boldest and loudest 'fuck you' to students in years."..#

AN EDITORIAL
Offensive speech

(Jan. 11, 1988) **UNIVERSITY PRESIDENT** Robben Fleming's code of non-academic conduct is a unilateral attempt to divide students by confusing the issues of administrative control of life outside the classroom and the problems of racism, sexism and anti-gay bigotry. Discrimination cannot be tolerated, but a code governing student life is a cheap power grab designed to cover up institutional racism and the racist views of the University administration.

Fleming's code designates the dean of each school the authority to punish any student who makes "discriminatory remarks which seriously offend many individuals beyond the immediate victim." Fleming's new administrative law usurps the role of existing civil and criminal court systems by fabricating a University court.

...

Fleming constructs a facade of rationality while dictating to the University community his own totalitarian morality. He claims the absolute right to control all portions of student life and says that those who believe he is wrong "have recourse to the courts to challenge actions which they believe contravene the law."

...

Proposing the code as a means to fight racism is an attempt to divert attention away from the patently racist attitude present in the administration. Even beyond refusing a mandatory class on racism and diversity, Fleming opposed canceling classes on Martin Luther King's birthday. Further, Black enrollment is barely half of the 1970 target of 10 percent and faculty representation is woefully inadequate.

...

LSA Dean Peter Steiner, who would be the dean responsible for the largest number of students under Fleming's code, demonstrated his incompetence to administer Fleming's code by recently declaring that the University should not aspire to be a place where Blacks would "flock." Steiner also said just last term that Blacks require a "revolution" in their values before they will gain proportionate representation in universities the way women have...

...

It is simply not credible for the University administration to target students for disciplinary action before it cleans its own house. Certainly Dean Steiner and Regent Deane Baker have offended "many individuals" with racist, sexist and homophobic remarks in the past, but thus far they have successfully gained "immunity from a campus disciplinary proceeding."

...

If the University were serious about creating an atmosphere free of bigotry, it would set aside money for litigation against bigots and publicity programs to inform students of the possibilities for litigation. Instead, Fleming has decided to devote resources to the aggrandizement of administrators' power over the rest of the University community.

Fleming's code is the most serious threat to student rights and will set back efforts to end discrimination by throttling freedom of expression... Students cannot allow the University to regulate their activities, speech, or written words outside the classroom. Students must raise one voice: no racism, no sexism, no anti-gay bigotry, **NO CODE!**#

Fleming's revisions

(March 3, 1988) **INTERIM PRESI-DENT** Robben Fleming's "Revised policy on discriminatory acts," issued this week, is an intelligent, but flawed proposal. Shorn of many of the outrages that prevented Fleming's last proposal from serving as an effective vehicle of discussion, the current proposal published in the University Record (2/29/88) is still provocative.

...

Fleming's new proposal distinguishes among three areas of the University-- public forums, educational centers, and housing. According to Fleming's new proposal, public forums--which include the Diag, Regents' Plaza, and the Daily-- should be "bound only by the limitations on freedom of speech enunciated by the courts..." Fleming allows for disciplinary actions by the University in cases of physical violence and/or destruction of property resulting from discriminatory harassment.

In contrast, according to Fleming, educational centers such as classrooms cannot be as tolerant of bigoted acts of speech because the University is duty- bound to see that no one is cruelly alienated in the educational process because of race, gender or sexual orientation.

...

In principle, Fleming acknowledges a heavy responsibility to see to it that prejudices concerning race, gender, and sexual orientation do not prevent anyone from succeeding in this University. Fleming should explicitly link this responsibility to minority recruiting and retention efforts for faculty, students, and staff. The paramount concern should be institutional racism, not punishment for individual acts of racist speech.

...

Underlying Fleming's whole proposal is a concern with the conflicting principles of free speech and educational responsibility. The flaw in Fleming's thinking that suffuses the operational parts of his proposal is that Fleming overdraws the conflict between free speech and the responsibility to fight bigotry.

The way out of this conflict is to use free speech to criticize bigotry. There is nothing more effective than public discussion and ridicule where necessary to handle the problems of bigotry. A good example is the WJJX incident of last spring. After having aired racist jokes on his show, disk jockey Ted Severansky was subjected to nationwide humiliation and attention. In response, Severansky volunteered for community service.

Instead of formal reprimands and little marks in people's academic files, Fleming should create and utilize anti-bigotry media and classes. The University's responsibility is to provide resources and access to information to those who will lend their energy to the struggle against bigotry on campus. A good example would be to create a newspaper and radio show to expose bigotry and promote diversity.

...

Fleming has clearly articulated that the University must promote two principles in the creation of its academic environment--free speech and anti-bigotry. However, instead of choosing one above the other in some places but not in others, Fleming should seek to reconcile the two by using free speech to fight bigotry.#

Fat chance for forced apology

FAT AL

(Jan. 14, 1988) Forced apology.

That is what old man Fleming wants to dole out as punishment under his "this is not a code" proposal. That made me throw back my fat head and let forth a championous chuckle. Step back from your outrage (for just a lickety split) and think about that phrase -- "forced apology."

What a bucket of bullshit.

A forced apology means about as much as a four year old's "polite" utterings. I remember when, as a chubby cherubic, I'd holler, "ma, give me some a'that buffalo steak." And ma'd smack my head and bellow, "say please fatso." This demand was always followed by a sincere "please." I figger that's about the equivalent on the sincerity meter of a "forced apology."

And this is what the administration boys offer up as a solution to racist and other discriminations.

Man, it's pathetic.

But let's back up for a second and give Pops Fleming the benefit of the doubt. I'm agonna sniff me some smelling salts (it's a good buzz anyhow, heh-heh-heh), clear my head, and try to take an objective look at this here code. Hmmm, I wonder, who's to decide if a forced apology is in order. The dean, huh? Well, I'm in LSA so my dean is...let's see...none other than...Peter "This is not Wayne State" Steiner.

Man, this is only getting more pathetic.

Of course, Dean Steiner understands my bellowings about forced apologies. That good ol' boy knows where I'm coming from. He himself refused UCAR's demand for an apology. Well, let's slow down, pop a Pabst, and ponder this here dilemma. Alright, the way I figger it, Steiner made a racist statement, was found guilty by a jury of his non-peers, and refused to cough up a forced apology. Hmm, I'm just a country boy but if I read the "a code by any other name is still a code" right, then Steiner ought to be...suspended for a term. Heh-heh-heh. See ya later, Pete.

Hey, y'all, wake up and smell the bacon lard frying on the fire. The inmates are running the asylum around here. In fact, it's not bacon lard that's frying, it's student's butts. Who opened the cages? Who let Fleming out of the nursing home anyhow? Go crawl back under your reactionary rock, Robben.

The administration is a bunch of honky bags 'o' wind. There I said it, I said it. Honky, honky, honky. Call me a racist. Come on and try to force an apology you pathetic, myopic foolish old men. heh-heh-heh...#

Students respond to code

By ANDREW MILLS
and JIM PONIEWOZIK

(March 19, 1988) Members of student groups gave mixed reactions yesterday to the University Board of Regents' approval of Interim University President Robben Fleming's proposed policy on discriminatory acts.

Some students backed the principle of a racial and sexual harassment policy, but said the policy needs to be considered further and revised. But other students reacted with "disgust" and called the policy "repressive."

Michigan Student Assembly members responded angrily to the vote, which MSA President Ken Weine called "a complete slap in the face of the students."

Weine criticized the regents for not giving students more time to respond to the proposal before they voted. He said MSA members would probably meet over the weekend to plan the assembly's response.

"The regents are in for a big surprise if they think the code battle is over," MSA Student Rights Committee Chair Michael Phillips said in a statement yesterday.

He and other anti-code activists yesterday announced that they would try to mobilize student opposition to the new policy.

…

But other students supported the policy in principle, while maintaining some reservations. "We would have liked for the Regents to have voted to wait until the April meeting to formally adopt a formal racial and sexual harassment policy," Charles Wynder, a 2nd-year law student and member of the Black Law Students' Alliance said yesterday.

…

Michael Nelson, president of the University chapter of the National Association for the Advancement of Colored People said the NAACP plans to work on suggesting revisions as well, but is "happy with the fact that a policy was proposed."..#

Regents approve code, 5-2

Regents call policy first step

By STEVE KNOPPER

(March 19, 1988) The University's Board of Regents yesterday approved a policy against discriminatory behavior, which many have called a code of non-academic student conduct.

The majority of regents, despite criticism from one regent that they were ignoring students' input, voted 5-2 to pass Interim University President Robben Fleming's proposal to deter sexual and racial harassment through academic punishments.

"Racism is a complex, multi-faceted matter," said Regent Paul Brown (D-Petoskey), who voted for the policy. "This is one step...to create a better climate on this campus."

But Regent Veronica Smith (R-Grosse Ile) said the policy was "vague," and did not create a clear distinction between harassment and constitutionally-protected free speech. During the meeting, she became emotional, criticizing Regent Deane Baker (R-Ann Arbor) for interjecting a statement during her speech.

Smith, backed by applause from several Michigan Student Assembly leaders, said, "This is a form of censorship. We are saying to students that this is how they're going to behave. We're instilling fear in their minds that they can't speak their minds for fear of being accused of harassment."

Baker also voted against the policy because, he said, "If the effect of this code is to chill free speech...we can do severe injury to the University."..#

EXTRA **The Michigan Daily** EXTRA

Ninety-eight years of editorial freedom

Vol. XCVIII, No. 115A Ann Arbor, Michigan — Saturday, March 19, 1988 Copyright 1988, The Michigan Daily

Regents approve code, 5-2

Regents delay AD decision

By STEVE BLONDER

Regents call policy first step

By STEVE KNOPPER

CODE TIMELINE

Smith — University regent
Weine — MSA president
Fleming — Interim 'U' pres.

Schneuler — Anti-code activist
Shapiro — Former 'U' pres.
Wynder — BALSA president

Students respond to code

By ANDREW MILLS and JIM PONIEWOZIK

See REGENTS, Page 3
See STUDENTS, Page 3

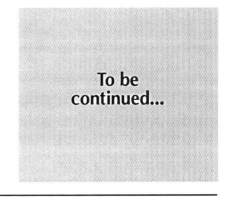

To be continued...

classified
research

'U' in Thailand:
Champions of the East

EDITOR'S NOTE: This is the first of a four-part series by a team of Daily reporters on military research at the University.

By ROGER RAPOPORT
Editor

(Oct. 17, 1967) "What the defense department does with our work is their business, we just go ahead and develop more technology," says Willis E. Groves, head of Project MICHIGAN, the largest of the University's $21.5 million worth of research contracts with the U.S. Department of Defense. About $9.7 million are classified and the remaining $11.8 million goes for unclassified projects.

1 9 6 7

Groves and over 900 other University professors, researchers, technicians and students working on defense department projects have done their job well. Dubbed by the Army, the "free leader in (combat) surveillance," the University is third only to Stanford and Massachusetts Institute of Technology in total defense department research funding.

...

The University's technological developments are basic to the nation's current military effort in Vietnam. At Willow Run, the dominant unit in the Institute of Science and Technology, University scientists have pioneered infrared reconnaissance techniques that make it possible for the U.S. military to pinpoint the enemy at night, or through partial foliage cover.

Willow Run Laboratories has made basic developments on a radar system that can see sideways (eliminating the need to fly directly over enemy territory for surveillance).

Other key military work is done at Cooley Labs and the Radiation Laboratory. The head of Cooley, Thomas W. Butler, says his unit serves as the "technical right arm" of the Army Electronics Command at Fort Monmouth, N.J.

At Cooley scientists have pioneered sophisticated means of jamming enemy radar, increasing radar capability, and improving communications. Many of these techniques have been made operational by industry and are used in Vietnam, according to scientists here.

Military research here will see fur-
ther applications in Vietnam. The University's developments in remote sensing will almost certainly be applied to the new electronic barrier in Vietnam, officials say.

President Harlan Hatcher's latest annual report on the University points out, "the importance to national defense of some of the present and past research programs of the Willow Run staff, especially in reconnaissance and surveillance technology, was brought into sharper focus by the situation in Vietnam, where allied forces rely heavily upon serial surveillance for military intelligence."

But much like the car designer who finishes his work on the 1970 models in 1967, the University's military researchers are hard at work on the military technology of the 1970's and beyond.

Consider these examples:

* The University is currently in the midst of a $1 million classified counter-insurgency project in Thailand. Under defense department sponsorship University scientists have helped build a "Joint Thailand - U.S. Aerial Reconnaissance Laboratory" with the Royal Thai military in Bangkok. Officials say the laboratory is the heart of a "fair-sized reconaissance program" to help the Thais "find clandestine Communist guerrilla activity." In addition to working with the Thais in Thailand, University scientists have been training "twenty to thirty" Thai military men in reconaissance techniques both at the University and in Thailand.

* This spring the University took a classified contract from the Army Ballistic Missile Agency to do research for the Strat-X project, which is developing a new Intercontinental Ballistic Missile for the 1970's.

* The University has begun operation of a $4.3 million infrared observatory in Hawaii to track Intercontinental Ballistic Missiles and Satellites.

* The University recently completed a $28,625 classified project on "Surreptitious Monitoring" for the Army Electronics Command. University scientists "looked at all available techniques for monitoring at a distance." The project was continued this fall for another year with a $51,000 grant and University scientists on campus will now concen-

trate on optical monitoring methods.

* The engineering school conducted a classified course in electronic warfare for 10 Army officers on campus last fall. This summer the school conducted a classified conference course in radar as well as an unclassified course in "military operations research" designed to help "engineers, operating managers and decision makers...in planning for next-generation weapons systems."

* University scientists helped plan and conduct a classified defense department conference on "Counter-Insurgency Research and Development" this summer. Willow Run scientists also continue to conduct the semi-annual classified meeting of the Anti-Missile Research Advisory Council and a classified symposium in advanced radar techniques under defense department sponsorship.

Thailand

Perhaps the most intriguing of these new projects is the $1 million counterinsurgency effort now going on in Thailand. The project is a joint venture between the defense department's Advanced Research Projects Agency (ARPA) and the Royal Thai Military.

Because the University has long experience in aerial surveillance, it was a natural place for the defense department to go with a $1 million contract for a reconnaissance laboratory.

"We know what parts to order, what systems to design, how to build it, how to interpret information and what to watch for," says George Zissis, head of the infrared physics laboratory at Willow Run, who worked with the project.

About half a dozen University scientists led by project director Joseph O. Morgan of the Infrared Physics Lab made numerous trips to Bangkok to help develop the laboratory, which will become operational shortly.

Currently James B. Evans, an engineer with the infrared physics laboratory, is "in Thailand advising them on the analysis of imagery," according to Zissis.

Zissis says that about 29 to 30 military officers were involved in the project and nine of them came to the University last fall for a special 10-week course. "A classroom arrangement was set up where we gave them basic instruction in engineering, physics, reconnaissance technology, etc." The courses were all taught by Willow Run staffers except "for one or two guest lecturers from the University faculty in meteorology," says

Zissis.

Returning to Thailand with a solid background in surveillance technology, the Thai military men went to work for their country. Under University supervision the Thais bought and outfitted a C-47 airplane for surveillance work.

Counter-Insurgency

According to Zissis, "This counter-insurgency work has two levels. First the Thais are using it to find clandestine Communist guerrilla activity." By using aerial surveillance techniques the Thai government can locate a group of Communists who have come in with military equipment. Then the Thai military will send in forces to capture the Communist ringleaders.

...

This surveillance work, which includes infrared techniques that make it possible to see at night, has also "aided the Thais in pinpointing and determining the extent of activity of Communist cells in the northern regions of Thailand," Zissis says.

Zissis says the second function of "this counter-insurgency work is to help tell the Thai government where it needs to send in its pacification workers to make friends with the natives.

"For example say some indigenous rebels are trying to get the people to revolt because of a water shortage. To halt the rebellion the teams will go in to try to correct the situation and sell the Royal Thai government to the people."

...

AMPIRT

Also in 1964-66, the school worked on a joint $2 to $3 million project with Cornell University called AMPIRT (ARPA Multispectral Photographic and Infrared Testing).

Under the $2 to $3 million ARPA sponsored contract University and Cornell scientists gathered data on the "effects of environment, crops, foliage, and terrain on detectability in Thailand," explains Zissis.

...

ICBM for the 70's

Not all the University military research is on long term projects. This spring the University completed another defense department contract dealing with ICBM's in only three months.

The University accepted a $12,660 classified contract for development work on the Strat-X project, which is developing an advanced ICBM being designed for the 1970's.

...

The University's contract was to "investigate seismic surveillance techniques." Long a leader in the development of seismic detectors to record earthquakes, the University was asked to determine the detectability of an ICBM launch with seismic equipment...

...

Probably the most sophisticated of the University's military research projects is the $4.3 million infrared observatory atop 10,000-foot Mount Haleakala on the Hawaiian island of Maui. The project is funded by ARPA and includes one 60-inch and two 48-inch reflector telescopes.

President Hatcher says the observatory "has very important military significance," and his 1963-64 annual "Report on the University" notes that "The observatory will study and track the midcourse flights of ballistic missiles and orbiting satellites with advanced infrared sensing, measuring and recording devices."

...

While the telescopes are for military work, University astronomers and visitors from other institutions are expected to be allowed to use them to do "fundamental research in application of infrared techniques to astrophysical and geophysical studies."

Surreptitious Monitoring

Sometimes the University's unique talents are called on for special kinds of classified contracts. For example at the first of this year the University completed a $28,265 contract on "surreptitious monitoring" for the Army electronics command at Fort Monmouth, N.J.

Butler, the project director, and principal investigator William B. Ribbens, an associate engineer in the electrical engineering department "looked at all available techniques for monitoring at a distance."

...

The work was renewed this year under a different title: "Optical receiver component techniques."

Asked why the name of the project was changed from "Surreptitious Monitoring" to "Optical Receiver Component Techniques," Butler explains: "The new name is more accurate. I don't know why they called it surreptitious monitoring the first time," says Butler. "That was an unusual name."#

Secret Research: Uncle Sam Wants 'U'

EDITOR'S NOTE: This is the second of a four part series by a team of Daily reporters on military research at the University.

By STEVE WILDSTROM

(Oct. 18, 1967) You walk through the door of the nondescript, converted Army building marked "Director's Office."

Just inside the entrance a uniformed security officer asks you to state your business. The party you've come to see is paged on the intercom and when your story checks out you sign into a register and are issued a numbered badge reading "Visitor--Escort Required."

...

Although more reminiscent of a spy movie than Angell Hall, this is the scene at the University's Willow Run Laboraties at Ypsilanti.

...

In recent years WRL's classified work has expanded to the Gas Dynamics and Aeronautical Engineering Laboratories and the IST building on North Campus. Classified work is also done at the Cooley Laboratories on North Campus and the Radiation Laboratory on Catherine St.

About $9 million of WRL's $11 million 1967-68 budget is classified work supported by the Defense Department, Evaldson said. According to director Thomas W. Butler, $600,000 of Cooley Labs' $1,090,000 budget is in classified work. The Radiation Laboratory has under $100,000 in classified work.

...

Classified work also involves closed courses, seminars, and conferences, classified and unclassified versions of some publications, widespread confusion and some complaining

Generally the University is not opposed to doing secret work. Explains Vice-President for Research A. Geoffrey Norman, "Some fields are totally classified. If you want to play the game, you have to play by the rules."

George Zissis, head of the WRL infrared physics laboratory added, "We hardly ever turn down government money for a classified project when it remotely fits into any of the programs we're working on."

The impact of the security measures extends from the electrical engineering department classroom to the highest echelons of the administration.

For example, last year the Army decided that it wanted 10 of its officers to "be aware of the latest talent and techniques in electronic warfare," explained electrical engineering department chairman Hansford W. Farris.

So for $23,000 the University set up a special, semester long course during the fall term last year. The men took a special classified course in jamming and penetration aids according to Farris.

...

Radar is one of the fields in which virtually all frontier work has military applications and radar research at the University, therefore, is almost entirely classified. Other fields in which University researchers work, such as infrared remote sensing and holography, the science of lensless, three-dimensional photography, are also heavily classified.

Because most frontier research in radar is classified the engineering school's 10 day summer conference on "Principles of Synthetic Aperture Radar" was secret. About 95 participants paid $300 to learn how radar can be used to resolve objects at great distances from the earth. The project was sponsored by the Air Force.

Similarly the national "Radar Symposium" which the University has conducted for the past 13 years is classified.

...

Security also presents some difficulties with students. Although students can and do work on classified projects, all these and dissertations must be public, that is, unclassified. According to Cooley's Butler, this may result in a student preparing two versions of his dissertation research report, a public one for his degree and a classified one for his government sponsor.

Nelson A. Navarre, assistant director of Cooley says a majority of doctoral students working on their dissertations there were doing work that was classified in some manner. Staff research likewise may result in dual reports for the government and the public.

For example, last year a student working on his doctoral dissertation at Cooley under Air Force sponsorship wrote a two-volume thesis on "A Study of Random Access Discrete Address Communications Systems," which dealt with computer theory. The first volume, which dealt with theoretical considerations, was public and constituted the actual dissertation. The second volume, which was classified, dealt with potential applications of the theories.

...

To work on a classified project or to get access to classified material, a person must do three things. First, he must be cleared by the Pentagon to the level of the material with which he will be working...

...

Second, the facility at which a person works as well as the person himself must be cleared.

Third, when a person seeks access to classified material, he must have "a need to know"...

...

Small Portions

Officials point out that often only a small portion of a project may be classified. However, under Defense Department security rules, if any part of a project is classified, the entire project must be classified. Also, a project which in itself has no military applications but which, for research purposes, must have access to classified material must be classified.

...

"For convenience's sake" an effort is made to obtain security clearance for all staff members at both WRL and Cooley, Evaldson and Butler said...

...

Butler said that of Cooley's staff of 80, including 48 students, all are cleared except for 10 or 11 foreign nationals who are unclearable.

John W. Wagner, security officer in the Office of Research Administration, has responsibility for processing of security clearance applications and for the physical security of research facilities on Main and North Campus.

Basic Qualifications

Wagner said the basic qualifications for clearance are that the person be a U.S. citizen or, under certain circumstances, a permanent resident alien, and that he be at least 18 years old. He said that, to the best of his knowledge, no University applicant who met those qualifications has ever been rejected.

...

Beyond the simple nuisance, security restrictions impose some real problems on researchers. A major problem is the transfer of knowledge gained on classified military projects to declassified civilian applications.

Because of military applications, much information needed to apply developments to civilian uses remains classified, researchers said.

Project directors at WRL expressed a concern for increasing the availability of research findings for civilian use and for speeding up the declassification process. "We like to think we are among the leaders in seeking increased dissemination of information," one said.

"Remote sensing led to a security problem," said Joseph Morgan, director of the WRL Infrared Physics Lab, citing a case where Defense Department security restrictions stymied development of a civilian application.

"The earth science people were very interested but they needed to know more than they were permitted to know," he added.

"Since 1962," Morgan continued, "we've made extremely slow progress" in speeding the declassification process.

...

Mixed Feelings

Researchers at WRL expressed mixed feelings about working under the restrictions imposed by classification. Marvin Holter, head of WRL's Infrared and optical sensing laboratory, said some restrictions, such as the need to lock up all files at the end of the day were "a nuisance.

"We'd be better off without them," he added.

Willis E. Groves, director of Project MICHIGAN, an Army sponsored $2.5 million-a-year project on battlefield surveillance research, said that doing work for the Department of Defense and accepting the attendant security restrictions "allows us to research on things that are important rather than things we can afford.

"Across the board," Groves continued, "we are proud of the fact that we have contributed to a stronger nation."

Total Support

"If we could have our total present support all from non-Defense Department sources, I don't think we'd elect it as an alternative," Evaldson said. "The Defense Department has been such a strong leader."

Defense research is "in the mainstream of historical science," Holter said. "Archimedes invented Greek fire and Leonardo Da Vinci designed tanks."

"The trend is toward much less classified work," said Hansford W. Ferris, chairman of the electrical engineering department. "Of course, that's not to say we don't want classified work; in many cases, you get much further along with classified work.

"Basic ideas are not classified," he continued. "When you get into development, lead time is the only thing you have against a potential enemy.

"In a technical field," Ferris added, "you can cut off your life blood and be two years behind without classified work. Some of our literary college colleagues aren't able to understand this distinction. We feel a technical man has the freedom to choose what he does or does not do."

"When people say 'don't do classified research'," said Groves, "they are talking about something that will be a long time in coming. Military research gives these guys (scientists and engineers) a chance to move and cash in."#

An Editorial

(Oct. 24, 1967) In universities across the country the relationship between academic communities and secret government military research has been undergoing re-examination. It is time for the University to begin this same reappraisal and make the inevitable changes that should accompany it.

...

These classified activities are now being conducted in a moral vacuum. There are no explicit guidelines describing the University's position on such work, only vague restrictions which can be easily circumvented.

The University is a far cry from institutions like Harvard which refuses to accept any classified contracts or the University of Minnesota whose president recommended to the board of regents that the school stop taking classified work.

...

Normally the university assumes research activities because they can make an academic contribution to the school. Research should be undertaken to advance the frontiers of knowledge, to provide a meaningful educational experience for faculty and students, and to find new and better ways of promoting human welfare.

The Thailand project accomplishes none of these. Much like the ill-famed Michigan State University work on Vietnam it is a service contract. It will aid Thailand in developing a "fair-sized reconnaissance program" to help the Royal Thai military "find clandestine Communist guerrilla activity."

...

Aside from the fact that University researchers may get a closer look at "clandestine Communists," the school is not learning anything from the contract. University scientists have pioneered aerial surveillance techniques with their own fleet of airplanes at Willow Run. The school continues to do reconnaissance throughout the world and does not need additional practice in Thailand.

Moreover, the project has no academic value to the University.

And most important, the project is only helping escalate the Thai situation into another Vietnam-style conflict.

...

We believe the University has no right reason or responsibility to get involved in secret counter-insurgency work.

The school should withdraw immediately from the secret Thailand project. And because this matter raises such serious questions about secret research, we believe the University should stop accepting all new classified contracts, pending establishment of clear guidelines that prevent University involvement in such projects.

THE SENIOR EDITORS

Electronic battlefield:
'U' and the Indochina war

EDITOR'S NOTE: The following article is the first of a two-part series examining the applications of University research to the Indochina war.

By DAVE CHUDWIN
Managing Editor

(March 9, 1971) University researchers are playing an important role in developing the technology for the military's electronic battlefield now being tested by U.S. forces in Indochina for use in future conflicts.

1971

This new concept of warfare, where advanced electronic devices detect enemy troops, lead soldiers and aircraft to hostile forces and evaluate combat intelligence, draws heavily on developments originated and refined at the University's Willow Run Laboratories.

...

Willow Run Laboratories, which receives about two-thirds of its funding from the Defense Department, is one of the primary university centers for developing this type of warfare. Its current activities in this area include:

--The measurement of heat, radar, sound and vibration characteristics of military targets, such as rockets, tanks and other vehicles. These measurements are used by electronic sensors to aid in identifying targets;

--The development of radar to take surveillance photographs, and the refinement of a "moving target indicator radar" which tracks convoys and troops;

--The testing of acoustic and seismic devices which provide means of detecting the sounds and vibrations of enemy troop movements; and

--The investigation of advanced countermeasures techniques to permit offensive aircraft to carry out bombings and strafings of targets.

According to comments prepared by Pentagon research director [John] Foster, "In these areas the University of Michigan has been continually in the forefront of research, making important contributions to the developments and to the state-of-the-art in these areas.

"These contributions have been invaluable in research leading to systems and equipments for battlefield surveillance and target acquisition."

University researchers perform about $10.4 million of military research annually, about half of which is classified.

...

The disclosure in 1967 of University participation in a counterinsurgency project in Thailand and other secret research led to a controversy over the participation of the University in military research.

Subsequently, all proposals for classified research have been reviewed by a committee of nine faculty members and three graduate students for their appropriateness under guidelines approved by the Regents.

The guidelines state that the University will not enter into contracts for research:

--"The specific purpose of which is to destroy or incapacitate human beings;

--"Which would restrain its freedom to disclose the existence of the contract or the identity of the sponsor;"

--For which it could not "disclose the purpose and scope of the proposed research;" and

--Unless the research will "make a significant contribution to the advancement of knowledge" or enhance "the research capability of the investigator or his unit."

A group of faculty members on Senate Assembly are planning to propose a change in the policy at the March 15 and 16 Assembly meeting...#

Secret research sent minus committee OK

By DAVE CHUDWIN
Managing Editor

(Sept. 23, 1971) At least two proposals for classified military research have been forwarded to the Defense Dept. by the University within the last six months without the approval of the Classified Research Committee (CRC).

...

According to the University's Standard Practice Guide, "Before a proposal for a classified research project is submitted by the University for a sponsor, the proposal must be approved by the Classified Research Committee."

However, on April 6, Vice President for Research A. Geoffrey Norman forwarded a proposal entitled "Target and Background Characteristics" to the Air Force requesting funding although the committee had reviewed and failed to approve the classified project.

And on Aug. 31, similarly without committee approval, Norman submitted to the Army a proposal on "Electronics Counter-countermeasures Techniques."

Norman, in an interview yesterday, justified his action on the basis of what a report on classified research, issued Tuesday by the Research Policies Committee, described as an "ambiguity" in procedures.

According to committee rules, seven votes of the 12-member CRC are needed to pass a proposal. A controversy has developed, however, over whether seven votes are also necessary to reject a project.

The vote on the counter-countermeasures project was 6 to 5 against approval. On the target characteristics project the tally was 5 to 2 in favor of passing the project with two abstentions, The Daily has learned.

In both cases the projects did not receive the necessary seven votes for approval. Norman claims the committee took no action on the two projects because at least seven votes were not also cast for rejection.

"The committee was unable to arrive at a decision," Norman said. "The deadline was reached and I exercised my responsibilities whether the project was within the guidelines (on classified research). I decided it was, and sent it out."

Norman said CRC is only advisory to him, and referring to the Standard Practice Guide statement, commented, "I don't regard that as correct."..#

SENATE ASSEMBLY REJECTS END TO CLASSIFIED RESEARCH AT 'U'

On classified research

(March 16, 1971) **IT IS ALWAYS** difficult to legislate morality for an entire University community, indeed for any community. Yet there are times when those in a position of authority have the responsibility to cope with moral issues, particularly when the question has considerably agitated and upset their constituents.

Three years ago, Senate Assembly, the representative body of the University's faculty, found itself in such a situation on the issue of military and classified research at this campus. And in Spring, 1968, Assembly accepted the principle that research "directed toward means for the destruction of human life or the impairment of human welfare is not consistent with the values of a university."

Acting on Assembly's recommendation, the Regents prohibited University researchers from engaging in projects whose "specific purpose...is to destroy human life or incapacitate human beings."

...

WE FIRMLY believe that Assembly should reaffirm its 1968 position that research directed at killing or impairing human welfare is not consistent with the values of a university.

To this end, we urge Assembly to consider recommending to the Regents a ban on all research which is classified.

The arguments against the presence of secret research at the University extend far beyond the mere fact that most military research is classified. Whatever its nature, secret research is inconsistent with the principles of an academic community for several reasons.

First, the aim of research at a university is the fostering of new ideas and concepts which can then be interchanged between all members of the community--not just between the researcher and his sponsor. When a faculty member signs a research contract which requires him to sequester his results, he is no longer able to fulfill the educational function of research, and might as well be working for a private firm; not a member of a university community.

Secondly, secret research is inconsistent with the principles of academic freedom so important to the dynamics of a university. The right to academic freedom entitles members of the community to absorb and intellectually benefit from the endeavors of other members of the community. When research is kept secret, however, this freedom is infringed upon.

...

...an even more compelling argument against classified research is that it makes the University part of the military establishment which enforces this country's foreign policy.

By virtue of its research, the University aids the government in waging better wars, in killing and maiming more effectively--all as part of an effort to maintain our world-wide military posture and our economic domination of other nations and peoples.

It is becoming increasingly important that the faculty take cognizance of the large number of community members who are violently opposed to this foreign policy. In the eleventh year of American involvement in the Indochina war, in the tenth month after the invasion of Cambodia, in the second month since the invasion of Laos, a growing majority of the community finds it difficult to accept the idea that the University is a prime instrument in these endeavors.

IN RECOGNITION of the relationship between classified research and U.S. foreign policy, and with the understanding that secret research in itself violates the principles of academia, we urge Senate Assembly to seek a broadening of the current University policy to clearly and effectively prohibit researchers from accepting contracts whose purpose is to facilitate the death and incapacitation of human beings...#

--THE SENIOR EDITORS

FACULTY SENDS DEBATE ON ISSUE TO COMMITTEE

By TAMMY JACOBS

(March 23, 1971) Senate Assembly, the faculty representative body, yesterday in effect rejected a proposal that it urge the Regents to ban classified research from the University, and asked two of its committees to make a further study of the controversial issue.

Meeting for the third time in eight days to discuss the question, Assembly declined to consider a motion submitted by faculty members who organized a week-long fast to protest the presence of classified and military research.

Instead, the faculty body called on its Research Policy Committee to undertake a three-month study of the issue and bring back recommendations to Assembly members at their June meeting.

In addition, the Classified Research Committee will investigate whether to change the methods it uses to implement current guidelines on classified research. The committee will report to Assembly on May 15.

...

Opponents of military and classified research have charged that the committee has not properly enforced the guidelines, and have asked that the guidelines be strengthened to effectively bar all military research from the University.

The motion approved yesterday by Assembly did suggest one change in the classified research guidelines. The proposed change would bar classified research whose "clearly forseeable purpose is to destroy human life or incapacitate human beings."

However, it remained unclear just what difference, if any, existed between this proposed guideline and the current one, which bans research whose "specific" purpose is killing or injuring.

An audience of about 350, most expressing vocal support for the proposals to ban classified research, listened as the various motions were discussed and voted on during the three-hour meeting yesterday afternoon...#

'U' classified warfare course revealed

By ALAN LENHOFF

(Feb. 16, 1972) As the Regents this week prepare to consider a revised policy on campus classified research, new information has come to the attention of The Daily which sheds further light on the University's close relationship to the U.S. defense establishment.

The recently-discovered text of a speech delivered by Prof. Thomas Butler, director of the University's Cooley Laboratories, has documented the existence of a "classified" course in electronic warfare techniques which was offered to military personnel at the University in the late 1960's.

The semester-long course, attended only by military personnel with top security clearances, specifically was designed to instruct the "students" concerning application of electronic warfare techniques to specific battlefield situations.

Many of the electronic weapons systems which were discussed had been developed by the University's Willow Run and Cooley Laboratories, which perform about $7 million worth of clas-

sified projects for the Department of Defense annually.

Engineering college officials last night would neither confirm nor deny the existence of such a course--past or present.

...

The course was initiated by Butler and others involved in the Cooley Laboratories in 1966, upon the request of the Army Security Agency (ASA).

A Pentagon spokesman yesterday described the role of ASA as "a world-wide monitoring and surveillance agency working to promote the security of the free world."

...

The program, which Butler claims has been discontinued, included standard graduate level courses in such areas as systems engineering, radiation, and computers, but also included a special class entitled "Fundamental Aspects of Electronic Warfare."

A note on the course description said: "This course has been specifically structured to meet the needs of the military attendees. Since some of the

lectures will be of a classified nature, it is anticipated the EW-1 (the course number) will be held in the Cooley Bldg."

The class included instruction on the history of electronic warfare and the use of electronic warfare devices in various battlefield situations.

In addition, the military personnel were given an update on "the state of the art" in electronic warfare devices, equipment and techniques.

"The sessions will give the students exposure to electronic warfare problems and solutions," the course description states. "It is anticipated that this portion of the course will be practical enough so that students can apply their knowledge to the solution of field problems."

...

Engineering college Associate Dean Hansford Farris, a former professor in the department of electrical engineering, yesterday declined comment on the classified course, terming it "not newsworthy."

"Don't you think all that stuff has been beaten to death?" Farris asked...#

Classified research project hit

By GORDON ATCHESON
and CHERYL PILATE

(Jan. 21, 1976) The Research Policies Committee will today review a classified research proposal that may violate regental regulations prohibiting the University from engaging in secret projects "the probable result of which...is to destroy human life or to incapacitate human beings."

The project outlines a highly sophisticated tactical radar system to be developed by two University professors and funded by the U. S. Air Force.

THE PROPOSAL, known as DRDA 76-815-KB1, has been questioned by Physics Professor Jens Zorn, one of three persons who screen classified research projects for the University.

In a memo obtained by The Daily yesterday, Zorn states that the proposal "appears to be a weapons engineering project that is more appropriate for the industrial than the academic sector."

Zorn told The Daily last night "I could be mistaken but I believe this is the type of device customarily used with guns."

...

Zorn states in his letter that the radar antenna plan violates Provision 3 of the Regental Policy on Classified Research that declares:

"The University will not enter into or renew any agreement

or contract, or accept any grant, the clearly forseeable and probable result of which, the direct application of which, or any specific purpose of which is to destroy human life or incapacitate human beings."

LSA Senior Elham Elahi, who also reviews classified research proposals, said he questioned the project because he understood that the radar could be used on fighter jets.

ENGINEERING PROF. Ralph Hiatt, one of the professors who authored the proposal, refused to confirm or deny Elahi's claim.

Thomas Senior, the other professor involved in the contract proposal, denied that the radar antenna system violates University guidelines.

"I am in no sense offended that the committee questioned this, but I feel it was misinterpreted," he said.

...

This is the first time in at least three years that a research proposal has been questioned as being in violation of Provision 3.

Senior last night discussed the...radar antenna system in very general terms, asserting that the project "was not sinister."

HE SAID the system would be used to detect objects in space but differed from those presently employed because it would be more difficult for the enemy to detect...#

Fighting defense research

By BARRY WITT
Second of a three-part series
(Nov. 19, 1981) Ten years ago, opponents of Pentagon research on campus had a much easier time. Over at the University's Willow Run Laboratories in Ypsilanti, researchers were developing "remote sensing devices" that the Army used to seek out battlefield enemies for destruction.

...today's critics find themselves protesting a far more nebulous evil--if it is an evil at all.

The fact is, defense research on campus today is of the most fundamental nature; it's nearly impossible to show any direct relationship between this basic research and the destruction of human life.

But the applications of this research concern many students and faculty members.

...

THE CRITICS believe that basic principles of scholarly work exclude defense research as a proper activity for the University.

...

Central to the debate is the issue of whether supporting the Pentagon is leading to the destruction of the world or saving the United States from its enemies.

...

[Medical School Prof. David] Basset and other critics of Pentagon-sponsored research question why the federal government chooses the defense department as its medium for supporting research.

Noting that much of the work being done for the Department of Defense is of an "innocent" nature, the critics question why other government agencies, such as the National Science Foundation or cabinet departments other than defense, are not sponsoring that kind of work.

Basset said he would like to see the Pentagon "keep to its purpose," rather than funding a variety of projects "that look good for the general public."..#

Students seize 'U' research lab

Activists call for end to defense projects

By JIM SPARKS and PETE WILLIAMS
(Nov. 8, 1983) Twenty-seven members of an activist student group seized control of a research laboratory in the East Engineering Building yesterday, vowing to "shut down" military research on campus.

The demonstrators, all members of the Progressive Student Network, blockaded the door to the radiation laboratory at 1:30 p.m. and refused entrance to the facility.

...

PSN members chose the radiation laboratory because Electrical and Computer Engineering Professor Thomas Senior, who runs the lab, regularly does research sponsored by the Department of Defense.

SENIOR'S current project, called electromagnetic pulse (EMP) research, uses microwaves to simulate the pulses given off to aircraft by lightning or a nuclear explosion.

Senior said he is working to develop sensors to measure the effect of lightning on planes but previous projects have specifically referred to simulating a "high altitude nuclear explosion."

The protesters demanded an end to the EMP project, stopping all military research at the University, extending classified research guidelines to non-classified research projects, and disciplinary or legal action against the participants...#

Moving a sluggish 'U'

(Nov. 9, 1983) **SHUTTING DOWN** a University research lab for one or two or however many days is a bold action. But often drastic actions are the only thing that moves this sluggish University.

Hundreds had to protest before the University would pull its investments out of companies which operate in apartheid South Africa. Thousands had to boycott classes in 1970 to force the University to set ambitious black enrollment goals. Students blockaded the LSA building just to get the U-Cellar bookstore.

And so the story goes, this time with defense department-sponsored research. Twenty-seven activist students blockaded a university laboratory Monday where they suspect weapon research is being conducted. They were still there at press time last night.

The sit-in is needed to make a point the University doesn't seem to want to acknowledge. Several research projects on campus are obviously questionable and should be examined thoroughly and objectively to determine if their purpose is to create better weapons.

The faculty is the most logical body to do this but up to now they have dismissed any investigation by claiming it would amount to a witch hunt. If they review these projects, they will have to review every research project, they say.

But this is not true. Official descriptions for many of these projects describe possible military applications for simulating bomb detonations, missile guidance systems, and the evasion of conventional radar. The faculty has every reason to single them out for closer examination, and should do so.

It is their responsibility to show the University community that either these projects are legitimate or they are not. Until such an investigation is conducted, the community is forced to guess, to rely on rumor and conjecture, and to act on little substantial evidence.

There are members of the community, both for and against weapons research, who want to act. They at least wonder about these projects. They deserve answers.

And if the research lab has to be closed for one or two or however many days to get those answers, it will be worth it.#

the
crusades

money
talks

'U' investment priority:
Profit or social concerns?

By MARK DILLEN
Daily News Analysis

(April 11, 1971) In an office on the fifth floor of the University Administration bldg. a small portfolio contains a list of 90 corporations. Occasionally, upon routine approval of the Regents, names on the list are replaced, signifying a change in what companies University investment officers think will yield the greatest return on their nearly $60 million worth of investments.

However, the expectation of profit will be the only thing causing the names to change--no consideration is given the rising criticism of certain profitable but unpopular investments on moral and social grounds.

This fact is the heart of the recent controversy over how universities and other large institutions decide where and how to invest; should these institutions subordinate profits and acquire and vote stock as an expression of their "moral" concern?

Increasingly, the University is among a group of many educational institutions being challenged on this question. Starting a year ago with consumer advocate Ralph Nader's "project on corporate responsibility"--Campaign GM--organized groups have tried, with no success, to revise the University's investment policy.

...

Nevertheless, many of the "approved" firms the University invests in are known to have dealings in the Union of South Africa--whose racial policy of apartheid has caused the United Nations to urge that its products and services be boycotted.

In addition, many firms on the list, University administrators freely admit, are also probably guilty of various kinds of discriminations within their own business. Still others contribute to pollution or contract heavily for the military.

Yet none of these grounds is sufficient to the administrators connected with the investment process to warrant recommendation of a policy change.

Wilbur Pierpont, Vice-President for Financial Affairs, would have perhaps the most influence in proposing such a change in policy. According to his subordinates in the University investments office, Pierpont must approve every transaction they recommend, and often consults with them on the wisdom of proposed investments.

However, Pierpont remains tight-lipped concerning his views on these "moral" questions. "It's a matter of policy for the Regents and I have no comment beyond that," he says.

...

Graham Conger, another University investment specialist, furthers the University view on investment, saying objections would be raised to a company's employe relations "only if it affected production and cost.

"The closest we ever came to making an investment decision on moral grounds was when we declined to invest in tobacco," Conger says. "And the decision that tobacco investment was not necessary was made not only because we felt it improper on public health grounds, but because it just wasn't good business."

Likewise was a previous decision not to invest in companies making alcoholic beverages, says Griffiths. "Most of those firms just don't have the growth."

Conger and Griffith sum up their opposition to groups like Campaign GM and the Angola Gulf Project--opposition shared by most of the Regents--by criticizing their "indirect approach."

"If Dow Chemical (a company in which the University currently owns $500,000 worth of stock) hadn't made napalm, someone else would," says Griffith. "These people have made the investment question a symbolism and they're trying to use it as a political lever."

...

...a more basic consideration might be the effect of such policy changes on the gift giving that forms the basis of University investments in the first place. Investment officials, like the Regents during the recruitment policy debate, are wary of making "social and mor-al" judgments lest alumni support drop off.

Drawing over $6 million in dividends on University investments in the last year alone--usually earmarked for a donor's special project or concern--University finances could be significantly handicapped by an investment policy which forced liquidation of securities more conservative alumni gave as gifts...#

Investments, The Daily, and the Board for Student Publications

(Nov. 22, 1977) The Daily staff was caught off guard when it realized last month that is own financial governing body, the Board for Student Publications, is indirectly investing funds--mostly Daily profits--in corporations which do business in South Africa.

Indignation was the first reaction. The Daily has repeatedly condemned such investments by the University, and the discovery that University investments included the Board's own prompted many staffers to feel hypocrisy had been forced on them.

AT THE NOVEMBER 10 Board meeting, a student member proposed that the group recommend to the Regents that all University investments be withdrawn from South Africa. The Board-- comprised of three professional journalists, three students, and four faculty members--discussed the proposal thoughtfully for some 20 minutes.

Neil Shine, managing editor of the Detroit Free Press, questioned the thoughtfulness of withdrawing the funds.

"If I was sure we could take something out of the hands of the white racists by withdrawing money, then I would support (the motion)," he said. "But I'm not sure." He said the withdrawal might force blacks out of work without hurting the minority regime.

OTHERS NOTED that the Board has no editorial jurisdiction over The Daily, and thus no political function, and should not take a political stand of any kind.

...

The Board rejected the proposal by a vote of seven to two.

AT A DAILY staff meeting November 13, firm objections were raised to the Board's vote. Despite the understanding that the staff is not responsible for Board investments, it was felt by many staffers that The Daily's editorial position had nevertheless been compromised. The thought of Daily profits being invested in South Africa, when the paper had condemned such investments, seemed totally incongruous and improper to many.

Some felt that a symbolic, one-day walkout should be staged to protest the Board's refusal to take action on the investments question. But a majority favored a special section in The Daily devoted to the issue--urging the Board to take action, making clear the paper's editorial stance, and detailing the issue at some length in a news story.

This is that special section.#

The Michigan Daily

MAYOR (L SCI I HEARINGS RESUME

Two city voters file new appeal

Sadat returns home to hero's welcome

IN EDITORIAL
The black hope

A SPECIAL SECTION:

The University's dilemma over South Africa stock

The pro and con of pulling out

Investments, The Daily, and the Board for Student Publications

Daily divestment request denied

By JULIE ROVNER

(March 18, 1978) The Board for Student Publications Thursday night turned down a request from the editors of The Michigan Daily to withdraw the paper's assets from the University's investment pool.

The request protested the Regent's decision not to divest University holdings in corporations operating in South Africa. A similar request was denied four months ago.

THE BOARD controls the finances of The Daily, the Michiganensian and all other student publications.

Irving Freeman, one of the two undergraduate students on the board, moved that the board ask the Regents to remove all of the board's assets from the University investment pool and return them to the board.

UNDER THE University's bylaws, the Regents have the authority to refuse the board's request to give back the funds. Many board members voiced objections saying it was not because they support apartheid, but because they fear that if the Regents return the funds it would leave the Board to administer some $300,000 on their own.

"It's terribly naive to think that this board could operate independently of the University," said Peter Ferren, an English professor and one of the faculty members on the board. "The first move I would make would be to resign," he said.

"If I were sitting where you were, I would probably be doing the same thing," Gratton Gray of the Monroe Evening News told the editors. "But since I'm sitting on this side of the table, I'm going to have to go against you."

The motion was defeated...#

Protesters halt Regents meeting

Angry group demands S. Africa divestiture

By MITCH CANTOR

(March 16, 1979) Providing one of the fiercest displays of activism on campus in several years, 180 shouting students, faculty members, and other citizens marched yesterday afternoon into the Administration Building where they forced the Regents to halt their meeting 45 minutes later after the Board refused to discuss the South African issue.

Several hours later 20 students, most of them black, received assurance from Regent Sarah Power (D-Ann Arbor) that she would submit a proposal today on behalf of James Waters (D-Muskegon)--who will be absent from today's session--calling for an action request to be added to today's agenda concerning the issue.

...

The group specifically demanded the Board reexamine the University's holdings in corporations which do business in South Africa. The protesters claim the Regents haven't yet accurately determined whether or not the corporations are actually instituting anti-discriminatory measures...#

Regents reject limited 'U' divestment proposal

By MITCH CANTOR

(April 21, 1979) It took nearly an hour of confused discussion about parliamentary procedure and alternative motions, but the Regents finally decided yesterday morning not to withdraw University investments from two companies doing business in South Africa.

Some 200 equally confused protesters sat patiently listening in the Union Ballroom while the eight policy-makers decided instead to direct University Counsel Roderick Daane to look into possible actions they could take to increase University influence in shaping anti-discriminatory policies for G. D. Searle and Black & Decker operations in the foreign country.

IN A RELATED decision, the Regents passed a measure calling for the creation of a committee on "socially responsible practices" for the University. The item was brought up at yesterday's meeting by members of the coalition who claim the University's policy on divestment is one example of an unresponsive action by the University...#

'U' to divest from firms operating in South Africa

By BILL SPINDLE

(April 15, 1983) The University Regents voted 6-2 yesterday to sell about 90 percent of the University's stocks in companies operating in South Africa as a statement against the country's apartheid policies.

At the same time they voted 5-3 to challenge in court a state law which requires the University to divest all of its stocks in those companies by 1984.

AFTER SEVEN years of rallies, demonstrations, and even a state law ordering the University to divest, the Regents yesterday reversed two previous decisions to retain stocks. By keeping the stocks, the board had hoped to encourage the companies to promote social change in the country.

The resolution came after 18 students, professors, alumni, and Ann Arbor residents, backed by a crowd of about 90 people, urged the Regents to sell University interests in that country.

In an effort to placate Michigan firms that have close ties to the University and to gain standing to challenge the state law in court, the University will retain about $5 million of stocks in Michigan-based companies which operate in South Africa. As of Dec. 31, 1982, the University owned a total of about $50 million worth of stocks in businesses operating in South Africa...#

University investments back nuclear weapons production

By BARRY WITT

(Sept. 9, 1982) The University has used its corporate voting power to support the production of nuclear weapons, the construction of nuclear power plants, and the sale of oil to the South African government, a review of proxy votes shows.

But at no level of the administration, from the Regents to the executive officers to the investment office, has there been discussion of the possible ethical implications of these investment decisions.

AS A SHAREHOLDER in more than 100 corporations, the University votes by proxy every year on a wide variety of shareholder resolutions concerning social issues. And almost without exception, these proxies are voted with management--against the resolutions, whether they come from the right, left, or center of the political spectrum.

That means, for example, that last spring the University opposed the efforts of a group of General Electric Corp. shareholders who were trying to stop the company from managing a nuclear weapons facility in St. Petersburg, Fla.

The University voted every share of its more than $1.5 million of GE stock for the management's position that it is not the place for private business to question the policies of the nation's elected officials.

...

UNIVERSITY administrators say the investment office votes with management because the Regents have never said to do otherwise. The only exception is for resolutions dealing with South Africa, but even there, the option to vote against management is restricted by a lack of breadth in the University's policy.

...

Unless the Regents or other members of the University community are shareholders in these companies, it is unlikely that they would know that the University has a voice in these issues. The voting procedure is a routine matter of the investment office, and the Regents customarily do not consider any of these issues.

Thus, members of [University Vice President James] Brinkerhoff's staff are among the few people in the community who know which specific issues the University is supporting. Several of these administrators receive monthly reports from the Investor Responsibility Research Center (IRRC), which explain the issues at hand and report on how institutions across the country are addressing them.

As possessors of that information, however, none of Brinkerhoff's staff feel the obligation to bring these issues to the attention of the Regents. Norman Herbert, the University's investment officer who casts the votes, said "It's not our role to introduce those issues other than to the extent that it is financial."

...

The faculty committee that watches over University investments addresses strictly financial issues (except for an annual discussion on South Africa).

...

THE UNIVERSITY remains politically indiscriminate in its social apathy; it opposes not only left-wing proposals, but also resolutions from the right.

One resolution asked Hewlett-Packard Co. to stop selling technology to the Soviet Union. Hewlett-Packard's management argued that the company is in full compliance with the government's export control laws, and the University, by virtue of its vote for management, agreed.

It is only for resolutions relating to a company's South African operations that the investment office can consider voting against management. The Regents' policy states that the University will vote its proxies in favor of resolutions supporting the enhancement of political, social, and economic rights for a company's employees in South Africa.

...

MOST universities with substantial investments have some sort of standing committee to advise their governing boards on questions of socially responsible practices.

Such a committee was suggested here in the late 1970s but the idea died before coming up for formal discussion, Brinkerhoff said. "The inference was we have a process that we're happy with," he said.

The University now stands as the only school with a large investment fund in the country that does not use any form of committee structure, said University President Harold Shapiro.

HARVARD University, with the largest investment portfolio of any school in the country, set up an Advisory Committee on Social Responsibility (ACSR) 10 years ago to make recommendations to Harvard's governing board on proxy issues.

The Harvard Corporation accepts ACSR's recommendations almost 80 percent of the time, said ACSR Secretary Candace Corvey...#

Regents 'unaware' of issue

By BARRY WITT

(Sept. 16, 1982) Although the University annually throws its multi-million dollar corporate influence behind the production of nuclear weapons, the individuals who decide the University's investment policy say they don't understand what's going on.

Last week the Daily disclosed that the University does not consider the ethics involved when it votes on dozens of corporate issues, covering a wide variety of social concerns--from nuclear weapons to affirmative action.

...

One Regent said she was "not informed," a second said he was "not aware," and two others said they "didn't know" that the University voted every share of its more than $16 million of General Electric Corp. stock against a resolution asking the company to halt its contributions to the nation's nuclear weapons arsenal.

...

Although the Regents said they welcomed the community's suggestions on which issues should be addressed, they all rejected the idea that a permanent committee or similar mechanism be formed to follow the issues. Most major universities across the country have such a mechanism, according to University President Harold Shapiro...#

the crit sheet

The following was submitted by Ivan Kaye, Sports Editor in 1954, through his successor, Phil Douglis, who writes: "He asked me to pass it on to you as his contribution, but asks that if it is published, it be published as it stands. 'If this proves impossible, then let them just throw the goddam thing away,' he asks." This is it, exactly as submitted.

I think it is the 'crit sheet' that I'll always remember. You could see it from forty feet away, even if you were as myopic as I was. It was two sheets of yellow paper tacked up on the Sports Department's bulletin board containing detailed criticism of every story appearing on that morning's sports page. A senior editor was assigned to write it, and I don't think that it is just a coincidence that the three who did the job during my years there each achieved the pinnacle in his chosen profession. One opted for the law, one for academe, and one for television journalism, and all three are listed in Who's Who. (That's nothing; I'm in What's This?)

The crit sheet was a marvelous way to train a staff, because you saw not only your own mistakes, but also those of everybody else. Sometimes the criticism was even longer than your story, and nearly always it was better written.

We were required to put our initials on the bottom so the editor could be assured that we had taken part in our own humiliation. If your spirit wasn't broken that first day, you eventually came out a pretty well-trained sportswriter.

Not everybody survived. I remember one guy saying, 'I don't hafta take this!' and storming out, never to be seen or heard from again.

Those of us who remained, however, became an inseparable band of battle-scarred veterans united by a common bond of shared misery. Somehow, we all knew in our bones that if we could get through three years of crit sheets, then whatever else life threw at us, we would not only endure, but even triumph over. We were half right.

--Ivan N. Kaye, '54

the Maynard Street wars

They say that if a newspaper doesn't make anyone mad, it's not doing its job. Measured by that standard, The Daily can claim a remarkable success rate over the last hundred years.

1929

the Maynard
Street
wars

The
Daily
vs
the board

Even the name has always been a red flag -- the Board in *Control* of Student Publications. And even now, when the name has been changed, the melody lingers on.

In 1929 the Summer Daily carried on a freedom of the press fight with the Board (in public) over the right of the Music and Drama column editor (Leslie Askren) to have unrestricted right to review University play production performances. Askren resigned, and the fight continued in print on the editorial pages for some time that summer, with Prof. Kenneth Thorne, who taught playwriting in the English Department, supporting Askren.

--Lawrence Klein, '30

"WEDDING BELLS"

Reviewed by R. Leslie Askren

(July 13, 1929) When critical reactions to a play differ so widely from the general audience reaction that a play which makes a whole theater rock with laughter seems only a tissue of glumness and horrors, then the critic has no right to criticize... It would be a trifle rash to call the entire audience braying fools, and yet no self respecting critic will admit himself to be one without some definite proof. Perhaps not enjoying "Wedding Bells" is proof enough, but there was no reason why I should not have enjoyed the show if it had been enjoyable; I suppose the only refuge is in the platitude that there is no accounting for tastes.

...

With such conglomerate characters it was fairly easy for the play to split the difference between comedy and farce; and the split was considerably widened by the directing. It is a little difficult to believe that Professor Wallace is entirely responsible for the direction; it looks much more like the work of an inexperienced zealot, afraid that his audience will miss the point. It would have been a relief if occasionally the point could have been missed. The sledgehammer technique becomes a bit tiresome after a while.

...

Of the play itself it is a little difficult to decide whether or not it is the worst that has been offered locally; "Take My Advice" was pretty bad. But then, the audience laughed, and these hot nights a good laugh is a worthwhile achievement, even if this is a University town.#

"CHILDREN OF THE MOON"

Reviewed by R. Leslie Askren

(July 20, 1929) An apology is due those who read in the publicity given this play that it had successful year runs in New York and London. ...[it] is certain that the play was a "flop" in New York.

Presented by a University group it becomes a good deal more than a flop. Judged by my own standards, producing it was an act of distressing immorality; but there are many who will not go that far in condemning it.

...

The theme of the play is the inescapable taint of hereditary insanity and the tragedy that it brings when the usual romantic complication sets in. With such material it is possible to conceive a good play, and Flavin has collected--I do not say conceived--some vivid characters, but the absolutely essential problem was to have made the tragedy inevitable as the outcome of human struggle with an inescapable, inhuman fact. Where Ibsen succeeded Flavin has overlapped this aesthetic distance and probed directly into the festering tissues of the neurosis itself. His conception becomes morbid and decadent, quite without the delicacy of treatment that...discovers an aesthetic of evil.

...

There are laws punishing fakirs for misrepresenting and pawning off false goods on a gullible public; a playwright suffers a "flop." But it is distressing to discover false coin passing through University hands, particularly when such splendid effort as the cast made is wasted upon it.#

A STATEMENT OF POLICY

(July 25, 1929) From this time forward it shall be the policy of The Daily to publish no more reviews of the Play Production efforts in the League theater. This action is necessitated by the resignation of Mr. Leslie Askren, editor of the Music and Drama column of The Daily. In the opinion of the editor there is no one at the present time on the campus eligible scholastically or critically to assume the direction of the column and to maintain on the high basis of sound, constructive critical judgment the work begun by Mr. Askren.

To those who know the state of campus drama there is little doubt of the value of Mr. Askren's work in connection with Prof. Rowe of the rhetoric department, and Valentine Windt of the speech department to take Play Production from a position of ridicule on the campus to their present laboratory in the League theater, where they are, after all, respected and patronized.

And because we are unable to find so capable a man on the campus at present, we are discontinuing the column and the reviews. To allow a writer who lacks Mr. Askren's background and critical, discerning viewpoint to continue with the work would be to undermine the splendid platform of policy for campus dramatics that Mr. Askren has erected.#

A COMMENT

To the Editor:
(July 27, 1929) ...Beyond any questions of what I or anyone else thinks of the content of Mr. Askren's articles, of whether we agree or disagree, principles which should be of concern in a university have been violated. Mr. Askren was exercising what should be a free creative activity, that of literary and dramatic criticism...

...

...To receive adverse as well as favorable criticism, if it is sincere and reasonably competent, furnishes valuable discipline to the student as well as material with which to work for improvement. Such criticism, to be of value, must be independent and unhampered; the university daily furnishes a medium of the same sort as that existing outside the university.

The relation of the Boards of Control to student publications in many universities is such as to interfere with the values which it is the business of a student newspaper to furnish both to its readers and to those who find in it a suitable field of activity, and further, to destroy what a university faculty should support as a fundamental right for the students as well as themselves. It would appear from the present case that such a situation exists in the University of Michigan. The American Association of University Professors stands for freedom of speech for teachers, and for public statement and substantiation of reasons for loss of position...

...

...That Boards of Control are necessary is probably true, in the light of the irresponsibilities that often appear in undergraduate editorial attitude. But control with purpose other than the development of the highest journalistic ethics in what constitutes professional training for the students engaged is itself unethical and tends to accustom the student to the idea of control by special interests such as we decry in the professional press...

...

It would appear to the writer that there has come about a misunderstanding of the functions of criticism, as well as of the purposes of an individual critic. Such a misunderstanding might have been cleared away and not have resulted in the present harm had it not been for the relation of the Board of Control to student publications...#

--Kenneth Rowe

Tilley and I and Pierce Rosenberg were the leading candidates for managing editor in 1929-30. Tilley was certainly the most brilliant. But the Board turned down all three of us. Tilley was considered too impulsive and irresponsible. I was considered only a little less impulsive and considerably less brilliant. Tilley got an editorial-writing job; my consolation prize was managing editor of the Summer Daily, and during the academic year I ran alternate books and Toasted Rolls columns and as a matter of fact continued the two columns during my graduate year. A grim put-down to the candidates was in drafting Ellis Merry from the Law School to be in charge as editorial director.

* * *

The Board in Control of Student Publications, headed by Professor Sunderland of the Law School, pretty much left The Daily to run things as the top staff saw fit. Sunderland's secretary, Eugenia Allen, sat in the business office like an empress. She had certain rules of conduct. No one on the day side could smoke, on pain of a dressing-down and a call from the Board if there were persistent indiscretions. The night staff could smoke, but Miss Allen would arrive at nine in the morning, sniff the air in disgust and throw open all the windows, even in zero weather. All this was during Prohibition, and what Miss Allen never discovered (or at least appeared not to) was the drinking in the conference room and the plying of their trade by bootleggers at night. Most of the salesmen were students.

--Lawrence Klein, '30

Neal Resigns With Charges Of Censorship

Accuses Board Chairman Of Direct, And Ruthven Of Indirect Suppression

(Mar. 20, 1937) Charging University censorship of the news columns of The Daily, Fred Warner Neal, '37, associate editor, resigned from his position yesterday.

Prof. William A. McLaughlin of the Romance Language department, chairman of the Board in Control of Student Publications, was charged in Neal's statement with direct censorship and President Ruthven was accused of indirect censorship.

...

Order for Deletion

Neal's action came, he said, as a result of Prof. McLaughlin's "order for deletion" of a portion of an interview secured in Lansing that day concerning a statement from a member of the Legislature, Rep. Harry Glass, Democrat from Grand Rapids, in which Mr. Glass changed his former position of opposition to the University appropriation bill, by pledging support of any appropriation for the University agreed on by the ways and means committee of the House.

Neal's statement reads as follows: "I am resigning from my position as associate editor of The Michigan Daily because The Daily was censored by University authorities.

"The censorship and order of suppression came the night of March 17 from Prof. William A. McLaughlin of the Romance Language department, chairman of the board in control of student publications. He ordered that a portion of a story concerning a statement from a member of the Legislature be deleted. President Ruthven said in a telephone conversation later that evening that he would not directly order the story out and 'that the Board in Control runs The Daily, and you will have to take your orders from it.'

Misunderstood the Rules

"The President further said that 'no student or no professor has the right to go to Lansing during the sessions of the Legislature.'

...

"I simply do not choose to work on The Daily under those conditions. I have misunderstood the rules of the game. I had labored under the misapprehension that The Daily was a newspaper, its news columns open to all news. I find that that is not so; that The Daily may not print material to which the University administration objects, that, although it does not speak for the University, it is a University organ.

Urges Clarification

"I regret to leave The Daily. There is absolutely no animosity between Professor McLaughlin and myself. He is acting according to what he believes to be the best interests of the University. I respect him, but his concept of The Daily simply differs from mine.

"As an employee of the Board in Control, after the order not to run the story from Lansing, I had no alternative but to obey. I do not choose, however, to remain subject to such orders in the future.

"I will be glad to be of any assistance to The Daily in the future, in an unofficial capacity.

"The status of The Daily with regard to the University was, to me, apparently, in doubt. I think it should be made clear.

"Fred Warner Neal."

One

To the Editor:

(Mar. 23, 1937) It is most unfortunate that Mr. Neal was forced to martyr himself that the students and faculty of the University might be made aware of a situation which seems to be completely out of line with the liberal ideas of education at times expressed by President Ruthven.

...If Mr. Neal is correct in quoting Prof. McLaughlin as saying that a part of a story had to be deleted because "President Ruthven would not like it," is there any possibility of The Daily's editors making clear the relation between President Ruthven, the Board in Control of Student Publications and The Daily?

Yet the students who read and support The Daily have a right to know whether or not the paper is just an enlarged Daily Official Bulletin.

...The Daily did not print the statement by Representative Glass which Mr. McLaughlin ordered deleted. May I be permitted to quote that statement from the Detroit Free Press:

"Certainly I do not like the arbitrary measures which Gov. LaFollette was forced to employ in order to bring the University of Wisconsin up to the liberal thinking and progressive ideals of the people of Wisconsin. I sincerely trust that nothing so drastic will be necessary for the State of Michigan."

As I understand it, the function of The Daily or any other newspaper is to print "all the news." Rep. Glass's statement was news...

As a body particularly interested in the well-being of the University, The Daily would seem to have severe and frank criticism as one of its prime functions. Otherwise it should be frankly recognized as just another University Publication, on a par with the monthly bulletins and the catalogue.

If the situation cannot be improved it should be clarified so that the students of the University may know how to interpret and understand the stories which they read in the columns of The Daily, and so that they may know whether or not The Daily is worthy of their support.

-- **An Interested Student**

Hardly anything the Board did caused a greater disturbance among Daily staffers than the notorious "Signed Editorials" directive in 1937.

This is how it looked when they got it all lined up on March 2, 1938:

The editorials published in The Michigan Daily are written by members of The Daily staff and represent the views of the writers only.

It is important for society to avoid the neglect of adults, but positively dangerous for it to thwart the ambition of youth to reform the world. Only the schools which act on this belief are educational institutions in the best meaning of the term.

Alexander G. Ruthven

The darkest hour for The Daily while I was there was a kind of inquisition by the Board. The Board, like the rest of the faculty and student body, was quite conservative. (In 1936, the year I arrived in Ann Arbor, there was a straw poll of the students and faculty on the presidential election, and Alf Landon, who in the actual election carried only Maine and Vermont, won an overwhelming victory!)

The Board simply didn't like the fact that the editorials in The Daily (like those about the German annexation of Austria) were liberal. It decided that the way to put a stop to it was to smoke out the radicals who were writing that stuff, who in their view were hiding behind the anonymity of the editorials. They ordered that the editorials be signed!

--Dennis Flanagan, '40

Looking back today, I'd say the fascinating thing about the board-staff conflict of the Thirties is the fact that it was so purely ideological. No campus issues were involved, only broad political ideology, which did not prevent the conflict from being sharp, bitter and meaningful.

--Joseph Gies, '39

A Statement Of Principle...

WE, THE EDITORS of The Michigan Daily, believe so thoroughly in the principles expressed by President Ruthven in his speech Friday, Feb. 25, in New York City, that we have selected a part of his address to serve as a guiding principle for those who are interested in greater freedom for student thought. This selection will appear in The Daily every day hereafter in this column immediately below the masthead.

Joseph S. Mattes
Tuure Tenander
Irving Silverman
William Spaller
Robert Weeks

At a meeting on November 8, 1937, the Board decided that henceforth all ed-itorials appearing in The Daily must be signed by the writer. In addition, the Board imposed the following statement to appear on the editorial page:
The editorials published in The Michigan Daily are written by members of The Daily staff and represent the views of the writers only.
Needless to say, all of the seniors and almost all juniors were most upset at this naked vitiation of the stance that The Daily staff might take on any given subject. We were all angered by this action which, we felt, was a totally unwarranted restriction on our editorial freedom.
At the time, one of the columns we were running every day was UNDER THE CLOCK - with Disraeli. (Written by Earle Luby, a voluntary contributor). In the November 11 issue Disraeli inserted the following below the column heading:
EDITOR'S NOTE
The editorials published in Under The Clock are written by Disraeli and they are not his at all, but just some things he picked up on the back of old beer skimmers at the Bell. You know how he does get around.
Although we were smarting under this restriction we didn't know how to fight back until opportunity knocked in a totally unexpected way. In late February of 1938 President Ruthven addressed the University of Michigan Club in New York.
The cover story of the speech was in the Saturday, February 26 Daily. We held strategy sessions over the weekend and on Tuesday, March 1, we ran an editorial in which we lauded President Ruthven, quoting extensively from his speech.
On Thursday, March 3, the boxed quotation from President Ruthven appeared under the masthead, above the statement concerning signed editorials, and it was run in every subsequent issue of that semester.
--Tuure Tenander, '38

Thanks Prof. Slosson...

To the Editor:

(Jan. 25, 1938) Permit a teacher of history to express his deep appreciation of the work which the editorial board of The Daily has for some time been doing in awakening the interest of the student body in important national and international problems. In this way you can be as truly an educative force as any department of the faculty, if not more so. That occasionally an editorial contains a statement that runs counter to my own opinions is not alarming; what would be alarming would be trite or conventional editorials always reflecting the opinions of older people. It would mean imitation in place of thought. I am glad that peace, civil liberty and economic justice are more interesting than "Poo," "Foo," frats and football...

--Preston Slosson

'Seven Old Men' Of Publications Board Sit In Judgment Today

(May 14, 1938) Seven men, each one carrying a portfolio, will file into a conference room on the second story of a red and gray brick building on Maynard Street at 8:30 this morning. For several hours they will discuss the contents of the portfolios around a highly polished table. They will come to decisions -- decisions that will be awaited by a group of students who have known during these last few days only dementia praecox in their waking hours and insomnia at night.

The seven men are the four faculty members and the three student members of the Board in Control of Student Publications. The expectant students are those palsied remnants of undergraduate manhood who are waiting for the announcements of next year's senior positions on Michigan's student publications.

...

Each member of the Board receives a copy of each petition and recommendation (about 46 documents in all) and is supposed to read each one before bringing them to the conference. There, staff votes, recommendations and petitions are discussed by the Board members before appointments are made...#

Student Senate Hits
Daily Appointment,
Asks New Hearing

Claims Publications Board Abandoned Past Criteria Of Merit In Selection

By ROBERT D. MITCHELL

(May 25, 1938) The Student Senate last night charged that the appointment of the managing editor of the Michigan Daily for the year 1938-39 was not made on a merit basis and demanded that the Board in Control of Student Publications immediately reconsider its own action.

...

The Senate further asked that President Ruthven, in making new faculty appointments to the Board "take into account the present Board's violation of its own established rules of appointment."

...

The Senate moved this action after evidence was introduced by Speaker Richard M. Scammon, who interviewed the chairman of the Board and the outgoing senior editors upon the petition of 10 members of the Senate. The seven criteria for the Board's appointments as enumerated by Prof. William McLaughlin, chairman of the Board, were reported by Scammon at the meeting to be: the recommendations of the retiring senior editors, vote of the entire Daily staff, grades, recommendations of the composing room staff, individual petitions of the applicants for the post, personal interviews and the general record of service of The Daily.

It was claimed that as far as could be determined the appointee led the field in only one of these respects, namely grades. However, Scammon submitted that he had discovered that four of the other five leading contenders for the position possessed better than a "B" average.

Prof. Louis Strauss, a member of the Board, was reported to have stated at the Spring Parley discussions that the recommendations of the retiring Senior editors were rated as 90 per cent of the basis for the Board's appointments. Scammon fur-ther reported that Professor McLaughlin told him that never in past years have the recommendations of all the outgoing senior editors been disregarded.

Senators claimed that the appointee was not named by any one of the retiring senior editors for any one of the three major senior positions, and thus maintained that the Board had ignored its own standards in making the appointments...#

The Spring of 1938 would be an interesting time to revive. Elections for the Board in Control were held in a pep rally atmosphere. We felt we could get control of the Board by electing three right-minded (read left-minded) students who would vote with one sympathetic faculty member and give us a 4-3 majority. Very exciting. Old-time election tactics, complete with telephone teams and taxicab pickup.

And that is what happened. But alas, one of the student winners was declared ineligible because his academic standing had suffered during the campaign!

--Robert Fitzhenry, '39

Publications Board Posts Won By Quick, Sizemore and Kahn

(May 25, 1938) George Quick, '38, with 713 votes, Roy Sizemore, '39F&C, with 524 votes, and Robert Kahn, '39, with 506 votes were chose above the eight other candidates running for the three coveted positions on the Board in Control of Student Publications, when more than 1,400 students, an unprecedented number, went to the polls yesterday in the annual all-campus elections.

...

Accompanying the election were the uglier features of politics. Several candidates are threatening to protest the election, and charges have been made that fraternities stuffed the ballot boxes with the blanks that were used when the regular printed ballots gave out early in the voting period. Charges of electioneering at the polls and double-voting have also been made... #

Official Statement About Expulsions Given By Ruthven

President Denies Action Taken Because Of Students' Political Views; Hearing On Dismissals Scheduled For November 9

At one point I, along with Al Sarasohn, the Editorial Director, were suspended for a week because of a letter we allowed to run in the Letters to the Editor column, from the American Student Union. Al and I had to fend off offers from such well-known rabble-rousers as Gerald L.K. Smith to come to campus and organize a protest rally.

—J. Hervie Haufler, '41

(Oct. 17, 1940) President Ruthven admitted today, for the first time officially, that nine University students had been asked not to return to the University for another year.

He said they had been banned for activities deemed "disruptive of good order in the University." He declined to elaborate on this clause.

He flatly denied that the action had been taken because of the students' political views, their stance on conscription, their membership in the American Student Union, or their opposition to governmental policies.

...

Explained Dr. Ruthven:

"It is the opinion of the University authorities that students in the University of Michigan and other State schools are guests of the State, and even if they do not respect this hospitality they should not in justice to other students be permitted to abuse it. As educators generally are aware, there are a few, and fortunately only a few, students in most institutions of higher education today who interpret their civil rights to include license to do anything they want to do on the plea that they are 'liberals.' This is a perverted concept of civil liberties and not 'liberalism' in the best sense of the term."

The President's statement...came in the heat of demands by the Michigan Committee for Academic Freedom for a public hearing on the matter...

...

About hearings the President said this in his prepared statement:

"It has been asserted that the students were denied the opportunity to be heard in their own defense. These are deliberate misrepresentations. All who have asked for conferences have been heard by proper University authorities and the others have been told that they would be heard if they so requested.

"Two or three asked for a public trial. This request was refused as contrary to the practice of the University and against the best interests of the students."..#

Davis Speaks At Trial Of 13 Students Told Not To Return

(Nov. 10, 1940) ..."President Ruthven told me that there was no such thing as academic freedom for students when I interviewed him several days ago," Prof. Jerome Davis of the New School for Social Research testified yesterday before 600 shivering people who had gathered in Island Park to hear the open "hearing" of the 13 students who were asked not to return to the University.

The "hearing," sponsored by the Michigan Committee for Academic Freedom, featured the testimony of Hugo Richard and Nat Rinzberg, former Michigan students who answered the queries put to them by Maurice Sugar, prominent labor attorney.

...

Remarking that in the 49 years of his academic career he had never head of such treatment to students, [American Civil Liberties Union chairman and University of Wisconsin Prof. E. A.] Ross declared that "if some of these students have given ill-conceived opinions it is the responsibility of others to refute them rather than deny the students the opportunity to express them."

Reichard Testifies

Reichard...read the letter which he received from President Ruthven in June stating, "It is the decision of the authorities of the University of Michigan that you cannot be readmitted to the University."

Neither before or after this note were any charges or complaints preferred, Reichard declared. In my interview with President Ruthven he intimated that it was I who had announced the dismissal, Reichard said in declaring that to keep quiet about the affair would have been an admission of being guilty of charges he had never been informed of.

...

...Nat Rinzberg...quoted from Ruthven's letter to him stating that he had been a disturbing influence among the students on the campus.

Rinzberg Speaks

What constitutes a disturbing influence on the Michigan campus has never been defined, Rinzberg said.

When the President was asked on what authority he expelled me, he told me that if he were expelling me I should have a hearing, but that he was not expelling me but only asking me not to return, Rinzberg related.

Then Roger Lawn, '43, testified that he had received a warning telling him he should go "right" and shouldn't spend so much time with a "certain group of students."#

The Little Red Schoolhouse...

(Nov. 12, 1940) OUR PRESIDENT DR. RUTHVEN has once again given the Michigan campus a moment to pause and think.

In Chicago last week-end Dr. Ruthven made a new address in which he advanced the somewhat befogged warning that "administrative officers and professors of colleges and universities should rid themselves of the notion that romanticism, sentimentalism and indiscriminate tolerance are essential constituents of democracy."

He also said that faculty members who countenance indiscriminate criticism of the democratic form of government should quit their profession.

...

THE CAMPUS has not yet forgotten that June Commencement address, wherein Mr. Ruthven informed the state of Michigan that:

"Michigan welcomes only students who are convinced that democracy is the ideal form of government for a civilized people. She will not be confused by sophistries built around meaningful but ill-defined phrases, such as 'freedom of the press' and 'freedom of speech' but will deal firmly, without fear or favor, with subversive or so-called 'fifth column' activities."

...

Then there's the case of the nine students who were asked not to reenter this fall. It's best not to play with this little nugget--it's full of dynamite. It isn't necessary, however, to discuss the background of the incident. It is sufficient to say that this simple action by the University has aroused varied reactions...

...

Now we have this Chicago address. Frankly, we don't know what Dr. Ruthven actually meant by his message saying that "freedom of independent thinking, expression, and assembly in our schools is not license for students and faculty to work against the very form of government which allows such rights to exist," but although we don't understand it, we are sure that it is being interpreted in a way which bodes no good for an educational institution which has always done its best to remain a seat of opportunity in which one may learn liberally and broadmindedly...#

--Paul M. Chandler

The Crime...

Letters To The Editor

A Reply To The Judiciary Council

(Nov. 26, 1940) In the Michigan Daily of November 19 a letter from the Men's Judiciary Council--a University selected body of conservative students--attempted to defend President Ruthven's dismissal of some thirteen University of Michigan students. The basic argument of the letter was simply and directly stated; in dismissing these students from the University, President Ruthven had "to forego his personal belief in academic freedom" so that he could erase the undeserved reputation of the University with its financial support.

...

To state as the Council does, that the University is faced with the 'demands of three or four students' is an unforgivable understatement. There are the thirteen students who were separated from their education, and a list of over 60 prominent Americans, who ardently desire the granting of an open hearing. The list includes such persons as Franklin P. Adams, James Truslow Adams, Franz Boas, Dashiell Hammett, Rockwell Kent, Max Lerner, Robert S. Lynd, R. J. Thomas, and 52 more. And to state, as the Council does, that nine students asked for no further publicity must be denied in the light of the fact that thirteen students have indicated that they would defend themselves if charges were made.

THE MEN'S JUDICIARY COUNCIL further states 'that a person is entitled only to rights which do not work ill upon the majority.' From this premise the council and the University is unequivocally led to the dangerous doctrine that the interests of the majority are best served by the suppression of a minority.

...

The 'ill upon the majority' in this instance, states the Council, is the tuition raise. They attribute the tuition raise to a state deficit and to the 'free tongue and free pen...which the Administration and the Council have permitted' (sic)!

....

WE DENY that the 'legislature' or the 'people' of the state effected the tuition raise and the expulsion of the Michigan students. We affirm that President Ruthven is not the person primarily responsible. We wish to point only to the make-up of the Board of Regents and let the implications speak for themselves. The University's Board of Regents contains, among its eight members, Michigan's former head football coach, Harry Kipke, who as a candidate for his post received the aid of Ford's anti-union personnel director, Harry Bennett. Since his election, Kipke has been given the luncheon concession at the River Rouge plant. Five of the Regents are corporation lawyers. One, a Democratic nation committeeman, was formerly legal counsel for Consumers Power, a subsidiary of Commonwealth and Southern. Another was chairman of a Garner-for-President Committee. The seventh is a retired banker. The eight is the wife of a General Motors executive. (S. R. Kays, The Nation, Sept. 14, 1940)

....

THE REAL SIGNIFICANCE of the case of Michigan may be summarized in these words: In the name of national unity for war, all opposition to moves which mean involvement must be silenced. Hence there will be a number of college presidents who will deny the existence of academic freedom in order to goose-step the weak and timid into another war. They seek to inoculate students with the stereotypes and superstitions of the dominant groups in control. They desire not free men but robots, weak and pitiful conformists clinging to the futile phobias of the past. They are the handmates of the interests that seek to break the backbone of labor, the CIO, emasculate the progressive measures of 1933-38, strike fear and apathy into the 'little people' and then plunge our country into a conflict on two oceans and two continents.

--Harold Norris, Chairman
The American Student Union

The Punishment...

For Dr. Ruthven And The Regents...

GENTLEMEN:

(Dec. 5, 1940) **WE TOOK OVER** management of The Daily last spring after it had been in what was charged were radical hands for five or six years prior. The Daily was in trouble because it had sung the praises of the American Student Union, had taken sides in strikes, had defended and, at times, fostered radical activities on campus. The Daily, it was said, had been one of the causes for the belief throughout much of the state that "Michigan is a center of subversive thought and a hotbed of radical activities."

However true these charges may be, last spring it seemed to us that the greatest service we could do for The Daily and the University was to stay clear of radical viewpoints and overemphasis of the activities of leftist groups. We did not want a censored paper, a "safe" paper. We held no brief against the American Student Union. We felt that we could publish a representative Daily without compromising our principles.

IF WE have done one job, however, we have fallen down on another; we have failed to keep as sharp a vigilance on campus matters as was needed. We know that you, Dr. Ruthven, have felt an occasional irritation with The Daily this fall. All we can say is that even though this is an ordered apology, we believe that you have tried to deal honestly and fairly with The Daily, and that, if through some possible errors on our part we have complicated your task still more, then we are sincerely sorry.

The ASU's letter, which has caused the trouble, made or implied charges against the Regents which are entirely foreign to the viewpoint of The Daily editors. Since letters in The Daily are often considered the expression of the paper's, and sometimes the University's attitude, this letter should either not have been run at all, or should have been supplemented by an explanation that the opinions expressed were entirely those of the ASU. For our remissness in this, we offer our apologies--again sincerely in spite of their being obligatory.

IF THESE PARAGRAPHS above are interpreted as meaning merely that we are running to cover, knuckling under, the interpreters are wrong. We are able, we insist, to say these things sincerely to Dr. Ruthven and the Regents. This apology seems to us the most just part of our penalty. But we do feel that some sort of disciplinary action could have been taken without subjecting us and The Daily to a lot of unhelpful publicity, and without making us the unwilling dupes of the many "civil rights" groups seeking to find an issue in such cases.

--Hervie Haufler
--Alvin Sarasohn

The Sting...

An Opinion On Freedom Of Speech...

(Dec. 20, 1940) Down at the University ultra-radical groups are finding that they are embarked on a real trail of trouble if they continue to defy or argue with constituted authority. No one seeks to deny students the right to "think for themselves," but when that thinking brings them to those radical conclusions entirely out of line with good sense and good taste in public expression, it certainly is time that these individuals picked some other sounding board than that of the state university.

We haven't a doubt but what President Ruthven's dismissal last summer of thirteen students for engaging in activities contrary to the best interests of the University, was entirely justified by the investigation which he and other University officials made before they took this action. President Ruthven impresses us as a man of real fairness and excellent judgment.

The fact that the so-called "American Committee for Democratic and Intellectual Freedom"--made up of assorted professed liberals, largely from the eastern states--is inclined to make an issue out of the affair isn't a matter of any particular moment to most of the people of Michigan...

The American Student Union has the reputation of being closely allied with the Communist endeavor. ...in a sort of blatant challenge to University authority, the local ASU chapter has been the latest to feel the hand of University discipline...

We believe that following through on President Ruthven's action of the summer, is just what is needed... If the freedom of speech of these individuals originates from some other place, if at all, the state of Michigan and its University are going to be considerably better off thereby.

--Isabella County Times-News
(reprinted in the
Ann Arbor Daily News)

'Packing' Of Publications Board Is Seen

By PAUL CHANDLER
(The Daily City Editor)

(May 2, 1941) President Ruthven will make public in the near future a new plan, approved already by the Board of Regents, that will "pack" the Board in Control of Student Publications with more faculty members.

This information was learned from well-informed sources by The Daily Editors yesterday. An official announcement of the action is expected to be given to the Board itself at a meeting with President Ruthven tonight.

...

The new Board will be composed of six faculty members, two alumni members, and three students, all with a single vote, it was learned.

President Ruthven has called a meeting of some of the Board members for Friday night, but he has not indicated what subject will be discussed...

Apparently the student members of the Board have not been invited to the meeting... James Tobin, '41, Phillip Westbrook, '42L, and Albert Mayio, Grad, said last night that they had not been asked to attend any such conference...#

An Editorial...

By HERVIE HAUFLER and ALVIN SARASOHN

(May 2, 1941) **LAST NOVEMBER** we editors of The Daily leaned over backwards in our attempt to work along with the University administration. After we had apologized and taken without protest a week's suspension from the staff for a deed of whose wrongness we are still not fully convinced, we felt that we had acted in good faith with them and had done what we could to improve relations with the University.

We do not believe that the University, now that its turn for fair play has come, has acted in good faith with us in the present issue of "packing" the Board in Control of Student Publications.

...

THE UNIVERSITY has known for five months that two alumni members and two Faculty Senate members would be added to the Board in Control of Student Publications. Yet it has waited until just before appointments--a period marked by the confusion and disorganization of changing staffs--to allow word of the "packing" plan to go before the public.

No time was left for any sort of discussion or protest. No chance has been left for supporters of the present set-up of The Daily to marshal the support of alumni, students and faculty. Even now, the plan has been learned of only through the piecing together of many small bits of information.

In a word, the Administration has not kept faith with us.

...

The Daily, we feel, in its best years has been the organ of the students... This action will take it out of the hands of the students who have worked it up into what it is today and--we have every fear--will make of it little more than a glorified house organ, singing emptily the praises of its masters. But no one will listen. No one will look. No one will want to read. That is the greatest tragedy, we feel. A Daily that is not the paper of students will be looked upon as a great Daily Official Bulletin. And that is what, in fact, it will be.

...

IT HAS BEEN SAID that freedom of thought and expression have been stifled on this campus during the past year. The Daily is the only organ in which all types of opinion have been expressible to a large audience--whether by editorial column, guest editorial, or a large-sized letter column which has always welcomed every intel-ligent contribution. If Michigan is to remain an institution where we are to gather some of the richness of the real University, The Daily must remain a student paper.#

1937-41 was a time of tense feelings between the Administration and The Daily editors. During the thirties the Daily editors were frequently more radical than the Administration liked. Daily stories were quoted on the floor of the State legislature to prove that the U of M (unlike Michigan's udder college) was a 'hotbed of Communists' and therefore unworthy of State funds.

The four faculty members who made up a majority on the Board were put there specifically to keep the lid on, and they frequently voted as a bloc against the three graduate student members. Came a vacancy among the faculty members, and the Administration goofed. They appointed Professor Calderwood who, at times, had the temerity to vote with the students. The Administration couldn't allow this, so they quietly planned to enlarge the faculty membership.

This plan to 'pack' the Board exploded in 1940-41 during my tenure as Managing Editor. My group of editors ended our tenure in banner-headline revolt against the packing plan, and the incidents leave scars in my memory.

--J. Hervie Haufler, '41

Faculty, Students Voice Disapproval
Of Publications Board 'Packing' Plan

Apparently prompted by news that the Board of Regents intends to "pack" the Board in Control... a prankster made a perilous journey yesterday down from a second story window to paste a piece of paper over the word "Student" in... the inscription over the entrance to the Student Publications Building...

Board 'Packing' Evokes Campus Protest

By PAUL M. CHANDLER
(The Daily City Editor)

(May 3, 1941) A rising storm of protest was expected to roll in from the campus today as the Board in Control of Student Publications convened in a tense meeting to consider a proposal that would leave Daily policy virtually in the hands of the faculty.

The Board was to meet at 9 a.m. to consider a resolution that would make its corporate laws conform to a by-law approved by the Regents which would "pack" the board with more faculty and alumni members.

Although meeting ostensibly to consider the "technicality" it is anticipated that the Board meeting will be devoted to a heated discussion of student versus faculty control of The Daily.

...

Students and faculty have united in protest against the "packing" since The Daily reported yesterday that the Board of Regents was about to make public the new by-law.

Leaders Submit Statement

Many campus leaders have submitted statements attacking the proposal, some of which are printed elsewhere in The Daily.

Other groups of faculty members were thought to be organizing to ask for a new hearing on the entire subject of student publications.

Early yesterday an unidentified prankster climbed through a second story window, a perilous journey, and covered with a piece of paper the word 'Student' in Student Publications over the doorway to the Student Publications Building.

The covering was later removed with sponge and water by a Daily janitor...#

(May 3, 1941) Protests against the proposed "packing" of the Board in Control of Student Publications have been coming in steadily to The Daily from all quarters on campus. Reproduced below are some of the most representative opinions:

Prof. John L. Brumm, Chairman of Journalism Department: "Believing that a widespread tolerance is the only quality which can save our democracy from defeat during this time of conflicting views, I should regret any authoritative action to limit the free expression of opinion at the University of Michigan...

"There may be marked differences between faculty and student opinion, but democracy requires that a free people or a free university shall risk what it may be needful to risk in avoiding anything which has the appearance of intolerance or censorship..."

Prof. Mentor Williams, English Department: "In view of the responsibility as shown by The Daily in the last two years and in view of the record it has made among other college papers the nation over, this action is inexcusable..."

Prof. I. G. Vander Velde, History Department: "I frequently disagree with The Daily, but I am always interested in it as an organ of student opinion. If the change in the composition of the Board in Control of Student Publications means that The Daily is to become an organ expressing not what the students think, but what the faculty would like to have them think, the real function of the paper will be frustrated..."

Tom Harmon, Number 98: "The Michigan Daily will be a better newspaper if the present ratio of four faculty members to three students is maintained on the Board in Control."

Charles Heinen, Secretary, Michigan Union: "The move to pack the Board in Control is, in my opinion, ideologically unsound, practically unfair, and tactically insulting to the intelligence of the Student Body.

"Threatening students, attempting to state the student point of view with an overwhelming of non-student control is certainly coercion. It can lead to nothing but nonthinking and sycophancy, certainly not aims of our democratic ideal..."#

Regents Stand Pat On Board Increase

Action Overrides Student Petitions Against Changes

(May 24, 1941) Disregarding the expressed opposition of more than 4,350 students, the Regents of the University went ahead yesterday in their determination to increase faculty control of the Board in Control of Student Publications.

Acting upon the report of the Committee on Public Relations, which met early in the afternoon with members of the Publications Board, the Regents announced that they saw "no reason to rescind or change their former action on this by-law."

Following the meeting, Regent Harry Kipke said that the proposed change in membership, as provided in the by-laws adopted at the December meeting of the Regents, was necessary to "improve relations between The Daily, the University and the public."

He explained that now the only action necessary to make the change final is the approval of the Publications Board itself.

"There is no doubt, however, that the members of the Board will agree to the increase. We shall probably appoint the two new faculty representatives at the next Regents' meeting June 20."

Add Two Faculty Members

The plan would not only add two faculty members, but would also give votes to the two non-voting alumni, thus making the ratio nine to three against the students as compared to the existing four to three set-up.

Nothing was said to indicate that the signatures of almost 4,500 students opposing the increase which were presented to President Alexander Ruthven before the meeting, were considered in the action. #

An Editorial...

(May 25, 1941) **SINCE FRIDAY** when the Regents voted once more that the "faculty must dominate the Publications Board" we have had time to reflect. We have reflected about the shallow conception of democracy that says that students may not participate in the responsibility of their own newspaper, (for the student members of the Board are to be in effect only "advisers" hereafter). We have reflected also on the conception of a University which allows so flagrant a disregard of the University's own constituents--the students and the faculty. The protests of 4,350 students were passed off like water off a duck's back, as were, what is asserted to be the "maturer" opinion, of a great many faculty members.

...

For the time being the reorganization plan is on the books--as securely as the draft. Histrionics now aren't going to remove it from the books. The plan--given with the pledge that it would never go further than administer the student formulated Daily Code of Ethics--is one of those givens under which we must continue to put out the same free and Pacemaker Award newspaper of the past...

...

If at any time the pledge of those who initiated the reorganization plan is broken, if the letter and editorial pages of The Daily are throttled and no longer represent student opinion, the campus will hear about it and can act upon it. As for the editors, we believe that a philosophy which would allow such a move is unworthy to be taught or learned. We would have to leave with the hope that our action would effect a better good.

* * * *

WE ARE CONFIDENT that such a move will not be taken. Though we will lend our influence to undoing what has been done, ours is the greater and more profitable task of continuing to publish a free and respected Daily. Given the situation, there lies the greater good. #

Robert Speckhard	Emile Gele
Albert P. Blaustein	Alvin Dann
David Lachenbruch	

1943

3 More Daily Editors Hand in Resignations

The Battle of 1943 started almost unnoticed, with a small, magnanimous gesture on the part of the outgoing senior editors toward the juniors. It escalated into one of the longest and most deadly battles in all the annals of the Maynard Street Wars.

(January 5, 1943) Three more Daily editors yesterday resigned their posts effective the first day of next semester.

Morton Mintz, Editorial Director, Will Sapp, City Editor, and George Sallade, Associate Editor, gave their resignations to the Board in Control of Student Publications to leave the five senior staff positions open next semester.

Homer Swander, Managing Editor, has already announced his resignation... Sports Editor Bud Hendel and Associate Sports Editor Mike Dann also announced their intention to resign yesterday...

All resignations were attributed to a desire to open positions to junior staff members who might otherwise miss the opportunity of getting a top job. #

AN EDITORIAL:
Board Cripples Michigan Daily

(Jan. 17, 1943) WE ALWAYS believed that hard work, initiative and competence were the criteria for promotion on The Michigan Daily and that your student newspaper, in the best interests of the University, was to be run for and by the students.

Yesterday a faculty-dominated Board in Control showed us once again that this is not true.

They refused to appoint to a senior position one of the most deserving applicants on the staff. They refused to appoint a student whose work both in quality and quantity led that of other Junior Night Editors, and who was voted in the top range by the staff he would have had to work with.

He was NOT appointed because he believed in telling the truth, because he believed that The Daily should be an active, constructive student newspaper unhampered by the whims of individual Board members, and, we believe, because of his religion.

The fact that Leon Gordenker did not receive an appointment is not all-important. The reasons why he did not, the haphazard manner in which the Board investigated the applicants and the general attitude of the Board throughout the past year ARE important.

The only time some of the Board members have shown a genuine interest in The Daily was when they were, through one means or another, attempting to stifle the student thought expressed therein. Representing a University which is sup-

posed to train young people to take their place in a democracy, Board members have time and time again shown that they are afraid to let students think for themselves. On every local controversial issue--and many national--which The Daily has discussed in its editorial or news columns, the students have had to fight for the right to reveal facts and express opinions.

...

One question, asked of Gordenker in a pre-appointment interview, illustrates how little some members of the Board know about The Daily:

The questioner wanted to know why, when Gordenker was night editor of a certain issue, he let an "objectionable" editorial appear. After a year and a half on the Board, the member should have known that the night editor has absolutely no control over what editorial appears in The Daily. The choice of editorials is entirely in the hands of the Managing Editor and the Editorial Director. Through inexcusable lack of knowledge on the part of a Board member, then, Gordenker's chances were jeopardized by something over which he had no control.

Although the majority of Board members certainly do not let questions of race or religion enter into their calculations, we believe this is not true of the entire Board. Last spring, for instance, when the newly-appointed Managing Editor, Homer Swander, presented his list of recommendations for junior night editorships, one of the questions asked him

was: "How many of them are Jewish?"

The Board has not confined its criticisms to questions of ethics, objectivity or accuracy. It has reacted innumerable times to the selfish pressures of various individuals and groups, rather than trying to obtain in The Daily a clear and unprejudiced perspective.

The stress placed by the Board on factors which have no place in fair and rational judgments inevitably results in an emphasis on servility rather than on competence.

To you, as students of the University and readers of The Daily, this means that your paper is in danger of losing every vestige of that freedom of expression which is essential to a democracy. It also means that the best student talent available will not necessarily be putting out The Daily.

And in the final analysis it means that a group of faculty men who have taken little interest in the real problems of the students, who are afraid to let students think for themselves and who know practically nothing about working journalism, will be telling you how to run your newspaper. #

Retiring Editors:	Incoming Editors:
Homer Swander	John Erlewine
Morton Mintz	Irving Jaffe
Will Sapp	Bud Brimmer
Chuck Thatcher	Marion Ford
George Sallade	Charlotte Conover
Bud Hendel	
Mike Dann	
Barbara DeFries	

Campus Backs Daily

(Jan. 21, 1943) **Arthur Maehlman, School of Education:** ...Our newspapers must be freed from petty censorship that now hampers them in their essential task of keeping the public informed of the progress of the war and of maintaining their struggle against greed, intolerance, and slavery and thus serve as reliable guides in adult education.

In my opinion you are publishing an outstanding student newspaper. More power to you.

* * *

Elsie Litman, '43SM; Betty Lefferts, and Gaye Locke, '43: The United Nations are now engaged in a war for the preservation of the Four Freedoms and the liberation of peoples throughout the world. This war entails more than just a military victory; it means we must live and practice those very ideals for which we are fighting. The actions of the Board of Publications are in direct contradiction to those aims...

WE CANNOT expect to win a just peace if we fail to practice democracy during the war. The students are indignant at this obvious violation of democracy. The requests of the Sunday and Tuesday editorials must be granted!

* * *

Jim Conant, '44: After the brilliant editorials in Sunday's and Tuesday's papers, this won't prove much. It might have a little interest, however, as coming from one who has written in objecting to the violent tone of a crusading Daily editorial, to what he believed was unjustified mud-slinging.

That editorial, I still think, slung mud. Other Daily editorials in the past have slung mud. Daily editorials in the future may indulge in it. But one who believes sincerely and vigorously in a cause always finds it difficult to keep his pen within the bounds of calmness; and, any-way, it would seem to me that when you disagree with somebody the thing to do is to address his arguments, rather than to exert pressure to prevent his having an audience in the future...

* * *

Norman Anning, mathematics department: I have been a friendly critic of The Daily and expect to be one as long as I am around to reflect light, resist pressure, and react to irritation. When I bring you a suggestion you take it out of my hand and then exercise your right to act upon it or destroy it as seems best. That's just one trivial aspect of free journalism.

...

If your path to the seven freedoms leads, as you seem to believe, by way of the thumbscrew and the stake, you can at least go down fighting, secure in the belief that nothing worth saving can be permanently lost.

I praise your grit.#

AN EDITORIAL:
Editors Ask Densmore to Resign Board Position

(Jan. 19, 1943) THIS EDITORIAL asks the resignation of Prof. G. E. Densmore from his post as chairman of the Board in Control of Student Publications.

As the Senior Editors of The Daily, we have been closely associated with Prof. Densmore during the past eight months and are now convinced that he does not possess the qualifications required for the important position of chairman of the Board.

Relations between the Board and the students on The Daily are today at an all-time low. We firmly believe that the responsibility for the present situation is largely attributable to Prof. Densmore. It is for this reason that, in the best interests of the University and The Daily, we ask for his resignation.

We believe, humbly, that a good Board member should have an active interest in the problems of The Daily; that he should have the respect and the friendship of the students; that he should attempt to the best of his ability to understand the organization of the paper; and that he should not allow his personal interests to influence his judgment.

Prof. Densmore fails to fulfill any of these qualifications.

His only interest in The Daily seems to be to make it a harmless and pacific newspaper so that it will cause him as little trouble as possible. He appears to act on the assumption that any protest--from whatever the source--necessarily means a flaw in The Daily.

...

...From the time of his appointment... his attitude has invariably been of the "we've-got-to-show-these-kids-who's-boss" variety. As a result, he has earned the bitter resentment of nearly every staff member with whom he has had any contact.

...After a year and a half in office he knows practically nothing about the organization of The Daily. He does not understand the relationship of the various editors and staffs, and is constantly placing blame on the shoulders of junior night editors when it should be placed on the senior editors, and vice versa...

...

Lastly, Prof. Densmore constantly injects his personal desires and interests into the official business of the Board. He magnifies out of all proportion what he considers "slights" to the Department of Speech, of which he is chairman. He has never forgiven one night editor who in a particularly small issue was forced to omit a story in some way connected with the speech department.

Recently he told a member of his department to demand from a sophomore reporter the written reasons why a certain story had not appeared. The young reporter, who was not at fault, was extremely frightened and thought she had done something terribly wrong. This is only one instance when Prof. Densmore has misused the power which is his as chairman of the Board.

We have not written this editorial in anger nor in haste. It represents our considered opinion arrived at after months of trying to work with Prof. Densmore and after hours of discussion on the advisability of making such a request for resignation.

We sincerely believe that the best interests of the University and The Daily can only be served with a new chairman of the Board in Control of Student Publications.#

--Homer Swander, Managing Editor
Morton Mintz, Editorial Director
Will Sapp, City Editor

A FAREWELL:
Outgoing Editors Urge A Never-Ending Fight

(Jan. 24, 1943) **RETIRING EDITORS** usually write a lot of sentimental tripe in their farewell editorial; all we will say is this:

FIGHT LIKE HELL FOR WHAT YOU BELIEVE AND FOR WHAT YOU KNOW IS RIGHT.

If you do this, people will either sneer or pat you on the head and tell you that you are young and "idealistic." They will tell you that the University must be "practical" and train students for a "practical world," that there is no place for idealism in a practical world.

They will tell you this because they are old and tired, dried up, stagnant both mentally and morally. They have lost all hope of getting a better world and they have lost their faith in the common people and in freedom.

Of course, they never put it in those terms themselves. They couch their feelings (or lack of them) in words like, "you can't remake the world overnight, you must be patient, you must take things easy." In other words, go under or around things--never through them.

These tired, old men--many of whom were never really young--picture themselves as the good people of the earth. Actually they are just the opposite: they are a drag on the progress of the world. And they try to force youth to side with them.

ONE of the greatest disappointments in our college life was to find men of this kind sprinkled through the faculty of as great a university as Michigan.

They will do their best to wear you down and make you tired along with them. They will find your every weakness and use it to their own advantage. They will alternately yell at you and pat you on the head; they will smile and hit you from behind.

The important thing to remember is that you cannot compromise with them, you cannot appease them, you cannot make peace with them. You have to fight, you have to fight every minute and all of the way. And you have to fight like hell.#

--Homer Swander, Managing Editor
Morton Mintz, Editorial Director
Will Sapp, City Editor
George Sallade, Associate Editor
Charles Thatcher, Associate Editor

A PROSPECTUS:
New Editors Reaffirm Free Editorial Policy

(Feb. 10, 1943) **WE THE NEW EDITORS**, are entering our positions at a particularly difficult time in the life of The Daily.

The tremendous disruption of University life caused by war presents serious problems in the managing of a college newspaper not encountered in peacetime. Not only is the actual running of the paper rendered more difficult, but additional functions are imposed upon the editors by way of having to serve a military as well as a collegiate community.

In adapting themselves to the swiftly changing conditions imposed by the war, the editors of a university publication are apt to lose sight of the liberal principles for which they fought in less confused times. With the gearing of a college paper to a war community, it is all too easy to forget that one very important function of such a paper is to serve as a forum for the intelligent discussion of issues which are fundamental to the democratic way of life.

We wish to affirm here that, although we will do everything we can to make The Daily an effective agent in furthering the war effort, we will also encourage the fullest airing of basic political and social issues in our editorial columns. We believe that the uninhibited discussion of such issues is as important to winnning the war as is a military victory, and we shall act on that belief.

...

As we assume our new positions, we are placing our faith in the statement of the Board in Control that our editorial decisions will not be interfered with, and we trust that the "business relationship" which we have been told is to exist between the Board and the editors will not invalidate their assurances that we will not be censored in any way.

It is our hope that the Board in Control and the new editors will be able to cooperate in order to put out the best Daily possible.#

--John Erlewine, Managing Editor
Irving Jaffe, Editorial Director
Bud Brimmer, City Editor
Marion Ford, Associate Editor
Charlotte Conover, Associate Editor

SENIOR STAFF RESIGNS
Protests Verdict On New Editors

(April 21, 1962) In an appointments session more heated than any in recent memory, The Board in Control of Student Publications last night overruled major recommendations by the present senior editors of The Daily.

The senior editorial staff, whose term of office officially ends in June, resigned in protest this morning. The business and sports staffs were not involved.

The Board's controversial action was in two parts:

* It changed three of seven recommendations for appointments.

* It re-structured the staff, choosing two Co-Editorial Directors in place of the traditional set-up of Editorial Director and Associate Editorial Director.

...

In a senior editorial announcing their resignation, the senior editors said the Board was unjustified in overturning the resignations. They contrasted their long appointments deliberation with the Board's action, which they called hasty and superficial.

...

As the paper went to press this morning at 3 a.m., Board Chairman Prof. Olin D. Browder was in conference with the newly-appointed senior staff and not available for comment.#

An Editorial...

(April 21, 1962) **THE MICHIGAN DAILY** is founded on a principle--the principle that students, given proper training and guidance, can be trusted to manage a great newspaper with maturity, responsibility and good sense. In defense of that principle--in full knowledge of the gravity of our actions--we, the Senior Editors of 1962, must resign.

...

THIS YEAR the Senior Editors went to especially great pains to insure that the recommendations were sound. We have, of course, known and worked with the petitioning juniors for two and three years. Since the beginning of the semester we have spent literally hundreds of hours discussing appointments. In addition, the Editor, City Editor and Editorial Director formally interviewed every petitioning junior for about one and one-half hours each. Our final decision was unanimous.

The Board in Control, in contrast, dealt with the solemn responsibility of appointments hastily and superficially. Its sole contact with the junior staff was a fifteen minute interview with each petitioner, plus written petitions and scrapbooks. Some members of the Board did not know the first name or even the sex of the juniors; at least one did not know the structure of the senior staff. After only a few hours of discussion, the Board approved a slate of appointments which differed importantly from the seniors' recommendations.

MUCH IS MADE of the need for responsibility on the part of students on The Daily, and students are quite properly checked by the ultimate authority of the Board in Control. But who will guard the self-same guardians? When the Board in Control behaves irresponsibly, taking actions which are not in the best interests of The Daily, students have no recourse but to resign--in the hopes that their pressure may prompt a reconsideration.

Our decision is the result of long hours of sober discussion, begun weeks ago. We are not moved by petulance or emotion. But by its action, the Board in Control has handed down a vote of no confidence in our staff. It has also exercised its unqualified right to make appointments irresponsibly and unjustifiably.

HERE WE STAND.#

The Senior Editors, 1962-63

JUNIORS DECLINE NEW POSTS
Would Continue To Publish Daily

(April 22, 1962) Seven of the eight petitioners for senior positions on the Daily Editorial Staff announced last night that they would not accept the appointments made Friday by the Board in Control of Student Publications.

After more than 24 hours of deliberation, Judith Bleier, Caroline Dow, Fred Russell Kramer, Cynthia Neu, Michael Olinick, Judith Oppenheim and Harry Perlstadt decided to remain night editors but continue putting out The Michigan Daily.

The eighth petitioner, Michael Harrah, has accepted his post as city editor.

The seven felt that the Board had attempted to disturb the workings of a free editorial policy "by an attempt to mold the tone and range of Daily editorials" through the appointment of co-editorial directors.

Explain Influence

The petitioners explained that the editorial director had no real influence on the editorials that appear in The Daily as they are individual, signed opinions of staff members. Thus the appointment of co-editorial directors, which ignored the recommendation of the former senior staff, was uncalled for. They condemned it as an "immoral" attempt to influence the editorial freedom of The Daily.

...

The seven petitioners will return as individuals to put out The Michigan Daily as a "task force" of night editors until new editors can be appointed or until an understanding can be reached with the Board.

"We believe that we owe the campus the best newspaper we can put out." Olinick said.

...

This decision was reached by the seven after a series of compromises proposed to the board proved unsuccessful. "We still believe we can reach some understanding with the Board..." Olinick said...#

An Editorial...

(April 22, 1962) **SEVEN OF THE EIGHT** Daily staff members who petitioned for senior staff positions refuse to accept the appointments made by the Board in Control of Student Publications; the eighth joins in our protest of the Board's decision.

...

The Board in Control...unanimously chose to slap down the seniors' recommendations in a crude attempt to mold the tone and range of Daily editorials.

...

IN TAKING ACTION, the Board violated fundamental principles of the freedom of the press and instituted, in one of the subtlest and vilest forms, pre-censorship of The Daily's editorial page. We believe that the Board has no right to decide which channels editorials should be steered into or to shuffle appointments to guarantee that a certain balance of interest and orientation will be represented.

Had we accepted the Board's appointments, we would have acknowledged its ethical right to step in and control the paper's internal policies, something which is incompatible with either the tradition of The Daily or our conception of its nature.

...

Our commitment to a newspaper to serve the University community, however, is a very great one... For this reason, we will continue to publish The Daily as an informal "task force." It is our intent to direct the production of the very best and very freest newspaper we can.

However, we sincerely hope that we can reach an understanding with the Board as we recognize their legal obligations and their distinguished record of service to the ideals of a free press. We will continue to make efforts to attain concordance with the Board.

We protest the Board's appointments. We cannot accept its attempt to deny us the freedom that would make us great. But we cannot turn our back on The Daily.#

--THE JUNIOR STAFF

LETTERS TO THE EDITOR:
Objects to Board's Interference

To the Editor:

(April 26, 1962) It is as you know often assumed in the world of the private universities that the big state universities such as Michigan, subject to legislative and budgetary controls, cannot be free and that their student papers must be house organs, carefully watched over by understandably cautious protectors, lest some segment of local opinion, not excluding influential student opinion, be offended.

Since the days of Henry Tappan over a hundred years ago, the University of Michigan has had an extraordinary record of vigor and freedom. And when I have read The Daily, which I regard as one of the two or three most vital, most distinguished and most interesting college papers, I am happily reminded of that tradition...

* * *

I am, of course, not qualified to enter into all the details of controversy and ambiguity in this particular case. But I can say that The Daily has a constituency outside of the State of Michigan which regards it as adding to the lustre of a great state university; and I also believe, as someone who follows pretty carefully the press in communities of the size of Ann Arbor, that the residents of that community are not ill-served by The Daily...

* * *

IT IS OFTEN SAID that students today are cautious and afraid to take risks, that they don't believe in free enterprise. Interference, heavy-handed or subtle, from adults who are put in a position of buffers between The Daily and its critics is not a way to encourage free enterprise at Michigan or anywhere else, and the long-run dangers of such interference would seem to outweigh whatever short-run alleviation it might bring.

--Prof. David Riesman
Harvard University

Board Fills Vacancies on Senior Staff

By GAIL EVANS

(May 23, 1962) The Board in Control of Student Publications announced new appointments to senor editorial positions last night.

After deliberating for six hours the Board named Michael Olinick, '63, editor; Judith Oppenheim, '63, editorial director; Caroline Dow, '63, personnel director; Judith Bleier, '63, associate city editor; Fred Russell Kramer, '63, associate editorial director; and Cynthia Neu, '64, and Harry Peristadt, '63, co-magazine editors.

Michael Harrah, '64BAd, retained his position as city editor. The new appointments will not become official until September.

...

Issues Statement

After new appointments were announced, the Board issued this statement:

"...Neither in these appointments nor in the earlier appointments of the Board was there any thought of exerting an improper influence upon The Daily editorial policy. We find the idea of censorship as repugnant as do any of the members of The Daily editorial staff. The Board however in its new appointments reaffirms its responsibility to exercise its independent judgment in the making of appointments..."

Speaking for the new editors, Olinick said:

"In making new appointments to the senior staff of The Daily, the Board has demonstrated that it had no intention to pre-censor the publication of editorial comment in any way. This was the main concern of the juniors and the prime motivation behind their protest of the Board's first set of appointments last month.

Save Face

"The Board did not make last night's appointments on the basis of what was best for the publication, but to save face and reaffirm its legal power to take such action..."#

BOARD REJECTS NEW EDITORS

Rapoport Considered Unacceptable

By MARK LEVIN

(Feb. 21, 1967) The Board in Control of Student Publications refused to accept The Daily senior editor's unanimous recommendations for next year's Daily editors early this morning.

The Board rejected the slate by a 7-4 vote because of the recommendation of Roger Rapoport, '68, as editor. The Board created no alternate slate of editors and will meet Thursday for further deliberation.

"We are unable to accept the slate of recommendations with Rapoport as editor," explained Board Chairman Prof. Luke C. Cooperrider of the law school. Cooperrider told the senior editors that the Board found "Rapoport unacceptable as editor."

The Board has overturned a slate of Daily editors only once in twenty-five years. No alternate slate of editors were created.

The Daily's editors released a statement following the meeting which said:

"The senior editorial staff has met and has considered the Board's statement. It believes strongly and unanimously that Roger Rapoport is the best candidate for editor and he alone deserves the post. We will not put him in another post. We cannot and will not consider substituting another candidate. The senior and junior sports staff, the senior and junior business staffs and the junior editorial staff fully concur in this belief."

At the conclusion of the meeting Cooperrider issued a statement.

"After very serious deliberation we found we were unable to accept the recommendations. According to normal Board procedure they asked the Seniors to submit a new slate of recommendations. The Seniors have refused to consider revising the recommendations. The Board then scheduled another meeting for Thursday to discuss the statement of the Seniors and have further deliberation."

Cooperrider said he hoped The Daily staff would continue to publish the paper in the interim.

...

Cooperrider added that although the recommendations of the senior staff are given great weight by the Board, "it is clear that the final responsibility in regard to senior appointments rests with the Board."

Vice-President for Student Affairs Richard L. Cutler and Vice-President for University Relations Michael Radock, both members of the board, would not comment on the proceedings.

...

Prof. John W. Atkinson of the psychology department, also a member of the board, commented that "a tired board found itself at an impasse. We leave in fatigue, not in anger."#

Michigan Legislators Call Board's Action 'Appalling'

See Adverse Effect on 'U' Reputation

By STEPHEN WILDSTROM

(Feb. 23, 1967) More than 35 state legislators yesterday sent a telegram to University President Harlan Hatcher saying they were "appalled" by the action of the Board in Control of Student Publications in failing to accept The Daily senior editors' recommendations for new editors.

The telegram stated: "We are all friends of the University who have defended and fought for the principles of academic freedom and freedom of speech. We wish to avoid seeing the University suffer from adverse publicity marring a great tradition and a great University."

The telegram was initiated by Rep. Jack Faxon (D-Detroit). Its signers included much of the leadership of both parties in both the House of Representatives and the Senate. Between 35 and 40 representatives signed the measure, including William Hampton of Birmingham, the Republican floor leader, William Ryan of Detroit, the Democratic floor leader, and Oak Park Democrats Daniel Cooper and Albert Kramer.

Nine senators signed the measure. They included... Harold Volkema (R-Holland), chairman of the Senate Education Committee... and Sander Levin of Berkeley, the Democratic floor leader.

He made it clear that the legislators who signed the telegram were acting as concerned individuals and were not attempting to use their legislative power to "blackjack" the University.

Faxon said he spent much of yesterday talking to people in Lansing, including people in the governor's and attorney general's offices.

"Everyone thinks very highly of Roger Rapoport," Faxon said. He also said that many of the people he spoke to were very favorably impressed by an editorial praising Rapoport's qualifications and abilities, which appeared in yesterday's Free Press.#

Rapoport Is Unacceptable To Hatcher

Tells Cooperrider And Regents of His 'Irresponsibility'

By MARK R. KILLINGSWORTH
Editor

(Feb. 23, 1967) President Harlan Hatcher told the chairman of the Board in Control of Student Publications before Daily appointments that he considers Roger Rapoport, '68, to be "irresponsible" and an "unacceptable candidate" for editor, a high University official said yestesrday.

According to the official, Hatcher privately informed the Regents and University vice-presidents of his meeting with Prof. Luke K. Cooperrider of the Law School last Friday morning before the Regents' monthly public meeting.

...

Hatcher reportedly called Coop-errider and asked him to come to the President's office. When they talked, Hatcher is said to have told the Regents Friday, "I was not my usual sweet, lovable self. I was very stern with him. I told him that I consider Rapoport irresponsible and unacceptable for editor because he would continue The Daily's present policies."

Then, according to the source, Vice-President for Student Affairs Richard L. Cutler and Vice-President for University Relations Michael Radock, both members of the Board in Control, spoke to the Regents.

Radock and Cutler reportedly told the Regents that "we can influence enough votes on the Board to secure a likely" rejection of The Daily's proposed slate of new senior editors with Rapoport at its head. Radock then read off a tally indicating how he thought each Board member would vote.#

Daily Editor Appointments Accepted Without Changes

Rapoport Takes New Editorship

By NEAL BRUSS

(Feb. 24, 1967) The Board in Control of Student Publications last night accepted without change the recommendations for senior editors of The Daily for 1967-68 submitted by the senior editors of 1966-67.

The action came three nights after the board turned down the same slate because they found Roger Rapoport, '68, unacceptable for editor, as recommended.

The Board's final vote was 7-4.

Rapoport said after the Board decision, "I think tonight's Board action preserves The Daily's traditional freedom and lays the ground for what I expect to be one of The Daily's best years."

...

During the Board meeting a majority of the recommended juniors announced seven points which they said they hope "to implement...to the best of our abilities in the following year."

The proposal said:

"--That the Michigan Daily add the American Society of Newspaper Editors to the existing code;

"--That the Board in Control set aside a specific time period at meetings to openly discuss with Daily senior editors newspaper editorial practices;

"--That The Daily contract with either a professional newspaper man or a professional service outside Ann Arbor to criticize the paper on a regular basis in writing. Such criticism should be distributed by The Daily editor to the entire staff... but would not be open to Board discussion;

"--That The Daily make use of the internal daily criticism sheet to properly evaluate each day's paper;

"--That all specific complaints about news stories be immediately directed to the attention of the managing editor..." and

"--That The Daily establish a forum on the editorial page where administrators and faculty members may contribute signed opinion."#

Hatcher Criticizes Daily for 'Youthful Harshness'

(Feb. 26, 1967) In his only public comment on appointments to The Daily senior staff, University President Harlan Hatcher yesterday criticized The Daily for "youthful harshness" and replied to a story on his relationship with the Board in Control of Student Publications.

...

In his statement yesterday, Hatcher said that one of his responsibilities as President "is to convey to the Board in Control of Student Publications the concern of the Regents. This I have done."

No Interference

Hatcher also said he has tried not to interfere with The Daily "pained as I have been at times by its youthful harshness, and by the occasional damage to the University which I and others have labored quietly to repair."

Rapoport, who was appointed editor late Thursday, said, "It's unfortunate given the events of the past week that harsh statements obviously injurious to the University's image cannot be ended on both sides."

Hatcher also said that questions "raised by the Board in Control" about The Daily are "pertinent" and "also of concern to the Regents."

"President Hatcher's statement neither confirms nor denies The Daily's story on his relationship with the Board, but I believe it virtually acknowledges its veracity," commented former Daily editor Mark R. Killingsworth, '67.

"As the author of the original news report I stand absolutely by its authenticity and its accuracy. As the past editor of The Daily I find hypocritical his remarks about conveying 'the concerns of the Regents' and his own 'non-interference' with The Daily," he continued.

"The fact is that President Hatcher conveyed his own 'concerns' to Board Chairman Luke K. Cooperrider and that his admirable record of 'non-interference' ended in a sordid attempt to smear an individual and subvert a great newspaper," Killingsworth concluded...#

Publications Board Requests Investigation Of Daily's Editorial Practices and Policies

Asks Faculty To Conduct Examination

By CLARENCE FANTO
Managing Editor

(Feb. 7, 1967) The Board in Control of Student Publications last night voted unanimously to ask the Senate Advisory Committee on University Affairs (SACUA) to undertake an investigation of The Daily's policies and practices.

The board passed a motion asking that SACUA, the executive committee of the Faculty Assembly...subject the newspaper to "an objective review by an outside group, uncommitted to the existing system and capable of bringing to the situation fresh points of view."

...

Faculty observers viewed the board's decision as a consequence of several controversial stories published by The Daily in recent weeks, as well as a history of deteriorating relations between the board and The Daily senior editors.

...

In a memorandum sent Thursday to board members, Prof. Luke Cooperrider of the Law School, board chairman, contended that a review of The Daily "conducted entirely within the board will inevitably lack credibility."

The memorandum emphasized that the review action by SACUA should be initiated before the selection process for a new set of senior editors begins.

Board members pointed out during their meeting that criticism of The Daily from other faculty members had contributed to their desire for immediate action.

The board told the Regents in a Nov. 30 report that "since there is a substantial question as to whether The Michigan Daily adequately answers the developing need for intra-university communication, an ad hoc committee be established...to study that broad question and propose solutions."#

SACUA asks Daily control over senior appointments

By ROB BEATTIE

(Oct. 22, 1968) The Senate Advisory Committee on University Affairs has recommended amendment of the report of its Committee on Communications Media to reaffirm the right of Daily senior editors to select their own successors.

SACUA is the executive arm of the Faculty Assembly.

...

The media committee interim report, issued last month, recommended that a revised student publications board appoint the Daily editor, managing editor and editorial director and that these three appoint the remainder of the senior staff.

...

The SACUA amendment would limit the board to an advisory role in the appointment of senior editors.

"The Daily staff shall consult with the Board on the appointment of senior editors," the amendment reads. "The details of the consultation shall be derived jointly by The Daily and the Board to the mutual satisfaction of both."

...

SACUA recommended adoption of the remainder of the report. The provisions of the report include:

--A restructured publications board consisting of three students elected by the student body, three faculty members chosen by Faculty Assembly and three professional journalists appointed by the President of the University at the recommendation of the senior editors...#

Regents revamp publications board

By STEPHEN H. WILDSTROM
Managing Editor

(Jan. 18, 1969) The Regents yesterday gave formal approval to a plan which will allow Daily editors to select their own successors.

...

Under the Regents' resolution, the publications board will maintain its present control over financial matters but "in all other matters, the board shall act in an advisory capacity. The Daily staff shall consult with the board with respect to the appointment of senior editors."

...

The Regents' resolution also calls for replacing the present Board in Control of Student Publications with a restructured Board for Student Publications.

The new board will consist of three faculty members selected by the Senate Assembly, two undergraduates and one graduate student elected by their respective constituencies, and three professional journalists, preferably alumni, chosen by the President at the recommendation of the student publications editors.

The board will also have a nonvoting faculty chairman, preferably from the Law School, who will be appointed by the President on the joint recommendation of the editors and the assembly.

A proposal made to the Regents by Fleming that the University hire counsel to study full financial independence for The Daily was not considered at the meeting.

...

Fleming also said he was not forwarding to the Regents a committee proposal that the University buy home-delivered subscriptions of The Daily for all faculty members and for members of SGC and other student organizations because "it would be bad for both The Daily and the University. It would make The Daily dependent on the University for subscriptions."..#

=== 1985 ===

Editorial restriction

(Jan. 29, 1985) **UNIVERSITY PRESIDENT** Harold Shapiro has taken a small but significant step toward inhibiting the editorial independence of The Michigan Daily.

A recent appointment to the Board for Student Publications, a group of students, professors, and professional journalists that oversees the financial affairs of the paper, was made in violation of the rules designed to protect that independence.

Regents' Bylaw 13.11 requires the Daily's senior editors, working jointly with the editors of the Ensian yearbook and the Gargoyle humor magazine, to submit a list of six nominees for the professional position on the board. Normally, this seat is filled by a person with a background in journalism. Preferably, the appointee is a University alumnus.

The most recent appointment to the board was not, however, on the list of editors' recommendations. Instead, the president ignored the recommendations as well as the regental guidelines in selecting a person to fill the seat. Allowing the students in charge of the Daily to determine these nominations is crucial to the formation of a balanced and effective board.

Although the president's office has assured the editors that the appointment was the result of a procedural mistake, there has yet been little effort to rectify the situation. Whether unintentional or intentional, an appointment to this board without consulting the Daily's editors constitutes a threat to the traditional student control of the Daily.

The board will hold its first meeting in nine months tomorrow night. Mistakes can happen, and if this appointment is merely an oversight by the president's office, we hope Shapiro will take steps to rectify the situation before an inappropriately constituted board is allowed to meet.#

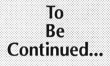

To
Be
Continued...

Shapiro denies Daily compromise

By ERIC MATTSON

(Jan. 31, 1985) University President Harold Shapiro yesterday denied The Michigan Daily's request that he promise to appoint the Daily's first choice to the next opening of the Board for Student Publications.

Shapiro said he could not guarantee the appointment of Urban Lehner, bureau chief of The Wall Street Journal in Detroit, because the next opening on the board will not occur until May.

SHAPIRO said that appointing Lehner to the board is ``not technically possible'' because it would ``fill a vacancy when none exists.''

The Daily said Lehner's appointment would rectify a mistake made by the administration in the selection of the newest member of the board.

...

``...**I REGRET** that, quite unintentionally, an appointment to fill a vacancy created by the resignation of a professional member of the Board went to an individual not on the list of journalists proposed by the Daily editors and without consultation with them,'' Shapiro said in a letter.

The board, a ten-member panel in charge of the finances of the Daily, the Ensian, and the Gargoyle, met last night to discuss the Daily's budget and publishing plans for the summer Daily.

The Daily had considered boycotting the meeting to protest the way [Frederick] Currier was appointed, but decided to attend because it was too important, according to Editor in Chief Bill Spindle.

AT THE end of the meeting, incoming Editor in Chief Neil Chase suggested that the board support the Daily's position in the matter, but Chairman Charles Eisendrath said the board should not discuss the matter until its next meeting because ``in any organization you have to set an agenda and stick to it.'' The issue was not on the board's agenda.

``This will not be a five-minute conversation. It will be a lengthy conversation, and I think we should do it justice,'' he said.

After 15 minutes of discussion about whether to address the issue, the board voted 6-3 to postpone the matter until next month's meeting.

Board member Patricia Montemurri urged the board to consider the issue, saying that ``the fact that it means so much to (the students) should mean something to us.''

Student representative Sam Slaughter also supported Chase's request. ``It just merits a five-minute discussion saying, `yeah, we support the students','' he said.

Currier argued that the issue wasn't important enough to warrant discussion. ``The president's office made a minor mistake,'' he said.#

The Daily vs the 'U'

When prohibition was repealed and the Michigan State Liquor Commission had selected an Ann Arbor outlet way downtown on the other side of Main Street, we ran a large picture of the store at the top of the front page. I as City Editor was held responsible and roundly chewed out by the assistant to the President.

--Norm Kraft, '33

Site Of Ann Arbor's State Liquor Store

(Feb. 13, 1934) Ann Arbor's State Liquor store, where persons over 21 years of age may buy liquor legally after 13 years of drought, is to be located at 113 West Huron St., adjacent to the Davenport restaurant. Charles H. Dawson, of Ann Arbor, will manage the establishment. The arrow points to the building, now being remodeled.

On The Daily's Policy...

(April 5, 1935) **IN A NEWS SENSE**, we believe this:

Principle: That a college newspaper should print the news as it comes, without the bias that both sides demand, and should endeavor to become more than a dull publicity sheet.

Therefore:

Corollary: This year The Daily has relegated free publicity to a position subordinate to news and interviews, although realizing that campus events should be given front page play on the day that they occur.

1935

Result: All the campus organizations are mad at us because we haven't acted as a group of errand boys putting out a supplement to their various organizations.

Conclusion: We still think that news and interviews make a more interesting newspaper than a front page D.O.B.

In an editorial sense, we believe:

Principle: Students should have some forum for free expression and The Daily should provide it.

Therefore:

Corollary: This year we have said what we wanted to say and not what the administration wanted us to say.

Result: The administration is mad as all get out at us and would like very much to get rid of us.

Conclusion: We still think we're right.#

Behind Closed Doors...

(Nov. 13, 1942) The Board of Regents met yesterday again behind closed doors after two Daily reporters had been ordered from the room by Dr. Alexander G. Ruthven, the Board's presiding officer.

The meeting had not yet been called to order.

Dr. Ruthven told the reporters that "there is a rule" against their staying and that "the Regents never allow outsiders in their meetings."

When asked for a copy of the rule, he said that there is such a thing as common law as well as written law.

After the doors closed behind the reporters, the Regents held their meeting.#

Hot Fertilizer Threatens 'U' Fertility

Soapy Succumbs To Deadly Piles

By JEAN BOLSHOI

(Feb. 9, 1953) Hordes of workmen arrived by plane from the Virgin Islands today to begin erection of a radioactivity-proof lead wall around the campus ordered by Atomic Energy Commission officials to protect the student population against mass sterility.

Source of the deadly radiation seems to lie in the mounds of cow manure used to fertilize campus shrubs and bushes.

Efforts to dissipate the deadly emanations by turning under the... clods failed yesterday although SL Boss Soapy Willens, toiling mightily, collapsed in a heap. No one has dared to drag him out.

...

Meanwhile, smelling sabotage, University President Handy Scratcher acted with alacrity to call for a full dress investigation of the matter by the Senate Committee. "The Committee will use kid gloves in investigating the matter," Scratcher said...

...

Latest reports indicated that as teams of University and city investigators dug further into the matter more and more evidence was piling up.#

Hip-Deep Prexy On Top of Heap

Special To The Daily

(Feb. 9, 1953) WASHINGTON--"I got to be the wheel I am by following the fine, upstanding principles my old man learned me down on the farm," Dr. John A. Humble said yesterday, with a straight face.

Humble is the new director of the Draft-All-Non-Agricultural-Students Bureau and the former strawboss of Michigan College for Bovines.

"What sort of studies would you recommend for a would-be wheel?" the nosey Daily reporter asked.

"Something in the classical line--sort of intellectual, like," Humble mumbled.

"Such as chicken farming?" our man suggested.

"Yeah, something hard like that," he snapped.

"ASIDE FROM your intellectual achievements in chicken farming, what else has led you to the prominent position you now hold?" The Daily reporter asked craftily.

"Just like all America's wheels, I started at the bottom and worked up the hard way," Humble declared and thumped himself on the chest.

"From a poor little barefoot lad lightly tiptoeing from one roost to the next collecting eggs"--a few misty tears began to patter down on the mahogany desk and he pulled a red bandanna from a hip pocket of his tux.

"I worked up the hard climb until I was stomping around with high rubber boots in the biggest cow college in the nation," he said.

...

"Your state college has shown considerable capital improvement during the last ten years. What facets of your administrative program contributed the most to this fact?" said our snooper.

‡ ‡ ‡

HUMBLE gasped a curse and a small, slippery figure, his administrative assistant Jim Hatchetman slipped out from behind the drapery.

"What did this guy say," Hatchetman rasped.

After several trips to the dictionary and three requests that the reporter repeat the question, the wily Hatchetman retired to a back room and a half-hour later emerged with a written statement from Humble.

"Thanks to the generous legislature of my state, the whole-hearted support of the citizens of this great state, my university has grown great," Humble read...#

ON THE BED

Beta Beta Pi fraternity will climax "Know-Your-Brother-Better Week" Friday by staging a stag dinner and slumber party for the neighboring Wee-Gees. The BBPi house will take on the appearance of a gigantic steamroom to provide atmosphere for the all-night affair.

‡ ‡ ‡ ‡

A Monte Carlo party, "You Bet Your Ace," will be featured Saturday night at the Kappa BB house, while the neighboring Tappa Thighs will dance to the music of Tommy Scabbard and his Blades.

‡ ‡ ‡ ‡

Rho Rho Rho and their dates will dance Saturday in an oceanic atmosphere for the "Navel Warfare Whirl." Tiny boats floating in punchbowls will emphasize the theme. During intermission, the dancers will participate in a group game called "Sink Your Navel."..#

New Addition To Daily Code Told by Young

(May 28, 1953) A new addition to The Daily's Code of Ethics was announced yesterday by retiring Managing Editor Crawford Young, '53.

...

The statement reads that the general standards of good taste required in regular publications apply to J-Hop extras and other supplements.

It was instituted as a result of certain articles in this year's J-Hop edition, in an attempt to avoid publication of articles in bad taste in the future, according to Young...#

Living the Kept Pledge

(EDITOR'S NOTE: This is the final segment of a two-part editorial.)

By THOMAS HAYDEN
Editor

(May 30, 1961) ONCE IT WAS warm blue sun and very grassy, and I was beaten in a putting match by Lyle Nelson, a man who is unfortunately leaving Ann Arbor after several years of successfully spanning the contradictions in both human and public relations man. Once Dean Rea found me some money, which made it possible to attend a summer session. Sometimes in class a professor turned a stirring phrase, sometimes I caught my mind changing or felt the deep-down chest heat that means a truth is forming there. And once I went to Michigras and liked the loop-the-loop.

So now it is tough to think all darkly of the University that has often been so nice. The criticisms I have made are not made without knowledge of the University's greatness or its frequent kindnesses...

My deepest fear about the University is the fear that we are adrift intellectually and humanly, and that responsible flesh-and-blood leadership has been replaced by the reign of an almost undiscussable tone which inhibits our whole perception of the possibilities of human achievement.

...

＊ ＊ ＊

A UNIVERSITY the size of the University of Michigan is inchoate, a congeries of the haphazard and in its very nature inimical to the development of driving leadership--not only are the members of the community too busy and too diverse to respond to anything but great brilliance, but even a brilliant leader or leaders would find it difficult to make a personality or an idea felt widely in the community.

Do we in fact have any brilliant leaders? Here and there exist Meisels or Frankenas or Eastmans or Kaufmans who occasionally turn a classroom intellectually ablaze. Here and there are the Lehmans or the Habers who, though you've never been in the classroom with them, have shown drive, commitment and flair. But the leadership of these men is limited; they are in the first place scholars, and in their functional position, cannot easily have wide effect.

The Administration, by and large, has provided a relatively steady maintenance of quality but not educational leadership, and the latter is necessary if quality is to be improved. Even if one sympathizes with the tremendous pressures bearing on the officials of a state institution, it is difficult to condone President Hatcher's confusion of bold action with unilateral action in the creation of the Commission on Year-Round Integrated Operation, nor can one be entirely pleased with the nobility of his stands during the Nickerson-Davis-Markert affair, or on fraternity and sorority discrimination, or on the Wayne State University speaker ban policy: in each case he hedged dangerously about education's twin responsibilities for promoting free speech and free opportunity.

...

Lacking structures for effective containment, power is dispersed not simply because the University consciously tries to decentralize but because it often is unwilling or unable to define the centers of responsibility. There is no bylaw delineating the philosophy of the operation of the Office of Student Affairs or its subunits. There is no clear bylaw on the rights and responsibilities of students, their legal and moral roles within the University, the due process to be accorded when charges of any sort are brought against them--and, it should be noted, such due process was defined for faculty only after the disastrous dismissals of "controversial" professors several years ago.

...

And so the University drifts, and within the general malaise arises the tone to which I referred earlier. The tone is generated by a deep conservatism--not political conservatism, but a conservatism of individual and institutional temperaments. It is seen in the inability of certain persons... to understand the relevance of new forms. It is fostered and sustained by the proliferation of committees which I sometimes suspect outnumber the ideas they claim to be exploring.

...

The emphasis in the University is on protocol and manner, not on enthusiasm or social vision; on the boat and not the shaking. Moderation becomes valued not merely as a better alternative than chiliastic messianism, but for its own sake.

Thus the boundaries of controversy, which in theory should not exist in a university, in fact narrow until moderation becomes one extreme to be compromised and reactionary conservatism the other.

The value of this temperament and habit of analysis lies in its emphasis on the sifting of opinion, in not moving too rapidly, in deliberately exploring consequences which might follow action. But the dangers are manifold. The greatest is the inevitable rise of what I have called "myopic realism." This is the tendency for realism to become insensitive to changed conditions.

In becoming rigid, realism not only limits its own powers of insight, but acts prohibitively against the injection of such insight by others into the process of decision-making. The fact that a faculty member is young is sometimes sufficient condition for an old faculty member to reject his opinion.

...

REALISM is evident in the Office of the Dean of Women, if non-direction is not. It is really not necessary to heavily document the attitude that Miss Bacon, her assistant deans and the housemothers (the latter represents the University's most-flagrant negation of the freeing aspects of university education) have taken toward change of any sort. Miss Bacon, for instance, has described culture as a "goldfish bowl" against which we (fish) bump our heads, never knowing that should we break the glass our life-giving context would run out. An attitude of this Office's kind--distrustful of students, opposed to the off-beat, circuitous in justifying itself--is deeply abusive to the University's internal freedom.

...

The failure of the University of Michigan has been in its glaring refusal to close the cleavage between ideal and practicality. Abstract support of free inquiry does not liberate the intellectual from the inhibitions imposed by the realism pervading the university. The University must give its ideals a human, realizable meaning. When it supports academic freedom, it should do it directly: abolish the lecture bylaw, prepare pamphlets on academic freedom for distribution to freshmen during orientation week, write rules relating to due process for students, cease tacitly cooperating with the state security police, get rid of any loyalty forms, politely tell the FBI that you do not keep information on a teacher's beliefs, stop emphasizing the superficial value of the grade and help turn the student's attention to the content of the course, initiate study periods before fall examinations, eliminate the "credit-hour."

Recognize that freedom to learn is freedom to participate: do not sustain discrimination of any sort in any living unit housing university students, develop positive means of providing interracial and intercultural relations within the campus housing and organizational units, actively seek student opinion where it is relevant in considering changes in the University, get behind a broad, critical and self-interrogating Conference on the University.

When the ideals of university education are ignored, when adherence is more admired than autonomy, when students are treated as immature, when institutional power is irresponsible to those who feel its impact, when all this is the image of the world which crystallizes in the still-forming mind of youth--then the University of Michigan has failed to discharge its duty as an educational institution: to exist in the tender balance between the postures of 1) toleration of individual whim and inquiry and 2) heresy in calling men to the historic task of radical examination and re-examination.

...

Much as it would like to believe so, the University's fundamental problems are not fiscal. They are moral and institutional. Morally, the University must decide upon the value it wishes to place on total human freedom--to read, write, say, and basically, to exist in the knowledge that society wants one to have such freedom. Institutionally, the University must find means to introduce the freedom of the spirit usefully into an arid bureaucratic mechanism. Only then will the University have opened the way for an end to realism and the great rise of the human spirit to its legitimate place.

Until that day comes, the student is left alone to pursue the critical dialectic between himself and the "realities" which the University and the society offer. The student should be asking the big questions which the bluebooks spurn but the world of living men raises endlessly: What things shall I think beautiful? What things are worth the trouble of wanting? What basis have I for my way of life and the way of life I call "best?"..#

HARSH CRITICISM OF THE DAILY
Regents to consider 'U' media

By HESTER PULLING

(Sept. 16, 1970) A proposal to expand free campus distribution of the University Record to include dormitories, libraries, and other student-related facilities will be discussed Friday at the Regents' regular monthly meeting.

...

1970

Vice President for University Relations and Development Michael Radock said the proposal has been under consideration for several years and was raised again by the Regents in July in conjunction with a discussion concerning The Daily.

At that time, the Regents aired many complaints about The Daily at a closed session with law Prof. L. Hart Wright, the chairman of the Board for Student Publications, and Daily Editor Martin Hirschman.

In interviews since then, several Regents have said regental complaints about The Daily include "frequent inaccuracy" and "bias" in news coverage. They said they hoped an expansion of the Record would allow students to get "another point of view."

"The faculty and students don't think The Daily is a good newspaper and the taxpayers don't want to support the filth which gets printed," said Regent William Cudlip (R-Detroit).

The Daily is run on a financially self-sustained basis and its physical plant was paid for out of profits made by The Daily and the other student publications. There is no University subsidy for The Daily but it enjoys tax-free status as a part of the University.

Regent Robert Nederlander said the question is not whether or not The Daily is a good or bad newspaper but "does the community need additional communications?"

Agreeing with Nederlander, Regent Gertrude Huebner (R-Bloomfield Hills), said, "This is merely another means for extending information to more segments of the community."

"The administration doesn't get a fair shot in the paper," said Regent Otis Smith (D-Detroit). "A competing medium is a good way to find truth and fact."

In addition to complaints about The Daily's news coverage, several regents said they objected to what they consider obscenities published in the paper and to editorials condoning or calling for violence.

"I would be most happy and it would help all of us if The Daily would eliminate some of its four-letter words," Mrs. Huebner said.

"I object to the utter vulgarity of obscene words," Smith said. "They serve no social nor useful value."

Defending the inclusion of "obscene words" in the paper, Hirschman said, "I think it's true that the student sub-culture increasingly includes the use of what people call obscenity as an accepted part of day-to-day language and even as a sign of anti-establishment sentiment.

"In dealing with stories where that factor comes into play, we may feel it necessary and desirable to quote words students have used so we do not substantially distort the tone of what's going on," Hirschman continued. "In general, though, we've tried to curtail the use of obscenities to minimize the possibility of offending a substantial segment of our readership."

Some of the Regents also disagreed with The Daily running editorials favoring violence as a means for change.

"We are all through with this business of violence and breaking things up," Cudlip said. "Yes, that's gone and we won't tolerate any more."

Responding to the sharp attacks, Hirschman said that it is the "traditional right and responsibility of newspapers to express their views on the issues of the day.

"There is, in fact, in this country and in this time," Hirschman continued, "debate over whether or not violence is an acceptable or necessary means for effecting change. I find indefensible the notion that we should shy away from this debate or refuse to print the views of those staff members or other writers who believe that violence will be necessary."

...

Throughout all discussions about the Daily, those Regents interviewed emphasized they were "not trying to threaten The Daily."...#

The memo reprinted here from Pres. Robben Fleming was not published in The Daily until January 14, 1988, but I am including it with the preceding Regents story to which it is related.

I am reprinting the memo in full primarily to emphasize Fleming's analysis of the status of The Daily vis-a-vis the University, as described in his point Number 1.

(Jan. 14, 1988)

THE UNIVERSITY OF MICHIGAN
REGENTS' COMMUNICATION

ITEM FOR INFORMATION

Subject: The Daily

You have repeatedly asked that we discuss the Daily and what might be done about it. We have devoted a good deal of time to discussion of this topic among the Executive Officers without very conclusive results. Nevertheless, I can tell you the nature of our thinking.

...

...College newspapers everywhere have always been, and probably always will be, a thorn. They are inaccurate, biased, often in poor taste, inflammatory and usually staffed by people who are considerably more radical than the student body. In most of these characteristics they find their parallel in commercial newspapers. Perhaps this is the reason the Daily is so vigorously defended by the public press anytime any effort is made "to do something about it."

Whenever the possibilities for "doing something about the Daily" are discussed three suggestions usually come to the fore. They are:

1. Dissociate the Daily from the University and make it wholly independent. The trouble with this solution is that it is not readily apparent what making it independent means. We do not subsidize it now. It operates out of a building constructed with the profits from the newspaper, the annual and the humor magazine. It makes enough on advertising to survive.

We could charge the Daily rent for the space it occupies in the building, but this would probably seem inequitable to both students and faculty in view of the way the construction was financed. We could withdraw the potential for subscriptions purchased by departments out of funds available to them, but there is no reason to believe that this would change the result. Wisconsin did both things this past year, and the paper is worse than ever and surviving solely on advertising revenues.

A further danger in pressing the Daily into totally independent status, whatever that means, is that we may then simply find ourselves with an underground newspaper which is much worse.

2. Appoint a professional editor to preside over the Daily. If such an editor were given genuine power we would precipitate a major fight, not only with the Daily, but probably with the entire press of the State on the grounds that we were censoring the paper. If he did not have power, it is hard to see what useful function he could fulfill. Schools which have tried this approach have no experience we know of which suggests any success. The job is a thankless one, and few people of worth are willing to consider it.

3. Replace the present Board of Student Publications with a Board which will exercise more power. It may be that the nature of the Board ought to be changed, but it is an illusion to suppose that such a board will stop the present difficulties. The same question of censorship will arise, and there is simply no basis for thinking that the Board will exercise effective control.

If none of these alternatives offer any chance of success, what can we do? Two possibilities occur to us:

1. Start publishing our own weekly newspaper this fall so that we at least get accurate information out to the University community on key questions. Some other schools have tried this, and it appears to meet with at least some success. It would cost us some money (we will have figures at the Regents' meeting), but we could do it and we believe it would be a positive step.

2. See whether we could establish for the Daily an ombudsman concept like the one reported in the Louisville Courier in a recent issue of Time. Hart Wright has made some further inquiries into this and will have more information on it. The Time excerpt is attached...

R. W. Fleming
President
July 8, 1970

Open salary list rejected
'Brown book' to
have little impact

By ALAN LENHOFF
Daily News Analysis

(July 22, 1972) Yesterday's decision by the Regents to release the University's "Brown Book" of salary statistics may cause a few ripples in faculty circles, but hardly compares to the potential impact of a complete release of all University salary data.

The booklet, officially titled "An Analysis of Salaries Paid to The University of Michigan Teaching Staff 1971-72," was previously a confidential document prepared by the University for its own use, and the use of several other agencies and organizations.

It lists the median and mean salaries at each professorial level paid by each school and college of the University. It also charts the minimum and maximum salaries paid by each unit at the various teaching levels.

It does not, however, disclose individual salaries, nor does it give departmental salary breakdowns.

In addition, the booklet includes no data on the numbers or financial status of women or blacks. Thus, it provides no clue as to whether the University's affirmative action hiring programs and salary equalization attempts are actually working.

...

The only potentially significant revelation from the "brown book" that has not already been widely circulated, is its listings of salary distribution, by unit.

These tables, while providing no names, tell how many professors are at various pay levels in each unit. For example, the Law School lists one professor making $36,000-$36,499, six professors making $34,000-$34,499, and so forth. This information is provided for each professorial level.

While previously disclosed information has allowed faculty members to roughly compare their own remuneration with that of their colleageus, this information will allow them to pinpoint exactly where they stand in their unit's pay scale.

Of potentially greater significance is that the distribution lists will allow some identification of faculty members and their respective salaries.

This is possible because in many departments one or two top professors are making $5,000-$10,000 more than their closest rivals...#

Regents vote
6-2 to refuse
Daily request

By RALPH VARTABEDIAN
(July 22, 1972) The Regents yesterday voted 6-2 to reject a request by The Daily that University staff salaries be released, along with corresponding names, sex, race, length of service and title.

As an alternative, The Regents voted to release a heretofore confidential booklet entitled "An Analysis of Salaries Paid to University of Michigan Teaching Staff, 1971-72." The booklet contains statistics on the mean and median salaries of academic personnel by unit, but does not list individual salaries or names...#

A protest...

(July 22, 1972) Despite the Regents' refusal to disclose full University salary information, The Daily is still strongly committed to obtaining the information, even if we must go to court for it.

The "Brown Book" which Fleming and the Regents saw fit to release yesterday tells us little more than we already knew.

We believe that full disclosure of the University salary information is in the public interest and would be the first step toward making our campus a more open academic community.

We feel it is the public's right to know the complete University salary listings by name, rank, sex, minority code and years of service, and we have decided to print salary information in protest.

--ALAN LENHOFF
--CARLA RAPOPORT

The following appointments and salary levels were approved by the Regents yesterday:

Robert Angell, professor emeritus in sociology, University year salary: $24,000

Eugene Arden, dean of academic affairs at Dearborn and professor of English, University year salary: $23,727

Florian Bartosic, visiting professor at the Law School, University year salary: $26,400

Peter Clarke, professor of journalism, University year salary: $20,000

David V. Ragone, dean of the engineering college and professor of material engineering, University year salary: $33,545

Jane Waterson, assistant dean and admissions officer for the Law School, University year salary: $12,272

John Witter, assistant professor in the natural resources school, University salary: $13,909

(We regret that this information is not complete, but we realize that no disclosure will be complete until all the University's salary information is released.)#

Daily, SGC sue 'U' over salary list

By DAVID BURHENN

(March 1, 1973) Student Government Council (SGC), the Daily, the local chapter of the National Organization of Women, and three other local organizations filed suit yesterday to force the University to make public complete lists of the salaries it pays to faculty, staff, and administrators.

The suit will receive a March 20 hearing before the State Court of Appeals. In his brief, SGC Legal Advocate Thomas Bentley asks that the following information be released to the public:

--The names and total number of University employes and the salary paid to each;

--The classification or title of each employe and the length of time he or she has been at the University;

--The sex, racial or ethnic background and occupational qualifications of University employes and

--The dollar amount and percentage of the budget that pays for employe salaries as well as the dollar amount and percentage of student assessments that pay for various University expenditures and funds, such as the athletic or building funds.

Eugene Robinson, co-editor-in-chief of the Daily, last night explained the position of the newspaper in asking for the release of the salaries.

"We seek," he said, "to force the Regents to disclose faculty salary lists because of what such lists may indicate-- possible discrimination by race or sex, or overt padding of the salaries of particularly prestigious but not so industrious professors.

"Since the University is funded primarily through funds from students and taxpayers, we believe the students and citizens of this state have a right to know exactly how their money is being spent."..#

---

letter from the editor
On suing the University

By CHRISTOPHER PARKS
Co-Editor

(March 1, 1973)...Yesterday, Gene Robinson and myself went to court to sue the University on behalf of The Daily. We are suing, along with SGC, Herself magazine and others, to force disclosure of the faculty lists.

...

THE DEEPER question, however, is why The Daily--or any other campus institution--has to take the drastic (and expensive) step of taking the University to court to accomplish its ends.

The answer, simply put, is that the University is among the most arrogant and secretive institutions ever to flourish in an allegedly democratic society.

Not a single member of this community of roughly 40,000 sits on its governing body--the Regents.

The Regents--none of whom live here--come to town once a month and make vital decisions behind closed doors. Often the only information available to them is that which comes from the executive officers whom they've hired.

They do hold so-called "public comment" sessions, but like the women in My Fair Lady, "they listen very nicely and go out and do precisely what they want," if they haven't already done it.

WHEN IT COMES to decisions, the Regents make all the big ones but a lot of the little ones are covered with the same veil of silence.

Most pernicious of all is the process for hiring and firing, or, as we say in the polite language of academia, "tenure."

Tenure decisions are made by a faculty committee. The membership of the committee is secret, their meetings are secret, the information on which they base their decisions is secret and their report is secret.

Almost everything of significance which the University does is secret until it becomes a fait accompli.

Except for a few token representatives in "advisory" positions, students who comprise the bulk of the University community and are its raison d'etre, are completely shut out.

Students have no power, little influence and in many cases not even the "right to know."

SO WE TAKE the University to court, and no carping about loyalty to our institution. It isn't our institution, it is an institution imposed on us. The distinction is important.

The University is not truly a community but a vast corporate octopus. It is the height of banality to talk about working within the University when we are not really allowed "in" the University decision making in the first place.

So we sue, because the only place a student can exert a reasonable influence on the University is in a forum not under its control.#

'U' salary list suit dismissed

By DAVID BURHENN

(May 24, 1973) A lawsuit demanding that the University make public the salaries, age, sex, race, job classification and qualification of all its employes by name, has been dismissed by the State Court of Appeals.

...

SGC Legal Advocate Thomas Bentley, attorney for those bringing the action, said that he expected an opinion would soon follow to clarify the reasons for the action.

According to Bentley, the dismissal may have resulted from questions dealing with court jurisdiction or the legal standing of the plaintiffs, and not from the points raised by the suit.

THE UNIVERSITY had claimed that the Court of Appeals was not the proper legal arena for action of the salary suit type. In addition, the defense brief had argued that SGC and The Daily, because of links with the University, could not sue that institution.

Daily Co-Editor-in-Chief Christopher Parks said last night that "We feel the State Appeals Court has made a highly regrettable decision.

"We do not intend, however, to let the matter drop here because we feel the central question of the suit -- the right of access to information concerning the use of public funds -- is vital."..#

State forces close to years of 'U' debate

(Dec. 12, 1979) ALTHOUGH the state legislature gave the University a final push by its passing a law forcing the University to publicly release name-linked salaries of faculty and staff, the internal debate over disclosure has raged for over seven years.

The discussion began in 1972 when some members of the University community, influenced by a judge's ruling that Saginaw Valley College should disclose its salaries, asked the Regents to follow suit.

In 1973, state Attorney General Frank Kelley issued an opinion supporting the idea of public disclosure. The issue came to the Regents again through one of its own--Regent Gerald Dunn (D-Lansing).

In February of this year, the issue came before the faculty Senate Assembly, and salary disclosure was rejected.

The University responded to a May request for salary information from State Sen. Jerome Hart (D-Saginaw), chairman of the Senate Appropriations Committee with figures by department and job title, but not individual names.

When Hart again requested a salary document listing individual names, the University "respectfully declined."

In mid-June, Hart introduced legislation--an amendment to the state's Freedom of Information Act--which would require the University to release the salaries of University faculty and staff upon request. The Senate unanimously passed the bill during the summer months, and it breezed through the House 100-1 in mid-October. Lt. Gov. James Brickley signed the measure into law Oct. 26.#

U-Club cancels meeting due to reporter

From staff reports
(Oct. 13, 1984) The University Club Board of Directors cancelled their meeting yesterday after learning that a Daily reporter was present.

Prof. Charles Lehmann, president of the board, told the Daily editor-in-chief and a reporter who came to attend, that the meeting was closed to the public.

THE DAILY considered this meeting especially important because the board was expected to decide how it will respond to several liquor license citations the club has received, said Daily Editor-in-Chief Bill Spindle.

Lehmann said that both the U-Club and the corporate board which runs it are private and therefore the board can hold closed meetings.

When the Daily representatives refused to leave the meeting room, however, Lehmann and several other board members consulted with a University lawyer who was to attend and decided to cancel the meeting rather than close it to the public.

"IF YOU (the Daily) are going to stay, then there will not be a meeting," Lehmann said...

Spindle said that the U-Club board meetings should be open to the public. The Daily considers the board to be a public, decision-making body which is prohibited from holding private meetings by the Michigan Open Meetings Act, he said.

The U-Club was cited for a violation of state liquor laws Aug. 28, after a state liquor control official was served a drink in late July.

...

The club was cited with a second, identical violation late last month for a liquor sale which occurred early in September.

...

Early this week [Lehman] said that the board would decide at yesterday's meeting how it would respond to the citations.#

Council Considers Motion on Daily
Proposal Expresses 'Grave Concern'

By JUDITH OPPENHEIM

(May 4, 1961) Student Government Council last night discussed in committee of the whole a motion to express "grave concern over the apparent trend towards irresponsibility in news reporting and editorial comment in The Daily."

NEWS.

(March 12, 1911) "What can we do to choke the DAILY?" asked a prominent senior literary student of a member of this publication's staff not so very long ago.

The other snickered.

It is strange that in a university the size of Michigan, with its liberal institutions and common tendencies, there exists an element so bigoted, so narrow, so reactionary in its thought and action that it must hold the rest back. In no better manner does this element make itself prudent than in its attitude toward the press.

..

The split in the senior literary class is one of the biggest news stories that the DAILY has handled this year. It is of tremendous local interest; every senior lit talks it at every opportunity; the faculty watches it; the other classes watch it and snort at the maneuvers of the various factions. All want to know more about it. And when THE MICHIGAN DAILY, doing its best to fulfill the functions of a newspaper, tries to tell in an impartial way what is going on in the literary class of 1911, someone wants to throttle it.

THE DAILY will continue to print news just as any other newspaper prints news. This is a newspaper, not an almanac-- at least, we are trying to make it a newspaper. If news hurts we are sorry. Often we throw out news stories that might bring about real harm. But this situation calls for no reticence.

Editorial opinion is another matter entirely. THE DAILY will continue to express itself through the editorial columns as seems fit and proper.#

The motion, introduced by James Yost, '62, states that The Daily has not met the standards set forth in its code of ethics. It urges The Daily to examine its present policies in light of its code and to take steps to ensure objective reporting of the news and institute "calm, fair and intelligent" editorial comment.

Not Condemnation

Yost explained that while his motion is not intended to condemn The Daily, he believes the newspaper has been neglecting its "responsibility to improve the image of the University, the student and itself in the eyes of the administration and other people."

He cited The Daily's code of ethics, in the form drawn up in 1940, which says that reporting in The Daily's news and editorial columns shall be as "calm, fair and intelligent" as possible. He said that recent Daily articles had not lived up to these standards.

Criticizing the motion's vagueness, Acting Daily Editor John Roberts, '62, emphasized that it does not specify when the alleged irresponsibility began, what particular points of the code of ethics have been violated, or which individual articles have violated the code.

...

Roberts also pointed out that the code of ethics referred to in the motion has since been revised and that the 1952 revision deletes the phrase "calm, fair and intelligent."

Union President Paul Carder, '62, answered the charges of vagueness by insisting that listing of specific grievances would constitute tampering with freedom of the press which is contrary to the stated aim of the motion.

But he did cite The Daily's handling of the Scheub report on the quadrangle situation as irresponsible as it raised doubts as to the quality of the quads in the minds of parents of incoming freshmen...#

An Editorial...

(May 5, 1961) **STUDENT GOVERNMENT COUNCIL** began consideration Wednesday night of a motion expressing "grave concern" over The Daily's apparent trend toward irresponsibility.

The Daily does not seriously question the Council's technical right to consider such a resolution. Nor, given the institutional independence of The Daily, do we believe such action constitutes a threat to academic and editorial freedom. But we are quite disturbed at what appears to be the Council's basic lack of understanding of The Daily's role on campus and, more fundamentally, of the qualities and practices which make a responsible newspaper.

The Daily is not a bulletin board, nor is it a passive reflector of campus events. It is not a partner of the administration. It is not the servant of any other organization, nor the captive of any particular campus interest. It does not essay to be an echo of the student voice.

The Daily is a newspaper, nationally recognized as one of the country's best college dailies. As such, it strives to report the news as honestly, as fairly and as completely as it knows how. It interprets that news with as much intelligence and sensitivity as it possesses.

BUT NO NEWSPAPER aspiring to greatness can merely report and analyze the news that lies on the surface. If it has a vision of things as they ought to be, and a perception of shortcomings that exist, a newspaper is obligated to work for improvement.

The SGC resolution appears to be part of a disturbing tendency to equate "responsibility" with leaving well enough alone. The Daily is not acting responsibly if it suppresses important information simply because publication would produce controversy. The Daily is not acting responsibly in "presenting a favorable impression" of the University or an organization if this entails distortion or omission of facts. And it is not acting responsibly if it devotes its pages only to superficial happenings and ignores more basic social problems.

The Daily, in fact, is most irresponsible when it fails to dig into issues, ferret out hidden problems, and press for their solution...#

--THE ACTING SENIOR EDITORS

LETTERS TO THE EDITOR:
The Daily and the Nation

To the Editor:

(May 10, 1961) **DURING** the last year I've become a one man Gideon Society for the Michigan Daily which seems to me one of the most alert, outspoken, and altogether interesting student dailies published anywhere in this country. Its coverage both of educational issues and of the world scene appear to me admirable--a model which I wish other student papers, more devoted to the trivial, the fraternal and the gossipy, might emulate. Furthermore, when my colleagues at private institutions such as Harvard aver that freedom to learn as well as to teach is difficult if not impossible at a state institution, I am apt to point to the Michigan Daily as an illustration that their view is mistaken. Any effort to censure the Daily should, in my entirely biased opinion, take account of your paper's national as well as its parochial audience--and consider the esteem that the Daily confers on the University that can attract such able and fearless students.

--David Riesman
Department of Social Relations
Harvard University

Congratulations...
To the Editor:

I WOULD LIKE to extend my wholehearted congratulations to the members of Student Government Council for their long overdue motion expressing grave concern over the Daily's editorial practices and news reporting in the past few months.

--J. Richard Pinnell, '64

Council Decides To Meet With Daily Staff

By JUDITH OPPENHEIM

(May 11, 1961) Student Government Council last night adopted by voice vote a motion by Acting Daily Editor John Roberts, '62, to have Council members meet with The Daily staff.

...

Panhellenic Association President Susan Stillerman, '62, and Assembly Association President Sally Jo Sawyer, '62, said that SGC, if it passed Yost's motion without first availing itself of the opportunity to discuss issues objectively, would be acting with greater irresponsibility than The Daily has been accused of.

Arthur Rosenbaum, '62, said he did not believe the Daily deserved the consideration of a meeting of the type Roberts proposed, since in the past The Daily has not shown a comparable willingness to discuss issues before publishing articles.

Nevertheless, Rosenbaum said he was willing to support Roberts' motion in hopes that the meeting could be conducted "in good faith."

Opposing the motion, Hanson said The Daily in instances including the Scheub report on residence halls, fraternity bias clauses and the Michigan Union policies had not consulted the student organizations involved before commenting on their activities.

Interfraternity Council President Robert Peterson, '62, said that in the past Daily editors have ignored protests regarding their articles and policies and "have shown no indication they will change their attitude now."#

Disgusting Quad Experience Calls for University Action

(May 3, 1962) **PERHAPS** the most disgusting experience on campus these days is a meal in the men's residence halls.

A recent lunch saw one student scrape the residue of his main course into his neighbor's milk glass, while a second student drank his soup directly from the bowl. What he didn't finish of it got poured alternately on the table and the floor.

It is nothing unusual to see dishes with food overturned on the tables, or milk soaked napkins flying through the air, or students spitting food and beverage at one another, or eating with their hands.

THE LANGUAGE is far from obscene--it is down-right pornographic; salt shakers fly through space with the greatest of ease, diners carry on their conversations audibly--between tables several yards apart.

Students precariously balancing trays make their way down the close aisle between tables while their seated cohorts make every effort to jostle, trip, poke, or otherwise upset them.

Dishes are broken, trays carelessly tossed about, and any woman who ventures in can hardly anticipate what type of reception she will encounter.

THE STATE OF UNDRESS of the diners is appalling. Shirts are often unbuttoned halfway to the wearer's navel; pants, tighter than the skin on a peach, are usually dirty. They often don't wear socks.

...

In a college community there should be no excuse for anyone to eat in an atmosphere that would disgrace a pigsty. Surely these same students who wallow in each other's food in the quadrangles would have a knock-down, drag-out fight on their hands if they attempted their antics at home.

...

In spite of the laissez-faire, "let-us-go-to-hell-our-own-way" attitude to which many members of the student body subscribe, the University must realize that it has a responsibility to the rest of the world, upon which it will soon thrust these social boors, to turn out something that might be half-way respectable.

And this responsibility the University must pursue even if it means the strictest type of discipline on record.

THERE IS NO REASON on earth why these swine of the meal line should be allowed to create an atmosphere that does discredit to themselves and the University. They do not own the University; nor is the University honored by their presence...#

--**MICHAEL HARRAH**
--Acting City Editor

--Daily--James Keson

MEALTIME MANNERS--Daily Acting City Editor Michael Harrah hangs in effigy on the Diag.

Besmirches Own Nest

(May 5, 1962)
To the Editor:

...Of the rare and isolated quad man who steps out of line, but also of him who with a gross lack of perspective sets up the occasional juvenile misfit as typical it may be said: It is a sad bird who besmirches his own nest.

--Prof. Frank X. Braun
Faculty Associate,
Wenley House

Disgusting...

To the Editor:

EASILY THE most disgusting experience on this campus is the use of the press for ill-informed and irresponsible editorials whose precepts do not fall far short of lies. The editor of any newspaper has the responsibility to at least make assertions in his editorials that have a reasonable probability of being true.

...

* * *

MR. HARRAH clearly implicates every man in the Quadrangles in his base indictment. Mr. Harrah clearly owes every man in the Quadrangles his sincere apology.

...

It is a sobering experience to learn that there are those who will use the precious freedom of the press to desecrate the integrity of individuals of the constituency that grant this right.

--James P. Starks
Administrative Assistant

Distortion...

To the Editor:

IT IS MOST unfortunate that at a time when so many people are fighting against encroachments on the Daily's freedom, Michael Harrah chooses to write an editorial which is a flagrant and malicious distortion of the facts. His editorial on meals in the residence halls shows a greater contempt for responsibility, truth, and accurate reporting than most others which I have seen since I came to the University.

...

Editorials such as this serve only those interests opposed to the kind of University which we all desire.

Daniel Gold, '63

BSU asks Daily suspension

By MARTIN HIRSCHMAN

(March 18, 1969) The Black Students Union (BSU) has called for the suspension of publication of The Daily pending a proposed investigation of its editorial policies.

The request, which was presented Sunday in a letter to University President Robben Fleming, came principally in response to the endorsements of Student Government Council candidates made by The Daily senior editors in Sunday's edition.

There will be a noon rally on the Diag today to protest The Daily's endorsement policy. The rally was announced in an unsigned leaflet distributed yesterday.

The senior editors listed Council candidate Darryl Gorman, a black student, as "unacceptable" for an SGC at-large seats.

Gorman received the unanimous endorsement of BSU.

Counter to The Daily endorsement, the black students contend Gorman does understand major University issues and could effectively represent black students.

BSU members also complained that inequities in the endorsement procedure also extended to other candidates. Specifically, they condemned the wording of the "unacceptable" listing given to SGC presidential candidate Roger Keats.

Several BSU members and the three top Daily editors met for two hours yesterday at the request of President Fleming, but the discussion failed to resolve the conflict.

At the meeting, BSU members attacked the "undemocratic" nature of The Daily's editorial policy and claimed the paper has misrepresented BSU actions.

BSU members charged The Daily emphasized only those actions by black students which involved violent action, ignoring peaceful, constructive BSU programs.

...

At one point BSU member Cynthia Stephens offered to provide The Daily with a weekly list of the organization's activities. Grix responded that this would be helpful in providing news coverage of BSU, but added that the paper would reserve the right to decide which items to publish.

BSU President Ron Thompson said the material would not be provided on those grounds.

Union members walked out of the meeting after Daily Managing Editor Ron Landsman said that the organization's closed meetings hampered news coverage of BSU activities.

...

Noting the hasty conclusion of yesterday's meeting, Cash suggested that the dispute is "more a personality clash than an issue clash." He said he sensed some antagonism between Landsman and Thompson.

Thompson declined comment last night. He said he would respond only if he was given a full page in The Daily for that purpose...#

BSU rally blasts Daily in endorsement dispute

(March 19, 1969) Black students lashed out at the editorial policies of The Daily yesterday at a noon rally on the Diag as about 250 students looked on.

Black Students Union President Ron Thompson called for "a newspaper that's responsible to everyone, not just 11 editors." He claimed The Daily is owned and subsidized by the University and said that therefore the paper's policies should be indicative of at least 50 per cent of the student body.

"Now The Daily just represents the views of 11 moral misfits," he said.

...

Thompson and Daily Editor Henry Grix will meet with Fleming today in an attempt to resolve the dispute.

At yesterday's rally, Thompson introduced Darryl Gorman, the SGC presidential candidate supported by BSU. Gorman was rated "unacceptable" by the Daily senior editors in their SGC endorsements printed Sunday.

Gorman attacked The Daily for asking increased black militancy. "We'll get militant when the time comes," he said. "We know what we want and we'll do it our way."..#

SGC unit hits Daily edit policy

By MARK DILLEN

(April 6, 1971) Student Government Council has become involved in a dispute with The Daily on whether the content of the campus newspaper can be regulated by SGC.

The dispute is focused on a rule passed by Council in February as part of the "election code" used in last week's campus-wide elections.

The rule states that "when a publication endorses candidates and states reasons for its endorsements, and there is no comparable media, then the endorsement and reasons should be publicized soon enough before the election that the candidates not endorsed can reasonably answer the charges in the time remaining."

In addition, the rule states that the publication should offer "at least equal and fair time or space" for the responses.

...

The dispute between The Daily Senior Editors and SGC emerged on March 28, the day The Daily published its recommendations for the campus-wide elections.

At a meeting of Council's Credential and Rules Board, later that day, SGC Elections Director Bob Nelson filed a complaint against The Daily charging it with violating the rule concerning endorsements. Noting that the next issue of The Daily was on Tuesday, March 30, the first day of the elections, Nelson said the Daily had not provided enough time for response...

At a hearing on the complaint last Sunday, the Senior Editors did not send a representative, and instead filed a statement with the Credential and Rules Board which denied that The Daily was subject to the rules of SGC.

"The Senior Editors feel...that the criticism...is quite sound, and we hope to be able to print future endorsements...several days prior to the election," the statement said.

"It is quite another matter to concede that Council or other governing bodies have the power or the right to impose such a rule upon The Daily, or indeed, upon any newspaper"...#

SGC, the First Amendment and The Daily
by robert kraftowitz

(April 6, 1971) **THE DAILY,** like all newspapers, has always cherished its freedom from being controlled by the institutions it reports on and evaluates in its columns each day.

This principle was adopted by the Regents in 1968 when they delegated to the Senior Editors the authority to determine this newspaper's editorial content.

Three years later, however, The Daily is experiencing the first attempt at curtailing its independence, an attempt being pursued not by the administration or the Regents, but oddly enough, by Student Government Council.

...

...it is not the content of the SGC regulation that is disturbing. Of greater concern is the precedent it sets for allowing SGC to make rules governing the content of The Daily. While the Senior Editors will continue to adopt ideas which would improve their service to the community, it is quite another matter for The Daily, or any other newspaper, to be restricted by a body on which that newspaper must independently report, comment, and provide constructive criticism.

The freedom of a newspaper to remain independent of existing governmental authority has always been recognized as an important element of a democratic society. Without editorial freedom, no newspaper could effectively fulfill its role to independently report on the activities of those in positions of authority.

Every democratic society has considered it essential that the public be served by a press which cannot be restricted by politicians, or political bodies. Armed with this freedom, newspapers become the most important check, and sometimes the only check on the powers-that-be.

...

It is important to recall that The Daily has for years been one of the strongest supporters of the proposition that Student Government Council should stand as the legitimate body exercising authority in areas which are the concerns of students at the University.

Editorially, we have fought side by side with SGC in this regard, and together, we have won many concessions.

But the mere fact that The Daily editorially supports the authority of SGC with respect to individual students, student groups, and student organizations should not prevent it from arguing against such authority being placed upon its own operation.

WE BELIEVE and will continue to believe, that the thrust of the SGC rule is sound, and a judicious way for this newspaper or any publication to handle election recommendations. But for all the obvious reasons, we would be acting irresponsibly if we did not oppose the establishment of any precedent that allows The Daily's editorial freedom to be restricted.

...

Thus, while the Senior Editors continue to support the authority of SGC as the appropriate governing body for students at the University, we cannot, as representatives of The Daily, recognize the legality of any proceedings relating to the content of this newspaper.#

...and finally,
The Daily vs. Itself

*Daily sports editor Al Fanger -- and the rest of his staff -- walked out after editor Mark Parrent told him they were taking the back page (usually reserved for sports) to put in a full-page photo of Bruce Springsteen on a football Saturday (Springsteen was in concert at Crisler that night). The news staff ended up doing the sports page -- and there were a **lot** of box scores! And the account of the football game was "from staff (whoever walked in the door who had happened to go to the game) and wire reports"*
--Joyce Frieden, '82

Bruce Springsteen
Crisler Arena — October 3, 1980

Daily Photo by LISA KLAUSNER

the Maynard Street wars

The Daily vs the world

(Dec. 9, 1890) [In reference to a "rush" at the Post Office] Now that the trial of Woodson has resulted in his acquittal, we feel prompted to make a few remarks relative to the duty of students in general, and those of the University of Michigan in particular. We make these remarks in deference to the sentiments of the people of Michigan, as voiced by the local press of the state.

1890

In the first place, no student should presume to appear at the post-office in the evening. Such conduct is reprehensible; it may excite the ire of some guardian of the peace, or of some military mayor. Then, too, when on the street students should carefully suppress all references to the University. The expression, "rah, rah, rah, U. of M." is almost criminal in itself, and when it is uttered in public, it justifies an outraged listener in proceeding to any extremity whatever. If a student should be on the street and be attacked by a tough, masquerading in the guise of a militiaman, it is his duty to get out of the way. If he doesn't he must simply take the consequences.

In short, a student is permitted to be on the street just long enough to go from his room to boarding place and recitation. He will do better to lock himself in the room. This may not make him a well developed man; but it will enable him to avoid the imputation of being a tough or a hoodlum. #

Conger incurred the adminstration's wrath in an editorial about the American Legion convention in Detroit. For punishment, the administration cut out the DOB and faculty subscriptions for a while.

--Norm Kraft, '33

Does The Legion Drink?

(Sept. 30, 1931) LAST YEAR, criticism was levied against the Harvard Crimson because of its account of an American Legion convention, which was termed "collegiate desire to show off" and "immature judgment," and was generally branded by Legion leaders as so much foolishness. Attendance at the American Legion convention in Detroit by members of The Daily staff, however, leads one to the conclusion that the undergraduate criticism was justified. Alleged college drunks are mere children's parties compared to some of the sights which were witnessed in Detroit.

1931

Why a city should ever consider inviting such a convention is beyond our understanding. Respectable citizens were afraid to venture into the heart of the city while the loyal defenders of the country were engaged in their annual brawl. Drunks of various sorts, in various stages of intoxication, littered the streets. Men strolled down the streets with steins of beer in their hands. Crap games were in progress in many a doorway in Washington boulevard. Cars attempting to pass on this street were severely shaken by men who rocked the automobiles on the bumpers. One pugnacious Legionnaire with a cane ferociously attacked bystanders because of some fancied injury.

All in all, we can see why the Legion voted predominantly wet on the prohibition question. Yet the feared return of the saloon would be nothing in comparison with the debauche staged at the convention. Leaders scornfully repudiated the public drunkenness by pointing proudly to the manner in which the Legionnaires marched in their parade. But the convention lasted four days instead of one afternoon, and the leaders rode around the city in cars protected, fortunately, by police and equipped with sirens... #

Socialists Storm Daily To Protest Straw Vote 'Fraud'

Mob Invades Publication Plant, Demands Expose Of A Practical Joke In Presidential Poll

---

'Free Speech' Advocates Threaten To Hold Up Presses In An Attempt To Coerce Editors

by KARL SEIFFERT

(Nov. 4, 1932) Hastily organized to demonstrate against "misstatement of fact" and "suppression of news" in The Daily account of the campus Presidential straw vote, more than 60 students and a handful of townspeople, led by Zeldon S. Cohen, '33, and Eugene Kuhne, '33, active members of the Michigan Socialist Club, stormed the offices of The Daily in the Student Publications Building shortly after 10 o'clock last night and threatened to "stop the presses until we get a full retraction."

While members of The Daily staff were attempting to reach Frank B. Gilbreth, '33, managing editor, at the Union, where he was attending a meeting, leaders of the mob occupied the editorial office and, amid much waving of arms and demands for "a fair deal," threatened violence unless alleged irregularities in the conduct of the poll were exposed.

Gilbreth Arrives

Gilbreth arrived in the office about 10:30 p.m., accompanied by James Inglis, '33, William Temple, '33, and Karl Seiffert, '33. Upon their arrival the mob quieted momentarily, allowing Cohen, who had organized them at Natural Science Auditorium after a lecture given by Fenner Brockway, member of the British Independent Labor Party, to act as spokesman.

Cohen charged that Inglis had voted illegally in the Daily-Union poll, and demanded that The Daily, which, he charged, had knowingly covered up the fact, publish a complete retraction on the front page. Gilbreth flatly refused to consider the program.

"We won't leave this office, and The Daily won't go to press, until you agree to publish an article as long, in the same position, and with the same size headlines as the one that announced the results of the vote."

Kuhne, who branded statements in The Daily to the effect that the poll had been conducted without any charges of dishonesty as "lies," asked Gilbreth "how much the Republicans paid him" to swing the vote for Hoover. Gilbreth explained to the members of the crowd that Inglis had cast several ballots illegally in a practical joking attempt to prove that he could evade the vigilance of Daily and Union staff members posted to conduct the poll. He declared that Inglis had immediately informed him of the fraudulent ballots, which were deducted from the total before publication.

Draws Deadline

Shortly after his arrival in the office, Gilbreth, in response to a threat from Kuhne that the mob would forcibly prevent The Daily from going to press, indicated a dead-line across the editorial room and ordered members of the mob to stay on their side. They did.

Little organization was evident in the conduct of the demonstration, few besides Cohen and Kuhne being sufficiently informed on the subject to voice their demands coherently. While the majority of those present lolled about on benches and chairs, occasionally crying, "Isn't this a student newspaper?" the leaders hurled threats and insults at members of The Daily staff.

Cohen Organized Mob

A member of the Michigan Socialist Club told The Daily that when the members of the mob were organized in Natural Science Auditorium, Cohen had promised them "that there wouldn't be any Socialist Club politics at the demonstration."

After an hour during which no action was taken and the leaders conversed with Gilbreth and other members of The Daily staff, less interested members of the mob began to leave the office, and by 11:15 p.m. only a handful of stragglers remained...#

Hot-Headed Puerilities...

(Nov. 4, 1932) ...They meant well, perhaps.

But they betrayed their cause abominably.

They gesticulated. They talked at length, all at once. Most of them were content to talk. A few favored violence. "We won't let them go to press 'till they print a retraction! We want a free press." Somebody suggested wrecking The Daily's machinery, all in the cause of a free press. The others laughed. Someone else was afraid the cops might come with machine guns.

They did more harm to their campaign on campus in one evening than they could make up for in weeks of constructive work.

They made themselves ridiculous, and very nearly did the same for their cause.

Martyrdom is sweet. Publicity is sweet. Going places in a big angry crowd is sweet.

The radical mob last night was Inferiority Complex on a bender.

The Daily has believed the Socialist platform to be an intelligent one, and the Socialist party to be an enlightened one.

It is disillusioning to find that terrorism, mob spirit, mass production of a moron voting body, are as typical of Socialism as of other political creeds.

Last night's demonstration was doltishly planned, stupidly carried out, and had asinine motivation.

If it had been directed at a privately-owned newspaper, it would have resulted in legal retaliation and would have alienated that paper to Socialist thought for all time.

The Daily, of course, does not intend to change its previously stated political stand, even under pressure from such back-handed allies.

The Daily still urges you to VOTE FOR NORMAN THOMAS if you believe that a protest against the established parties is needed.

The Daily believes that it is more liberal than the radical mob of last night -- if liberality means democracy and defense of Constitutional rights...#

I Killed The President

(Jan. 15, 1952) (EDITOR'S NOTE: The following is an abridgement of an article which appeared in the Soviet magazine "Krashdna Sovietski." ...The story is apparently Russia's answer to the welter of inflammatory fiction published recently in various American magazines. Those U.S. citizens responsible for Collier's "War Issue," Esquire's "I Killed Stalin," and the many other hate articles should read the Russian piece in its entirety. Then they should reflect on the obviously detrimental effect their products have had upon the world's uphill struggle to peace...)

Edited by RICH THOMAS

SYNOPSIS: Gen. Eisenhower was forced upon the American workers by "warmongering Wall Street" in the fall of 1952. From this point on, "Our Great Stalin" realized the decadent capitalist-imperialists of the U.S. would force the world into a war they did not want... As a means of immediately punishing the foremost war criminal... a raid was planned upon Washington... 25 commandos safely crossed the Atlantic... and chugged serenely up the Potomac...

* * *

PART III OF WASHINGTON RAID

The trip up the Potomac was as uneventful as the rest of the voyage had been. The audacity of our venture had evidently caught the stupid imperialists off guard...

...

Our boat nosed gingerly into the shadow of the Potomac Memorial Bridge. The second trawler followed and the commandos jumped quickly overboard and waded ashore. The shock of the icy water staggered us.

...

AS WE WALKED along in the darkness, each man's gorge rose up in hate of the decadent soil he trod on. We marched a hundred yards out of our way to trample a flower bed full of young buds. (It was a tribute to the worst enemy of the people of all -- Theodore Roosevelt.)

...

We had anticipated resistance in trying to enter the White House grounds. But only one guard was awake, even the Pentagon bombing had not aroused four other sentries from their drunken stupor. Broken likker bottles lay all around. We knifed the four sleepers and shot the other as he knelt and whimpered for mercy...

We left the soldiers bleeding in the filthy streets and ran up the White House lawn towards the bomb shelter... We felt no fear, only doubt -- would we find Eisenhower?

* * *

DOWN WE PLUNGED into the gigantic concrete structure. Our submachine guns spewed death to the guards who tried to stop us. A sixth begged for mercy and we spared him so he could lead us to our objective.

As we rushed up the subterranean corridor we kicked down each door and tossed in a grenade. The place was packed with admirals, generals and Wall Street financiers. In one room I caught a glimpse of fat men in black silk hats gleefully running their hands through an enormous pile of gold. Then the grenade went off.

Now we were in the tyrants' apartment. When we burst in he was swilling from a 25-ruble bottle of white lightning. He had his arm around a half naked woman. His glazed eyes did not understand what was happening as we seized him and shot her. In another room we found his wife, who was being visited by her son and two grandchildren.

We lined them all against the wall. An argument broke out among the men over who would get to execute the president. Before it could be settled, however, all ten of us fell with a vengence upon the quaking family. It was the wrath of century-long suppression pent up in the workingmen.

The horrible Eisenhower lived to see his entire family slaughtered. A sublime moment of the peoples' justice.

His wife was bayoneted twice before she fell writhing to the ground. Her blood spurted out on the grandchildren, painting them sunset red. His son, cowering in a corner, was kicked to the ground by three of us and was cut into two pieces by a magnificient bayonet slash.

Meanwhile the Commandos had spied the grandchildren and were swinging their guns at them like peasants flailing wheat. The children were quick on their feet, however, and the rifle butts missed them several times.

Throwing away their weapons, our entire force assailed him with their bare fists. He fell immediately but was dragged up and killed while justice continued to be meted out.

Outside we rejoined the other groups (one of which had successfully blown up the Washington monument) and...so we returned; mission accomplished and not one of us had been injured.#

Sequel to 'Assassination'

(Jan. 16, 1952) Satire, by its very nature, can easily be mistaken. Often, however, it is the only means, or the most effective means, by which a condition may be pointed out or a hypocrisy bared.

Yesterday, we ran a piece in these columns entitled "I Killed the President." It was devised by Rich Thomas, and was intended to show, as indicated in the editor's note, the monstrosity of some magazine fiction on this side of the ocean.

Nothing further was meant. The reaction, however, which met us -- by telephone and letter -- yesterday afternoon, was of such a curious nature that it deserves to be mentioned in its own right. A total of perhaps 25 phone calls asked if the source was really true. A certain number of others, perhaps five, vociferously claimed that the article was the sturdiest piece of libel against the Soviet Union ever to appear in the pages of The Daily. One gentleman, who believed the story to have actually appeared in a Russian magazine, explained that Americans should take warning.

It is personally repugnant to me to have to explain the point of a satire. But since such confusion evidently exists, it might be well to rephrase the issue in ordinary language. It is simply this: scare fiction can do nothing but harm. Orientation of hatred is an extremely drastic propaganda measure, and one which should never be employed lightly. Those examples of scare fiction already in print (and we may presume, in the growing number yet to come), flaunt this basic condition in an appalling way...#

--Chuck Elliott

Daily Editorial Satire Draws Russian Blast

By CHUCK ELLIOTT
Daily Managing Editor

(March 26, 1952) Daily editorials, long a local target for criticism, finally hit the big time yesterday when the Russian magazine Literary Gazette labeled one "a slanderous attack" against the USSR.

The editors hailed the announcement as "proving almost beyond the shadow of a doubt that The Daily's editorial policy is consistently ambiguous."

* * *

RICH THOMAS, '52, author of the attacked article, was somewhat elated that his work had been chosen "for special condemnation of Moscow." At the same time, however, he expressed dismay at the fact that they had completely missed the point.

...

The Literary Gazette angrily...claimed that Thomas' article was "yet another intentional slanderous attack on the Soviet Union." Swinging wide, the Russians also hailed the University as an institution which "exists on gifts from Wall Street and U.S. government subsidies."

Arthur Brandon, University public relations head, was quick to rejoin, "Those are two sources we don't get support from."

* * *

TO THE RUSSIAN statement that the editorial was "a crude forgery" editor Thomas retorted that it was not crude. Shaking his head sadly, he remarked "Satire would seem to be as dead as Dean Swift, these days..."

...

A look at some old Daily files reveals that Radio Moscow attacked the Michigan football team on about the same grounds in the Summer of 1950. The "bestial instincts" of the University athlete were being aggravated at that time by "profit-hungry Wall Street bosses."

Daily reaction to the Literary Gazette blast was pretty well summed up by a University authority (who asked to remain anonymous) when he said, "It's nice to be remembered."#

Daily Called 'Warmonger' In UN
Satiric Editorial Quoted in Session

by ZANDER HOLLANDER
Daily Feature Editor

(Oct. 31, 1952) The Daily tucked away a new laurel this week -- it was blasted by the Soviet bloc in the hallowed halls of the United Nations.

Source of the attack was Mrs. F. A. Novikov, Byelorussian delegate to the UN Social, Humanitarian and Cultural committee, who Tuesday singled out The Daily as an example of the "warmongering" of the American press.

* * *

MRS. NOVIKOV'S onslaught was part of a battery of Red-satellite attacks backing up Soviet delegate Arkady A. Sobolev's earlier charge that the United States press was "monopolistic-controlled" and trying to incite world conflict.

The attack came during a session discussing the drafting of a controversial global pact on freedom of information.

Mrs. Novikov claimed that The Daily had accused the White Russian Soviet Republic of building submarine bases at Minsk. But Minsk, she pointed out triumphantly, is far inland.

The Byelorussian charge provoked at first only mystification locally but racking of memories dredged up the recollection that The Daily had once referred to Minsk. The mention came in a satire called "I Killed the President" by Rich Thomas, '52, a former senior editor.

...

LOCAL misunderstanding of the satire's purpose brought an explanatory note the next day from Managing Editor Chuck Elliott. But even this did not prevent an Ann Arborite from forwarding the piece to the Moscow Literary Gazette -- minus the explanatory note and with the hint that the article was a deliberate forgery added.

The Gazette fell for it. They came out with a scathing excoriation of the article, The Daily and the University. For the Ann Arborite who had deliberately misled them (initials D.L., according to the Gazette), they had nothing but praise.

The rehashing of the old lie brought swift response from the United States delegation which wired The Daily last night for full particulars on the case. The material is now on its way...#

Daily Defended By UN Delegate

Special to The Daily
(Nov. 2, 1952) UNITED NATIONS, N. Y. -- The Byelorussian Soviet Socialist Republic got a belated lesson in American satire yesterday when Charles A. Sprague of the United States informed the Communist satellite that The Daily was being funny and not warmongering in an editorial last January.

...

...Sprague, armed with several relevant copies of the paper, spelled out -- in simple words with few syllables -- the facts which The Daily has communicated to the Soviet bloc at least three times before: the editorial, entitled "I Killed the President," by former senior editor Rich Thomas, was intended as a takeoff on the rash of anti-Soviet fiction then current in American magazines.

Sprague pointed out, moreover, that the "editors felt the editorial was not fully understood and an explanation was printed by the newspaper the following day." That explanation was in the hands of the Byelorussian delegate when she made her original attack -- but she did not mention it at the time.

Mrs. Novikov's onslaught had charged that The Daily accused the While Russian Republic of building submarine bases at Minsk, a well-known inland city.

In rebuttal Sprague explained once more that The Daily had assured him this obvious impossibility "was inserted in the editorial purposely to add to the ridicule intended by the satire and with the knowledge that there could be no such base in Minsk."#

An Apology

To the Editors:

(Feb. 8, 1966) **RUMOR HAS IT** that The Daily has been accused of sponsoring **THE AD**. We apologize for any condemnation The Daily may have incurred on our account. To set the record straight, five boys, working inde-pendently, motivated by a love of excite-ment and a belief that warped standards prevail in the Selective Service proce-dure, collected $168 from over 200 students, faculty and others to finance the **AD**. We feel sorry for those readers who took offense at our "serious" efforts to subvert the academic excellence of the University.

We, the undersigned, are the spon-sors.

--Dick Berman, '69
--Joe Breines, '69
--Marty Lieberman, '69
--Jim Murphey, '69
--Larry Ruhf, '69

Ad Wasted

To the Editor:

(Feb. 8, 1966) ...it would do men on campus no good were the girls to sac-rifice their grades.

In Hershey's proposed guidelines, part of the criteria for determining Selec-tive Service classifications of college men is the rank in the male part of the college class...

THE AD was a waste of money, fellows!

--Robert R. Simpson, Jr., '68

ASKS REPRIMAND:
TV Editorial Lashes Daily Ad

By CLARENCE FANTO

(Feb. 11, 1966) An editorial broad-cast Wednesday night by a Detroit tele-vision station called on the University to "reprimand" The Daily for publishing an anonymous advertisement of "scurri-lous" character.

The advertisement, which appeared in Sunday's Daily, asked female students to sacrifice their academic averages to allow more males to enter the upper half of their class...

...

There have been reports that the Selective Service System will return to the Korean War standards for determin-ing student deferments. At that time, freshmen had to be in the upper half of their class, sophomores in the upper two-thirds and juniors in the upper three-fourths in order to receive a 2-S defer-ment, unless they passed a special exami-nation given by Selective Service.

...

WJBK Blast

The editorial, broadcast on WJBK-TV, channel 2, owned by the Storer Broadcasting Co., mentioned the stu-dents' letter of explanation but added "that does not excuse the loose practices at the student paper or the silence from the University administrators."

Prof. Luke K. Cooperrider of the Law School and chairman of the Board in Control of Student Publications said last night "the ad appears to have been someone's idea of humor. The humor was perhaps misguided, but I'm certain no one need fear the students will take the proposal seriously."

Cooperrider reported that while the ad did not violate any specific rule, the Board and The Daily business staff are considering instituting a policy requiring identification of such announcements as paid advertisements.

Vice-President for Student Affairs Richard L. Cutler last night termed the incident "laughable" although he urged that all advertisements in The Daily be identified as such.

...

Cutler said he did not view the ad as a "serious effort by University men to avoid serving their country."..#

The mighty wolverine, Michigan's own answer to the cow and rising beef prices, gobbles down an unidentified but undoubtedly tasty morsel.

Meat shortage got you down? Try Wolverine

By ALBERT FOXLER
Daily Science Writer

(Aug. 16, 1973) Though weak stomachs may find it revolting and University purists may call it sacrilegious, the wolverine, symbol of both the state and University, can be used as a beef substitute in these days of food shortages.

1973 According to officials from the state wildlife department, the small but vicious little rodents make a pretty fair meal for those hunters clever enough to catch them.

"PEOPLE ON farms have been eating them for years," reports Larry Dogman, director of the wildlife department. "The meat can be a little stringy, but with hamburger at $1.50 a pound who can afford to be choosy."

About two and one half feet long, with brown hair and two yellow stripes running down its back, the wolverine inhabits wooded rural areas around the state, some as close as 10 or 15 miles from the city.

SOME INEXPERIENCED gamesmen have tried to trap the animal, but they soon learned the wolverine is just too smart for that.

"They've been known to pull the bait out of traps without being caught," comments Dogman. "If you want to get one your're just going to have to shoot it."

Even hunting the animals is no easy task. Despite their small size--generally around 20 or 30 pounds--wolverines can be among the most dangerous of opponents. Their razorsharp teeth have discouraged more than one greenhorn hunter.

IF A HUNTER is fortunate enough to bag one, he has got himself enough meat for seven or eight meals. The Outdoor Gourmet, a popular camper's cookbook, lists several ways to prepare the meat.

The authors recommend broiling, but hamburger-like patties or meat-loaf variations are termed acceptable. Organic vegetables come highly recommended as side dishes and red wine is considered a must.

According to University natural history Prof. Harold Katz, wolverines have been used for food during other times of economic deprivation.

"DURING THE depression in 1893," Katz reports, "the governor himself ate wolverine for dinner to show the citizens that it would be all right."

Though no such gestures are coming out of Lansing today--this not being an election year--consumption of wolverine around the state is definitely on the rise.

So for those hearty souls who aren't about to let a little local patriotism stand in the way of their stomachs, we can only say--bon appetit.#

Media confused by Daily menu suggestion

(Aug. 22, 1973) LANSING (UPI) -- It sounded like the ultimate sacrilege--eating wolverines, the Michigan state symbol, as a substitute for beef.

It began in Ann Arbor, where the University of Michigan student newspaper even quoted a state wildlife department spokesman on how wolverines taste.

...

That touched off a mild flap, and a lot of confusion, at the wildlife department.

Relax, everyone.

"THERE HAS NEVER been, as far as anyone knows, a wolverine in the state of Michigan," said Fred Stuwer, senior biologist at the department.

"And if there were wolverines," he said, "there probably isn't a man, woman, or child in the country who could stand to eat one. They would taste about as bad as anything you can imagine."

...

MICHIGAN IS CALLED the "wolverine state," giving many persons the idea that state is in fact inhabited by that member of the weasel family.

Not true. Michigan got that nickname because of the number of wolverine furs shipped south by eighteenth century trappers in the Hudson Bay area.

"If anyone finds a wolverine," Stuwer said, "I sure hope he tells me before eating the evidence."

Sorry

Alas, we must admit our story about eating wolverines was indeed a hoax. The names, dates and 90 per cent of the facts were fabricated.

But judging by a number of calls we've received as well as Mr. Stuwer's description of the UPI correspondent handling the story, we wonder how many people were aware of the joke.

Hopefully, no one has spent the last week looking for wolverines as a result of our story. And for those who genuinely need a beef substitute, well, you'll just have to stick to armadillo.#

Editorial Freedom

The Michigan Daily

Sixty-Eight Years of Editorial Freedom

VOL. LXIX, No. 368   ANN ARBOR, MICHIGAN, WEDNESDAY, AUGUST 12, 1959   FIVE CENTS   SIX PAGES

When I joined the staff in the fall of 1954, the masthead boasted 'Latest Deadline in the State.' It warmed us as we stayed up late six nights a week, helping Arch or Earl put the paper to bed about 1:30 a.m. so Loren could run the presses at two. My disillusionment came when, as the 1956 staff was retiring, I decided to tap the fertile brain of Editorial Director Murray Frymer for any leftover ideas about the future of the paper. He startled me by suggesting that we scrap the time-honored motto. He pointed out that most of the state's dailies were afternoon papers, whose deadlines could be considered later, depending on when you started the clock. We really had the 'Latest Deadline of Any Morning Paper in the State' -- surely not a battle cry to make an army march. Even worse, there was only one other morning paper in the state, so we were really down to 'Later Deadline than The Free Press' -- at which point the army sits down and plays cards.

Murray's suggestion was that we cite instead the paper's editorial freedom, since reinforcing that tradition might make it harder for the university administration to move against it in some future crisis.

The next year, when our senior staff took office, one of my first suggestions was that we scotch the old motto. In

September, 1957, when our names at last appeared in the staff box, the first paper made the shift without fanfare, proudly proclaiming 'Sixty-Seven Years of Editorial Freedom.' Angry crowds did not gather outside the Publications Building that night, so it seemed successful.

We left it to the good judgment of the staff of 1960 to deal with whatever minor embarrassments it might raise for them. They responded discreetly with 'Seventieth Year...' And so it remains, raising a standard for each subsequent staff and drawing a line in the sand for each subsequent administration.

--Peter Eckstein, '59

One of the things that comes to mind from my time at The Michigan Daily was the year that we did not celebrate 69 years of editorial freedom... I was on the staff during the year that we commemorated 'Sixty-Eight Years of Editorial Freedom.' The following year would have been 69, but I recall hearing Bob Junker, the incoming city editor, remark that he was not about to have 69 on his front page. So we went from 68 years to 'Seventieth Year of Editorial Freedom.'

--David Lyon, '60

FRESHMAN EDITION

The Michigan Daily

FRESHMAN EDITION

Seventieth Year of Editorial Freedom

SIXTY PAGES   ANN ARBOR, MICHIGAN, TUESDAY, SEPTEMBER 15, 1959   SIXTY PAGES

How much is a full page, anyhow?

Ad for non-meeting draws 150 to Diag

By DAVID SPURR

(Nov. 8, 1968) It all started with a two-page, $400 ad in Thursday's Daily, proclaiming the death of SDS with McLuhanesque effect.

The ad, placed by an unidentified person, drew 150 people to the Diag last night for what was billed as a "mass meeting of the Campus Americans for Democratic Action."

The people came. The ADA did not.

The ubiquitous Students for a Democratic Society also showed up, and finding a crowd with no leaders, promptly took charge.

SDS leader Bill Ayres said, "Let's go to the Fishbowl and discuss politics!" As the crowd followed him, bewildered students who had come to support ADA could only mutter, "Wait a minute...I thought it was supposed to be the death of SDS."

In the Fishbowl, all was amok. Rumors ran rampant that SDS had run the ad as an expensive joke.

ADA sympathizers accused Ayres and James Mellen, both of SDS, of pulling off another "irresponsible maneuver."

...

Another student got up to exhort the crowd. "Take the platform before that jerk takes control of the whole organization," someone said...

At this point, Ayres and his colleagues nobly announced, "Well, we don't want to horn in on this if it's really an ADA meeting, but if anyone wants to discuss politics, come with us." And off they went.#

SDS's

Ann Arbor, Michigan, Thursday, November 7, 1968
Help fill these pages with tomorrow's news.
A United U of M
Working for Peace
TONIGHT
at the Campus Americans for Democratic Action
Mass Meeting 7:30 p.m. on the Diag

chapter 6

arts & letters

The first appearance of "The Victors"

COMEDY CLUB TONIGHT

Arrangements All Made for a Successful Production.

(April 5, 1899) Every indication points to a most successful rendition of Daly's comedy "A Night Off" by the Comedy Club this evening in the Athens Theatre. Rehearsals have been held every day for the past two weeks and the play will be put on in professional style.

...

Special music will be rendered by the orchestra under the direction of Prof. Louis Elbel. The following is a program for the music:

Overture-- "Raymond"....A. Thomas
(a) Prelude and Intermezzo from Cavalleria Rusticana ......Mascagni
(b) "Dance of the Bayaderes" from Opera "Feramors".....A. Rubinstein
"Babbie" Waltz from "The Little Minister".....Furst
(a) "Narcissus"...Arr. by Richard Elbel
(b) "The Victors" March.....Louis Elbel
Dedicated to '98 U. of M. Football Team.#

SCORES A HIT.

"A Night Off" by the Comedy Club a Great Success.

(April 6, 1899) At its performance of "A Night Off" last night at the Athens Theatre, the Comedy Club was greeted by a packed house. The faculty and fraternities attended in large numbers and the play was made the occasion of a society event...

...

But the play was even a greater theatrical than social success. Considered from all points it was the most successful production the Comedy Club has yet given. The costuming, staging and mechanical effects were much superior to those of past years. The company was unusually well balanced and the acting was uniformly good throughout. All of the players had the ease and command which mark the professional actor.

...

Mr. Louis Elbel arranged all the music for the play. His latest composition "The Victors' March" was greatly appreciated and an encore was called for after its rendition...#

CAMPUS FABLES.

by our own George Ade
He Who Rusheth Not.

(Oct. 20, 1911) Once there was a Stude. He had a 14 Three B Pipe and an English Hat, and he thought himself Some Cheese. There was another stude who smoked a Corncob and wore Corduroys. He knew he wasn't much and wondered at the Price of that English Hat.

The Day of the Rush came, the Cheese decided that being a Sophomore it would not go to the Rush. The Corncob figured that as he was a Soph, he would go to the Rush.

Now the Cheese had a Swell Dame, who watched the Rush from the Bleachers. She saw the Big Doings of the Corncob and said to the Cheese, who stood at her side, "Who is that Swell Guy in the Corduroys? Ain't he Brave?"

So she got a knockdown to the Corncob and gave the Cheese the Icy Mitt. Then the Corncob married the Swell Dame, and they lived happily ever afterwards.

Moral: Go to the Rush.

GAS METER RHYMES

by our own Walt Mason.
I'm Not in the Whirl.

(October 20, 1911) I shave my neck; I part my hair in the middle, I wear "pants" not trousers, and call a violin a "fiddle." I don't smoke the pill; I don't know the Varsity yell. I haven't a bubble duster, or even a six-cylinder smell. I speak plain English not rah-rah slang; and, although I'm a pretty good fellow, I don't suit the college gang; for I haven't a hairy hat or a hobbled girl, and besides my coat's too long; so I'm not in the whirl.

When I ponder over my grievances, I find there's something wrong that hurts. I'm rated in class 2, compared with mollycoddles who should be wearing skirts. Fate is dealing aces from the bottom of the deck--cheating in a most underhanded way. At home 'tis said I'm a youth of "much promise" but here--well, I'm not in the whirl.#

Official Song Sheet -- The Michigan Daily

"THE VICTORS"

(Nov. 12, 1904) Now for a cheer, they are here, triumphant;
Here they come with banners flying,
In stalwart step they're nighing, with
shout of victory crying
On! Hurrah, Hurrah, we greet you now
Hail!
For we their praises sing for the glory and fame they bring us,
Loud let the bells then ring,
For here they come with banner flying,
Here they come, Hurrah!

CHORUS:

Hail to the victors valiant,
Hail to the conquering heroes,
Hail, hail to Michigan,
Leaders and best.
With pride we hail the victors valiant,
Hail to the conquering heroes,
Hail, hail to Michigan,
The Champions of the West.

We cheer them again, we cheer for Michigan,
We cheer with might and main.
Hail to the conquering heroes,
Hail, hail to Michigan,
The Champions of the West.#

New Field Song Goes on Sale.

(October 20, 1911) "Varsity," the new field song by Lawton and Moore, has been published by the University Music House. The cover, in three colors, was drawn by J. H. Meier, winner of last year's opera poster contest, and shows a be-megaphoned cheer leader, starting in front of the twenty-yard line, with an Irish terrier for an assistant.#

WILL ROGERS

A review, by Robert Henderson

(Nov. 26, 1925) What will you? ... He is funny, the subtlest comedian on the American stage, much cleverer than Al Jolson with his semite bathos, surely funnier than Raymon Hitchcock and Fanny Brice -- I have never seen Fred Stone. And he is possessed of devils: something there is in him that can twist any hero into a zany; he is pregnant with an impudence, American and of Butte, Wyoming.

There is that in him which is growing far too rare in our land and glory -- a zest for gaucherie, a homely, biting unmorality. Today, with all our clans for virtue, with our zealots for stamped efficiency, his clear-eyed irony and clean disillusionment can still stagger our national dragbags and their sawdust manners.

His is a satire that can picture President Calvin soused, the University a tomb of Nordic hopes, the cinema queens in moral perversions for the publicity of their films and the Senate a chest of pompous derelicts. His is a humor unmannered and ungodly -- a vast Rabelasian wit.

...

Each effect planned as skillfully as it was hidden, his best points were those of general excitement: Colonel Mitchell and the Prince of Wales became much more familiar ground than the new champions of the west -- with a wry smile -- and President Little. This odd talent, sophisticated and naive, could hold an absolute attention for all its illiteracy. It has created a prophet and a smasher of Rotary shams, cogent and acid and disarming.#

Valentine Davies won an Academy Award in 1947 for the screenplay of "Miracle on 34th Street" and nominations for "The Glenn Miller Story" and "It Happens Every Spring."

The Theatre Ascendant

II. Norman-Bel Geddes, by Valentine Davies.

(Editors Note: This is the second of a series of six articles on contemporary personalities in the modern world theatre.)

...

(Feb. 22, 1925) Norman-Bel Geddes is perhaps the most spectacular scenic designer of the new generation, but he is also the most practical. His vivid, unbounded imagination pictures new and beautiful things; and his practical sense works them out to the minutest detail. He binds himself by no laws or conventions of the theatre. He does not even let the physical limitations of the stage interfere with his conceptions. First he conceives; then he proceeds to work out the practical problems. Nothing daunts him; he will even build a theatre to suit his ideas. This was what first brought him into the field of which he is one of the leaders today.

...

Each one of his sets is modeled to scale and completely worked out by his staff, whether it is actually to be used or not. When I visited his studio they were at work on his set for the Players' Club revival of "The Rivals." Later I saw the actual set, which was one of the most beautiful ones that he has ever designed.

...

Those who expect to see in Geddes a man as striking as his work are disappointed when they meet him. He is not at all unusual looking. He is for one thing quite young, blond and quite short. His clothing is about equal to that of an average college student. He has a strong disliking for vests and rarely wears them. He is given to slang and speaks with a typical mid-western accent. He has no pose -- or perhaps that is his pose. He shows no conceit, either openly or by conscious modesty. One would never picture him as an artist -- perhaps the only sign of his active mind is a constant movement -- brushing his hands through his hair -- hitching up his belt, etc., etc. Even his name though it sounds artistic is not really so. It is Norman Geddes. The "hyphen Bel" part was added through a peculiar chance. When he first began submitting sketches, he worked in collaboration with his wife. Her first name was Belle, and so the drawings were signed Norman-Bel Geddes. The name stuck and all his work is signed Norman-Bel Geddes...#

SHOW OF OPERA SCORES HIT

DANCING AND COSTUMES ARE STRIKING FEATURES

(By Thomas E. Dewey)

(Dec. 10, 1921) From the brilliant, varied dance that gave the 1922 production of the Michigan Mimes, "Make It for Two," a send-off which would satisfy the most critical follower of Mr. Ziegfield's production, to the stirring lines of "The Victors," at the close, the fourth night of the show went through its spectacular numbers last night with a snap which lagged seldom, and which carried the production into the lasting memories of every member of the audience.

Most striking in the show is, of course, the costuming, of which Lester can well be proud. Such scenes as "Garden of Girls" and the final denouement which breaks into a laugh at the tragic, "Betrayed!" of Nemo the king, will give this year's opera a prestige on the road for splendor not equalled by many of the productions on the road today.

The dancing this year is the best ever shown in an opera, without question, with the Dagger Dance in the last act as the most striking and professional act of the show. The songs and rhythmical music of Cyrus N. Tavares, '24, and Dwan Y. Tang, '24E, who, decked in native costume, opened the second act with the most unique scene of the evening.#

RADIO *Gang Busters*

By DAVID LACHENBRUCH

(March 30, 1941) (Today The Daily inaugurates a new feature--radio criticism--to be run in much the same manner as a column of drama criticism...)

GANG BUSTERS -- For my first review, I'm giving myself an easy job. There probably aren't many on campus who listen to the program (WWJ--9 p.m. Friday), since the majority of the audience are not college types. Still, because of the influence this type of program exerts, it is well to discuss the feature, which PTA organizations have been railing against for years.

...

Friday's dramatization sponsored by liniment, concerned the heroic adventures of Charleson and Rodgers, the "nickel and dime bandits." They seemed like real nice boys. Charleson, at the beginning of the play, tells Rodgers that he has a "new idea to get a lot of dough" -- namely that they drive around the Mississippi Valley holding up small retail establishments. "We'll make as much as if we robbed a dozen big banks," he says twice. They speak of their scheme in such glowing terms that it would inspire practically any weak-willed kid to think seriously on the scheme. Another time, one of the crooks says, "Boy, dis is de life. Newspapers screamin' about us all over de country. Nothin' to do but sit down an' take it easy." So they go south, robbing every gas station along the way, and obtain expensive silk shirts, new cars, liquor, guns, pin money. Not one word is spoken against the criminals until the very end--that makes the play more interesting.

...

Gang Busters is definitely hopped up to make it exciting. Characters are reinforced and the result is a militant, brave brand of gangster whom it is not difficult to admire. No matter with what intentions these programs are written and aired, they contribute greatly to the child's and adolescent's intriguing admiration for crime. Some first-offender reformatory cases have admitted that the ideas for the perpetration of their offense came directly from the radio crime dramas...#

SEE THE COUNTRY:
Seeger Discusses Music Appeal Change

By MARGE PIERCY

(Oct. 11, 1955) "Folk music has undergone a tremendous revival since I went to college when it was something for sticks, hicks and a few esoteric scholars," Pete Seeger remarked Sunday.

Interviewed in Detroit where he gave a concert Friday night and a children's concert Sunday, Seeger expressed optimism about the new interest in folk music, a revival and not a survival, he stressed.

The major trend in American life is toward mass production for low cost consumption, but it has produced a countertrend in the form of the do-it-yourself movement.

"The Sunday painter, the basement toolshop handyman, the wife making ceramics or hand block prints are all part of a healthy movement," he continued.

Seeger speaks readily in a low, even voice about his music but only reluctantly about himself. Every bit of biography extracted reminds him of something else about folk music.

Though both his parents were professional musicians, Seeger wanted to be a journalist. But when he left Harvard after two years in a depression economy there were no jobs for journalists. "I did change singing in saloons, on back porches, street corners, revival meetings, learning songs and seeing the country."

"The ages between 18 and 24 are the one time you can really see the country, before you settle down." The most valuable way for college students to spend the summer, he insisted vehemently, is "hitchhiking around the country."

See the People

"Students tell me they have to earn money for the fall semester, but taking a year off from school, seeing the 48 states and meeting people is the most valuable thing you can do. The one way to see a town is to drift in broke. You have to meet the people."

Seeger spent three and a half years in the army, ending up in the Pacific. "We have a family joke about my army career. My son asks me, 'What did you do in the army?' and I tell him, 'I played

SINGER PETE SEEGER
... part of folk music revival

the banjo.' I organized shows and entertained troops mainly."

Seeger feels one of the best things about the folk music revival is that "It's creating a new tradition of popular folk songs out of the best of old traditions," which has an influence through the whole field of music.

Not Low Class Music

"For centuries fine arts composers have swiped folk tunes, but today folk music is no longer a lower class music. The same person can like to sing folk tunes, dance to good jazz, and listen to symphonic music. It's music for different purposes without being on different social levels."

The ancient definition of folk music as anonymous doesn't hold. "Today's folk music is written by city people on typewriters. It takes a very unusual work of art to last beyond the period of history that created it originally, but a few of these will last hundreds of years."

Discussing the recent House Un-American Activities Committee Seeger remarked, "Our grandchildren will look back on this period and shake their heads. I stated under oath I'd never done anything conspiratorially and they never questioned that, and I offered to sing any song I'd ever sung anyplace."#

'THE COOL WORLD':
We Dying All the Time

(Sept. 23, 1959) **AN IMPORTANT** novel dealing with juvenile delinquency was published in America this year-- Warren Miller's "The Cool World." The book is quite remarkable as a work of fiction but will probably go unnoticed since it is not sensational enough, in the profitable sense, to merit the publicity that would be given a "Peyton Place" or a "Lady Chatterly's Lover."

* * *

"THE COOL WORLD" ...is Warren Miller's second novel...set in Harlem, the principle protagonist being Duke Custis who is fourteen years old and a prominent figure in the Royal Crocadiles, a teen-age gang whose chief activity is "rumbling" with the Wolves, a rival hoard.

Duke's ambition is to buy a gun and become leader of the gang. He states it nakedly: "Someday I come walkin down the street they all look at me with respect and say, 'There goes a cold killer. Here come Duke Custis. He a cold killer.' Then everybody pay attention--and listen when I talk--I be at the top of the heap and when I push they stay push..."

* * *

THE CROCADILES move into an abandoned tenement flat and are joined by Lu Ann, a fifteen-year-old girl, who becomes the club prostitute. Blood, an older boy who is leader of the gang, announces, "She dont put out for nobody but Crocadiles hear?...One dollar fifty. One dollar for Lu Ann and 50 cents for the treasury. 50 cents is the club cut...We have money soon to buy some pieces."

...

Through Duke's descriptions, we are given pathetic insight into the sparse upbringing of these youngsters. "...We lay on the bed an read the comic books. ...She read the one about the monster an askin me to tell her whut is this word an whut is that word. Some of them I knew an some of them I dont know. I read the Mighty Mouse. But they was only one Mighty Mouse an which I finish it I didnt feel like readen anymore."

...

Warren Miller has written a brilliant novel. Its language is colloquial because the author thought it the most effective way to write of his characters. Duke's narrative is warm and clear, occasionally approaching the rhapsodic, and not without humor.

What is most commendable about "The Cool World" is that it mirrors the life of these neglected boys, growing like weeds, in a way that points no finger at anyone but teaches much...#

--Al Young

Dylan Delights Public

(April 24, 1962) **AS COLORFUL** as his red-checkered shirt, as lively as his skipping fingers, as dynamic as his wild harmonica and as ethnic and varied as his audience, Bob Dylan proved his reputation as one of the most promising new stars in folk singing Sunday night.

Short in stature but tall in talent, Bob Dylan had the audience in hand the moment he stepped on stage. Unlike many of the "rising young artists" Bob Dylan steers clear of the tried and trite folk songs that are now altogether too familiar.

* * *

THE TWO FINEST songs of the performance were both his: "Walk in my Shoes" a serious ballad on the present American emphasis on death and bomb shelters and "Talking John Birch Society Paranoid Blues" a comic-parody of high degree. The poetry of his language and the naturalness of his style add another facet to his talents.

While his guitar playing was intricate and strong it was the combination of his frantic harmonica and his trance-like, searching voice that most enthralled the audience. Catching a note, Dylan would wrestle with it and squeeze every meaning and emotion from it only to go after another and another.

Asked how he likes singing as a career, Bob Dylan answered that it was fine but that he'd rather be riding his motorcycle around the country. With his talent, and the hearty approval he receives wherever he performs he's not likely to ride that cycle for a long, long time. Bob Dylan is bound for other roads right now.

--Hugh Holland

PP&M:
Soft-Style Folksinging

(March 3, 1963) **PETER, PAUL** and Mary: three names of religious significance. Peter and Paul indeed look the Christian part; and Mary: well, more Magdalene than Madonna.

The Magdalene bit is perfect, too, just "come hither" enough to interest, but pure enough to let the men in the audience know it's hands off. and so said men, duly pacified, turn back to their dates, and all are happy.

And happy is what PP&M aim at, as entertainers. What they aim at as folk singers seems dubious, but the entertainment comes through strong.

* * *

MARY IS the pro entertainer of the outfit, as she swings a subtle twist through her songs, her skirts flaring just high enough to escape cheesecake.

...

Besides offsetting their female partner's appeal with what they call "grotesqueness," Peter and Paul bring laughs. Paul, the tall one, is a master of sound effects--from a boat to a toilet down to a Michigan State football player. And Peter offers group participation and intellectual appeal: from splitting the audience into "in-group out-group" to chanting pacifist songs.

The humor varies from such cornball as laughing at their own jokes to a classic burlesque on rock n' roll singing to a subtle "We're glad to see you at least identify with America" aimed at collegiate politics.

And so as entertainers PP&M rate. Their folk singing is another question. Their vocal restraint leads one to believe they lack the strong voices necessary for folk singing. Their belabored beat and emphasis on harmony leads one to believe that they believe the same, and are content to entertain.

But the only time their vocal virtuosity interferes with enjoyment of the program is when they bravely attack such pieces as "This Land," voices rasping full force. They sing their best on their well-practiced hits like "Where Have All the Flowers Gone?" which the audience appreciates for familiarity and perhaps nostalgic memories they evoke...#

--Burton Michaels

McCartney dead; new evidence brought to light

To the best of anyone's knowledge, this was the first, true, original Paul-is-dead story.

By FRED LaBOUR
Copyright 1969 The Michigan Daily

(EDITOR'S NOTE: Mr. LaBour was originally assigned to review Abbey Road, the Beatles' latest album, for The Daily. While extensively researching Abbey Road's background, however, he chanced upon a startling string of coincidences which put him on the trail of something much more significant. He wishes to thank WKNR-FM, Louise Harrison Caldwell, and George Martin's illegitimate daughter Marian for their help. Mr. LaBour says it's all true.)

(Oct. 14, 1969) **PAUL McCARTNEY** was killed in an automobile accident in early November, 1966 after leaving EMT recording studios tired, sad, and dejected.

The Beatles had been preparing their forthcoming album, tentatively entitled Smile, when progress bogged down in intra-group hassles and bickering. Paul climbed into his Aston Martin, sped away into the rainy, chill night and was found four hours later pinned under his car in a culvert with the top of his head sheared off. He was deader than a doornail.

Thus began the greatest hoax of our time and the subsequent founding of a near religion based upon Paul as Messiah.

The Beatles as a whole had considered seriously what would happen to them if one should meet with death as early as 1964 when substitute drummers were utilized to fill in for an ailing Ringo Starr. However, it should be emphasized for the sake of religious records, that they had no definite premonition of the death of Paul. From all accounts, it appears to have been simply an unforeseen accident.

When word of Paul's untimely demise was flashed back to the studios, the surviving Beatles, in a hurriedly called conference with George Martin, decided to keep the information from the public for as long as possible. As John Lennon reportedly said, "Paul always liked a good joke," and it seemed that they considered the move an attempt to make the best out of a bad situation. As will be seen shortly, however, the "good joke" soon took on terrifying proportions.

George Harrison was called upon to bury Paul, Ringo conducted services and John went into seclusion for three days. After his meditation, Lennon called another meeting of the group, again with George Martin, and laid the groundwork for the ensuing hoax. Lennon's plan was to create a false Paul McCartney, bring him into the group as if nothing had happened, and then slowly release the information of the real Paul's death to the world via clues secreted in record albums.

THE PLAN WAS adopted, although Ringo expressed skepticism as to its possible success, and work began. (Brian Epstein was informed of the group's plan, threatened to expose it all and mysteriously died, leaving five men who knew of the plot.)

First, a Paul Look-a-Like contest was held and a living substitute found in Scotland. He was an orphan from Edinburgh, named William Campbell, and his picture before joining the Beatles can be found in the lower left-hand corner of the collage distributed with the Beatles album.

Minor plastic surgery was required to complete the image, and Campbell's mustache distracted everyone who knew the original McCartney from the imposter's real identity. The other Beatles consequently grew mustaches to further integrate the "new" Paul into the group.

Voice print studies have confirmed the difference in voice timbre between the original and phoney Paul, but the difference was so slight that after studying tapes of Paul's voice and singing style, Campbell nearly erased entirely his own speech patterns and successfully adopted the late McCartney's.

...

Lennon and Martin worked closely throughout the spring of 1967 on Sgt. Pepper. Their goal was an artistically and monetarily successful album filled with clues to Paul's death.

It was decided that an appropriate cover would include a grave and so it does. At the lower part of the grave are yellow flowers shaped as Paul's bass or, if you prefer, the initial "P." On the inside of the cover, on the fake Paul's left arm, is a patch reading "O.P.D." which

is the symbol used in England similar to our "DOA" meaning Officially Pronounced Dead. The medal upon his left breast is given by the British Army commemorating heroic death.

On the back cover, Paul's back is turned to us. The others are facing us.

THE SONGS ON the album contain numerous references to Paul's accident, "A Day in the Life" being the most obvious example. "A crowd of people stood and stared. They'd seen his face before...etc." When the top of a man's head is sheared off his identity is partially obscured.

...

While Sgt. Pepper was being recorded, Lennon worked on a song called "Strawberry Fields Forever" and inserted at the end of the recording after the horn freakout, a distorted voice saying "I buried Paul." Play it at 45 rpm and check it yourself.

...

Lennon had been doing a great deal of reading on the ritual of death in various cultures around the world (documented by Hunter Daves' authorized biography of the Beatles) and presented his knowledge graphically in Tour.

One instance is the constant appearance of a hand behind Paul's head in nearly every picture in the record album. The hand behind the head is a symbol to mystics of death. Another is the picture of Paul (Campbell) on page three with the poster saying "I YOU WAS" indicating change of identity. Another is the appearance of surgeons and policemen, both involved in Paul's car crash, on page five.

On page ten and thirteen Paul is shown wearing black trousers and no shoes. Dead men are buried in black trousers and without shoes. Empty shoes, as appear next to Ringo's drums on page thirteen, were a Grecian symbol of death. And finally, on page twenty-three where the group has just descended a long, curving staircase, Paul is shown wearing a black rose while the other three are wearing red roses.

THE SONGS again are paramount. "Magical Mystery Tour" implies the hoax in its entirety and marks Lennon's developing suspicion that the plot is out of hand. They are "dying" to take us away. "The Fool on the Hill" sits "perfectly still," as though dead, and grins a dead man's "foolish grin."

...

...Played backwards, a favorite ploy of the Beatles as early as "Rain," the words "Paul's dead" can be plainly heard.

...

Thus we come to Abbey Road. (Monks live in abbeys.) On the cover is John Lennon, dressed in white and resembling utterly an anthropomorphic God, followed by Ringo the undertaker, followed by Paul the resurrected, barefoot with a cigarette in his right hand (the original was left handed), followed by George, the grave digger.

AND IF YOU look closely, they have just walked out of a cemetery on the left side of the street. Thus, Paul was resurrected, given a cigarette, and led out of the tomb, thereby conquering death with a little help from his friends.

The real Paul is still dead, of course, but his symbolic resurrection works fine without him.

The album itself contains clues to his death and now, clues to his resurrection. "Maxwell's Silver Hammer" is a tale of religious justice, with a dashed in head for punishment. "Octopus's Garden" is British Navy slang for the cemetery in England where naval heroes are buried. "I Want You (She's So Heavy)" is Lennon wrestling with Paul, trying to pull him out of the earth...

The second side announces the principles upon which the religion will be based: beauty, humor, love, realism, objectivity...It analyzes inter-personal relationships in "You Never Give Me Your Money," explains Paul's part in the ritual in "Sun King" ("Here come the sun king. Everybody's laughing") humorously, never cruelly inspects money grubbers and fad-followers in "Mean Mr. Mustard" and "Polythene Pam," and realistically looks at life with "Boy, you're gonna carry that weight a long time."

AND AT THE END, Paul ascends to the right hand of John and proclaims, "the love you take is equal to the love you make."

But in the VERY end, they are joking about the Queen. The Beatles are building a mighty church, and when you emerge from it, you will be laughing, for Paul is the Sun of God.#

News startles McCartney fans

Thanks Silvio

To the Editor:

(Oct. 17, 1969) I READ and immensely enjoyed Mr. LaBour's article. As a student of the law of evidence, I can tell you that Mr. LaBour's conclusion is the result of piling inferences upon inferences and a certain amount of post hoc propter hoc reasoning.

But all of this is irrelevant for even if Mr. LaBour's conclusion is incorrect he has succeeded in achieving what all rock music reviewers strive for: namely, the creation of an album review which is as beautiful and meaningful as the album itself...

All you need is love.

--Silvio Nardoni
'70 Law

More truths

To the Editor:

A VERY INTERESTING article indeed by your Fred LaBour concerning the death of Paul McCartney. It is unfortunate that he did not check into the matter a little farther (as we did) and learn the truth of the matter instead of foisting his hoax of a purportedly true story upon your readers. Three years ago (the precise date is unascertainable), Bob Dylan was killed when his motorcycle smashed into a corner drugstore just outside of Hibbing, Minnesota. ...his family was immediately notified and according to a plan Dylan had made known to them in case of accidental death, they paid off the occupants of the drugstore to keep quiet and then the family buried the body in secrecy.

...

AT THE TIME, in accordance with Dylan's plan, McCartney was flown over and his face changed by plastic surgery to resemble Dylan's. You might notice the original resemblance between the two. So McCartney actually was replaced and the clues in the albums of the Beatles are intentional, but this is only part of the greater plan to mask Dylan's death....

...

If Mr. LaBour is interested we can direct him to the story of the death of Joan Baez eight years ago, and perhaps the most bizarre story of all, the death of Richard Nixon three years ago and the hoax where no one has been used to take his place...

--Fargo Berman
--T. Falconridge Blake

Going to Rio

Del Rio
122 W. Washington
Hours: 11:30 a.m.-2 a.m., Monday-Friday; noon-2:30 a.m., Saturday; 5 p.m.-2 a.m. Sunday

By Julie Hinds

(Nov. 19, 1982) 1969–THOSE were the good old days. Where have all the radicals gone? Where is that tough, cocky attitude? Where are the real places to drink beer?

1982--we're drowning in a sea of pink and green as students try to outconform each other. we sup our beer at Charley's or Dooley's, where happy, peppy, preppy plasticity is the order of the day.

That's o.k.--if you're good at that sort of thing. But if you long for a time when the hair was longer, the clothes more rumpled, and the drunken statements more profound, there's still an oasis on the Ann Arbor bar circuit. This haven of authenticity? Del Rio.

...

The prices run from convenient to damn cheap. Del Rio knows that if you're slightly counterculture, you probably don't have a lot of money. For hard-core poverty cases, the plain, but filling, burrito is a mere 85 cents. The $1.95 deluxe burrito can easily feed two. Other staples on the menu are pizza, nachos, and the beer-steamed Detburger (created, according to the menu, by J. Detwiler, jazz musician and former bartender).

...

It's fun being a student. But it's a tough image to keep up. Just think of all those Shetlands and Oxfords you have to keep clean. When looking nice and acting nice and going out to a nice place is just too much to bear, let your hair down and go to Del Rio. Real people are welcome.#

A hometown girl named Gilda finds the time's prime to make people laugh

By JAY LEVIN

(March 26, 1978) **ON THIS PAR-TICULAR** Friday, little Gilda has plopped herself on a pink shag rug; stuffed toys and dollhouses at her fingertips. She is playing with her Looking For Mr. Goodbar Sleepytime Playset, and an impish grin of delight crosses her face as she dances her Diane Keaton doll around an imaginary singles bar with a plastic businessman.

But little Gilda misses the point of this game. Rather than have her dollies boogie the night away, Gilda is told that the object is for Diane Keaton to pick up as many strange men as possible before being killed.

...

This is a rehearsal for the set of NBC's Saturday Night Live, and little Gilda is Gilda Radner--a once obscure weathergirl for Ann Arbor's WCBN who is now a somewhat obscure TV crack-up. Unless you watch Saturday Night Live, you probably haven't the foggiest who Gilda Radner is. If that's the case, then you've probably never heard of Emily Letella, Rhonda Weiss, Roseanne Rosannadana, Lisa Leubner and Baba Wawa. Gilda Radner is all those people.

But, more than anything else, Gilda Radner is your little sister, or the nerdy girl down the aisle in Hebrew School or the funny kid with the big mouth.

...

Inside the small, spartan dressing room that she shares with fellow Prime Timers Jane Curtin and Laraine Newman, Radner curls up on a sofa and reaches for a tray of cheese and crackers. She lights up a Virginia Slim. She offers her guests Tabs. And she commences to tell how a pudgy Detroit girl--a University of Michigan drop-out, no less--has managed to establish herself as a cult heroine among late-night TV addicts.

Much of what she does, Radner says, is drawn from her youth.

"What I do in comedy I call bedroom comedy," she says. "It's like the stuff you did in your bedroom with your girlfriends during a slumber party. I also used to shut myself in my brother's room and pantomime to records and do stuff in the mirror."

...

Everything Radner does during the week is in preparation for the 90 minute show broadcast live Saturday nights at 11:30. "I think of it as an opening night," she says of the actual show, one of the only live programs left on network TV. "Each show is like the opening night of an under-rehearsed off-Broadway show...and we're never getting to do it again."

She credits her stage experience with preparing her for the rigors of Saturday Night Live. And she credits Saturday Night Live with preparing her for what lies ahead in her performing future.

"Before I did this show I never performed alone, I always performed in groups," she says. "Now I have monologues and characters that work alone. I cannot believe it, but I have enough material now that I do by myself that I can now go (somewhere else) and do it."

What will you be doing at age 41, Gilda? Stage? Perhaps. Movies? Maybe.

Like a preoccupied child, she has no idea where she'll be ten years from now.

But, she says, she'll always be in show business. "I have no fears of being unemployed," she says confidently.

Though Radner says she dared never fantasize about stardom, she admits having fleeting premonitions of celebrity.

"I never thought this would happen," she says, "yet I remember coming down the stairs of my house one day and saying to my boyfriend at the time 'Someday I'll know kings and princesses.' I didn't know why I said it."

And kings and princesses she has known. Despite the sweat, Gilda enjoys a good measure of glamor. TV guest shots. Rubbing elbows with a different Saturday Night Live guest host each week. An occasional evening at Studio 54.

"I even met a Beatle," she chirps with all the enthusiasm of a teenager crashing the backstage of a concert. "It was George--and he knew who I was!"

Undoubtedly, Gilda's gotten a lot of press recently--in good places like New Times and People (cover story), and not-so-good places like the National Enquirer. Such exposure is threatening to blow her cover as a well-kept secret. Because of the show's appeal to a predominantly young viewership, Radner is a little-known entity among the older set and the early-to-bed generation. That means she can roam her adopted New York unmolested, but such splashy magazine coverage--People called her the "Darling of Saturday Night Live"--worries her.

For one thing, Radner says she's been unfairly compared with Chevy Chase...

"The media divided him from us, called him a star and made him leave too soon," she says. "People use that comparison, but the thing is, I refuse to believe it or live by it or let (the press) divide me from the group."

Radner says she's worked with her fellow Prime Timers too long to let the media single her out.

"I can never feel like a star around here."

✱ ✱ ✱ ✱ ✱

GILDA RADNER has a theory about her acting technique: She hasn't any. "The best thing I do," she says, "is pretend, and that's what acting is to me--pretending. Like we did the Video Vixens, a punk rock group, so I was really pretending that I was Patti Smith and I was pretending that I could sing and that I'm hot and dirty and a rock star. And then I see the tapeback, and it's me!...But if people like what I do, it may be because they know they're seeing me pretend."#

arts
&
letters

we
get
letters

Students Express Disappointment

(May 11, 1960) **To the Editor:**

                we
being of all purposes
                eager to see
                        mr cummings etcetera
        bought tickets
                at eight
        on monday morning
we love you, union and english dept
our faces lit up
                onetwothreefourfiveetcetera
                        Jesus,
        we were happy
                we sat in row c
we love you, union and english dept
we came
        and asked who sat onstage
                only to find ourselves
                        there
studying the
        wrinkles on
                cummings' neck etcetera
his voice
        drowned out
        som
        E
          wh ere and nowhe
                        Re
we love you, union and english dept
                during the second half,
                unless statistics
                                lie,
                not a soul was left
                behind mr cummings
studying the
        wrinkles on
                his neck etcetera
his voice
        drowned out
    by
som
E
  wh ere and nowhe
                Re
and what we want to know is
                who
                        the h....'s to blame--
we're disgusted, o union and english dept
                                --Merrill Waitburn

Letters to the Editor:

How About Shay's Rebellion, Mr. Yost?

To The Editor:

(Jan. 24, 1932) If not the 18th Amendment, then what? For one hundred and forty years our governments, national, state and local, attempted to regulate the manufacture and sale of liquor, beer, wine, etc., under the license system. Under this system the saloon was condemned by everyone. Does anyone know of a saloon keeper that did not in some way violate the law? Thousands of those who could not or would not pay the liquor license entered the speakeasy, bootleg, and moonshine business. Call the new place of sale whatever you please, it will still be a place where liquor is sold, and the same problem as of old will return. The first rebellion our country had was the Whiskey Rebellion in western Pennsylvania during Washington's administration, and all those who have sold liquor ever since have been in "rebellion" against the laws that have been made to regulate, prevent or control the sale of alcohol.

Fielding H. Yost.

Analogy?

To the Editor:

(May 26, 1938) Coincidence!

On the same day this week, two widely divergent political bodies entered upon a similar course of action. The Reichspropagandaministerium of the resurrected Greater German Empire and the Ann Arbor City Council were in accord:

BERLIN, May 24--(AP)--The American magazine Ken was banned from sale in Germany.

ANN ARBOR, Mich., May 24--(U.P.)--The American magazines Ken and Esquire were banned from Ann Arbor.

--R.W.

Give Him Air...

To the Editor:

(May 23, 1954) ...Just who is this Tom Arp anyhow that is a campus legend? I have never heard of Tom Arp and I have been to school here ten years as an undergraduate and graduate in steam engineering. I have lived in Ann Arbor for ten years now and I never heard of any Tom Arp...

...

...Now another thing, I think something should be done, like a long series of stories, about the poor ventilation in the steam compression lab in the second basement of the engineering building. Five other people and me have been working in this damp place for seven years now, ...and the air conditioning is not working and never did... Instead of writing long stories about publications people like Tom Arp, why don't you try and do something about the ventilation down here? I would like to see a few editorials someday about this place.

...Just happened to think; somebody told me you forgot to mention me in the honors supplement. I won the Ezra W. Thatchbody award in steam engineering last month for my design of a steam powered trombone. This prize was an unabridged set of the steam tables in eleven volumes in greek. I think this should have been mentioned if it wasn't. And get busy on that story about the ventilation down here. Forget about Tom Arp. I never heard of him anyway.

--Dave Kessel

Readers Deprived Of 'Right to Know'...

To the Editor:

(Oct. 27, 1961) **ONCE AGAIN** The Daily, exercising the much-abused franchise of so-called "editorial freedom," has deprived its readers of their right to know. With what has become customary in its approach--so-called "liberalism," "progressivism," and the like--The Daily has disregarded the dictates of taste and of propriety, and in a spirit of over-ambitious modernization, has most cruelly and unthinkingly seen fit to omit a long-standing campus tradition, one dear to the hearts of all who have trod these hallowed halls.

Last Sunday, groping up to the nadir of mediocrity, The Daily failed to print the Slippery Rock score in its traditional place of honor above the masthead.

--Mason Wyxun, Jr., '60

The conspiracy of the Ohio State 22,000...

To the Editor:

(Nov. 26, 1969) **THE PUBLIC SAFETY** and respect for the law have been violated again by a small group of extremists, waving banners, taking over the streets, and creating a riot which engulfed the whole of Ann Arbor last Saturday, Nov. 22. This must not go unchallenged by the Department of Justice. The disorder and violence which swept this town on Saturday had been carefully planned months in advance, by a small group operating across state lines; a major base from which rioters were recruited was in another state, and the actions of Nov. 22 clearly centered on violence, inside and outside of the stadium.

AS WAS ONLY to be expected, the publicly proclaimed moral standards of the American people were flouted by acts of gross indecency, and the lives of everyone who attempted to use the roads were endangered by the crazed and drunken mob which took them over. The police were utterly unable to prevent or control these flagrant violations of law, decency, and public order, nor could we expect them to have done so in the face of an interstate conspiracy of this magnitude.

The Ann Arbor-Columbus conspiracy cries out for prosecution!

--Prof. Rhoads Murphey
Center for Chinese Studies

A Study
of the Motion Picture

(By William M. Randall)

(Oct. 8, 1922) During the past ten years a new medium has been added to the repertoire of art's interpreters...

Unfortunately for the form itself and for the race of man, the artists do not know of it. And so we have the astounding and sorrow-provoking spectacle of a great opportunity for wonderful accomplishments going to waste...

Of course, it is true that the so-called prostitution of art is no new thing. We find it in every artistic field -- in the trashy novels and the trashy plays that clutter up our libraries; in the trashy pictures and the trashy marbles in our art stores; and in the trashy music in our cabarets and concert-halls. But in no other field has there been such an absolute dearth of worthy effort, such an absolute waste and misdirection of energy, and such an appalling effect upon the public taste and, I believe, upon the public morals, as has resulted from the first decade in the history of the Motion Picture.

Last year somebody or other presented Mae Murray in "The Gilded Lily." This picture might be taken as typical of the sort of thing with which a major part of the exhibitors are seeking to amuse their public.

First of all let us examine the "star" whose name appeared in letters at least as large as those announcing the title of the attraction, and therefore must be held forth as an inducement of at least as great weight for seeing the picture.

She is introduced to us in the picture as Lily, the cabaret girl. She comes dancing into the middle of the spotlight in as little as will get by the censors, and continues to dance for a few feet of film. So far, so good. She can dance. We must give her credit for that. And then she goes back to her dressing room. Now -- far be it from me to insinuate that I have seen the inside of all the cabaret dressing rooms in this great United States. But you can take it from me the inside of a dressing room was never like that! If it was,

there would have been no need for the Actor's Equity. As a matter of fact, it is not a dressing room into which she goes; it is a cross between the best room in an artistic Sultan's harem and the showroom in a Fifth Avenue "Maison des Robes."

...

Now what does Lily do? Very little, I assure you, my friend. By actual count she dances twice, drinks one glass of wine, walks in the park once, weeps twice, laughs three times, and lies around in graceful positions the rest of the time. In other words, she is not there to act; she is there to be looked at. The work is done by the poor supporting cast, who have to scurry around and scrape together a semblance of a plot to give Mae an excuse to be charming. The plot they manage to evolve bears a family resemblance to Camille, except that it comes out happily after all, due to the thoughtfulness of the author in providing a man for Lily-Camille to fall back on when Armand went home to mother. They are much more thoughtful in the movies than they are in the plays.

Well -- that's that. It represents the contribution of that month from one of the largest studios. It will be seen by probably eight or ten million people. What will be its effect? What will the young girl in the large city or the small town think when she sees this wonderful lady with the Lily-white Soul find Love and Happiness in a cabaret (and at the same time have a wonderful time)? Is it going to make her any more contented to pound her typewriter or weed the beans? Obviously not. Probably it will not move a single person to go and do likewise. We are not so gullible as that. But it will give a distorted image of life; it will make for discontent and unhappiness; and all because it chooses, like ninety-nine out of a hundred other moving pictures choose, to tell lies instead of the truth.

That's what's the matter with the Moving Picture! It's a Liar -- that's all!#

STUDENT HURT IN RIOTING

SHOWS ORDERED CLOSED

(March 9, 1927) One student was reported to be in a rather serious condition late yesterday, and is still confined to the University hospital, as a result of the riot which followed the basketball game Monday night. Henry Blakely, '27, of Rockford, Ill., the injured student, was burned and cut about the face by the explosion of a tear gas bomb and by blank cartridges...

...

A request was made late yesterday afternoon by Mayor Campbell that the Butterfield management institute free entertainment in one or both of their campus theaters, to begin immediately after the general pep meeting which was held last night in the assembly room of the Union... This request was not complied with by the managers of the theaters, due to the fact that they could not make arrangements on such short notice.

Mayor Campbell then issued an order officially closing the theaters after their first evening performance, in order that the city might not be held responsible for any damages which might result...#

INDISCREET

(March 9, 1927) Michigan students have again been regrettably involved in a movie rush and a subsequent encounter with the officers of the law. Rather than the students, however, the members of the local police force located in the vicinity of the Arcade theater were the chief offenders in the disturbance.

In driving the students and townspeople from the sidewalks for a block from the theater, and in chasing them off the adjacent parts of the campus, the officers showed considerable indiscretion and obviously exceeded their rights. Their use of night sticks and tear gas bombs was carried much farther than was necessary. On two occasions, at least, the glass cartridges were fired at such close range and in such a manner that the faces of students were cut by the fragments...

The students, of course, were not entirely blameless for the affair. The "hoodlum" action of a certain class on the campus, which has been exhibited upon previous occasions, was the fundamental reason for the presence of the officers...

This, however, does not excuse the unwarranted action of the police. Their excessive use of weapons and their indiscretion should be severely condemned.#

PROMISE FREE SHOWS AFTER CHAMPIONSHIP GAMES

THEATER MANAGERS OFFER TO GIVE ENTERTAINMENT IN HILL AUDITORIUM

(March 13, 1927) Free shows in Hill auditorium following the winning of a Conference championship in any major sport are promised the student body in a statement issued yesterday by Gerald Hoag and James S. Helsdon, managers of the Majestic and Arcade theaters.

Stating that it is almost impossible to arrange for free shows on short notice and expressing a desire to cooperate with the Student council, the managers of the local Butterfield theaters cite the fact that they have long given passes to members of Varsity teams as evidence of their cooperation with the student body. Any picture being shown at the Arcade, Majestic, or Wuerth's theaters will be presented in Hill auditorium, according to the statement. Hill auditorium is suggested because of the limited seating capacity of the Majestic and Arcade theaters...#

Theatres

THE MICHIGAN OPENS

(Jan. 6, 1928) The Turkish bath school of theater architecture has a new and overwhelming triumph in the new Butterfield gift to the world of popular amusement, the Michigan. Rising nobly to the skies, behind a facade of shops and shop windows, this palace of the movie is the epitome of all efforts of its kind. It is unique in Ann Arbor, for the sole reason that it is more nearly like a theater than any other of the converted skating rinks which have served the intellectual audiences of the city for so long.

...

The one unfortunate result of the new theater, if you call the rest fortunate, is that there will be no more vaudeville at the Majestic... Now that there is something better, I must confess to a romantic attachment for the Maj, where I've so often had my ribs nearly bashed in, and to see it sink to the level of the Arcade -- a level low indeed -- is a bit saddening to one who, in spite of an intellectual conviction that the movies are stupid and not worth while, finds himself regularly at the show four nights a week.#

R. LESLIE ASKREN

Campus Gets Dose Of Bad Taste...

(March 29, 1942) WELL, Ann Arbor can settle down to the sweet and simple again. Having had two glimpses of the better life at the State Theater opening and Zoot Suit Stuff the campus may once more resume the prosaic course of everyday existence.

The gigantic pinball machine on S. State St. has bowed in to the applause of a duly impressed populace, a populace so dazed by a bare-faced multi-colored sign that it couldn't fight back.

Capacity crowds sat submissively through a picture whose moments of vulgarity were exceeded only by the appointments of the theatre. A Phineas T. Barnum ceiling that clashed with every color in the interior (and there were plenty of them) and carpets that were garish in the extreme combined to give the general effect of an architect's opium pipe-dream.

Zoot Suit Stuff was an improvement only in degree, not in kind...#

--HALE CHAMPION

AT THE MICHIGAN

(Oct. 20, 1931) By this time those who haven't heard or seen the Marxian antics are few indeed. "Monkey Business," the Michigan's current output, is the latest of the triad. "The Cocoanuts," probably the funniest of them all (because Harpo ate the hotel clerk's telephone and washed it down with the contents of an ink-well) was succeeded by "Animal Crackers," an absurdity which most people saw twice and more... Some critics have said that "Monkey Business" is below the other two. True or untrue, it's still twice as funny as any other movie in the last twelve months.

Harpo is at his very peak what with the additional situations and the chance for pantomime highly magnified. Once he gets mixed up in a nursery Punch and Judy show aboard a transatlantic steamer and augments the childrens' delight by appearing side by side with the dummies. Again, he comes upon a harp, frightens the performer away, plays beautifully amid distorted grimaces while scratching the sole of his shoe.

Chico is trying to persuade a gang leader that he and Harpo are worth hiring as body guards. "We're tough," says Chico. And he tells Harpo to hit him in the jaw just to prove it. Harpo does so, but Chico doesn't think it's hard enough so he tries to get Harpo by pushing him all over the room. Harpo takes it just so long, begins to breathe impassionedly, bares his teeth and crosses his eyes to show his intense anger. Then he winds up and knocks Chico clear off his feet. They get the job.

Harpo isn't any funnier, however, than Groucho whose chatter is as idiotic as ever. Zeppo and the villain are battling in a barn straw pile and Groucho broadcasts the fight into an old lantern while clambering around in the beams. He is at his best when he is encouraging a cow, whose stall is at the ringside, to "go in there and fight."#

R. L. T.

THE AFRICAN QUEEN, with Katharine Hepburn and Humphrey Bogart.

SUFFERING MOSTLY from an incredible story, "The African Queen" nevertheless appears to be one of the better adventure films to be made recently. Most of the praise belongs to the two Hollywood veterans who allowed themselves to be messed up almost beyond recognition for the sake of the picture.

Notwithstanding the recent Academy Award announcements, this reviewer prefers the work of Katharine Hepburn to that of Bogart. It is hard to imagine anyone doing a better job of portraying the prim, naive missionary, completely innocent and yet alive with physical desire. It isn't necessary to make a trip to Africa to feel the acute discomforts she experiences; seeing her go through it all is quite enough.

When we come to Bogart the problem of evaluation becomes more difficult. Perhaps his "Oscar" is the result of the different type of role he assumed; "Casablanca" was never like this. He is aptly suited for the part, but he doesn't quite approach the excellence we might expect. It is the novelty that sells him.

C. S. Forester's story is the weakest point. Too many lucky coincidences can ruin an adventure of this sort. Perhaps the best thing that can be said is that director John Huston emphasizes the personalities rather than the events or wonders of the African interior.

And the cartoon is a gem.#

--Tom Arp

CENSORSHIP GHOST HOVERS OVER MOVIES

(March 3, 1928) Censorship is about to invade our fair city! Gerald Hoag, manager of the Majestic theater, has recently intimated that in the future all pictures presented at his theatre will be placed on probation for a period of one day and that all scenes calling forth from the male attendance such exclamations as "Ah," "Oh," or other such remarks will be cut out before the next performance...#

NIAGARA, with Marilyn Monroe, Joseph Cotten and Jean Peters.

(March 19, 1953) **IT MUST** certainly be conceded that Marilyn Monroe has proved herself a one-role actress. That she will ever be able to play anything but a loose, over-sexed blonde is doubtful. But when a picture is built around her meagre talents, when she is called upon to do nothing more than she is able, then she can fill her role as fittingly as any of Hollywood's best dramatic actresses have ever done.

"Niagara" has been filmed along these lines. Within the framework of this picture Miss Monroe does exactly what she should, and consequently her performance is completely satisfying. This is really her best movie to date.

Joseph Cotten, as her neurotic and ever-alert husband, is driven almost insane just trying to keep her from being the bad girl she must be... Cotten has a tendency to overplay his part a bit; it is too bad that film neurotics cannot be content to be just slightly abnormal, but always find it necessary to seem like complete lunatics...

Much of what is good in the picture can be attributed to the fact that it was actually made at Niagara Falls; while there is a trace of obtuseness in the continual equation of Miss Monroe's fatal attraction and the wonderful power of the water, still it is not a bad idea. Two such awesome natural phenomena are at times almost too exhausting.

Unfortunately for Miss Monroe's reputation as an actress, the most exciting part of the film occurs after she has bowed out. The trip down the Niagara River with Cotten and Miss Peters in a small motor launch is really quite good, and by the time we reach the end of the picture there is nothing to do but admit that despite all its advance publicity and the fact that it stars Marilyn Monroe, it is nevertheless a thrilling and entertaining film.#

--Tom Arp

Students React to Movie Price Increase

By MICHAEL JULIAR

(Jan. 18, 1965) There is a growing reaction among students to the recent ticket price increase at the three motion picture theatres in Ann Arbor.

--The Lawyers Club Board of Directors called on Student Government Council Wednesday night to represent the students in protesting the increase.

...

--Interquadrangle Council unanimously passed a motion last night supporting any SGC action regarding the price rise.

--The International Students Association has given its support to any SGC action.

...

Raise Prices

The three area theatres, the Michigan, State and Campus, raised their nightly and Sunday admission prices over Christmas recess from $1 to $1.25. The daily prices were raised from 75 cents to $1.

Gerald Hoag, manager of the Michigan Theatre and spokesman for the managers of the State and Campus Theatres, said Tuesday that the price rise "is a result of inflation." He pointed out that overhead costs, such as renting the films, paying rent on the building and paying the projectionists, ushers and other workers, have gone up. He emphasized that advertising costs have substantially increased in the last few years.

He noted that other theatres in Michigan owned by the Butterfield chain which owns the three Ann Arbor theatres had raised their prices "long before."

Protest Movements

Michael Mathews, '66BAd, president of the Lawyers Club, said last night that "the 25 per cent increase has no apparent economic justification and until this is demonstrated to the contrary, we hope that all movie-goers will protest it."

Mathews said that many of the members of the Lawyers Club would support a boycott of the theatres.#

Demonstration by 600 Protests Price Increase

Set Meeting With Theatre Management

By MICHAEL JULIAR

(Jan. 23, 1965) More than six hundred students went to the Michigan Theatre at 6:30 p.m. yesterday, paid their $1.50 and stayed to see "Mary Poppins" a time and a quarter to protest the recent movie price rise.

Student Government Council called the "stay-in" Wednesday night to demonstrate student support for a meeting between SGC and the W. C. Butterfield, Inc. representatives in Detroit now scheduled for Monday.

...

At the same time, pickets from Voice Political Party, the Independent Socialist Club and the Young Democrats marched in cold and rain in front of the Michigan and State Theatres. The State Theatre was boycotted. No demonstrations were held at the Campus Theatre. All three theatres are owned by the Butterfield chain.

...

The picket leaders said that they were carrying the demonstrations further than SGC had urged because they feel "that SGC will be in a better bargaining position if demonstrations continue. We need more than one demonstration to get a reaction from Butterfield," one student said.

'Having Fun'

Gerald Hoag, manager of the Michigan Theatre noted that the students were "having their fun." Asked if prices would be lowered, he replied, "No, there is no chance."

...Charles Herbert, manager of the theatre, said that several hundred tickets were sold for both performances, "a better than usual turnout for a show at the end of its run on a rainy night."..#

'Stay-In,' Boycott Fails At Two Local Theatres

Students Demonstrate Against Price Increase

By MICHAEL JULIAR

(Jan. 24, 1965) Efforts by three student organizations to hold a "stay-in" and boycott at the Michigan Theatre last night collapsed.

An estimated 200 students held a "stay-in" after the 6:30 p.m. show ended to protest the recent admission price increase at the three local movie theatres.

The boycott of the 9 p.m. show failed as the theatre filled up for the performance.

Picket State Theatre

The pickets also marched in front of the State Theatre, asking for a complete boycott. Charles Herbert, manager of the theatre, said that he was surprised at the "good" turnout. The Campus Theatre was not picketed. All three Ann Arbor theatres are owned by Butterfield.

The three organizations, Voice Political Party, the Young Democrats and the Independent Socialist Club, picketed outside the theatres in cold, snow and slush for several hours.

...

Not Enough Support

The groups that demonstrated last night said they felt SGC had not gone far enough to rally student support to convince Butterfield of student sentiment against the price rise.

SGC President Douglas Brook, '65, and Council Member Thomas Smithson, '65, will represent the students at the Detroit meeting. Several student leaders do not expect Butterfield to lower its ticket prices. They only expect Butterfield representatives to clarify their reasons for the price rise.

Gerald Hoag, manager of the Michigan Theatre, said Friday night that he saw no chance of the prices being lowered.

If prices remain the same after the meeting SGC is expected to take further action at its regular Wednesday meeting.

...

The protests both nights were watched by Butterfield representatives. The Ann Arbor police also observed the proceedings...#

'Jailhouse' Shook Up

(Nov. 19, 1957) THE LATEST Elvis Presley movie, "Jailhouse Rock" is not even as good as "Love Me Tender." We might also say that cancer is not as good as leprosy, and that "Kiss Me Deadly" is not as good as "I, the Jury."

An Elvis flick should at least be funny, but "Jailhouse Rock" can't even boast that. It is dull. It drags along, plodding through its plot (?), compelling the audience to sleep. It's so dull that I had to buy an extra box of Jujyfruits to stay awake. That way, I keep so busy picking my teeth that it's impossible to snooze.

Even Elvis doesn't seem to have his heart (or other portions of his anatomy) in this one. Occasionally, he will slam about and grunt, revolving and rolling in the style that made him infamous. But that stuff is at a minimum, and we don't know whether that's to the good or not.

...

THE PLOT of "Jailhouse Rock" might well have been a writing assignment for students in Ding-Dong School. At the opening, Elvis is in a bar and sees a lady (hah!) get insulted. His wrath mounts and he slashes out at the insulter, finally killing him with bare fists. Pretty cool stuff.

So Elvis goes to jail where, in the picture's high point, he gets his hair cut. His cellmate is a whiny hillbilly singer who foresees a great future for the Pelvis. "Aw," says the unbelieving hero, "I never heard of anybody payin' money to hear guitar playin'."

In one of the most implausible events since the birth of Fats Domino, a network coast-to-coast television show emanates from the penitentiary. Sure, happens all the time. In this little sing at Sing-Sing Elvis appears, is seen by the world, and skyrockets to success upon his release. It's very poignant stuff.

...

...The songs are all based on the same three chords, done in the usual way, and the Jailhouse Rock number is, at least, well staged.

Poor Elvis. He just doesn't seem happy in Hollywood. Maybe it's all above his head.#

--David Newman

The saga of 'Putney Swope': Harvard Lampoon of the screen

By NEAL GABLER

(Oct. 26, 1969) Putney Swope, currently playing at the Fifth Forum, has been called a lot of things. (I refer you to Vincent Canby for a complete listing.) And it is a goulash of everything-- snappy lines, a few duds, and a moral on top of it.

I get the feeling that writer and director Robert Downey thought up some good jokes and some wild situations, then proceeded to build a film around them. He gives us a pack of one liners and a zoo of weird characters. President Mimeo, a pot smoking midget with a construction helmet atop his head and an advisor telling banal stories, is such a brilliant creation that I am thankful the film was made, if just for this.

The plot itself is thin and disjointed. The head of a staid Madison Avenue advertising firm dies and the firm's members must pick a new chief. But there is one catch--according to the rules, no one may vote for himself. So each one votes for the man least likely to win, Putney Swope, the agency's black music director. When elected, Swope, a combination Groucho Marx-Fidel Castro, begins the Truth and Soul Ad Agency--no cigarettes, no liquor, no war toys.

...

Despite the hilarious commercials and the total insanity that provokes uncontrollable laughter, Putney Swope has a lot of dead air. Frequent scenes in which Putney is confronted by the Arab, an agency dissident, become tiresome. But, this really doesn't hurt the film severely. I don't think anyone takes it seriously enough to get bogged down by the klinkers. The bombs bomb, and the audience waits for the funny line it knows is just a few minutes away.

Putney Swope should be seen by anyone who enjoys sophomoric humor. It may not be the year's best comedy, but you can still bust a gut. It is the kind of thing you don't often see, a sort of Harvard Lampoon of the screen.

And, yes, Virginia, there is a moral--that deep down, black or white--we're all the same, greedy, little bastards.#

Daily Critic

--Daily--Allen Jackson

(Oct. 7, 1952)

Ode to 'what used to be a good country'

This trip goes nowhere

By NEAL GABLER

When I heard that Peter Fonda was making a "serious" film about two itinerant motorcyclists I snickered. Come on! Peter Fonda, graduate of the Roger Corman School of Acting, makign a serious film? But somehow either he has transcended his former self or the film transcends him, because Easy Rider is one of the best films I've seen this year.
...

The protagonists, Wyatt-Captain America (Peter Fonda) and Billy the Kid (Dennis Hopper) make a fortune smuggling dope and stash the bankroll in their cycles' tanks. Then off they zoom for the Mardi Gras, carefree. Or are they free? Sure they have long hair and wear wild clothes and smoke pot. But what Easy Rider tells us is that they aren't any freer than Mr. Suburbia or even the Southerners who hate them. Wyatt and Billy are Americans, caught in the American culture. What Wyatt comes gradually to realize and what Billy never realizes is that all the money crammed in the gas tank can't buy them freedom.

Not only is he an American, but Billy is middle-class America personified: only his clothes and manners are different. When he says to Wyatt, "We're rich. We did it. We're retired in Florida," he could just as well have been talking to his platinum blonde wife, in his suburban ranchhouse with the two-car garage and his kids at the U of M. The point is, we shouldn't go around feeling so superior to those dullards of the silent majority, because we're all in the same fix. That's why Captain America says, in those now famous words, "We blew it."

...I didn't even care that a large part of the film is filler to get Wyatt and Billy from one place to another. And somehow it is appropriate that, like many of their fellow Americans they are always going somewhere.

Dennis Hopper's direction is sharp and innovative. He has a good eye for composition, he juxtaposes shots nicely, and he uses some ingenious transitions. Above all, he is able to get some wonderfully natural performances, especially from the bit players, who occasionally give the film the air of a documentary.

I talked about the new style of nonacting when I reviewed Alice's Restaurant. Some of the best scenes in Easy Rider use townsfolk whom Hopper and Co. happened to find along the way. In one classic scene, guaranteed to boil the blood, a group of crackers in a diner brandish some Southern wit. "I think she's cute." "Put 'em in a cage and charge admission." "Looks like a bunch of refugees from a gorilla love-in." The remarkable, and frightening, thing is that these are not actors; they are just folks speaking their own minds.

Dennis Hopper is perfect as Billy--crude, dim-witted, funny, lovable. His feat is extraordinary considering the genuine affection the audience comes to feel for this loud-mouthed pothead. Peter Fonda may be nice to look at, girls, but he has all the range of a Steve McQueen. Always cerebral, every line gets the same dispassionate treatment, he's got no soul. He had me hoping someone would get the guy just to show he was human after all.

Jack Nicholson as George Hansen, an alcoholic lawyer the boys meet on their journey, gives the film's outstanding performance. Nicholson has been stuck in a lot of Corman horror flicks, and here he finally gets a chance to show his talent. He is brilliant in creating a whole character from a few characteristics. I found in his cornpone ACLU lawyer, a simple wisdom that came not so much from his dialogue as from his whole presence.

For all this, Easy Rider is not a flawless film. For one thing, there is Fonda's unfeeling acting. For another, there are some very affected lines. Finally, there is an LSD scene, flashy camera work and all, that seems right out of a pseudo-hip Film About Young People. But these are small faults in what is otherwise a very good film.

Easy Rider must be seen, but not as the story of an unorthodox life style in an intolerant land. It should be seen as the story of a nation that, in George Hansen's words, "used to be a hell of a good country."#

| **Flashback** |
| dir. Franco Amurri |

BY MARK BINELLI

(Feb. 6, 1990) "This was a different kind of role for me," said Dennis Hopper, speaking, of course, about his latest film, *Flashback*, in which he plays a radical hippie fugitive. Now, a sly reader might say, "Wait a minute, Mr. Hopper, didn't you write, direct and co-star in *Easy Rider*?..."

Well, if Dennis Hopper himself were here, he would probably have to admit that, yes, there are some basic similarities between the two works. *Easy Rider* is one of the few films able to adequately document the free spirit of the sixties, while *Flashback*, 20 years later, is likewise able to sum up the '80s --albeit inadvertently-- by completely exploiting everything that the '60s stood for. The movie takes what could have been a sort of nostalgic and funny film and makes it into something offensive to anyone who has even a remote respect for what happened in the flower power era. It's modern greed in its most primal and beautiful form.

The plot is pretty simple. Hopper's character is basically a more annoying version of Abbie Hoffman who's wanted by the pigs for "malicious mischief with intent to do bodily harm to the Vice-President of the United States." That's Spiro Agnew. Hopper's been on the run for 20 years, and he only let himself be arrested so he could get into the public eye again and get his book published.

The problem is, now he's captured, and he has to escape from Keifer Sutherland, who is a real tight-ass FBI agent, so he convinces Keifer that he dropped some acid in his mineral water ...the reason Keifer's character is so anal, it's because he grew up in this hippie commune, and to sort of rebel against his parents, he ran away from the peace farm and joined the FBI, only to be ordered, years later, to arrest the King of the Hippies, Hopper, dancing over that fine line between irony and stupidity.#

arts
&
letters

The
Daily
discovers
sex

LADY CHATTERLEY
& Censorship
A New Impetus To An Old Controversy

By GORDON MUMMA

(Sept. 9, 1959) **CENSORSHIP** controversy over D. H. Lawrence's "Lady Chatterley's Lover" first arose in 1928, immediately following publication of the book in Italy (in the English language). Attempts were made to import the book into this country, but confiscations by the United States Post Office discouraged free market publication of the book.

On May 4 of this year the Grove Press of New York City came forth with the complete book. They handled the situation discreetly, first by distributing the book prior to publication date and second by shipping the book by truck, bus and air freight to avoid conflict with the United States Post Office.

THE STORM broke when the Readers Subscription mailed circulars advertising the book as a part of their book club series. On April 30 the Post Office seized 20,000 circulars from Readers Subscription, and one week later it impounded 164 copies of the book itself...

...

The Post Office case against the book is against the four letter words, the descriptions of the sexual act, and the adultery. The Post Office maintains that "the effect of the book...considered as a whole...upon all those whom it is likely to reach...would arouse sexual desires or sexually impure thoughts...and with its numerous obscene and filthy terms and passages, does offend the common conscience of the community by present day standards."

...

The Supreme Court decisions have established ineffective precedents concerning the freedoms of Speech, Press, Religion and Assembly. They are ineffective because every work censored or suppressed must be laboriously, expensively and exhaustively challenged by the defendants...

The issue is not being properly considered, or rather, the wrong issue is being considered. The question is not one of obscenity or artist's intentions or political, social and artistic offense to the common conscience of the community by present day standards. The question is one of freedom to write and read, think and speak. It is a freedom which cannot be limited by the constraints of special groups.

...

It is unfortunate that obscenity always clouds the issue of freedom of the press. Censorship on moral grounds is but a small fraction of that which confronts the American citizen. Political censorship is a far worse problem. Until one has battled with the Post Office, Customs, or the State Department to receive newspapers, books and works of art which have been legally purchased, there is no way to imagine the extent of trouble, cost and discouragement involved.

IN RECENT years the meaning of "political propaganda" has been expanded so far that the Protestant Council of Churches has been forced to send delegations to New York City and Washington, D. C., to free religious literature from abroad which has been recklessly confiscated by the Post Office and Customs. A senator from New Jersey was forced to use the diplomatic courier service to obtain articles from a London newspaper because the Post Office thought the whole affair was "suspect." Not only literature, but a considerable portion of first class mail from the Communist bloc countries is sent to Washington, D. C. or San Francisco by the Post Office for "inspection" before it is delivered to the intended receiver. And, except by devious means, it is impossible to receive any literature, political, social, cultural, whatever, from any country which does not have diplomatic relations with the United States. That includes nearly one third of the land area of the Earth.

We are not in a time of war, and freedom of the press is not concerned here with military secrets, a problem all its own. The Grove Press may or may not win its battle for Lady Chatterley. It does not really matter. If they win, every book which follows will still have to be fought in the same way...#

Police Seize Cinema Guild Film;
Protestors March on City Hall

Incensed Audience
Blocks Officer's Exit
But Violence Avoided

By CLARENCE FANTO
Managing Editor
and ROGER RAPOPORT

(Jan. 19, 1967) The Ann Arbor police halted the showing of "Flaming Creatures" at Cinema Guild last night and seized the film on grounds that it was "obscene."

About 100 students subsequently marched to the city hall in ten-degree weather and staged a sit-in at the police station lobby to protest.

...

Capacity Crowd

Lieut. Eugene Staudenmeier, chief of the Ann Arbor Police Detective Bureau viewed the movie during the 7 o'clock performance as part of a capacity crowd of 300 in the Architecture Auditorium. He left the auditorium about 8 p.m. after the vivid depiction of a rape scene, entered the second floor projection booth and seized the film.

Staudenmeier said he took the film, which had been playing about 20 minutes because a "misdemeanor had been committed before a police officer."

The police officer was reportedly acting on a formal complaint filed earlier this week by an Architecture School professor who contended the film was obscene. The professor had never seen the movie.

The incensed audience blocked Staudenmeier's exit from the projection booth for a short time.

'Don't Be Afraid'

When the way cleared Staudenmeier hesitated before setting out into the hostile crowd. "I'm not leaving until you get all those people out of the way," he told Cinema Guild officials.

"Oh, come on," Assistant to the Vice-President for University Relations Jack Hamilton told Staudenmeier. "You know--sticks and stones."

Staudenmeier rushed down the staircase to a chorus of boos and insults from the crowd.

There was no violence, although a compact police squad car was kicked by several persons in the crowd as it drove away.

March on City Hall

The crowd which gathered in the police station lobby of City Hall demanded an explanation for the confiscation of the film.

"I declared it was obscene because of my previous experience," said Staudenmeier.

...

University Vice-President for Student Affairs Richard L. Cutler had told Cinema Guild leaders Tuesday afternoon, "You know you're responsible for anything that happens tomorrow..."

...

The film was delivered from New York by freight to avoid possible difficulty with federal postal regulations... When the film arrived, it was screened by the Cinema Guild advisory board, which decided the film had "redeeming social value" and considerable artistic merit...#

Movie Seizure Endangers Academic Freedom at 'U'

By CLARENCE FANTO
Managing Editor
Daily News Analysis

(Jan. 20, 1967) The furor which has developed over the Ann Arbor police's seizure of the experimental film "Flaming Creatures" at Cinema Guild Wednesday has grave implications for academic freedom as well as civil liberties and first amendment freedom.

Regardless of an individual's opinion of the artistic merit of the film, the sudden action of a local police lieutenant in stopping the film mid-way through its performance and creating a near-riot among the assembled viewers raises the spectre of more incidents of this type in the future.

Ann Arbor Police Chief Walter E. Krasny has indicated that if the municipal court hearing on the seizure of the film upholds Lieut. Eugene Staudenmeier's action in halting the performance, similar attempts to stop future showings of experimental films at Cinema Guild can be expected.

Cinema Guild has scheduled experimental shows on Jan. 25 and twice next month. One of the films on the program next week, "Scorpio Rising," reportedly will be viewed by several classes in the University as part of their assigned work; in fact, the showing of "Flaming Creatures" Wednesday was reportedly attended by a cinematography class of the architecture school.

Thus, the prospect is that police officials will be attending future showings of experimental films and other movies considered to be questionable. In a sense, the situation resembles a prior censorship of material presented in an academic setting or framework.

Prior censorship of printed, spoken or visual material has been declared unconstitutional by the Supreme Court. Furthermore, there may be a strong legal case against a judgment that a film is obscene on the basis of an individual scene rather than by means of an evaluation of the entire film and an assessment of its literary or social value.

...

But the most important issue by far, one which may not be determined immediately, is whether a self-appointed public censor in the form of a police officer can legally roam the University at will, halting the presentation of material which he considers "objectionable." There are a number of well-known attorneys who argue that prior restraint of this nature has already been declared unconstitutional by the nation's highest court.#

Sex: Mailer's ball and chain

By WALTER SHAPIRO

(March 10, 1971) SHAPIRO first became aware of the latest Norman Mailer Extravaganza when the cultural hucksters at Harper's in the media's self-aggrandizing tradition announced to the assembled literati that "the favorite target of women's lib chooses his weapon-- Harper's Magazine" and then carried this adrenal self-glorification one consciousness level further by adding, with nary a visible wince, "Pick up a copy. Before your newsstand is picketed."

Alarmingly susceptible to the blandishments of the Current, but deeply offended by Harper's marketing strategy in merchandizing Mailer, Shapiro, reflecting the amorality of the age, compromised by picking up--but definitely not paying a dollar for--a misaddressed copy of Harper's which was lying untended in a public place without a picketer in sight.

...

As he held--nay fondled--his "hot" copy of Harper's, suddenly there was the flash of insight, the gasp of an idea, the Kilimanjaro of the Soul. Shapiro would climb out of the mire of indolence and write a reaction to Mailer's "The Prisoner of Sex." But deep, darkling doubts remained. Was he man enough to attempt to take on Norman Mailer at the typewriter? Could the Magazine-Swiper even attempt to discuss women and their liberation in response to Mailer--a Mailer who noted modestly in Armies of the Night that "he (like all novelists) prided himself on his knowledge of women."

...

With Mailer, substance as well as style is important. And here parody fails us. For despite the arid gaps between subject and predicate in so many of his long and convoluted sentences, Mailer is taken seriously. Both Kate Millett and Mailer himself agree that he is one of our leading mythologists of sex. And when Mailer writes, thousands of male sexual fantasies answer.

...

THE UNACKNOWLEDGED fellowship of the spirit between Mailer and [Irving] Howe extends to a mutual failure to understand why Women's Liberation does not limit itself to political action toward such reformist goals as vocational equality and free day care centers. Both male critics whine, why should women feel oppressed since they have so much

NORMAN
THE PRISONER OF SEX
MAILER

power over men already?

Mailer expresses this quaint notion in personal terms using the military imagery he cannot seem to avoid when writing about women. "Four times beaten at wedlock, his respect for the power of women was so large that the way they would tear through him...would be reminiscent...of German tanks crunching through straw huts on their way across a border." Presumably women should abandon their struggle for liberation and devote all their energies to tearing through Norman Mailer.

...

Although Mailer seems blithely unconcerned about his own reification of women, he has an almost neurotic fear of a sexual Brave New World "of vibrators and plastic dildoes" in which men are expendable and women are freed from the burdens of childbirth. Utilizing some of the prose left on the cutting room floor of his moonshot book, Mailer likens Millett to a "technologist who drains all the swamps only to discover that the ecological balance has been savaged."

BUT WHAT MAILER really fears are not test-tube babies, but the demystification of sex. For Mailer is our leading sexual mystic, a self-appointed guru in the carnal wilderness, who can oppose birth-control because it would deprive "women forever...(of) the existential edge of knowing that to become pregnant, might mean their death, yet not to be pregnant might bring on the worst of illness..."

Sex is the road to self-awareness, that's Mailer's gospel. Waxing lyrical, he writes, "For when a man and woman conceive would it not be best that they be able to see one another for a transcendent instant." Yet sex is also the ultimate testing ground, the veritable mirror of the soul. "Give meaning to sex and one was the prisoner of sex," the self-described Prisoner intoned, "until every failure and misery, every evil of your life, spoke their lines in its light."

With these spiritual insights it is almost as if Mailer believes that his entire life is just a long and arduous preparation

for that one transcendent fuck, that orgasm which will rattle the pillars of heaven, and God will come out and write in flame across the sky, "Norman, this is what it's all about. Only You did I make in My image. For who could fuck like that except a God."

There is an undeniably romantic appeal to this concept of transcendent sex, but the ideology becomes oppressive, as well as banal, when one realizes that women are merely convenient vessels through which men can attempt to achieve their self-awakening eternity-rattling orgasms.

...

In terms of understanding the sexual politics which afflict us all, it is not enough to merely understand what Mailer is trying to say. Perhaps even more significant is the role played by Mailer and other talented sexual gurus in creating and nurturing masculine erotic fantasies.

FOR MANY, novels provide the earliest and most lasting source of vicarious sexual experience. It is the novelist's desperate search for the ultimate sexual metaphor which has led many men to become victims of all sorts of destructive, plastic myths about all-consuming sex.

The novelists have succeeded too well. They have left too many men with the lurking suspicion that the sexual myth-makers are having erotic experiences which bear almost no relation to their own. How many men have the gnawing fear that Norman Mailer is having better sex than they are? How many men are disappointed upon achieving orgasm to discover that in real life thunder doesn't roll and the heavens don't light up with fire?

Given this peculiar masculine insecurity, it is a logical next step for males to begin to regard women as almost Stations of the Cross which one penetrates at will while striving with almost religious fervor to duplicate the sexual feats of Norman Mailer and those other talented chroniclers of sex.

SMALL WONDER that the dialectics of this "notches on the bedpost syndrome" remain unfathomable to Mailer. For rarely has a writer become more securely entangled in a web of his own sexual myths. Poor Norman, it's just a terminal case of too much Army, too much ego and too much talent.#

DIONYSUS CAST ARRESTED

By STEVE NISSEN
and JIM NEUBACHER

(Jan. 27, 1969) Ann Arbor Police Chief Walter Krasny said last night he will seek warrants this morning for the arrest of the ten-member cast of "Dionysus in 69" on charges of indecent exposure.

The play, a modern adaptation of Euripides' Greek classic "The Bacchae", was performed with two nude scenes before an overflow crowd in the Union Ballroom last night as part of the Creative Arts Festival sponsored by the University Activities Center.

...

The players were detained briefly following the performance while police fingerprinted and photographed them. They were allowed to remain free on personal recognizance--no bond money was required.

...

The charge of indecent exposure is classified as a "high misdemeanor" and carries a maximum sentence of one year in jail and a $500 fine.

The players arrested last night performed two scenes of the controversial play in total nudity.

In the first nude scene, five men and four women stripped off their clothes on stage. With four of the men lying on gym mats the women formed an arch over them.

A fifth man was shoved through the gap to the sound of grunts and groans in the symbolic birth of Dionysus, or Bacchus, the Greek and Roman god of wine.

Following the "birth," the nine actors performed a frenzied dance, all of them still nude.

A similar arch was formed at the end of the play as cast members doused one another with red fluid symbolizing blood. A man was forced into the arch, which fell into a heap on the floor, in the enactment of the death of Pentheus, king of Thebes.

Early yesterday afternoon, a representative of the performers met with Krasny and UAC senior officers to discuss standards of conduct for the play.

Krasny then told the players that nudity would be grounds for arrest.

But the players decided to go ahead and perform the play "according to the script," said Pat McDermott, one of the performers.

However, McDermott said the actors adjusted the script to rule out portions of the play which encouraged members of the audience to disrobe and join the cast...#

'Dionysus,' Fleming and 'U': The paradox of obscenity

(Jan. 28, 1969) ONE OF THE best passages of Kurt Vonnegut's God Bless You, Mr. Rosewater describes Senator Rosewater's bout with pornography. The Hoosier Republican had introduced legislation which defined obscenity as "any picture or phonograph record or any written matter calling attention to reproductive organs, bodily discharges, or bodily hair."

...

Later, cooing over his triumph, the Senator boasted "other people say, 'Oh, how can you recognize it, how can you tell it from art and all that?' I've written the key into law! The difference between pornography and art is bodily hair!"

No law journal article, however carefully researched, could better capture the absurdity of attempting to define the obscene. Objective standards for obscenity are inherently unattainable, and the existing criteria are ambiguous and ludicrously unfair.

...

THE MEMBERS of the Performance Group who put on Dionysus in 69 Sunday night are charged not with obscenity but with indecent exposure. This charge allows the prosecution to consider the nude scenes as isolated incidents rather than integral parts of the entire play. The defense will undoubtedly argue that the verdict should be decided by applying the Supreme Court's criteria for obscenity.

If these criteria are bypassed and the issue made one of deciding whether the nude scenes actually occurred, the distinction between disrobing on a public thoroughfare and disrobing as part of an artistic presentation will be completely blurred. Given the provincial conservatism of the Ann Arbor bench, the distinction will undoubtedly remain blurred until the case reaches an appellate court...

...

OF THOSE WHO have played unfortunate roles in this affair, University President Robben W. Fleming is especially culpable. Certainly no one would deny his contention that "the University is not a sanctuary," and "therefore the law applies on campus as well as in the community."

Yet surely Fleming would agree that whether the law applies at all in this case must be determined in the courts. And the University, by a consideration of its own best interests, should be assisting the arrested players in their litigation.

Until the notion of contemporary community standards is finally deleted from the statute books, the University must insist that it is a separate community, not subject to the standards of any other community.

...

IF ACADEMIC freedom is at stake, so are future artistic experiments sponsored by student groups. Motion pictures as explicit as Flaming Creatures have run at local commercial houses without police interference. Plays having nude scenes have been performed. The authorities seem to pick weak opponents--student groups like Cinema Guild and University Activities Center and obscure Off-Off-Broadway companies like the Performance Group. Perhaps clear University determination to intercede on behalf of pushovers would deter police harassment.

Yet President Fleming has made no move to assist the group legally. And he has indulged in extraneous comments which could prejudice the actors' case in court. For example, it is not for Fleming publicly to decide, as he did Sunday, that "They don't have much of a case if they performed clothed on Saturday."

We expected better.#

THE SENIOR EDITORS

EXTRA **The Michigan Daily** EXTRA

Vol LXXIX No 95A | Ann Arbor, Michigan—Monday January 27 1969 | FREE ISSUE | Four Pages

DIONYSUS CAST ARRESTED

Play creates fiscal, legal issues for 'U'

By DAVID SPURR

The performance of "Dionysus in 69" and the subsequent arrest of ten actors drew quick reaction last night from University and community leaders.

University President Robben W Fleming said he stood by his statement Saturday defending the performance of the play while warning that "the law applies on campus as well in the community"

But he added, "They don't have much of a case if they performed clothed on Saturday"

"Dionysus" ran Saturday night in Detroit without incident Police said the actors "kept their clothes on."

When asked whether he thought last night's incident would hurt the University financially, Fleming said, "There are many state legislators who are quite concerned about this sort of thing"

However, one legislator who attended the play, Sen. Gilbert Bursley (R-Ann Arbor) reacted favorably to the production. "The dramatic techniques were most unusual and interesting," he said "I enjoyed it"

However, Bursley said the performance "could have financial repercussions for the University."

"I will try to give my colleagues in the State Senate a factual account of what happened, but they will read the news reports and may make their own opinions," he added.

Bursley recently signed a resolution calling for the formation of a special legislative subcommittee to investigate student activism in the state universities.

An American Civil Liberties Union spokesman said the case might be defended on the same grounds as the "Flaming Creatures" case two years ago.

"In any case this incident potentially raises a first amendment issue that the ACLU might get involved in," said Ann Arbor ACLU chairman Lawrence Berlin

"In the new theatre a good deal of the way in which actors perform is based on the mood and effective feeling of a particular moment. I feel that's a legitimate kind of statement they can make to defend their disrobing one night and not another" Berlin explained

Prof Joseph Sax of the Law School was critical of the University's role in the controversy "The University has an interest in the whole range of criminal law concerning the first amendment," he said.

"If the University were to stand by and do nothing, we might find many individuals subjected to arrest who were not in a position to defend themselves," Sax added.

He explained that a trial would center on whether the nudity was in fact obscene

UAC hits action by city police

The senior officers of University Activities Center, which sponsored "Dionysus in 69" as part of its Creative Arts Festival, reacted angrily to the arrests last night of ten members of the play's cast

"We believe "Dionysus in 69" is a serious dramatic effort and should be accepted as such," the UAC senior officers said in a joint statement released at 3 a.m today.

"The production was brought to the University community as legitimate, topical, experimental theater," they explained

"We reaffirm the right of the University community to view such theater We regard the arrests as a serious violation of the basic freedom of artistic expression"

It will not be clear until after the warrants are issued today whether the officers of UAC will be liable for prosecution for sponsoring the performance

However, the fact that Prosecutor William Delhey and Police Chief Walter Krasny chose to charge the performers with indecent exposure indicates that the UAC officers may not be affected.

The Michigan Daily

Celebrating the birth of Dionysus

theatre

Toward a new environment

By DANIEL OKRENT
Feature Editor

To censor the nudity out of "Dionysus in 69" would be to deprive it of its sinews

Two nude scenes, coming at beginning and end, make the perfect frame for all that passes in between the birth and the death scenes with the entire case arrayed in a ritualistic tableau of raw sexuality —raw "being" are such quintessential elements, it is hard to understand how the company performed the same scenes clothed in Minneapolis last week

It is equally hard to understand how the guardians of the public morality could find any appeal to prurient interests whatsoever "Dionysus" is not that type of play

And it is the type of play, rather than the play itself, which redeems "Dionysus" and makes it important. It sits nestled between Euripides and Julian Beck, picking the best of both, and keeping enough of an internal fit to make it both startling and noteworthy

The concept of environmental theatre often suffers in practice, and for much of last night's performance, the suffering showed as the "Dionysus" audience offered an incredible mess of false responses which enabled them to feel they were "participating"

But even though each cliched epithet hurled at Pentheus was almost inevitably followed by an embarrassed flush, the important thing was the fact the audience bothered to take part at all

In his review of "Dionysus" in the Aug 10 issue of The New Republic, Robert Brustein of the Yale Drama School bemoaned the state of an avant-garde theatre movement which, he felt, was moving toward "self-indulgence and accident"

While Brustein may have been right about the seeming lack of intended, coherent, and worthwhile content, he nevertheless misses the entire point that such theatre is trying to make that the self-indulgence represented by cast members who physically carry a member of the audience to his seat practically without regard for the spectator's own wishes scores heavily against the restrictions of the complacent drama we have grown up with.

Nevertheless, for the walls of convention that the play knocks down, for the spontaneity and truthfulness and the sheer artistic chutzpah that Director Richard Shechner's company pulled off, much of the evening was unfulfilling. It seems that there must be a limit to the display of narcisssistic self-praise that the play and the company lavish upon themselves. And, at various times this updated version of "The Bacchae" was simply and unforgiveably, boring

Technically, there is little fault to be found. Shechner is a virtuoso at creating a perfectly ordered chaos As his players fan out into the audience, mumbling gibberish and droning chants that consist of equal parts of the Gregorian and of those of the asylum each part meshes with each of the others

The company itself, cloaked in all the anonymity of modisn theatre, is equally good The men perform first-class ballet as well as fine theatre, and the four female cast members control the entire spectrum of emotion and non-emotion

Furthermore, one girl in particular looks particularly fine when undressed. And believe me—there's nothing in the world wrong with that

Police book performers

By STEVE NISSEN and JIM NEUBACHER

Ann Arbor Police Chief Walter Krasny said last night he will seek warrants this morning for the arrest of the ten-member cast of "Dionysus in 69" on charges of indecent exposure.

The play, a modern adaptation of Euripides' Greek classic "The Bacchae", was performed with two nude scenes before an overflow crowd in the Union Ballroom last night as part of the Creative Arts Festival sponsored by the University Activities Center.

None of the UAC officers were immediately arrested. However, Krasny indicated that County Prosecutor William Delhey would be responsible for the final decision in any further arrests.

The players were detained briefly following the performance while police fingerprinted and photographed them. They were allowed to remain free on personal recognizance — no bond money was required.

The ten performers were ordered to report to District Court at 10 a.m. this morning. Formal arrests will be made after the issuance of warrants in the court, Krasny said.

"They have assured us they will stay in town until tonight at least," the police chief said. If the players left the state, no extradition would be possible, he explained.

Attorney Peter Darrow has offered his legal services to the group, and is expected to represent the players today.

The charge of indecent exposure is classified as a "high misdemeanor" and carries a maximum sentence of one year in jail and a $500 fine

The players arrested last night performed two scenes of the controversial play in total nudity.

In the first nude scene, five men and four women stripped off their clothes on stage. With four of the men lying on gym mats the women formed an arch over them.

A fifth man was shoved through the gap to the sound of grunts and groans in the symbolic birth of Dionysus, or Bacchus, the Greek and Roman god of wine.

Following the "birth," the nine actors performed a frenzied dance, all of them still nude.

A similar arch was formed at the end of the play as cast members doused one another with red fluid symbolizing blood. A man was forced into the arch, which fell in a heap on the floor, in the enactment of the death of Pentheus, king of Thebes.

Early yesterday afternoon, a representative of the performers met with Krasny and UAC senior officers to discuss standards of conduct for the play.

Krasny then told the players that nudity would be grounds for arrest.

But the players decided to go ahead and perform the play "according to the script," said Pat McDermott, one of the performers.

However, McDermott said the actors adjusted the script to rule out portions of the play which encouraged members of the audience to disrobe and join the cast.

Following the performance, as rumors spread that arrests were about to be made, an angry crowd of several hundred gathered in the corridor leading to the ballroom.

Richard Shechner, producer of the play, after conferring with Krasny behind closed doors, emerged angrily from the room and led the group into the lobby on the second floor. There he confirmed that the arrests were going to be made. He asked for support from the spectators, but ruled out violent action.

"What we did we did partly for ourselves, but most of all for you," he said. "For if there is to be political freedom in this country, there must be artistic freedom." However, he added, "We did not come here seeking confrontation."

The crowd drifted away after Shechner finished speaking, and the threat of an immediate confrontation was ceased.

However, at a 2 a.m. meeting at Canterbury House, Shechner changed his tone.

"To be neutral is to be on the side of the oppressors," he told a group of about 50 playgoers who met with several actors to consider further action.

Shechner said the "censorship" displayed in the arrest of the cast has raised serious questions with regard to artistic freedom.

He said the group chose Ann Arbor for a "frontal exposure" of censorship because the atmosphere of the University was better than that of Detroit, where the group performed the play without the nude scenes Saturday night.

He said the group had not been prepared to confront the Detroit police.

"You have to pick your battles," the director explained. "We're interested in guerrilla tactics, and not interested in getting into fights we can't win."

Shechner insisted that the central issue is "not the simple question of nakedness, but of freedom of expression."

He indicated that at least two, and maybe all of the players are interested in appealing the case on Constitutional grounds if convicted. He hopes to make it a test case to establish a broad legal precedent in the area of free expression.

Most of the actors indicated they would probably not perform "Dionysus" tonight as planned. Shechner said he felt a discussion of censorship with the second night's audience might be more appropriate.

One actress, however, suggested the play be put on as planned because "we didn't come to mobilize the campus, we came to do our show." She said the show had merit even when performed without the nude scenes.

MEETING IN AUD. A TONIGHT

Crisis approaches in LSA dispute

By RON LANDSMAN

The controversy over the literary college's language and distribution requirements appears headed for its climax this week

The mass meeting scheduled for tonight will be held in Aud A of Angell Hall instead of the Union Assembly Hall It was moved to the larger room because of the expected turn-out

Students will decide then what action should be taken on the requirements

Proposed action ranges from a disruptive sit-in in the office of literary college Dean William Hays to waiting for faculty action, which may come as early as next week.

On Thursday the college faculty meets to consider changing the language requirement and whether to open their meetings

The mass meeting tonight follows months of petitioning and organizing by Radical Caucus and Student Government Council.

The meeting was first suggested by the caucus on Jan 14, the day the college faculty abruptly adjourned their meeting after some 25 students, mostly from the caucus, refused to leave.

The next day, the executive committee of the college called for a special open forum the following Tuesday to discuss the language requirement.

Radical Caucus leaders initially decided not to attend the meeting, charging that it side-stepped the issue of open meetings

They changed their minds the next day, though, but added the proviso that some faculty member must move that the meeting be made a regular faculty meeting with decision-making power

The forum went on as scheduled and the demand was not met

The day after the announcement of the forum, SGC voted to back the caucus initiated mass meeting. However, an SGC resolution prohibiting disruptive sit-ins barred their further support of the caucus

The forum last Tuesday to discuss the language requirement was quite a surprise Over 1000 students and faculty turned out for the meeting, forcing it to be moved from Natural Science Aud to Hill Aud

However the meeting was inconclusive Both students and faculty spoke on both sides of the issue

After the meeting Hays announced a special faculty meeting for this Thursday to discuss only open meetings

Student leaders criticized him for limiting the issue, and Hays later reworded his proposal, adding the question of language requirements to the agenda

Hays' move was not without effect on the students' action. At their meeting that night caucus members decided to move the beginning of the sit-in back one day to noon Wednesday

On Thursday Hays suggested a compromise. In an open letter to the student body, Hays called for elected, voting student representatives on the curriculum committee and came out in favor of open meetings

The move forced the caucus to shift its position. Caucus leaders indicated they would probably move the sit-in from Wednesday to Thursday and that it would not be disruptive—pending what the faculty did at their meeting

That same night, SGC defeated an attempt to suspend their rules barring disruptive sit-ins, which would have left them free to support the caucus' position. The move was not related to Hays' letter

The press of events in the last two weeks tends to obscure what happened the previous year. As long ago as September, 1967, Prof Roy Pierce of the political science department, then chairman of the curriculum committee cited revision of the language requirement as one of the major goals for the year.

Other important issues kept the committee from delving deeply into the requirement this year. But late last year the committee told Hays their report would be ready by the March faculty meeting, and it is a commitment current committee chairman Prof. James Gindin says he can meet

But by last semester, students were on the move, too. In September the caucus began its petition drive against both the language and distribution requirements which was to net some 3,500 signatures.

SGC started its own petition drive a short time later

In late November more than 150 students joined in presenting the petitions to Hays

Hays later turned the petitions over to Gindin, who in turn informed the faculty officially of the petitions at the Dec 2 meeting

The student demand at the time was for a decision by the end of January, although no specific action was threatened if the demand wasn't met

The issue of open meetings was not ignored either In November, Prof E Lowell Kelly of the psychology department moved that meetings be open

A similar motion in the 1967-68 academic year had been defeated in an informal vote

Kelly said he thinks the chances of passage now are overwhelming

The issues now before the faculty are very clear, but what they and the students will do is not. Thursday should be the decisive day

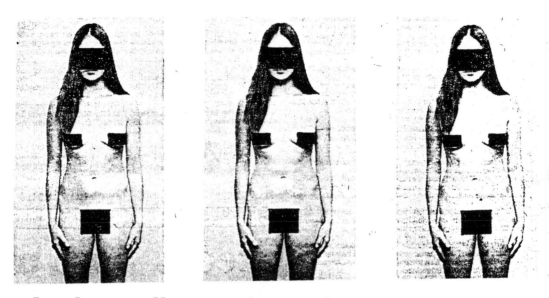

an essay

A short discussion of obscenity in society, or, censorship as a way of anti-life

by daniel zwerdling

> Obscene literature is wanton, depraved, nauseating, despicable, demoralizing, destructive and capable of poisoning any mind at any age...
> Obscenity menaces the whole society, and all who care about the survival of the nation, and indeed civilization, should be concerned about it.
> --Chicago Police Department Training Bulletin

(Sept. 28, 1969) **WHEN PAGAN** Israelites recently delivered from wracking bondage in Egypt revelled and made love around the Golden Calf, their God-fearing brethren smote them for the sin of obscenity.

Now, in the 20th century, Americans simply imprison people for it.

Obscenity has aroused the entire nation--obsessed it even before the "hippy" culture first started worshipping natural sex in the early 60's. Mothers for Moral America write Congressmen about obscenity, and massive Rallies for Decency inspire the wholesome young to fight it.

Since last spring a special squad in the Justice Department has tried to root out obscenity from the American cultural soil--and local courts and police prosecute people who sell it.

These anti-obscenity crusaders, like Chicago's police, are out literally to save

the world--from pictures and words of sex that may poison and corrupt, goading the populace, especially the young, into perversion and grotesque crimes against humanity.

...

THE HUMAN BODY has failed historically to muster much social respect--although it occupies much of our lives. Men have chained the body, mutilated it and obliterated it--and passed laws against it. Procreation in marriage has been acceptable, but society has seldom condoned physical pleasure for pleasure's sake.

People just don't believe they should see or use their own bodies. That's why painters portrayed the Son of God wearing a loincloth on the cross to hide his penis.

The imperative for this self-degradation is something no one completely understands, but it has its roots in the established church which revered the soul and spirit, and decried the body as a carnal prison which death and salvation would ultimately cast off.

Industrial societies absorbed the same concept, and added more practical reason for suppressing the body: people who spent their time enjoying their bodies spent less time producing in the factories.

THIS IS WHERE history has brought the United States today: to a society

which makes physical exposure a crime except behind locked doors, and which forbids words and pictures and speech-- all symbols--which arouse sexual thought.

And it is a society, say psychiatrists, which makes many of its citizens sick.

"The sickest patients a psychiatrist sees--adults and children--are those who have been stringently conditioned by the society to suppress from their minds a comfortable awareness of sex and their bodies," says Dr. Donald Holmes, one of the nation's foremost adolescent psychiatrists...

...

American culture, says Holmes, "unteaches kids there is such a thing as the body." The job of psychotherapy is precisely to help them "unburden themselves of the sickening but undeserved sense of guilt and the crippling anxieties" they feel about sex.

Can anyone doubt what Holmes is talking about? They remember fearing to ask teachers and parents questions about sex, giggling when a girl's slip was showing; they remember the tight knot which clenched in their chests at the words "penis" and "vagina"; and the social taboos against letting anybody--often including members of the same family-- see them undressed.

SOCIAL IGNORANCE about sex, says Holmes, is astounding: 50 per cent of a large sample of medical students in

1961 believed masturbation caused mental illness, and more than half wanted psychotherapy to resolve sexual problems.

Society, regrets Holmes, forbids its people to "promote the pleasures of being alive."

And that, say psychiatrists, is exactly why the society has "pornography" and "obscenity." Deprived of free physical contact, guilt ridden about sex, and horribly frustrated sexually, people must seek relief in cheap picture magazines, graphic verbal descriptions and grubby peep show joints--all merely paper symbols of the real thing.

Here the society makes another crucial mistake, argues Holmes: rather than permit people the secondary relief of reading about sex after suppressing sex itself, the government outlaws it.

THE TRAGIC irony is, all the usual justifications for suppressing "pornography"--corruption of the mind, sexual perversion, incitement to sexual crimes--have no scientific basis whatsoever. No tests anywhere have ever proven them.

But there are overwhelming refutations:

- Eighty-four per cent of mental health professionals in a recent national poll said persons exposed to "pornography" are no more likely to commit violence, rape or other antisocial behavior than persons not exposed.

- In Denmark, where pornography has been legalized, sexual crimes have not increased--they have dropped markedly.

England may follow Denmark's lead, if Parliament listens to a top level committee of judges, lawyers, psychiatrists and artists who urged this summer that obscenity laws be abolished.

"The so-called permissive society may have its casualties," reported the committee, "the repressed society almost certainly has a great deal more.

"Repressed sexuality can be toxic both to the individual and to society.

"Repression (of obscenity)," the panel concluded, "can deprave and corrupt."

In the ideal society which does not foster sexual guilt but promotes a healthy, natural respect for the body and all its functions, the need for pornography would probably disappear.

But until then, psychiatrists like Holmes urge that exposure to what we call pornography not only doesn't harm us, but is actually educational and even essential for mental health...#

Learning to do it by the book

By HENRY BURLINGAME
Sex Expert

(The Photographic Manual of Sexual Intercourse, by L. R. O'Connor, Pent-R-Books, Inc., $12.98 (way, way too much)

(Oct. 12, 1969) THERE IT IS, sitting right there in front of you on your desk, "America's first complete Sex Course in one volume." No one is born with a working knowledge of sexual intercourse, as the dustjacket so gracefully tells you, but this little honey is just what you needed to find out all about it.

Just Think!!! Over One Hundred and Fifty Actual Photographs of a man and a woman (a "married couple") are presented for your perusal and emulation.

...

And what this review is trying to say (in its own humble way) is that you should forget the whole thing because this book is REALLY STINKO, unless, of course you're sitting home with Martha and looking for a good ha-ha.

...

O'Connor's style sweeps radically from purple prose--the sort that seems always to use "penned," instead of "wrote"--to early high school. Although this would seem on the surface to detract from the book it often provides some of its more interesting highlights. For example, the sentence which begins the chapter on female oral-anal sexuality: "We now enter into the nether world of sex, that area in which most discussion is conducted in deepest secrecy, not to mention under the conditions of the darker shadowings of night."

...

The chapter entitled "Positions for sexual intercourse" and accompanying pictures depict, according to the author, better than 150 possible postures for doing "what comes naturally."

Solely in the interest of our readers I dedicated myself to the task of proving out, by rigorous testing, each of the alternatives pictured and described.

...

The first set of positions is fairly standard--the only difficulty is trying to emulate the stony faced expressions of the people in the pix. Throughout the depiction of their amorous contortions neither of the two pictured (a married couple) shows the least emotion (except once in the "Sitting Face to Face" position the girl has this vague sneer). Initially we thought the guy in the pix was merely uninterested or maybe drunk but a thorough study revealed that he is stuffed.

In fact, his being stuffed seemed to explain for a while his ability to maintain all of these positions standing on his head. However after one hour and twenty-three minutes of futile attempt, we discovered that some of the pictures are intended to be viewed with the book rotated approximately 90 degrees. (It was real hard to tell because the captions were still at the bottom of the page and the pix are those kind with no backgrounds.)

BUT HAVING resolved that problem new ones developed. Among them pain and agony. But that's not so bad--at least they can be passed off as exotic positions with hidden spiritual qualities. They prove only mildly impossible for the extremely athletic who are able to resolve the adverse physics of facing in opposite directions, having absolutely no leverage, and thus being reduced to excrutiating immobility.

More disturbing however are the positions that just don't work. Apparently O'Conner or his models discovered at some point that his goal of 150 positions was a bit ambitious. On top of using a considerable number of precisely duplicated poses and very slightly changed positions (like moving one hand about three-eights of an inch), The Photographic Manual of Sexual Intercourse stoops to showing entirely fictional postures. In the words of the Graduate Ben to Mrs. Robinson's husband, "It was just like we were shaking hands." That's about as close as a few of the positions come to sexual contact. (Unless, of course, the man in the pictures is mighty damned endowed.)..#

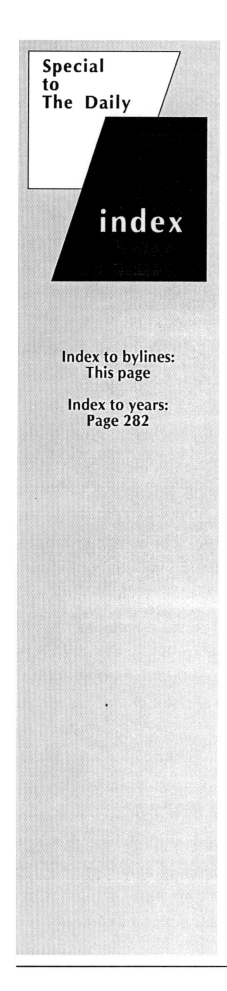

Special to The Daily

index

Index to bylines:
This page

Index to years:
Page 282

Index of Bylines

(Page numbers in standard text refer to reprints of bylined material; page numbers in italics refer to comments and anecdotal material.)

Index of Years